# The

**AMA**

# Handbook of

# MARKETING FOR THE SERVICE INDUSTRIES

# The

# AMA

# Handbook of

# MARKETING FOR THE SERVICE INDUSTRIES

Carole A. Congram, Editor

Margaret L. Friedman, Associate Editor

**amacom**

**American Management Association**

This publication is designed to provide accurate and authoritative information in regard to the subject matter covered. It is sold with the understanding that the publisher is not engaged in rendering legal, accounting, or other professional service. If legal advice or other expert assistance is required, the services of a competent professional person should be sought.

Library of Congress Cataloging-in-Publication Data

The AMA handbook of marketing for the service industries / Carole A.
    Congram, editor, Margaret L. Friedman, associate editor.
        p.   cm.
    Includes bibliographical references and index.
    ISBN 0-8144-0104-X
    1. Service industries—Marketing.   I. Congram, Carole A.
    II. Friedman, Margaret L.   III. American Management Association.
    HD9980.5.A53   1991
    658.8—dc20                                                    90-55204
                                                                      CIP

Printing number

10 9 8 7 6 5 4 3 2 1

# Contents

# Contributors

Carole A. Congram, Congram Associates; Bentley College
Margaret L. Friedman, University of Wisconsin-Whitewater

Rita Abent, *Hollywood* (Florida) *Sun*
Pamela V. Alden, Dun & Bradstreet Business Credit Services
John E. G. Bateson, London Business School
Kristine J. Bean, Peterson & Co.
Nancy L. Brenner, Brenner Consultants
Mary Cain, U S WEST
Rusty Campos, Sundel Research, Inc.
Craig E. Cina, NTS, Inc.
John A. Czepiel, New York University
William M. Dawson, Consultant
James H. Drew, GTE Laboratories
Ruth J. Dumesic, Suby, Von Haden and Associates
Michael J. English, GTE Telephone Operations
Thomas J. Fitzgerald, ARA Services, Inc.
William R. George, Villanova University
Christian Grönroos, Swedish School of Economics and Business
    Administration (Helsinki)
Evert Gummesson, Cicero Executives
Donald A. Hughes, DePaul University
Fred O. Jensen, Jensen Associates
Jane Kingman-Brundage, Kingman-Brundage, Inc.
Dennis Lefond, Eastern Michigan University
A. Dawn Lesh, J. P. Morgan & Co.
Donald H. Light, D. H. Light Consulting Services
Robin Scott MacStravic, St. Anthony Healthcare Corporation
Dave Masterson, Masterson & Associates
Kent B. Monroe, Virginia Polytechnic Institute and State University
Adrienne Margules O'Hare, The Marketing Company
Michael J. Pessetti, Foremost Insurance Group
Thad D. Peterson, Eureka Bank
Charmaine L. Ponkratz, Valley Bancorporation
K. Shelly Porges, Porges Marketing, Inc.
Timothy W. Powell, FIND/SVP

(*continued*)

Susan S. Prince, GTE Telephone Operations
G. Lynn Shostack, Joyce International, Inc.
Laurence N. Smith, Eastern Michigan University
Douglas C. Snyder, IBM Canada, Ltd.
Fletch Waller, Jr., Consultant
Michelle A. Yakovac, GTE Telephone Operations
Barbara M. Zuppinger, Ontario Training Corporation

# Editors' Preface

Service marketers face unique challenges when compared with their counterparts in goods-producing organizations. That is why, although marketing is marketing wherever it happens, marketing is being transformed in some subtle and not-so-subtle ways to accommodate today's service economy.

Among the unique challenges facing service marketers is the fact that marketing does not have a long history in most service organizations. Not only is there an absence of tradition, but also the environment is posing immediate threats to many service organizations—threats that require a speedy marketing-type response. For example, years after it occurred, deregulation of the airline industry is still creating marketing headaches. There was no such thing as a marketing function in the airline industry before deregulation. Almost overnight, there had to be. And what marketing meant, at the beginning of airline deregulation, was simply price cutting—to the dismay and demise of some competitors. Other threats come from foreign competition, new forms of competition, and rapidly changing technology. The bottom line for the service producer is that he or she frequently must start from scratch when it comes to marketing and must perform well very quickly to ensure survival.

The second set of challenges facing service marketers is that services are different from products; they are not simply an industrial by-product. The *Fortune* Service 500 attests to the unique and important role of services in our economy. The unique nature of services stems primarily from the fact that services are sold and then produced and consumed simultaneously, whereas products are produced, sold, and consumed sequentially—at different places in time and space. Services, therefore, are largely intangible and experiential. To name a few of the marketing implications, this intangibility makes the "product" development process more complex, means that the concept of inventory is largely irrelevant, and suggests that consumers probably have a more difficult time evaluating among service alternatives. Hence, what we know about what works in marketing tangible products needs to be adjusted for services.

The experiential nature of services means that they are inseparable from the service provider, as well as the service consumer. The implications for distribution are tremendous. No longer is distribution a matter of moving physical goods from here to there; instead, it primarily concerns accessibility. In addition, the fact that services are largely labor-intensive makes human resource and personnel issues of great concern to marketers. More will be said about this later under the topic of internal marketing. Also, the burden of helping the consumer participate appropriately in the service delivery process falls to the service organization. Services cannot be delivered well if consumers cannot, will not, or do not cooperate; it is the responsibility of the service organization to enable the consumer to do so.

Finally, the intangibility of services and their inseparability combine to create a situation where whole new conceptions and measures of quality and quality control are needed. Quality control is not an engineering problem, where tolerances can be physically measured, as they are with products, but is largely a behavioral issue. The nonstandard nature of services begs for nonstandard, unique marketing responses.

A final critical challenge facing service marketers is internal marketing, that is, using marketinglike activities to create satisfied, motivated employees who are seen, or ought to be seen, as internal "customers." In goods-producing companies, the marketing department directly controls 80 to 90 percent of the marketing function. Employees in other departments focus on their department's function; for example, factory workers direct their efforts toward operational productivity and quality.

In service organizations the percentages are different. Marketers manage only 15 to 25 percent of the marketing function because the responsibility for marketing is diffuse: Everyone relates directly or indirectly with a customer during the service delivery process. For example, the telephone operator may be the first person a customer speaks with in a service organization. The customer's first impression of the operator generalizes to the organization and its level of service quality. Another example is the way customer-contact people interact with the customer as each employee "produces" the service. Every experience a customer has with a service organization represents a basis for evaluating the organization.

In successful service organizations, then, marketing permeates the organization, and everyone focuses on the customer. Thus, one of a service marketer's major responsibilities is to help people throughout the organization—the chief executive officer, functional managers, customer-contact people, "back-room" staff—become customer-conscious. Internalizing marketing in a service organization is a prerequisite for success in the marketplace.

Of course, the service marketer also faces some of the same new challenges now encountered by manufacturing marketers. To succeed, both types of marketers must change the marketing activities and techniques that developed in response to the industrial revolution and the mass baby-boom market so that they can be effective in heterogeneous micromarkets in our new economy.

## Organization of the *Handbook*

In this *Handbook* we have assembled for the first time the basic concepts and practical guidance a service marketer needs to succeed in meeting these challenges, as well as myriad other unique demands posed by services. The volume's six parts will help you learn how to:

- Be market-oriented from the top down and the bottom up through customer- and quality-focused leadership.

- View your business from a radical new perspective—from the outside-in rather than from the usual inside-out.
- Plan for the future and position your organization with a strategic focus on your customer.
- Translate your strategic plans into practical approaches for reaching and satisfying your customers.
- Implement marketing programs and tactics that address such necessities as service development, relationship building, pricing, distribution, and communication.
- Use service as a basis for product differentiation in an economy where products are looking more and more alike.
- Think creatively beyond what the marketing norm is in your particular service industry.

We have gathered an extraordinary group of practitioners and academicians who provide a comprehensive, state-of-the-art perspective on services marketing. The academicians offer the perspective of the spectator who is able to generalize across the various specific situations observed and studied, whereas the practitioners take you right down into the ring where the theories and analytical frameworks are fleshed out and used. The contributors to this *Handbook* are drawn from all areas of services marketing, leading to the unusual breadth of this volume. We hope you will find it to be an invaluable and trusted reference.

The diversity among contributors was planned to make the *Handbook* useful to a broad readership, whether those readers are experienced service marketers or are new to services marketing, coming to services marketing from goods-producing organizations or from other functional areas, like operations or human resources. If you are a product marketer who looks to service as a source of differential advantage and added value, you will find the *Handbook* useful. If you are a service entrepreneur or are responsible for marketing activities in large service organizations, you will also find guidance in the *Handbook*. Finally, leaders of seminars and courses in services marketing should gain valuable insights from this volume that they can share with their students.

The *Handbook* is organized around six areas of interest, ranging from broad-reaching strategic issues to tactical concerns in service businesses in general and in specific service industries. The first five parts of the *Handbook* cover what we consider to be "generic" marketing topics—generic in the sense that they address issues of importance to all service marketers as a group. The final part of the *Handbook* contains chapters that address specific marketing issues and practices in particular service industries, because different service industries pose somewhat unique marketing challenges. We hope that these final chapters will encourage and help readers to find innovative marketing solutions that go beyond standard marketing practices in their own industry.

The volume is introduced, in Part I, with a chapter on the link between service quality and effective leadership. The most innovative and creative marketing program in the world cannot work if service quality is lacking. Quality issues are of particular interest in a service organization because providing quality service implies mobilizing *people* to achieve results. Leaders in service businesses do not have machinery they can rely on to achieve consistent results. It is human fallibility that complicates the leader's job in a service organization where such fallibility has a direct impact on consistency of service and on consumers' perceptions of service quality.

With the importance of the quality-leadership connection clearly stated, the volume proceeds, in Part II, to address the strategic thinking/planning components of a customer-focused organization. You are taught how to break out of your tunnel vision to achieve a whole new perspective on what you do and whom you do it for.

The third part of the *Handbook* deals with what goes on inside the market-focused service business. The intricacies of an internal marketing effort are spelled out and a case example is provided. The importance of organizational structure to a customer focus is also covered.

Part IV is devoted to planning—the foundation of effective marketing. The importance of consumer research and accurate, timely information to the planning effort is stressed, and the option of engaging outside consultants to aid in this effort is covered. Applying the reality test of effectiveness—whether we have achieved what we set out to achieve—is the content of the chapter that completes this part of the book.

Part V gets down to the nuts and bolts of marketing. Here, the traditional marketing mix variables are covered, carefully customized to accommodate the unique nature of services.

The final part of the *Handbook* considers state-of-the-art marketing in various service industries: information services, telecommunications, transportation, financial services, professional services, educational services, the arts, retail, health care, and hospitality. These chapters represent an opportunity for real creativity to evolve in services marketing, as we break through our own industry boundaries and borrow new techniques to market our own services. Part VI concludes with a look at marketing in the entrepreneurial service business. This chapter is probably of interest no matter what the size of your service organization, as we all try to move away from the slow-moving bureaucratic methods to reap the benefits that accrue when you ''act small.''

Following Part VI is The Service Marketer's Bookshelf, a collection of books and references that we have found to be particularly helpful in studying and practicing services marketing.

C. A. C.
M. L. F.

# Acknowledgments

A volume of this magnitude is obviously the effort of many minds, whose owners we would like to thank at this time. We are, of course, indebted to our many contributors, who have been uniformly generous with their expertise, patience, and persistence. We deeply appreciate their willing support. And we thank our many friends and colleagues who led us to just the right contributor.

We are grateful to the chief executive officers of major service organizations who took the time to respond to our questions about quality and effective leadership in service organizations. Henry Bloch (H&R Block), M. Anthony Burns (Ryder System), Larry Horner (Peat Marwick Main & Co.), Fred Smith (Federal Express), and Orville Wright (MCI) shared their views and experience with us. It is clear to us why they and their companies are leaders in their industries.

We appreciate the support and advice given to us by the AMACOM editorial and production staff.

Finally, we thank Raymond P. Fisk and James B. Shanahan for their respective reviews of the final manuscript. It must have appeared to be an overwhelming task to them on the basis of the weight of the manuscript alone. Their insightful, specific suggestions added greatly to the quality of the *Handbook*.

# PART I

# QUALITY: THE ESSENTIAL MARKETING STRATEGY

# 1

# The Quality-Leadership Connection in Service Businesses

Carole A. Congram
Margaret L. Friedman

*Quality is the only patent protection we've got.*

James D. Robinson III
CEO, American Express

*High-quality service is the best marketing device ever cre-*
*ated, and mediocre service is the surest way to deserved*
*oblivion.*

Larry D. Horner
Chairman, Peat Marwick Main & Co.

Leaders of service organizations are discovering that quality is a critical but intractable element in their organizations' success. Quality is critical as a source of competitive advantage because services, in a manner similar to what is happening to tangible products, are becoming commodity-like, and, apparently, lack quality. Consumers are crying out for common courtesy and caring in service delivery.[1] Why? Quality is intractable due, largely, to the complex nature of services. The more complex operating and delivery environment that services present begs for innovative solutions from service organization leaders.

What is this "complex nature" of services? First, services are intangible. This characteristic poses major problems for service customers. How do you, as a customer, evaluate something that you cannot taste, touch, smell, or feel? Prior to purchase, most customers seek out personal, word-of-mouth recommendations because the quality of a service can only be evaluated as it's experienced—after it has been purchased.

The opening quotation by James D. Robinson III is from John Paul Newport, Jr., "American Express: Service That Sells," *Fortune,* November 20, 1989, 80. Throughout this chapter, you will also find other quotations from chief executive officers (including the above quotation from Larry D. Horner that opens the chapter) who represent a number of service organizations. These quotations are excerpted from written responses to questions that we posed.

The authors are indebted to Lucinda H. Gerhard and Michael S. Epelman for their insightful comments on drafts of this chapter.

Intangibility poses such complex questions as these: How do you help customers understand what to expect from your service? How do you manage quality so that customers' expectations are met and they are satisfied? The answers depend on in-depth understanding of customers' perceptions of quality, and this outside-in perspective is not known in many service organizations.

A second characteristic of services is that they are produced and consumed simultaneously (as opposed to products, which are produced first and consumed later). During the service-delivery process, customers and service providers interact, often repeatedly. Customers participate in the delivery process and have contact with several different parts of the organization; all these experiences color their perceptions of the organization's quality. In every interaction, service providers frequently influence customers' perceptions of quality. As a result customers know these organizations well and are aware of the degree to which quality is valued.

From the organization's perspective, the simultaneity factor means that employees must be supported in ways that help them become truly sensitive to customer's needs. In their dealings with customers, employees embody the organization's regard for quality.

A related characteristic concerns the fact that, within a service organization, no two customer-service provider interactions are alike. Customers and service providers vary in their personalities and needs, so their interactions vary considerably, as well. As a result, it is difficult for an organization to impose rigorous quality standards on such heterogeneous interactions. And it is almost impossible when the service offered involves some degree of judgment (e.g., legal or investment banking services).

Services, then, represent complex environments in which leaders must establish quality on an organization-wide basis because quality is the responsibility of the entire organization. Quality control cannot be delegated to a group of engineers or technicians, but must be of concern to every employee, at every level. The broad-scale approach to quality mandated by the complex nature of services must begin at the top because that is where, presumably, the necessary broad-scale perspective resides. It is also where the long-run perspective should reside, and quality requires a long-term commitment.

The long-term goal of any organization is, of course, to obtain and keep customers. Without quality neither customer acquisition nor retention is possible. In the pages that follow we consider how an organization must ''look'' and ''act'' to be considered quality-conscious and how the organization's leaders affect quality consciousness in the quest to obtain and keep customers.

This chapter begins with a ten-point profile of the successful service organization, the one that distinguishes itself because a consistent level of quality is promised and delivered. The sections that follow describe three perspectives on quality. The first concerns definitions of quality and discusses the assessment challenges that must be addressed. The second perspective concerns customers and their point of view regarding the service organization and quality. The third perspective represents the organizational issues that must be resolved in embracing quality as an organizational imperative. These issues are organizational integration, culture, and empowerment of employees. The chapter ends with a look at the role of the leader in creating a quality-conscious service organization.

## Profile of a Successful Service Organization

How can you describe a service organization or unit that is successful? The successful organization has at least ten characteristics. The first three relate to defining quality:

1. An understanding of its customers' needs
2. A differentiated market position that is articulated clearly and consistently
3. A vision or mission statement that captures the essence of exactly how the organization serves customers

The next two focus on the customer's perspective:

4. A customer-driven, research-based definition of quality
5. Customers who believe that the organization is responsive to their needs, committed to quality, and ethical

The remaining five characteristics address organizational issues in delivering service of consistent quality:

6. Employees who fulfill the organization's service promise to customers, whether they are front-line or back-office personnel
7. Employees who believe in what the organization stands for—its mission, strategies, services, and inner workings
8. Employees who are empowered to assist customers in any reasonable way and, sometimes, in ways that go beyond the call of duty
9. Service delivery support systems that consistently do what the organization promises
10. An ongoing evaluation system to ensure that the organization stays on track

Leaders of successful service organizations know that "Quality is . . . closely linked with efficiency and profitability. . . . Quality contributes to profitability by positioning a company strategically, thus defining its service concept and the associated market segment while simultaneously helping to define a suitable service strategy."[2] If a service organization is to be successful, its leaders must embrace quality and continually seek to understand its pervasive, yet elusive nature. Service providers and the service development and delivery processes must be saturated with a quality perspective so that customers perceive quality on the receiving end of service.

## Three Perspectives on Quality

Corporate executives are recognizing that there is a link between quality and productivity that affects profits. In organizations of all types—both service-producing and goods-producing—management is recognizing the significance of quality improvement as a corporate strategy.[3]

One example is Xerox Corporation, a recipient of the Malcolm Baldrige National Quality Award.[4] In the face of intense competition from Japanese manufacturers of photocopy machinery, Xerox personnel looked for ways to cut costs; they found that cost cutting and quality improvement could be done simultaneously. Xerox's chairman, David T. Kearns, described the potential of a zero-defects approach this way: "Pretty early in the process, we realized the cost of non-conformance was 20% of revenues. . . . The opportunity was enormous." Although financial performance suffered in the short term, the company has regained significant market share from the Japanese. This example illustrates that quality requires the "long-haul" perspective.

Developing and implementing a quality improvement process in a service organization is complex. Consider the multifaceted quality service process developed by American Express and based on the strategy that "quality service . . . is the most powerful way we can differentiate our product in the marketplace," according to Louis V. Gerstner, former president of American Express.[5] The company's quality assurance program combines a philosophy that has quality service as its core, input from customers and employees, strong management, customer service requirements that are measurable, and more than 100 programs to recognize employees and increase internal awareness of service quality. The success of American Express indicates that leaders who are serious about integrating quality into their organizations must work on several "tracks" or "levels" simultaneously, owing to quality's pervasive nature.

We have identified three perspectives that are crucial:

1. The definition of quality
2. The customers' perspective
3. Organizing for quality

These perspectives, which also relate to the profile of a successful service organization presented earlier, are covered in the next three sections.

## Quality: What Is It?

As customers, we all know what service quality is. Or at least, we think we do. Describing service quality is difficult. We tend to describe service quality in terms of our experiences, especially interactions with customer-contact employees. Positive experiences, particularly those that are better than expected, may be retold in glowing detail. We are even more vocal when an experience does not meet our expectations. Research shows that we are twice as likely to recount bad experiences as good; furthermore, the impact of word-of-mouth on consumers' repurchase decisions is twice as important as corporate advertising.[6] Such findings attest to the importance of defining service quality, which we attempt to do under the five headings that follow.

## The "Quality Is Philosophy" Definition

One commonly held view is that "quality is a philosophy and it cannot be defined." Quality seems to result from management example at best and by osmosis at worst. Although a quality-minded philosophy is needed to inspire programs that promote quality, too often the attitude never leads to programs of substance. You can spot this cheerleader approach to service quality when employees receive mugs imprinted with a slogan about quality and advertisements that feature "our commitment to quality." The lack of substance causes knowing employees and customers to roll their eyes when they hear these messages.

## The Technical-Functional Definition

From this perspective, quality is divided into two parts. The technical aspect relates to the procedures followed by the service provider to ensure that the technical component of a service is performed correctly. In other words, do the service providers have the necessary expertise, and do the supporting computer systems work to provide the technical solution the customer desires? The functional aspect concerns the customers' dealings with the service organization; functional activities that promote satisfactory experiences include returning telephone calls, delivering reports on time, holding planning sessions with the client, and eliminating surprises.[7]

## The Product-Attribute Definition

A third approach links quality with certain attributes of the service.[8] This approach, derived from product marketing, posits that service quality is controlled if management establishes discrete performance standards for specific points in the service delivery process. If "helpfulness" is an important attribute to hotel customers, for example, management can develop a set of "helpful" activities (e.g., registration clerks may describe to guests the services available from the concierge, who is helpful by definition, or an electronic checkout system may reduce checkout to two minutes or less).

Focused on the outcome of the service process, attribute-based definitions of service quality do not serve management well because they ignore the service process itself. Additionally, these definitions may cause employees to concentrate on procedures, thus neglecting the process of serving customers. Customers, in turn, are aware when employees' behavior is "automatic," and so the effort to provide quality service backfires.

One of the benefits of this approach is that a service organization can use these attributes and standards in communicating with customers. For example, an airline may tout its on-time performance record as an indicator of a desirable attribute, reliability.

## The Process-Based Definition

The premise of approaches emphasizing process is that quality permeates the service process. This approach takes into account the customer's participation in the service and the customer's perception of his or her interaction with the service provider (in addition to the service provider's perceptions).

One process-oriented approach to service quality focuses on the customer's satisfaction with the service experience.[9] A service quality model focuses on the gap between consumer expectations and perceptions. The size of this gap depends on the nature of four potential gaps occurring within the service organization and within management's control:

> *Gap 1*—the difference between consumers' expectations and management's perceptions of their expectations
> *Gap 2*—the difference between management's perceptions of what consumers expect and service quality specifications
> *Gap 3*—the difference between service quality specifications and the service delivered
> *Gap 4*—the difference between what is delivered and what is communicated about the service to consumers

The challenges management must meet in order to use a process-based framework are considerable. Measurement is one significant problem. How do you assess quality without reducing it to a set of procedures at a particular point in time? Another challenge concerns priorities. How do you decide which gaps warrant significant investments of resources? The answers are not easy.

## An Integrated Definition

For many service companies, one of the major areas that must be addressed is the concept of quality as a moving target. That is, customers and service providers bring to the service delivery process a host of constantly changing contextual variables having differing degrees of influence on the process. As a result, the customer's expectations and definition of service quality are always changing.

One framework, based in social psychology, focuses on the service encounter, the interaction between the customer and the service provider.[10] These two individuals interact to achieve mutual gain and, over time, their interactions become stable, thus representing a basis for understanding quality empirically.

By focusing on the customer–service provider encounter, service managers can acquire a great deal of knowledge about what factors are most important to customers' decisions to continue the relationship. These factors might include clients' attitudes toward and experience with the service, clients' and service providers' behaviors during meetings, or cultural influences on service providers. Once service managers understand the salient contextual elements of the service relationship, they can begin to plan and control encounter outcomes.

Effective service leaders work hard to define quality in meaningful and measurable ways. Let's consider several of these working definitions of quality.

## Defining Quality in the "Real World"

Chief executive officers of leading service organizations see quality as fundamental to their success, both philosophically and practically. "Quality service is the first issue with customers, and value is next," according to MCI's vice chairman and CEO, Orville Wright. Henry Bloch, president and CEO of H&R Block, defines quality service as "providing the customer with more satisfaction than he expected. The key to good service is emphasis on training—knowledge and courtesy." [11]

Yes, quality is a philosophy, a way of doing business. It also extends into every action you take. At Federal Express, Fred Smith, chairman, president, and CEO, explains the relationship between quality and how one does business like this: "People-Service-Profit. Simply stated, it means that if a company takes care of its employees, they will take care of the customers, providing a superior service which results in profit." [12] Given the link between quality, productivity, and profit explicitly stated here, it is imperative that leaders in service organizations take pains to deal with this "slippery" factor.

Does this discussion sound like you should attempt a zero-defects approach to service? Yes, you should. Many service organizations accept something less than 99.44 percent as the standard, but consider this. If we accepted a 1 percent error rate, it would result in:

- More than 200,000 wrong drug prescriptions annually
- Water that is undrinkable four days per year
- No telephone service for almost 15 minutes every day [13]

As new approaches to the definition of quality are developed and as our measurement tools become more sophisticated, other approaches to the assessment of quality will evolve. What we can conclude at this point is that quality must be defined from an outside-in perspective.

# The Customers' Perspective

The marketing concept holds that an organization can achieve its goals by determining its markets' needs and satisfying them better than the competition does. For a service organization, the basic questions to answer are these:

1. What do our customers need and want?
2. What does service mean to our customers, our employees, and our competitors?

The first question is best answered through research because it is company-specific. Formal research programs are necessary, but leaders should conduct research informally as well. Talk with important customers, and find out what they like about your organization, what improvements they would like you to make, what their plans are, and how you can help them meet their objectives.

Attend focus groups, and learn how customers evaluate your organization and your competitors. Leaders must have firsthand knowledge of customers' perceptions.

Research can be useful in answering the second question, but there are generalizations to be made, too. According to Orville Wright, service at MCI means "complete satisfaction of our customer with every contact with the company, including the service he buys, the providing of information, the solution of problems, and the price he pays." [14]

The MCI definition implies that employees play a crucial role in determining service levels. M. Anthony Burns, CEO of Ryder System, agrees. He defines service at Ryder as "delighting our customers by meeting their expectations, and measuring and rewarding good service delivery on the part of our employees." [15]

Meeting customers' needs and expectations is a complex process. Larry D. Horner, chairman of Peat Marwick Main & Co., the large accounting and management consulting firm, describes the broad range of considerations:

> We define service in terms of consistently meeting client needs. There are all sorts of preparation and investment subsumed in that definition. We hire the best and have continuing education programs that span our people's whole careers; we invest in information technology so that our people have the leverage to provide services efficiently; and we support research on every major phase of our operations. We do all this in the name of professionalism and equally because it makes good business sense. High-quality service is the best marketing device ever created, and mediocre service is the surest way to deserved oblivion. [16]

Horner's description of the "preparation and investment" involved in delivering quality service underscores the complexity of implementing the process. Consider how many different clients your organization has. They all have different needs at any one time, and a single client's needs can change dramatically over time. As the number of clients, service providers, and services increases in an organization, understanding those needs and the degree to which your organization is meeting them becomes more and more difficult.

One way to facilitate understanding is to gather information about customers' perceptions of your organization through an ongoing quality survey. One company that is committed to a broad-scale survey process is GTE Service Corporation. [17] Through the survey process, GTE management assesses whether corporate strategies align with customer needs, whether service delivery specifications are being met, and how GTE's service compares with that of competitors. Survey usage extends across the organization, including strategic planning, operations planning, market planning, problem diagnosis, network planning, public affairs and advertising, internal communications, and service operations. GTE is using the survey process to focus on the customer; in so doing, the organization is addressing another facet of service quality, organizational integration, covered in the next section.

What is critical is not the specific "definition" of quality that you live by, but rather that you have one and that it is driven by customer perceptions. Having a "definition" helps you maintain your focus on quality.

## Organizing for Quality

As you set your organization's quality standards, you must put in place the organization to make it possible to meet them. Your imperatives are the subject of the next three discussions.

### Move Toward an Integrated Organization

The founders of many service organizations have a technical background—banking, medicine, graphic arts, and repair services, for example. Having limited experience in management, they designed their organizations after manufacturing's functional model, for want of something better. In today's marketplace, the functional model works against success for services. It encourages an inside-out approach to the market, as opposed to an outside-in perspective, representing the customer's view of the organization and its services.

One key to success is internal integration. Heskett suggested, as a rationale for organizational integration, "a definition of psychological integration: the organization of various traits, feelings, attitudes, etc., into an harmonious personality." He continued: "We in services are beginning to learn the significance of some reasonably intuitive relationships between such factors as employee satisfaction, employee motivation, service quality, customer satisfaction, and, indeed, increased volume of business or profitability."[18] Your organization's "personality" derives from organizing this set of complex and interrelated factors, many of which are organizational and within management's control. Marketers tend to be the facilitators of this integration process, and it is especially important to minimize any barriers between operations and marketing so that everyone's focus is on the customer.

How can you break down the turf barriers between functions? By focusing on the customer, leaders of service organizations can begin to eliminate the functional barriers that impede internalizing the marketing concept. When every functional area is expected to assess its relationship with the customer, interdepartmental barriers fall. The GTE service quality survey process (described earlier) has increased interaction between functions and departments. For example, when survey results indicated a decline in customer satisfaction with billing services, interfunctional teams were formed to identify solutions. Representatives included customer service, finance, and information systems. These teams met with operating units as well as customer focus groups. As GTE's approach has grown more sophisticated, intergroup cooperation also occurs in survey planning because employees recognize that their goal is the same throughout the organization: satisfy customers.

Consider facilitating the internal integration process through incentive compensation. For example, Hyatt Hotels implemented a detailed point system through which the "top level of management in a hotel can earn up to 30% of annual income in a cash bonus. . . . A manager cannot achieve the maximum number of points unless there is cooperation with other functional managers."[19]

As you examine your organization's structure, you must decide where responsibility for quality resides. On the one hand, quality is everyone's responsibility, but we have shown that employees need assistance in understanding the customer's perspective and meeting quality expectations. Your choices range from a centralized quality group to a decentralized approach. The GTE approach is based on the premise that the customer defines quality; the measurement function is centralized, but implementation is the responsiblity of the operating units.

Metropolitan Life Insurance takes another approach.[20] Each division or operating unit is responsible for assessing its customers' perceptions and taking action on the results. A central consulting group advises and coaches the divisions and maintains a semi-supervisory relationship with each division's quality manager. Whatever approach you take, it should proceed in tandem with an internal marketing process to help employees become more sensitive to customers and more productive by doing the right thing the first time.

### Create a Quality-Conducive Organizational Culture

Every service organization has a culture that influences its success. Smart leaders understand their organizations' culture and nurture it if it is influencing results positively or change it if it is out of sync with objectives. There are many approaches to describing and assessing different cultures. Here is one description as an example: "Entrepreneurial in style, [baseball-team companies] seek out talent of all ages and experience and regard them by what they produce. . . . Managers . . . perceive themselves as free agents, much like professional athletes. If one company doesn't give them the freedom or rewards they think they deserve, they'll leave for a company that does—or form their own."[21] Many baseball-team companies are professional service firms or software-development companies.

For leaders of service organizations, the role of quality in the culture is significant. If quality is an integral part of the culture, build on it; if it is not, your objective is to shift the culture toward a quality orientation through an effective internal marketing process, our next topic.

### Empower Employees

Empowerment has become a popular buzzword—easy to say, but very difficult to translate into action. Consider first the results of empowering employees. Employees who are empowered:

- Understand their relationship to the customer.
- Articulate the essence of the organization.
- Understand the organization's basic strategies.
- Speak knowledgeably about the firm's basic services.
- Take responsibility for a broad range of customer-service activities.

- Believe that the organization is a good place to work.
- Feel involved and have fun.

You can empower employees in three basic ways. The first is to define the organization's commitment to its employees—in the firm's mission statement or in some other way. This point is extremely important. Research has demonstrated that the way employees are treated is consistent with the way customers are treated.[22]

A second major way to empower employees is to involve them in the planning process. According to Federal Express' Smith, "The biggest obstacle to achieving marketing objectives in any organization is promising the customer more then you can deliver. You avoid that by involving on the front end and throughout the objective-setting process all groups who have a role in meeting the objective. Effective communication with all players is the key."[23] At Ryder, Burns states it this way: "Let people know what is expected and agree on agendas for action."[24]

The third major way to empower employees is to give them the support they need to do their jobs properly. MCI's Wright characterizes MCI by its employees' "flexibility and responsiveness."[25] What constitutes support? Training is a primary tool; some of the most successful service organizations—Merrill Lynch, for example—consider educating their employees a major investment that produces results. Support also means breaking through some bureaucratic barriers. For example, one common customer complaint is that employees do not have responsibility for handling simple transactions that may be a little out of the ordinary. Find out what those transactions are, and do what is necessary to help employees assume added responsibilities that result in improved service.

Technology is another means of helping employees serve customers well; for example, supermarket receipts now spell out each purchase, by brand, and graphics software gives customers a rendering of a new facility's interior speedily and economically. Training and technology are two significant areas of support, but there are others related to your industry, organization or particular task at hand.

Some people would question the cost of this support. However, one objective in providing support is to deliver your service defect-free. In so doing, the productivity of service employees improves. If that idea seems implausible, consider the amount of time it would take the U.S. Postal Service to trace 2 billion pieces of mail, or 2 percent of the 100 billion pieces that go astray each year.[26] Isn't it more productive to do it right in the first place?

The quality revolution described here requires enlightened leadership. The kinds of attitudes and behaviors that result in the delivery of consistently high-quality services must be valued and nurtured by the person at the organization's helm. The leader of a service organization must lead by example as well as rhetoric.

It is important to understand the role of effective leadership in promoting sound management: "The difference between managers and leaders is fundamental. The manager administers, the leader innovates. The manager maintains, the leader develops. The manager relies on systems, the leader relies on people. The manager counts on control, the leader does the right thing."[27] The purpose of differentiating between leadership and management is not to undermine managing. Rather, the purpose is to start with a clear understanding of the significant impact leadership has on a service organization and the attainment of its objectives. Sound management is a prerequisite to achieving objectives, but if the "right things" are not being managed, then management is wasted.

Also important is the realization that the changing terrain of the business world, for product and service producers alike, is creating new challenges for leaders. Rapid growth and technological developments, diversification, consolidation, and globalization all test "yesterday's" leadership axioms and skills.[28] These realities, added to the complex nature of services, make leadership issues in service organizations especially critical.

In the final sections of this chapter the characteristics of effective leaders are discussed.

## The Four Components of Leadership

Leaders at any position or "level" in an organization have four basic competencies. They:

1. Create a vision, or focus for the organization.
2. Communicate effectively.
3. Develop a consistent position for the organization.
4. Possess distinctive personal characteristics.*

Each of these components has strategic implications, and thus each deserves a closer look.

### Create a Vision

Leaders have a clear vision of what their organization or unit will be at some point in the future. Formulating a vision involves judgment, creativity, intuition, analysis, and risk taking. This vision focuses on goals; it is easily understood and can be described simply, perhaps in a mission statement or a department plan.

Once the vision is formed, leaders focus on results. They know what they want, and they need the guidance and support of others to follow and complete the activities that are part of achieving the vision. A leader and his or her fol-

---

*A great deal has been written about the characteristics of leaders. Observers of leaders generally agree that there are four components of leadership. Our summary of the components, as well as the discussion of the relationship between leadership and power, is based upon Warren Bennis and Burt Nanus, *Leaders: The Strategies for Taking Charge* (New York: Harper & Row, 1985). The authors conducted interviews with ninety leaders, and we recommend this book for the many quotations, anecdotes, and examples presented.

lowers engage in an exchange process in which both parties collaborate and reinforce each other's activities.

Consider the example provided by Fred Smith at Federal Express. His vision started with the basic need for fast delivery of goods and information, the basic concept of a switching system, and has resulted in an efficient and valued worldwide delivery service. His ability to envision the finished system at its conception, despite ridicule and nay saying, is what vision is all about.[29] Furthermore, his vision was backed with the nuts-and-bolts know-how and follow-through to make the system operational. Vision is not pie-in-the-sky dreaming, but is the ability to take a long-run perspective in determining how consumer needs and producer capabilities will be matched profitably.

## Communicate Effectively

It is one thing for a leader to articulate a vision. It is quite another for employees, customers, and other significant audiences to understand the vision.

If everyone in the organization is to understand and integrate the vision into both individual and team efforts, a leader must communicate what actions and attitudes are needed clearly, creatively, and consistently. These communications are part of the core internal marketing process. Substance is key, but style helps, too—whether that involves visiting employees at their work stations and talking about customer service issues or other scheduled and unscheduled meetings with employees.

A leader also must understand the organization and its inner workings—not just the organization chart. At the Disney Corporation, this type of understanding is accomplished in part through the cross-utilization of employees.[30] Employees trade roles for certain periods of time to get a firsthand knowledge of exactly what goes on within all levels of the organization. This type of lateral communication is valuable because it helps to break down the functional barriers that interfere with delivering quality service to customers.

Bottom-up communication is one of the most valuable, but overlooked, communication routes. When employees understand their roles in serving customers and the service company's strategies, they become a valuable source of information about such components of service quality as customers' expectations, gaps in the service delivery system, ways in which service can be improved, and the support employees need to serve customers well. Peat Marwick's Horner wants "ideas from the people who are going to implement them" and wants those ideas "to be thought through and challenged by individuals in daily contact with clients."[31]

When internal communication systems are complementary and reinforcing, communications improve with outside audiences, such as clients, potential clients, stockholders, the press, and potential employees. Many service organizations suffer because they present such diffuse messages (in effect, "We can do anything . . .") that their audiences become confused and unsure of what the service organization represents or does—the organization has no identifiable position. An organization's leaders must understand communication principles and use them effectively.

## Position the Organization

Positioning involves charting a course and staying with it. The process begins with defining a position, or niche, and then establishing and maintaining it. "Defining a position" means specifying exactly the market segment you serve, how you serve that group uniquely, and how you define quality. For example, Charles Schwab has tapped the price-sensitive investment market with no-frills investing services. Each department or unit, and the organization as a whole, must focus on what is critical to the attainment of that position—in the case of Schwab, efficient service delivery systems.

The organization's internal consistency is integral to positioning. The left hand (e.g., marketing) needs to know what the right hand (e.g., operations) is doing as they work toward a common goal. The degree of internal consistency correlates with the organization's corporate integrity—making sure promises to customers are fulfilled and that standards are upheld. The degree of correlation is another indication of quality.

## Four Distinctive Personal Characteristics of Leaders

The effective leader possesses three interrelated characteristics dealing with strengths and one involved with getting results. The first characteristic is knowledge of his or her strengths. The second is the capacity to develop these strengths. The third is the ability to see how these strengths mesh with the organization's needs. A symbiosis between the personality of the organization and the personality of the leader is required.

A fourth characteristic shared by effective leaders is their ability to focus on achieving objectives. They are not afraid of making mistakes; they view them as part of learning. The critical point is that they do not allow themselves to be distracted by thoughts of failure. Their passion and optimism prevail.

The effective leader creates a vision, communicates well throughout the organization, positions the organization, and manages himself or herself. Jan Carlzon, who effectively led Scandinavian Airlines System out of the red in just a year's time, offers the following anecdote:

> There is no better way to sum up my experience (with leadership) than with the story about the two stonecutters who were chipping square blocks out of granite. A visitor to the quarry asked what they were doing.
>
> The first stonecutter, looking rather sour, grumbled, "I'm cutting this damned stone into a block."
>
> The second, who looked pleased with his work, replied proudly, "I'm on this team that's building a cathedral."
>
> A worker who can envision the whole cathedral and who has been given responsibility for constructing his own portion of it is far more satisfied and productive than the worker who sees only the granite before him. A true leader is one who designs the cathedral and then shares the vision that inspires others to build it.[32]

## What About Power?

You are probably wondering how a leader's ability to inspire others relates to power, an attribute many associate with leadership. In many ways, though, power is antithetical to effective leadership.

Power is an attribute many of us associate with leaders. Bennis and Nanus define the relationship this way: "Power is the capacity to translate intention into reality and sustain it. Leadership is the wise use of this power."[33] The way effective leaders are wisely using power today is by *empowering* others to create the means of attaining a vision and sustaining it. Kenneth Olsen, CEO of Digital Equipment, says, "I've got no power. All I can do is encourage people, motivate people to do things. I've got no power over them."[34] In a service organization, it is not "Do as I say," it's "Do as I do."

By empowering others, the effective leader helps people:

- Believe that they are doing something significant not only for themselves, but also in a larger sphere.
- Develop their competencies on the job.
- Experience a sense of community by working together to achieve common goals.
- Have fun and enjoy what they are doing.

When employees are empowered, the effective leader can depend on the support and goal-directed activities needed to sustain the vision. People are not being forced to do things against their wills. Rather, they believe in what they are doing—they are part owners of the vision. It actually involves trust—"You can't expect them (your employees) to go all out for you if they think you don't believe in them."[35] The potential to provide quality service is within people. It is the leader's challenge to tap that potential.

## Notes

1. "Pul-eeze! Will Somebody Help Me? Frustrated American Consumers Wonder Where the Service Went," *Time*, February 2, 1987, 48–55.
2. Richard Normann, *Service Management* (New York: Wiley, 1984), 112.
3. "Biting the Bullet," *The Quality Review*, American Society for Quality Control, Milwaukee, 1987, 32–36.
4. John Holusha, "Stress on Quality Lifts Xerox's Market Share," *New York Times*, November 9, 1989, D1 and D11.
5. Steve Blickstein, "It's in the Cards," *The Quality Review*, American Society for Quality Control, Milwaukee, 1987, 4.
6. John Goodman, Arlene Malech, and Theodore Marra, "I Can't Get No Satisfaction," *The Quality Review*, American Society for Quality Control, Milwaukee, 1987, 10–14.
7. Christian Grönroos, "Internal Marketing—Theory and Practice," in *Services Marketing in a Changing Environment: Proceedings*, ed. Thomas M. Bloch, Gregory

D. Upah, and Valarie A. Zeithaml (Chicago: American Marketing Association, 1985), 41–47.

8. Theodore Levitt, "The Industrialization of Service," in *The Marketing Imagination* (New York: Free Press, 1983).

9. Valarie A. Zeithaml, Leonard L. Berry, and A. Parasuraman, *Communication and Control Processes in the Delivery of Service Quality* (Cambridge, Mass.: Marketing Science Institute, 1987).

10. Peter G. Klaus, "Quality Epiphenomenon: The Conceptual Understanding of Quality in Face-to-Face Service Encounters," in *The Service Encounter: Managing Employee/Customer Interaction in Service Businesses,* ed. John A. Czepiel, Michael R. Solomon, and Carol F. Surprenant (Lexington, Mass.: Lexington Books, 1985), 23–28.

11. Written correspondence.

12. Written correspondence.

13. Examples are from a letter by Don McNeill to "Dear Abby," *New York Post,* August 2, 1988.

14. Written correspondence.

15. Written correspondence.

16. Written correspondence.

17. John F. Andrews, et al., "Service Quality Surveys in a Telecommunications Environment: An Integrating Force," in *The Services Challenge: Integrating for Competitive Advantage,* ed. John A. Czepiel, Carole A. Congram, and James B. Shanahan (Chicago: American Marketing Association, 1987), 27–31.

18. Carole A. Congram, John A. Czepiel, and James B. Shanahan, "Achieving Internal Integration in Service Organizations," in *The Services Challenge: Integrating for Competitive Advantage,* ed. John A. Czepiel, Carole A. Congram, and James B. Shanahan (Chicago: American Marketing Association, 1987), 5.

19. Congram, Czepiel, and Shanahan, "Achieving Internal Integration," 6.

20. John J. Falzon, "Met Life's Quest for Quality," *The Journal of Services Marketing* 2, no. 2 (Spring 1988): 61–64.

21. Carol Hymowitz, "Which Corporate Culture Fits You?" *Wall Street Journal,* July 17, 1989, B1.

22. Ben Schneider and David E. Bowen, "Employee and Customer Perceptions of Service in Banks: Replication and Extension," *Journal of Applied Psychology* 70, no. 3 (1985): 423–433.

23. Written correspondence.

24. Written correspondence.

25. Written correspondence.

26. From a letter by Don McNeill to "Dear Abby," *New York Post,* August 2, 1988.

27. Warren Bennis, "Leadership From Inside and Out," *Fortune,* January 18, 1988, 173.

28. John P. Kotter, *The Leadership Factor* (New York: Free Press, 1988).

29. Stanley M. Davis, *Future Perfect* (Reading, Mass.: Addison-Wesley 1987), 206–219.

30. N. W. Pope, "Mickey Mouse Marketing," *American Banker,* July 25, 1979; and "More Mickey Mouse Marketing," *American Banker,* September 12, 1979.

31. Written correspondence.

32. Jan Carlzon, *Moments of Truth* (New York: Ballinger, 1987), 135.

33. Warren Bennis and Burt Nanus, *Leaders: The Strategies for Taking Charge* (New York: Harper & Row, 1985), 17.

34. "Not Power But Empower," *Forbes,* May 30, 1988, 120.

35. Kenneth Labich, "The Seven Keys to Business Leadership," *Fortune*, October 24, 1988, 58–66.

\*    \*    \*    \*

***Carole A. Congram,*** *Ph.D., is the principal of Congram Associates, a consulting firm based in New York City and specializing in services marketing. She assists clients with a broad range of planning and implementation services. She also holds the position of associate professor of operations management at Bentley College in Waltham, Massachusetts. A frequent speaker on services marketing topics, she was on the national marketing staff of Touche Ross & Co. for eleven years, most recently as director of marketing communication planning.*

***Margaret L. Friedman,*** *Ph.D., is assistant professor in the marketing department of the College of Business and Economics, University of Wisconsin-Whitewater. She teaches courses in consumer behavior and personal selling and has developed an undergraduate course in services marketing. She previously served as director of service sector marketing programs at the university's Management Institute, the continuing education unit of the School of Business at Madison. She has worked as a consultant with a variety of service sector businesses.*

*The authors contributed equally to this chapter.*

# PART II

# CUSTOMER-FOCUSED STRATEGIES FOR SERVICE ORGANIZATIONS

# About This Part

A focus on customer needs and customer satisfaction is fundamental to effective marketing. Sounds easy enough. What it requires, however, is seeing the world from your customers' point of view, and that is not easy. Many product marketers can be criticized for focusing on products and their features and ignoring the benefits customers are hoping to obtain from purchase and product use. We experience this perspective firsthand as consumers when we have to deal with the overzealous salesperson who "pushes" products with little regard for our needs. Similarly, service marketers run the same risk—focusing on what they do, what expertise they have, what processes they perform—losing sight of what benefit customers are trying to obtain by purchasing a service. It is the customers' perspective of service quality that has to drive marketing programs.

The chapters in this part address the issues involved in saturating and permeating your conception of your business with a customer focus. And so, although we hesitate to label the three chapters in this part *the most* important chapters in the *Handbook,* lest you stop reading after Chapter 4, we put them first for a reason. The issues addressed are basic and fundamental. If your attitudes and perceptions about what you do are not infused with a customer focus, there is no way—barring dumb luck—that your marketing actions will have the customer focus required for success.

Chapter 2 takes a deceivingly trivial question—"What Business Are We In?"—and makes you fully appreciate the effort needed to answer it adequately, in a way that propels your marketing efforts in the right direction. A six-step process is explained that clearly specifies what you need to do to answer this "simple" question. The process takes account of the unique nature of services and, therefore, speaks to the exceptional aspects of producing an intangible. Critical to the six-step process described is research—research inside the service organization (a sort of soul searching) and, perhaps more important, gathering information from customers. There is not a single chapter in this *Handbook* that does not talk about research, and so there is no better time than the present to begin to see how it can work for you.

This chapter may shake you up a bit, because it suggests that you question the old, comfortable ways of finding the answer to the question "What Business Are We In?" The process described not only gets you focused on the customer, but on the future as well so that you are sure to be a contender in the competitive ring.

Chapter 3 discusses the relatively new but proven marketing tool, positioning. Positioning concerns how you communicate with your customers about your service. The power of positioning lies in its ability to cut through the information overload that bombards consumers. It is a way to give your marketing message a better chance of being heard and retained. The intangible nature of services precludes the shelf-space visibility products enjoy. Therefore, for services, the mental space in consumers' minds established through an effective positioning strategy is all the more critical.

Chapter 4, "Developing Strategies in Service Organizations," discusses the fundamental role of strategic planning in business development and operation, and provides special provisos for service marketers. Prerequisites to strategic planning are covered, particularly a clear mission statement, position statement, and objectives. An interesting portion on how to organize the planning effort and how to identify the key players in the planning process is provided. The relevant environmental context for strategic planning is presented on both the macro and micro levels, followed by an in-depth description of the steps in the strategic planning process. Tangible products of this process are discussed as well as the implementation plan, including tactical plans, which must derive from the strategic plan.

As a package, these three chapters provide the strategic foundation upon which tactical planning and implementation depend. The advice and guidelines provided in the chapters that follow will "work" only if the organization is strategically focused on the customer.

# 2

# "What Business Are We In?"

Dave Masterson

It's a simple question, one that gets asked at various times in practically any organization. For some, it's asked once a year during the allotted time for strategic planning. For some, it's asked when a new entrepreneurial effort is budding. For some, it's asked when merger or acquisition debates are raging. And usually the answer seems obvious! "We're in the hotel business, restaurant business, insurance business, airline business, banking business," and so on. But this industry-classification answer is seldom adequate, and the simple question gets asked again. This time more deliberate answers emerge: "We're in the business of providing dining experiences" or "We're in the business of helping people reach their financial goals." Not-for-profit endeavors also have their answers: "We're in the business of raising money for the underprivileged." But somehow these answers are also inadequate as a marketing statement. It's a simple question. Depending upon the tenacity of the person assigned as devil's advocate, answers can sometimes reach lofty levels of esoterica: "We're in the people business! We're people. Our employees are people. Our customers are people. . . . We're obviously in the people business." It's a simple question.

## A Not-So-Simple Answer

For a service industry marketing practitioner, the question may be simple, but it requires complex answers. And there are no "right" answers. The answer to this question is based on the perspective of the person (or group) creating the answer. Unless senior managers are arbitrarily forcing "right" answers, various constituencies will have differing opinions as to what business the organization is in. The challenge for the marketing practitioner is to elicit the various answers, remove the corporate "party line," and synthesize an answer that gives the organization strategic marketing direction.

## A Critical Question and Answer for Service Organizations

The marketing differences between providers of goods and providers of services received considerable attention during the 1970s and 1980s.[1] Providers of goods have the luxury of fairly discrete functions of inventory, manufacturing, and distribution. Here the marketing function is positioned comfortably between these functions and the customers.

Providers of services have no such luxury, however. Inventory, manufacturing, and distribution all blur into a single function of "doing" or "performing." Additionally, this doing or performing is in concert with the customer and, to a large extent, under the control of the customer. The next time you get your hair cut, have your tax return prepared, call long distance, or travel to Washington, ask yourself what the service provider would be providing if you were not participating! Here the marketing function is uncomfortably homogenized into the entire service organization.[2]

Service organizations essentially deliver two things—customer interface experiences and customer capability. A few examples help. Insurance companies provide customer interface experiences when the customer deals with an agent or files a claim. Insurance companies then give the customer the capability to externalize and mitigate some form of risk. Hair stylists provide customer interface experiences while the client is in the shop or when the client calls to make an appointment. Hair stylists then give the customer the capability of functioning in society with a more positive self image. Airlines provide interface experiences to customers when the customer reclaims baggage, gets bumped from an overbooked flight, or reads from an airport monitor a new "on time" schedule that is mysteriously fourteen minutes later than the previous "on time" schedule. Airlines then give their customers the capability of conducting some portion of their lives in a different part of the world.

Because service entities provide customer interface experiences and customer capabilities, our simple question needs a two-part answer. For us, the focus of our answer must be on the customer experiences and the customer capabilities we deliver.

But it is in getting to this two-part answer that we encounter difficulty. Usually we obtain our answers through some form of strategic planning or marketing planning. This process can simply involve notes jotted on the back of an envelope or results from a specialized staff's computer-assisted analysis. Regardless of methodology, the perspective and assumptions[3] of the planners involved will affect the planning process and hence "the answers." The process involves accumulating data from which management draws predictive conclusions about the future. Ideally, these data should be quite broad, very timely, accurate, and free from methodological bias. They aren't. Furthermore, the various pieces of data should carry the "correct" relative importance in management's decision-making process. They don't.

The underlying data are seldom complete, let alone methodologically unbiased. And managers frequently dwell on only a few facts. More planning processes today also generate income statements and balance sheets for each year of the planning horizon. These financials usually carry the requisite "return on . . ." performance ratios.

With all of the best intentions in the world, a process originally designed to answer our fundamental "simple" question frequently degrades into an iterative number-crunching cycle to generate numbers that "build stockholder wealth at a rate superior to our industry peers." The process focuses on the scorecard instead of focusing on the game.

# Six Steps in Defining Your Business

How does the service sector practitioner deal with services differences, normal human bias in data and processes, and the tendency to plan the financial scorecard rather than operational causes? A six-step process is recommended to deal with these service sector marketing difficulties:

1. Document your company's "inside-out" perceptions.
2. Research the market's "outside-in" perceptions.
3. Sketch the future of the company-to-customer interface and the customer capability.
4. Predict competitor focus.
5. Define culturally dependent causative factors.
6. Adjust and refine your plans. (Focus on operational causes, not financial scorecards.)

If there is a formal planning process and resultant plan in place, this proposed procedure can be used as a fairly quick critical review of both the process and the plan. If no formal planning process is in place, this procedure can also be used as a basic structure to arrive at some strategic plans. Service organizations create customer interface experiences and customer capabilities. This process focuses on these two critical parts of our answer to "What business are we in?"

## Document Your Company's Inside-Out Perceptions

Have you ever dealt with a service company's employees who obviously knew more about the company's PR slogans than they knew about your needs? They're everywhere. "We're the largest firm in this business." "We were the first organization to offer . . ." or "Our chef graduated from the best schools."

If you deal with commercial business-to-business service providers, you've heard it in different ways. "But we'll stand by you over the *long* haul" or *"Our* service is excellent." Then there are those whose internal marketing is working better than their external marketing. "It's our people that make us better!" And, once in a while, we're graced with the classic marketing contradiction of our time: "But quality costs more!" Normal customer reaction to these insults ranges from "Who cares?" all the way to expletives that can't be printed here.

Why are prospects and customers subjected to these meaningless exhortations? It's because the speakers, and probably the firms they represent, have an "inside-out" perspective. For them, market reality is defined in terms of their perceived priorities and their standards, almost always in terms of their perceived strengths.[4] Seldom do these exhortations add anything either to the customer interface experience or to the customer's delivered capability.

## "Inside-Out-Itis"

Unfortunately, we are all susceptible to this "inside-out-itis."[5] We simply have more information, more insight, and more day-to-day experience with our own organization than we have with the marketplace at large. Additionally, we cultivate and cherish organizational pride as a source of organizational strength. But this pride can also be blinding. If we are big, we think big is good for the customer—stability, you know! If we're small, we think small is good for the customer—responsive and flexible! We even begin to believe that balance-sheet strength, technological capability, or established customer relationships ensure us de facto success in any endeavor. Not so. We need to learn this lesson from our manufacturing predecessors. General Electric and Xerox represent just two examples. They are both strong and proud organizations with large customer bases. Both companies entered the data processing/computer business and tried to compete with IBM. Both failed.

We need to separate internally defined perspectives of market reality from customer-defined perspectives of reality. We must proactively identify our internal biases, get them out on the planning table, and keep them in front of us.

To do this, you need a Columbo-like detective. You need someone to ask a lot of seemingly stupid questions of a lot of knowledgeable employees and managers. You need to ask the obvious of your organization. Assign an "ignorant" interviewer or group of interviewers to ask good probing questions of a cross section of your organization. This process works for large companies or divisions, and smaller, independent service companies, as well as not-for-profit service organizations. The idea is to get a clear understanding of the blinding and misleading biases defining the organization's answer to our simple question.

This interviewing is a job for someone who is little attuned to internal bias and who is ignorant of the party line. It is a job for people with fairly good questioning and listening skills. Corporate naïveté is a plus. In fact, company naïveté is a bigger asset than questioning skills because you can give your interviewer good questions to ask. You can't give your interviewer nonbias. For interviewing candidates, look to your youngest or newest ranks. The newest sales trainee or the most recently hired marketing analyst frequently works out well. Consider hiring a college intern for a few months. Don't hire the owner's son or the founder's granddaughter! (You need to find bias, not create more!)

Design an interview structure for your detective. Here you want a sequence of questions that will make sense to virtually any employee or manager. Questions should be open and nonthreatening. Closed, yes/no questions capture almost no perceptual bias. Threatening "gotcha" questions destroy the whole process. Since your interviewees will see your Columbo-like detective to be somewhat uninformed, your questions can be brilliantly ignorant.

## Thirteen Suggested Questions

As a catalyst for creating your interview, consider these few sample questions:

1. Who are our customers?
2. Why do people pay us to do whatever it is we do for them?
3. What do we (our division, company, etc.) do?
4. If you couldn't use the word *customer,* how would you describe the people who spend their money with us?
5. What do our customers receive from us?

6. When a customer is interacting with us, what is important to him or her?
7. What causes the timing of customers' purchases?
8. Who influences our customers in their choice of our services?
9. Who are our competitors?
10. What role does your department/area play in satisfying our customers' needs?
11. What is our "product"?
12. How do we add value?
13. What capability do we provide to our customers?

These are only ideas. Use these questions or others as you see fit. A word about apparent redundancy in your questions. "What do we do?" sounds a lot like "What do we do for our customers?" and "How do we add value?" Don't be too hasty to be "efficient" with your questions. "What do we do?" will usually elicit a process answer or a customer interface answer. "What do we do for our customers?" will usually elicit customer capability answers or a list of customer benefits. "How do we add value?" will sometimes elicit blank stares but will usually draw out the organization's party line. These differences are the exact things you're looking for. They will define your inside-out perspective, discover any "watch my lips" management "right" answers, and alert you to departmental and divisional myopia.

Also, don't be overly concerned about asking directly about your organization's strengths and weaknesses. Perceived strengths and the organizational ego will be glaringly evident in the answers to your questions. And the organizational weakness you're looking for will be quite apparent as inside-out bias and organizational party-line answers surface. Keep your questions open-ended. Concentrate on perceptions concerning customer interface experiences and delivered customer capability.

## Whom to Interview

Those you interview should be people from a diverse cross section of the organization—diverse across function and diverse across rank. Be sure to interview some representative of every customer interface function. Obviously this includes your direct contact personnel—salespeople, waitresses, pilots, tellers, hair stylists, and such. But be sure to include your not-so-obvious indirect contact areas too. Include personnel such as receptionists, switchboard operators, garage attendants, doormen, reservationists, and busboys.

Keep your interviewing campaign low-key. Open managers' doors for your interviewer, but this is no time for Fourth of July promotions. Get your interviewer with your salespeople, but don't make a recognition program of it. Visit with your back-room operations, but this is not an organizational design review. You want to document normal everyday perceptions with as little Hawthorne effect as possible.

After your interviews are complete, group the responses based upon whether the respondents have or do not have direct customer interface. Then document frequently used terminology and responses that are similar. Cross-group differences in your answers reflect the functional myopia and internal biases for which you are looking.

### Research the Market's "Outside-In Perspective"

Regardless of internal perspectives, it is the customers' perceptions of service offerings and the market that influence purchasing behavior. The customer defines reality. Once you have documented your internal perceptions and biases of the market, you must acquire the customer's perceptions and biases of your offerings and your competitors' offerings.

Measuring Multiple Issues. This is a place for multi-attribute quantitative research—not focus groups, traffic interviews, or simple attribute-ranking customer surveys. Since you will project your findings to the market at large, you want a statistically valid handle on the following five issues:

1. Which attributes of the customer interface experience and delivered customer capability are most discriminating for the buyer?
2. Based upon these attributes, how is your company or service perceived to be positioned?
3. How are your competitors or their offerings perceived to be positioned relative to these attributes?
4. How is your company or service perceived to be positioned relative to your competitors?
5. What combinations of attributes do various segments of the market want, and who is perceived to be delivering those combinations best?

A service organization has more difficulty addressing these issues than does a manufacturing organization. All buying is based upon buyer perception, but buyer perceptions for services are more volatile and arbitrary. Lack of tangibility and difficulty of prepurchase comparability are the main causes of this difficulty. Therefore, research methodologies and research competency are even more important for services research.

A Place for "Advanced" Statistics. Whether you use in-house research staff or purchase services from a market research firm, I suggest you use some of the more advanced statistical methodologies. Attribute discriminations, perceived relative positioning, customer trade-off decisions, and clustered segmentations require some research sophistication. Simple importance rankings and top box/bottom box-scoring processes won't do here. Consider either pair-wise or full-profile conjoint analysis reported via perceptual mapping. With competent execution, these methods work well for services marketing research. These methods deal with the complex attribute interplay associated with services. Additionally, they can deliver actionable information out of megatons of data.

A few words of caution. Be sure your research design encompasses both the customer-delivered capability and the customer interface experience. Also, because prepurchase comparison is so difficult for services, be sure to analyze perceived benefits as well as objective attributes, such as price.

To measure delivered capability, include attributes of services in the design. In transportation, for example, ask about perceptions concerning departure and arrival schedules, destination cities, and en route beverage service. In the insurance industry, for example, ask about perceptions concerning breadth of product line, dividend performance on policies, and policy upgrades. To measure interface experiences, ask about perceptions concerning how customers are treated. Are customer-contact people courteous, knowledgeable about products, willing to render assistance, responsive to inquiry? Are people and facilities convenient for the customer? Do incoming phone calls get rerouted multiple times before the customer receives the assistance needed?

A valid design must address both delivered capability issues and customer interface issues. In addition to documenting the market's outside-in perspective of your firm or service, this type of research can be used for strategic and tactical decision making as well. (For application of mapping to positioning strategy, see Chapter 3.)

## Sketch the Future

Once you've done your "inside-out" interviewing and completed your "outside-in" marketing research, you have two somewhat contrasting views of the situation. In order to either test an in-place marketing plan or create a new marketing plan, some judgments about the future must be made. Normally, this endeavor would encompass projecting industry trends as well as estimating future impact of macro issues, such as the globalization of markets and the shift of our economic base away from manufacturing.

In addition to these macro issues, service firms must pay particular attention to both the customer interface experience of the future and the delivered capability of the future. The more difficult of these issues is the customer interface. The focus here is on describing *how* the customer will interface with your organization of the future. This aspect of services marketing is quite dynamic, and miscalculating the interface of the future can be costly.

Examples of customer interface changes are everywhere. Not long ago, fast-food restaurants delivered their service across stainless steel counters. Then, in many locations, drive-through windows appeared. Then came a series of two drive-through windows. Presumably the delivered customer capability, subsistence for the next period of time, has not changed significantly, but the customer interface has. What used to be an exchange with a single human being who took your order, took your money, and presented your food is now a separate three-step process. Today, customers stay in their cars, "communicate" with a speaker/microphone, give their money to one human being at the first window, and receive their food from another at the second window. Changing from small fries to large fries is a whole new adventure under this system!

A banking customer used to visit a local branch or telephone a customer support representative in order to get account balances or find out whether a check had cleared. Today this interface is done via Touch-Tone telephones and talking computers.

The media entertainment customer interface has changed as well. Seeing the latest Hollywood production used to involve standing in line at the box office, paying popcorn and candy prices that gave "captive audience selling" a bad name, and laughing at jokes because everyone else in the audience was laughing. Today the interface is with video rental clerks or catalogs. Now you're on your own for ambience.

What will your customer interface experience be like in the future? Although interfaces will vary drastically from one industry to another, a few questions can help you to sketch possible future scenarios.

<u>What to Look For.</u>  Try to imagine possible changes as you answer the following five questions:

1. *What role does two-way communication play in the delivery of the customer capability?* If it is small, customer interface changes are likely.

2. *What role does technology play (or could it play) in delivering the information component of the customer capability?*

3. *How much of the delivered customer capability is delivered and absorbed concurrently via the customer interface process?* The offering of an elegant dining experience is more likely to remain brick-and-mortar intensive than is the offering of pizza. Takeout and home delivery of pizza can obviate the need for on-site brick-and-mortar.

4. *How could customers avoid the need for the delivered capability entirely, or how might the capability be acquired with no direct interface at all?* Retailers might not need check-verification services if their customers were to go entirely to debit cards.

5. *How might your "selling" customer interface overlap or be delivered concurrent with that of a noncompetitor?* Airline reservations, rental car reservations, and hotel reservations are frequently accomplished via one customer interface. Are similar noncompetitor alliances possible in your business?

Attempt to be imaginative and generate various scenarios of what your customer interface might look like.

## Predict Competitor Focus

One remaining set of external information is needed before you can create or adjust an in-place strategic marketing plan: What do you think your competitors will do? It's important to consider this before committing yourself to a course of action, because there is no customer-perceived differentiation if two or more organizations do the same thing.

<u>Look at Direct and Indirect Competitors.</u>  If you have not done so already, divide your competitors into two groups: direct competitors and indirect

competitors. For the sake of this discussion, direct competitors are those who are in your line of business and who compete directly for your customers. Indirect competitors are those who can circumvent entirely the customer's need for your service, or they can be those who are not in your line of business but compete for your customer's money. These two groups of competitors will probably act differently in the future.

If you are in the banking business and make commercial loans to large companies, you have direct and indirect competitors. Your direct competitors are other commercial banks making commercial loans to large companies. Your indirect competitors are those who can give commercial companies direct access to the paper markets and circumvent the intermediary banking function entirely. If you are in the overnight courier business, your direct competitors are other air couriers. Your indirect competitors may be those who manufacture and sell facsimile machines. These two rather obvious examples of indirect competitors make a point. Paper brokers and facsimile manufacturers will probably behave differently in the future than will banks and air couriers. It's important to identify these two different groups of competitors. Direct competitors will typically fight for, and influence, market share. Indirect competitors can, and frequently do, influence the total size of the market as you define it. They frequently shrink it!

What are your competitors likely to do in the future? A normal tendency here is to study the strengths and weaknesses of each competitor and predict action accordingly. Follow these normal tendencies, but also try to estimate your competitors' perspectives of the future. Their perspectives of strengths, weaknesses, and future markets will be different than your perspectives. What are their internal management biases? What syndicated or proprietary research has been done recently? If a research firm has been busy asking questions, someone has been paying to obtain answers. If a syndicated study is available, chances are that some competitor or competitors are reading the results and recommendations of those syndicated studies. If they are, how are they likely to conduct themselves?

Trends Are Not Strategies.    As you look at your information, be sure to separate competitor strategies from industry trends. Your strategy needs to incorporate how you will deal with your industry trends, but mistaking a trend for a strategy can be costly. Occasion expansion in the fast-food industry is an example. Burgers-and-fries establishments realized that there was a growing customer need for on-the-way-to-work breakfast service. They also realized that adding the breakfast occasion would increase revenue per fixed asset. This quickly became an industry trend. But being open for breakfast is not a competitive strategy per se. Both customer experience differentiation and customer capability differentiation exist within this relatively new breakfast occurrence. McDonald's Egg McMuffin was different from Bojangle's Bo-To-Go. Both differed from Kentucky Fried Chicken's Open for Breakfast strategy. Two were pursuing differentiation strategies, whereas one was following an industry trend.

Another example of competitive strategy versus industry trend is found in the current vogue of "Quality" and "Service Manner." Service quality is generally considered to be relatively poor in the United States.[6] Because of this, and the obvious competitive advantages good service generates, many American service industries and service companies are stressing service quality. "We will compete based on the quality of our service," or "Our service will be the standard of our industry" are frequently heard in management meetings and read in annual reports. Although this is progress in an environment where customers are pleading for quality service, competing based upon quality will only keep you even with the competition. It's a trend, not a viable differentiation strategy. From the customers' perspectives, you must be different.

If those in your industry are looking at comparable data and drawing comparable conclusions, various "strategies" will simply homogenize into industry trends. Predict competitor strategies and identify probable trends. Accommodate the trend, but find some positive way to be perceived differently by the market you serve!

## Define Culturally Dependent Causative Factors

By the time you have explored probable competitor strategies, you will have a fairly good idea about which particular strategy you may want to execute. But before you begin to review your in-place plan or start to write a new one, look for your cultural hurdles.[7] Regardless of what strategy you choose, it will either be executed, or not executed, based upon two things: your delivery of the customer's interface experience and your delivery of customer capability. Both depend on employee behavior. From the customer's perspective, your organization *is* what your customer-contact people *do*. The rubber meets the road when your people are eye-to-eye, telephone-to-telephone, letter-to-letter, and handshake-to-handshake with the customer.

Precious Opportunities.    Everything within a service organization must be focused on that precious opportunity of interfacing with the customer. Albrecht and Zemke said it well: "If you're not serving the customer, you'd better be serving someone who is."[8] Behaviorally, strategic execution in this setting depends upon three interdependent constituencies: external customers, internal customers, and employees. Obviously, external customers' needs and expectations must be met. But in order for this to happen successfully, your customer-contact employees must be the internal customers of every other functional area of the organization. For this to become a reality, employees as a whole must be management's "customers."

Enter culture. It's reasonably easy to understand that your external customers rely on customer-contact employees, who in turn rely on every other functional department, whose employees in turn rely on their management to empower them and to lead them. Executionally, this is a much trickier concept. Go back and look at your results from step 1—Document your company's inside-out perceptions. When you asked a manager or a departmental employee about "customers," how often did you hear about other employees or your customer-contact people?

What is your organization's culture, and how does it affect employee behavior? Is management's style autocratic or influencing? What is the balance of internally focused effort and measurement, and externally focused effort and measurement? What drives decision making? Chances are that your Information Management Systems area is managed by data processing professionals, your accounting function is managed by accounting professionals, and your personnel function is managed by personnel specialists. Extend these functional perspectives into your management team's style.

Herein lie cultural hurdles. Whatever your chosen strategy, success will depend upon employee and management behavior. Behavior is very sensitive to culture and management style. A former IBM executive had a saying that highlights this fact well: "Managers and employees don't need to be told; they need to be allowed." Deciding what behaviors are needed for success is the easy part. Empowering and "allowing" that behavior is much more difficult. Strategically, you want to decide what can and must be done to loosen the cultural harnesses and free your organization to focus on the precious opportunities of customer interface.

## Adjust and Refine Your Plans

Having completed the five previous steps in this process, you are now ready to adjust your in-place plan or create your new one. You've dealt with the "difference" issues of services marketing. Your Columbo detective has documented your internal biases. Market research has given you the market's perspective of your offerings and your competitors' offerings. You've estimated the customer interface of the future. You've estimated competitor strategy and separated viable strategies from industry trends. And you've taken a hard look at how your organizational culture might impede strategy execution.

So, "What Business Are You In?"  Before you answer our "simple" question for your organization, some before-and-after examples may be of interest. Prior to using this process, a certain downtown high-rise hotel was in the "upscale hotel business" for business clientele. After using this process, the hotel's answer became, "Through every employee's behavior toward our guests, we help reflect a success image to our guests and we help them positively position themselves with their prospects and clients in our city." Notice how this answer focuses on everyone's responsibility to *behave* toward, and for, the customer. Everything in the environment and every interaction with guests reflects success on the customer. In addition, the "positively position themselves with their prospects and clients in our city" phrase focuses on a point of differentiation for this hotel. The nuance of "we help" also has significance. There is no lofty "we *will* help" in this answer. "We help" focuses on here, now, today! It also reflects the fact that the customer is ultimately in control and that some customers are impossible to please. This caused good "buy in" with front-line employees who had previously rejected earlier absolutes about the customer always being right. This answer improved on some internal departmental myopia, got away from "be friendly" directives for staff, and broadened the definition of customer needs. Obviously, this answer is neither right nor wrong. It is simply a "better" answer for this particular organization.

A second example of a before-and-after answer centers on an insurance company. This company's "before" answer simply placed it in the business of selling insurance policies to individuals in order to mitigate financial risk. After this process was used, the answer became, "Through working with our customers, we enrich their lives by lowering certain anxieties and by helping them to better meet their responsibilities to loved ones." Here the answer focuses on "working with" rather than "selling to." The company believes that this is shifting employees toward long-term relationships and an advisory role with customers. This answer also stresses life enrichment, anxiety reduction, and helping that, in turn, has focused a new and healthy attention on such issues as legal jargon in policies, data overload on sample insurance programs for prospects, and misrouted telephone inquiries at headquarters. It also casts light on the customer's customers—their loved ones. This is helping to resensitize the firm to the ultimate beneficiary. As in the preceding hotel example, the answer is neither right nor wrong. But for this company, the answer's simplicity is helping to hasten some much needed change and facilitating some internal streamlining.

Once you have completed this six-step process, you probably will have a more satisfying answer to our "simple" question. Usually by this point, one or two new facets of a desirable strategy have surfaced, and they usually appear to be almost self-evident. Frequently, there are differences between a new plan and your original, in-place plan.

Time for Safety Checks.    Check for the focus of your plans. Ensure that it is based on those precious opportunities of customer interfaces of the future. Everything in both your plan and your organization must peak at these occurrences. Check your plan for proactive management of cultural issues. Be sure to help your functional specialists—for example, data processing and finance professionals—understand their customers' needs. Check for tactical plans that focus on causative behavior. You want to manage the processes, not the accounting scorecards.

Document the gaps between your organization's internal perspective, the market's outside-in perspective, and your original plan. Review your original plan for "strategy," which may in fact become a homogenized industry trend. Check your plan for definitions of desired employee behavior in the future. What will your people *do?*

Take another look at your direct and indirect competitors. Now that you've tried to anticipate how each will act in the future, review your original plan in this context. How will the customer of the future see differences between you and your competitors? If you have indirect competitors who may shrink the size of the market as you know it, how will your plan deal with this possible shrinkage?

Review your in-place plan, taking into account your estimate of possible changes in the customer interface experience. How are you planning to apply technology changes to your customer experiences? How does your plan accommodate possible changes in cost structure, such as the possible elimination of brick-and-mortar facilities? Perhaps there are some noncompetitor alliances that your original plan overlooked.

In short, review your original plan in light of your results from this process. Most clients who have used this process find "holes" in their original plan and make subsequent adjustments to their plans.

## Summary

Service organizations essentially deliver two things: customer interface experiences and customer capability. The customer interface is the service company's most precious resource. It is through these experiences that the company delivers capability to the customer and the customer forms experiential impressions of the company.

Virtually any attempt to answer the simple question of "What business are we in?" is laden with bias, data imperfections, and future unknowns. This six-step process is a method that can help service organizations with these common planning difficulties. This process can be used as a relatively quick critical review of an in-place strategic marketing plan for any service organization. It can also be used as a relatively simple structure to initiate a strategic plan if one is not yet in place. It challenges internal party line and blinding corporate ego. It can thus mitigate a major planning risk. It uses research methodologies that measure the customer's perspective of reality, and thus helps you to see your plan through the customers' eyes. It helps sketch the customer interface of the future while looking for trends within competitor strategies. This prevents surprises two years hence, when trends can mask attempts to differentiate. Additionally, the process reminds the user that organizational culture will affect any strategy's implementation. Culture has inertia, and awareness can help overcome it.

In the words of one user, "This process hasn't eliminated our 'old' planning process, but it has certainly enhanced it. It makes us focus on the real customer of the future."

## Notes

1. Christian Grönroos, *Strategic Management and Marketing in the Service Sector* (Cambridge, Mass.: Marketing Science Institute, 1983), 6.
2. For a discussion of the marketing function in the service sector, see Paul N. Bloom, *Knowledge Development in Marketing—The MSI Experience* (Lexington, Mass.: Lexington Books, 1987).
3. For a formalized method of discovering assumptions in planning, see Richard O. Mason and Ian I. Mitroff, *Challenging Strategic Planning Assumptions* (New York: Wiley, 1981).
4. For a lively discussion of "inside-out" thinking, see Al Ries and Jack Trout, *Positioning: The Battle for Your Mind* (New York: Warner Books, 1986).

5. For a conceptual model of perceptual gaps and service quality, see Valarie A. Zeithaml et al., *Communication and Control Processes in the Delivery of Service Quality* (Cambridge, Mass.: Marketing Science Institute, 1987).

6. For a frequently cited article on service quality in America, see *Time*, February 2, 1987, 48–57.

7. For a discussion of proactive management of corporate culture, see Ralph H. Lilmann, *Beyond the Quick Fix* (San Francisco: Jossey Bass, 1984).

8. For an expansion on the need to have all employees focused on the customer, see Karl Albrecht and Ron Zemke, *Service America! Doing Business in the New Economy* (Homewood, Ill.: Dow Jones-Irwin, 1985).

*   *   *   *

**Dave Masterson** *is principal of Masterson & Associates, a Memphis-based management consulting practice that specializes in sales and marketing productivity. He previously served as senior vice president of strategic marketing with First Tennessee Bank, where his responsibilities included strategic planning for technology-based commercial services. Prior to working in the financial services industry, Mr. Masterson spent nine years in sales and marketing with IBM. His experience encompasses strategic marketing, sales management, product development, and training.*

# 3

# Positioning Strategies for Differential Advantage

Margaret L. Friedman

Our minds are able to accept and understand information best when the information is presented in a form that relates it to things we already know. That is the simple but powerful premise upon which the marketing tool positioning is based. Consider a geographical analogy. If you want to tell someone where Chicago is, and he or she already knows where Milwaukee and Lake Michigan are, you are able, with relatively few words, to communicate Chicago's position in space. Taking account of what your audience already knows makes your communication job easier, whether you are trying to explain where Chicago is, or what the Avis car-rental company offers that is unique and superior.

In this chapter on positioning you will find out where the idea came from, why it is important, how to do it, and its relationship to the marketing communication function. Although positioning is a relatively new marketing tool, it is one that has been used in sophisticated ways with glowing results—the archetypal success story being Avis's strategy to position itself "against" Hertz; second, surely, but therefore, the company that tries harder.

## The Origins of Positioning as a Marketing Tool

Jack Trout and Al Ries introduced the concept of positioning in the early 1970s in a series of three articles describing the origins of the idea.[1] They described the 1950s as the "product era": If you could build a better mousetrap and had a lot of money to promote it, you would be successful. At that time a product's unique selling proposition (USP), the unique feature offered, was the major component of marketing messages. Over time, however, as advances in technology made it possible to copy so-called unique features relatively easily and quickly, it became more and more difficult to develop unique features that would endure.

The 1960s were described by Trout and Ries as the "image era": The overall or composite image that customers held toward a product and company was key to communication in the marketplace. Hence, a barrage of ads about friendly, helpful, conservative products and companies. Soon the market was flooded with friendly, helpful, and conservative companies that all looked alike from the customer's perspective. Now there were me-too images instead of me-too products.

The 1970s were described by Trout and Ries as the ''positioning era.'' They argued that it is imperative that marketing messages be designed to communicate clearly a product's and/or company's *position relative to the competition*. The buzzword Trout and Ries coined is ''overcommunicated society.'' Because we (consumers) live in an overcommunicated society, the only way for one company's message to be heard above the advertising clutter is to talk about one's own product relative to what the competition has to offer. Furthermore, it is crucial that the *customer's* perspective be considered when determining how products or services are perceived relative to one another.

Recall the ''position'' of Chicago analogy. If your ''customers'' already know where Milwaukee is, where Lake Michigan is, and that Chicago is more populous than Milwaukee, then instead of trying to describe where Chicago is in abstract terms (a large city in a central U.S. location), why not explain it in terms that your customer will accept, in terms that he or she already understands and therefore will accept more easily? Chicago is that large windy city to the south of Milwaukee on the shore of the same beautiful Lake Michigan.

Similarly, instead of Avis touting that it has the most streamlined checkout and check-in procedures in the business (features) or that they are the warmest and friendliest car-rental company in the business (image), why not accept what customers already know in their minds (that Hertz is the largest car-rental company, and that Avis is not number one). Then you have a better chance of breaking through a person's natural psychological defenses against information overload using your known number two position as an asset (we try harder).

You might crow about all the features your service offers until you are blue in the face, or shout about the warm and friendly atmosphere you provide until you are green, but to no avail. You are not telling the customer anything different than he or she is hearing from a dozen other service providers, and so you are tuned out by the consumer.

On the other hand, demonstrate in your communications that you understand what the customer knows about the competitive marketplace and exploit the position you own, or create the position you desire, and your message will make sense to the customer and be less likely to be ignored. Burger King has positioned itself as being more responsive to customer needs, recognizing who its major competitor is in the customer's mind and one of that competitor's vulnerabilities.

What positioning boils down to is a way to make your marketing messages work harder. It is a tool to help you grab ''share of mind'' from your customer—share of mind in terms of attention to your message and space in his or her memory.

Our minds work in a networking fashion. Associations help us remember. Instead of ignoring what customers think of your competition, understand customers' perceptions thoroughly, because only then will you be able to figure out where there is a position for you to claim in customers' minds. It may be that customers perceive your competitor to be the leader on price, or quality, or ability to customize, and so on. The point is to know thine enemy and especially how your customers see thine enemy, because only then are you able to talk to your customer in terms that he or she will accept, understand, and believe. If consumers believe Hertz is the market leader, you are wasting your communication dollars trying to convince them otherwise.

In the 1980s, marketers were urged by Trout and Ries to fine-tune their positioning strategies, but with a greater focus on the competition. The terminology of conflict is used a lot in marketing—warfare, attack, guerilla, defense, offense, and so on. For example, Trout and Ries now claim, "To be successful today, a company must become competitor-oriented. It must look for weak points in the positions of its competitors and then launch marketing attacks against those weak points."[2] Positioning is being developed beyond its initial focus on consumer perceptions of the marketplace to include even additional consideration of competitors' positions and actions.

## Why Positioning Is Important to Service Marketers

Positioning is important to service marketers for several reasons:

1. It addresses the issue of differentiation and the goal of removing your service from the realm of commodity.
2. It forces tough decisions regarding what you do, whom you do it for, and whom you are going to compete against.
3. It has the potential for easing the shopping burden for consumers of services where that task is generally more difficult and complex than for products because of the intangibility and related characteristics of services.
4. The "firstest with the mostest" can establish the enviable leader position as IBM has done in the computer market, Xerox in the photocopy market, Coca-Cola in the soft-drink market, and McDonald's in the fast-food market.

Let's look at each of these factors in turn.

### Moving From Commodity to Differentiated Service

Is toothpaste just toothpaste? Definitely not, because of the various positions that have been carved out in that market. Crest is the cavity fighter, Close-Up is the toothpaste for the person who desires fresh breath, and Aim with its visible, multicolored striped appearance has positioned itself between Close-Up and Crest as offering both good taste and cavity prevention. Viadent, a relatively new entry in the market, is recommended by dentists for plaque control. So, is all toothpaste basically the same, a soft abrasive with an inoffensive flavor that is squeezed onto the brush for the purpose of rubbing onto your teeth to keep them clean? No! Different brands "own" very different places in the market, do different things for different people.

It is important to note as an aside that because branding is not common in services marketing, when we talk about positioning we are talking about positioning the entire organization and its services. In product marketing, the relationship between corporate or institutional positioning and specific product positioning can be more complex when a company uses brand names that are different from the company name. For example, the Procter and Gamble *company* is positioned as the high-quality and trustworthy producer of consumer packaged goods. Each of its many detergent products is positioned very specifically in terms of *what it does* and *who it is for*. The "practical washer," "convenience washer," "traditional washer," "economy-minded washer," and "expert washer" have been identified as target consumers for the different brands of detergent. So although all-temperature Cheer is positioned to meet the needs of the convenience-oriented washer, it is a high-quality product, fully guaranteed by trustworthy P & G, supporting the corporate position.

In contrast, Arthur Andersen & Company, one of the nation's top public accounting firms, puts the AA & Co. name on every service it markets, worldwide, as do Citibank, Federal Express, and the United States Postal Service, as is the case for most services. Although this may appear to make the positioning job easier because you do not have to worry about reconciling multiple positions, it makes it all the more important to develop a versatile, yet consistent and enduring positioning strategy. "It's a good time for the great taste of McDonald's" has endured in many forms, launched many new service additions, and has appealed to many different market segments.

Milwaukee and Chicago are midwestern cities located on the shores of Lake Michigan. So far what we know indicates that they are undifferentiated commodities. But consider this: Chicago is the largest midwestern city on the shores of Lake Michigan. So for the market segment that likes big cities and all they have to offer, it is the place to go. So, what can Milwaukee do? Should it try to become bigger so that it can compete with Chicago in attracting customers? Or should Milwaukee stress its city-quality dining facilities at small-town prices for those in the market who prefer good food but in a more relaxed and economical atmosphere? You cannot be what you are not, but you can understand your strengths, your competition, and your customers well enough to be able to develop a successful position for yourself.

## What Do You Do and Whom Do You Do It For?

The unique characteristics of services, especially their intangibility and labor-intensive versus machine-intensive production process, make it appear relatively easy and desirable to be all things to all people. Let's say I am a psychologist. I can counsel children or teenagers, or adults, or elderly people, or families or blended families, or divorced families in the areas of stress, suicide, alcoholism, eating disorders, and on and on and on. The point is, that with some extra effort on my part, some time, and perhaps a licensing exam or other such legal requirement, I am in business. I do not have to make large capital investments in plant and equipment to add a new service. If someone calls and asks if I do counseling on dealing with the death of a pet, I can easily say yes, and probably will, because more business is better, isn't it?

We have all been told that there is a difference between working harder and working smarter. Positioning helps you work smarter. It forces you to clarify what you do, whom you do it for, and who else is trying to do what you do. Furthermore, it prescribes very specific methods for communicating what you do, whom you do it for, and how you fit in with your competitors. For example, let's say that consumers evaluate airlines on the basis of two characteristics—friendliness and on-time service. Furthermore, customers have an idea where the various airlines are positioned in this two-dimensional space, just as we all understand where cities are positioned on a map according to the two-dimensional space defined by the axes north-south and east-west. United Airlines apparently found that many customers wanted more friendly service but did not find it among existing carriers. So United has positioned itself as the airline in the "friendly skies."

American Airlines has attempted to position itself as the reliable carrier using the headline, "What Makes the On-Time Machine Tick?" American apparently recognized that many consumers wanted on-time service and did not find it among existing carriers. The positioning promise, of course, must be backed up by actual delivery of the benefit promised, be it friendliness or on-time service. In short, American Airlines is promising the traveler who is most interested in on-time travel that he or she will receive just that. American wants to be the first to claim a position that a sizable segment of consumers values.

## Positioning Can Ease the Shopping Burden

Products and services are said to possess three qualities to help consumers evaluate them: search, experience, and credence qualities.[3] Search qualities are those things that can be evaluated prior to purchase. You can try on a suit, you can test drive a car, and you can often taste the pizza in the supermarket before committing to purchase.

Experience qualities are those things that you can only evaluate in actually using the product or service over time. For example, the amount of satisfaction you derive from consumption or the durability of a lawn mower can only be known over time. The same is true of the purchase of a vacation. I have recently returned from a vacation in the Grand Teton Mountains. I could only anticipate and imagine the fun I might have when I made my reservations for a place to stay, a raft to paddle down the Snake River, and a horse to ride in the wilderness. It was only during and after the service delivery that I could evaluate whether I was served well or not. At the time of purchase, only promises can be made regarding experience qualities.

Credence qualities are those things that can never be evaluated, because we do not have the expertise or simply cannot see physically what was done or produced. For example, how can you tell whether your triple bypass surgery was done well, or that the tune-up on your car was quality job? It is interesting to note that many auto mechanics now show you the parts they take out of your car to help you evaluate some tangible evidence of the quality of service.

Generally, services exhibit few search qualities, some experience qualities, and relatively numerous credence qualities. That is why shopping for services is so hard and why consumers often rely largely on personal sources of information when trying to choose among services. Information from a trusted source who has had some experience with the service you are evaluating provides vicarious experience and helps to reduce the risk involved in the decision. Most of us shop for professional and personal services in this manner—for our doctors, our lawyers, our hairdressers, our lawn-care service, and others.

Although consumers certainly discount mass advertising messages because of their biased source, nevertheless, in choosing services, consumers have so little to go on in evaluating services prior to purchase that testimonial support for a positioning claim might be seen as at least some information input to the prepurchase evaluation of service. If I have to attend an important business meeting and am very concerned about getting there on time and I see the American Airlines ad that positions the carrier as the "on-time machine" accompanied by testimonials from real customers as to the veracity of this position, my decision might be made simpler.

### The First to Own a Position Has an Advantage

IBM owns the dominant position in the computer industry, which gives the company a lot of latitude in its actions, a bit of a cushion if times get bad. Despite its technological and financial strength, IBM failed in its attempt to enter the photocopy market. Xerox was first to own the dominant position there. Trout and Ries stressed the importance of being first in a position by asking simple questions—who was first to walk on the moon? Who was second? Who was the first to fly solo across the North Atlantic? Who was second? We can all answer the first questions easily, but have considerable difficulty with the "seconds." Being first to occupy a position is enviable because everything that follows is related to what already exists in our minds and experience. It is difficult to think or talk about computers without the big block letters IBM being activated in our minds.

Because marketing is a relatively new business function in many service businesses, those who learn it and practice it first have a definite advantage when it comes to something like positioning, where timing is of the essence. Positioning can obviously add real power to your marketing program. McDonald's, Hertz, and American Express have set the rules by which all other competitors must play. That is not to say these leaders do not have vulnerabilities. Rather, it is those vulnerabilities that mark the boundaries of the arena in which other competitors vie for position.

The general caveat to remember is, Don't create for yourself a position that looks good on paper but that has nothing to do with your capabilities and resources. Positioning is not a way to trick consumers into thinking you are something that you are not. It is a means to communicate more effectively about exactly what you do stand for and exactly what customers can expect from you that they cannot get from anyone else. A large university hospital housed in the largest brick building in the state where I live, a labyrinth of allegedly color-coded paths, cannot position itself as the friendly, concerned health-care facility. Rather, this hospital has positioned itself as the provider of "strong medicine" in keeping with the organization's image, strengths, and capabilities.

# Needed: Impetus From Top Management

Everyone in the service organization should have an understanding of why positioning is important, because everyone has to behave in a manner that supports the position. It is absolutely imperative that top management have this understanding. It is too tempting for service businesses to lose their focus and to start getting into businesses that they have no business getting into, as we've seen in numerous corporate restructurings.

Federal Express provides a good example of vision and focus. Overnight delivery of small packages is guaranteed. All of its staff and delivery systems are designed and geared to fulfill that promise to their customers. The Federal Express management team has created and nurtured an environment in which people and systems are given latitude and support to fulfill the positioning promise. Federal Express has become the generic in the industry it created, as Xerox is the generic in the photocopying industry.

Management must demonstrate commitment to a position so that an organization has the time and resources to fully exploit that position. Jumping around from position to position in a frenzied attempt to stay competitive simply drains resources, demoralizes employees, and confuses customers. Mr. Whipple has been announcing the squeezably soft position that Charmin holds to several generations of bathroom tissue users.

It is the onerous task of top management to define an organization's mission or purpose. As you learned in Chapter 2 of this *Handbook,* this task is much more difficult than you might initially believe it to be. The danger is defining an organization's purpose from the inside looking out, rather than from the outside looking in—that is, from the *customer's* perspective. Tom Peters and Nancy Austin[4] used the term *smell* of the customer to capture just how far you should go to know your customers intimately and how they see you.

Effective positioning demands that an organization take the perspective of the customer in evaluating the marketplace. Remember, the value of positioning is that it works to break down consumers' natural psychological defenses against information overload. It rests on the premise that you have to understand how the customer perceives the marketplace before you can speak to him or her effectively.

A mission that suffers from an inside-out perspective—based on what you can do, the needs of the customer be damned—will cause you to say things that customers will not find useful or accept. A temporary help agency might advertise that it can provide typing skills, filing ability, and telephone answering service. That's what we have—want any? An outside-in perspective would be the temporary agency communicating the ability of its people to listen and to make sound decisions regarding clients' staffing needs. This outside-in perspective has the advantage of forcing you to be responsive to customer needs. If an outside-in perspective is found in the mission statement of an organization, the stage is set for effective positioning to follow. You need also to find out how the customer views the relative ability of various competitors to meet his or her needs, the topic of the next section.

# How to Plan a Positioning Strategy

In planning a positioning strategy, you are generally either starting from "scratch" if you are a new business or have a new service to offer; or you are faced with a repositioning task, if you are not satisfied with your current position, if your position has become outdated, or if your position has acquired negative associations. Honda, for example, found its sales suffering from the negative connotations associated with people who ride motorcycles—gangs. So Honda creatively moved its product away from this position with the theme, "You meet the nicest people on a Honda," and were rewarded with increasing sales. A local hospital in its initial positioning efforts communicated that it was the "place where babies come from." Over time as the hospital's marketing strategies have evolved, its management presumably thought that this position was too confining and have since repositioned the hospital as the place to go "because life is good," showing smiling service providers at every turn in the hospital who are enhancing patients' lives.

## Positioning Starts With a Perceptual Map

Regardless of whether your task is to position or to reposition a service, the procedure to follow is similar. The place to start is with consumer research and development of a perceptual map. A perceptual map is very much like a geographical map. A geographical map positions cities according to their distances from one another on the dimensions north-south and east-west. On a perceptual map the "psychological" distances between services are reflected on whatever dimensions consumers deem relevant in evaluating the service being studied—dimensions like friendliness, economy, or convenience.

One method for obtaining perceptions from consumers is the form of similarity judgments. Let's use a simple example first. You might ask a group of subjects to evaluate the similarity of various sports such as football, basketball, swimming, tennis, sailboarding, and golf. You would present subjects with all combinations of two of the sports under consideration and ask them to rate the similarity of each pair. Your instructions would *not* include telling subjects on what attributes to evaluate similarity. Rather, you require only that they use some consistent rule in making their similarity judgments. These data then are input to a computer program called multidimensional scaling. This program processes the data so that a map is produced that reflects the relative positions of the objects rated based on the psychological distances revealed in the similarity data obtained. Figure 3-1 illustrates hypothetically what the map for the sports example might look like.

How do you attach descriptive labels to the axes that the computer program produces? Remember, you told subjects to be consistent in their evaluations, but did not tell them upon what characteristics to base their evaluations. Sometimes when you simply look at the map and see where the computer positioned the objects, it is intuitively clear what the names of the axes should be. For instance, in our sports example the positions of the sports in two-dimensional space might make it clear that people made their evaluations based on whether

**Figure 3-1.** Hypothetical perceptual map for sports example.

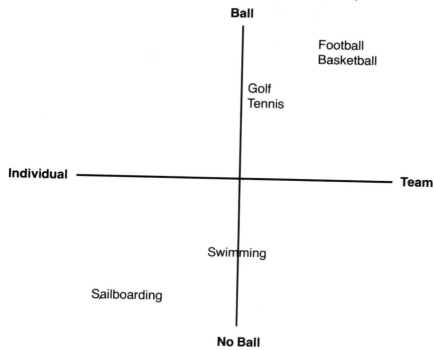

or not the sport involved using a ball and whether it was strictly a team sport or could also be played individually. The map shows that golf and tennis, like football and basketball, depend on a ball, but unlike football and basketball, they do not depend on an assortment of team members. The map also shows that sailboarding is perceived as an individual sport in which a ball is not used.

An alternative way to find out what characteristics subjects used to judge similarity is to ask a different group of subjects what characteristics they would use to evaluate the similarity of certain objects, without actually having them judge similarity. The reason for using a different group of subjects is to avoid biasing the group giving you similarity judgments to see the market the way *you* see it rather than the way *they* see it.

Figure 3-2 illustrates hypothetically what a map for rapid mail services might look like. In this example the subjects from whom similarity judgments would be gathered should be consumers in the target market for the service, for example, businesses rather than households.

Again, in our sports example, some people might naturally base their similarity judgments on whether the sport is played in summer or winter, or indoors or outdoors, in which cases the perceptual map produced would look different than the map in Figure 3-1. Other dimensions upon which consumers might judge rapid mail services might be economy or convenience and, again, the resultant perceptual map would appear different than that shown in Figure 3-2. It is important that the consumers' perceptions of reality are captured in this

**Figure 3-2.** Hypothetical perceptual map for rapid mail services.

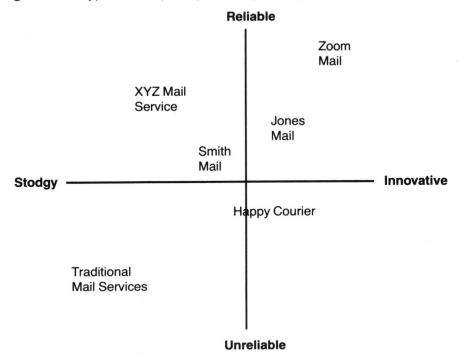

effort, not your perceptions, or mapping loses its value in helping you know how to position your service in terms that consumers will believe and accept.

If you are starting from scratch, the objects that you ask subjects to rate may simply be concepts that you are testing to see how consumers might evaluate them relative to what is currently available in the market in which you plan to compete. When Sears was considering introducing the Discover Card, they might have tested the idea by pitting a written description of what the card would offer and how it would fare against such competitors as American Express, Visa, and MasterCard. If you are working with an established service, then it should be clear what services other than your own need to be evaluated by consumers. Visa, for example, is most interested in knowing how consumers perceive their card relative to American Express, MasterCard, and the Discover Card—that is, whether it is more or less prestigious, costly, accepted, or whatever is important to consumers.

The perceptual map, then, is used to look for gaps or areas where there is open space and, therefore, a possible new position. I say *possible* because a gap may indicate a need that is not being met by current offerings or it may indicate no need. The gap in the northwest corner of the sports map (Figure 3-1) may mean there is nothing people want to do with a ball by themselves or that there is a need for a sport like Hacky Sack, where an individual attempts to keep a small ball airborne by having it ricochet off his or her feet and legs.

You should also look for cluttered areas on the map, where services are too close together, which indicates an undifferentiated position. In Figure 3-2, the proximity of Jones Mail, Smith Mail, and Happy Courier means that they are not differentiated from each other. Furthermore, the mid-map position of these three services indicates the absence of a clear, distinctive image in the marketplace.

You may find that your position is unique but undesirable; that is, you have your own space on the map, but it is space that consumers view negatively. If your car is seen as a gas guzzler that is hard to handle, you probably want to do something. One possibility is to reposition it by user category, that is, by appealing to larger families who need a bigger and safer car and who expect to have to fill up more often.

Although part of perceptual mapping is science, part of it is also art. It is interpretation of the map that is the artistic part. The more you know about your customers and how they see the marketplace, the better your ability to make sound decisions about positioning. As with every other marketing tool, positioning is definitely not a magic wand. You do not go through all the steps described and then pull the answer to your positioning questions out of a hat. Effective positioning starts with a challenging information-gathering task and ends with good judgment.

## Tactical Positioning Considerations

In planning to develop a position or to reposition, you can look to your marketing mix to see where your strengths lie and on what basis you can develop and sustain a viable position, based now on what you know about consumer perceptions of the market. I cannot stress enough that you have to look for a fit between what you do well and what it is the customer wants. If Burger King has enough flexibility in its service production process to be able to cost-effectively customize the finished service, a positioning program based on this benefit is valid only if customization is seen as a benefit *from the customer's point of view*. Do not consider your strengths in a vacuum, but always in the context of what is important to the customer. You can also look to your competition for positioning opportunities. Where are they vulnerable? Also, consider your consumers and their behavior as a source of positioning ideas. Finally, you can position yourself with the help of a positive cultural or social symbol. We will consider each of these factors in turn.

<u>Consider Your Marketing Mix.</u>   First let's look at the service itself. Ask yourself, is there a new benefit we can offer (on-time service), a new application we can fulfill (recipes using concentrated soup as an ingredient), a new product classification we can enter (margarine as a substitute for butter or writing checks on an interest-drawing savings account)?

Chapter 13 of this *Handbook* describes the procedure for blueprinting. This procedure is a method for rationalizing and visualizing the service production and delivery process and provides an excellent opportunity to look for positioning opportunities. Can we make it faster, cleaner, easier? Can we add value or enhancements either behind the scenes or up front where we have face-to-face contact with our customers?

Second, consider price. Retailers have done a good job of positioning along the lines of price-quality perceptions. We all have a very definite idea where Saks, Sears, and K mart are positioned along price and quality dimensions. In the early 1980s Sears was quite successful in repositioning itself away from its traditional value position to a more fashionable position (Cheryl Tiegs and designer clothes). This move was billed "the biggest single success story in memory" at Sears.[5]

If you are in a position to offer special deals on a regular basis, perhaps you want to position yourself as the "dealingest dealer" in town. In my community we have a large appliance dealer who does just that and every spring gives away more bicycles as a sales promotion than any bicycle outlet in the state of Wisconsin sells. His competitors then position themselves as offering individualized attention and aftersale service, which the dealingest dealer is not known for, of course.

The place or distribution element can be considered in terms of accessibility, the use of technology in delivering services, and the physical evidence that accompanies most services, since the concepts of a traditional channel of distribution—transporting, inventorying, and warehousing—are not applicable for services. Banks have positioned themselves as being much more accessible to the customer through various means. They have more convenient hours, offer services that make them more accessible (banking by mail, direct deposit), and have generally attempted to create a more flexible and approachable atmosphere. Similarly they have used technology to make their services more available (ATMs).

Physical evidence includes such things as the facility itself, any physical objects that accompany the service and more peripheral things like parking. The advent of marketing in the legal profession has spawned a rash of legal clinics positioned as being much more accessible to the middle- and lower-class consumer. The positioning promise has been carried out in their neighborhood locations, the more casual manner and dress of their employees, their lower prices, and the no-frills design of their basic services.

An added element in the marketing mix for services is the people who deliver the service. People are an especially resilient factor upon which to position your service because it takes time to locate, hire, and train good people. A local health maintenance organization positions itself as the one "where the doctors make the difference." If then the doctors actually do behave as caringly as they are portrayed in the advertising, a position can be established that is very hard to imitate quickly.

We all have a retail outlet we frequent because we get special attention there. We will go out of our way to patronize that outlet, perhaps paying a little more or being inconvenienced a bit because we receive caring attention. Midwest Express Airlines cameos its employees in its ads conveying "The Best Care in the Air," and has typically had the employees ad lib the script, talking about how committed they are to serving customers. The carrier, in the first four years of its existence, enjoyed an 85 percent growth rate.

<u>Your Competition's Position in Your Thinking.</u>  With the positioning era of the 1970s grew the prevalence of comparative advertising, where competitors are actually named in advertisements and compared directly. Citibank has positioned both its Visa and MasterCard against American Express by lining up all three cards and then asking "Guess which card will get rejected 3 million times more than the others?" Of course, the answer is the American Express card. Citibank is positioning itself against the ubiquitous position of American Express and setting the record straight, claiming superiority on what they call the most important feature of any credit card, acceptance. The Avis "We Try Harder" position accomplishes the same objective, only more subtly.

<u>Consider Your Customers and Their Characteristics.</u>  You can position along age lines, lifestyle, usage rate, or usage occasion. For example, Canada Dry is for the more grown-up palate, Revlon's Charlie cosmetic line is for an active, young-at-heart lifestyle, and Jif is the peanut butter for choosy mothers. Johnson & Johnson baby shampoo has been successfully repositioned along age and usage rate lines—for the older shampooer who shampoos often, and therefore needs a very mild product.

<u>Consider Using a Symbol to Position Your Service.</u>  Some products and services have been positioned using a symbol that has positive connotations. For example, we have the Pillsbury doughboy, the Green Giant, Betty Crocker (whose image has been subtly changed over the years to stay current), the Prudential rock, and the Merrill Lynch bull. Probably the most successful example of using a symbol to position a product has been the Marlboro cowboy, who is known globally.

# Positioning and Marketing Communications Go Hand-in-Hand

Positioning and marketing communications are inextricably linked. Remember the whole point of positioning is to increase your chances that your message will be heard and accepted by consumers. It is a way to increase the efficiency and effectiveness of your communication dollars.

We need to discuss two kinds of marketing communications, internal and external. Internal communication has to accompany and actually precede external communications (see Chapter 5), because if your internal "customers" (employees) do not understand the positioning promise being made to external customers, there is no way that the promise will be fulfilled, except perhaps through dumb luck. If Avis is going to position itself as the "We Try Harder" car-rental company, then every employee had better be trying harder either to serve the customer or to serve the employee who is actually serving the customer. It is preferable to promise nothing than to promise what you cannot deliver. If you promise that I can have it "my way" and I ask you to give me extra tomatoes, your people had better be prepared to give me the tomatoes.

Keep your external communications with your customers simple and consistent. Plan your positioning strategy carefully so that you have confidence to stick with what you commit to. The Doublemint twins have been around for a long time positioning Wrigley's gum as a flavorful addition to any good time. One of the keys to successful positioning is consistency and longevity. Plan your strategy to give you some room for keeping up with the times, but also provide for a constant, unchanging message that makes sense to consumers, and therefore, is heard. Even though you and the creative people working on your message may become bored with the messages you have been using, do not change them if they are working for you. Rather, keep the core position and change the details in small ways. It is always a "Good Time for the Great Taste of McDonald's," the theme that we have all seen and heard many times.

## Summary

What have you learned in this chapter? You have learned that positioning involves talking with your customers in a language that they understand. It forces you to understand yourself, your competition, and most important how your customers see you and your competition. Proponents of positioning argue that it is the marketer's only hope for breaking through the consumer's natural barriers to information overload to get the message across, because it takes account of what customers know about the market. We all know "Coke Is It" and so 7-Up took this perception into account when communicating to consumers what differentiates it, the "Uncola."

You have learned that positioning is important because it relates to differentiation, the touchstone of successful marketing, forces tough decisions that keep you focused on what you are supposed to be doing and not diluting your resources, potentially makes the consumers' shopping task easier, and, if you are quick and clever, can help you own the position of market leader in your industry.

What positioning requires to be successful is top management support, not just in words but in action. Management has to provide the market-oriented mission and purpose for the organization that avoids an inside-out perspective but promotes an outside-in perspective.

Finally, you have learned about the important role that perceptual maps play in the whole process, the basics of how to develop such a map, and how to use it. You can look at your marketing mix, competitors' positions, and the characteristics of your customers for positioning ideas. All that is left is to communicate your position, first internally, and only then externally, to your customers. If you have done a good job of tuning in to customers' perceptions, they will be more likely to tune in to your messages.

## Notes

1. Jack Trout and Al Ries, "The Positioning Era Cometh," *Advertising Age,* April 24, 1972; "Positioning Cuts Through Chaos in Marketplace," *Advertising Age,*

May 1, 1972; and "How to Position Your Product," *Advertising Age,* May 8, 1972.

2. Al Ries and Jack Trout, *Marketing Warfare* (New York: McGraw-Hill, 1986), 4–5.

3. Valarie A. Zeithaml, "How Consumer Evaluation Processes Differ Between Goods and Services," in *Marketing of Services: Proceedings,* ed. James H. Donnelly and William R. George (Chicago: American Marketing Association, 1981).

4. Tom Peters and Nancy Austin, *A Passion for Excellence* (New York: Warner Books, 1985).

5. Donald Katz, *The Big Store* (New York: Viking Penguin, 1987).

*       *       *       *

*Margaret L. Friedman, Ph.D., is assistant professor in the marketing department of the College of Business and Economics, University of Wisconsin-Whitewater. She teaches courses in consumer behavior and personal selling and has developed an undergraduate course in services marketing. She previously served as director of service sector marketing programs at the university's Management Institute, the continuing education unit of the School of Business at Madison. She has worked as a consultant with a variety of service sector businesses.*

# 4

## Developing Strategies in Service Organizations

Michael J. Pessetti

As a proactive service marketer, you are rarely short on ideas for enhancing or adding to your company's offering in the marketplace to achieve better results for both your customer and your organization. The leap from idea to implementation, however, can often be long and treacherous. Customers shift attitudes and preferences quickly. Competitors are constantly attacking your position or building strong ones for themselves. Innovation seems to change the face of your industry almost daily. Your own organization is all but impossible to get moving on new insights. Yet the call of your intuition is strong. What an opportunity!

Strategic development and planning provides you with tools that will help you forge a path through this jungle of uncertainty. It's an approach that identifies and accounts for variables in your marketplace that impact your ability to succeed and lets you take advantage of them. It allows you to build some logical structure from the swirling shades of gray presented by today's business environment. It moves you from idea to implementation.

The purpose of this chapter is to give you a front-to-back view of the strategic planning process and provide specific suggestions to make it work for you in your organization. It starts with an overview of the concept in terms of the role and value of strategic planning and the special perspective needed by service marketers. Second, you'll look at strategy development in the larger environmental and organizational contexts in which you must build plans to compete effectively and operate efficiently. Third, as the focal point of the process, you'll get a feel for the importance of and some simple steps for "planning to plan." Fourth is the situation analysis approach for gathering information about the variables in your environment and ways to identify and focus on those that are most critical to address in your plan. Fifth is a building-block process to give you answers to questions related to who you are, where you are, where you want to be, and the recommended way to get there. This is the nuts and bolts of the strategy development program. Sixth, you'll learn about the necessary outcomes or goals of the strategy development process and the crucial role they play in making the transition from plan, to action, to results. Seventh is the aspect of planning where many great strategies have fallen: implementation. If you are going to overcome organizational inertia and get commitment to a strategic view of the future, this is arguably the single most important step in the process. Finally, you'll face the realization that the development and implementation of your plan are only the beginning. Success is measured by your ability to monitor and adjust for long-term strategic effectiveness and results.

Don't feel overwhelmed. Although there is a lot going on here, you will see as you proceed that somewhere within your organization you already have most of the information and resources needed to mount a winning strategic development program.

# Strategic Planning Concept Overview

Strategic planning tends to be more or less in demand primarily in relation to the rate and extent of change that is taking place in the business environment. It has become a mainstay of the management of companies today as a result of the realization that companies that consistently provide a competitively superior offering to the customer produce better results at the bottom line. Acknowledging that those companies that find the most efficient means to operate competitively in their business environment, whatever its rate of change, will be the most successful, the challenge for the service marketer lies in the need to integrate the management of the internal environment where service is created and performed with the external environment where it is demanded and consumed.

## The Role of Strategic Planning

The function and role for strategic planning are often most readily observed in situations where an effective job has *not* been done. How many times have you seen a product or service introduced in a market that had changed by the time the product or service got there? Have you seen or experienced, in the absence of a well-defined and accepted strategic plan, a frenzy of activity that is more related to putting out little fires than to achieving company objectives? Do your budgets reflect planned investments in strategies or the power and influence of functional specialties in your organization? The role of strategic planning is to provide an objective framework within which the resources and activities of the firm can be directed. The only goal for that direction is the superior delivery of customer services in a manner that provides you with a defendable advantage over your competitors.

The understanding, acceptance, and use of strategic planning are not as universal as you might expect. Its inconsistent application is what may provide you with your largest advantage. Many times winning with the customer is more a function of better execution than in finding some unique and unrecognized need or in devising a strategic breakthrough. Couched in an understanding of your organization's mission, objectives, and resources, the function of the strategic plan is to: (1) identify competitive positions that are valued by the customer and are both obtainable and defendable by your company, (2) define and develop strategies to achieve that positioning guided by the results required and resources available, and (3) serve as a guide for the policy decisions of top management and the day-to-day operating plans and decisions of the functional groups that make up the company. The strategic planning process is summarized in Figure 4-1, which also serves as an outline of the following sections of this chapter.

## The Benefits of Strategic Planning

In the simplest terms, those companies that most effectively and efficiently take advantage of the opportunities available achieve the best business results. The evidence to support this position comes from the research work conducted over a fifteen-year period by the Strategic Planning Institute of Cambridge, Massachusetts. Their findings show that those companies that are perceived as providing high-quality products and services enjoy higher average growth rates, stronger profits, larger market shares, and better return on investment than those companies perceived as average performers.

There are two basic principles behind this result. First, when you have established a position based on consistently high quality, you are ultimately able to charge a premium price for your offering. The relationship here to profit and return on investment is clear. Second, the provider of high quality rarely has to expend resources to replace an unimpressed or dissatisfied customer. This allows you to focus on building your customer base instead of just maintaining it. Here you see a clear connection to growth and market share, but there is also a less obvious but equally direct effect on financial results. Numerous studies have focused on the costs of replacing a lost customer. In general, they have found that it costs about four times more to attract a new or replacement customer than it does to keep one you already have. The average- to low-quality performer pays a high price and adds significantly to the underlying cost of doing business because of the customer turnover that results.

You will also generate tangible organizational benefits from a commitment to strategic planning. In many firms, you will find both a serious lack of common understanding about what is being offered in the marketplace and real concern about the number of separate decisions that are based on those different views. To overcome the difficulties of such misunderstandings, your strategic initiative must incorporate and communicate the fundamental components of: (1) the mission of your company, (2) your objectives and strategies for achieving them, (3) the specific and agreed-upon plans for implementing the strategies, and (4) the roles to be played by the functional units to execute the plan. This approach helps to clarify perception about what the customer really wants, allows you the ability to analyze your assumptions about your offering and their validity, and encourages a broad-based and common understanding of what you are actually providing and how it will be accomplished. If nothing else, you will reap benefits from more efficient deployment of resources and effective action.

A final benefit comes in relation to the longer-range management and operation of your company. A well-documented and understood strategic plan mediates the interruption of ongoing operations that can occur when personnel turnover occurs at either the management or functional level. Transitions are made more smoothly, and the efficient execution of your plan in the marketplace is less subject to costly starts and stops.

**Figure 4-1.** The strategic planning process.

```
              ┌─────────────────────────┐
  ────────▶   │       Market and        │
              │ Organizational Direction │
              └─────────────────────────┘
```

1. Define mission, position, objectives.
2. Consider information needs/sources, resource needs/availability, current market position, customer and competitor profiles.

```
  ┌─────────────────────────┐
  │  Planning Preparation   │
  └─────────────────────────┘
```

1. Identify participants and build team.
2. Define roles/expectations/goals.
3. Lay out the game plan for planning.
4. Maintain focus on goals of the process.
5. Define information needs in detail.

```
  ┌─────────────────────────┐
  │  Strategic Plan Proposal │
  │       Development        │
  └─────────────────────────┘
```

1. Communicate mission, position, objectives.
2. Evaluate environment.
3. Perform customer analysis.
4. Develop and evaluate strategy.
5. Select strategy.
6. Do contingency planning.

```
  ┌─────────────────────────┐
  │      Plan Approval      │
  └─────────────────────────┘
```

1. Present plan to executive management.
2. Amend/adjust as needed.

```
  ┌─────────────────────────┐
  │   Implementation Plan   │
  │       Development        │
  └─────────────────────────┘
```

1. Expand team.
2. Set the stage with mission, position, objectives.
3. Outline the strategic plan.
4. Develop implementation alternatives.
5. Consolidate the proposal for management approval.
6. Finalize plan.
7. Execute.

```
  ┌─────────────────────────┐
  ◀ │  Execution Management   │
  └─────────────────────────┘
```

1. Monitor, control, adjust.

## Special Considerations for Service Marketers

Special challenges are a large part of your task as a service marketer. First, your product is intangible. The outcome of the service event and the customer's perception of its adequacy are all that really matter. This invisibility of all that you do to satisfy your customer can make it difficult for you to identify and improve the aspects of your support process that will allow you to provide better service. You can't simply change packaging or add a new and secret ingredient in order to satisfy the requirements of your customer. You deal in a world where perception is often more important than reality. Second, services can't be inventoried on the shelf. You can't stockpile during slow periods in order to meet the peaks of demand. Third, the service is defined principally by the person providing it, which results in variations in quality. Employees aren't production lines and their behavior can't be standardized. Their action in providing service is less manageable by classical quality control methods. It's easy to see why many service firms are confused about the role of planning. Here again is another real opportunity to succeed if you can face these challenges and conquer them with your strategic plan.

To achieve consistently superior levels of service quality, you have to work hard. This type of performance is difficult to produce in service industries, because the interaction between customer and employee is the largest piece of your product. The effective delivery of service and the degree of efficiency with which it is done depend directly on your employees. Your planning then must recognize and enable your organization to handle several particular characteristics of the service environment:

1. *Service problems are often invisible.* Dissatisfied customers many times won't complain; they just never come back.
2. *Service encounters are made up of a multitude of individual events.* Because your entire organization must be focused on the outcome of those encounters, management must be clearly focused on common objectives and in tune functionally at every level of the company.
3. *Service breakdowns are difficult to eliminate.* Since everyone in your organization should be responsible for serving the customer or supporting someone who does, pinpointing the direct cause or optimal solution to a service breakdown is especially challenging.
4. *Service-level consistency is not easy to maintain.* You need a day-in and day-out focus on the customer and an understanding of what that customer needs from every employee involved in supporting or delivering your service.

It looks like a tall order, but the payoff is there if you can deal with these issues. More focused attention and understanding by both the management and employees of your company on the actions that make up your interaction with the customer and the roles that each must play to perform effectively is the central purpose of a strategic plan. It can get you an improved perception of service quality, more satisfied and repeat customers, and better bottom-line business results.

Your plan revolves around a few basic principles that are directly related to delivering high-quality service. First, you must have a clear understanding of who your customers are and what they want from you. Second, you need to communicate effectively to all of your employees that understanding and the details of your commitment to acting upon it: your service strategy. Third, as you design and plan the actions that make up your offering, always keep the customer as your first consideration. Finally, but perhaps most important, you must have a strong organizational commitment to structure the alignment of your people (e.g., organizational structure, management span of control, functional role definition, physical location) and provide comprehensive training (education about both the customer and the job) focused on the desires of the customer you have chosen to serve.

## Strategic Planning Perspectives and Inputs

So, just what is strategic planning? What isn't it? Where do you start? What do you need to know? All very pertinent questions, and here is where you start to deal with them. The most important thing for you to accomplish at this point is to gain some perspective on the process you are about to undertake. In addition, it's critical to understand the role and function of strategy in the larger corporate business plan.

### Plan Components and Roles

The first stop in the planning process flow needs to be at the largest corporate or organizational level available, because it is here that the decisions about where you will play, what position you will take, and what you expect to get for it are made. This is the basis of Chapters 2 and 3. The mission statement, which crystallizes your thinking on the business you have chosen to be in, provides you with guidelines from the organizational perspective about what you do, for whom you do it, and why. In effect, the mission statement tells you basically what game you are being asked to play. Objective and positioning statements help develop further definition for your task. Positioning statements tell you what ground you want to hold in the competitive landscape. They define how you want to be perceived by customers, competitors, and your own employees in terms of the way you conduct your business. Statements of objectives tell you what is expected for that effort. They can be performance- or perception-oriented. Objectives related to profit or market share are equally as important as those more focused on reputation and mind share. It is to the fulfillment of the mission, position, and objective statements that the balance of this process is directed. Business, division, or unit level strategies and plans must now be developed to create an optimal plan for satisfying the needs and requirements of the organization through satisfying the needs and requirements of potential or existing customers.

Without the guidance provided by these organizational-level directions, individuals are often left to their own devices to decide what to do. The fundamental role of strategic planning is to create a common interpretation of the goals to be met, definition of the market opportunities or alternatives through which they can be met, and communication of realistic expectations for how it will be done. Here you are developing the story that you will tell both inside and outside the organization. Your story will be effective to the extent that it convincingly and realistically explains what the customer wants and why what you have to offer should be perceived as competitively superior. It must also target or focus the firm's resources and attention on markets or customers where you have the best chance to meet and exceed organizational goals, both today and in the future. The strategic plan guides the investments you make and actions you take today toward the competitively advantageous position you want to hold tomorrow and beyond.

Whereas strategies deal with positions to be taken or held with regard to customers and competitors, tactical and implementation planning are focused on how it will be done, who's responsible for doing it, and when it will be accomplished. It is here that the best strategy can meet an unfortunate and undeserved demise. It's the first internal reality check for the strategic story that you have written. The functional experts in your organization on whom you as strategic planner rely to transform concepts into reality will let you know if your plan is understandable and actionable. To the extent that you have clearly defined the goals that everyone is responsible for meeting and built a compelling case for the strategic plan that you have developed as the best way to accomplish it, you can achieve buy-in from the operational side of your organization. Don't expect this aspect of plan development to pass without modification and adjustment, however. Look on it as an opportunity to tap into different viewpoints, additional relevant expertise, and the hard-won experience of people charged with making it all happen. Course corrections identified and made now can save you from costly delays in implementation or unsatisfactory, if not disastrous, market introduction. Learn everything you can about what it will take to do the best job possible.

## Information and Inputs

This beginning phase of the planning process is also your best time to identify, pull together, and verify the types and sources of information that you need. Make certain that you have the correct view of the organization's mission and objectives. Know the extent and adaptability of resources, both human and financial, and organizational structure that are available for use. Understand not only where and who you want to be perceived as by the market, but also what your position is now and how far you have to go to get where you want to be. Have the best possible working knowledge of who your potential customers are and what they actually buy, not just what they say they want. Be intimately aware of your present and potential competitors, their strengths and weaknesses; project their strategies; and anticipate their reactions to your moves. The list goes on, and what is on it depends largely on the type and extent of positioning movement you're after. Although the actual task of gathering and interpreting this kind of information is a functional step covered later, do yourself the favor of spending some time thinking seriously about all the things you'd like to know and how you might go about getting answers or organizing those that you already have before you get started. Work on thinking before, but not instead of, doing.

## Getting Organized to Plan

Strategic planning seeks to develop a logical approach to dealing with the uncertainties and variables in the market. This step in the process is directed at doing the same thing for you within your organization. It is the plan for how you're going to plan and includes four necessary components.

### Identifying Participants

Given the insight and understanding that you have developed up to this point related to the business challenges and opportunities that you are going to tackle, determine whose participation and assistance will be most valuable. At the very least, you should build a team made up of those managers who control and are responsible for the resources you will need. Their role in the organization is to manage a function efficiently and effectively, and you should expect them to have well-grounded opinions and to demand participation. Involving them now and making them part of the team can eliminate surprises or lack of cooperation later on. Additionally, if other specific expertise is required, you should add to the team to the degree that the participation required is long run. One big caution here: Don't fill up auditoriums with a planning team. Attempt to keep your focus on higher level managers with the authority to make decisions and call in other players temporarily as needed. You'll never manage the development of the plan if you can't manage the actions of the team.

### Definition of Roles

This is the most important planning team management factor. People need to know why they are on the team and what is expected of them in terms of participation and decision. Take the leadership role immediately, but understand that you are a facilitator rather than a dictator. Your job is to keep the team and its individual members focused on the objectives of the process, the game plan that you're using, and their expected and needed contribution. Keep the process moving, keep the players actively and effectively involved, make certain that everyone has a chance to be heard, seek agreement rather than consensus, and get decisions made within the team about the recommendations you are making through the construction of the plan. How you get that done is less through control and authority than through helping everyone understand his or her importance and influence in developing the plan with the method you have chosen.

**Figure 4-2.** Strategic planning game plans.

| | Customer | |
|---|---|---|
| | New | Existing |
| New | Total Team | Total Team + Directed Subteams |
| Existing | Directed Subteams + Total Team | Subteams |

*Service* (label on left axis)

## Laying Out the Game Plan

Roles will be better understood and accepted when they are explained in the context of a game plan or sequence of steps that will achieve the desired outcome of a strong strategic plan. Your choice of that game plan is a function of the extent of change you need to accomplish. Figure 4-2 provides a quick overview of the basic development situations that you will face and the recommended use of team members to best address them. If your strategies are more related to adjustments or fine-tuning of programs already under way, individuals or small subteams most familiar with the technical or operational aspects of the changes will be most effective, whereas the larger team serves as a sounding board and coordinating device. If your strategies involve providing new services to existing customers or offering existing services to new customers, you will need a balance between large team and subgroup activity. There will be much new information for everyone to learn and in turn communicate, so you will spend a lot of time as a whole team. On the other hand, not everything that you are now doing will be changing, so again the smaller subgroups can be used to develop the detail that can then be presented to the larger team. If your strategies lead you to new services and customers, keeping the larger team operating as an intact unit is crucial. In this case, no one knows everything but everyone has some insight to contribute as new internal and external relationships that need to be formed are identified, defined, and planned for. This overview perspective is needed by functional managers so that they can better explain and execute on required roles.

*Maintaining Focus on Goals*

Your biggest challenge in managing the strategic planning process will be in keeping your team and its members focused on the outcomes that you are responsible for producing. Remember that in the early stages of plan development, it is very easy to wander down the path of infinite detail in the name of gaining knowledge. Here you have to decide what is to be done, rather than how. Beware of paralysis of analysis. If you think enough has been discussed and is known, move for closure on a decision and proceed to the next one. Use a planning schedule or timetable to full advantage, because everyone on your team can relate to deadlines. Open team meetings with a review of the "planning plan," a summary of where you've been and are now, and a check against your planning calendar. For each working session, develop an objective that is directly related to making progress on your timetable, and let everyone know that it is going on. All the pieces are in place so now your job is to communicate, communicate, communicate.

# Information Requirements: What You Need to Know

You've already done some thinking about what you need to know and where you can find the information. Now is the time to begin doing something about it. Before you present your team with the task of developing a situation analysis, document what you've already done to establish a starting point for the process. Introduce it in the context of the mission, objective, and positioning statements that you already have. Your focus is to build a common base of understanding and direction so that you can proceed quickly to adding to what is already known to fill in the gaps. This allows you to define those additional requirements in relation to the mission and general strategic direction that you are pursuing.

Ultimately, your strategic plan must reflect and respond to your anticipation of changes or adjustments that will occur in the environments in which you operate, the industry you are part of, the customers you do or may serve, your competition, and your own organization. From this analysis will begin to emerge the opportunities available to you in the market and the foundation for the development of your plan. Again, the types and extent of changes you anticipate making in your market positioning will help you define which areas need to be most thoroughly examined and the relative importance of taking the time to do comprehensive research. Following are some of the basic information topics you'll most likely use and some ideas on how to find information.

*Your Environments*

Identifying the environmental factors that will have an impact on your efforts or influence your ability to succeed is always your first step. Few things are more discouraging or potentially dangerous to your firm than introducing a product or service to a market that has changed substantially from the one that it was designed for. If that introduction dealt with a major piece of your efforts, it could be a blow from which the organization would be unable to recover financially or in terms of customer perception. The types of environmental factors that you should consider and develop projections of the future for include economic climate, social trends, legal or regulatory climate, and so on. These are factors typically out of your control but not all that difficult to learn more about. The business periodicals that you and your team usually read contain a wealth of insight about these factors, since they tend to present issues of concern to all businesses. Beyond that, a trip to your local library and a short conversation with someone at the reference desk should provide you with more than enough information leads to follow up.

## Your Industry

Although trends and developments for the business you are in are related to changes in your operating environments as discussed previously, fundamental changes in the way business is conducted in an industry can also occur. For example, those financial institutions that had a solid understanding of the potential and uses for automated tellers enjoyed a distinct competitive advantage, whereas others struggled to catch up. Your analysis must identify such potential changes and how you might best take advantage of them. While trade journals from your own industry will give you after-the-fact insight into new developments or ideas, watching what's going on in industries that you use as part of your service offering or that provide major support to it are more likely to lead you to break-through ideas. Again, a good library is your most readily accessible source.

## Your Customers

Here again, your preliminary insights on the social environment will provide you with some starting points for thinking about your present and potential customers. If your strategic direction is pointed at more comprehensively servicing your present customers and those like them, in the absence of any major change anticipated in the environment, you have all the information sources you need within your own organization. Sales records, accounting records, customer service logs, and such will give you a clear picture of who your customers are, where they are, and what they buy. Conversations with your sales and service personnel can also help you clearly define what your customers like and don't like. You could even ask your customers for their own opinions. The point is that, in this case, the customers you already have and what you already know about them are your most reliable sources of information.

If your strategic direction is open to the possibilities of new types of customers, the job becomes a bit more difficult. You will have to define as much as possible who you expect these new customers to be, where they are, what they want, and how you'll find them. Once that is accomplished, your first search for information should still be internal. Your salespeople may immediately recognize the customer you describe as a prospect they know or even a present customer who is also a competitor's customer for what you're now proposing to offer. Use this source to clarify and refine your picture of this new customer before you embark on external market research to speed up that process and improve the utility of the information that it will provide you. In either case, don't discount the value of this step. You can never know too much about the customer; whenever the opportunity is available to learn more, grab it.

### Your Competitors

Building a real and reliable working knowledge about your present and potential competitors is one of your most difficult tasks in this area for two primary reasons. First, no competitors, yourself included, are in the practice of making information about their plans and strategies openly available. Second, if your competitors are competent, they are involved in a process much like the one you are; they will be a moving target, at best. This does not mean that you can't or shouldn't build a dossier on each viable competitor. You're just going to have to be a little smarter to do it.

Several sources of worthwhile information about competitors are available to you. One is your own staff. Your salespeople compete with them every day and will often have a very good operating knowledge about what your competitors are or may be planning to do. You should also identify and talk to any employee who previously worked for a competitor to gain any insight he or she may be able to provide. A second source is your customer base. Many of your customers may also be your competitors' customers and, if they think that helping you may provide them with the benefit of something better, will have information useful to you. Third is history. For all major competitors, you should document the moves and countermoves that they have made in the past as at least one way of predicting their future behavior.

The important point here is to remember that the actions you take do not happen in isolation. Your competitors will respond, and your strategy must include your best estimate of that response so that the strategy you invest in and implement is not rendered suboptimal as soon as your competitors react.

### Your Resources

Finally, do yourself the favor of using your team to identify, document, and quantify the organizational resources that will be available for use in constructing your strategic plan. Know in advance where the constraints as well as the flexibilities are. Market opportunities that you identify in the planning process become real opportunities for you only if you have the necessary resources and expertise to pursue them. If the basic strategic direction that has begun to emerge at this point is in conflict with your resource expectations, now is the time to find out if adjustments can be made before you've developed a strategy proposal that the organization simply cannot support. There will never be enough resources at your disposal to address all the opportunities available. Your challenge is to identify and develop strategies that make up the most effective competitive front given the limited resources available. If you have chosen the right players for your team, this should come together quickly. If it doesn't, evaluate your roster because you are missing someone important.

### Your Next Step

You've now done most of the preparation to do an effective job of strategic planning. You've laid out a plan, built your team, gathered pertinent information, and gotten everyone tuned in to what it is you're all there to accomplish. It's time to make some decisions and build a strategic plan.

## Steps in the Strategic Planning Process

The process of developing a strategic proposal is made up of a series of interrelated steps that all the work you have done up to now has prepared you for. Your team's focus is now on such activities as understanding the goals and objectives of the organization that your proposal must satisfy, assessing the environments in which you operate and identifying business opportunities, evaluating your resources and internal capabilities in relation to the opportunities seen, making choices among alternatives to produce the optimal strategic plan, and moving toward development of an integrated plan to implement your strategy throughout the organization.

Surrounding all the work you do to build your plan is a constant awareness of the requirement that your plan works. Each step should be checked against three basic performance dimensions. First is effectiveness, which is based on your estimate of the success of your service or program in relation to those of your competitors. Second is efficiency, which evaluates the expected outcome of your strategy in relation to the resources used to implement it. Third is adaptability, which projects your ability to adjust your strategy over time in response to changes in the marketplace and opportunities that emerge. Although you don't know the answers at this stage, making these performance factors part of your process of identifying, defining, and selecting strategic alternatives will dramatically improve your probability for success.

Following is a series of steps, supported by the work you have already done, that lead to a strategic proposal. Remind yourself and your team before you get started that your objective at this point is strategic. You are not trying to figure out how it can all be done, just what the best things are to do.

### Step 1: Mission and Directions

As in several of your previous activities, take the time now to once again make certain that you and your team have a correct and common understanding of the mission and objectives of the organization. The only valid outcome of your planning efforts is in a strategic proposal that best satisfies those requirements. Stay in the business that your organization has said it is in and provide for it the types of returns it most values. Keeping your proposal couched in this context will make its presentation, acceptance, and implementation a much smoother procedure.

## Step 2: Positioning Requirements

The positioning objectives of the organization provide a second set of guidelines for your efforts. These statements give you a clear definition of what the organization wants to be or how it wants to be perceived in the marketplace. Understanding and acceptance of these directions are especially useful in the steps involved with the evaluation and selection of strategic alternatives. For example, if your desired position on the competitive map is that of a low-cost provider of basic services delivered with consistency, a market opportunity that requires special attention or customized offerings is inconsistent with what management wants your organization to be. Your attention goes first to opportunities that match the organizational guidelines that you have been provided. It is only when the performance objectives of the organization cannot be met under those circumstances that you embark on the major effort to adjust or amend mission, objectives, and positioning. It is a step that should never be taken lightly because of the far-reaching effects it will have in your company and in the market. Your positioning is best developed and strengthened when you can take advantage of internal synergies that result from your strategies. This is accomplished when the investment you make or action you take to execute on one strategy supports one or more other existing opportunities or allows you to pursue a new one. For example, an investment in automated mail-sorting and distribution equipment to support a target marketing strategy employing direct mail communication with potential customers will also be likely to provide cost-reduction benefits to other strategies you are pursuing.

## Step 3: Environmental Evaluation

The situation analysis that you developed previously now comes very much into play. It is from your knowledge, assessment, and projections of the environmental situations that you will face that strategies are derived. Your analysis has given you the basis for determining whether your organizational guidelines are realistic; for understanding relevant economic factors, regulatory trends, and ethical issues; for developing a keen awareness of your competitors and the customer's buying behavior; and for evaluating your own strengths and weaknesses. A thorough and reliable environmental forecast is especially critical in the following situations:

1. Factors in your environments that you can't control have historically been or are expected to be subject to frequent or large shifts;
2. You are proposing major financial investment to implement and support a strategic move;
3. You will be entering new geographic markets for the long haul;
4. You will be introducing new services or programs that are expected to have reasonably long life cycles; or

5. The fundamental health of your business could be severely impacted by a change in one or a small number of those factors.

Your challenge here is to identify and isolate those environmental factors that influence your ability to operate or affect the makeup of the marketplace that you serve. To the extent that you can accomplish this, you have enabled yourself to identify and develop strategic initiatives that will provide you with real competitive advantages. Examples of shifts in critical environmental factors abound in what we've seen in just the last few years. The regulatory environment for providers of telecommunication services has seen dramatic change. The stock market crash, failure of parts of the thrift banking system, and the ongoing problems with the federal deficit have caused displacements in everyone's economic environment. The trends in the legal environment related to the tort system pose real and potentially dangerous liability issues. The growth in the mature market and its buying power has generated both market opportunities and policy challenges for those affected by this social trend. Globalization of markets and the accelerated adoption and use of these methods of strategic planning are causing fundamental changes in many competitive environments. Your success will be less determined by finding some unique new insight than it will by your ability to structure a plan that recognizes the critical environmental variables, anticipates changes that are likely to occur in them, and can be adapted quickly and correctly when those changes occur. The only safe assumptions that you can make are that your environments will change and that your competitors are all going to be outstanding marketers. Your advantage lies in understanding and ongoing execution.

Once you have identified the pertinent environmental considerations, you should pose the important questions related to them. What if the consumer need you have identified is a fad rather than lasting? What if the market opportunity you are pursuing is suddenly deemed to be in the public interest, and legislation or direct government intervention occurs? What if you or your competitors find it difficult, if not impossible, to operate profitably and they flee the market, leaving you to deal with a serious business problem? These questions go to the heart of a strategy in terms of your ability to sustain an effort begun or defend a position held. It is the answers to this series of "what if's" that are readily supplied by your best strategic alternatives. You might go so far as to get them down on paper and pin them to the wall during the balance of your development work.

## Step 4: Customer Analysis

What you are really dealing with here is market segmentation. You've gathered much data on present and potential customers. You have data on the whens, wheres, whys, and hows of their buying behavior. It's time to turn those data into strategic information. Your data become information when they enable you to develop a strategy or design a program that appeals to the needs and expectations of a viable segment of consumers that you desire.

If you can identify what your customers really buy—as opposed to what they accept in accompanying baggage—you have found the potential for competitive advantage. Do customers buy special mail-forwarding services or do they buy "absolutely, positively overnight"? Are they really interested in financial planning or are they simply looking for peace of mind about their future? You must understand the expectations of your customer. In simplest terms, it is what they get for what they are willing to pay. What they get is directly related to the need they are trying to satisfy with any extra features looked on as niceties. What they are willing to pay can be time, money, effort, and so on. Value is created for the customer and success for the organization when you consistently meet or exceed the customer's expectations.

A fair question at this point asks that if it's so straightforward, how come so few companies do it effectively? First, organizations will tend to resist the ongoing commitment and hard work that are required if acceptable results are otherwise generated. Surely you recognize the shortsightedness of that view. Second, it is hard to surrender your organization to the customer. This is an everyday, every-employee focus on accepting the satisfaction of the customer's needs as the common cause. It's scary, but it is also the stuff of which the winners in the marketplace are made.

## Step 5: Strategy Development and Evaluation

Finally! It certainly has taken a lot of time and effort to get here, but stop for a second and look at where you are. You know where your organization wants to go and what it wants to be and expects to receive when it gets there. You have a solid working knowledge of your environments, the critical variables in them for your business, and an insightful assessment of how they will behave in the future. You understand what your customers really want and what they are willing to pay for it. You have anticipated your competitors' reactions to your moves in the market. Most important, you have a team of experienced people who know all this as well as you do. How can you lose?

Let this knowledge be the only limitation to your search for strategies at this stage. Encourage open discussion and brainstorming with your team. Don't be evaluative or judgmental about any contribution. Emphasize that the only bad ideas are the ones that didn't get expressed. Each member of the team has distinct experience and expertise from his or her position in the organization. Use it and build on it. Let one thought add to the one before it until an avenue is exhausted and then move on. During the strategy identification phase, your only concern should be in generating as many ideas as possible that can help you gain or hold the position you want. Because the people on your team do have some idea of what they are talking about, there will inevitably be some screening of ideas. Do your best to keep that focused on suggestions that are in conflict with your organizational guidelines.

Now you have a list of ideas, but it's still not time to evaluate them. Have the discipline to take each one of the potential strategies or opportunities identified and document and quantify it. Gather the data you have and turn them into strategic information. Spell out who the target customers are, where they are, how many there are, what they want, who you'll have to compete with, the stability of the market, potential sales and profits, and so on. Each of these opportunity outlines is your working document for the next two phases of the development process, so do a complete job of documenting the information and make certain that each member of the team has a copy of the same writeup for each idea. At least you'll be sure that you are all singing out of the same hymn book as you proceed.

It's still not time to make decisions about the strategic alternatives you have identified and documented. Your focus now is on assessing your organization's ability to support the execution of each alternative you have defined. This relates directly to resource adequacy and organizational expertise. It is why you built your team the way you did. Work now to define what parts of the organization would be involved in implementing the strategy, whether or not they have the expertise to execute that role, and what degree of their available resources would be taken up if the alternative is accepted. Remember, there are no right or wrong answers here. You're just trying to add to the strategic information you have about each alternative. The functional experts on your team can provide answers about what it will take to effectively and efficiently pursue the idea. Another outcome of this phase, and a good reason for paying attention to it, is that it lays the groundwork for the implementation planning you will do for those strategies accepted as part of your plan.

Now, make some decisions. Look at each one of your idea sheets. Does it fit with the organization's mission, objectives, and desired positioning? If the answer is no, reject it and move to the next one, but don't throw it away. Who knows, next year it could well be the answer you're looking for. If the answer is yes, evaluate the stability of the opportunity. Will it still be there tomorrow or are its environments volatile? Uncertain or unstable opportunities should be moved aside but not discarded. They may still be needed to meet objectives or might take on a different look when combined with an acceptable alternative. What you're now working with are opportunities that fit your guidelines and look like they will be around for a while. So how do you choose? First, does it have enough sales or profit potential to justify consideration? Big isn't necessarily better, but big enough to justify the investment required is mandatory. If the potential appears to be inadequate, set it aside. Again you may find later on that it carries little or no incremental cost to pursue in conjunction with a more attractive strategy. Second, given that the potential exists, can the resources and expertise of your organization support it? If not, set it aside. Again you may find that you need it later on to meet objectives, or one of your recommended strategies might be to develop the resources and expertise now so that a good opportunity can be pursued in the future. Third, gather up the survivors from this step and go to the next. You're almost there.

## Step 6: Strategy Selection

All of the alternative opportunities left on your list meet your evaluation criteria, so two more cuts at it should be made. But first you need to refresh everyone's memory with respect to the quantitative and qualitative objectives of the organization. The strategies you select to make up your plan proposal must accomplish those objectives.

With this in mind, your first pass with all of the acceptable opportunities is to rank or prioritize them. As noted earlier, the hallmarks of good strategy are effectiveness, efficiency, and adaptability. With respect to effectiveness what you're really asking is if it will get you where you want to go. Here you're rating the strategy's contribution to the objectives you are charged with achieving. This may be sales volume, profits generated, perceptions built, and so on. Be realistic with your assessment. Next is efficiency, where you are evaluating the projected return against the investment required. Here you could look at the organization as a customer because it wants to know what it's going to get for what it's being asked to pay. Carefully identify both this relationship and the percentage of available resources that would be used. You want to maximize the return-to-cost relationship, but you can't overdraw your resources account. Finally you need to assess adaptability. You know that change is a certainty, so how difficult or costly will it be to adjust or modify the strategy in relation to the probability that you will have to do it? Be very careful about strategies that appear to paint you into a corner. There is no one best way to score strategies on these measures. Find one that makes sense to you and your team, and stick with it.

Having set your priorities, you now need to start adding them up to see if you have met your objectives. You also need to keep track of how you are doing with respect to resource capacity. Start with your number-one priority and add the second and the third and so on until you have what you need to meet your quantitative objectives. If the fates are with you, this is done within the resource constraints you must accept. If you meet the objectives but exceed your resources, develop alternative scenarios for strategy combinations that both recognize your priorities and balance your resources. If the list you are working with does not add up to meet your objectives, return to the less attractive alternatives that you set aside previously, rank them according to priorities, and go through the cycle again. Repeat the procedure until you have what you need. If you still can't get there, go back to the idea generation stage and forge on to a conclusion.

### Step 7: Contingency Planning

While all this is still fresh in your mind, lay out, for each strategy that is now part of your plan, your expectation of environmental changes or competitor reactions that are likely to occur and a basic outline of your recommendation of what will need to be done to adapt. Make this a documented part of your plan so that if the need arises to react quickly, you already have a head start. The best-laid plans can go awry so one of the best measures of the quality of your plan is in its ability to anticipate those points of deviation and preparedness to deal with them. You're not looking for a great deal of detail here, but at least identify the most likely changes that you would have to respond to, what parts of the organization would have to be mobilized to react, and a general idea of what they would be asked to do.

Congratulations, you've got a plan. Now you really get to go to work!

## The Expected Outcomes

The assumption is made here that you and/or your team do not have final decision-making authority with respect to acceptance of your plan and the commitment of the requested organizational resources to it. As you move forward, several different audiences inside and outside of your organization will need to be influenced by your strategic proposal, from executive management to functional units and ultimately to customers. Your task is to develop one strategic story that, with minor adjustment, can be used with any audience to explain all or part of your plan.

Executive management wants to hear a bottom-line kind of story. You are asking for their approval and commitment to proceed, and in return they want to know two basic things. First is the extent to which your proposal meets or exceeds the organizational requirements represented by the mission, objective, and positioning statements they provided you. Second is the degree of effectiveness of the competitive front that you will build for the resources you will use. The conceptual part of this story has already been developed in all the work and thinking that you documented during the strategy development process. The tangible part, beyond a writeup, still needs to be done. This is best accomplished by developing a prospective pro forma for each component of your strategic plan that builds to an overall financial projection for your plan. Although much of what you use here may be ballpark estimates, you have generated enough strategic information to make it much more than an educated guess. At this point, you should go ahead and do the same thing for the alternatives you did not accept, with whatever information you have available.

When you make your management presentation, expect a lot of questions. You've done your job well, so answering them is not a problem. Expect issues to be raised about the assumptions you have made to make your decisions. This group does have a different perspective on the organization and its business than do you and your team. What you all share is a desire for the best possible results. Use this interaction for all it is worth for adjusting and fine-tuning your plan. Flexibility and compromise now can save a lot of frustration later. Concurrence on strategy will lead to commitment of action, and you do need their concurrence. Who knows, even some of the strategies you passed on might come back into play. It wouldn't be the first time that "new" resources were suddenly found to pursue an attractive but unplanned for opportunity.

Once agreement is reached, you are ready to start telling your story to the rest of the organization that will be affected by your plan. This is important for two reasons. First, you still owe management a detailed implementation plan that you will be asking the functional units of the organization to help you put together. This is the focus of a later step in this process. Second, employees are going to do a better job executing on your plan and feel better about doing it to the extent that you can help them understand why they are doing it, who they are doing it for (the customer), and how it will benefit them (the customer and the organization). You may be asking people to take on new roles or serve different customers. You need to be certain that what you are telling your customers externally is consistent with what the organization understands and is prepared to deliver internally.

The third version of your strategic story is the one that you are going to tell the customer. This should be the easiest of all, because everything that you have developed stems from your understanding of what that customer needs, wants, and expects. Your planning is directed toward matching your actions with your words. This will, however, be the true test of the quality of your strategic plan. Will the customer respond?

Your presentation to the customer is made up of the parts of the marketing mix that you manipulate to best match the needs and expectations of your target in the marketplace with the requirements of your organization. For the service marketer, the standard mix components of product, price, place, and promotion are the foundation of your offering. Product must clearly define to the customer what you are offering or are prepared to do, so that it can be easily checked against the need you have found to exist. Price tells the customer not only what you expect to be paid for what you provide, but also communicates more subtle messages about perceived quality. Place tells the customer where and how your offering can be accessed and the extent to which it meets requirements that may exist for convenience or perhaps even exclusivity. Promotion is then the basic package you use to communicate all of the salient features and benefits of your offering to the customer and potentially its competitive advantage.

As a service marketer, however, you know that the standard mix components are not enough. As you have already noted, the people of your organization and their understanding and commitment to taking up the cause of the customer are crucial to your success. This suggests three additional components that the growing body of knowledge about services marketing indicates must be a part of your presentation to your customer. First are the participants. They are the employees of your organization who come in direct contact with the customer or directly support those who do, enabling them to provide superior performance. Their understanding of, commitment to, and excitement about their role is one of the most telling aspects of your offering. Second is physical evidence. One of the major challenges you face is the intangibility of your product. Success is dramatically influenced by your ability to ''tangibilize,'' or create physical evidence. This may be as simple as the comfort and decor of a waiting room. The benefits you can gain are well worth any effort. Third is the process you have designed to do what you do. You engineer a system to perform consistently with effectiveness and efficiency. It gives the customer no less than expected every time and responsibly utilizes the resources of the organization. You get benefits here from elimination of waste or duplication in your delivery system and reduction of the degree to which your people must throw themselves into the breach to make up for system deficiencies or glitches that impede serving the customer. Taken together, you have seven components that can be linked to communicate a powerful and persuasive message.

You now have two steps remaining in the strategic journey you embarked on, which at times seems like years ago. They are the real outcomes of all of the work you have done. Very simply, implementation planning is organizing the organization to make it happen. Strategic control is making sure that it works. These are the subjects of the last two sections.

# Implementation Planning

Excitement is running high. You can almost see everything you have planned for actually happening. But you can't do it. Your team can't do it. It takes the people of your organization to help you develop an action plan and timetable. That is when strategy can change to reality. It is only when the specific tasks to be accomplished are defined, the deadlines for those activities established, and the monitoring and control points are put in place that you can begin to move forward. Your objective in implementation planning is to identify the functions involved, develop detailed plans for the roles that they play, and manage the needed relationships and cooperation among functions that support successful operation and satisfied customers.

Your focus here is on the empowerment of the people who serve the customer to execute the strategy you have developed. Empowerment is evidenced by a commitment on the part of the organization to both the satisfaction of the customer and the development of its people by making available the opportunities and resources that allow them both to see a return on the investment they are asked to make. Empowerment means pushing authority, responsibility, and ownership in your objectives to the levels of the organization that are closest to the customer, so that you can tap into their knowledge and effort. For your employees, it means removing any obstacle they identify that prevents them from doing their job and playing their part in creating and keeping satisfied customers.

## Step 1: Expanding the Team

The core strategy development team that you started with must now identify the remaining managers and employees of the organization who will be needed to formulate an effective implementation plan. They may play any one or all of three different parts. The first is in providing the functional knowledge and experience that will be required to identify the tasks that must be performed to achieve your objectives and the detail of how it can best be done. The second is in providing a reality test for your strategies, their expected results, and estimates of resource utilization. The third and perhaps most critical part is in communicating the plan and everyone's role in it throughout the organization. Implementation planners should be the people who manage or influence day-to-day activity and the employees who do it. Again, don't fill an auditorium. You need valid input and the consistent communication of your strategic story. The larger this group becomes, the more difficult that is to accomplish.

## Step 2: Setting the Stage

Just as with your core strategy team, you start your work with the implementation team by using the mission, objective, and positioning statements of the organization to serve as the focus for this level of planning and as both the basis and goal for the implementation effort. This allows you to establish the superordinate goal(s) that everyone can buy into because it is everyone's responsibility to achieve them. It helps you settle differences of opinion that occur when people try to maximize the performance of a function rather than optimize the results of the overall effort. This approach also provides for the legitimacy of your strategic plan.

## Step 3: Outlining the Strategic Plan

Now you can tell your strategic story to this audience but from a different perspective than the one you used with executive management. Their concerns are more related to what they will be asked to do and what results they will be held responsible for. Keep the focus in this step on the expected outcomes of the strategies that have been accepted rather than on how they will be accomplished. You have to know where you are going before you can figure out how to get there. Use the members of your core team (to whom many of these people likely report) to explain the individual strategic elements of your plan and provide their perspective from the standpoint of the function they represent and are responsible for. Doing an effective job here accomplishes three things. First, it shows the larger implementation team that there is a common understanding and spirit of cooperation at your level, which will make it easier to develop at theirs. Second, it identifies the relationships that must be fostered between different parts of the organization and management's commitment to direct cooperatively and systematically the activities and resources of the various functional units involved. Third, it gives everyone the necessary information to communicate strategy effectively and consistently further down in the organization.

## Step 4: Developing the Implementation Proposal

Once this team has gained a clear understanding of the expected outcomes of the strategic plan, you can get on with the business of identifying what specifically needs to be done to reach the desired destination and defining how best to do it. This is done in two stages, one still as a group and the other within functional units.

At the group level, have the implementation team identify the relationships and dependencies that are created by the plan. These exist at three levels. First is the relationship between the function and the organization, which addresses the role played and the flexibility the unit is allowed in allocating activity and resources to achieve its goals. Second is the relationship between functions with respect to who is responsible for doing what things to make the strategy happen or which units rely on each other for support or execution in order to perform their role. Third is the relationship between the function and the strategy that looks at the degree of similarity of the role they are being asked to play and the existing programs and policies of the unit. This stage identifies inconsistencies that must be dealt with before you can proceed and interdependencies that must be factored into the implementation planning process.

When these issues have been identified and settled, you can move to the functional unit level for the development of detailed operational plans. Let the managers you added as part of your implementation team head up these efforts. They and their people, who ultimately are charged with making things happen and who tend to be closest to the customer, deserve the chance to advise you on the best way to accomplish the task at hand. You've provided the organizational and strategic perspectives; now charge these groups with coming back to the table with a detailed plan and timetable for how they will communicate, prepare for, and execute their role. You and your core team should be available as consultants, but you must resist the temptation to tell these groups what to do and how to do it. You need their ideas. Concentrate your activities on providing reinforcement of strategic information, defining goals and expectations, explaining roles, helping to bridge organizational gaps between functions that are dependent on each other or that must act in concert to be effective.

## Step 5: Consolidating the Proposal

With your implementation planning team pulled back together, review the plans that have been developed. You can do this either by function for all strategies or each strategy for all functions, whichever works best for your group. The emphasis is on all the functions hearing others' plans and making sure that they are not working at cross-purposes.

What you are aiming for here is a comprehensive implementation plan. Each functional plan must be evaluated for its own efficiency of operation and marketplace impact as well as its compatibility with and contribution to a unified plan. Here again expect some issues to be raised and disagreements to occur, but if you stayed on top of the process with your team, there should be no surprises. Use the whole implementation team to sort out the real issues, effect acceptable compromises or adjustments, and present a final proposal that spells out roles, eliminates overlaps, uses resources to their best advantage, establishes accountability, and provides a workable timetable for execution.

## Step 6: Finalizing the Plan

As stipulated in a previous section, you still owe executive management a presentation of your implementation plan proposal before you will receive final approval on the whole strategic plan package. You should be confident for several reasons. One, everything that you have done has been focused on the customer, who is the ultimate arbiter of the success you will enjoy. Two, your plan is firmly grounded in the expectations and requirements of the organization. Three, your strategic approach has already met with approval. Four, your plans have been developed with the involvement of all functions who have a role to play. Five, your implementation proposal was built from the ground up and has a firm understanding of what can realistically be accomplished. Fine-tuning may still take place in this step, but that should be accepted and taken advantage of for all the same reasons as noted before. Finally, you have the approval to go.

### Step 7: Executing

Don't pop the champagne corks just yet. There is still some important work to do before you celebrate. You must prepare for the successful introduction and ongoing implementation of your plan. You need a systematic approach aimed at enabling the organization to execute effectively. Use an internal marketing process to make certain that all the players in the organization are on the same strategic wavelength. They must know what they do, why they do it, who they do it for, and what everyone gets out of it. Educational programs related to that knowledge and the skills required to fulfill the roles must be developed and delivered. Lines of communication must be established and opened across, up, and down the organization. This is one of the ongoing tasks of your strategy and implementation teams. Monitoring points and feedback mechanisms, which are the subject of the last section, must be put in place to assure that the information needed to successfully adapt and extend your strategies is being collected and communicated. Execution begins. Okay, now you can pop the corks!

## Strategic Planning Is a Process, Not an Event

Throughout this process you have thought about, identified, and planned for change. In many ways, change is the only constant in the business world and one of the few things that you can absolutely rely on. The reason that you spent the time developing a thorough situation analysis and contingency plans to back up your strategies is that you have anticipated the changes that are most likely to occur and determined how you will respond to them in order to hold or develop an advantage in the marketplace. Now make it happen.

The plans that have been developed will readily indicate the components of your strategic and implementation plans that must be watched closely. The teams you put together to implement those plans, and who by now understand the strategies and their expected outcomes as well as you do, provide a multitude of eyes and ears spread throughout the organization. Keep those channels of communication open and the information flowing. Don't let people fall into the comfortable trap of focusing on just their function or role, forgetting that it is part of a larger plan. Determine what information you need, how often you want it, and who is responsible for getting it to you. Maintain an ongoing meeting schedule with both your strategy and implementation teams to review results, discuss changes, and activate contingency plans as appropriate.

Remember that the implementation of your strategic plan does not happen in isolation. There are uncontrollable factors in your environments and competitors in your markets that insist on moving around and muddying up the water. The good news is that you anticipated that this would happen and you prepared for it. Watch what happens, verify that it is what you expected and use your contingency plans, or that it isn't and put new ones into play. The effectiveness with which you monitor, evaluate, and adjust to change will determine a large part of your ability to deliver consistently good results.

Finally, realize that superior performance is a double-edged sword. Few things motivate strong competitive reaction like conspicuous success. Just keep in mind that a hit today won't be quite so easy tomorrow because of the competition you have invited in. Given the tendency of consumers to be a somewhat fickle lot, today's winner can be tomorrow's flop. On the other hand, superior performance and successful results are what you and your organization are striving for. A strong commitment to an effective strategic planning process keeps that sword in your hands.

## Summary

At the beginning of this chapter it was proposed that strategic development and planning would provide you with a systematic approach for dealing with the uncertainties of your business environment and a means to move effectively from idea to implementation. If that is what happened, then the "plan" for this discussion was a success. Now you recognize and understand the extent of commitment that an organization must make in attention, time, resources, and support to mount an effective strategic planning effort.

Refer back to Figure 4-1 on page 58 for a schematic picture of the process that has been proposed here. The schematic is a quick reference, but more important, it helps to show the building-block approach recommended and takes some of the intimidation out of the challenge.

You start with organizational and market direction. Your plan is going to be built to satisfy a consumer, but it must also recognize and address the needs and expectations of your organization. You must identify and verify the requirements of both these customers for your strategic plan. Second, you prepare yourself for planning. The quality of the time spent and work done in this phase will have a lot to do with the degree of success you will enjoy. Building the right team, defining roles and expectations, laying out the process to be used, maintaining focus on the goals of that process, and comprehensively identifying information needs all contribute to putting you into position to plan effectively. Third, a strategic plan recommendation is developed. Starting with the organizational requirements defined by the mission, direction, and positioning statements of the company, you explore your environment to look for market opportunities for which customers exist and on which you can plan for and execute to fulfill your organization's needs. Fourth, through presentation, explanation, and discussion with executive management, you transform your strategic proposal into a plan that the company is committed to acting on. Fifth, with the help and participation of the organization at large, you construct an implementation plan that most efficiently and effectively deploys the resources available to maximize performance on the strategic objectives that have been accepted.

Here is where you turn ideas into actions. Finally, you manage the ongoing execution of your strategic and implementation plans to assure continued successful operation in the marketplace.

*       *       *       *

***Michael J. Pessetti*** *is business planning manager for the Foremost Insurance Group, a provider of personal lines, property and casualty insurance products. In this capacity he focuses on long-range planning for developing businesses, as well as products and channels of distribution for standard and preferred customer groups. He previously worked for Foremost in areas including market planning and sales management. Currently he also serves on the advisory board for the insurance education program at Olivet College.*

# PART III

# HOW TO MARKET INSIDE YOUR ORGANIZATION, OR HELPING EMPLOYEES ACHIEVE SERVICE EXCELLENCE

# About This Part

The three chapters in this part consider what has to happen *inside* a service organization to make a customer focus possible. Because services are largely experiential, requiring consumer-provider contact, the conduct of service employees is crucial in providing a consistent level of quality to customers.

Chapter 5 (the lead chapter in this part) discusses internal marketing, a concept new to marketing to accommodate the labor-intensive nature of services. Internal marketing concerns how to create dedicated employees, the rationale being that if you have dedicated employees, you have the potential for creating satisfied customers. The one-on-one provider-customer relationship typical of most service businesses makes internal marketing a necessity. The "moments of truth"* that take place when the customer has contact with the service organization must be effective for customer satisfaction to result. Disgruntled employees do not create satisfying moments of truth for customers. All of the components of an effective internal marketing program are discussed in Chapter 5. Short case histories are provided to show how the components produce the desired result—motivated, sensitive employees who serve the customer well all of the time.

Chapter 6 is a case history describing how a service organization makes the shift from an operational perspective to a customer orientation. Ten key actions in effecting such a shift are discussed and then illustrated through an example. In the example, a mid-size public accounting firm is considering whether to develop or drop a particular segment of the market. The ten key actions are applied to this situation to illustrate how it would be approached using a customer perspective, rather than a "we-know-what's-best-for-the-customer" approach.

Chapter 7 looks at how the structure of the service organization supports employees in carrying out a customer orientation. The specific issues involved in organizational design in a service business are discussed. An array of organizational possibilities is provided, together with a discussion of the practical implications of each organizational arrangement.

These chapters make clear the diffuse nature of marketing in a service organization. Everyone's focus has to be on the customer. The relative autonomy across functions in goods-producing organizations is not appropriate in service organizations where every department and every employee has direct or indirect responsibility for customer satisfaction and service quality. "Customer service" is not a separate function or department in a service business; it is everywhere.

---

*This term was popularized by Jan Carlzon when he led the repositioning of Scandinavian Airlines System in the early 1980s.

# 5

## Developing Customer-Conscious Employees at Every Level: Internal Marketing

William R. George
Christian Grönroos

If you want your service organization to be successful in the marketplace, you must adopt an internal marketing strategy in order to develop customer-conscious employees. The first section of this chapter raises questions and provides answers about the essentials of internal marketing. This part of the chapter will help you evaluate internal marketing as part of strategic management. The second part presents guidelines to help top management determine the significance of this management strategy. In the third section you will find tactical steps for developing and implementing an internal marketing strategy. Two brief case histories illustrate this emerging management strategy. Sanger-Harris Department Store is the subject of one case. A freight-forwarding transportation company provides the setting for a more comprehensive case on internal marketing.

## How to Evaluate Internal Marketing as a Part of Strategic Management

Internal marketing operates as a holistic management process to integrate the multiple functions of the firm in two ways. First, it ensures that the employees at all levels in the firm understand and experience the business and its various activities and campaigns in the context of an environment that supports customer consciousness. Second, it ensures that all employees be prepared and motivated to act in a service-oriented manner. The premise of internal marketing is that internal exchanges between the organization and its employee groups must be operating effectively before the organization can be successful in achieving its goals regarding its external markets. Thus, employees take priority as the initial market of the organization.

### Internal Marketing Essentials

Answers to several questions help to explain the basics of an internal marketing program.

<u>What Is Internal Marketing?</u>   Internal marketing is a philosophy for managing the firm's human resources based on a marketing perspective. This philosophy must be transformed into an internal action program that becomes a continuous process so that a lasting motivation for service and customer orientation among the personnel is achieved. The internal marketing concept states that *the internal market of employees is best motivated for service-mindedness and customer-oriented behavior by an active, marketinglike approach, where marketinglike activities are used internally.*

Certain aspects of an internal marketing program have been in place in many organizations for a long period of time. What is new with the internal marketing concept as described in this chapter is the introduction of a unifying concept for more effectively managing a variety of established activities and adding new activities as part of an overall program. The importance of internal marketing is the fact that it allows management to approach all of these activities in a much more systematic and strategic manner.

<u>Why Is Internal Marketing Needed Today?</u>   The increasing attention to internal marketing is due to the movement from the industrial era to the new competition of the service economy where the logic of the manufacturer has to be replaced by a "service know-how."[1] The single most critical issue in this transition away from the logic of the manufacturer is the notion of employees as the scarce resource. The skillful, service-oriented employees, rather than the raw materials, the production technology or the products themselves, are vitally important in most businesses today. These employees will be even more critical in the relevant future.

Employees remain the key to success at the "moments of truth"[2] when the service provider (the so-called contact person of the company) and the customer meet and interact. Service organizations, such as banks, insurance companies, hotels, restaurants, telecommunication companies, and professional firms, cannot easily differentiate their services on the basis of mere technical quality of the outcome rendered to their customers. Instead, how the organization manages the buyer-seller interactions—that is, the quality of the service production and delivery process—is much more important to success in the marketplace.[3] The growing importance of technology, which increases the effectiveness and efficiency of the service process, means that the decreasing number of employee contacts becomes even more crucial.[4]

These same developments are apparent in the industrial sector as well. Manufacturers of goods are recognizing that what now counts is their ability to add various kinds of services to enhance their exchanges with customers. Skillful and service-oriented employees must provide a variety of service elements during the organization's exchanges with its customers. Such service elements, including technical service, repair and maintenance, customer training, consultancy, billing, claims handling, telephone receptionists, and so on, are often necessary in the selling of both goods and services.

*Relationship and interactive marketing.* Services marketing is changing, especially in the areas of the marketing mix and order-taking selling. More emphasis is now being placed on keeping customers and cross-selling to existing customers. The concepts of relationship marketing and interactive marketing[5] have been developed in order to describe marketing programs that emphasize the service providers and are directed toward the existing customers of a company.

In both relationship and interactive marketing the role of the employee is vital. Moreover, it is not the marketing specialists of the marketing department who are the most important human resources. During customer contact these specialists are frequently outnumbered by a variety of employees whose main duties are production, deliveries, technical service, claims handling, and other tasks that traditionally are considered nonmarketing. However, the skills, customer orientation, and service-mindedness of these employees are of critical importance to customers' perception of the company and to their future patronage behavior. Gummesson has introduced the term *part-time marketer* to describe the status of such employees.[6]

Indeed these part-time marketers must meet the challenges of marketing to existing customers or the company will have to buy its market share more expensively by trying to get new customers. Thus, the company must consider its employees as a *first, internal market* so that they fulfill their tasks as part-time marketers. Systematic internal marketing is the mechanism for developing and maintaining service-minded customer-contact employees.

<u>What Situations Call for Internal Marketing?</u>   In principle three different types of situations can be identified where internal marketing is called for:

1. When creating a service culture in the company and a service orientation among the personnel
2. When maintaining a service orientation among the personnel
3. When introducing new goods and services as well as new marketing campaigns and marketing activities to the employees

Each of these situations will be discussed.

*Developing a service culture.* A service culture exists when a service orientation and an interest in the customer are the most important norms in the company. The Walt Disney organization, SAS Airlines, and Nordstrom Department Stores are examples of businesses with established service cultures.

Today a service culture is lacking in most businesses. In such cases, internal marketing is often viewed as a means of achieving a service culture. Internal marketing programs alone are not sufficient to achieve such a culture in the company, however. Four areas must be developed for the establishment of a service culture. First, there are organizational requirements for good service. The organization's structure, both formal and informal, has to support good service instead of counteracting it, as is far too common today. Second, there are strategic requirements for good service; that is, good service and the development of human resources must be recognized as strategic variables. Third, there are managerial requirements because the managers and supervisors must believe that these variables can position the organization for competitive advantage. They must actively support a service orientation and customer-conscious employees. Finally, there are attitudinal requirements for good service. Every employee has to understand and accept the importance of relationship marketing and the interactive marketing function. Indeed, employees must be committed to dual responsibilities—that is, responsibility for their "main duties" as well as their "part-time marketing" duties. Each of these four requirements is needed to achieve a service culture.

Clearly, the preceding four requirements mean that internal marketing programs in a vacuum cannot establish a service culture. However, these programs are a powerful means for developing such a culture in connection with other activities. The internal marketing goals for helping to achieve a service culture include: (1) to enable the employees—managers, supervisors, and all others—to understand and accept the business mission, the strategies and tactics, the goods and services, and the marketing campaigns of the firm; (2) to develop a service-oriented management and leadership style among managers and supervisors; and (3) to teach all employees service-oriented communications and interaction skills.

*Maintaining a service culture.* Once a service culture has been created, it has to be maintained in an active manner. Otherwise the attitudes and behaviors of the personnel and the norms in the firm will easily revert back to a bureaucratic culture where only technical efficiency is the guiding principle. The internal marketing goals for helping to maintain a service culture include: (1) ensuring that the management methods are supportive and enhance the service-mindedness and customer orientation of the employees; (2) ensuring that the employees receive continuous information and feedback; and (3) marketing new goods and services as well as marketing campaigns and activities to the employees before they are launched externally. The most important internal marketing issue here is management support of every single manager and supervisor. When they are able to encourage their subordinates, when they can open up the channels of communication, and when they make sure that feedback information regularly reaches their subordinates, an established service culture can be expected to continue.

*Introducing new goods and services as well as new marketing activities.* Internal marketing originally emerged as a systematic way of handling these types of introductions. Note that this level of internal marketing is interrelated with and reinforces the other two situations calling for internal marketing. These introductions, however, form an internal marketing task in their own right. The internal marketing goals for helping with these introductions include: (1) making employees aware of and accepting of new goods and services being developed and offered to the market; (2) making employees aware of and accepting of new traditional marketing campaigns and activities that are mostly mass marketing; and (3) making employees aware of and accepting of new ways in which various tasks influencing relationship and interactive marketing performance of the company are to be executed.

<u>What Are the Prerequisites for Successful Internal Marketing?</u>   If internal marketing activities are implemented as a program without connections to other management factors, the risk that nothing enduring will be achieved is overwhelming. The three prerequisites for successful internal marketing are: (1) internal marketing has to be considered an integral part of strategic management; (2) the internal marketing program must not be counteracted by the organizational structure or lack of management support; and (3) top management must constantly demonstrate an active support for the internal marketing program.

In order to be successful, internal marketing starts with top management. Next, middle management and supervisors have to accept and live up to their role in an internal marketing process. Only then can internal marketing activities directed toward customer-contact employees be successful. The contact employees' ability to function as ''part-time marketers'' depends to a large extent on the support they get from other employees and functions within the organization. Often there are large numbers of support persons who do not come in contact with customers themselves, but who nevertheless indirectly influence the service the ultimate customers get. These supporting personnel are, in fact, ''part-time marketers'' as well, because they should recognize the contact employees as their internal customers. The support personnel should perform marketinglike activities for the customer-contact employees (i.e., their internal customers) in order to assist the contact employees in servicing the company's ultimate customer.

# How to Determine the Significance of Internal Marketing

Guidelines to help top management understand the significance of internal marketing in achieving organizational goals will be needed by the person(s) who champions the adoption of an internal marketing program. A considerable commitment in resources is necessary for internal marketing to become successful. Top management needs to understand the costs and benefits of an internal marketing strategy. The following directives provide the internal marketing champions with the agenda for reviewing this management approach with the top decision makers.

## Document the Current Situation

There are many signals that indicate internal marketing may be an appropriate new strategy. Basic causes that support the adoption of an internal marketing program include: customer dissatisfaction about their interactions with the company; longtime tensions between functional areas; low employee awareness about the firm's mission, direction, new offerings, and marketing campaigns, as well as their own role in each of these; employee morale problems; complex or extensive service encounters; and so on. These particular basic causes must be presented in an objective way with all available research data to support each cause.

*Assess the Internal Marketing Concept*

Begin by informally discussing the basic causes noted earlier and the idea of a new management approach to address these problems. From these discussions determine a small group of allies who meet informally to learn more about internal marketing as a possible solution. Enlarge this support base and use a creeping commitment approach to develop a following. Hold a top-level meeting to discuss: (1) relevant basic problems, (2) the substance of the internal marketing concept as discussed previously, (3) the costs and benefits of an internal marketing program.

The Costs of an Internal Marketing Program.   Internal marketing entails numerous costs. It requires a major commitment of resources, including time demands at all levels of the organization, significant changes in thinking and behaving at all levels of the organization, a team to develop and implement the program, and a budget to support this development and implementation. Note, however, that in some cases the new budget may be more of a redirection of existing resources and costs (e.g., training programs).

The Benefits of an Internal Marketing Program.   The major benefit of a successful internal marketing program is its synergistic impact on the contributions from the individual units of the organization. It is a strategic approach that optimizes the return from the company's investment in its personnel. It ensures the development of long-term customer relationships with the by-product of continuing improved profitability. These outcomes are so rare in the corporate world that a competitive advantage can be achieved from the adoption of an internal marketing program. The next section of this chapter discusses development and implementation of an internal marketing program.

# How to Develop and Implement an Internal Marketing Strategy

The following guidelines are the tactics necessary for developing customer-conscious employees at every level of the organization. These tactics include structural issues and internal activities, such as research, strategy analysis, and implementation factors. These tactics follow from an understanding of the internal marketing essentials discussed earlier.

*Structural Aspects of an Internal Marketing Program*

Internal marketing works best when implemented in a sufficiently large arena, for example, a geographic location, a division of a company, a strategic business unit, or the entire organization for a small company. The selected unit should encompass a number of groups whose total efforts represent the output of the unit rather than just employees of a single department. The more self-contained the unit is, the greater the likelihood of positive outcomes.

Most important is the continuing involvement in the internal marketing program by the senior executive of this unit. Close participation is needed between this top person and the one designated to carry out the actual development and implementation—that is, the manager of the internal marketing program. This manager cannot be a tactical-level person, because strategic issues must be resolved. This manager should function as the champion of the internal marketing program, the idea person, the implementor and monitor of the program. The senior executive must function as the defender of the internal marketing program and share the role of visionary with the manager of the program.

Developing a new program of this magnitude is a fragile undertaking. Resistance is likely, because change is often uncomfortable. Many employees and even some departments may be threatened by this program and/or its manager. Therefore, a project setting or a task-force approach is recommended where the various groups within the unit are brought together. In this way all functional areas are involved in the internal marketing program from the start. Note that the functional area of the internal marketing manager is not important. However, this manager must have power and influence and be able to establish acceptance and trust. The process that is overseen by this group and managed by the internal marketing champion involves the internal activities discussed next.

## Steps in the Internal Marketing Process

We have used the phrase "marketinglike activities" to describe the steps followed in establishing an internal marketing program, because these steps parallel the traditional procedures for establishing an external marketing program. Research should be the starting point.

<u>Market Research Activities.</u>　The likelihood of success with an internal marketing program increases significantly when it is research-based. An early assignment for the project task force is to determine their information needs and initiate collection and analysis of relevant data. A situation analysis is suggested to review the available information. Collection of primary data will be necessary to fill in any gaps in the available information. The collection and analysis of the internal data can help to focus the external research. These two processes will take at least several months each.

*Internal focus.* Employees sense the organization views them as important when they are allowed to participate in the research process. Taking the perspective of "ways for us to improve," the task force should solicit suggestions and advice from all employees. Small groups of employees should be assembled to talk about "how we can better serve our customers." Note that the task force need not talk about internal marketing per se.

The task force must understand the capabilities of the employees—their attitudes, know-how, and skills to participate in an internal marketing strategy. Qualitative methods are as important as quantitative methods here. Note that this research becomes a promise to the employees for future improvements. Minor problems and suggestions can be dealt with immediately, and plans should be developed to deal with the major changes.

The employee information and the perceptions of the project team should be considered from the perspective of internal problems and opportunities. For example, Systems Barrier discussion groups could be formed to identify what organizational procedures and problems inhibit employees at all levels from providing good customer service on a daily basis. In essence, the task force must document the organizational climate. Employee perceptions of the company environment and its impact on their output is needed. Finally, these employee perceptions and other internal information should be analyzed based on employee segmentation, for example, differences between contact employees and support employees or between middle management and operations level employees.

*External focus.* Information on the perceptions of the company by its external publics regarding the effectiveness of relationship and interactive marketing programs is needed. This research about the company and its major competitors should focus on the service orientation of "part-time marketers" as well as on the quality of the service production and delivery process itself, physical resources and technology, and so on. Collection of primary data is necessary if the available marketing research data have not included this service orientation focus. There are two sources for the data—customers and competitors.

Information may be needed from former, current, and potential customers. The analysis should consider the various segments within each of these customer groups. Price perceptions from former customers should not be accepted at face value. The research must uncover the more basic causes of dissatisfaction, which price perceptions so often conceal. Finally, information from current and potential competitors can provide another very useful perspective on the company's service orientation.

Internal Marketing Strategy Analysis. The team can develop the goals and select the target markets for the internal marketing program, once consensus is reached on the meaning of the data.

*Employee segments.* The wants and needs of various employee groups will differ. Therefore, targeted strategies to these different employee segments will be more effective than a mass internal marketing approach. Of course, all employee segments should share both a common sense of the firm's mission and receive the same information about the internal marketing program.

Four general segments of employees can be targeted for internal marketing—top management; middle management and supervisors; and the two groups of "part-time marketers" who are the contact and the support personnel. It should be noted that the same person occasionally may move among the segments. For example, a support person may sometimes be a contact person. Or, supervisors, whose jobs are to encourage and motivate subordinates in customer consciousness, may themselves be contact people serving ultimate customers.

The department store marketing case history at the end of this chapter illustrates strategy analysis of the four general segments and of the specific employee segment of store buyers. The marketing mix for the Sanger-Harris buyers is described.

Implementation Components. Five important components for implementing an internal marketing process require attention:

1. *Management support.* The most important component in the internal marketing process is *continuous management support.* This support must be provided by every manager and supervisor as a normal part of their jobs. Managers must continue the internal training process where the formal courses and seminars stop. They must demonstrate how subordinates can combine new ideas and routines concerning customer service and marketing with their everyday jobs. Their challenge is to create an open internal climate where the marketing and customer service aspects of their subordinates' jobs are considered important. Regular feedback to subordinates is a requirement for an open climate. This employee feedback can be used as a powerful motivating tool. In essence, for the internal marketing process to succeed, managers and supervisors must be active leaders rather than mere technicians who see themselves primarily as "paper pushers."

Personal involvement by managers and supervisors with the internal marketing program can take many forms. These people should provide encouragement and support to individual subordinates who risk being more service-minded. These new service-mindedness behaviors should be recognized, communicated, and rewarded in a timely fashion.

Employee recognition is an excellent mechanism for promoting the internal marketing program and its outcomes. The internal marketing plan can bring together the disparate parts of existing recognition approaches. Some departments may be conscientiously recognizing employees for stellar performance, while many employees are quietly performing in an outstanding manner without any recognition. This lack of uniform recognition was overcome in one organization by a program called "Extra Step." An "Extra Step" form can be filled out by any employee to recognize that extra measure of effort on behalf of another staff person. The personnel department recognizes these "Extra Steps." This internal recognition from one peer to another has proven to be very popular. Rewards, bonuses, and incentives for excellent customer service, when properly planned and administered, are other possible ingredients of an effective recognition system. Employees should be asked for their input regarding what qualifies for extraordinary performance and how it should be rewarded.

The internal marketing program will fail if it is viewed as being just tactical and is initiated only at the customer-contact level. This level alone cannot engender a service culture for the company nor reach the many support personnel who must function as part-time marketers.

The remaining four implementation components function to support the managers and supervisors in doing their internal marketing tasks.

2. *Training.* Training activities should be developed to explain the ideas about marketing as a continuous process that must be carried out by the employees outside of the marketing department.[7] They must understand and accept their roles as part-time marketers. Internal marketing training goals include: (a) making the business mission and strategies known and accepted; (b) creating favorable attitudes toward marketing; (c) developing an understanding of everybody's responsibility for customer relations and customer satisfaction; (d) creating interest in giving good functional quality; and (e) improving communication and customer service skills. This training should start with top management and may be done best with small group discussions. Note also that such a training

program is a promise to the employees, indicating further activities and improvements.

Training can provide the forum for discussions about mutual problems and opportunities among the personnel. Quality circles are a training activity that engage the employees in defining quality standards and in monitoring performance. Quality circles require regular feedback and give more responsibility to the employees. In summary, the overall goal of the training program is to create a favorable attitude toward marketing and a service orientation among all employees.

The transportation company case history at the end of the chapter illustrates a comprehensive training approach that was implemented as a part of an internal marketing strategy.

3. *Internal communications.* Internal communication programs can function as a mechanism for carrying out the company's internal marketing strategy. Of course, these programs cannot substitute for the substance of the internal marketing strategy itself. The pieces of the internal communication program may include an employee newsletter and other feedback loops, an employee annual report, and sales promotion items such as posters, booklets, brochures, videotapes, and buttons. The selected pieces must be viewed as a system and considered as only one small part of the internal marketing strategy.

The internal communications system at Transamerica Corporation illustrates how these pieces can come together over a period of time.[8] In the 1960s a typical house-organ newsletter was established. It took a top-down approach, with top management providing their information to the employees. This house organ evolved into *Transamerica Magazine*. By the 1980s the vice president of corporate communications described it as a vehicle used "to market our companies, our strategies and our direction to our employees." It communicates the corporate spirit, style, and values. By the late 1980s *Transamerica Magazine* served several purposes: (1) to provide information about the corporation and its business environment; (2) to help employees get to know one another; and, (3) to inform employees about the role the individual can play in moving Transamerica forward. Thus it has become a forum for management and employee views. Since 1981 one issue a year of *Transamerica Magazine* is designated as the employee annual report. This issue focuses primarily on the human resources area with an emphasis on employees' contributions to the corporation and the corporation's contributions to the employees. A readership survey was done in 1987, and the magazine got high marks in most areas. It was found, however, that readers wanted a lot more information about certain topics. These topics included: Who are our competitors? How are we doing against our competitors? What is happening in the industry? and requests for more success stories and employee profiles.

A direct written feedback program between the employees and top management exists in most of Transamerica's operating companies and at corporate headquarters. This program is administered by the human resources director with assistance from employee communications. The employees also have the opportunity to meet with their senior management twice a year.

The communications staff at Transamerica believes that face-to-face communications will become increasingly important. Employees want the word *first* from their supervisors. This will necessitate additional communication training for managers as the traditional forms of written communications are supplemented. Also, managers will be held accountable for their communication responsibilities with employees.

4. *Personnel administration.* In a firm oriented with a service culture, marketing is understood to be a conglomeration of functions in which everyone in the employ of the company participates.[9] Thus the marketing and personnel administration functions cannot be separate in a service company. Policies for these two functional areas must be prepared simultaneously, with each policy document containing ideas about the other area.

Traditional personnel administration topics may need to be reconsidered. For example, one service organization now includes customer contact and customer relations responsibility in every job description. Recruitment may take a market segmentation perspective to match more effectively the requirements of the job with all the skills needed to succeed in that employee assignment. This means that all part-time marketers must have customer relations skills to assure that qualified people are hired in the first place. Career planning and development, the compensation package (e.g., salaries, wages, incentives, and bonuses), and job rotation plans also may have to be reviewed when service orientation is the company's driving force.

5. *External activities.* Activities such as advertising, personal selling, publicity, public relations, and other mass-marketing support have a significant impact on the internal marketing process. It is important that the internal and external perspectives be integrated closely. For example, such integration assures that realistic promises are made to the company's external publics. The external communications can be used to mold and reinforce desired employee behaviors. In this situation the employees are considered a secondary audience of the advertising. Finally, the mass communications can be a powerful motivator for employees. Employees may be a source of ideas and input for these communications. They should see all mass communications before such communications are released to the external publics.

The two cases that follow use real-world settings to illustrate the many ideas presented in this chapter.

## Case History: Internal Marketing at Sanger-Harris

Positively impacting on the conditions or factors within the organization that influence individuals to improve their performance is how George Wilson, vice-president of personnel, Sanger-Harris of Dallas, describes the personnel approach there.[10] Building a positive work atmosphere includes traditional techniques such as recognizing and rewarding performance, offering opportunity for growth, and encouraging open communication. Promotions are recognized through internal media and gifts (attractively styled briefcases) for those reaching the buyer or department manager level. Growth opportunities include career path alternatives available to the new executives and training and development opportunities. Sanger-Harris is clearly committed to growing their own: 87 percent of all buyers were promoted internally in 1980.

To encourage a healthy flow of information to and from management, all executives are involved in the business by scheduling quarterly updates on the company's financial performance. Senior management time is made available for employees. Their feedback, in anonymous form, is invaluable for the personnel department. Regular feedback is also given to executives on their performance through the formalized review system. All of the preceding are examples of the application of traditional internal marketing management in a retail organization.

A more exciting example of internal marketing at Sanger-Harris is the commitment to examining jobs themselves and to changing the structure of these jobs to make them viable and effective. Buyers were selected as the original target market for several reasons. First, there was clear evidence that many buyers felt harried, overworked, overwhelmed, and unappreciated. Second, buyers were considered to be a key line position at Sanger-Harris because of the company's aggressive growth plans and the anticipated environmental changes in the 1980s. The strategy for marketing to the buyers started off with research on the buyers themselves and their jobs. Implementation included solving immediate problems, changing the physical workplace, and restructuring the job itself.

Immediate solutions to problems uncovered by the research included the implementation of standard job descriptions for buying office positions, standard guidelines for buying office information management, optimal office-staffing models based on job complexity, and a structured assistant buyer training program. These are components of the ''services offering'' part of the marketing mix.

A second major change was recognition of the importance of physical comfort in the workplace. New buying offices were built to give the buyer privacy and a sense of importance. All offices were standardized to give everyone equal space, but personalization in decor was left up to the individual. Adjacent space was provided for the buyer's support staff that is superior to what was available in the past. Access to word processing and telephone answering service was provided. Vendor showrooms and conference rooms were built in each buying complex. These are examples of the ''place'' and ''physical evidence'' marketing mix variables.

To restructure the job, a new concept was tested that impacts on the buyer's span of control. It relieves the buyer of by-location planning and adjustments. The objective was to free the central buying organization from traditional and peripheral activities so that they can concentrate on the key elements of the job (i.e., assortments and margins). The buyers' priorities have been narrowed to those things that only they can do best and that tend to be the most exciting elements of the job. This is a better ''price'' for the target group.

This marketing strategy aimed at buyers has had a significant impact on buyer turnover. In the first year the average time for a buyer on the job increased by 40 percent. Turnover at the assistant buyer level has dropped in a similar way. More seasoned buyers will ultimately affect the overall profits of

Sanger-Harris. The strategy began by researching the customers (buyers) and then developing a new internal product for the corporate buying function with a new mix of elements, which was more meaningful, more professional, and more fun.

## Case History: Internal Marketing as a Prerequisite for Successful External Marketing

Internal marketing started in John Nurminen Co. a decade ago with the idea that the employees were a first internal market of the firm.[11] Service orientation and marketing-oriented performance of the contact employees were believed to be at least equally as important to market success as sales and advertising campaigns.

John Nurminen Co. is a Finland-based international forwarding and transportation company, with more than 600 employees. Billing/sales amounts to approximately half a billion U.S. dollars.

A 1979 corporate image study of users of freight forwarders indicated partly positive results: John Nurminen Co. was considered financially sound, experienced, large, versatile, and good in import forwarding, customs clearance, ocean transport, and warehousing. However, there were important negative findings as well: The firm was viewed as being stagnant, uneconomic (i.e., no real value added), old-fashioned, inferior in customer service and in giving information, expensive, rigid in its credit terms, and inferior in some forwarding functions. Management realized that the corporate image was vague and without highlights. Moreover, it observed that the "moments of truth" where customers and employees meet were not handled in a customer-oriented manner.

Five overall objectives of an internal marketing program were set forth and eventually achieved:

1. *Attitudes.* Marketing had to be seen as playing a role in everyone's work.
2. *Information.* Internal and external information had to be improved.
3. *Corporate image.* The company had to be regarded as the best freight forwarder in Finland with a high-quality image.
4. *Market share.* Increase of the market share was to proceed according to plans.
5. *Profitability.* ROI should be at least 13 percent before interest and taxes.

By 1984 these objectives were achieved.

The steps of the internal marketing program included creation of its structure, internal activities, and external activities. Creation of structure included four parts: organization, guiding principles, definition of marketing functions, and definition of service quality. Sales was decentralized to the line organization. The centralized marketing department became much smaller. As one guiding principle, marketing and personnel policies were combined. Marketing was redefined as a conglomeration of functions in which everyone in the employ of the company participates. It was formally stated that production of the company's services is part of marketing.

Service quality was defined and the importance of the functional quality of the process was stressed. Every single customer contact was realized to be a "moment of truth" where service quality emerges.

Activities of the internal marketing program included training, internal information, and management support. The training was multifaceted, starting off with extensive management training, including four sessions of one-week duration each for top management and three sessions of three days' duration each for middle management. Vocational training included basic courses, professional skills courses, language courses, and special theme sessions. In 1985, for example, 1,000 training days were accomplished. Such training was recognized as an investment in the staff.

The marketing courses focused on teaching sales and communication skills. For psychological reasons, however, they were labeled Active Customer Service courses. These courses were divided into two parts. The first part consisted of two-day courses for the entire staff—from the managing director and his top management team to truck drivers. Lecturing took three hours, with fifteen hours of group work. Problems and opportunities related to customer service, handling customer contacts and operational systems as well as routines were discussed. The group sessions focused on tracking problems that could be solved immediately and listing other problems or actions to be attended to in the near future. Deadlines for actions were assigned. The second part consisted of three-day courses intended for contact persons immediately involved in the "moments of truth."

The internal information component of the internal marketing program focused on internal memos (circulars) and the internal magazine. The role of management was extremely important here, as were the congruence with personnel policy and the integration with the external marketing.

Mass marketing was considered a part of the internal marketing program because of the need to integrate both the external and internal perspectives. The main vehicle to do this was the *Nurminen News,* which is published once or twice a month. It is factual in nature and includes no advertisements. It circulates to 4,000 Finnish import and export companies and also to other potential customers. The customer-oriented information in this magazine was intended to become the best available about import- and export-related issues. This goal seems to have been achieved. In addition, extensive advertising campaigns in the press were undertaken.

Another component of mass marketing was exhibitions and sponsoring special events. Public relations involving the press was also used. Seminars on special issues were arranged for CEOs. Finally, external marketing included talks in business schools and other colleges of higher education. Note that the external advertising campaign was intended for employees equally as much as for customers. The advertising stressed employees' skills and the importance of marketing and customer service.

The impact of the internal marketing program was measured by a corporate image study done in 1984 and 1985. The following results were of interest:

1. Employee attitudes and customer service skills have improved and are considered good.
2. John Nurminen Co. was considered the best by far in giving relevant information to the customers.
3. The respondents considered John Nurminen Co. the best freight-forwarding company in Finland.

That market share and profitability objectives were achieved is another measure of success. Also, in 1984 John Nurminen Co. was recognized as the best training organization in the country.

In summary, the experience from this internal marketing program suggests the following guidelines:

1. Be strong in your faith and secure the support of top management.
2. Do your homework well and define the subject comprehensively (changing the corporate culture, combining and coordinating personnel administration, training, management methods and the use of internal and external information).
3. Make your own applications; do not just imitate what others have done.
4. Set your planning objectives on a yearly basis and include measuring of results.
5. Remember, it will take years.

## Summary

For a service organization to be successful in the marketplace, its management must develop customer-conscious employees. This development process, called internal marketing, focuses on ensuring that:

- Employees fully understand the business—its mission and practices.
- Employees have the preparation and motivation to serve customers well.

Internal marketing uses a marketing perspective for managing an organization's human resources. This chapter presented guidelines to help top management understand the reasons why an internal marketing strategy is needed and the prerequisites for successful implementation of the strategy. The specific steps in developing and implementing an internal marketing approach were presented, and two case histories provided examples of successful implementation.

## Notes

1. Christian Grönroos, ''Assessing the Competitive Edge in the New Competition of the Service Economy: The Five Rules of Service,'' working paper, Helsinki, Swedish School of Economics and Business, 1987; Evert Gummesson, ''The New Marketing—Developing Long-Term Interactive Relationships,'' *Long-Range Planning*

20, no. 4 (1987): 10–20; and Christian Grönroos and Evert Gummesson, "Service Orientation in Industrial Marketing," in *Creativity in Service Marketing: What's New, What Works, What's Developing,* ed. M. Venkatesan et al. (Chicago: American Marketing Association, 1986).

2. Richard Normann, *Service Management* (New York: Wiley, 1984); and Jan Carlzon, *Moments of Truth* (New York: Ballinger, 1987).

3. Christian Grönroos, "An Applied Service Marketing Theory," *European Journal of Marketing* 16, no. 7 (1982): 30–41.

4. Leonard L. Berry, "The Employee as Customer," *Journal of Retail Banking* 3 (March 1981): 33–40.

5. Relationship marketing is discussed by Leonard L. Berry, "Relationship Marketing," in *Emerging Perspectives on Services Marketing,* ed. Leonard L. Berry et al. (Chicago: American Marketing Association, 1983), 25–28; and Theodore Levitt, "After the Sale Is Over," *Harvard Business Review* (September–October 1983): 87–93. Interactive marketing is discussed by Christian Grönroos, "A Service-Oriented Approach to Marketing of Services," *European Journal of Marketing* 12, no. 8 (1978): 588–601; and Christian Grönroos, "An Applied Service Marketing Theory," *European Journal of Marketing* 16, no. 7 (1982): 30–41.

6. Gummesson, "The New Marketing," 10–20.

7. The following articles describe training approach examples for internal marketing programs: N. W. Pope, "Mickey Mouse Marketing," *American Banker,* July 25, 1979, 4, 14; N. W. Pope, "More Mickey Mouse Marketing," September 12, 1979, 4, 5, 10, 14; and William R. George and Fran F. Compton, "How to Initiate a Marketing Perspective in a Health Services Organization," *Journal of Health Care Marketing* 5 (Winter 1985): 29–38.

8. William R. George, "Internal Communications Programs as a Mechanism for Doing Internal Marketing," in *Creativity in Services Marketing,* ed. M. Venkatesan et al. (Chicago: American Marketing Association, 1986), 83–84; and personal interview with Beth L. Quartarolo, Director of Employee Communications, Transamerica Corporation, October 2, 1987.

9. Fran F. Compton et al., "Internal Marketing," in *The Services Challenge: Integrating for Competitive Advantage,* ed. John A. Czepiel, Carole A. Congram, and James B. Shanahan (Chicago: American Marketing Association, 1987), 7–12.

10. Adapted from William R. George, "Internal Marketing for Retailers: The Junior Executive Employee," in *Developments in Marketing Science,* VII, ed. Jay D. Lindquist (Academy of Marketing Science, 1984), 322–325.

11. Adapted from Compton et al., "Internal Marketing," 7–12.

\*       \*       \*       \*

**William R. George**, *Ph.D., is professor of marketing at Villanova University. His publications have appeared in leading periodicals, and he is a marketing consultant in accounting, credit union, health services, and volunteer circles. He is a frequent speaker before management groups.*

**Christian Grönroos**, *Ph.D., is a professor at the Swedish School of Economics and Business Administration in Helsinki. In addition, he is chairman of the board of Nordic Service Institute Ltd. and a member of the board of a number of other companies. Dr. Grönroos also acts as a consultant to many major corporations in Scandinavia and Finland and has spoken to management groups in such American corporations as AT&T and S. C. Johnson & Sons.*

# 6

## Shifting to a Customer-Driven Organization: A Case Study

Margaret L. Friedman
Ruth J. Dumesic

How does an organization position itself to be distinguished from its competition when service offerings appear similar? The professional marketer would probably respond: Focus on customer service. Yet, "Surveys repeatedly show that poor service or the lack of it is one of the major consumer complaints of our age."[1] A *Time* magazine cover story was entitled " 'Pul-eeze! Will Somebody Help Me?' Frustrated American Consumers Wonder Where the Service Went."[2] The buzzwords "The customer is always right" and "The customer is king" are often just verbiage—the majority of customers who are looking for service of any kind feel abused because they are treated as "nuisances" who get in the way of doing business.[3]

Focusing on customer service is no small feat. Why? Because for most organizations, focusing on the customer would require a complete organizational restructuring and cultural change. A customer orientation requires an integrated, consistent, and holistic approach to serving customers, which is a far cry from the fragmented, inconsistent, and piecemeal approach we consumers are fed up with . . . being given the "royal runaround," being put on infinite hold, being told, "That's not my job."

In this chapter we will examine the activities involved in making the shift to a customer focus. First, we identify ten actions that are key in guiding a service organization through the cultural shift to a customer-driven business. The second section illustrates their application in a midsize public accounting firm. The real-life example is provided to make sure that the actions are not just platitudes to you—so that you see how the process works, given time, patience, and determination.

## Ten Key Actions for Creating a Customer-Focused Organizational Culture

What follows are "executive summaries" of what each of the ten proposed actions entails. It is important to keep in mind that the actions can be thought of as occurring on a global, organizational level as well as simultaneously on a specific service-line level. Acting on either level alone will not accomplish the goal of becoming customer-focused in a comprehensive way. If you try to become customer-focused solely on a global organizational level, you run the risk of spouting lofty platitudes without ever demonstrating the attitude in your day-to-day encounters with customers. If you operate simply on a service-line level, you run the risk of creating a disjointed approach to the customer, where it is more luck than design if the customer gets served well consistently.

1. *Understand the organization's philosophy of doing business.* This first point prescribes an activity that needs to be carried out on a continual and on-going basis in any organization that is trying to change its focus from an inward one to an outward one. You have to constantly question the status quo. If you are about to begin your organizational shift, look for areas where you can begin to introduce change, where resistance will be minimal and acceptance will be relatively easy. Then move on to bigger challenges.

2. *Engage the entire organization, including top management, in a customer-focused mission.* Your toughest job in moving an organization toward a customer orientation will be to educate people about the merits of such an orientation and need for the marketing tools required to implement the attitude. Although it is important to educate people at all levels in the organization, it is critical that top management embrace marketing so that the new or renewed commitment to customers is credible both inside and outside the organization. Chapter 2 of this *Handbook* outlines for top management the process of formulating a customer-focused mission statement.

Most service providers have considerable technical training in their respective areas of expertise, and traditional business practice has capitalized on offering this technical expertise, not on identifying and satisfying customer needs. Marketing programs need to entice the service providers out of their technical shells and to train them in the behaviors and skills needed in their roles as part-time marketers (see Chapter 5 of this *Handbook*). Service providers must understand that their technical skills alone are not enough to enable them to serve the customer well.

3. *Determine internal perceptions of the organization and of the services it offers and whether the organization is fulfilling customer needs.* Examine the products, services, and programs in existence in your organization. The experiences of the management team and front-line personnel, their vision for the future, and their perception of customer needs must be analyzed in order to determine the direction of the marketing program.

4. *Determine customers' perceptions of the organization and of their service needs.* No successful marketing can happen until customers are consulted about their perceptions of your image, of the level of quality of your service, of what they need from you and of their level of satisfaction with your service. These are key elements in determining what you need to do to meet your customers' needs in a satisfactory manner. Customers' perceptions must be studied by top management to keep the needs of the customer, rather than the needs of the organization, at the forefront.

5. *Compare your internal evaluations with customer evaluations.* Upon completion of internal and external evaluations, look for similarities among the

responses, ideas that seem to be on everyone's list. Also, look for discrepancies between your employees' perceptions of your operation and your customers' perceptions of your operation. This comparison exercise reveals what needs to be built upon and expanded in your current business and what needs to be changed. Remember, the customers' perceptions should take precedence, within the constraints of current and anticipated resources and expertise available to the firm.

6. *Use the discipline of marketing: Analyze the market, analyze service offerings, set objectives, develop and implement marketing plans.* The marketing planning process is intended to move you from the realm of good intentions toward customers to the practical realm of living what you profess. It is easy to claim to have a customer focus, but so much harder to act it out.

The marketing plan depends on the strategic direction provided by the customer-focused mission statement and the organizational attitude it promotes. The marketing plan builds and expands upon the internal and external analyses discussed previously. Formal planning includes a detailed market analysis and service portfolio analysis, proceeds with a statement of objectives, and ends with a plan of specific actions to achieve objectives.

7. *Use a team approach in planning.* The labor intensity of services necessitates a team approach to planning. The recommended marketing programs are doomed to failure without internal support. We are not talking about making it possible for people to stand on an assembly line and to add a part to a standard product that some unknown customer will eventually buy in some faraway place. We are talking about mobilizing people to behave in a competent, consistent, and caring manner toward customers with whom they interact directly. The real-time nature of service delivery allows little margin for error despite the fact that the real time is filled by real, fallible people. It is easier to get people to buy into a plan they have had a hand in developing.

8. *Develop an operations system to support the plan.* A well-oiled operations system is needed to assure a project's success and acceptance within the organization, outside of the group planning the project. Without the establishment of the internal structure prior to service implementation, success may be severely hampered. The operations system must be designed with an intense focus on the market rather than around traditional business functions (e.g., personnel, accounting, finance, marketing). You want to blend functions so that employees' actions are driven by concern for customer needs rather than defense of "turf."

9. *Use feedback to encourage and motivate continued support.* Communication of progress and results, both formally through established channels and informally, is an important element to continued support and motivation. Without it, a program, even if it is working effectively, loses its momentum. It seems to be basic to human nature that we find it easier to criticize when mistakes are made and harder to praise when performance is high.

10. *Assess results and progress against objectives.* This is where most planning efforts begin to fall apart. We seem to be able to get into the planning and the doing, but when it comes to measuring whether we have accomplished

what we set out to accomplish, we often tend to avoid the issue. Part of the problem is that we do not think about how we will measure results when we set objectives. Often the systems needed to measure results are not available or not developed.

Critical to the whole process of shifting to a customer culture is the idea of measuring results in terms of whether the customer feels he or she is being served well. Customer satisfaction surveys must be a part of the assessment procedure.

Lest you think it all sounds okay on paper but wonder whether the actions can really help your organization, let's turn to an example where a service organization attempted to use a marketing approach to deal with a client development problem (and succeeded). Note throughout the example how the entire process is driven by the customer, rather than by the internal expertise of the firm.

## The Ten Actions in Action

The example that follows shows how a customer-focused approach was used to determine whether an accounting organization should develop or eliminate the community financial institution as a target market. The example deals with a particular service line. Remember that you should be implementing these ten actions simultaneously at various levels in an organization. What is not discussed explicitly, but should be assumed, is that a customer focus was being implemented on other service lines as well as in firmwide programs. For example, we will be talking about a specific customer-focused mission the firm developed relative to the community bank market. The firm was simultaneously reassessing its encompassing global mission, shifting its vision of itself as a technically driven organization toward a customer-driven orientation.

### Actions 1 and 2: Understanding the Organization's Philosophy of Providing Service and Engaging the Entire Organization, Including Top Management, in a Customer-Focused Mission

The question raised, whether to develop the community bank as a target market or not, was ripe for a client-oriented approach to its answer. The partner involved in this area had been serving community banks for ten years. Recently, the client base was decreasing due to acquisition of smaller banks by larger financial institutions.

Realizing that the way things were done in the past was simply not working anymore, the partner involved was quite open to any suggestions as to how to deal with the environmental forces at work. This was one of those opportunities where a customer-oriented approach could be implemented relatively easily (with minimal internal resistance), quickly, and with positive results so that it would begin to become the preferred approach throughout the firm.

Our mission in this market was "To provide financial and consulting services to establish the firm as a specialist to the community financial institution market.'' Instead of focusing on technical expertise, this mission stresses a tailoring of service to meet unique needs.

### Actions 3 and 4: Determining the Internal Perceptions of the Organization and of the Services It Offers and Whether the Organization Is Fulfilling Customer Needs and Determining Customers' Perceptions of the Organization and of Their Service Needs

Internal interviews revealed that firm personnel felt there was a decline in the level of service offered to community banks. As the market was shrinking, the firm appeared to be backing off from the clients who remained.

The community banks that remained our clients were brought into the planning process early. We solicited their input on exactly what help they needed from us. This not only gave us sound information from which to develop our new approach to this market, but also helped us establish even stronger relationships with those clients because the firm and the client were actually working together and the benefits were obvious to both parties.

### Action 5: Comparing Internal Evaluations With Customer Evaluations

The research indicated that there were no accounting firms positioned to serve this market. There was no one accountant or accounting firm identified within the banking community that had any special expertise in this industry. Within the firm, no special effort was being made to market to the needs identified by this segment. This indicated that if accounting services could be repackaged to provide a broad consulting perspective, the market potential was strong.

### Action 6: Using the Discipline of Marketing: Analyzing the Market, Analyzing Service Offerings, Setting Objectives, Developing and Implementing Marketing Plans

Analyzing the Market. There was a steady but slow decline of community banks. Those remaining independent, however, made up a large enough market to be an attractive growth area for the firm.

Specific targets within the community bank market were selected on the basis of referral relationships and geographic territories. Referral relationships were those community bankers who had business relationships with our present clients. Community banks that were geographically close were also selected based on the firm's ability to provide better service closer to the organization's headquarters.

Analyzing Service Offerings. Services were reexamined and repackaged specifically with the community banker in mind. For example, instead of describing services as ''accounting, financial, tax and management information,'' new descriptions were developed: ''Pre-loan Evaluations, Trust Department Reviews, Holding Company Debt Service,'' and so on. Of course, it is not enough to change descriptions alone; the service and supporting expertise has to be developed as well.

Setting Objectives.  Specifically, the goals for the first year were to (1) reorganize the community bank group services to be more client-oriented, (2) begin establishment of the "banker's accountant" image, and (3) define and implement a communications program for bankers.

Developing and Implementing Marketing Plans.  With goals defined and target markets and their needs identified, developing the marketing program was the next order of business. A plan was formulated that covered all elements of the marketing mix. We will describe here how we developed the promotion element in the marketing mix.

It was beyond the firm's budget to reach community bankers through advertising. Examining the other communication sources community bankers used gave us two alternatives.

First, the most obvious source was the state's independent bankers association. We became very visible at association meetings as well as in the pages of its newsletters and announcements to members. Working with a state-sponsored, independent banking association was beneficial in lending a form of "official" support to the type of assistance the firm could offer community bankers.

Also, the firm initiated a newsletter strictly for community bankers that contained timely and informative articles. This effort also communicated the commitment of the firm to serve community banks.

## Action 7: Using a Team Approach in Planning

To serve community banks, the firm assembled a team consisting of a partner, two managers, three accountants, the marketing director, and an administrative assistant, who coordinated assigned tasks and monitored follow-up activities. This team refined objectives and identified the internal support system required to meet the objectives.

## Action 8: Developing an Operations System to Support the Plan

As the independent banking group grew, assuring clients of personalized attention was going to be a problem as professionals became more involved with ongoing projects for various banks. A program, therefore, was developed to assure that all banking clients were contacted on a bimonthly basis. This involved scheduling work with clients in advance, planning who, when, and why contact would be made with the growing number of bankers, and designing a process to monitor the system's effectiveness.

It is because of the systematic approach developed that the administrative staff was an integral part of the planning team. The responsibility for tracking, evaluating, and general support of the effort was accomplished at the administrative support level, so that the professionals spent their "marketing time" effectively and efficiently.

### Action 9: Using Feedback to Encourage and Motivate Continual Support

An internal newsletter was published every Friday to keep the staff informed of upcoming projects and the status of various ongoing projects. Quarterly meetings involving the entire staff kept employees aware of marketing events. Monthly reports to management were provided by the marketing representative.

The firm's internal communications recognized those individuals who were participating in the community bank program. Instead of using special incentives, this approach laid the foundation to make marketing a part of the "expected" behavior and not a special effort that was needed only at certain times.

### Action 10: Assessing Results and Progress Against Objectives

A number of tracking systems were developed to measure progress toward objectives. A marketing section was added to the new-client form that needed to be processed for billing purposes. It required the accountant to ask the banker why he/she had chosen to do business with the firm. Using the computer, we were able to analyze why the firm was obtaining new clients. This system helped to evaluate why we lost clients as well.

Customer satisfaction surveys were conducted on an individual basis as well as in the firm's community bank newsletter. The questions were designed to provide actionable data. For example, regarding a specific service, we asked for detailed information on what attributes of it were satisfying and what attributes needed change and what sorts of changes were desirable.

This customer-focused marketing effort was very successful. Within two years, growth in this area alone was 20 percent. A before-and-after research survey within the same period resulted in recognition of the firm as a leader in offering the banking community customized accounting services. Internal motivation and morale increased substantially as the success of the program was recognized throughout the organization.

## Summary

A customer-focused organizational culture involves an interplay between attitude and action. Too many service organizations claim to have the attitude, but do not demonstrate that attitude in their actions. They're "all talk and no action."

The ten actions carry you through a process that includes: (1) in-depth internal and external analyses, (2) a plan that gives purpose and direction to actions, (3) a plan to harness human resources to implement the actions, and (4) an assessment and communication of results.

The situation described illustrated an opportunity where there was initial receptivity to trying a new approach, where the time frame was not long and where the risk of failure was relatively small so that success could start to propel the shift. Remember that the actions described do not happen in serial fashion, but should be happening in different stages and at different levels in the organization. Do not expect to reach a point when the actions become unnecessary, but rather hope to reach a point where they are internalized and are the standard practice in your organization.

## Notes

1. John Cuniff, "Service Is Often Promised, But It's Rarely Delivered," *Marketing News,* June 6, 1988.
2. " 'Pul-eeze! Will Somebody Help Me?' Frustrated American Consumers Wonder Where the Service Went," *Time,* February 2, 1987, 48–57.
3. Jim Mitchell, "Service With a Smile? Not by a Mile," *Wall Street Journal,* October 9, 1984.

*     *     *     *

**Margaret L. Friedman,** *Ph.D., is assistant professor in the marketing department of the College of Business and Economics, University of Wisconsin-Whitewater. She teaches courses in consumer behavior and personal selling and has developed an undergraduate course in services marketing. She previously served as director of service sector marketing programs at the university's Management Institute, the continuing education unit of the School of Business at Madison. She has worked as a consultant with a variety of service sector businesses.*

**Ruth J. Dumesic** *is director, marketing and business development, for Suby, Von Haden and Associates, CPAs, in Madison, Wisconsin. She previously served as marketing director for Auto Glass Specialists, also in Madison, where she was responsible for developing strategic marketing plans for service centers in a five-state region. Prior to that, she held the position of marketing director with Williams, Young & Associates, CPAs.*

# 7

## Organizing for Marketing and the Marketing Organization

Evert Gummesson

This chapter provides guidelines for organizing the marketing of a service company. Little research has been done in the area—researchers seem to duck the tricky issues of organizational structure in marketing. Therefore, this chapter is primarily based on my own research and practical experience.

A service company can be anything from a local one-person operation to an international corporation with tens of thousands of people; it can be anything from the highly professional, custom-designed services of hospitals and management consultancy to highly standardized and routine banking or cleaning services. Obviously, I cannot suggest a single organizational solution that would satisfy this diversity. I can, however, give guidelines for the approach to and structuring of a marketing organization. In each instance a contingency solution is necessary, meaning that knowledge of the specific conditions of a particular service firm and its markets is necessary to design a proper marketing organization.

In order to organize marketing we have to recognize the unique characteristics of service operations. Other chapters present differences between services marketing and product marketing, so here I stress those factors that relate to the structuring of the marketing organization.

The chapter is outlined as follows: (1) The reasons for organizing marketing and the marketing tasks that the service business must organize for are identified; (2) the notions of an organizational dilemma and the part-time marketer are presented; (3) the necessity of understanding the service production and delivery process is made clear and the point-of-marketing concept is introduced; (5) the division of organizational roles in order to be supportive to marketing is explained; (6) twelve dimensions and types of organizational structures are shown. The chapter ends with nine rules for organizing the marketing of the successful service operation.

## What Reasons and Tasks Are You Organizing For?

You are organizing your marketing for the following reasons:

1. To get the right customer
2. To sell more to a customer

3. To keep a customer
4. To get the customer to recommend you to others
5. To get more customers
6. To get the right price from the customer

Marketing is a matter of creating and strengthening relations with customers in such a way that the business makes a profit. To achieve this you will have to perform the following tasks:

1. Establish marketing strategies, plans, and programs.
2. Design the service production and delivery system.
3. Design after-sales services and support (important in some service companies like insurance).
4. Develop new services and redesign existing services.
5. Establish and implement the "right" quality standards.
6. Establish pricing procedures.
7. Plan and implement personal selling activities: sales calls, telephone selling.
8. Plan and implement mass communication activities: advertising, sales promotion, public relations.
9. Build image and position yourself in the mind of the customer.
10. Carry out marketing research.
11. Create customer access to your services ("the distribution system").
12. Implement internal marketing programs (particularly important in service companies).

In summary, there are six reasons for organizing marketing and twelve major tasks that have to be carried out. The reasons and tasks outlined here carry different weight, depending on your type of service operation and its life cycle.

## The "Organizational Dilemma" in Service Firms and How to Use the "Part-Time Marketer"

In service companies especially, only part of the marketing is handled by the marketing and sales department. In fact, the department is not able to handle more than a limited portion of the marketing, because its staff cannot be at the right place at the right time with the right customer contact.

This poses an organizational dilemma! The organizational dilemma is created by the fact that those who produce and deliver services carry out marketing activities for that service, whether they know it or not.[1]

In order to make this dilemma manageable I use the distinction between the marketing department (including sales) and the marketing function (Figure 7-1). The marketing department is the unit designated to work solely with marketing and sales activities. Add to this all other activities that influence customer relations and the generation of revenue. Such activities are carried out by top

**Figure 7-1.** The marketing department and the marketing function.

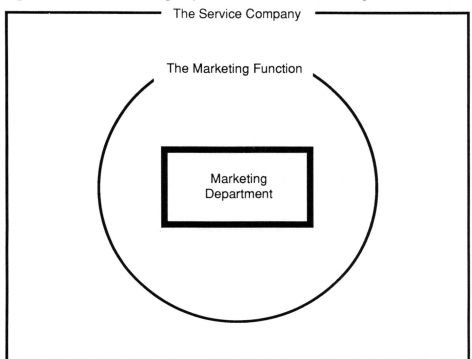

management and by all the different departments of the company. Include distributors and outside consultants (such as advertising agencies) and you have the marketing function.

The distinction between the marketing department and the marketing function is relevant in any type of company, but in service businesses it is particularly important. Two examples illustrate.

The first example concerns the marketing organization of a bank (Figure 7-2). The full-time marketers are those belonging to the marketing department; its role may be limited to handling marketing research, advertising, sales promotion, and part of public relations. The shaded areas in the other boxes of Figure 7-2 indicate that marketing activities are carried out part-time at different levels by different organizational units. Marketing strategy can be designed by the board, the top executives, the "service line" management, and the regional management. The sales force consists of those people who are in direct contact with customers, among them branch office managers and cashiers. With the exception of the members of the marketing department, however, the staff is not hired for its marketing know-how, but for its ability to produce bank services.

Professional service firms—management consultants, CPAs, architects, and others—constitute the second example. It is common for a professional to spend the most time on service delivery and negotiate contracts for a limited part of the time. In smaller professional firms marketing is handled by partners and

**Figure 7-2.** The marketing function in a bank.

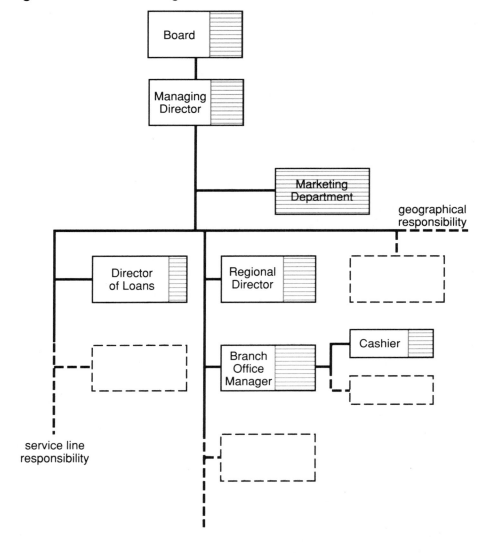

*Note:* Shaded areas refer to the marketing function. The dotted-line boxes indicate that the positions may be replicated as applicable.

senior professionals, and is often regarded as a nuisance that steals time from "productive" work. In larger professional service firms, however, a specialized marketing and sales department usually exists. This department also has to include people who have had client service responsibilities, and thus have an understanding of the service production and delivery process. In order to get leads and introductions to prospective clients, information on competitors, and such, the department has to draw on the skills and contacts of the professionals who do not belong to the department.

For CPA firms different combinations of the following four possible "positions" have been suggested:[2]

1. *Partner in charge of marketing,* representing the know-how of the production and delivery of auditing services
2. *Marketing director,* with a background in services marketing, but not necessarily in auditing services
3. *Marketing coordinator,* with a general background in marketing
4. *Marketing assistant,* with some experience in administrative work

The first two are senior positions concerned with marketing strategy, planning, and resource allocation, whereas the last two are geared toward implementation and monitoring of marketing programs. Finally, *outside consultants* can be used as reinforcement. Although this is suggested for CPA firms, it may give guidance to other professional service firms as well.

The examples of the bank and the accounting firm illustrate that service companies have full-time marketers but also have many part-time marketers. This has to be recognized by management as well as by each individual employee. Both recruitment and training have to be geared toward this fact: All employees must learn to look at their job through marketing glasses.

However, what may at first glance be considered a dilemma could be turned to your advantage: The fact that so many people in a service business have customer contact creates multiple opportunities to influence customers. In order to take advantage of those opportunities you have to implement the following six activities:

1. Identify where the full-time marketer would be superior in fulfilling the marketing tasks, and where the part-time marketer would be superior.
2. When the need for full-time marketers has been established, one or several marketing departments could be organized.

In order to use the opportunities of the part-time marketers—who often form the core of the service company's marketing—do the following:

3. Recruit employees who have a potential to assume the role of part-time marketer as well as the professional role of their core job.
4. Train them to understand their role in influencing customer relationships.
5. Motivate them to strengthen customer relationships and use sales opportunities.
6. Design the service production/delivery system to support marketing activities.

## How to Identify the "Points-of-Marketing"

The product company has a sales force that is responsible for direct contacts with customers. Some service companies have sales forces as well (e.g., insurance companies). In services marketing, relationships and interaction, created by direct contact between the customer and the service provider, are key phenomena.[3] These face-to-face contacts are necessary in order to produce and deliver the service or part of it; for example, the contact between a waiter and the guest, and moreover, the customer partly consumes the service at the same time as it is produced and delivered. During this simultaneous production, delivery, and consumption process, a number of natural marketing opportunities emerge, and these must be recognized and utilized. The direct contacts between the customer and an employee of the service company are usually referred to as the service encounters or moments of truth. For marketing purposes I would like to rename them points-of-marketing. A point-of-marketing is an opportunity to influence favorably the customer's present and future purchases.

In order to identify the points-of-marketing I divide the "service product" into two distinctive elements:

1. The service production and delivery process
2. The future benefits of the service to the customer

The customer will judge the quality of the service and form an attitude about the service provider both from experience of the process and anticipation of future benefits. It is during the process that you stand a unique chance of influencing the customers' present and future purchases because you are in direct contact with them. During the process natural points-of-marketing can be created.

In Figure 7-3 four types of contacts in the service production and delivery process are shown; these contacts provide points-of-marketing. They are described as follows:

1. *Interaction between the service provider's contact person and the customer*. For example, the interaction between a doctor and a patient, an advertising agency account manager and a product manager, a flight attendant and a passenger. The customer is a *co-producer* and a *prosumer* (*pro*ducer plus con*sumer*).[4] If the customer does not cooperate—the patient does not take the prescribed medication, the product manager does not brief the account executive properly, the passenger does not appear at the airline gate on time—the service cannot be properly produced. The quality of the service—the process as well as the future benefits—is often greatly enhanced if the service is produced in close interaction between a knowledgeable customer and the service provider. The contact is sometimes extremely intense and intimate and includes enormous stakes for the customer, such as in surgery, counsel in a divorce case, or financial advice for an investment decision. The shared experience can cement—or prevent—long-lasting relationships. In other services, each service encounter can be less complex but regular—such as hair styling, taxi services, and postal services—and, because of the repeated need for the services, is considered very important by the customer. All these contacts provide opportunities to influence the customer's perception of the service. The customer may find the service provider friendly, professional, and may feel at ease—or the opposite. The experience of this contact can be totally decisive for future purchases and referrals to other customers.

2. *Interaction among customers*. Customers partly produce the service between themselves if the seller provides the right systems, the right environment,

**Figure 7-3.** Identification of points-of-marketing during the service production/delivery process.

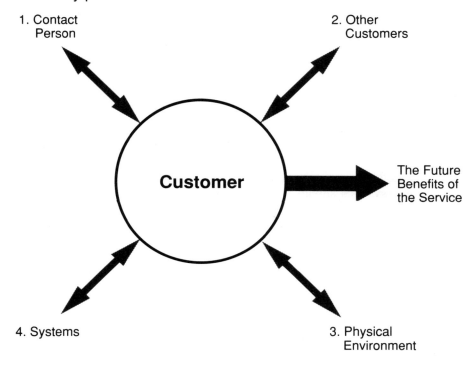

1. Contact
   Person

2. Other
   Customers

**Customer**

The Future
Benefits of
the Service

4. Systems

3. Physical
   Environment

and the right staff. An obvious example is a nightclub. If the customers refuse to dance with each other there will be no service produced; if the setting is right, the customer will be stimulated to coproduce—by dancing, for example—high-quality services and thus come back as well as recommend the place to others. When customers line up in front of a box office, travel business class, or listen to a concert, they interact and jointly influence the image of the service provider and the perceived quality. The choice of customers is important as a segmentation factor, for example, business travelers and tourists (different sections in the aircraft, special lounge for the business traveler), or a law firm only accepting prestigious clients. In waiting lines customers become dependent on each other. The interaction among customers is sometimes nonexistent, for example when the service is carried out on the customer's premises, such as cleaning services. On the other hand, the waiting time for a service may be dependent upon the other customers and the number who want the service at the same moment. This is particularly significant for emergency services: Downtime of computers can keep an entire factory still, or the rapid delivery of security services could be a life-or-death matter.

3. *Interaction between the customer and the provider's physical environment.* One example is a supermarket where the positioning of the merchandise, the way it is displayed, and the attractiveness of the premises, including such things as the parking lot, influence the buyer's purchases. The marketing director of a hamburger chain stated that his most important marketing staff is a

group of architects who design the restaurants. They influence the visibility of the restaurant through the architecture of the building and the signs, attract the desired customer segment through the appropriate interior decoration, determine the number of customers that can be seated, and so on. The physical access is important: Is the service operation conveniently located for the customer? The physical environment is also perceived as evidence of the price class and of the professionalism of the service provider.

4. *Interaction between the customer and the provider's systems, machinery and routines.* This man-machine or man-system interface is equally important as the person-to-person interaction—for example, a bank customer and an automated teller machine, the taxpayer and the taxation system, the credit card user and the system for credit clearance, the checking in and checking out procedure at a hotel, the system of ordering tickets to a play. From a marketing point of view systems should be customer-friendly. The ease of access to the system is important: location, opening hours, the know-how needed to enter the system, and security. Systems sometimes scare away customers and make them avoid the services even if they really need them.

In the preceding paragraphs four types of points-of-marketing have been identified. These are unique to the way that services are produced and delivered. In these points there is an important marketing opportunity, either through direct or long-term influence on sales; we want to maximize customer retention and create positive word of mouth.

The customer's style of participation, particularly in the most intense phase of the service production/delivery becomes important, as well as the seller's ability to design and produce the service so that the buyer's contribution becomes effective. The customer should feel welcome and find the provider responsive to customer needs. (Some customers are difficult, however, which adds an extra burden to the contact person's job.)

The service production/delivery process is actually designed-in marketing. The more marketing is built into the service production/delivery process the less you have to worry about the marketing organization—the major part of the marketing is already prepared for at the design stage.

The four types of contacts and interactions explained in this section show marketing opportunities that can be handled by the part-time marketers who are present at the points-of-marketing. The part-time marketers can contribute to the fulfillment of several marketing tasks, for example:

- *The design of the service production/delivery system, new service development, redesign of existing services.* Because of their hands-on experience of the process, they can assist in giving advice and ideas, suggest improvements, and test new ways of operating.
- *Quality and image.* All the points-of-marketing influence the customer's perception of the quality of the service and the image of service providers. Especially in the face-to-face contacts they can influence perceived quality through friendliness, professional conduct, and such.
- *Personal selling.* Additional sales can be made, such as increased sales of merchandise by flight attendants.

- *Marketing research*. The contact person can learn about customer attitudes, behavior, needs, and complaints.

# An Organizational Structure
# That Supports Marketing

As the marketing function is spread throughout the service company, it is essential that the entire organizational structure is supportive to marketing. There is extreme interdependence between the traditional departments of a service firm— production, delivery, personnel, administration, finance, and so on—and marketing. Therefore, it is more appropriate in the service firm to talk about marketing-oriented management than to use the traditional label "marketing management." An example of an organization that is based on marketing-oriented management, thus giving total support to marketing, is Scandinavian Airlines System, SAS.[5] The airline went through a major turnaround into a customer-oriented company in the 1980s. From posting a loss, it went into the black within one year and has remained there. A basic change was that *the organizational structure was turned into a structure that supports excellence in customer relations*. The differences between the old limiting organization and the new supportive organization are shown in Figure 7-4.

The old organization suffered from several deficiencies that hampered cus-

**Figure 7-4.** The old and new organization at SAS.

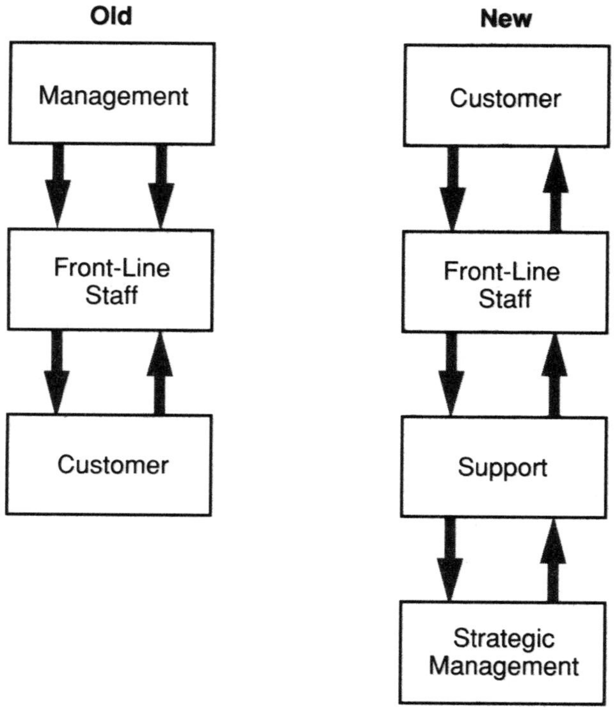

tomer contact and the continuing adjustment to market needs. The organizational structure was centered around the technology of operating and maintaining aircraft. Further, there was one-way communication from management down the organization, and thus neither the experience of front-line staff nor customer reactions were fed back to decision makers. The passenger became a residual in the system, maybe even a nuisance.

To overcome these deficiencies an organization was introduced that focused on the following roles:

- The role of the *customer*. The customer is now seen as part of the production/delivery process and as the most important person in the organization. To emphasize this the customer is placed on top of the organization instead of at the bottom.
- The role of the *front line*. Front-line staff are put in the spotlight and given increased authority to make decisions. One-way communication is banned and two-way communication is actively encouraged.

Both these roles have been discussed earlier. The other roles in the organization and their relations to the front line and the customer have not been explicitly defined. Two specific roles of management were identified and tasks that did not fit into these roles were made redundant:

- The role of *support functions*. Each service organization needs support functions, sometimes referred to as the back-office. These are people who give support to the production/delivery process but are usually invisible to the customer; they work in the kitchen of the restaurant, they service the car-rental company's vehicles, they maintain the computer systems. Their jobs support the service production/delivery system and they are essential both to the front-line staff and to the customer.
- The role of *company management*. Management focuses on strategic issues, company policy, the provision of resources, and other long-term and structural issues. The task of management becomes to provide a platform for the front-line and the support functions, based on both the know-how of these two categories and on other conditions, such as company mission and long-term goals. Management should delegate authority and make sure that the operating conditions are known throughout the organization. This requires communication up and down the hierarchy. If the communication chains are broken, the company will abound in silly policies, curbed support, and missed marketing opportunities. The behavior of contact personnel, the interaction between customers, the physical environment, and the systems can only be partly changed by the front-line and support functions. Management is needed, because they have decision power on those issues.

The following lessons can be learned from the new organization:

- See the customer as part of the organization.
- Give the front line freedom to make those decisions that can only be

made in the service encounter, and use them as points-of-marketing. Make sure front-line staff know the mission of the firm, but do not restrict them with unnecessary and stifling regulations.

- Listen to the hands-on experience of the front-line and the support units, encourage their suggestions, delegate assignments to them, make quick decisions. Don't dream up fancy solutions based on reports and research. Use the knowledge within the organization.

## Types of Organizational Structures and How to Apply Them

This section presents twelve organizational dimensions and approaches that can be used in structuring marketing. These are complementary to each other and may guide any type of company in organizing its total operations as well as its marketing. These approaches must always be applied with deep insights into the specific company and its market. In service companies they must also be applied with insights into the uniqueness of services and with the use of the part-time marketers and the points-of-marketing. The dimensions and approaches that will be presented are:[6]

- Functions
- Types of services: "the service line"
- Geography
- Customer segments
- Matrix approach
- Holographic approach
- Franchise
- Project approach
- Network/partnership approach
- Available people approach
- Profit center/cost center approach
- Hybrid

In describing the types of organizations it is neither entirely possible nor useful to separate marketing from the rest of the company, because the dependence among tasks is so great. Most companies are some kind of blend between these dimensions and approaches; they are hybrid organizations, as the last item in this presentation is called.

Functional Organization (Figure 7-5).   The service company may organize one or several specific marketing activities in functions such as sales, advertising, marketing research, and marketing planning.

Service-Line Organization (Figure 7-6).   The notion of the product (or brand) manager from manufacturing industries can also be applied to service companies. Instead of talking about a product line we will use the term *service line*. A special manager can be appointed to each of these lines—for example

**Figure 7-5.** Functional organization.

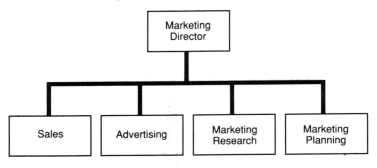

**Figure 7-6.** Service-line organization.

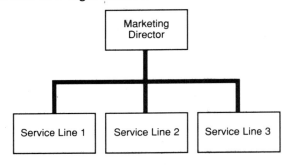

**Figure 7-7.** Geographical organization.

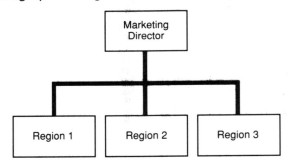

in banks as illustrated in Figure 7-2. The service-line manager becomes a coordinator of all aspects of the service line.

Geographical Organization (Figure 7-7). Companies that produce and deliver services locally must establish local units. These may be independent but their marketing may also be coordinated through a regional and central organization.

**Figure 7-8.** Customer segment organization.

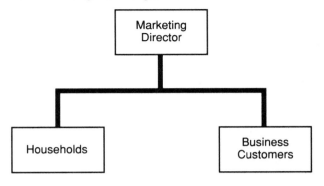

**Figure 7-9.** Matrix organization.

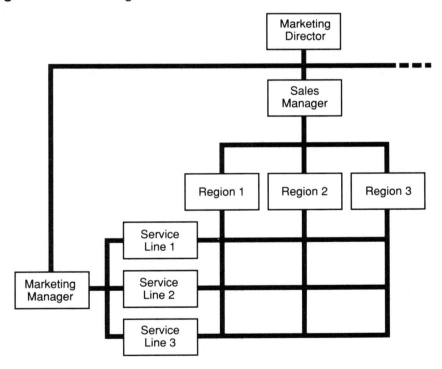

Customer Segment Organization (Figure 7-8). If the service business addresses itself to different types of customers, it may use an organization based on these segments. For example, a hotel would market services differently to corporate customers than to tourists.

Matrix Organization (Figure 7-9). The four dimensions mentioned earlier are traditional ways of organizing, but the dimensions are usually used in some kind of combination. The most frequent type of matrix organization is one in which marketing responsibilities are shared between a service line and a region. The product (brand) manager often works in an organization of this kind. Figure 7-2 shows a bank application having this principal layout.

Holographic Organization (Figure 7-10).   This method of approaching organization is inspired by the hologram, a picture best known for being three-dimensional. However, the hologram has yet another property: If you cut it into a number of pieces, each piece will be a new, complete picture, not just a fragment of the original. I use this metaphor to stress the need for integration, the interdependence between departments in a service company, and the need for all those with customer contact to represent the company well. In other words, all employees should represent the entire company and what it stands for. Imagine the small service company—a restaurant, a one-man consultancy— where the founder is able to do all the jobs. As the business grows, the new employees have contacts with customers. What the founder really wants is to reproduce the company and ensure that the new employees understand the company's goals and strategies and that they understand the service production, delivery, and marketing process. Expanding a service company is a matter of reproducing the service concept either to more employees so that more customers can be served, or reproducing it into new locations. In Figure 7-10 the founder has reproduced the company into eight more units, and he wants the company to perform the same service in all nine locations. For example, Hyatt legal services devised the concept of "legal advice for ordinary people." In order to reach these people a large number of "legal stores" had to be reproduced with convenient access in suburban shopping centers throughout the country. Internal marketing programs[7] are necessary to implement the holographic organization.

Franchising (Figure 7-11).[8]   This is an application of the holographic multiplication of a service concept to new locations without *directly* employing additional personnel. The franchisor licenses the franchisee with a business concept and a tested method of operation, including such things as a name, a system for service production and delivery, promotional activities, financial practices, and training. The franchisor earns money through fees and royalties. Franchising has become a popular form for expanding service businesses and exists in such diverse areas as equipment rental, real estate, motels, educational services, dental care, and weight-loss clinics. The franchisor centrally develops marketing strategies, plans and programs, and the design of the production/delivery system. The implementation rests partially with the franchisor and partially with the local franchisee. Franchising is a practical way to apply the holographic approach to expansion in service businesses.

Project Organization (Figure 7-12).   A project is a temporary organizational unit that is established for a specific purpose when the base organization is insufficient. For example, in their efforts to get a contract from a prospective

**Figure 7-10.** Holographic organization.

The One-Man Service Operation

The Multiplication of the Operation to Eight New Locations

**Figure 7-11.** Franchise organization.

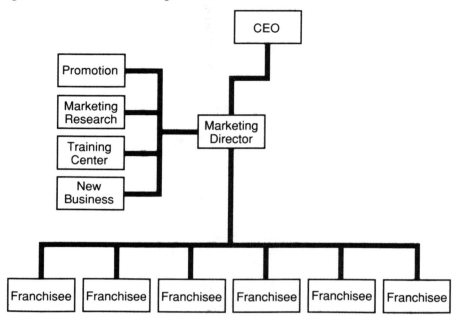

**Figure 7-12.** Project organization.

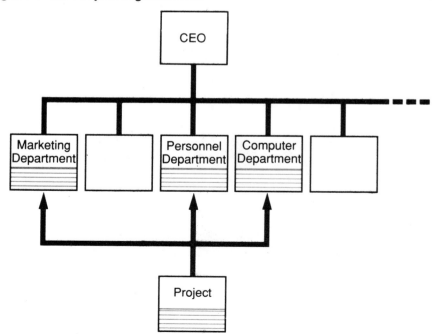

**Figure 7-13.** Network/partnership organization.

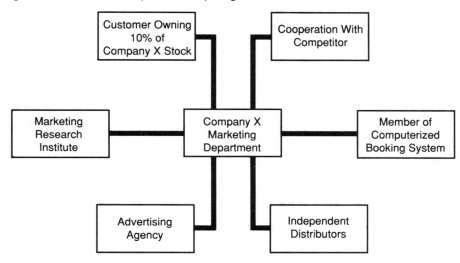

client, a construction company may form a temporary team that deals with the client. In these cases each job is usually carried out by a different team, which is dissolved when the job is completed. A person can be a member of several project teams simultaneously.

The Network/Partnership Approach (Figure 7-13). This is a way of operating with other independent organizations. Networking is likely to become increasingly important; for example, a hotel may be part of a network of other hotels, travel agencies, and airlines through which reservations are made; if it is not in the network, few reservations will be received. This is a good example of designing marketing into the service production and delivery process; being in the system generates business continually. The network/partnership approach is also a distribution system. Other members of the network can be outside consultants who reinforce the marketing function. These constitute a large number of professional specialists today: management/marketing consultants, advertising agencies, public relations consultants, marketing research institutes, recruitment/executive search agencies, legal advisers, and providers of training and education (such as sales training). The modern technology of computers and telecommunications within service companies is particularly important for these networks.

Availability of Suitable Personnel (Figure 7-14). Sometimes you cannot get the people you want, or maybe not for the right price. You may solve this problem by using less staff and more equipment, or design your service production/delivery system for more customer participation or self-service. Service businesses are sometimes based on a personnel concept,[9] for example, the hiring of young people during a brief period of their lives (fast-food establishments do this), and homemakers or retirees in need of part-time work. Available personnel are crucial for a family business so common in retailing, as well as for the

**Figure 7-14.** Organizing around the available people.

hospitality industry, dry-cleaning, and many other areas; new businesses often start this way. Says Casson in his study of the entrepreneur: "The origins of the firm lie in the family—specifically in the family of its founders. Admittedly, some firms begin life as fully-fledged joint stock companies with many share-holders. But the vast majority of firms are founded by just one individual, and their early development is very much tied up with the founder's family."[10] If you have people with particular skills, use them; do not let the (alleged) logic provided by organizational principles and the squares and arrows of organization charts curb your business.

Profit Center/Cost Center Approach (Figure 7-15).   Marketing means satisfying customer needs and wants—but at a profit. Therefore financial aspects of marketing have to enter the marketing organization; you need to control the three factors that determine the bottom line: revenue, cost, and capital. This is done by appointing certain units as profit centers, or cost centers. The head of a profit center is responsible for revenue, cost, and the amount of capital utilized (the provision of capital is usually centralized). This is a common way of or-ganizing local units and service lines; it requires managers to become business executives instead of just administrators. Functional units—advertising, market-ing research, marketing planning, and such—support profit centers but have no revenue of their own and thus become cost centers with the responsibility for budgeting and monitoring their own costs.

Hybrid Organization (Figure 7-16).   Most organizations are a combina-tion of several of the listed dimensions and approaches—they are hybrid orga-nizations. One such combination of two dimensions was the matrix organization

**Figure 7-15.** Profit centers and cost centers.

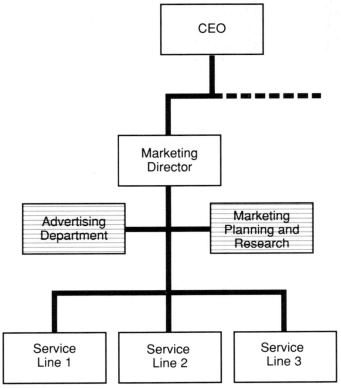

Note: Shaded boxes indicate cost centers; unshaded boxes indicate profit centers.

shown in Figure 7-9. Figure 7-16 shows the hybrid principle in an organization influenced by several of the preceding dimensions and approaches.

New innovative forms of organizations are appearing, but they have not yet been well investigated and the general conclusions have not been drawn. This should not discourage you from devising unorthodox solutions; it should inspire you to be inventive.

The twelve dimensions and approaches could be summed up in this three-step action plan:

1. Identify which dimensions and approaches strike you as relevant to your particular business.
2. Combine them with consideration of the specific features of your company mission, your service, and your market.
3. Make sure that the organizational structure makes efficient use of the full-time marketers as well as the part-time marketers.

**Figure 7-16.** Hybrid organization.

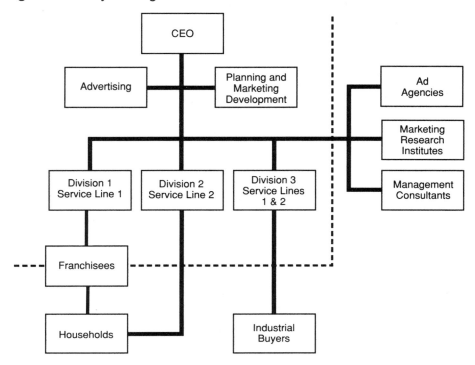

# How to Organize Marketing of Services— Nine Rules for Success

These nine rules summarize the chapter:

*Rule 1*    Recognize the most important reason why you need to organize your marketing.

*Rule 2*    Identify the most important task that your marketing function should be able to fulfill.

*Rule 3*    Identify possible points-of-marketing in the service production/delivery process, and design in marketing activities as a natural part of the process.

*Rule 4*    Decide what tasks should best be carried out by the full-time marketers and organize these into one or several marketing and sales departments.

*Rule 5*    Decide what marketing tasks should be carried out by the part-time marketers.

*Rule 6*    Recruit, train, and motivate both the full-time marketers and the part-time marketers, so that their tasks are carried out efficiently.

*Rule 7*    Make sure that the total organizational structure of your company is supportive to marketing, that marketing is designed in.

*Rule 8*    Review the types of organizational structures and select the combination of dimensions and approaches that strike you as being appropriate for the unique features of your business.
*Rule 9*    Be innovative; look for unconventional solutions.

## Notes

1. Evert Gummesson, "The Marketing of Professional Services—An Organizational Dilemma," *European Journal of Marketing* 13, no. 5 (1979), and "The Part-Time Marketer," Service Research Center, University of Karlstad, research report no. 3, 1990.
2. The CPA example is taken from Carole A. Congram and Ruth J. Dumesic, *The Accountant's Strategic Marketing Guide* (New York: Wiley, 1986), 66–68.
3. Evert Gummesson, "The New Marketing—Developing Long-Term Interactive Relationships," *Long-Range Planning* 20, no. 4 (1987).
4. See Alvin Toffler, *The Third Wave* (London: Pan Books, 1980).
5. See the book by SAS President Jan Carlzon, *Moments of Truth* (New York: Ballinger, 1987).
6. Some of these organizational structures are discussed further in Eugene M. Johnson, Eberhard E. Scheuing, and Kathleen A. Gaida, *Profitable Service Marketing* (Homewood, Ill.: Dow Jones-Irwin, 1986).
7. For a discussion on internal marketing, see Christian Grönroos, *Service Management and Marketing* (Lexington, Mass.: Lexington Books, 1990), chapter 10.
8. The significance of franchising for service companies is discussed further in James Cross and Bruce J. Walker, *Service Marketing and Franchising: A Practical Business Marriage,* Tempe, Ariz., First Interstate Center for Services Marketing, Arizona State University, working paper, no. 3, December 1986.
9. The notion of the "personnel concept" is discussed further in Richard Normann, *Service Management* (New York: Wiley, 1984), chapter 4.
10. Mark Casson, *The Entrepreneur* (Oxford, Eng.: Martin Robertson, 1982), 299.

*        *        *        *

*Evert Gummesson, Ph.D., is currently senior consultant for Cicero Executives in Sweden. His consulting involves market-oriented management including corporate strategy, organization, and quality management. Dr. Gummesson is also professor of service management and marketing at The Service Research Center, University of Karlstad, Sweden, and conducts seminars in this field both in Europe and the United States.*

# PART IV

# MARKET PLANNING: PREPARING TO SERVE THE CUSTOMER

# About This Part

In this part the various activities involved in fleshing out a customer-focused strategic framework (see Part II) are covered. The chapters here address what information is needed, how to obtain that information, and how to use that information for market planning.

It is fitting that the first chapter in this part examines consumer behavior, the most important category of information to be considered. Consumer behavior, whether it involves business consumers or end users, is especially important in a service business because when a consumer buys a service, he or she must be viewed as a partial employee, due to his or her participation in the service "production" process. You can talk about being customer-focused but cannot *be* customer-focused until you know your customer. Consumers' perceptions and expectations are the starting point for any marketing effort. Chapter 8 presents a model of consumer decision making that outlines how consumer perceptions are formed and how they relate to purchase decisions and satisfaction. Further, the model suggests actions that you can take to influence consumer perceptions, thereby increasing your chances of being the service provider of choice. The chapter ends with a listing of specific, high-priority questions to consider in order to understand your customers.

Chapter 9 gets down to the nuts and bolts of information gathering—conducting a research project. The common steps that are required in any research effort are presented, together with illustrative examples of how to implement each step. Included are a discussion of problem definition, research design alternatives and factors to consider in choosing among them, sampling considerations and, finally, analysis, interpretation, and presentation of results. The chapter also includes discussion of the question of whether to use an outside supplier of research services and how to choose the right supplier.

The next chapter, "How to Develop a Marketing Plan," describes the steps in a comprehensive marketing planning process, where you make use of and analyze all the market information you have gathered. The author argues, as do those who have preceded her, that market-driven services have a much greater chance for success than "internally conceived" services. A marketing plan is the mechanism for achieving a market focus. It ensures that all marketing efforts are complementing one another and working harmoniously to achieve a customer focus not only in outlook, but in action. The four parts to a marketing plan are presented—goals, situation analysis, strategies (both internal and external), and action plans. The key players in the planning process are identified, and the type of research you need for well-grounded planning is discussed.

Chapter 11, "Information: The Next Battleground," explores the important role that information plays in any service business. The chapter is organized around four opportunities for performance improvement provided by information: in marketing decision making, in marketing operations, in providing service to customers, and in differentiating your service. The author provides a section on where to find useful information, discussing both internal and external sources. Guidelines for using some of the attractive new information-handling technologies are provided as well.

Chapter 12 discusses the role that outside consultants might play in helping you satisfy your need for information. The chapter covers the kinds of consultants available, what each can do for you, criteria you might apply in choosing among consultants, what you should expect from your consultant, and what your consultant will expect from you.

This part concludes with a chapter on using information to measure marketing effectiveness. Key issues affecting services marketing effectiveness are covered, recognizing that the clear, functional lines drawn in manufacturing businesses are inappropriate in service businesses where, according to the author, "everybody sells." A case history is used to illustrate a comprehensive system for measuring marketing effectiveness. The author concludes by stressing the importance of effectiveness in three critical areas: customer satisfaction, front-line management, and key marketing specialists, whose role is to be especially tuned in to the pulse of the market.

# 8

## Understanding Services Consumer Behavior

John E. G. Bateson

A consumer orientation is the heart of the marketing concept. We are urged to understand consumers and to build organizations around them. This is particularly true for services that in the past have tended to be operations-dominated. This is hardly surprising, because for services the operation is the product. Without a successful operations department there can be no service firm.

In the absence of competition operational efficiency is enough to generate success. As soon as competition arrives, however, the rules of the game change. Consumers now have a choice. If the choice goes against you, then you go broke—however efficient your operation seems to be. Now mere operational efficiency is not enough; now it is important to make sure that the operation delivers what the customer wants. Now marketing effectiveness can become as important as operational efficiency.

Suddenly it is important to understand consumers—to understand how they make their choices and evaluations. This is by no means simple, because consumers make evaluations *during* the consumption of the service, not just afterward as is the case with goods. Consumers are part of the process and are called upon to play a "production" role; their behavior can influence the efficiency of the entire operation. The purpose of this chapter is to provide a framework for understanding the consumer. It first draws the distinction between preconsumption choice and postconsumption evaluation. It then goes on to introduce a series of ways of thinking about consumers; none is perfect, but each can provide insights that can yield competitive advantage.

## The Consumer's Choice and Evaluation Process

Marketing managers need to understand the evaluation process used by consumers for two broad categories of problems: the preconsumption choice between alternatives and the postpurchase evaluation. In the first case the objective is to understand why a consumer chooses to use a particular service or service outlet. In the latter we need to understand the sources of customer satisfaction or dissatisfaction.

### Prepurchase Evaluation

We can think of a consumer trying to decide which restaurant to choose for lunch. The first question we would ask might be "What is the occasion?" It is often possible to segment consumers into homogeneous groups based upon the occasion. It is clear that the choice of restaurant will be different if our consumer is planning to eat a quick lunch alone rather than have a business lunch with colleagues and a client. The same individuals often eat in McDonald's at lunchtime and in a French restaurant in the evening.

Once the occasion for the meal has been specified the next question becomes "Which restaurants are on the list?" For banking this question might become "Which brands in which locations are on the list?" It is clear that in all consumer decision making we seldom consider all feasible alternatives. Instead we have a limited list chosen on the basis of past experience, convenience, and knowledge. This list is often referred to by the theorists as the evoked set—the set of "brands" that will be evoked by the consumer and from which the choice will be made.

Even if we have specified the occasion and the evoked set, it is clear that the consumer still has to choose where to go for lunch. That choice process is the focus of this chapter. We can never truly know the process being used by any individual. As will be discussed later, however, we need a model to structure our thinking and to guide our market research.

### Postpurchase Evaluation

Customer satisfaction is the key outcome of the marketing process. It is an end in itself but it is also the source of word-of-mouth recommendation. As will be discussed in a later section, "The Consumer as a Risk Taker," a lot of evidence suggests that buying a service is a big risk for a consumer, and this makes word-of-mouth recommendations very valuable. But how does satisfaction arise? A number of approaches have been suggested, but perhaps the most simple and most powerful is shown in Figure 8-1.

The heart of the model is very simple. It argues that consumers evaluate services by comparing the service they perceive that they have received with their expectations of what they should have received. If the perceived service is better than or equal to the expected service, they are satisfied. It is crucial to point out that this entire process takes place in the mind of the customer. It is the perceived service that matters, *not* the actual service.

Once this simple idea is established, two subsidiary questions emerge: "What is it that drives expectations?" and "What is it that drives perceptions?"

Expectations are important for two reasons. It is crucial to understand consumers' expectations in order to try to meet them. It is also feasible to manage expectations to produce satisfaction without altering in any way the quality of the perceived or actual service delivered.

Expectations come from many sources, such as from past experience or from word-of-mouth communication from friends. Both of these sources are beyond the control of management. A number of controllable factors also influence expectations, however. Advertising can create expectations. The advertisement that promises the consumer a particular benefit in order to influence the preconsumption choice process will also set a benchmark against which that

**Figure 8-1.** The relationships among sources of consumer satisfaction with services.

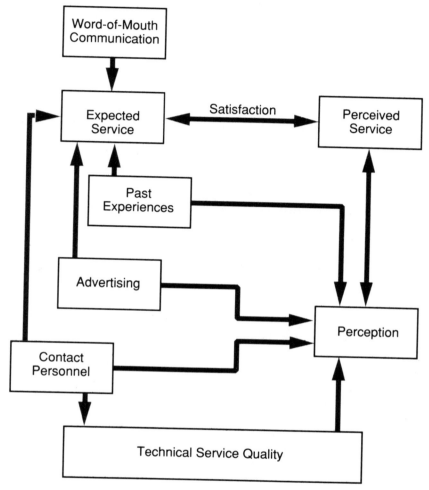

service is evaluated during and after consumption. Contact employees who interface with the consumer also set expectations. They make promises or commitments that can become part of an implicit "contract" in the consumer's mind.

Perceptions in turn are not driven merely by technical quality, which can be thought of as the reality that is measurable using a stopwatch or video camera. It is the real and objective world in which the operations people of the service firm function. Unfortunately it is the consumer's perceptions of that reality that are crucial. Waiting time may have been reduced by thirty seconds, but there is no reason why consumers should perceive the difference. Past experience may have shown them that there is always a long wait. The staff members may be surly and rude and this will be reflected in the perceived service time. Many things can interfere with the perception.

# Models of the Consumer's Mind—The Black Box

Within both the prepurchase evaluation and the postconsumption evaluation process the consumer must be using a model to make the evaluation. There are many versions of those models, some of which will now be described. Before continuing, it is important to point out that no model is correct. The consumer's mind is still closed to us; it is a black box that is sealed. We can observe inputs to the box and the decisions made, but we can never know how the process actually happens.

Why, then, should we bother with such models? The problem is that the heart of marketing is consumer orientation. Whether marketing managers like it or not, every time they make marketing decisions they are basing them on some model of how the consumer will behave. Quite often these models are implicit and are seldom shared with others—they are the marketing manager's "experience." However, every time a price is changed, a new product launched, advertising shown, some assumption will have been made about how the consumer will react.

Models are therefore needed as a way of structuring marketing decisions. They may not be totally accurate, but many are the result of much research in marketing and psychology. They can provide frameworks. They can provide formats for the structuring of market research, which is the heart of the marketing process. All of the perspectives to be described have both strengths and weaknesses. These perspectives should therefore be considered as complementary rather than mutually exclusive. Some are more relevant to the prepurchase choice process: the risk-taking perspective and the multiattribute model. Others are more powerful when trying to understand customer satisfaction: the control and script theory models. Managerial insights, however, can be developed more effectively through a combination of various perspectives.

## The Consumer as a Risk Taker

The idea of perceived risk as an explanation for customer purchasing behavior was first suggested in the 1960s.[1] The idea is that consumer behavior involves risk in the sense that any consumer action will produce consequences that he/she cannot anticipate with any certainty, some of which are likely to be unpleasant. Each purchase can therefore be thought of as the taking of a risk. Bauer, who first suggested this idea, proposed that perceived risk is actually composed of two structural dimensions:

1. *Consequence*—the degree of importance and/or danger of the outcomes derived from any consumer decision; and
2. *Uncertainty*—the subjective probability of occurrence of those outcomes

As the idea was developed four types of perceived risk were identified based on the different kinds of outcomes: financial, performance, physical, and social.[2] Financial risk relates to the monetary costs of something going wrong. Performance risk relates to the idea that the item or service will not perform the task for which it was purchased. The physical risk of a purchase can emerge should something go wrong and injure the purchaser. Social risk is interesting because it suggests that there is a negative outcome associated with being the person who made the purchase—"Who bought this?!"

A number of people have shown that services have a higher perceived risk of purchase. Much attention has been focused on the fact that it is extremely difficult to standardize the service product.[3] Because a service is an experience involving highly complex interactions, it is not surprising that it is very difficult to replicate the same experience. As a result the customer may find that it is difficult to predict precisely the quality of the service he/she will be buying. Because Brown's Auto Repair shop did a good tune-up for your neighbor, there is no guarantee that they will do the same for you.

Other authors have argued that the higher risk level is due to the limited information available before the purchase decision is made. One group of authors,[4] for example, draws on the economics literature to suggest three different properties of services:

1. *Search attributes*—those that can be evaluated before purchase
2. *Experience attributes*—those that cannot be evaluated until after a service has been received
3. *Credence attributes*—those that cannot be evaluated confidently even immediately after receipt

Because of the nature of services, it is often extremely difficult for consumers to evaluate a service objectively before it is bought. Services thus have very low search attributes. A large proportion of the service properties (e.g., how friendly are the attendants of a certain airline?) can only be evaluated by consumers after the consumption of the service (experience attributes). Finally, some of the properties of many services (e.g., how well a car has been repaired) may not be assessed even after the service is completed (credence properties).

The consumer's involvement in the "production process" of services is another source of increased perceived risk. One cannot take the service home and use it in private where one's mistakes would not be visible. Instead, the consumer must take part in the ritual. To be part of such a process and not to know exactly what is going on clearly increases the uncertainty about the consequences, particularly the social consequences of doing the wrong thing.

### Risk-Reduction Strategies for the Purchase of Consumer Services.

If we start from the premise that consumers do not like taking risks, it would seem obvious that they will try to reduce risk during the purchase process. Many studies have been conducted to determine how consumers attempt to reduce high perceived risk.

One strategy is to be brand or store loyal; having been satisfied in one high-risk purchase, consumers are less inclined to experiment with others. There is then an obvious trade-off made between the risk inherent in returning to one uncertain service business and the even greater risk of trying something new.

Research has also shown that in the communications area, word-of-mouth references often take on increased importance over company-controlled communication. A reference from a friend assumes more importance when the purchase to be made has a greater risk. A visit to a new hairdresser can be stressful because the outcome is so visible. That stress is reduced by a recommendation from someone whose judgment you trust.

In the same way some evidence suggests that opinion leaders play an important role in the purchase of services. An opinion leader in a community is an individual whose advice is sought. Within the perceived risk framework an opinion leader can be viewed as a source of reduced social risk—"Don't laugh at me, because I used this hairdresser whom X recommended" (and X is well regarded by everyone).

Risk-Reduction Strategies for Industrial and Professional Services. In the same way a number of authors have used the risk idea to study the purchase of industrial services. Their approach is shown in Figure 8-2.

This simple grid depicts the risk-reduction strategies available for considering uncertainty and/or consequences—the horizontal axis. The vertical dimension focuses on how to approach uncertainty or consequences using internal and external information sources.

Dealing with consequences is relatively staightforward. It can involve minimizing the financial consequences by making initial purchases small. This implies trials and pilot projects for professional service firms. Such a strategy can

**Figure 8-2.** Risk-reduction strategies for industrial and professional service firms.

|          | Uncertainty | Consequences |
|----------|-------------|--------------|
| External | Reputation Advertising References Articles | Pilot Projects Investigations |
| Internal | Past Experiences | The Decision-Making Unit |

also be thought of as the heart of the multiple source argument, because the consequences of any one supplier's failure are minimized.

Minimizing uncertainty requires collecting information. That information can come either from inside or outside the organization. It can be of a general nature as would be represented by "general reputation," or as specific as a reference from a current user of the service.

Consequences can be used as an explanation by a buying committee or decision-making unit (DMU), which is often described as the formal or informal committee involved in purchasing goods or services in organizations. The rational explanation for the emergence of such committees is the need to provide interested parties with relevant information or expertise. Users need to be involved as do engineering, finance, and other departments, because everyone experiences the consequences of the decision.

Using the risk perspective, however, a different explanation can be hypothesized. It is the committee or DMU that makes the decision and therefore suffers the consequences of a bad decision. DMU members can, if necessary, deny their involvement, or claim that it was in fact minor. Alternatively, each member of the committee can in turn claim that he or she wanted to select professional service firm X but was overruled and the service of firm Y contracted.

Recognizing this risk perspective, it is important for the supplier to offer as many opportunities as possible for clients to reduce their risk. Competitively it could be argued that the client will choose the supplier with the lowest risk, which implies either minor consequences or low uncertainty. Selecting a well-known firm can help, but the clients are always seeking other ways to reduce their risk.

## Multiattribute Models and the Service Experience— The Rational Mathematician Model

Marketing theorists have made extensive use of multiattribute models to simulate the evaluation process of tangible goods.

According to these models a number of salient attributes or dimensions are employed by consumers as the basic references for the evaluation of a service. Consumers compute this preference for the service by combining the scores of the product on each individual attribute.

In the prepurchase evaluation process, consumers are assumed to create a matrix similar to that shown in Table 8-1. This example uses the choice of airline to fly across the North Atlantic. Across the top of the table are two types of variables. This first is the evoked set of brands that will be evaluated—in this case four airlines. Generally, this selection does not include all possible choices. The second type of variable is an importance rating with which the consumer is supposed to rank the various attributes that constitute the row heads of the table. (A rating of 10 in this example signifies *most important*.) In this case the consumer rates safety as the most important attribute followed by such factors as time of flight. To complete the table the consumer rates each brand on each attribute and then weights the attributes.

Various choice processes have been suggested in using this type of table.

**Table 8-1.** A typical multiattribute choice matrix.

|  | Evoked Set of Brands | | | | |
| --- | --- | --- | --- | --- | --- |
| Attributes | Airline A | Airline B | Airline C | Airline D | Importance Weights |
| Safety | 10 | 10 | 10 | 9.9 | 10 |
| Time of flight | 10 | 10 | 9 | 9 | 9 |
| Type of aircraft | 10 | 9 | 10 | 10 | 8 |
| Flight time | 9 | 9 | 9 | 9 | 7 |
| Cabin crew | 10 | 8 | 8 | 10 | 6 |

The "linear compensatory model" proposes that the consumer create a global score for each brand by multiplying the rating of that brand name on each attribute by the importance attached to that attribute and adding the scores together. Airline A would score $10 \times 10$ (safety) + $10 \times 9$ (time of flight) + $10 \times 8$ (aircraft) and so on. The brand with the highest score is chosen. Various other combinatory or decision rules have been suggested, but they are all rooted in the basic table.

The same kind of model can be applied to the postpurchase evaluation process. In this case the brands are replaced by two columns. The first is the score expected by the consumer on each attribute. The second is the perceived score on each attribute obtained by the consumer after purchase. The satisfaction score is then derived by creating a global score of the comparisons between perceptions and expectations weighted by the importance of each attribute. This is shown in Table 8-2.

In this example the consumer has chosen to fly on Airline A, using the Multiattribute Choice Matrix shown in Table 8-1. The expected levels on each attribute are therefore taken from that matrix. In reality the flight was delayed and the cabin crew was not very helpful under the circumstances. The consumer therefore downgraded their performance on those attributes.

Given the popularity of the multiattribute models, it is obvious why they

**Table 8-2.** A postpurchase evaluation model for an Airline A flight.

| Attribute | Expected Scores* | Perceived Scores | Importance Weights |
| --- | --- | --- | --- |
| Safety | 10 | 10 | 10 |
| Time of flight | 10 | 9.5 | 9 |
| Type of aircraft | 10 | 10 | 8 |
| Flight time | 9 | 9 | 7 |
| Cabin crew | 10 | 8 | 6 |

*From Table 8-1

have been used to describe and explain the consumer's service decision processes. Based on the results of twelve focus-group interviews, the following generic dimensions of service quality were identified: reliability, responsiveness, competence, access, courtesy, communication, credibility, security, tangibles, and understanding/knowing the customer.[5]

The merit of these multiattribute models lies in their simplicity and explictness. The attributes identified cover a wide range of concerns related to the service experience, and are easily understood by service managers. The job for management using this model is relatively straightforward.

First it is necessary to identify the criteria used by consumers. This can often be done by using focus groups in which consumers are asked to talk about a particular service. The kind of words consumers use and the criteria they use for evaluation become apparent. Importance scores can be elicted directly or by using such procedures as conjoint analysis. Evoked sets and brand scores are elicted directly. It should be stressed that such a model must be used at the individual level. Groups of consumers can, however, be combined.

Once managers understand the process, obvious actions can be taken to improve a firm's competitive position—to improve the share of consumers' choices. If the full-fare service package does not contain the appropriate mixture of attributes, then a new service can be developed. To return to our airline example, if consumers demand an executive cabin, this can be built into the aircraft and the system. Alternatively, advertising can be used to highlight a particular attribute on which the firm's service appears weak to consumers. An airline may have had a poor on-time record in the past, but still be perceived that way by consumers. If necessary, an airline can also try to reduce consumers' attribute scores by engaging in a competitive advertising campaign. For example, when it was first launched, Federal Express featured the result of market research about ''on-time delivery,'' which showed that it outperformed existing competitors.

The same logical process can be applied to managing customer satisfaction. Because satisfaction is the result of comparing expectations with perceptions, two different routes are open to improve satisfaction. Consumer perceptions of the service can be improved by stressing in communications how good the service is, relative to the competition, on the key attributes. Alternatively, communications can ensure the accuracy of customers' expectations on key attributes. Returning to the Federal Express example, communications must clearly distinguish between Priority Service (guaranteed overnight delivery) and Standard Air (second day delivery).

Modeling a Dynamic Interaction With Static Attributes. The first shortcoming is that such models impose a static perspective on an experience that consists of a series of dynamic interactions. A defect in one aspect of the service encounter may adversely affect the customers' perceptions on a wide array of attributes, and thus there is no way to determine the real source of the problem.

For example, a crowded bank may not only convey to customers a perception of poor service, but also jeopardize the relationship between the tellers and the customers. The customers may feel that the tellers are unfriendly and rude when actually they are rushing to accommodate the large number of customers.

Conversely, when tellers are working under pressure, they may feel that the customers are too demanding. In this case, it may be unwise for bank management to focus solely on training and regulating their tellers' manners and behavior; rather, the managers may have to identify the real source of the problem—the crowded environment.

Similarly researchers in the area of human touch have demonstrated the existence of a "Midas touch." [6] In a library setting they determined whether or not the librarian touched borrowers' hands when they checked out books. They identified the sex of the librarian and borrower, and found that the touch was so casual that only 57 percent of the respondents who had actually been touched claimed that they had been when asked. Respondents were intercepted after leaving the library, and asked to evaluate the librarian, the library environment, and their own emotional state. All of those touched, regardless of whether they noticed it, responded more positively on all scales. A single touch was therefore able to influence apparently concrete attributes of the environment as well as customers' emotional states.

<u>Relating Consumers' Attributes to Managerial Actions.</u>   The second major shortcoming is the lack of correspondence between a service company's effort to improve its operational standards, such as increasing the number of branches of a bank, and its customers' rating of such service attributes as convenience. One reason for this is that the attributes are frequently abstract in nature (reliability, friendliness). Second, the atttributes are rarely under the full control of the service organization. The service delivery process is open to the influence of the customers and to environmental factors that are usually beyond the service manager's control.

In response to the insufficiency of multiattribute type models, theorists have proposed a number of new perspectives on the service encounter. New concepts, originally developed in various disciplines of the behavioral sciences, have been suggested.

## *The Perceived Control Perspective—Who's in Control Anyway?*

The concept of control has drawn considerable attention from psychologists. They argue that in today's society people no longer have to worry about satisfying primary biological needs, so the need to control situations in which people find themselves is a major force that drives human behavior.

The concept of control was first introduced by Bateson to explain the service employee and customer responses to the service experience. [7] Rather than being treated as a service attribute, as implied by the multiattribute models, perceived control can be conceptualized as a super-factor, a global index that summarizes an individual's experience in the service. The basic argument of the perspective is that during the service experience, the higher the level of control over the situation perceived by the consumers, the stronger will be their satisfaction with the service. A similar positive correlation is proposed between the service providers' experience of control and their job satisfaction.

In a slightly different way it is equally important for the service company itself to maintain control of the service experience. If the consumer gets too much control, the company's economics may be destroyed—consumers tip the value equation in their favor to such an extent that the company loses money. If the service employee takes control, the consumer may be unhappy and take his or her business elsewhere. Even if this does not happen, if an employee takes too much control, the operational efficiency of the company may be ruined. This three-cornered conflict is shown in Figure 8-3.

Services can be thought of as the exchange of cash and control by the consumer for benefits. But it would appear that no one can truly win such a contest. In fact the concept of control is much broader than implied. Behavioral control—the ability to control what is actually going on—is only part of the concept. Much of the work that has been done suggests that cognitive control is also important. If consumers perceive that they are in control, or if they can predict what will happen to them, then the outcome can be the same as achieved with behavioral control. In other words, it is the *perception* of control that is important, not the reality.

Managerially this raises a number of interesting issues. The first is the value of information to consumers during the service experience to increase their sense of being in control, and that what is happening to them is predictable—they know what will happen next. This is particularly the case with professional

**Figure 8-3.** The perceived behavioral control conflict in the service encounter.

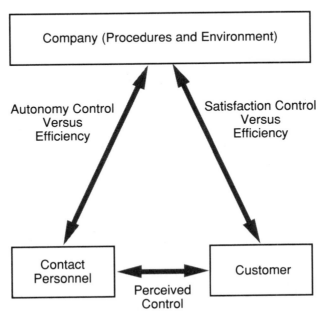

service firms, which assume that simply because they are doing a good job their clients will be happy. They forget that their clients have not heard from them for more than a month and are frantic about lack of information.

Similarly, if the company is due to make changes to the operation that will impact on the consumer, it is important to forewarn those consumers. If not, they may perceive themselves to be "out of control" and therefore change suppliers or be dissatisfied with the poor service received.

The control perspective raises interesting issues about the trade-off between predictability and choice. One of *the* strategic operational issues is the amount of choice to give the consumer. Since both choice and predictability (standardization) can contribute to a sense of control, it is crucial to determine which is the more powerful source of control for the relevant consumers.

### The Script Perspective—All the World's a Stage and All the People Players

A number of alternative theories within psychology and sociology can be brought together under the idea of a script and role. An alternative but similar theory from social psychology is role theory. A role is generally defined as "a set of behavior patterns learned through experience and communication, to be performed by an individual in a certain social interaction in order to attain a maximum effectiveness in goal accomplishment."[8] The principal argument proposed is that in a service encounter, customer satisfaction is a function of role congruence, whether or not enacted behaviors are in agreement with role expectations. Thus, the focus is on the postpurchase phases. Because the interaction is two-way, role congruence is expected to impact on the customer as well as on the service provider. In other words, both parties are likely to be satisfied when the customer and the service provider enact behaviors congruent with each other's role expectation; otherwise, both performers may be upset by the interaction. The result of role discrepancy may be a dissatisfied customer and a dissatisfied employee:

> **Teller** [*annoyed about having to fill out a deposit slip when many customers are waiting in line*]: "Next time, please fill in the deposit slip before you come to the window; it's not my responsibility to do that for you."
> **Customer:** "The teller is not helpful and is unfriendly."

The key managerial tasks implied by the role theory perspectives are: (1) designing roles for the service encounter that are acceptable and able to fulfill both the needs of the customer and the service provider; and (2) communicating the roles to the customer and the employee, so that both have a realistic perception of their role as well as that of their partner in the interaction.

Role is assumed to be extra-individual; that is, every individual is expected to display the same predetermined set of behaviors when he/she assumes a certain role, for example, as a customer or a service provider. Role theory is not directly concerned with the perception of the participants in the service encounter, and thus is incompatible with the concepts of service evaluation and customer satisfaction. For example, two customers—one an introvert and one an extrovert—may have completely different perceptions and evaluations of inter-actions with the same chatty provider. In this case, intra-individual variables have to be used in order to explain the differences in customer evaluation and satisfaction.

The same idea can, however, be adapted for use in such situations. This draws on the psychological idea of a script. The script theory and role theory perspectives appear on the surface to be extremely similar. Script theory argues that rules, determined mainly by social and cultural variables, exist to facilitate interactions in daily repetitive events, including a variety of service experi-ences.[9] These rules shape participants' expectations in this type of event. Fur-thermore, the rules have to be acknowledged and obeyed by all participants if satisfactory outcomes are to be generated; if one participant deviates from the rules, the other co-actors will be uncomfortable. Therefore a satisfied customer is unlikely with a dissatisfied service provider, whereas a dissatisfied customer is rarely associated with a satisfied service provider.

Two basic differences exist between the two perspectives, however. First, the script theory perspective has a wider range of concerns (e.g., the impact of the service setting) and hence is concerned with the service experience rather than just the interpersonal service encounter. Second, scripts are by definition individualistic and are subjective. Scripts exist for each individual and are a function of that individual's experience and personality. Part of the service pro-vider's job is to uncover the script and either enact it (if appropriate) with the customer, or revise it with the customer. Conversely, the content of a role is defined in a more objective sense, by means of a social position or title (doctor, waiter) rather than the perception and cognition of an individual. Part of the job of the service provider who has a defined role is to manage customers' expec-tations by educating them about the service process.

In this section, four different perspectives that attempt to describe the psy-chological processes influencing consumer choice among service alternatives have been described. In the following section, the focus shifts to consumers' actual *behavior* relative to service consumption.

## The Consumer as a Partial Employee

A radical view of consumers' behavior in services is to consider them as partial employees. Consumers derive the benefit they receive from services from an interactive experience of which they are part. Following the script analogy, con-sumers *must* obey the script; otherwise they will destroy the whole experience. Classic examples of this occur when "novice consumers" appear in services. Foreign tourists on their first visit to a McDonald's, or the tourist in a foreign bank, do not know the script. As a result they can ruin the experience for themselves, for those trying to serve them, and for other customers.

Such a perspective presents an opportunity for marketing to improve the profitability of service firms in nontraditional ways. At the heart of marketing is the idea that consumer behavior can be changed to induce more consumers to buy or each consumer to buy more. In services a third option is available—to change the consumers' behavior as a partial employee.

## Managerial Implications

A number of authors have drawn an analogy between marketing and warfare. The enemy is the competition. The market is the battlefield, but what are the weapons? They could be thought of as the elements of the marketing mix: product, price, promotion, and channels. I believe it is more appropriate to think of competitors competing with their knowledge of the consumers. The competitor who best understands the consumer wins. This chapter was designed to help in that battle by offering insights into the services consumer.

From the chapter, a number of questions emerge that every manager should answer:

1. *What model of consumer behavior is currently being used?* The easiest way to discover this is to look at recent market research reports dealing with consumer behavior. The nature of the questions used in the questionnaire provides the best clue to the model used.

2. *Would one of the other models described in this chapter offer more insight?* It is worthwhile to take a group of marketing and market research people to a one-day workshop to discuss this issue. It is important initially to suspend disbelief and force the group to try to use the ideas and frameworks *before* evaluating them.

3. *Which is the current key problem—prepurchase choice or postpurchase evaluation?* These two key consumer behavior processes are both important and related. The process is circular, with prepurchase choice leading to purchase and evaluation, which in turn can lead to repurchase. Consumers can, however, drop out of this process at either stage; they do not choose your firm or use it once and then leave. It is important to pinpoint which is the key problem.

4. *What expectations are being set for consumers using your service?* Many firms forget that the generation of customer satisfaction is a two-stage process. Consumers compare their perceptions with their expectations. It is important to realize that this provides two opportunities to improve satisfaction and that expectations can be managed. To do this it is important to know customers' current expectations and the source of those expectations. Satisfied customers return *and* tell their friends.

5. *What important role should the consumer play as a partial employee?* The behavior of the consumer as a partial employee can dramatically affect operational efficiency. This in turn can give the company a competitive cost advantage in the marketplace. To achieve this it is important to define the ideal script *from the operations perspective.* Operations managers can be presented with a simple idea. If marketing could control consumers like puppets, what

would you want them to do to make your life easier? It is important, like a brainstorming session, to forestall the ''but it wouldn't work'' reaction.

The list that is produced from such an exercise is often amusing. Many items are simply not feasible. Buried in the list are some items to which marketing can respond. For example, a distribution business was about to install new telephone systems to cope with the peaks in the telephone ordering done by customers. The operations managers' ''wish list'' included getting customers to call only at certain times (i.e., to flatten the peak). Marketing took this idea and developed a promotional campaign to inform customers that it was in their interest to gather their orders and call once a day. The telephone operators were also trained to convince customers to call only at certain times. The new telephone exchanges were not needed.

Because consumers participate actively in the ''production'' of a service, it is crucial for service providers to understand consumer motivation, expectations, evaluation processes, and perceptions. As a service provider, you are depending on consumers to create, with you, a well-delivered service. The more you can understand consumer behavior—with the help of models like the ones we have discussed—the greater an asset you can be to the consumer in ensuring that he or she is getting the service desired. When you truly understand the consumer's perspective, you are differentiating your service organization from the competition. In this way, you will win—and keep—more customers.

## Notes

1. Dennis Guseman, ''Risk Perception and Risk Reduction in Consumer Services,'' in *Marketing of Services: Proceedings,* ed. James H. Donnelly and William R. George (Chicago: American Marketing Association, 1981), 200–204; and R. A. Bauer, ''Consumer Behavior as Risk Taking,'' in *Dynamic Marketing for a Changing World,* ed. R. S. Hancock (Chicago: American Marketing Association, 1960), 389–398.
2. L. Kaplan, G. J. Szybillo, and J. Jacoby, ''Components of Perceived Risk in Product Purchase: A Cross-Validation,'' *Journal of Applied Psychology* 59 (1974): 287–291.
3. Guseman, ''Risk Perception and Risk Reduction.''
4. A. Parasuraman, V. Zeithaml, and L. Berry, ''A Conceptual Model of Service Quality and Its Implications for Future Research,'' *Journal of Marketing* 49 (Fall 1985): 41–50.
5. Parasuraman, Zeithaml, and Berry, ''A Conceptual Model of Service Quality.''
6. Parasuraman, Zeithaml, and Berry.
7. John E. G. Bateson, ''Perceived Control and the Service Encounter,'' in *The Service Encounter,* ed. John A. Czepiel, Michael R. Solomon, and Carol F. Surprenant (Lexington, Mass.: Lexington Books, 1984), 67–82.
8. Michael R. Solomon et al., ''A Role Theory Perspective on Dyadic Interactions: The Service Encounter,'' *Journal of Marketing* 1, no. 49 (Winter 1985): 99–111.
9. Ruth A. Smith and Michael Houston, ''Script-Based Evaluations of Satisfaction With Services,'' in *Emerging Perspectives in Services Marketing,* ed. L. Berry, G. L. Shostack, and G. Upah (Chicago: American Marketing Association, 1982), 59–62.

*     *     *     *

**John E. G. Bateson,** *Ph.D., is a senior lecturer in marketing and Ernst & Whinney Research Fellow at the London Business School. Previously, he was affiliated with the Stanford Business School. He consults extensively in the service sector, and his clients have included American Express, Citibank, and Price Waterhouse, as well as many other leading companies.*

# 9

## Applying Market Research Techniques in Service Industries

Pamela V. Alden

Incorporating market research techniques into any aspect of services marketing is a challenging task for the marketing professional.

In this chapter, you will see how practicing market research professionals in service industries prepare a research design, evaluate different research approaches, select research suppliers, and use market research data in their day-to-day marketing activities.

## Services Marketing—How to Get Started

Whether you are working on the marketing of a product or service, the basic principles of marketing and research apply. What varies is how you apply them and on what factors you place the greatest emphasis in your decision-making.

Several features of services marketing complicate the process for the marketing and marketing research professional. As a result, services marketing research is often more challenging than projects you may have tackled in the past. These differences spring from differences between products and services themselves.

First, in most cases a service is intangible. You can describe it and its benefits, but you can't touch it, taste it, or look at it without experiencing it, and that generally means purchasing it. A customer's expectations about a service and the image a company conveys in being able to deliver it are usually as important in the sale of the service as the service itself.

Second, a service is often developed to replace or supplement a process or procedure that is currently being performed by some other method. The company or person buying the service may receive a quantifiable benefit (e.g., cost savings due to efficiencies); however, this may also mean a change in how a task is being performed. If this change is not introduced carefully, it can lead to resistance or outright rejection of the service instead of ready acceptance. This potential impact is emphasized here to reinforce the need for the market research professional to view all variables affected by a service with uncertainty.

Third, the use of a service is usually repetitive versus a one-time occurrence. This requires a thorough understanding by the researcher of how a customer's behavior will change as a result of continued use of the service.

To the services marketing research professional, these factors translate into an uncertain market environment that one must approach with few preconceived notions. It requires a rigorous yet flexible research approach because of the experiential nature of most services.

As we move through the rest of this chapter, we'll illustrate how market researchers use a wide variety of techniques to answer different research questions and needs.

## How to Define the Research Problem

As in any market research project, you have to start the process with a clear understanding of the research problem—"Exactly what am I expected to find out and why?" In services marketing, the research problem will vary with every project and may range from measuring customer satisfaction or perceptions, to determining levels of demand for a new service, to gaining specific feedback on a new service's features, benefits, and value. There will be more than one question to be answered. Therefore, it is critical that as much time as possible is spent, up front, to identify all of the relevant questions.

Let's look at an example to illustrate this point. The marketing vice president has a new service idea initiated by the president of the company. She feels that "a real market exists" for a service that home buyers and real estate brokers could use to shop for mortgage rates and different types of mortgage instruments. No such service exists today. The service would be available "online" through a personal computer and would be updated weekly. Your company would be responsible for gathering the data, updating them, providing the network for accessing the data, and the overall marketing of the service. This service would be the company's first offering to the real estate community. The vice president would like you to conduct research to define the service and to determine the level of market demand. You should be prepared to present a go or no/go recommendation to the president in six months. You must submit a budget request and research plan to her in two weeks.

The first place to start is to write a project plan that outlines "the problem" and the questions that will have to be answered. Also included will be your initial recommendations on obtaining a sample, the methodologies for getting the answers, the timetables to accomplish key action steps, the budget required, and the actual anticipated deliverables.

STOP: Before submitting a project plan for approval, first spend some additional time defining what is known and not known about this situation—a major shift may occur in the way you decide to approach this problem as opposed to others you may have researched in the past.

Take a few minutes to think about the questions that must be answered in our example. Now, refer to Table 9-1, which lists the key questions to be answered in our case study in a format useful for organizing your thinking about the real estate information service mentioned earlier. It is by no means an exhaustive list. As with any research project you tackle, your initial list of questions about consumer behavior, the market, and the service should be equally long. Information must be obtained not only about the level of market interest in this new service, but also about sources of information, updating procedures, interest by multiple customer segments, how the potential need met by this service is being provided today and, of course, possible pricing scenarios. In addition to the different types of information needed, the customer segments "with the answers" vary, as do the appropriate methods for obtaining these answers. Table 9-1 illustrates that at least four sources will have to be tapped to address the questions in this research project.

To solve this "problem," or a research problem you are facing, the research plan will probably be multifaced, and different research phases and approaches will be needed to obtain the end result—the answers! Let's quickly review the *key* questions we have identified:

- What need will I be serving?
- Who is the customer?
- Who is my competition?
- Is the service or strategy viable?
- How will I know?
- What can I expect?

Many researchers make the mistake of immediately focusing their attention on the features of a marketing campaign or service—applications, packaging, costs, marketing—and forget the key ingredients: the customers and their motivations for purchasing the service and the benefits they will receive. Also important is the feasibility of your producing the service to meet customer expectations or carrying out your plan as proposed. Although the latter may be beyond your direct area of responsibility in the research area, in order to adequately address the "research problem," all factors that could influence the success or failure of your project must be considered.

As you get started on any new research project, you will need to prepare a project plan that summarizes the objectives and scope of the project. Each company prepares a research project plan to its own specifications. At most companies, a standard format to receive approval to proceed is used.

A research project plan should at minimum include the following:

- Project description
- Statement of objectives
- Why project is being performed
- Description of market opportunity
- Description of service to be tested
- Description of research methodology
- Cost breakdown for each step of the process
- Total budget
- Statement of deliverables
- Gantt chart indicating key checkpoints and deliverable dates

Often, the cost of the "ideal" research methodology will exceed the budget available for a project. In meeting with your manager in seeking budget ap-

*(Text continues on page 156.)*

**Table 9-1.** Key questions to be addressed for a real estate information service.

| Question | A. Who Has the Answer? (see key) | B. How Will I Get It? | | |
|---|---|---|---|---|
| | | Primary Research | Secondary Research | Internal Research |
| **A. Consumer Behavior** | | | | |
| 1. How is this information obtained today? Is it free? Is it obtained the same way nationwide? | 1, 2 | X | X | — |
| 2. How well does the service meet the needs of the market? | 1, 2 | X | | — |
| 3. Does a service like this exist? | 1, 2, 3 | X | X | — |
| 4. Do consumers express a need for this service? | 1, 2 | X | | — |
| 5. Are they actively looking for alternatives? | 1, 2 | X | | — |
| 6. Are they willing to pay for an alternative? | 1, 2 | X | | — |
| 7. How many consumer segments are there? How do they differ? How are they alike? | 1, 2, 3 | X | | — |
| 8. What is the real cost to the consumer of getting this information today? | 1, 2 | X | | — |
| 9. Will this service have a negative impact on any groups involved in this marketplace? | 2, 3 | X | | — |
| 10. Will consumers buy the service—why or why not? | 1, 2 | X | | — |
| 11. How often? At what price? | 1, 2 | X | | — |
| **B. The Market** | | | | |
| 1. How does this service fit in with other services used by these groups of consumers? | 1, 2, 3 | X | | — |
| 2. What is the overall relationship among potential buyers? | 1, 2, 3 | X | | — |
| 3. Will this service change the marketplace in any way? | 2, 3 | X | | — |

## C. The Service

| Item | Question | Codes |
|---|---|---|
| 4. | What is the overall measure in the market to which the potential of this service will be compared? | 2, 3 |
| 5. | Is there an identifiable set of lead users? | 2, 3 |
| 6. | Is the market computerized? To what extent? | 1, 2, 3 |
| 1. | What are the specific elements of the service to be tested? | 1, 2 |
| 2. | Will testing vary by customer segment? | 1, 2 |
| 3. | Can the service be prototyped? | 4 |
| 4. | How will it be delivered? | 1, 2, 3, 4 |
| 5. | How will it be priced? | 1, 2, 3, 4 |
| 6. | How will it be sold? | 1, 2, 4 |
| 7. | Who are the data sources? Will they cooperate? | 2, 3 |
| 8. | What is the incentive for the data sources to cooperate? | 3 |
| 9. | How will the data be collected and updated? | 2, 3 |
| 10. | Is this a local, regional, national, or international service? | |
| 11. | What network will be used? | 1, 2, 3 |
| 12. | What hardware is required? | 1, 2, 3, 4 |
| 13. | What software is required? | 1, 2, 3, 4 |

## D. Marketing

| Item | Question | Codes |
|---|---|---|
| 1. | What sales approach will be needed? | 1, 2, 4 |
| 2. | What advertising and promotional support will be needed? | 1, 2, 4 |

## E. Finance

| Item | Question | Codes |
|---|---|---|
| 1. | What ROI is required? | 4 |
| 2. | What are the expected development costs and on-going expenses? | 4 |
| 3. | What are the five-year customer penetration, revenue, and ROI projections? | 1, 4 |

*Key:* 1 = Consumer   2 = Real estate broker   3 = Financial institution   4 = Internal departments proval, be prepared to discuss several variations of the research plan at reduced costs. Additionally, if changes in design will reduce the projectability of results or the ability to test multiple variables, be sure this is made clear during the approval process. Follow up this conversation in writing or by revising the project plan altogether.

As we have seen in this discussion so far, making the research variables operational (i.e., clearly defined and measurable) and ensuring they are the correct variables is not a simple task in services marketing. Therefore, for most projects, the definition of the problem and agreement that the project plan will appropriately address the relevant variables is often the most important part of your research project.

## How to Construct a Research Design

Now you are ready to begin thinking about your research design—your blueprint for getting the answers. After defining the specific information needed, the most likely sources of this information, and the number of different groups to contact, it is time to consider research approaches that will become an overall research design.

There are four major approaches to consider:

1. *Secondary research*—Data that are not derived directly from the target customer
2. *Qualitative research*—Responses that are obtained directly from the target customer, usually in a group setting, with small samples that are not projectable to the target market
3. *Quantitative research*—Responses that are obtained directly from the target customer groups with sample sizes of sufficient magnitude to be projectable to the overall market
4. *Market testing*—Following sufficient implementation of research using one or more of the preceding methods, the actual creation, sale, and fulfillment of the service for a set period of time with a target group of customers

Each of these four approaches has strengths and weaknesses that must be evaluated before selection. These fall in the areas of:

- *Turnaround time/speed of research* to completion
- *Cost* of project
- *Projectability* of research data to predict overall target market or consumer behavior (e.g., does it represent the target group sufficiently?)
- *Reliability* (e.g., is the variable well-defined and clearly understood so that the research can be replicated?)
- *Depth of data* (e.g., amount of specific information) that can be collected from each respondent using a particular approach

- *Type of data* (e.g., attitudes, perceptions, purchase behavior) that can be collected from each respondent using a particular approach

Let's review the strengths and weaknesses of each in terms of these factors.

## Secondary Research

Secondary research is the *fastest* of all the approaches mentioned. It involves using a combination of existing resources found in the corporate library, publications, purchased market studies, and literature searches (manual or online) of published sources. The cost of using secondary sources can range from being free (no incremental cost other than your labor, depending on your internal resources) to thousands of dollars for database searching, reprints, and purchased studies. A secondary search is usually a part of every research project. The extent of its use varies by project as does its importance.

A secondary literature search is used to locate consumer, market, and industry data already gathered, which may be used as a framework for defining the research data to be collected. It is usually not available in a format that allows easy manipulation. Secondary data are usually limited by the depth of data (e.g., did they ask the question you are interested in?) that were collected and the type of data collected (e.g., are they projectable to your target group?) This limits their value.

## Qualitative Research

Qualitative research involves primarily the use of focus groups, customer advisory panels, delphi groups, and in-person interviews. Other research methods can also be considered qualitative or exploratory if the sample sizes used are too small to be projectable or if the questioning tends to be indirect and flexible and is likely to vary from respondent to respondent.

Qualitative research is relatively fast and can usually be completed in a four- to six-week time frame with the greatest amount of time spent on developing the questions to be used and recruiting respondents for participation.

The cost of qualitative research is controllable and relatively inexpensive in total, but expensive on a per-respondent basis. Primary variables influencing cost include: number of groups, number of participants, incentives used, fee for proper facility, moderator (if hired), travel, and fee for results analysis.

Qualitative research is often used at the start of a project to test initial hypotheses and to establish the direction of the questioning used later in quantitative studies. Most qualitative data are not projectable due to the size of the samples, although many companies do use them for this purpose when results are either extremely positive or negative.

If we return to our real estate information service example, you can see why qualitative research would be helpful in determining how consumers and businesses are getting this information today and their initial level of interest in a complete service.

Qualitative research is strong at identifying "top of mind" perceptions and attitudes. Most respondents will not answer every question. A participant who overparticipates can overshadow others and bias the results. Nothing can be more disappointing than a focus group dominated by a "nay-sayer" or "know-it-all" who can sway the perceptions of a group pro or con in the first ten minutes.

Finally, because participation in qualitative research is usually uneven, it is difficult to quantify responses and draw meaningful conclusions.

## Quantitative Research

Quantitative research is used to gather very specific data in answer to specific questions. Respondents are selected for their representativeness of a segment of the target population and every question is asked of every respondent, if appropriate. Results are projectable to the target market if proper sampling techniques have been used to ensure that respondents in each group sampled are representative of their universe.

A variety of quantitative techniques is available to the researcher, including: telephone, mail, scripted computer/based, or in-person interviews. The cost of quantitative research varies according to the method of interviewing used, the size of the sample, the difficulty in reaching the desired respondent, the number of questions asked, the use of closed or open-end questions, incentives, turn-around time, travel, and cost of data analysis and report preparation.

Quantitative methods allow the researcher to capture the precise type and depth of data needed if the questions are asked properly and thoroughly without biasing the results. When selecting a quantitative method, put yourself in the shoes of the respondent. Is it interesting? Am I motivated and able to respond to the questions?

## Market Testing

Market testing is the least talked about research method, yet probably the most accurate. Market testing involves creating a version of the actual service and bringing it to the market for customers to purchase and use on a trial basis. Market testing frequently follows extensive market research and is usually the most costly of all methods described because of the production requirements.

A properly designed market test gives the researcher feedback not only on the service, but on how it will be used, frequency of use, and appropriateness of pricing, marketing, and sales methods. A market test usually lasts from three months to one year. Consumer reactions are usually taken at the start of the test, at least once in the interim, and at the conclusion. Often, components of the market test, like price or fulfillment, are varied in different segments or regions of the country to determine impact on buying and usage behavior.

Projectability of a market test varies, again, by the sample size used. Your objectives for selecting a market test will vary as well. If you have a strong set of projectable data from a quantitative study that answers your primary questions, you may use a market test to concentrate on obtaining performance and marketing effectiveness feedback. If you want to verify that your research results will be duplicated within a range of confidence after market introduction, a projectable sample of your target customer set should be used.

In either case, a market test comes closest to simulating real customer behavior and serves as a final "reality check" on all other research data.

Now let's get back to our real estate information service example. Referring back to Table 9-1, notice the two columns. Column A indicates "Who has the answer?" and Column B indicates "How will I get it?" In this example, there are at least four segments with "the answers": the potential home buyer (a consumer or business), the real estate broker, the financial institution, and your internal departments such as sales, marketing, and finance.

Now you are ready to select your research approach. Table 9-1 reveals the five specific areas that you will need to study in detail. They are consumer behavior, the market, components of the service, marketing approaches needed, and financial outlook. Information about market structure, trends, and behavior should be available through library searches, government sources, professional associations, and published studies or reference materials. To test the hypothesis that there is in fact a "real opportunity for this new service," and to gain some immediate background on the subject, you may decide to conduct a limited, online data base literature search to familiarize yourself with the market and to determine how successful this type of search can be. Any of the commercial data base distributors or the services of an information broker can help you in this search.

## How to Select the Right Methodology

In the previous section we discussed a variety of methods that can be used to find the answer to a specific research question. How do you select the appropriate method? Table 9-2 summarizes the strengths and weaknesses of each approach, including a breakout by the most commonly used methods in each approach. Table 9-3 summarizes the types of information that each approach is used to gather. As you can see, you have many choices.

Let's return to our specific example. How do we determine if we should introduce this new real estate information service? In Table 9-1 the information needed was summarized and the likely respondents identified. The B column in this table shows the type of research that is needed to gather this information. Tables 9-2 and 9-3 describe the strengths and weakness associated with "getting the answers" using each of these approaches and the type of information that is usually gathered by each approach.

Now, take a few minutes to study Tables 9-1, 9-2, and 9-3 together and to work up a research approach for each of the segments in the example—the property buyer, the real estate broker, and the financial institution. How does this approach compare to your original thinking about the problem?

*(Text continues on page 163.)*

**Table 9-2.** Evaluating research approaches by strengths and weaknesses.

| Benefit of Approach | Secondary — Literature Search/ Gov't Data/ Business Indexes | Secondary — Company Records | Secondary — Internal Surveys | Primary Qualitative — Focus Groups | Primary Qualitative — Delphi Approach | Primary Qualitative — Customer Advisory Groups | Primary Qualitative — In-Person/ PC Interviews | Primary Quantitative — Operational Audits | Primary Quantitative — Telephone Surveys | Primary Quantitative — Mail Surveys | Market Test — Prototyping | Market Test — Market Tests |
|---|---|---|---|---|---|---|---|---|---|---|---|---|
| Fast turnaround/immediate results | ✓ | ✓ | ✓ | ✓ | | ✓ | ✓ | | | | | |
| Cost-effective | ✓ | ✓ | ✓ | ✓ | | ✓ | | | | | | |
| Quick "read" on market | ✓ | ✓ | ✓ | ✓ | | | | ✓ | | | | |
| Sets direction for quantitative approach | ✓ | ✓ | ✓ | ✓ | ✓ | ✓ | ✓ | ✓ | | | | |
| Opportunity to interact/modify service | | | | ✓ | ✓ | ✓ | ✓ | ✓ | | | ✓ | |
| Confidentiality of respondents ensured | | | | | ✓ | | | | | | | |
| Allows for application of multiple analytical techniques | | | | | | | | | ✓ | ✓ | | |
| Comprehensive | | | | | | | ✓ | ✓ | ✓ | | | |
| Provides information on perceptions/image | | | | ✓ | ✓ | ✓ | ✓ | | ✓ | ✓ | | ✓ |
| Establishes benchmarks | | | | | | | ✓ | | ✓ | ✓ | | ✓ |
| Measures behavior | | ✓ | | | | | | ✓ | ✓ | ✓ | | ✓ |
| Reliable | | ✓ | | | | | ✓ | | ✓ | ✓ | | ✓ |
| Projectable results | | | | | | | ✓ | | ✓ | ✓ | | ✓ |
| Can be transferred to predictive model | | | | | | | | | ✓ | ✓ | | ✓ |
| Demonstrates actual purchase behavior | | ✓ | | | | | | ✓ | | | | ✓ |
| Provides concrete feedback on the actual service/allows for refinement before launch | | | | | | | | | | | ✓ | ✓ |

| Weakness of Approach | Secondary | | | Primary | | | | | Quantitative | | Market Test | |
|---|---|---|---|---|---|---|---|---|---|---|---|---|
| | Literature Search/ Gov't Data/ Business Indexes | Company Records | Internal Surveys | Focus Groups | Delphi Approach | Customer Advisory Groups | In-Person/ PC Interviews | Operational Audits | Telephone Surveys | Mail Surveys | Prototyping | Market Tests |
| Limited to data available | ✓ | ✓ | ✓ | | | | | | | | | |
| Data not always in form desired | ✓ | ✓ | ✓ | | | | | | | | | |
| Can't ask "new questions" | ✓ | ✓ | | | | | | | | | | |
| Not projectable/representative | ✓ | | | ✓ | ✓ | ✓ | ✓ | ✓ | | | ✓ | |
| Can be influenced by "group think" | | | | ✓ | ✓ | ✓ | ✓ | ✓ | | | | |
| Very structured questioning required/loss of flexibility | | | | | ✓ | | ✓ | | ✓ | ✓ | | |
| Service must stay "as is" throughout test | | | | | | | | | | | | ✓ |
| Investment required to create service/support fulfillment during test | | | | | | | | | | | ✓ | ✓ |
| High nonresponse error possible | | | | | | | ✓ | | ✓ | ✓ | | |
| High number of terminated interviews due to amount of data desired | | | | | | | ✓ | | ✓ | ✓ | | |
| Not available for brand new service | ✓ | ✓ | | | | | | | | | | |
| Responses cannot be transferred to predictive model of behavior | ✓ | ✓ | ✓ | ✓ | ✓ | ✓ | ✓ | ✓ | | | ✓ | |

*Note: Internal research may be primary or secondary.*

**Table 9-3.** Evaluating research approaches by type of information.

| Type of Information Needed | Secondary | | | Primary | | | | | | | | |
|---|---|---|---|---|---|---|---|---|---|---|---|---|
| | | | | Qualitative | | | | | Quantitative | | Market Test | |
| | Literature Search/ Gov't Data/ Business Indexes | Company Records | Internal Surveys | Focus Groups | Delphi Approach | Customer Advisory Groups | In-Person/ PC Interviews | Operational Audits | Telephone Surveys | Mail Surveys | Prototyping | Market Tests |
| Industry data | ✓ | ✓ | | | | ✓ | ✓ | ✓ | ✓ | ✓ | | |
| Industry trends | ✓ | ✓ | | | | ✓ | ✓ | ✓ | ✓ | ✓ | | ✓ |
| Industry structure | ✓ | ✓ | | | | ✓ | ✓ | ✓ | ✓ | | | |
| Use of your service | ✓ | ✓ | | ✓ | | | ✓ | ✓ | ✓ | ✓ | | ✓ |
| Use of competing services | | | | | | ✓ | ✓ | ✓ | ✓ | ✓ | | ✓ |
| Perception/satisfaction with existing services | | | | | ✓ | ✓ | ✓ | ✓ | ✓ | ✓ | | ✓ |
| Evaluation of new service | | | | ✓ | ✓ | ✓ | ✓ | ✓ | ✓ | ✓ | ✓ | ✓ |
| Buying intent | | | | ✓ | ✓ | ✓ | ✓ | ✓ | ✓ | ✓ | | ✓ |
| Value of new service | | | | ✓ | ✓ | ✓ | ✓ | ✓ | ✓ | ✓ | ✓ | ✓ |
| Estimation of demand | | | | | ✓ | ✓ | ✓ | ✓ | ✓ | ✓ | | ✓ |
| Sources of supply | ✓ | ✓ | ✓ | ✓ | | ✓ | | ✓ | ✓ | ✓ | | |
| Cost of supply | ✓ | ✓ | ✓ | ✓ | | | | ✓ | ✓ | ✓ | | |
| Estimated financial impact | | ✓ | | | | | | ✓ | ✓ | ✓ | ✓ | ✓ |
| Best marketing approach | | | ✓ | ✓ | ✓ | ✓ | | ✓ | ✓ | ✓ | ✓ | ✓ |

*Note:* Internal research may be primary or secondary.

## How Can a Research Supplier Help Me?

The research approach for our example calls for secondary research, qualitative and quantitative research with potential customers, an internal analysis of your company's capabilities, and an evaluation of the results of these efforts at critical points in the process. To complete each activity requires that you either ''make or buy'' the resource to accomplish it.

Market research suppliers and consultants are readily available to assist you in any or all of these activities. However, their capabilities and experience vary widely from supplier to supplier. Selection of the correct supplier(s) will be a pivotal decision in the overall scope of your project.

An appropriate supplier will have to be selected for each component of the research design. Many of the large, nationwide research houses can complete the entire project. By breaking it into separate projects, however, experts or specialists can be used, often at a reduced cost!

Figure 9-1 provides a checklist of the essential information you will need to begin to evaluate suppliers for bid solicitation. Most companies have policies in place regarding the number of written bids that must be submitted for each project or spending level. In selecting a research supplier, the ability to do the project in-house should also be quantified and evaluated in the same way.

**Figure 9-1.** Research supplier checklist.

---

Name of Supplier: _____

*Yes No*

— — Has experience in service industry research
— — Has experience with target customer group
— — Has experience with both consumer and industrial research
— — Is capable of conducting *all* aspects of research design
— — Is capable of conducting *parts* of research design
— — Has experienced, permanent in-house staff to perform
    desired research techniques
— — Has a standing working relationship with second vendor to
    provide desired research capability
— — Has references
— — Has appropriate staff support
— — Has experience in advanced statistical applications
— — Has ability to assist client in selecting appropriate
    techniques
— — Is geographically accessible
— — Has ability to meet targeted deadlines
— — Has ability to perform task within specified budget
— — Has ability to deliver desired end result (tape, tabulations,
    or final report)

---

Most research suppliers will consult with you at no charge on methodology and approach before the bid is submitted. However, the supplier should not be expected to "give" this service away. If you need help in preparing a research design and the specifications for a bid, be prepared to pay for this service.

Once the basic capabilities the supplier will perform have been identified, *you* must define exactly what you want done with the data when they have been collected. This will be a critical determinant in vendor selection.

## Sampling Considerations

Once you have selected your research approach, you are ready to select your sample(s). As mentioned earlier, your sample size will be influenced by the research method you have selected, the projectability and reliability you must deliver, and your budget. In other words, what margin of error will your management tolerate around the findings of your research? Most trained statisticians or researchers would be surprised by how much error is tolerated by the business community because of budget limitations! If you are doing qualitative research (nonprojectable), your sample may include as few as twenty respondents to get a "quick read" on the level of market interest. If you are fortunate enough to know the size of the potential customer universe (e.g., the total number of real prospects in this demographic group, such as annual number of home buyers) from other published or purchased research or secondary sources, you will probably select a sample representative of the universe within limits agreed upon with your management or dictated by your budget. If you must undersample due to budget limitations, it is important to try to capture at least fifty complete responses from each potential customer group you will be addressing in your final projections.

## How to Analyze and Interpret Results

There are many types of data analysis that can be performed on the data obtained. They range from a write-up of major findings from a focus group, to cross tabulations of answers to each question, to calculations of means, to drawing of perceptual maps and modeling of results under different conditions. The types of data analysis you perform beyond routine tabulations will influence the cost and length of the project and may eliminate certain research suppliers from the process. Therefore, it is essential that you clearly articulate your analysis plan *before* selecting a research supplier.

To prepare a proper analysis plan, identify the specific data elements required to perform the final calculations needed for projecting final results. Turning back to Table 9-1 by section and question, the types of data needed are listed. Within each type, specific data elements must be identified. For example:

- Number of residential and commercial property purchases each year (B4)
- Number of customers who shop for mortgage rates annually (B4)

- Level of interest in purchasing the service at various price points (A10, A11)
- Impact of changes in features of the service on purchase intention (C1, C2)
- Number of banks that would cooperate in supplying information to support the service on a recurring basis (C7)

Next, identify precisely where each piece of data will be derived and from what methodology. If the only way a particular piece of data can be reliably collected is by using sophisticated statistical techniques, then the research supplier selected must be able to execute these techniques competently.

A thorough analysis plan in conjunction with the research design and budget will be the key components in narrowing down choices for a research supplier to the most appropriate candidate. It is imperative that the analysis plan be completed *before* any data are collected to be sure all variables have been included. Nothing can be worse than getting to the end of a project and finding that a key piece of data is missing!

One of the most exciting times in any research project is the receipt of the first computer printouts of data. This can also be a time when you are overwhelmed with the task of determining "how good are the data" and "what do they really mean?" It therefore is necessary to be sure that the data are clean and have been run correctly. One of the easiest ways to do this is to go immediately to a concise, closed question (e.g., Yes/No) where you are very confident about the answer, and check the responses. Do they add up with few "don't knows"? Do they make sense? Does the tab summarizing your sample check with the actual profile? Additionally, sampling problems, nonresponse errors, and completeness of responses by question must be examined to determine how reliable the data are on each question. Are there many "don't knows" on a key question? Also, any problems encountered during the research, such as high terminations at a specific point in the questionnaire or a specific question that may have been misinterpreted or large deviations around the mean responses, must be documented.

Research practitioners analyze data in many different ways. Some choose to go directly to the decision-making questions identified in the analysis plan. Others like to get a "feel" for all of the findings and review the results, question by question, following the flow of the questionnaire.

Each research method used in a project has different strengths and weaknesses. It is important to keep the range of projectability in mind as findings are taken from each research method. Some research methods have built-in constraints around their projectability; for example, focus group results cannot be projected at all.

In using research results to project potential customer behavior and overall market potential, most companies have their own formulas and "rules of thumb" that have been finely honed to a science after years of experience. It is rare to find a textbook with a definitive approach to making projections, particularly for a service that currently does not exist! Some companies will simply extract the proportion of potential customers expressing *definite* interest (i.e., those very interested) in the service and will extrapolate this interest to the market at large. Others will take a more sophisticated approach and construct a model of how customers will behave under different conditions. Both methods have been proven effective.

## Summary

Now we would like to briefly review our discussion of services marketing research in this chapter. See Figure 9-2 for a review of our process.

We started with our *idea*. As we found in our example, putting the meat on the skeleton is the hardest and often the most important part of the process. Don't skimp for time in this stage.

Next, we moved to *defining the research problem*. This consisted of identifying all the questions you will be expected to answer from all parties and establishing boundaries or parameters around what you will (and won't) do. Taking the time to read between the lines with *all* of your audiences during this stage can save you a lot of "catch-up work" at the end. Watch out for hidden agendas and unrealistic expectations.

Once you have defined the problem and laid out the project specifications in a *project plan*, take the time to gain consensus on the plan. Be wary of those who won't agree upfront to your approach—it may give them too much leeway to discount your findings later if they disagree!

Now you're ready to *evaluate research approaches* in detail. Even if you think you know the best way to get the answers, take time to consider different approaches. Each has its strengths and weaknesses. Even if you are an experienced researcher, there is always value in trying a new technique or method of questioning in each new project. Your research supplier can assist you and will help to keep you current on the latest techniques.

Once you have *selected a research approach*, you are ready to get started. That means finalizing *the budget, obtaining the sample,* and *preparing an analysis plan*. This often overlooked step is *the most critical*. Do a final check. Have you asked all of the key questions? Can you put them together in a meaningful way to get the answers? Take time to do this sooner, not later!

Now you can *select your research supplier*. Can they really perform or do they just sound that way? Make an effort to visit their facility and observe them in action before you commit. Remember, you only get to do it once.

You are ready to begin. Your survey instrument is ready and you are ready to start. Pay close attention on day one to the interviewers. This is your pretest and your last chance to make a correction. Be sure to allow adequate time to brief the supplier and the interviewers, and build in flexibility for last-minute changes. They will happen!

The interviews are completed and the data are in. You are ready to *analyze* the results. Did you remember to clean the data? Have you clearly documented the source of each data point? Are you sure the respondents understood the questions?

Finally, you are ready for *findings, recommendations,* and *conclusions*. Are

**Figure 9-2.** An overview of marketing research for services.

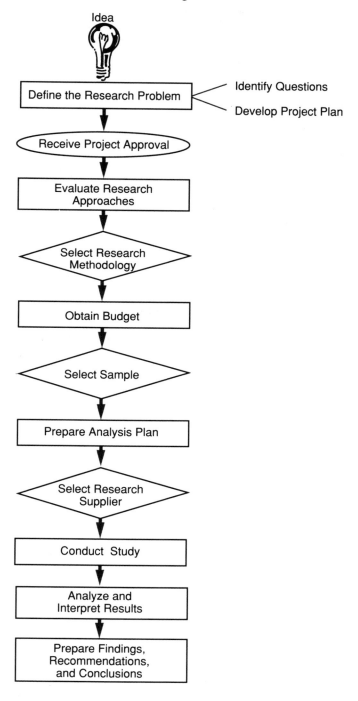

your findings supported by the data? Are they projectable? Do they make sense? Make sure you clearly articulate any data limitations.

This project is complete. You are ready for the next challenge, using research to monitor actual consumer behavior now that the service exists, and to evaluate and fine-tune your marketing strategy. Back to step one!

## Further Resources

Ackerman, Laurence D. "What Makes Successful Service Companies Distinctive?" IABC Communication World, 1986.

Total Research Corporation. "Advanced Research Seminar on the Utility of High Technology Research for Strategic Planning Decisions," 1986.

Uttal, Bro. "Speeding New Ideas to Market." *Fortune* 115 (March 2, 1987): 62.

Vichas, Robert P. *Complete Handbook of Profitable Market Research Techniques.* Englewood Cliffs, N.J.: Prentice-Hall, 1982.

\*     \*     \*     \*

***Pamela V. Alden*** *is the vice president of new customer services for Dun & Bradstreet Business Credit Services, where she is responsible for the development, marketing, and fulfillment of a variety of products, services, and technologies that are designed to help customers automate their risk assessment decision processes. She also managed the market research and product development activities for D&B's Business Credit Services.*

# 10

## How to Develop a Marketing Plan

Kristine J. Bean

It's always easiest to find your destination if you use a map. And that's what a formalized plan will do for the marketing of your services. Developing a marketing plan forces you to think about where you are and where you want to go, and marks the signposts of accomplishments along the way. If you put your plan in writing and follow through on each action step, you will increase sales.

In this chapter, we'll discuss different types of services and how they're most effectively marketed. Then we'll cover the development of a services marketing plan, including the various parts of the plan and how to create each one. You'll also receive some tips on what marketing techniques and tools have and have not been effective.

## Types of Services—What's Out There?

Hundreds of thousands of services are delivered every day—renting a hotel room, performing an audit, managing a checking account, designing a building, renting a car, collecting the garbage, insuring a house, and writing a will. Each of these services can be placed in one of three service categories based on the following factors:

- Risk of purchase
- Intensity of personal relationship
- Who sells and who does

### Professional Services

The first category of services is professional services, including the work performed by accountants, financial consultants, attorneys, doctors, stockbrokers, and others. These services are generally intangible, relying on the expertise of the professional to be successful. They have a high risk of purchase to the buyer, an intense relationship between the buyer and seller, and because of that strong relationship, the professional who sells the work is also involved with doing or delivering the service.

The "people factor" and relationship building are extremely important in the successful marketing of these services. Professional services marketing is, in fact, "relationship marketing"—recognizing that people will only buy your services if they believe that you are competent, qualified, trustworthy, and likable.

Assuming the market knows you're in the business, these marketing plans must focus on training your staff to be "trusted advisers" for their clients, generating a good target list, and convincing potential clients that your employees are competent and able to deliver.

## Balanced Product/Services

The second type of service is actually a balanced combination of product and service. Balanced product/services include such businesses as insurance, printing, and banking, where the benefits of the "product"—that is, the rate of return, quality of the printed document, cost of the checking account—are as important as the service that supports the product. These services have (1) a medium risk of purchase (the buyer has reduced the risk by comparing the features of the product with the competition and making an informed choice), (2) a relationship between the buyer and seller that is less intense than professional services, and (3) a seller and deliverer of the services who are not always the same person. The benefits and features of the product are probably as important as the personal relationship in the marketing of these services. Marketing plans need to focus on creating opportunities to demonstrate the qualities of the product to targeted buyers. The timely and effective services support the benefits of the products but cannot stand alone as a marketing tool.

## Consumer Services

The last type of services, consumer services, includes such things as renting a hotel room or car, using a credit card, and traveling on a commercial airline. These services are usually bought by an individual and are more like consumer products (soap, toothpaste) than other services. In most cases the risk of purchase is low (the effects of a buying mistake are short-lived); the personal relationships are superficial (ticket agent, flight attendant); and the seller is rarely the doer of the services. Consumer services include both product and personal service elements, but the intense, one-on-one personal relationship doesn't exist, and these services are marketed like consumer products. Because the risk of purchase is low, consumers can be persuaded to try alternative services; therefore, mass marketing techniques such as promotion, couponing, discounting, and advertising play major roles in the marketing of these services. In this chapter we emphasize marketing for the first two services categories; marketing planning for consumer services will be covered in less depth.

# Market-Driven vs. Internally Conceived

Services are developed from two different points of view. A market-driven service is one that has been developed to fill a need identified in the marketplace. It is based on discovering what buyers want and creating a service that meets their needs. A new service that is internally conceived arises when a firm has an idea, turns that idea into a service, and then attempts to find a buyer.

It is always best to try to develop a market-driven service line, because you are catering to the needs of the market rather than trying to build or change the market. Obviously, an internally conceived service is more difficult to market because it may take a significant marketing investment to discover exactly who needs your service. As you begin to conceive your marketing plan, analyze the characteristics of your service—is it market-driven or internally conceived? Certainly, you can launch a successful internally conceived service, but because the buyer's needs are less defined, it usually takes more time, effort, and investment before significant results are realized. Adjust your marketing expectations to reflect the outside world's general need for your service.

## Getting Started

You have already done some preliminary work to put your marketing planning into perspective. By this point, you should know whether you are dealing with a professional service, a balanced product/service, or a consumer service, and you should have some sense of whether the service was developed as a response to the market or as a result of an internal capability. Now you are ready to start developing the plan. This is going to require good, solid, intuitive, and creative thinking (which is the fun part); the discipline involves writing it down and following it through.

## Four Parts to a Plan

A good services marketing plan includes four separate parts:

1. *Goals for the service*—what we want to accomplish
2. *Situation analysis*—where we are now
3. *Marketing strategies/objectives for the service*—positioning
4. *The action plan*—how we get there

The "perfect" marketing plan has no particular format or length. The key is to give it serious thought and to develop the plan with the ideas of all the interested parties. The resulting marketing "map" will be an effective living document capable of surviving change.

## Who Is Involved in the Planning?

Who should be responsible for developing the marketing plan? It depends on the kind of service you're considering. Professional services need to receive input from all of the professionals who will be involved in the selling and delivering of the service, with assistance from a professional marketer. Because personal relationships are so important in selling professional services, the professionals must also be actively involved in the marketing.

An ideal situation for developing a professional services marketing plan is a group of three or four of the professionals most committed to the marketing, selling, and delivering of the service and the professional marketer, collaborating and writing the first three parts of the marketing plan. The marketing professional may then be responsible for developing the first draft of the action plan because of his or her familiarity with the most effective marketing techniques and tools. But the service professionals need to approve of all the assumptions and the plan as a whole. As a group they need to commit to following through and holding themselves accountable for accomplishing the action steps.

For other services, the professional marketer can take a more independent role in developing the plan. Less seller/doer involvement is required, because the personal relationship aspect of the service is less important in these marketing and selling situations. The professional marketer is more likely to work with division or product/service management to develop the plan.

## How to Set Objectives

The service marketing team needs to address the question: What is our objective for this service? Examples of objectives are:

- Generate $2 million in profit in two years.
- Develop a door opener for other parts of our business.
- Grab significant market share (even at the expense of profitability).

You should develop three or four short statements to define the service objectives; it's helpful if they are measurable so that later you can evaluate results. The objectives define what's most important about the service opportunity and guide the decision making in the remaining parts of the planning process.

## Attacking the Situation Analysis

The purpose of this part of the plan is to define where we are:

- What is the market for this service?
- What do the buyers know about us?
- Who are our competitors?
- How do we stack up against the competition?

A thorough situation analysis will provide us with an overall concept of this service.

## Economic and Environmental Background

It's important to detach yourself from the details of your markets and competition and look at the overall business and economic trends that generally support the needs for your services. An example of a long-term trend is the increasing shift to a service economy in the United States, which has resulted in the need for many more white-collar employees. This trend suggests a ripe market for white-collar productivity consulting. Relating economic trends to your service helps you determine whether or not your service is on the leading edge of developments. Obviously, the closer you are to the leading edge of a new trend, the greater your chance of opening the window of opportunity and closing out the competition.

## Segmenting the Market

Now look at the buyers of your specific service and group them into as many different buying segments as there are significant buying differences. Ask yourself:

- Who will buy our service (segmented by industry, size, geography, and so on)?
- What needs will they have? Why buy this service?
- How will people buy our service? What will be most important to them?
- What is their spending power? What is affordable?

People buy to satisfy a need of some kind—including an emotional need such as prestige. That need can be as basic as getting from here to there, requiring the purchase of an airline ticket; or as sophisticated as decreasing manufacturing time, requiring the development of a major integrated information system. By segmenting your buyers based on the most significant buying differences, you have an opportunity to evaluate the level of the "critical need" of the various groups. As you set marketing strategies and develop the action plan, you can focus your efforts on those with the most critical needs—in other words, those most likely to buy. Reaching for the "lower-hanging fruit" is important in increasing your marketing and selling success. Before reaching for the fruit that is out of reach (the more difficult sale), concentrate on the close-at-hand opportunity, which may be easier to convert into a sale.

## Identifying Important Trends Within Each Segment

As you look at each of your market segments, you need to identify important trends that they are experiencing, which will influence what they buy from you or how much they will buy. For example, a law firm provides services to a number of banks that are active in the mergers and leveraged buyout market. An important trend to that law firm is the change in the level of these types of deals in recent years. By trying to identify these trends, you can build them into your marketing strategies and then exploit them as a key part of the marketing action plan.

*Assessing the Competition*

Unfortunately, not many of us operate with a monopoly on the market, and in many ways maybe that's fortunate. Dealing with the competition sharpens our edges and keeps us focused on providing excellent services to our customers and clients. So we need to know our competition in order to address questions such as:

- Who else does this?
- How are they perceived by the buyers?
- What are their strengths and weaknesses?
- What are our strengths and weaknesses compared to the competition?
- How does the competition differentiate its service; that is, how does it "position" its service in the markets?
- How can we differentiate our services from the competition?
- What are the competitors' marketing strategies, themes, and tools?

An honest investigation and assessment of the competition is an excellent "reality check" for any services organization. And this doesn't apply only to new service lines. A services organization that is already successful—that is now providing quality services to a number of satisfied customers and clients—can tend to become self-satisfied and complacent. When you discover that your competition is providing some of the same services on a more timely basis, less expensively, and more creatively, you'll have a tendency to focus aggressively on your marketing once again.

How do you find out about the competition? Through what is known as primary or secondary research. Primary research involves going directly to your market to find answers. A professional research firm is necessary to help you choose the proper type of research for your purposes. Telephone interviews with the appropriate sample of people and a correctly designed questionnaire can help, or you may require the expanded qualitative information learned through focus groups.

Secondary research is using anything else that is out there—statistics from trade groups; brochures, ads, and other information of your competitors; intelligence gathering from within your organization and its network; credit reports, SEC filings; anything within the public domain. If you have access to a good business library with on-line database capabilities, you can find out how your market is served. You can also supplement this research with your own "quick-and-dirty" primary research by interviewing a number of your clients about your competitors.

# Developing Marketing Opportunities/Strategies

When you've completed your situation analysis, you will have accumulated information that addresses major trends in the economy that affect your service; segmented your market according to significant buying differences; identified important trends within each of your market segments; and assessed the strengths and weaknesses of your competition.

Based on your analysis of these factors, you can now draw some conclusions on marketing opportunities and strategies for your service. These strategies include:

- Target market
- Target volume
- Differentiation strategy—positioning
- Internal marketing strategy
- Communication strategy

## Target Market

This is the opportunity to prioritize your market segments from "most critical needs/most likely to buy" to "least likely to buy." The level of marketing effort will be significantly different for those at the top of the list versus those at the bottom of the list and, in fact, some of those "least likely to buy" segments at the bottom may receive no sales attention whatsoever for a few years.

## Target Volume

The situation analysis will give you enough information to make an intelligent projection of the target volume you plan to accomplish. That volume can be defined in one of many ways: dollars of sales, new clients, hours billed, and transactions processed. Frequently, this projection would be stated in two parts; for example, a minimum of $1 million in fees and five new clients.

## Differentiation Strategy

How do you differentiate your service from the competition? What position do you want to occupy in the mind of your buyer? If you are a new or unknown company with a brand new service line, you can probably position yourself wherever you would like in the buyer's mind. If a service line is new to you but not new to the market, you need to position your service in relation to the competition. You want to occupy a unique position in your buyer's mind.

A more established firm may already be positioned in the buyer's mind, but can be even more successful if a new service line attempts to occupy the same position in the buyer's mind. For example, if your company is perceived as being high quality, top-of-the-line, and expensive, it would be counterproductive to attempt to position a new service as average quality and inexpensive. Either your buyers won't believe it, or if they do, your current position for the company and its services will be jeopardized.

When you address differentiation points, you may consider factors such as price, quality, and method of distribution. As you understand how your competitors have positioned their product, you define a strategy that positions you to capitalize on your competitive strengths. In their book *Bottom-Up Marketing*, Ries and Trout describe this as developing a "competitive mental angle."[1]

### Internal Marketing Strategy

For a new service, your best opportunity for building business short-term is by selling to existing clients. For professional services and balanced product/services, that means you have to market the benefits of your service internally, to those people in your organization who have the primary relationship with the customers you want to reach. This is sometimes referred to as cross-selling.

In these cases there is actually a two-step sales process—first to sell the internal person who will introduce you to the clients for whom they are responsible, which provides your second sales opportunity. In these situations you need a strategy to accomplish the internal marketing.

Your success at getting introductions to clients is directly proportionate to the aggressive personal effort invested internally. A face-to-face meeting with the key client-relationship person will be most successful in getting referrals and introductions to clients. You must make it happen. You cannot expect internal contacts to sell your service for you. It is reasonable to expect introductions to their clients, however, and you should be tenacious in requiring them to do so.

### Communication Strategy

You need to identify the best way to get your message out to your target markets. What are the best and most efficient ways to generate selling opportunities? First, determine the general communication strategy for your service. This means pinpointing one or two marketing techniques you want to use to generate selling opportunities. For professional services this could involve using round tables or seminars that provide opportunities to explore with your prospects topics relevant to your service line. In balanced product/services you may follow a combined program of advertising in specifically targeted locations, coupled with speeches and demonstrations to that market through trade association opportunities. In consumer services, you may combine extensive advertising with a couponing program.

This communication strategy defines the big picture, the general direction, but it doesn't include the detailed step-by-step plan to accomplish each of these activities. That comes later in the action plan.

## Testing Assumptions—The Need for Research

You've just finished identifying your marketing opportunities/strategies and have written a series of statements about what you're going to do. Those opportunities were based on certain assumptions that you drew from the situation analysis. Before you proceed further in developing the action plan to implement the strategies, you may believe that it's necessary to test those assumptions through research. The primary research techniques previously discussed would be appropriate here. The objective of market research is to confirm, clarify, or redirect your planning.

The need for research depends on several factors. In particular, your knowledge of the buyers, competition, and other situation factors is critical. If the level of the knowledge involved in your situation analysis is very high, you will probably have confidence in the assumptions you draw, and won't feel a need for research to confirm. Also, the level of investment required to launch or build a service affects the research decision. The higher the investment, the stronger the justification for research to test assumptions so that your marketing plan proceeds in the most efficient manner.

If you are concerned about the accuracy and quality of the marketing assumptions in your plan, now is the time to test them. Postponing this will only end up costing you time and money.

## How to Decide What to Do

You're now about ready to create the action plan—a document that contains a number of "to do's" with time frames and responsibilities. So, what kinds of things do you need to do? That depends very much on where you stand with your buyers. Do your buyers:

- Know you're in the business?
- Consider you qualified?

Or, have they:

- Selected you previously for another service?
- Kept you on after you were selected?

Buyers go through a regular progression in their purchasing cycle, so your action plan needs to determine your buyers' position in that cycle. First, buyers must know you're in the business, then believe that you are qualified to help them. They need to select you and, finally, keep you on after you've been selected.

Different stages in the cycle require different marketing techniques. For example, to increase awareness that you are in a business, you might want to use some "broadcast" marketing techniques, such as extensive direct mail, media relations, and advertising. To begin building buyers' confidence in your qualifications to provide a service, you may want to obtain speaking engagements before key groups and then distribute the speech as an article or direct mail piece, or issue a newsletter containing recent developments and successful client stories.

Once you have been selected, your clients or customers want continued assurance that you are committed to their industry or specialty area—round tables that provide an opportunity for satisfied customers to talk with each other, significant industry or technical papers and articles, and high-profile positions in trade organizations. How do you make sure they keep you after you have been selected? By following through on all the promises made when you sold them, continuing to use timeliness and creativity in delivering your service, and nurturing the personal relationship. Remembering to thank customers for the business with a personal note, dinner, or party on occasion is a thoughtful and appreciated gesture.

There are any number of marketing technique combinations that can help to bring your buyers through this cycle. The most important thing as you write the plan is to have an understanding of their position in this cycle.

### Creating the Action Plan—Some General Advice

The action plan is upon us. You're going to write the "to do's" and assign the responsibilities. Here are some helpful hints learned through experience.

Keep a Short Horizon.    Keep your detailed planning horizon short. Make your Year-One plan very specific; Year Two more general, perhaps indicating only the market segments you're going to pursue more aggressively; Year Three should be a very general "possible scenario."

Year One Should Be Very Specific.    The plan for the coming year should include dates, specific steps, individual responsibilities, due dates, and key milestones.

Follow Through.    Action plans will produce results if people follow through on the specific action steps and if they are held accountable for their pieces of the plan. "Hold accountable" usually means that marketing performance is an integral part of evaluation and compensation.

Pluck the "Lower-Hanging Fruit."    As previously mentioned, pursue those market segments or target buyers where you are more likely to be successful. Postpone the tougher sales opportunities until the following year. Respect your clients. If you are an established firm introducing a new service, focus on selling to your existing clients first. They already know you, your qualifications, and your ability to deliver, and it's easier to transfer that advantage to your new service than trying to sell to new entities that don't know you firsthand.

Lead With Your Best Foot.    If your marketing focus is to attack a new industry or a functional/geographic market, proceed with the service that you're known for and excel in. You already have that position in the marketplace, and it's easier to extend that position to a new segment of buyers than to introduce a new service in a market where you're unknown.

Focus Your Action Steps on Results.    The ultimate objective of all marketing plans is to generate sales opportunities—preferably as fast as possible. Focus your efforts on activities that will quickly provide face-to-face selling opportunities, such as round tables and surveys, where the result of the activity is a face-to-face meeting with a buyer. Avoid dwelling on marketing activities that require a lot of time and money, give you a sense of accomplishment, but don't actually move you any closer to the sales opportunities. (An example of such an activity is direct mail distribution of brochures and newsletters.)

Be Realistic.   In a perfect world with unlimited resources you could do everything you've identified for marketing through your situation analysis. If you include all those things in your action plan for the first year, it becomes a wish list rather than an action plan. Include what can reasonably be accomplished by the resources you're certain will be available. Also, address other factors, such as internal obstacles to accomplishing your plan.

## Actually Writing the Plan

The marketing action plan, like the rest of the planning process, has no magic answers. The marketing activity should be appropriate to the market, but other than that simple rule, there is more than one way to do something. As long as you have given the action plan some good thought, it's counterproductive constantly to second guess yourself. There are usually several different ways to approach your objective; if some planned activity doesn't produce the expected results, try one of your other alternatives. It's important to formulate the plan and start implementing it so you get consistently closer to your goals. As General George S. Patton, Jr., put it: ''A good plan violently executed now is better than a perfect plan next week.'' His words are appropriate for marketing warfare.

## What Are the Marketing Techniques and Tools?

Your marketing action plan is going to rely on marketing techniques and tools to publicize your service. Some of the tools for producing marketing results are:

| | |
|---|---|
| Brochures | Direct mail |
| Advertising, print or electronic | Media; Public relations |
| Speeches | Newsletters |
| Articles | Speech and article reprints |
| Couponing, promotion | Specific target identification |
| Telemarketing | Seminars, round tables |
| Special events sponsorship | Surveys |
| Trade/professional society activities | Personal phone follow-up |

Although no magic combination of these marketing techniques and tools exists, some are more appropriate to the marketing of one type of service than others. Table 10-1 shows a breakdown of these techniques. Generally, the marketing techniques and tools that focus on presenting qualifications to a target market—such as speeches, speech and article reprints, article placement, seminars, and round tables—are appropriate to professional services marketing, because they provide an opportunity to showcase the expertise that the professionals possess.

As previously mentioned, some techniques and tools are more appropriate to one phase of the buying cycle (e.g., knowledge building and qualification)

**Table 10-1.** Marketing techniques and tools appropriate to different types of services.

| Marketing Technique/Tool | Professional Services | Balanced Product/ Services | Consumer Services |
|---|:---:|:---:|:---:|
| Brochures | X | X | X |
| Direct mail | X | X | X |
| Personal telephone follow-up | X | X | |
| Telemarketing | X | X | X |
| Speeches and reprints | X | | |
| Articles and reprints | X | X | |
| Trade or professional society activities | X | X | |
| Newsletters | X | X | X |
| Specific target selection | X | X | |
| Seminars, round tables | X | X | |
| Product presentations/demonstrations | | X | |
| Surveys | X | X | |
| Media, public relations | X | X | X |
| Advertising—print or electronic | | X | X |
| Couponing, promotion | | | X |

than others, and some are better suited for selling new services to existing clients/customers than others. Remember that the ultimate goal of any marketing action plan is to provide the greatest number of sales opportunities. For professional services, this must mean a great number of opportunities for face-to-face meetings between buyers and the seller/doer. In balanced product/service your marketing must include numerous opportunities to highlight the benefits and demonstrate the features of your product.

### A Few Practical Tips on Marketing Tools

The following things we've learned about some marketing tools may prove helpful to you.

"I Need a Brochure."  One rallying cry in every marketing plan is "I need a brochure!" This is true, you do. Regardless of what your professional or balanced product/service is, you need a brochure to use as a "calling card" for your service; the brochure demonstrates your commitment to the service. Brochures, however, don't sell anything. A great amount of marketing time and dollars are frequently expended, particularly in professional services, in creating eye-catching, "coffee-table" quality brochures, which are rarely necessary. Generally, a well-written, attractively produced brochure (left behind at the end of a sales call), highlighting the benefits of your services, will be just as effective and easier and less expensive to produce. And using such a brochure will allow you to move on to the important part of your marketing plan—developing sales opportunities.

<u>Personal Follow-Up.</u>  Seminars, round tables, and similar events are often good ways to market professional services one-on-one to buyers. Personal follow-up by phone after the invitation has been sent significantly increases positive responses to these events. A reminder call immediately before the event always increases attendance.

# Evaluating Your Marketing Plan, or It's a "Living" Document

You should build into your marketing plan certain points at which you evaluate the activities to date and their success versus your anticipated results. Your marketing action plan should be a living document and modified accordingly to eliminate activities that aren't effective, and to maximize the impact of those that are. As you proceed, you'll learn which strategies affect your goals and marketing tactics. The plan should reflect the most accurate and up-to-date information.

The points that should be difficult to change in a marketing action plan are the "due dates." Once due dates start slipping and accountability disappears, the likelihood of implementing your plan in an effective and timely way is seriously diminished. Someone must be ruthless, holding people accountable, moving the action plan forward. Frequently this responsibility rests with the professional marketer.

# Summary

In this chapter we've discussed the different types of services—professional services, balanced product/services, and consumer services. We've also included the elements of a marketing plan and how to go about developing them. We've touched on the effectiveness of the various marketing techniques and tools and shared some hints based on experience.

The marketing plan is a living document, which should be adjusted for changes, insights, and experience. The only things that shouldn't change significantly are due dates and personal accountability. In fact, follow-through and accountability are essential to the success of any marketing action plan for professional services and balanced product/service marketing.

The most effective marketing plans focus on activities that lead to the end result—increased sales opportunities. Avoid spending too much of your marketing time and dollars on activities that don't generate specific sales opportunities.

Look at the example starting on page 183 of a marketing plan for a new service in professional services. Keep in mind that it's only an example; it's intended as a road map, with specific responsibility and signposts for accomplishment. Marketing is an art as much as a science, and because marketing nonconsumer services is so new there are no pat answers. Developing a services marketing plan requires thought, a willingness to take a chance, and flexibility. And a well-prepared plan, faithfully implemented, *will* build sales.

## Note

1. Al Ries and Jack Trout, *Bottom-Up Marketing* (New York: McGraw-Hill, 1989).

\*    \*    \*    \*

***Kristine J. Bean*** *is currently director—business development for Peterson & Co., a Chicago consulting firm that provides litigation support to the legal community and information management services to various industries. Previously, she served as director of marketing and planning for Winston & Strawn, one of the largest law firms in Chicago. She also started and developed the Marketing Services Group of the Chicago office of Arthur Andersen & Co.*

# Example of a Marketing Plan for Productivity Improvement Consulting *

## Goals

- To become known by buyers of this service in the coming year
- To "buy" opportunities to do this work and therefore refine our techniques
- To develop sound delivery skills in ten people in the organization in the first year

## The Situation Analysis

Trends

With increasing pressures on companies in the Midwest to stay viable and be more profitable, there is a strong interest in improving productivity in such areas as transportation, the office, and purchasing in order to control the number of employees and costs. As a result, the market in the Midwest is favorable for productivity improvement consulting, which results in the controlled reduction of head count and control of costs.

Segmenting the Market

The techniques we've developed for implementing productivity improvements are sound and are applicable to companies in various industries. With an effective use of listening skills, the techniques can be applied effectively by our deliverers to any industry.

From what we know, however, those industries having the most significant investment in physical resources and having been most affected by the downturn in the Midwest are our best prospects. These are primarily medium- to large-size manufacturing companies.

Smaller companies could also benefit from this service; however, our intelligence indicates that at this point they are less likely to have the cash available to hire us and will probably want to obtain these benefits by doing this themselves.

Competition

From our review of the coverage of this topic in the trade and local press, conversations with clients, discussions with trade association groups, and such, it appears that only two businesses—ABC Company and XYZ Company—have any market presence in this field. The other competitors or sole practitioners are obviously limited by their own time capacity and are not significant competitors in this market.

ABC has developed a reputation for providing one or two good hits in reducing the work force on each of its projects, and it charges less than the other companies. From what we can tell, they seem to do only one job at a company, which implies that their quality is inferior. XYZ gives introductory seminars, during which they discuss their ability to do a "checklist," or review of four or five standard departments for opportunities. Although XYZ doesn't charge a great deal, they're more expensive than ABC.

---

*A new professional service developed in response to market trends

# Marketing Strategies

### Target Market

We will pursue large to mid-size manufacturing companies, primarily those that are already clients of our firm. We will not turn away any opportunity, however, because we are trying to gain experience in this service; we will respond to all requests and inquiries that we receive.

### Target Volume

In the first year, we will sell work with fees of $500,000 to at least eight companies, two of which are not now clients of our firm.

### Differentiation Strategy

We will position this service in line with the general reputation of our firm for delivering quality, responsive, high value, and expensive service. We will be the customized Cadillac in this market. We will provide one-day, free evaluations to each potential client and use that time to build an understanding of the value of our customized approach, looking for the greatest payback opportunity. In addition, the hiring of Joe Smith, who's regarded as the leading expert in this field on the East Coast, will give credibility to our skills in this area.

### Internal Marketing

The highest priority target market for this service consists of clients who are manufacturing companies. Therefore, the internal marketing effort to generate introductions will be significant. We will send something in writing to announce this service to our people, we will have Joe Smith demonstrate his credentials in speaking before various division groups, and we will have one-on-one conversations with those client-relationship people who deal specifically with manufacturing companies.

### Communication Strategy

We want Joe to become well-known as the expert in this field representing our company and this practice. We will use public relations and speaking engagements to attempt to develop awareness of him in this market.

In addition to the internal marketing efforts to build sales opportunities, we will hold a number of seminars to meet with potential buyers who are not clients.

# The Action Plan

| Broadcast Activities<br>Action Step | Responsibility | Due Date |
|---|---|---|
| Broadcast—to let our market know that we're in this business by highlighting Joe Smith and his experience in programs attended by our buyers. | | |
| 1. Speeches | | |
|   A. Compile a list of the most appropriate trade associations—manufacturing, local chambers of commerce, specific industry, and determine their schedule for speakers or seminars. | Johnson | 4/1 |
|   B. Work with each group to get Joe on agenda in as many places as possible during the next six to nine months. Report to group on status each month. | Johnson | Continuing |
|   C. Develop a generic speech that can be easily customized for a number of different venues. | Smith | 4/1 |
|   D. Prior to first speaking engagement, team to meet and review attendees; make assignments for personal contact and expected level of follow-up based on quality of targets. | Smith | As required |
| 2. Public Relations | | |
|   A. Article placement—review key publications for manufacturing trade; work with PR counsel, determine opportunities for article placement in each. Write an article and include byline by Joe Smith. | Jackson | 6/1 |
|   B. Article reprints—after the article has been published, order reprints and send with a personalized letter to all existing contacts and interested prospects. | Jackson | 6/15 |
|   C. Media interviews—using public relations counsel, discover an effective angle for productivity improvement that will generate a general business interview with the local paper. | Smith | 5/1 |
| Internal Marketing—communicate the benefits of service with internal client relationship people in order to obtain introductions to clients who are potential buyers of this service. | | |
| 1. Brochure—write and produce a brochure that is effective, focused, reasonably priced, and suitable for internal selling and external distribution. | Hopkins | 6/1 |
| 2. Brochure distribution—together with a cover memo, distribute brochure to key | | |

*(continues)*

| Broadcast Activities Action Step | Responsibility | Due Date |
|---|---|---|
| relationship people, announcing the service. | Hopkins | 6/10 |
| 3. Get Joe Smith to talk about the service during each division monthly meeting (to be held by July 1). | Smith | 7/1 |
| 4. Target companies—review the firm's client list, and select those clients most likely to buy this service. Distribute the list to all people on the team. Each person is responsible for visiting with each of his or her relationship people to explain the service and set up introductions. | Jackson (for list) All make calls | 7/1 |
| 5. Follow-up—Continue to follow up with internal people until the introduction is made. Reporting against this goal each month is critical. | All | Monthly meeting |

External Marketing—to develop face-to-face selling opportunities with companies that are not currently clients.

| | | |
|---|---|---|
| 1. Setting up seminars—establish dates for two seminars in the next eight months, about three months apart. Assemble mailing list from reasonable sources, design invitation, make facility arrangements, and prepare invitations for mailing. | Seminar 1—Johnson Seminar 2—Hopkins | 8/1 11/1 |
| 2. Personal phone follow-up—when invitations are ready to go out, phone those persons who are invited to let them know the invitation is on the way. Follow up with those who haven't responded. Also reconfirm attendance prior to seminar. | All | 6/15 & 7/26 |
| 3. Preseminar planning—assign individual attendees to service team people to establish contacts, collect business cards, and begin establishing relationships. | All | 7/26 |
| 4. Follow-up meeting—immediately after seminars, review notes and ideas that each person on the team obtained from the prospects who attended the seminar. Prioritize the prospects and then begin individual follow-up and sales efforts. | (Overall) Jackson (Implementing) All | 8/2 |
| 5. Continual follow-up—with each person who attends the seminar or who has demonstrated any interest in our service, at least once every three weeks send him or her an article or a speech rewrite or some other point of possible interest. Report on status at monthly meeting. | All | Continuous |

| *Broadcast Activities* Action Step | Responsibility | Due Date |
|---|---|---|
| Monitoring and Assessment | | |
| 1. Progress meetings will be held at 7:30 A.M., on the third Monday of each month. Each person will report about his or her specific assignments, progress on sales opportunities, and sales made. | All | As indicated |
| 2. Assessment—about seven months into the program we will formally assess our progress against our goals, review the propriety of our strategies, and make any directional changes or marketing technique changes that seem appropriate. This will be a half-day meeting. | (In charge) Joe Smith All | 10/1 |

# 11

# Information: The Next Battleground

Timothy W. Powell

The Age of Information is fast upon us. There is more business information available than ever before, it is becoming easier to use, and managers are beginning to realize its value as a strategic asset. Marketing managers in particular are beginning to exploit the potential of information technologies to (1) improve marketing decision making, (2) rationalize and improve marketing operations, (3) improve service to customers and clients, and (4) differentiate their services in the marketplace.

This chapter is directed at the services marketing executive who wants to do more with information, and who doesn't want to waste time and money in the process. It includes background on the information explosion; thoughts on the role of information in corporate strategy; ways to assess the value of information; two information models; a survey of information sources; a description of the information component found in every service, and how to use it to best advantage; pitfalls to be avoided; a checklist of information tools; and tips on working with your data processing department.

## The Information Opportunity

Opportunities to apply information in competitive ways are uniquely rich at this time. From each of three perspectives (the historical, the managerial, and the technical) I'll describe why that is.

### Historical Perspective: The End-User Revolution

During recent decades, the installed base of computers has grown exponentially. Managers have had to become more familiar with computers in order to remain competitive. And the management vision of what computers are has evolved from a *control and monitoring* orientation to a *strategic* orientation. Managers are increasingly recognizing computers as tools to compete, rather than only as ways to reduce back-office costs.

Much of this growth has come from the introduction of personal computers in the late 1970s. This has fundamentally changed the way we use computers. Before that time, a computer user typically submitted computing jobs to be run in *batch* mode (i.e., at the convenience of the computer and the computer staff, and with no direct interaction with the end user). In contrast, PCs are built to be interactive. They depend on user input to work—in technical terms, they are *interrupt driven*. It is this man-machine interaction that is driving the productivity of computers ever upward.

### Managerial Perspective: The Underutilized Asset

By far the single biggest application of PCs in most organizations is word processing. They have virtually replaced typewriters in many organizations, and have substantially added to productivity in the process. This has created a tremendous opportunity for PC applications of other kinds, which run on the same equipment. PCs are software-driven and can do many functions depending on the software loaded at the time. A PC can be used to type a document, then create a budget on a spreadsheet, then download electronic mail, then create mailing labels. No other piece of equipment in the modern office comes anywhere near this kind of flexibility.

In thinking of new ways to use PCs in our organizations, we should keep in mind the tremendous installed base of computing power that probably already exists. In many companies, this installed base now represents a substantial corporate asset, from which only a fraction of the potential return is being realized.

### Technical Perspective: Information Is More Than Facts and Figures

The term *information* in a management context is usually used to mean facts and figures, which have been organized or interpreted to a greater or lesser extent, and which are then used by decision makers to evaluate alternatives and make "better" decisions. This definition, although certainly valid, is limited; it unnecessarily restricts managers trying to use information in competitive ways.

Many kinds of sensory stimuli can now be coded and manipulated digitally. Sounds can be recorded in digital form on compact disk or tape. Computer manipulation of visual images, both in the context of desktop publishing and in computer-aided design (CAD), is another new and productive application. The addition of sounds and visual images put computers in a new communications arena, where the only "computing" going on is in support of end-user benefits, and is (at best) invisible to the user.

## Strategy and Information: A Paradox

It is becoming a management cliché that "information is a competitive weapon." Most modern managers would agree, and add that information is most useful to the organization when it can be harnessed in the service of the strategic goals of the organization. As a general rule, this would lead us to develop new information applications by first examining business objectives, then setting information objectives, then developing applications to meet them. For example, a business objective could be to "improve our customer relations." This could drive an information objective of "providing more convenience to our customers through on-line ordering and inventory availability information," out of which the specifications for such an application could be developed.

This model, although eminently reasonable on the face of it, ignores the potential role that information could play in developing business strategies and objectives. As we will see later, information can be used to change rules of the competitive game, and thereby in effect can become a key determinant of business strategy (together, of course, with a number of other factors).[1]

So although it may be comforting to intone that information strategies should serve the organization's strategic objectives, the opportunity to use the "tool" as a "driver" should not be ignored.

## The Value of Information

That information has value is demonstrated by the recent blossoming of the information industry, currently valued at more than $20 billion and still expanding rapidly. But the economic nature of information is paradoxical, in that it has characteristics of both goods and services. Like a good, it can be inventoried and usually has a limited shelf-life. Like a service, it is intangible, and its value may be less obvious than for a good.

### Information in Financial Markets

Modern financial markets are the clearest example of an information-intensive market environment. Wall Street has spent more on information technology than any other industry, and its demands continue to fuel developments in the information business. The laws and regulations that surround the fair use of information in the securities business, and the penalties for abuses of privileged information, are other emblems of the economic value of information.

Such developments are not so new. During the early nineteenth century, the European financial markets rose and fell with the successes and failures of Napoleon in his various campaigns abroad. During one such campaign, the Rothschild bankers were known to hire a relay chain of scouts across Europe. In this way they could be the first to possess the latest information from the front, and could trade on the Bourse accordingly.

### Marketing Warfare

Information about financial services is, of course, an extreme example, in that information plays such a central role in the production and delivery of the service. However, any service can be shown to have some role for information in its marketing. Information is being used in a sales and marketing context as follows:[2]

1. *Show the customer the benefits of the service.* Example: an insurance agent who uses a computer to model various premium and cash-value scenarios under a life insurance policy.

2. *Respond quickly to customer needs.* Example: using electronic mail and spreadsheets to quickly prepare and revise business proposals.

3. *Stay close to the customer.* Example: using one-way video teleconferencing to sell interest-rate sensitive financial instruments in times of financial volatility.

4. *Improve the effectiveness of the sales force.* Examples: using on-line searches and electronic publishing to improve the quality of proposals; using electronic mail to coordinate sales force activity.

5. *Formulate marketing strategies.* Examples: using computer graphics to better analyze sales performance; using electronic searches to identify and evaluate potential new markets.

6. *Identify prospects.* Examples: using statistical analysis to improve the return on direct-mail campaigns; using an on-line database to identify new prospects.

7. *Time sales calls.* Example: a real estate broker who uses electronic mail to coordinate the sale of mortgages and insurance to home buyers.

8. *Build a public image.* Examples: using word processing to quickly prepare "customized" press releases for insertion in regional and local media; using electronic mail to coordinate statements made to the press.

## Measuring the Value of Information

The value of information is important, because it usually has a cost, and we would like to know how much we should be willing to pay for it. All business decisions are made in an environment where there is uncertainty—either greater or lesser—about the outcome. Information is often used to reduce the amount of uncertainty. The value added is the change in the *expected value of the outcome* (i.e., the economic value of the various outcomes weighted by the probabilities of their occurring). A business school professor of mine used to ask, "How much would you pay to talk to the Oracle?" (i.e., to eliminate the uncertainty altogether and have perfect foresight of the outcome). It is possible, using mathematical decision modeling, to arrive at some calculated estimate of the value that would be added by additional information. The real question here is, "What would you do differently if you had the information?" If the information is not "actionable," chances are you're wasting time and money in trying to get it.

Another way to explain information value is simply the *net present value of cash flows* generated by the implementation of some new information technology or procedure. Negative cash flows include the incremental investments in hardware, software, and personnel. Positive cash flows include cost savings, and, more important, additional revenues generated.[3]

Yet another way to measure information value is to gauge the *replacement value* of the information provided. This is especially germane when a transfer of information media occurs. For example, the value of information provided on compact disk could be compared to the price of that information when provided on-line from a mainframe.

# Two Information Models

We must always ask the question "What information are we talking about?" Presented here are two different, but compatible, ways to look at this question: a structural model, and a functional model.

## A Structural Model

One way to categorize information is to consider whom or what the information is "about." This approach could use industry structure as a framework. (The following questions are intended to illustrate this approach, not to serve as an exhaustive checklist.)

About Our Markets.   What comes to mind first here, of course, is information about our current or potential markets. Relevant data might help us answer questions like:

1. What is the size of the market, by segment?
2. Who are the market leaders? What are their market shares?
3. What is the outlook for the market?
4. What unmet market needs are there?
5. What other markets might exist?

About Our Customers/Clients/Prospects.   To stay close to our customers, we might want to monitor:

1. What are their recent operating results?
2. What are their business plans?
3. Who are their key executives? What are they like?
4. How are purchasing decisions made?
5. Which ones would be especially interested in our services?

About Ourselves/Our Services.   This is a big one, and all too often it's overlooked. Data might include:

1. What services do we offer, by "line of service" category?
2. Who is buying each one?
3. What are the sales and margins of each one?
4. What are the sales and margin trends of each one?
5. What returns are we getting on media and promotional spending?
6. How are our company and our services positioned and perceived in the marketplace?

About Our Competitors.   Currently there is a big demand for "competitive intelligence," especially the kind that can be gathered quickly, inexpensively, and legally. Every marketer/planner wants to know certain things about the competition:

1. What is their current and recent past market performance and operating results?
2. What are their service lines? How do they differ from ours?
3. What are their business plans, especially regarding new service introductions and media campaigns?
4. Who are their customers or clients? Where are they located?
5. How large is their sales force? How is it organized and compensated?
6. How are they using technology in their service delivery and marketing efforts?

## A Functional Model

Another way to look at information is to consider its function; that is, what are we trying to achieve with the use of the information? There are two very different approaches here, and we'll look at each in turn.

The "Better Decisions" Approach.    This is the perspective usually taken in the current literature on using information in marketing. The underlying question is "How can we use existing information, or purchase new information, to make better marketing decisions?" This, of course, helps us attain the uncertainty-reduction goals described earlier. The decision maker is implicitly at the center of the "information universe" in this model.

The volume of information available for purchase by marketing decision makers has grown rapidly in recent years. The ability to gather and manipulate this information electronically has also grown, to the point where many businesses will not move without first consulting the databases. The competition is usually using them, and they are much less expensive than conducting research directly with customers.

There are, in fact, at least two segments of the information industry devoted not to producing information, but simply to making it available to decision makers in a timely, organized way. The first of these is the *information vendors,* through whom you can purchase information on-line. The other is the *information brokers,* who are devoted to knowing where to find the most appropriate and accurate information most quickly and at the lowest cost.[4]

The "Better Service" Approach.    Another way to think about information is to consider it as a service adjunct, which somehow enhances the value of your service to your customer or client. Here the customer is at the center of the "information universe." Electronic home banking, for example, is an information-driven enhancement to an existing service.

There are two variations on the better service theme—one is the explicit or "front office" approach, where the customer is aware that information is being actively provided to him or her. The options here are either to provide new information or to deliver existing information in new ways. (Home banking contains elements of both these options.) The new ways of delivering information could involve anything from a simple reformatting of existing information to make it more usable to the use of a completely new medium to deliver the information. (It's especially important here to keep the "more than facts and figures" perspective in mind.)

The other variation is the *implicit* approach to better service, where the customer does not directly perceive the information per se, but rather the effects of an information enhancement on service improvements. The Federal Express package tracking system is an example of this. The customer does not receive information directly about the whereabouts of the package. If a package is late, however, a company agent is able to access that information, which adds value to the service.

## Information Sources

Knowing where to get information is always a challenging job. Dedicated personnel with training in library science and computer searching increasingly inhabit corporate libraries and information centers. Specialists in this field are able to start their own businesses as consultants and information brokers.

The full value of information as a decision-making tool is realized when internal data (e.g., sales by service line) are linked with external data (e.g., overall market size estimates) to create a total marketing support information system.

### Internal Sources

Using internal information can be extremely cost-effective in marketing situations. This can be information produced by another system and redirected for use in marketing, or information produced specifically to support marketing goals.

Leveraging Existing Transaction Systems. This is usually where an information-savvy marketer begins. There is usually a wealth of marketing intelligence hidden within the existing data processing systems of the organization. If they can be harnessed, they can be leveraged into powerful business development tools. For example, a promotional mailing list could be linked to a customer/client file to approximate *database marketing,* a tailored and "intelligent" approach to direct marketing. Accounting systems often hold sales and profitability information, although it may take considerable reformatting and analysis to make the data useful to marketing decision makers.

Building Dedicated Systems. Eventually, dedicated systems can be built that can also generate marketing information. This is increasingly less expensive to do, both in time and money, because of the advent of powerful personal computers. A large professional services firm built a PC-based system to automate the generating of form letters and mailing labels used by its headquarters staff to respond to requests for technical and promotional publications. The system essentially paid for itself in the time saved in this fulfillment process alone. Simultaneously, though, the information was captured in a central file, and subsequently routed to branch offices for follow-up calls. Follow-up on selected leads positioned the firm as interested and responsive, and in several cases resulted in new business relationships. It also became much easier to measure the demand for various types of publications.

### External Sources

Much information relevant to marketing activities is not available internally. The following is a brief outline of external sources of available information.

Commercial Sources.    When time is short and budgets permit, electronic access is usually the preferred method. All you need are a PC (preferably with a hard disk), a modem, telecommunications software, and a subscription to an on-line vendor. A vendor (Dialog, for example) owns the marketing rights to various databases, and makes them available to its subscribers. Charges often exceed $100 per hour, plus phone costs. Getting the right information quickly and at lowest possible costs is a skill that usually requires considerable training and experience. Most vendors offer training in accessing the information they provide.

Moreover, the indexing and abstracting power of a good on-line vendor can make effective searching relatively easy and affordable. An increasingly greater percentage of information that appears in print also appears in electronic form, and the lag times for this to happen are often very short or nonexistent. The *Wall Street Journal,* for example, is available electronically in full text at 6 A.M. every day it is published.

A number of on-line sources of information are of special interest to services marketers:

1. Periodicals, especially the general business press *(Business Week, Forbes, Fortune, Wall Street Journal, New York Times)* and the trade press (industry-specific magazines and newsletters)
2. News wires (e.g., Dow Jones, UPI, AP)
3. Market research reports on individual products or product lines
4. Investment analyst reports on companies or industries
5. Financial data and annual reports on key customers, prospects, or competitors
6. Executive biographies (for business-to-business marketing)
7. Company listings (for prospects or competitors) that can be searched by various criteria (e.g., industry, size, location)
8. Registered trademarks
9. Press releases

Each of these sources may be used to monitor customers, competitors, suppliers, and other companies of interest. An ever-increasing amount of international trade information is available from these sources.

Free Sources.    Even on a restricted budget, valuable information can be gathered. Industry trade associations, many of which are based in Washington or New York City, often have publications and knowledgeable personnel. Government agencies, especially at the federal and state levels, may also be helpful. Some federal agencies are beginning to maintain electronic bulletin board systems, which may be accessed by modem at no charge (beyond telephone rates). Others are beginning to publish data on inexpensive CD-ROM disks.

It pays to persist—the rule of thumb is that it takes an average of seven call referrals to find the right person in the federal bureaucracy—because the people are usually helpful and accurate, and always inexpensive. There are also published directories of federal agencies and of lobbying and trade groups. Government Printing Office bookstores are full of inexpensive information; these items can also be ordered by phone.

Libraries, of course, are a great source of information, if one has the time and/or personnel to make use of them, and if the information has a relatively long shelf-life. Public libraries in larger cities may be depositories for federal agency publications. Some federal agencies also maintain their own libraries, as do some trade associations and independent groups.

## The Information Component in Service Delivery

Just as there is a service component to every product, there is an information component to every service. Depending on the service, this component plays something between a peripheral and a central role in the delivery and marketing of the service.

### Information as Peripheral to the Service

At the very least, the information component of a service includes its nature, its price, and its availability. Even the local shoe-shine stand (often singled out as the "primal" services marketing environment) must communicate, either explicitly or implicitly, these fundamental information elements.

### Information as Central to the Service

Conversely, there are some services in which the role of information is much more central. For instance, in financial services, where no less an authority than Walter Wriston said, "Information about money is almost as important as money itself." Indeed, an ever-increasing number of financial transactions rely not on money or on paper surrogates for money (like checks), but on electronic information transfers between parties.* This is possible because the financial industry has been a leader in applying information technologies, originally to cut costs and later to provide additional customer benefits.

Some modern financial services literally could not exist without advanced information technologies. Convenience accounts that link banking, brokerage,

---

*This may not qualify so much as *information about money* as it does *a new form of money*.

and credit services are one example. Home banking and on-line securities brokerage services are another.

Let's look at another information-intensive industry in which the information component is more distinct from the service itself—the airline industry. American Airlines is widely credited with pioneering the use of "channel systems," which are information systems provided at favorable costs to distribution channels (in this case travel agents) to help them in their work, and which provide strategic benefits to the provider (in this case, switching costs and system bias toward American flight listings).

Because American was so successful in doing this, several other airlines tried to do the same thing, most with limited success. As a result, though, the role of information became more central to the ongoing war for the consumer's air-fare dollar. In effect, the rules of the game were redefined by one vendor. This system in turn enabled other tools of competitive warfare to be more easily implemented, such as demand-based pricing and promotional discounts.

### Information as a Stand-Alone Service

Information can become so important that it can be offered as a service on a stand-alone basis. This development is driving the growth of the information industry. Information producers such as Dun & Bradstreet or Standard and Poor's originate or compile the information. Electronic distribution is typically handled by a separate vendor, which is the company with whom the user has an account. Prominent examples of companies selling business information are Knight-Ridder (Dialog), Mead Data (Lexis/Nexis), and Dow Jones (which is also, of course, an information producer). Stock market information has its own specialized set of producers and vendors.

It is not unheard of for an information resource to start within an organization as a supporting cost center, to become a freestanding profit center, and even to be spun off as a separate business. Some information companies got their starts as efforts to use slack time profitably on industrial companies' computer systems (General Electric Information Services and Dialog, originally owned by Lockheed, are examples).

# Using the Information Component for Competitive Advantage

The real strategic leverage of the information component of your service comes from (1) its ability to provide customer benefits, and (2) its ability to differentiate your service in the marketplace.

### Customer Benefits

The clearest way for an information technology to pay its way is to *provide a customer benefit,* either directly or indirectly. What are some of the ways in which information technology can provide such benefits?

Reduce Costs and Prices. For years, the typical justification for the implementation of a new information technology was that it would reduce the cost of certain operations. To the extent that is true, and to the extent that reduced cost can be passed on to the customer, technology clearly provides a competitive weapon in price-sensitive markets.

Enhance Convenience. As the installed base of computers continues to grow, and as computer software becomes increasingly intuitive to use, the convenience factor will become a more potent strategic weapon. For example, the convenience of using an automated teller machine for getting cash and making other transactions, thereby avoiding waits in teller lines, was clearly a selling point. (The banks were simultaneously able to reduce their per-transaction processing costs.)

Provide Personalized Service. Computers make it possible to regain some of the personal touches that many people complain have been lost from services. Personal customer profiles can be stored in a computer and used to quickly tailor the service to the user's specifications. Airline travel agents, for example, record seating preferences, and car-rental companies maintain customer identifiers and preferred vehicle types. Hotels are beginning to try the same kind of approach for frequent guests.

Although I have used examples from consumer services, essentially the same concepts apply in business-to-business situations when you substitute "critical success factors" for "benefits."

## Differentiation

It is one thing simply to enhance customer value, still another to actively use this as a differentiating point in the marketplace. Advertising campaigns are beginning to tout uses of information as providing customer value. Campaigns for American Express card accounts use the value of enhanced financial statements as selling points; MCI has a similar pitch for its phone services. Federal Express has used its package-tracking technology as the focus of a campaign. This is particularly interesting because, although this technology application is inherently implicit (as described earlier), here it is publicized as a differentiating point. Aside from selling package delivery, express services are also selling peace of mind, and this technology reinforces that value.

The way in which information is packaged and presented can have a major effect on its usefulness, regardless of the actual content involved. Several major retail financial service providers have changed their monthly statement formats to be both more informative and more attractive. The recent affordability of desktop publishing and other presentation technologies has opened up the possibilities here immensely.

## Changing the Rules

It is possible to change the rules of the game by redefining information from a peripheral to a more central component of the service package. A procedure for doing this can be summarized as follows: (1) identify your market constituencies, (2) assess the "information values" of each (i.e., how the provider's information adds, or could add, value to the users' operations),[5] (3) provide that information in a way consistent with the users' value structures, and (4) do so in a way that a sustainable competitive advantage is achieved.

Competitive advantage can be sustained by creating barriers to entry for the information component—creating switching costs related to investments in information hardware or user training, or media promotion of the benefits of the enhanced information to the user, for example. McKesson, the pharmaceuticals distributor, was able to win the buying loyalty of drug retailers by giving them on-site order entry terminals. Each of its accounts had invested considerable employee time in learning to use the equipment and the associated procedures, and thus an entry barrier was created for McKesson's competitors.

## Five Technology Pitfalls

For most information-savvy managers, the honeymoon with information technology is over. People are not as dazzled about the "miracles of technology" as they once were, and they are more aware that the costs—both in money and in time—can be staggering. Watch out for these pitfalls as you embark on technology-driven projects: the "gee whiz" factor; missed budgets and deadlines; the shifting landscape; "infoglut"; and garbage in, garbage out.

### The "Gee Whiz" Factor

The latest front-page technologies, although exciting to contemplate, often do not pay off in a business context, for several reasons: (1) a high position on the cost curve, (2) lack of an established user base, and (3) the often unsteady fortunes of the vendors. It may not pay to be first, unless by so doing you can preempt other entrants.

Similarly, technology-based solutions are sometimes not as effective as revising the current manual systems. "Low-tech" solutions, or low-tech components of total solutions, should always be considered.

### Missed Budgets and Deadlines

Technology solutions, although eventually integrated into the routine of doing business, are designed in a creative environment. Here it is difficult to measure productivity, and therefore difficult to control it. Costs often run higher than anticipated, and deadlines are often missed. Problems seem to appear out of the blue, and a solution to one problem may create another in a least-suspected place.

### The Shifting Landscape

Because information technologies are evolving so rapidly, any technology plan may be outdated by the time it is implemented. There is no way around this, because it is very risky to build plans that rely for implementation on the delivery of developing technologies.

By doing nothing, however, you risk moving farther back relative to your competition. This is often the bottom-line justification for technology projects, and is very real in the marketplace—but nonetheless very hard to plan around.

### "Infoglut"

This is the new affliction of the Information Age, the availability of too much information to absorb and act upon. One more piece of information is always there to be gathered and sifted. The real question, of course, is what that buys you in terms of uncertainty reduction, versus the cost of getting it. Costs considered must include out-of-pocket expenses, personnel time, and the "opportunity cost" of waiting to make a decision until the information is gathered and analyzed. (On the other hand, there are information tools on the horizon that will make this retrieval and analysis faster and easier.)

### Garbage In, Garbage Out

Data integrity is critical to the usefulness of any information system, and can be won through the building in of checks along the way, as well as periodic audits of system validity.

## The Marketer's Toolbox

The following is a checklist of some of the types of office-based information technologies available to marketing people at this writing. Some examples of how they are being applied are included:

| Technology | Sample Application(s) |
|---|---|
| Word processing | Proposals, brochures, and presentations |
| Desktop publishing | Proposals, brochures, and presentations |
| Graphics (hard copy) | Proposals, brochures, and presentations |
| Imager | Produce 35 mm slides; presentations |
| Projector | Display PC screen for a large audience; presentations |
| Telecommunications (with modem) | On-line research; electronic mail |
| Electronic bulletin board | Electronic mail; customer/channel information networks |
| FAX board | Send instant hard copy from a PC |
| Voice mail | An intelligent answering machine |
| Spreadsheet | Media budgeting; sales forecasting; data analysis |
| Statistical software | Data analysis |

| | |
|---|---|
| Database manager | Customer lists; mailings; lead management |
| Project manager | Planning and monitoring projects and campaigns; producing peripherals |
| Sales support software | Prospecting and follow-up |
| Mailing list manager | Merge and purge; test mailings |
| Computer-assisted telephone interviewing (CATI) | Scripting of phone interviews; on-line data entry; automated tabulation |
| On-line database | Secondary research |
| CD-ROM | Secondary research |
| Knowledge-based system (artificial intelligence) | Personality analysis; sales training; customer support; product names; data analysis; advertising strategy |

Clearly there is an explosion in the volume and variety of information technologies, which can be harnessed in the service of marketing.

## Working With Your Data Processing Department

It is important for marketers to develop and maintain good relationships with the company's data processing department. As mentioned, in-house data can often be invaluable to a marketer but often they must be analyzed or at least reformatted before they can become useful as a basis for marketing decisions. Systems enhancement projects, which any data processing department undertakes periodically, can be opportunities to have marketing information needs directly addressed. An authoritative marketing person should have direct input to whatever task group is drafting the new design, because data processing people typically have little exposure to marketing practices and priorities.

Some organizations have clearly identified the strategic value of information, and do not have to be sold on the concept. Most, however, are not utilizing this resource as much as they could. Some of this may be due to inertia in the data processing operation: Most computer applications of the past twenty years have been driven by financial or operational needs, and the internal machinations required to change this rarely occur overnight.

Large systems by nature do not lend themselves to rapid change, because in effect they tend to operate as information-processing "factories." That is, they have a set production schedule to meet each month, and meeting it requires most of their available resources. Deviations from the norm are often seen as problems, not opportunities, and may therefore be overlooked. Mainframe applications are by nature mediated applications; that is, they require the intervention of programmers and support personnel to maintain and run.

The good news is that personal computers are becoming increasingly powerful, and can usually be operated by end users with little or no intervention from support personnel. This is probably the most significant thing about the "PC revolution." To continue the analogy, small information "job shops" can be set up that apply the functional expertise of user personnel (marketers, for example). This is not to imply that company-wide information systems are obsolete or not potentially competitive, but simply that there are many competitive information applications that are best suited to end-user computers and that in fact may not be feasible on mainframes.

In the best of both worlds, PCs can be linked via a local area network (LAN) to a larger server (often a mainframe or a minicomputer) that houses the raw data. In this way, the integrity of the raw data is maintained, and the end user retains the flexibility and uniqueness of his or her own application.

## Summary

Information is playing an increasingly important role in all facets of marketing. The sheer volume of marketing-related information that is available practically mandates that computers be used to collect, sift, and analyze it prior to its introduction into the decision-making process.

Information is also being used to enhance the "marketing infrastucture"— those tactical and operational supports that are invisible to customers and clients, and that do not serve as inputs to the decision-making process. These are often opportunities for cost-cutting, rationalization and better organization, and enhanced effectiveness.

Finally, information can be used to enhance the value of services to your customers, provided that you use customer benefits as a guidepost. These enhancements can in turn be used as points of differentiation between you and your competitors.

Information will play an increasingly important strategic role in positioning services in the minds of customers and prospects. Information *is* the next battleground in the continual warfare that is marketing.

## Notes

1. This idea was initially developed by F. Warren McFarlan, "Information Technology Changes the Way You Compete," *Harvard Business Review,* May–June 1984.
2. The examples here are summarized from N. Dean Meyer and Mary E. Boone, *The Information Edge* (New York: McGraw-Hill, 1987). See especially the two chapters on applications of office automation to selling and marketing. Other examples, especially related to sales support, are found in Louis A. Wallis, *Computers and the Sales Effort* (New York: The Conference Board, 1986).
3. Meyer and Boone's book contains many examples of how to use this method of valuing information-based projects.
4. Probably the best published introduction to using on-line databases is Alfred Glossbrenner, *How to Look It Up Online* (New York: St. Martin's Press, 1987). This contains the basics, as well as tips that may be valuable to more experienced searchers.
5. A related concept, that of value chains, is developed by Michael Porter, *Competitive Advantage* (New York: Free Press, 1985). He in fact includes an entire chapter called

''Technology and Competitive Advantage.'' This treats technology in general, not specifically information technology, but I highly recommend it as background reading.

\*     \*     \*     \*

**Timothy W. Powell** *is a research director at FIND/SVP, a business information and research company located in New York City. He supervises strategic consulting projects on behalf of financial institutions and information companies. Previously, he served as a national marketing manager with Coopers & Lybrand, where he specialized in applying information technologies to marketing problems. Mr. Powell was formerly a management consultant with Peat Marwick.*

# 12

## How to Manage
## Outside Consultants

Michael J. English
Susan S. Prince
Michelle A. Yakovac
James H. Drew

There are a number of occasions where it is desirable and advantageous for service companies to obtain professional services from outside their organizations. One often needs the specialized expertise and talents that are difficult to develop and maintain within the company. Because the service company will place top priority on developing the technical knowledge and expertise for its *core* service business, it is in *support* services where it is often desirable to obtain professional services from an outside consulting firm.

There are many instances in which a consulting firm can be useful to the service company. One might retain a market research firm to assess the acceptance of a new customer service. An advertising consultant might be hired to develop a new theme, or a public relations agency might be brought in to recommend broader ways of making the company better known to customers and the general public. Top management may use a management consultant to assist with long-term strategic planning. Finally, academic consultants may help develop long-term goals in any of these areas, often in the guise of evaluating systems for currency.

Clearly, for a company to remain competitive it must perform these sorts of functions at least periodically. Yet the option of creating a year-round in-house market research or advertising staff may not be cost-justified. These periodic functions are often found to be better performed by a contracted agency.

Cost, however, is not the only reason to go outside. Innovation is another reason to seek an external consultant. It is healthy to import fresh and new ideas periodically. In addition, an outside "expert" consultant offers objectivity, independence, and credibility. These characteristics can be compelling reasons, especially when there are "turf" struggles over delicate issues within the company.

Sooner or later, the issue becomes how a service company manages the processes associated with the contracting of outside services. This chapter provides proven practical steps and processes for the reader to draw upon like a handbook. The remainder of the chapter discusses the types of outside consultant services available and when to use them, how to decide to use an outside consultant, how to select the company, and how to get the desired results. Finally, the chapter closes with how to "live" with a consultant, including how to evaluate his or her performance.

## Types of Consultant Services

This section identifies five types of consultant services generally needed at some time by the service company. Although there are other types of very specialized services, the 80/20 rule (80 percent of consulting services are performed by 20 percent of all consultant types) caused us to narrow the discussion to advertising and market research agencies, management and marketing consultants, and public relations and academic consultants.

*Advertising agencies* develop and implement advertising campaigns. Usually the services provided range in any negotiated combination from creation, production, casting, and direction, to media planning. Few service companies can justify the cost of maintaining an in-house staff of professionals to perform all these specialized professional services. Besides, the intangible of creativity is neither easily obtained nor is there a year-round need.

A full-service *market research agency* will provide qualitative or focus group research, interviewing or quantitative data collection (sometimes referred to as fieldwork), tabulation, analysis, and presentation. It is not uncommon for many service companies to perform some of these services in-house. One of the key advantages of obtaining these services from a market research agency is the independence and objectivity by which the information is obtained, tabulated, and interpreted. The agencies provide expertise in designing and completing research from which service companies can decide courses of action in markets in which they compete.

*Management and marketing consultants* consist of two groups: generalists and "boutiques." The first group tends to be large companies that do consulting with senior-level executives in companies for strategic planning. This may involve assessing objectively the strengths and weaknesses of key processes within the company. Many of the questions posed are of a marketing nature: How to develop a competitive edge? What are the strengths and weaknesses of this process? Another service provided by these consultants is that of "facilitating" senior-level meetings where large amounts of data or information must be processed, interpreted, and integrated. Clearly, independence, objectivity, and expedience are prevailing arguments for using these consultants.

The second group of these consultants consists of "boutiques" that specialize in a particular niche marketing function or industry. Smaller in size than the first group, these companies have a specialty (e.g., in price strategy, product planning, organization development, or strategic planning). Some specialize in specific industries like banking, telecommunications, or travel and leisure.

*Public relations consultants* are typically agencies that offer an array of services in two distinct areas. Similar to an advertising agency, enhancing corporate image or service recognition is one of the areas. Whereas the advertising agency limits its specialized services to media messages, however, the public relations agency looks across the entire spectrum of how the client creates impressions with the public. Such things as charity sponsorship, community activities, public appearances, and interviews can be designed to fit a client's strategic plans.

The second area is investor relations. Here the objective is to get the public interested in the client's stock and enhance its value over time. This can involve arranging security analyst briefings and issuing bulletins to the media regarding the client's earnings, as well as significant decisions that create interest and followers of the stock.

*Academic consultants* are typically marketing or management science professors who, as research contributors, are considered experts in the field. There are leading academics within services marketing who specialize in such topics as new service development, the service encounter, internal marketing, positioning, and measurement. Academics can be helpful to a service company by identifying current tools and techniques for solving problems. Generally speaking, the cost for academic consultation can be significantly below other alternatives. The client should be aware, however, that such consultants often have an idealistic perspective and may not be as familiar with business organizations as other professional consultants.

## Guidelines for Using Outside Consultants

When is it best to go outside? Obviously, the answer to the question will depend upon specific needs on a case-by-case basis. So to be helpful, we address the need for a practical framework to aid the decision process. Start with listing the What? Why? When? and Where? for the service needed. This exercise will sooner or later lead to the question, How? The answer will require brainstorming to develop a list of all the options.

As a separate step, specify the evaluation factors considered relevant to the decision of performing the service in-house versus using an outside consultant. Use Figure 12-1 as a starting framework. In this figure, we have listed four options for the help you need. Since this matrix will be filled out prior to vendor selection, distinguish between the Ideal Delivery and a Realistic Delivery for both the internal and external consultant.

This matrix should be filled out in the following way: In the early stage of thinking about the proposed work, consider the ideal delivery you would anticipate both from an in-house team and from an outside consultant. You may wish to ignore the possibility that the in-house team members may not be available, or that the consultant you seek may not have the correct package of skills you want. Under these conditions, fill in the matrix columns labeled Option 1 and Option 2 with the pros and cons for each relevant Evaluation Factor. Each of these columns constitutes a profile for the associated option. By informally weighting each of these factors by its Importance, it would be possible to form a conclusion about using internal expertise versus going outside.

Based on this level of thinking, you should be in a position to make a preliminary decision to either go inside or outside. (One might, of course, decide to pursue both options to some extent.) As a result of this decision, you

**Figure 12-1.** Deciding whether to use an outside consultant.

| Evaluation Factors | Importance | Ideal Delivery | | Realistic Delivery | |
|---|---|---|---|---|---|
| | | Option 1 Inside | Option 2 Outside | Option 3 Inside | Option 4 Outside |
| Technical Competence<br>• Knowledge<br>• Problem Solving | | | | | |
| Innovativeness<br>• Originality<br>• Creativity<br>• Ingenuity | | | | | |
| Credibility<br>• Reputation<br>• Candor | | | | | |
| Objectivity | | | | | |
| Confidentiality | | | | | |
| Availability | | | | | |
| Legal Considerations | | | | | |
| Costs<br>• Start-Up<br>• Project | | | | | |

will begin either to gather an in-house team or to initiate the vendor selection process outlined later in this chapter. At some point during each of these selection processes, review Figure 12-1 to fill in the Realistic Delivery columns labeled Option 3 and Option 4. Using the same form as for your Ideal Delivery decision, compare your new knowledge of in-house staff availability and consultant identity to fill in the pros, cons, and cost for the Realistic Delivery columns. The completion of this form should clarify your final thoughts on the in-house versus outside consultant question.

### An Example

A large, diverse corporation intends to apply for a national award that requires the careful completion of an extensive application form. The complex problem of finding, accessing, coordinating, and integrating corporate information into a coherent application to be completed according to a strict schedule could be assigned to an ad hoc in-house project team, or contracted to an outside consultant. In the matrix of Figure 12-2, Option 1 is the creation of a corporate team of six handpicked, highly qualified managers. Option 2 is the use of ABC Consulting Company, which has recent experience in the construction of this kind of document. On the basis of preliminary conversations with the six internal managers and with ABC, the cells of the first two profile columns of the matrix are filled in as in Figure 12-2. Note that not every cell is used, and the importance ratings are informal.

Because both the in-house managers and ABC Consulting do not have enough time to complete such a demanding project, an Option 4 is created, in which the corporation used the DEF Consulting Company, which, although it is highly innovative, has little useful experience in constructing the needed document. Its profile is shown in the right-hand column of Figure 12-2. Option 3, the use of a less highly qualified in-house team, is not seriously considered and its profile column is not completed.

## How to Select an Outside Consultant

If you have made the decision to buy outside expertise, you will not be at a loss in locating firms that market their ability to provide the expertise you need. There is an abundance of independent consultants in existence today. Your challenge, therefore, will be to narrow down the prospects to the individual, agency, or company that can best satisfy your needs.

An objective, thorough, and competitively based selection process is recommended for making the best decision and for providing your internal organization with confidence in your final selection. A particularly effective five-step process to be considered for accomplishing this is provided here.

### Step 1: Identify Potential Suppliers

An appropriate starting point in your selection process would begin with a search for those individuals, agencies, or companies that can provide the expertise you

**Figure 12-2.** One company's use of the matrix to compare options.

| Evaluation Factors | Importance | Ideal Delivery | | Realistic Delivery | |
| --- | --- | --- | --- | --- | --- |
| | | Option 1 Inside | Option 2 Outside | Option 3 Inside | Option 4 Outside |
| Technical Competence • Knowledge • Problem Solving | Medium | Best Technical | Best Knowledge | | Least |
| Innovativeness • Originality • Creativity • Ingenuity | Medium | Good | | | High |
| Credibility • Reputation • Candor | High | | Highest | | |
| Objectivity | Medium | Least | Highest | | Low |
| Confidentiality | High | | Low | | |
| Availability | High | No | No | | Yes |
| Legal Considerations | | | | | |
| Costs • Start-Up • Project | Low | $10K $10K | $20K $50K | | $10K $30K |

need. A realistic objective at this stage would be to generate a list of at least three but no more than ten firms that appear to best meet your requirements.

You can narrow your candidate list immediately if you define your specific needs and/or preferences. For example, you may only want to work with a local consultant who knows your market, or you may prefer to work with a nationally recognized (i.e., top ten) consultant who specializes in your industry. In most cases, you will have a preference for the type of consultant you wish to retain, whether it is based on reputation, industry ranking, location, or area of specialty. The more specific you are in determining these up front, the more time you will save later on.

Many valuable sources may be consulted during your preliminary search process. Those that should be considered include:

- Internal sources/Supplier lists
- Recommendations from other companies/Competitors
- Professional associations (e.g., the American Marketing Association, the Council of American Survey Research)
- Professional directories *(Standard Registry of Agencies)*
- Special publications *(Ad Age* ranking of top 50, *Marketing News)*
- Companies/Advertising agencies

The more experience you have in dealing with outside consultants, the less time you will need to devote to this initial search stage. Even if you are an "old pro," however, don't completely skip this stage, because the number and expertise of consultants change over time.

### Step 2: Prequalify the Best

If your initial search uncovers a fairly lengthy list of potential candidates (more than three would qualify as lengthy in our opinion), a simple screening process can be used to narrow your options to those best qualified for your needs. Aside from being a time-saver, preliminary screening of potential suppliers can help to ensure you are working with the right people from the start. This step is particularly important if you have no firsthand experience with the individuals or firms you are considering.

Surprises can be uncovered and confidence gained fairly quickly by interviewing firms and talking with their clients, past and present, those provided as references and those not. Ask about the firm's capabilities, qualifications, and experience, particularly as they relate to the type of assistance you are seeking. Ask current and previous clients about the firm's track record on projects handled to include their reliability, responsiveness, competence, and delivery of a quality service on time, within budget, and as expected.

Be candid with prospective suppliers during the screening process. Tell them they are one of several firms being interviewed, the most qualified of which will be invited to submit a proposal for the project you have in mind. Be consistent in the questions you ask of each. Know what factors are important to you and judge each accordingly. By the end of this process you should have a good preliminary feel for those you would like to do business with and those who would like to do business with you.

The remaining steps will provide guidance for the final selection process.

## Step 3: Choose a Vendor Selection Panel

No one person will have experience in every aspect of the research task the consultant will have to perform. Gather a team of internal experts from a variety of backgrounds. For consistency, ensure that each member of the team can participate in most of the discussions where the selection criteria are set, and require that the team attend each vendor presentation/interview. Scheduling the presentations/interviews on consecutive days will help increase attendance. It is best to agree on specified question areas that each team member is responsible for during the presentations.

## Step 4: Identify and Weight the Selection Criteria

The vendor selection panel has the responsibility for translating the needs of the company's clients into a set of selection criteria. After meetings or telephone conversations with key internal users of the consultant's output, panel members should convene to decide on the final selection criteria and their relative importances.

After agreement on these criteria (which will generally take at least two rounds of talks), the panel chairman should prepare a form on which the panelists can rate the vendors, using a consistent scale.

Figure 12-3 is an example of such a form. In this case, each of the three vendors was a finalist in bidding on a contract to perform the data collection, analysis, and reporting for a large, preexisting longitudinal survey of telecommunications customers. The Overall Weights for the four main sections of Business and Financial Qualifications, through Cost Competitiveness were agreed on prior to the actual rating. After all the finalists had given daylong presentations of their proposals, the rating blanks were filled in by each panelist using the agreed-on scale 1–5, where "1" was Poor and "5" was Excellent.

Of course, the weights, the rating criteria, and the rating scale will vary depending on the project and the consultant, but the form here covers many standard issues. Use of the ratings can be as quantitative as desired, depending on the project and the selection panel. One selection process might carefully average ratings within panelists and section categories, weighting them by the importance weights, whereas another selection process might just use the ratings and weights as informal guides.

## Step 5: The Final Selection Process

From the previous four steps, the vendor selection panel will have made a recommendation to the appropriate internal decision makers. (For some small projects, the panel and the decision makers may be the same people.) By making the panel deliberations apparent through the form shown in Figure 12-3 (or

*(Text continues on page 216.)*

**Figure 12-3.** Vendor rating form with selection criteria.

Evaluator:_____

I. Business and Financial Qualifications     Overall Weight_____%

|  | Vendor A | Vendor B | Vendor C |
|---|---|---|---|
| **A. Financial Stability** | | | |
| 1. Years in business | ____ | ____ | ____ |
| 2. Industry ranking | ____ | ____ | ____ |
| 3. Profitability | ____ | ____ | ____ |
| 4. Growth | ____ | ____ | ____ |
| 5. Client dependence* | ____ | ____ | ____ |
| **B. Full-Service Capabilities** | | | |
| 1. Experience | ____ | ____ | ____ |
| 2. Operations capacity | ____ | ____ | ____ |
| 3. Staff qualifications | ____ | ____ | ____ |
| 4. Use of technology | ____ | ____ | ____ |
| 5. Flexibility | ____ | ____ | ____ |

II. Technical Competence/Appropriateness     Overall Weight_____%

|  | Vendor A | Vendor B | Vendor C |
|---|---|---|---|
| **A. Program Management Plan** | | | |
| 1. Staff qualifications | ____ | ____ | ____ |
| 2. Number/dedication of professional staff | ____ | ____ | ____ |
| 3. Location of staff | ____ | ____ | ____ |
| 4. Understanding of client program needs | ____ | ____ | ____ |
| 5. Ability to work with multiple entities | ____ | ____ | ____ |
| 6. Ability to respond to special requests | ____ | ____ | ____ |

* Client dependence refers to the extent that a vendor's financial viability seems to depend upon continued business with a small number of clients who generate a large part of its revenue.

*(continues)*

**Figure 12-3,** con't.

|  | Vendor A | Vendor B | Vendor C |
|---|---|---|---|
| **B. Research Design Plan** | | | |
| 1. Understanding of technical issues | ___ | ___ | ___ |
| 2. Research enhancement plans | ___ | ___ | ___ |
| **C. Data Collection Plan** | | | |
| 1. Understanding of requirements | ___ | ___ | ___ |
| 2. Sample management plan | ___ | ___ | ___ |
| 3. Plan for complete use of sample | ___ | ___ | ___ |
| 4. Staff assignments | ___ | ___ | ___ |
| 5. Facility location | ___ | ___ | ___ |
| 6. Facility capacity | ___ | ___ | ___ |
| **D. Data Processing/Reporting Plan** | | | |
| 1. Understanding of requirements | ___ | ___ | ___ |
| 2. Turnaround time | ___ | ___ | ___ |
| 3. Report content | ___ | ___ | ___ |
| 4. Report format | ___ | ___ | ___ |
| **E. Data Analysis Plan** | | | |
| 1. Understanding of requirements | ___ | ___ | ___ |
| 2. Staff background | ___ | ___ | ___ |
| 3. Appropriateness | ___ | ___ | ___ |
| **F. Implementation Plan** | | | |
| 1. Maintaining administrative consistency | ___ | ___ | ___ |
| 2. Maintaining methodological consistency | ___ | ___ | ___ |
| 3. Schedule of required events | ___ | ___ | ___ |
| 4. Start-up time needed | ___ | ___ | ___ |

III. Quality Commitment           Overall Weight_____%

| | Vendor A | Vendor B | Vendor C |
|---|---|---|---|
| A. Quality of Data Collection | | | |
|   1. Interviewer selection and training | ___ | ___ | ___ |
|   2. Interviewer procedures and controls | ___ | ___ | ___ |
|   3. Interviewer monitoring and standards | ___ | ___ | ___ |
|   4. Interviewer rewards and compensation | ___ | ___ | ___ |
| B. Quality of Data Processing | | | |
|   1. Commitment to accuracy | ___ | ___ | ___ |
|   2. Commitment to timeliness | ___ | ___ | ___ |
|   3. Cleaning/editing | ___ | ___ | ___ |
| C. Experience/Expertise | | | |
|   1. Large, longitudinal tracking programs | ___ | ___ | ___ |
|   2. Customer satisfaction measurement | ___ | ___ | ___ |
|   3. Telecommunications research | ___ | ___ | ___ |
| D. Added Value | | | |
|   1. Interpretation of results | ___ | ___ | ___ |
|   2. Suggestions for service improvements | ___ | ___ | ___ |
| E. Protection of Proprietary Information | ___ | ___ | ___ |

IV. Cost Competitiveness           Overall Weight_____%

| | Vendor A | Vendor B | Vendor C |
|---|---|---|---|
| A. Start-Up Costs | ___ | ___ | ___ |
| B. Ongoing Costs | | | |
|   1. Per specifications | ___ | ___ | ___ |
|   2. Other | ___ | ___ | ___ |

perhaps a summarized version), the decision makers will be able to make an informed selection.

Whatever the final selection, it is important to communicate the decision quickly to all the consultants who were finalists. Clearly stating why the runners-up lost might make them better prepared and more sensitive to your needs. Some of these firms may have inspired enough confidence to warrant future consideration for a smaller project. They should be so informed.

## How to Get the Results You Want

Obtaining the results you want is dependent upon:

1. Knowing the objective(s) for obtaining the service and specifically what you want from the consultant to begin with
2. Communicating this in documented terms to the consultant
3. Translating your needs and expectations into quantifiable measurements with specified performance levels
4. Negotiating agreement on the specified performance levels, to include possible rewards for performance beyond these levels and penalties for performance below them
5. Designation of the key people on both sides who will be the communication "points of contact"; include a process to identify those who would address and resolve issues, review and sign off on deliverables
6. Joint scheduling of "checkpoint" status meetings and/or calls to monitor progress and prevent the missing of objective(s)
7. Evaluating the consultant's performance, and deciding the future course of the relationship

The preceding process has been simplified to the essence of what it takes to get what you expect and need. Some would say that it all comes down to three critical things: communication, communication, and communication.

## How to Develop a Results-Oriented Plan

"If you don't know where you're going, no road will get you there." If a plan isn't developed and well thought out to get the desired results, you probably will not achieve them. Since we have covered the main points of the client-consultant relationship in discussing the selection process and its antecedents, and because selection of the proper consultant is itself a major part of getting the results the client wants, the rest of this section sketches a series of general outstanding points.

As a starting step, the company as a client must specify the objective(s) and document its needs and expectations into some sort of *requirements document*. This need not be too detailed: The key is to reach mutual understanding. Care must be taken to ensure that both the consultant and the client have the same understanding of the words of this document. Language can be a barrier. Esoteric industry terms and acronyms contribute to confusion and thus should be avoided. When it comes to designing the plan and the designated points of contact for communication, only the most skilled and effective people should be handpicked. This is an absolutely essential step.

Thus, it is suggested that the consultant be required to have a plan that addresses the key processes, including steps 3 through 7. Some of the general foundations of these steps warrant further discussion. First, the document must acknowledge that the consultant works to reach the goals set by the client, and not vice versa. There can be no confusion about this.

Second, the plan should clearly define the roles and responsibilities of the specific people on both sides of the consultant-client relationship. This will provide the structure by which interaction can prove effective. A few general responsibilities of both the consultant and the client deserve special attention.

## Responsibilities of the Consultant

Simply, these responsibilities are to translate customer needs and expectations to internal specifications, and to deliver what's needed and expected on time and within budget. This simplistic formula has two salient points. First, the consultant must not promise to deliver more than is possible for his organization or for the current state of the art. When legitimately unforeseeable obstacles arise, though, he must promptly notify the client and negotiate a solution.

In addition, the consultant must designate a principal contact person who commits to using the designated command chain in the client organization. From the client's viewpoint, it is a "sin" to circumvent the agreed-upon client contact by escalating discussion above the level at which the client's principal contact thinks that they should be addressed.

## Responsibilities of the Client

The customer of the consultant's services must conform to certain guidelines. At each point in the consultant selection process, he must describe the project objectives and any restrictions or special problems as clearly as possible. It is important to do this more than once, because the selection process often changes goals or uncovers pitfalls. Whenever the client's needs require a change in the project, this must be promptly and clearly communicated to the consultant. In that case, the client should ensure that the consultant clearly understands which study changes can be made unilaterally, and which require negotiation with the client.

In particular, the client is responsible for furnishing an organization chart of those individuals who may be involved with the project. A principal contact person should be designated, and any protocol in discussing issues or resolving problems should be clearly communicated to the consultant.

Many studies require the client to furnish information, data, procedures manuals, or other documents. Delivery must be timely, of course, particularly when these are prerequisites to consultant's work. Such delivery delays can manufacture an excuse for a study's lateness! Finally, prompt payment for services rendered is a legitimate expectation of the consultant.

If all these steps—largely planning considerations—are addressed at the onset of a project, needs will likely be met and there will be no surprises.

## Evaluating the Consultant's Performance

Conducting an evaluation of the consulting firm's performance will provide managers with useful information. The information can be used to:

1. Determine the overall effectiveness of the firm in meeting (a) the objectives of the project and (b) the needs of the client.
2. Provide documentation for future reference to managers in the client organization regarding the capabilities of the consulting firm.
3. Provide a summary of performance that can be the basis of a discussion with the consulting firm to facilitate feedback to it about its performance. (*Note:* Some firms have self-evaluation vehicles in place to obtain feedback from their clients. The client, however, needs to conduct and maintain an evaluation for internal uses as well.)

Figure 12-4 is provided as a guide to assist the practitioner in developing a format to standardize evaluations. This particular questionnaire was designed for use with market research firms; the items to be evaluated will vary with the type of consulting being evaluated. Although the first seven questions of this form are applicable only to consulting projects requiring extensive data collection, analysis, and reporting, questions 8–18 should be applicable to most contracted research projects. It is suggested that the person responsible for the project within the company complete the evaluation, together with input from at least two of their internal clients benefitting from the service.

## Nurturing Long-Term Consultant Relationships

In many cases, there will be only a short-term relationship with a consulting agency. The consultant is hired for a specified project, and his services end at its termination. Many long-term or repeated needs will be met by an in-house organization because of that organization's familiarity with the company's evolving structure. Some projects, however, may require an outsider's independence and objectivity, whereas others may endure and evolve more efficiently through the use of a single consultant. Also, a consultant's expertise and personal relationships may grow over time and result in repeat business with the client. For these and other reasons, some client-consultant relationships may last beyond the framework of a single study.

There are benefits and disadvantages to such long-term relationships. Consultants may become complacent and inflexible in their plans. Their practices may become entrenched, and time previously spent in enhancing the quality of

*(Text continues on page 222.)*

**Figure 12-4.** Consultant evaluation form.

Consulting Firm _____

Project Manager _____

Date of Project     Start: _____ Finish: _____

Objectives of Project _____

_____

_____

_____

_____

_____

_____

_____

_____

_____

_____

_____

Tasks Assigned to Consultant _____

_____

_____

_____

_____

_____

_____

_____

_____

_____

_____

_____

_____

_____

_____

_____

*(continues)*

**Figure 12-4,** con't.

### Ratings of Consultant

Rate the consultant on each item by using the scale A, B, C, D, F, or N/A, where A = Excellent, B = Good, C = Average, D = Below Average, F = Poor, and N/A = Not Applicable, and writing comments in the space provided. (Comments are particularly helpful if the ratings are either "D" or "F.") Note that the last three questions require a yes or no response.

1. Quality/quantity of contributions and suggestions made by the consultant at the beginning of the project to clarify the problem statement, objectives, or methodology:

   Rating: _____ Comments: _____
   _____

2. Quality of secondary research effort carried out by the consultant:

   Rating: _____ Comments: _____
   _____

3. Quality of qualitative research (focus groups, interviews) conducted by the consultant:

   Rating: _____ Comments: _____
   _____

4. Ability of the consultant to design effective quantitative survey instruments:

   Rating: _____ Comments: _____
   _____

5. Quality of the consultant's field survey work and procedures:

   Rating: _____ Comments: _____
   _____

6. Quality of data editing and coding:

   Rating: _____ Comments: _____
   _____

7. Data analysis capability of the consultant (list analytical techniques used in the space for comments):

   Rating: _____ Comments: _____
   _____

8. Quality, quantity, and creativity of effort exhibited by the consultant in thinking through the data collected and analyzed in order to derive "marketing insight" (please provide comments on this item):

Rating: _____ Comments: _____

_____

9. Acceptability of recommendations made by the consultant:

   Rating: _____ Comments: _____

   _____

10. Clarity and quality of written reports:

    Rating: _____ Comments: _____

    _____

11. Quality of oral presentation of results:

    Rating: _____ Comments: _____

    _____

12. Ability of the consultant to adhere to the project plan and schedule:

    Rating: _____ Comments: _____

    _____

13. Flexibility of the consultant in dealing with any midterm changes to the project:

    Rating: _____ Comments: _____

    _____

14. Ability of the consultant to adhere to cost estimate:

    Rating: _____ Comments: _____

    _____

15. Quality of work by any subcontractors used by the consultant (list subcontractors in the general comments section below):

    Rating: _____ Comments: _____

    _____

16. The value received from the consultant (relationship of quality/quantity of output to fee paid to the consultant):

    Rating: _____ Comments: _____

    _____

17. Overall rating of the consultant as a market research supplier:

    Rating: _____ Comments: _____

    _____

*(continues)*

**Figure 12-4,** con't.

18. Overall rating of the project manager assigned by the consulting firm to this project:

    Rating: _____ Comments: _____

    _____

19. Would you use this consultant again for a similar assignment?

    Yes _____ No _____ Comments: _____

    _____

20. Would you use this consultant again for a less complex assignment?

    Yes _____ No _____ Comments: _____

    _____

21. Would you use this consultant again for a more complex assignment?

    Yes _____ No _____ Comments: _____

    _____

    General comments (also include comments on any items not listed earlier, as well as comments describing the consultant's particular areas of expertise, such as data communications or field survey work)

    _____

    _____

    _____

their work gets spent in defending their intellectual turf. Consistency takes precedence over appropriateness, and the work may fail to evolve with the client company or with the technical state of the art. These problems are especially likely to occur when the client's contact people are inexperienced in consultant selection or state-of-the-art research techniques and findings.

Conversely, the eased financial pressure of a long-term bond works to both side's advantage. Without the nonreimbursable costs of proposal writing, the consultant is freed to spend time on the relatively invisible aspects of good service (such as interviewer training or survey design in market research), and the client has leverage to demand process improvements, such as automated interviewing systems. Then, the consultant can take time to learn enough about the client to ensure the usefulness of his or her recommendations.

In sum, the benefits of long-term relations can outweigh the disadvantages if a few common-sense rules are followed by the client company:

1. Take time to gain some familiarity with several consultants before committing to an ongoing relationship.

2. Carefully select a long-term consultant; involve a spectrum of company experts in the selection process.
3. Agree on a detailed service plan in advance; this should spell out communication processes and procedures for dealing with evolving technical service strategies and changing personnel.
4. Require the same regular communication with the long-term consultant as you require with other suppliers.
5. Regularly review the consultant's practices, perhaps with an external academic evaluator, to ensure the currency of the methods being used.
6. Evaluate the consultant's performance regularly, even though there may be no postproject time at which this is appropriate to do. Remember that the consultant's adherence to the negotiated budget is a part of this performance.
7. Establish and maintain relations with other consultants with other projects, if possible.
8. Competitively bid the long-term contract periodically, and require the consultant to rebid.

Adhering to these guidelines helps ensure that the comfort of ongoing personal and professional relationships will not stagnate into presumed advantages and mediocre research.

## Summary

Choosing a consultant is an important process, but it can be tricky and frustrating without proper guidelines. Both small and large companies rely heavily on consultants: Advertising and market research agencies are often part of one's daily life, while management, public relations, and academic consultants play a large role in setting companywide standards and objectives. It is thus vital to choose carefully and systematically the consultants with whom so much of company operations and policy is implicitly entrusted.

Some projects are best performed by in-house staff, whereas others should be contracted to outside vendors. The choice between the two is dominated by questions of the need for independence, objectivity, and credibility, occasionally by specialized technical competence and, of course, by cost. These and other issues must be addressed in the abstract, before serious vendor selection, and in reality, when specific vendors are compared to specific in-house experts.

Selecting an outside consultant should be a careful, systematic, multistep task, involving several levels and types of internal staff. At each step of the selection process, immeasurable pain can be avoided by continually refining your notion of what the project is and what kind of consultant can best complete it. After the first level of such thought, three to ten possible suppliers should appear on a preliminary list. These should be prequalified through informal conversations and references. The three (or more) finalists should be interviewed after an internal panel sets up a selection criteria list that is applied consistently to the candidates. This careful planning makes the panel's recommendation easy to translate to top management, and helps all the finalists by clarifying the client's expectations.

Consultants are like other humans: They require periodic feedback to perform effectively. Regular evaluations are a good way to provide that significant feedback and to identify problem areas. They can also be useful in guiding the company's future use of a particular consulting firm.

Such intensive nurturing, following the painstaking selection of the most appropriate consultant, is the key to properly managing the client-consultant relationship. When it is done well, the high quality of the consultant's work and its value to the company will repay the selection and management process manyfold.

*    *    *    *

***Michael J. English*** *is director of quality positioning in the operations section of GTE Telephone Operations in Dallas, Texas. He has held a variety of positions within GTE Telephone Operations during the past seventeen years, the most recent of which was director of quality measurement and assessment.*

***Susan S. Prince*** *serves as manager of design and methodology in the operations section of GTE Telephone Operations. During her twenty-year career at GTE, she has held positions of increasing responsibility in service operations and human resources.*

***Michelle A. Yakovac*** *is manager of quality positioning at GTE Telephone Operations. She is responsible for developing and administering the methods, procedures, and systems for measuring the quality of services provided by GTE to both its external and internal customers. Prior to this, Ms. Yakovac was affiliated with Walker Research.*

***James H. Drew,*** *Ph.D., is a principal member of the technical staff in the Network Architecture and Services Laboratory of GTE Laboratories in Waltham, Massachusetts. Dr. Drew's research interests have focused mainly on survey design and market research.*

# 13

# Measuring the Effectiveness of Services Marketing

Thomas J. Fitzgerald

The premise for this chapter, based on more than twenty years' experience at ARA Services, is simply that *services marketing is different from product marketing*.

Although the marketing functions are similar, there is a significant difference in how they're organized and implemented. Therefore, evaluation of the effectiveness of marketing in a services business has to be different from the established approaches for a product business.

In this chapter, we'll review our experience, sharing what we believe is generally applicable to a broad range of other service businesses. We'll give you some specific guidelines for measuring the effectiveness of services marketing that should be applicable in your own services organization.

## ARA Background

ARA Services is the largest employee-owned diversified service management company in the United States. In 1989 it recorded revenues in excess of $4 billion. Established in 1959 as a food and vending services company, it expanded to cover health and education, textile rental, periodical distribution, and maintenance services. The ARA work force of 125,000 employees provides services to 10 million people daily at more than 400,000 locations.

From the very outset, it was clear in terms of strategic marketing that the company was in the service business even though initially it was in only one small segment of it. It was also clear that if the company were to grow, it would have to broaden its service offerings and move into other carefully selected areas that met some very basic criteria. ARA's initial success was based on the fact that it developed a system for providing a direct service to business and to the people working for those businesses. The demand was constant. The service provided could not be postponed or inventoried. And the need for such services would grow.

This philosophy led quickly to some basic conclusions about ARA's service business—the expertise was transferable. Procedures and systems that proved to be effective in one business often could be used in another. Each business, however, no matter how large or small, represents a unique challenge. No two are identical. Each demands specialized solutions. Each provides a unique service. (See Table 13-1.)

**Table 13-1.** ARA matrix of services.

| Major Business Segments | Primary Service | The Client* | The Customer† |
|---|---|---|---|
| Business dining | Employee food service | Major employers—Human resources/plant management | Employees |
| Campus dining | Student dining service | Deans and business managers of colleges and universities | Students, faculty |
| Health care nutrition | Patient/staff food service | Administrators of hospitals and retirement facilities | Patients, staff |
| School nutrition | Student food service | Superintendents/school boards of elementary and/or secondary school districts | Students, faculty |
| Vending | Food/beverage service | Human resources and facility managers of large employers | Employees, staff, visitors, students |
| ARA/CORY refreshment | Beverage/snack service | Office management/ employee groups in smaller companies | Employees, staff, visitors, students |
| Leisure | Food, gifts, souvenirs, concessions | Major sports or recreational facility management | Sports fans |
| Convention centers | Banquet, catering, and specialty services | Large convention center management | Convention attendees |
| Magazine and book distribution | Wholesale distribution of periodicals | Supermarkets, drugstores, newsstands, convenience stores | Reading public |
| Aratex | Uniform and dust-control rental | All kinds of businesses, large and small | Employees |
| Environmental services | Housekeeping and maintenance services | Educational, health care, and corporate facility managers | Facility and its occupants |
| Living Centers | Management of long-term care facilities | Families | Elderly or disabled people |
| Spectrum emergency care | Staffing and management for emergency departments | Hospital medical staff | Patients |
| Children's World | Educational child care | Families | Children |

*The *client* signs and administers our contract.
†The *customer* is the consumer of the service. In the contract services business both clients and customers must be satisfied for complete success. The challenge is that their objectives are often different. For example, in food service we must satisfy the client (such as the hospital administrator, college business manager, or corporate human resources director), whose objective might be good food without a cash subsidy by the organization. The customer's objective might also be good food but at a price requiring a subsidy by the organization.

# Key Issues Affecting Services Marketing Effectiveness

Over the years as we tried to apply basic marketing principles to our businesses, it became clear that product concepts reported in the literature were not relevant. It has been only in the last few years, thanks to a handful of scholars and practitioners, and the American Marketing Association's Services Marketing Division, that the subject has received proper attention.

In the services business, the traditional marketing functions—planning, research, development, pricing, selling, merchandising, advertising, and customer relations—cannot be relegated to a separate marketing department. At ARA's business unit levels, many of these functions are the responsibilities of operations.

Services marketing's main distinction is that production occurs at the point of sale. One must distinguish between the marketing *department* and the marketing *function*. Len Berry got to the heart of this distinction when he wrote, "The most effective staff marketing departments in services enterprises are not those that are exceptionally clever in practicing marketing; rather, they are those that are exceptionally clever in getting everyone else in the organization to practice marketing." [1] At ARA we have, during recent years, referred to this concept as "Everybody sells." We use this theme to emphasize the point that, in a service business, everyone is responsible for the client/customer, no matter what the job title.

Although this theme might be applicable in a product business, it's essential in a service business. In a product business, many marketing functions can be carried out by a separate marketing department but in a service business most of the traditional marketing functions (pricing, selling, merchandising, customer relations) are the responsibility of "operations." "Operations" are those people who are responsible for the day-to-day creation and delivery of the service—people who don't have sales or marketing titles.

Using ARA food service business as an example, operations people include the regional VP, the district manager who supervises a number of food service accounts, and, most important, the food service director (whom we call the "front-line manager") we have in residence at each account.

We can see the major differences between product marketing and services marketing more clearly by comparing four key areas where operations people perform marketing functions:

## The Focus—Service Delivery vs. Product Manufacturing

In the product business, manufacturing is clearly a key process. A pharmaceutical firm manufacturing drugs for use in a hospital focuses its resources on product quality control in that key process. Contrast that with the management and staffing of a hospital emergency room where the doctor and the patient participate together in the service delivery function. The considerations for evaluating effectiveness are obviously quite different.

### Channels of Distribution—Many vs. None

In a product business many channels of distribution are often available with many middlemen involved—wholesalers, retailers, brokers, agents, jobbers, distributors. In a service business there are usually no channels! For example, the teacher at a child-care center is manufacturing the "product" and delivering a service at the same time in a direct personal relationship with the children. Contrast evaluating that "channel of distribution" with that of a textbook publisher.

### Objective vs. Subjective Measures of Satisfaction

In a product business, fairly objective measures can be developed and applied. It's possible to use well-defined specifications checking all the tangibles, such as size and weight. Contrast this with measuring the service in a nursing home when the family's specification is very subjective "good care for my mother." Think about the implications for evaluating marketing effectiveness with that specification.

### Restricted vs. Complete Flexibility—Effect on Feedback

In manufacturing products, businesses require a long period of time to move from the first blueprint to the final production run. They are also generally restricted in making changes by significant investments in expensive tooling. Therefore, it may take months, even years, for marketing managers to gauge their effectiveness.

In a service business the feedback is, by contrast, almost instantaneous. In building maintenance and housekeeping, a manager can alter his service delivery process to meet the changing needs of the client/customer often in one day—from the planning step to the customer feedback step. If one area needs special cleaning, or additional labor, it's relatively easy to modify the necessary work schedules and review the results of that service the next day. This area of timing and flexibility is important in evaluating service marketing effectiveness, because "responsiveness" is such an important attribute of the successful service provider.

Recognizing these significant differences and working within this kind of environment, we need to agree on a definition for marketing and a responsibility for the functions before we can establish measures for effectiveness.

### Definition of Marketing

The definition with which I'm most comfortable I call the *3 D's:*

1. *Discipline of analyzing client/customer needs.* Understanding the needs of the clients and customers is obviously the first part of the definition—and there should be a discipline to it to help sort out and prioritize all that is involved in this critical step.
2. *Design of services/systems to meet the client/customer needs profitably.* Once we think we know what the client/customer needs (or wants) we

can design the appropriate response. Using food service as an example, this response could range all the way from a simple change in service (adding another cashier to reduce waiting time) to designing an entirely new system (converting from a cafeteria line to self-service).

3. *Development of selling methods to activate demand.* Finally, when the first two steps are in place, we need to tell people that we do have what they're looking for.

## Current Responsibility

As stated earlier, many of the traditional marketing responsibilities in a services business belong to operations. A marketing-specialist function, however, can facilitate the process of ensuring the organization is responsive to its markets.

The role of the marketing specialist is determined by those particular factors that drive each business. In some cases a complete change in culture may be required—from a "production" orientation to one of "service." In other cases it may be fostering a "marketing mentality" so that marketing is understood not as a function but as a philosophy that requires sharper focus on the customer. In all cases, however, this effort has to be fully integrated into operations both strategically and tactically.

At least three things can be done to help accomplish this integration:

Don't Have a "Marketing Plan." Just using the term *marketing* often provides the opportunity to divide the organization rather than unify it, primarily because so many people (or departments) say, "That's not my job."

It's much better to have a total business plan that integrates marketing, financial, human resources, and operations plans in one document. The plan should include objectives that can be measured *and* tracked. The tracking system should be in place at the start of the planning cycle so that corrective action can be taken when needed.

Don't Have a Large Marketing Department. In a services business there is no need for one! (This will raise the eyebrows of some people with a product marketing background.) Like the Marines, you do need a few good people— people who understand the organizational culture and who will help keep the business believing that the customer comes first! These specialists, regardless of where you place them in your organization, should serve as catalysts between the field and headquarters functions, assisting in the development of new services and improving present ones.

Based on the premise that every market is changing every day (along with competitive situations in these markets), these specialists should be "advocates of change" to help achieve the business plan objectives. Christian Grönroos visualized the relationship of the marketing function and department size quite well, as shown in Figure 13-1.

In recognizing this important distinction, it became clear that successfully marketing a service requires not just the implementation of a set of business functions. It also demands a state of mind—that a *"marketing mentality" be*

**Figure 13-1.** The relationship between the marketing function and the marketing department.

Marketing Function for Goods          Marketing Function for Services

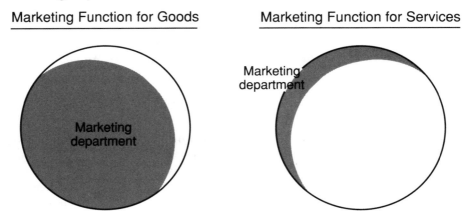

*Source:* Reprinted with permission from Christian Grönroos, "Designing a Long-Range Marketing Strategy for Services," *Long-Range Planning* 13 (April 1980), copyright 1980, Pergamon Journals Ltd.

*created in those who are, at the same time, creating and delivering the service.* A marketing point of view is required that asks everyone to think first of the service user and only then of the service provider.

Don't Have "Market Share Mania." Any business certainly needs to know where it stands in the marketplace relative to its competitors. In services, however, market share leadership doesn't drive sales and profits. Services don't fight for shelf space or for the attention of distributors. Services don't rely on market share dominance to establish pricing and margin leadership. Services are driven by service reputation and segmentation.

For example, in ARA's dining service group we don't solicit every business or hospital or college (similar, I'm sure, to accounting firms, legal practices, and advertising agencies). We are after those prospects who are genuinely interested in, and willing to pay for, quality service. Because we're really in the people business with our "product" being our "front-line manager," we need to be selective about where we place our people to satisfy both the client's needs and our own.

## The Critical Role of the "Front-Line Manager"

The special nature of the service product makes the human resources issue especially critical to quality in services. Because services are produced and consumed simultaneously, it's nearly impossible to prescreen and pull a substandard "product" before it reaches the customer. Our product *is* the service process itself. Therefore, quality control has become an integral part of the process based on three principles:

1. Every worker must know his or her job completely.
2. People can, and will, accept responsibility for managing their own work if that responsibility is given to them in the proper way.
3. Intelligence and creativity exist at all levels of the organization—particularly at the field or unit level, which we at ARA call the "front-line" (not as an adversarial term but simply to emphasize that's where the real action is).

The performance of employees in delivering quality service depends largely on the caliber of their unit manager and supervisors. Because of the geographical dispersion of more than 3,000 profit centers at ARA, we give a lot of autonomy to our managers. Tip O'Neill, the famous politician, once said, "All politics is local"; the same can be said for the service business: "All service is local." Therefore, we look for managers who are able to meet the challenge of running their own business and tailoring it to the needs of their clients and customers. It's right at this "front-line" where local managers must have a marketing orientation, not just control and production orientations.

## Measuring Effectiveness—Emphasize Retention

In a service business, both new-business development and client retention are needed, but retaining clients is more important. Losing a client means not only losing revenue, but also developing, possibly, a reputation for inferior service. Present clients are the lifeblood of the business. New business is a transfusion. Ted Levitt reminds us that in services ". . . the customer doesn't know what he's getting until he doesn't."[2] When that happens, the customer becomes susceptible to the appeals of the competition.

### Techniques for Protecting Your Business and Finding Out "How You're Doin' "

Here are two techniques that will promote client retention:

1. *Make sure you have a counterpart or "zipper" relationship in place.* In our contract services businesses (and others that I have observed, for example, law firms and advertising agencies) there is seldom just one buyer of the service, or more important, just one person who must be satisfied to retain the business. In business service situations there is usually the direct liaison and at least two levels above plus one or more staff functions, such as finance or human resources, which may play a role.

We have found it effective to make specific assignments from our appropriate levels so that each "counterpart" person is covered, for example, our manager to their manager, and our VP to their VP. This is also referred to as the "zipper" process with the various counterparts in touch with one another like a zipper to maintain a constructive working relationship.

2. *Don't let "students" mark their own papers.* We rely on the organization to deliver quality and listen to our employees tell us how well they're doing. Like many other companies, however, we also use a variety of tech-

niques to check on the quality of our services. These include mystery shoppers, independent quality assurance teams, client/customer interviews, and focus groups. The results are used primarily to give the front-line manager an objective view on how he or she is doing. Through these objective evaluations we've been able to quantify quality. Over the years as each of our businesses surveys its clients, we have been able to better define our clients' expectations. We ask them to tell us how we're doing on a point scale for the services we provide. We now know where we rank compared to last year and compared to other locations providing similar services. This process also helps us determine where we need to improve and by how much. This whole process compensates for the normal human response to filter out negative feedback from clients and customers. More important, it enables our managers to respond more quickly to potential problems.

### The Key Element in Measuring Services Marketing Effectiveness— "It's How You Do Things, Not What You Do"

There's been a great deal written about the *work* ethic. In our business we call it the *service* ethic. The attitude of the people providing the service is crucial to the perception of value received. At ARA we've trademarked an internal program we call the ''Spirit of Service'' to help develop our employees' care and concern in the delivery of service—focusing primarily on the end-user of the service. One excellent case in point regarding that philosophy is what we do at ARA Living Centers—240 facilities located in thirteen states and licensed for 26,000 beds.

When ARA Living Centers wanted to know the factors important to quality of life in its facilities, we asked the people who know best—our residents. In combination with specially designed resident focus groups, ARA set out in June 1986 to examine quality of life ''close up,'' from the residents' point of view.

Five focus groups were conducted in different locations across the country, with participants representing residents in twenty-four ARA facilities. A total of fifty residents participated in the five groups, which ranged in size from nine to eleven persons.

### Resident/Staff Relationships

When asked how facility staff should treat them, residents said that the ideal staff member greets them by name and uses pet nicknames; initiates conversations; gives love and hugs; and anticipates needs, offering assistance. An ideal staff member expresses interest in residents and listens, pats them on the shoulder, straightens their collar, and combs their hair. He or she helps put on sweaters, treats residents with respect, acts fairly, and listens to both sides of resident disputes.

Asked how they could tell if a nursing assistant was well trained, residents listed staff attitude, knowledge of care techniques, and willingness to take the initiative in anticipating resident needs. Residents dislike staff members who raise their voices when irritated, lecture forgetful residents, gossip about residents' medical conditions, and are too busy with paperwork to talk with residents. They also disapprove of the staff member who bumps residents without saying, "Excuse me," when pushing them in a wheelchair.

Residents want staff to tell them in advance when activities such as physician visits or baths are scheduled, so they can plan for them. When questioned regarding respect for their privacy, residents reported more privacy infringements from other residents than from staff members. They are particularly sensitive to privacy issues during bathing and prefer help from same-sex attendants. Residents also want privacy in bathing areas.

## Putting Quality to Work

Residents and their needs as expressed in the five focus groups are the goals of ARA Living Centers' Quality Assurance Program. As the quality assurance director says, "Our new quality assurance manual has a resident and client focus instead of a paperwork compliance approach."

Comments from the resident focus groups were used by ARA Living Centers' quality assurance staff in writing a new manual of policies and procedures that emphasizes resident outcomes, staff process, and quality-of-life issues. When ARA's quality assurance staff visit facilities, they review residents' health, appearance, and attitude—the outcome of quality care—as an indication of how well a facility operates.

Through these modules, ARA Living Centers' quality assurance manual outlines more than 500 criteria to be evaluated during each facility visit. The quality assurance review procedure includes: evaluation of residents to determine the outcome of facility care; evaluation of all areas of operation such as physical plant and environment, nursing, dietary, activities, social services, and documentation; administrative self-assessment review; and review of previous state/federal surveys. Results of these quality assurance reviews are then used to improve problem areas and maintain ARA Living Centers' high standards of quality care.

## Take Time to Care

ARA has also implemented a company-wide in-service program designed to sensitize employees to residents' needs. The Take Time to Care (TTTC) program teaches employee skills in caregiving, problem solving for residents and families, understanding residents' feelings, touching positively, and expressing friendliness and concern. Employees also learn effective teamwork, self-care, and positive recognition. The administrator of each Living Center has been trained to teach TTTC to his or her facility staff members, and the five-part program is taught in one-hour sessions.

Many positive developments have resulted from TTTC: increase in morale and service; decrease in employee turnover; improvement in census through new admissions and retention; improvement in employee self-esteem; and increase in positive feedback from health departments and communities. There have also been greater team efforts by staff members and improvement in resident care, as noted by residents and families.

# Guidelines for Evaluating Effectiveness

With these differences between product and services marketing, what should you look for? Certainly I would review the basics. The dictionary generally defines effectiveness as "producing a desired result." The conventional business wisdom takes the dictionary approach a little further by asking you to do the following basic steps during the business planning process (see also Chapters 4 and 10):

1. Establish measurable objectives.
2. Assign responsibilities.
3. Set timetables.
4. Agree on budget.

Kotler suggests that you look at five key classifications and rate your own marketing effectiveness on (1) customer philosophy, (2) integrated marketing organization, (3) adequate marketing information, (4) strategic orientation, and (5) operational efficiency.[3]

In addition to these basics, I suggest you evaluate your performance in three important areas:

## Client/Customer Satisfaction

Although one says "the customer comes first," what evidence do you have that your people actually believe it? If your organization says "customer satisfaction drives our business," then I hope you're measuring it. Most service organizations simply don't measure what the customer thinks of their service. I think we learned a long time ago you can't rely on just the cash register ringing to tell you how well you're doing. When it stops ringing, it's usually too late to find out why.

## Focus on the Front-Line Manager

The front-line (or first-level) managers are very important in the success of a service business. To deliver your services effectively, they must be given the proper responsibility for managing your services—responsibility for personnel, operations, purchasing, finance, and marketing.

Several important questions to ask are: To what degree is decision making decentralized? What kind of tools do you provide to your local managers to hold and expand the business? How much recognition/reward do you give them?

## The Role of Your Marketing Specialists

As much as we have emphasized that marketing is everyone's job in a services business, we have found it effective to employ marketing specialists whose main mission is to make sure we stay tuned into the market. They facilitate the process we defined as marketing earlier in this chapter. They recognize they can't completely control all the marketing functions as they would in a product business. They use their interpersonal and persuasive skills to act as "advocates of change" within the organization. Most important, they build their own credibility and gain the respect of those who must approve their recommendations as well as those who must carry them out.

## Other Issues in Effectiveness

On a more tactical level, your specific marketing program needs to be evaluated according to what I call "the M's approach to services marketing effectiveness":

| | |
|---|---|
| Merchandise | What are the benefits of our service? |
| Market | Who are we trying to reach? |
| Motives | Why do they buy? |
| Message | What key ideas must be communicated? |
| Media | Which methods are most effective? |
| Money | What budget is required? |
| Measure | What results do we expect? |

These seemingly simple but really quite robust questions need to be addressed on an ongoing basis. You can count on the fact that your markets are dynamic and so continuous evaluation of effectiveness is needed.

In closing, here are seven danger signals of services marketing inefficiency so that you can benefit from our hard-earned wisdom at ARA:

1. Expecting a separate marketing department to be responsible for all the traditional marketing functions in a services business
2. Hearing your operations people say that they are not marketing people—that's somebody else's job
3. Focusing the majority of your marketing efforts on new business instead of present client/customer retention
4. Thinking you need a separate Marketing Plan rather than an integrated Business Plan
5. Centralizing more than decentralizing marketing responsibility
6. Relying on your own organization to tell you how well the clients/customers are being served
7. Finding that your CEO and/or division presidents don't focus on present clients/customers because they have "too many other things to worry about"

## Summary

To evaluate the effectiveness of your service organization's marketing process, begin with your company's business plan, which should reflect the best strategic thinking of the marketing, operations, finance, and other functions. Achieving the measurable objectives specified in the plan represents the first criterion of effectiveness.

The complementary evaluation area is customer satisfaction. You must understand what the customer values about your organization and how well your services meet customers' needs.

It is also important to evaluate how well your organization supports front-line managers, who direct the service delivery process and lead customer-contact personnel. Ongoing evaluation is a critical element in maintaining an image of providing high-quality service in the marketplace.

## Notes

1. Leonard L. Berry, "Big Ideas in Services Marketing," *The Journal of Consumer Marketing* 3, no. 2 (Spring 1986). Used by permission.
2. Theodore Levitt, "Marketing Intangible Products and Product Intangibles," *Harvard Business Review,* May/June 1981. Used by permission.
3. Philip Kotler, "From Sales Obsession to Marketing Effectiveness," *Harvard Business Review,* November/December 1977.

## Further Resource

Rhoades, F., and J. Harris, "ARA Residents Set Management's Agenda." *American Healthcare Association Provider,* July 1987.

\*      \*      \*      \*

***Thomas J. Fitzgerald*** *is vice president of corporate marketing for ARA Services, Inc., where he is responsible for coordinating marketing efforts across all lines of business. He concentrates primarily on the cross-selling of services and quality assurance. Since joining ARA in 1967, Mr. Fitzgerald has served as sales promotion manager in the food services group, followed by regional director and then vice president of the school nutrition services division.*

# PART V

# IMPLEMENTATION: MAKING IT HAPPEN

# About This Part

The chapters in this part of the *Handbook* provide the specific tools to help you move in the strategic direction you have charted, according to the specific marketing plans you have developed. Discussion of the tools is organized into sections around the traditional marketing mix variables—product, price, distribution, and promotion—customized according to the unique requirements of the service marketer. Part V concludes with a chapter on how to implement a service-based product differentiation strategy. Service is rapidly becoming *the* source of differentiation, as products become more commodity-like.

# THE SERVICE DEVELOPMENT AND DELIVERY PROCESS

This section begins with Chapter 14, "How to Design a Service." The intangible, experiential nature of services calls for a method that imposes a degree of rationality and consistency upon the design process—what has been coined the "industrialization" of service. The process of rationalizing service design, "blueprinting," is an integral part of the iterative service development model presented. Beyond initial service design, the monitoring of service performance over time and design modification are discussed. This chapter provides a gold mine of immediately applicable techniques you can use to help you get a handle on all of the complex, interrelated parts of your service system.

The next chapter in the section focuses on the lifeblood of service delivery— the customer–service provider relationship. The customer's participation in service production necessitates that this relationship be managed carefully. Your goal is to build strong relationships that last, what product marketers call "brand loyalty." This chapter offers practical steps you can take at critical points in the service delivery process to facilitate customer retention. Also included is guidance on how to evaluate the results of your retention program, and how to support and promote the relationship sensitivity of employees.

Chapter 16 describes the service management process from beginning to end. Included is discussion of the service life cycle, how you can recognize each stage, and what you need to consider in navigating successfully through each stage. Key operational components of service planning are covered, including evaluation of your current service mix, establishment of objectives and goals, generation and screening of new service ideas, business analysis of alternatives, and service development, testing, commercialization, and monitoring.

# 14

# How to Design a Service

G. Lynn Shostack
Jane Kingman-Brundage

Service design can be thought of as a form of architecture, but an architecture dealing with processes instead of bricks and mortar. The objective is the creation of a complete blueprint for a service concept that can be translated into a soundly functioning service. What makes service development unique is the number and complexity of issues that must be dealt with in order to plan and manage a service concept from conception to realization.

## Why Service Design Is Different

A service is not something that is built in a factory, shipped to a store, put on a shelf, and then taken home by a consumer. A service is a dynamic living process. A service is something that is executed on behalf of, and often with the involvement of, the consumer. A service is performed. A service is rendered. A service is motion and activity—not pieces or parts. The "raw materials" of a service are time and process—not plastic or steel. A service cannot be stored or shipped—only the means for creating it can. A service cannot be held in one's hand or physically possessed. In short, a service is not a thing.

The important fact about a service is that it cannot be disassembled. Every part of the system is interrelated. A service is a "real-time" occurrence. In a metaphysical sense, the service only "exists" when it is being rendered. Otherwise, a service is simply a collection of machines, paper, or bodies at rest.

## Planning the Total System Is the Key

Every service is a complex system. To design and manage any service, all parts of the system must be addressed simultaneously. It is important to know that most of the needed methodologies already exist in the managerial tool kit: The methods are not themselves exotic. What *is* rare is a new managerial perspective—the habit of looking at a service as an integrated whole.

Consider the simple service of the corner shoeshine stand. In Figure 14-1, we can see that four actions, proceeding left to right in time, constitute the primary processes of the service. But clearly there is more to the service than

**Figure 14-1.** Blueprint for a simple service: the corner shoeshine.

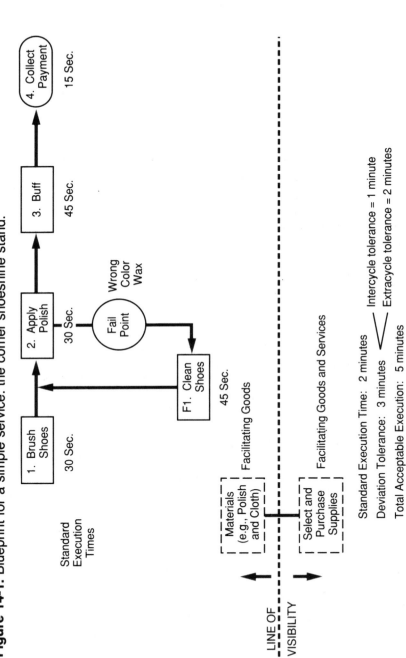

*Source:* Reprinted from "How to Design a Service," G. Lynn Shostack, *Proceedings From the American Marketing Association Services Marketing Conference* (Orlando, Florida), published by the American Marketing Association, 1981. Also reprinted by permission of *Harvard Business Review*, exhibit from "Designing Services That Deliver" by G. Lynn Shostack, January/February 1984 issue. Copyright © 1991 by President and Fellows of Harvard College; all rights reserved.

simply these functional procedures. Every service requires *setup,* even so simple an action as purchase of supplies and arrangement of the shoeshine stand. Many services also require *follow-up,* actions taken to complete the service after the customer departs.

In Figure 14-1 a "line of visibility" separates actions observable to the customer from those which, although necessary to the functioning of the service system, are nonetheless invisible to the customer. In large service systems, these "back office" or "invisible" parts of the system can have enormous impact on quality, image, and function.

If, for example, a computer program is redesigned in such a way that a different account statement is produced for banking customers, this new piece of evidence may affect service image and other perceptions of price/value as well. Thus, even invisible processes must be planned and monitored by the marketer.

A facilitating good—wax—is necessary to the rendering of shoeshines. If this good is not selected and managed with care, the overall service will suffer.

The system also includes a person who renders the service. This person not only must be functionally competent, but also must be socially competent. Thus, his or her manner and appearance also are part of the system, representing physical "evidence" of service quality to the customer. The system has time and material costs, and it has "fail points," where potential breakdowns in service execution are most likely to occur. The service has an environment in which it is performed and, finally, the entire service system has a result or benefit, which we can describe as "shiny shoes" or perhaps "a smile on one's face."

This "simple" service can take many unique forms. Figure 14-2 shows a different "design" with different constraints, prices, and marketability.

Not only can shoeshine service take many forms, whole new constellations of services or service "packages" can be created by combining various designs, including products. Figure 14-3 shows three different service "packages," derived from arrangement of basic service elements: additional service (repair) and product (shoe-care items and even shoes themselves).

Similarly, as Figures 14-4 and 14-5 show, the service of flower arranging can have as many unique designs as there are providers. In Figure 14-4, every arrangement is unique. The variability is infinite—constrained only by the imagination of the flower arranger. In Figure 14-5, the service design *predefines* the eight outcomes (arrangements).

From a service design perspective, it is harder to control for consistent, high quality on a discrete number of known outcomes than to control for quality by securing the service of a single master performer. The sources of difficulty are numerous. First, it is not easy to define standard outcomes, which are also desirable to consumers. Second, it is not easy to plan the *means* (goods and tasks) by which specified outcomes are to be achieved. Finally, variability in the skills of individual service providers may, at the last moment, thwart the best design. Trade-offs in quality, volume, and price follow naturally. For these reasons, service design demands a comprehensive approach to planning all elements of the service system.

**Figure 14-2.** Modified design for shoeshine stand, incorporating new service cycle, service evidence, and product elements.

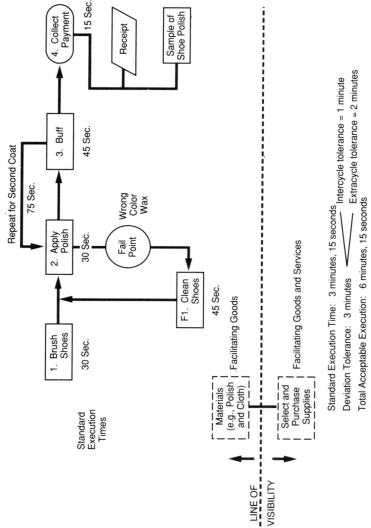

*Source:* Reprinted from "How to Design a Service," G. Lynn Shostack, *Proceedings From the American Marketing Association Services Marketing Conference* (Orlando, Florida), published by the American Marketing Association, 1981. Also reprinted by permission of *Harvard Business Review,* exhibit from "Designing Services That Deliver" by G. Lynn Shostack, January/February 1984 issue. Copyright © 1991 by President and Fellows of Harvard College; all rights reserved.

**Figure 14-3.** Three alternative product/service combinations for a shoe-shine operation.

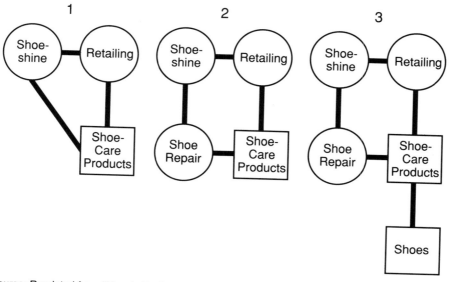

*Source:* Reprinted from "How to Design a Service," G. Lynn Shostack, *Proceedings From the American Marketing Association Services Marketing Conference* (Orlando, Florida), published by the American Marketing Association, 1981.

# How to Use the Planning/Development Model

Figure 14-6 shows the stages involved in designing and introducing a service. The model is a progressive step-by-step process that results in a fully defined, operational service.

## Five Steps to Success

Five primary activities constitute the service development process:

Step 1: Design.   Design is a mental plan or scheme in which means to an end are laid down. Service system design is the iterative act of defining and refining an initial service concept. As shown in Figure 14-6, reaching a master design involves repeating the cycle of definition, analysis, and synthesis many times. Even after a master design is finalized, the design function remains a permanent part of managing any service system. Design modifications and adjustments are a continuing necessity, based on consumer input, competitive conditions, and operational change.

Step 2: Implementation.   Implementation means translating a master service design into the operating tasks, functions, and requirements that are necessary to introduce and operate the service. These tasks are ultimately performed by others who constitute the living service system.

**Figure 14-4.** Service design for a Park Avenue florist.

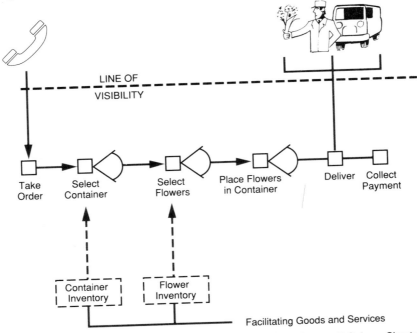

Take Order · Select Container · Select Flowers · Place Flowers in Container · Deliver · Collect Payment · Container Inventory · Flower Inventory · Facilitating Goods and Services

*Source:* Reprinted from "Service Positioning Through Structural Change," G. Lynn Shostack, *Journal of Marketing* 51, no. 1, published by the American Marketing Association, January 1987.

**Figure 14-5.** Alternative service design for the florist.

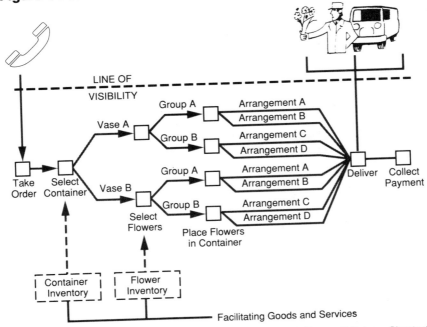

Take Order · Select Container · Vase A · Vase B · Group A · Group B · Arrangement A · Arrangement B · Arrangement C · Arrangement D · Select Flowers · Place Flowers in Container · Deliver · Collect Payment · Container Inventory · Flower Inventory · Facilitating Goods and Services

*Source:* Reprinted from "Service Positioning Through Structural Change," G. Lynn Shostack, *Journal of Marketing* 51, no. 1, published by the American Marketing Association, January 1987.

**Figure 14-6.** Service design and development.

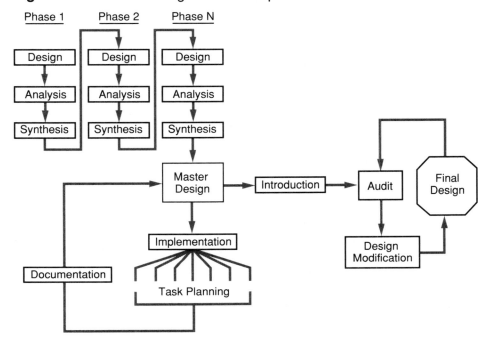

Step 3: Documentation. Documentation represents specification, at the detailed level, of all the operating standards, instructions, schedules, rules, and outputs of the service system, so that other people know how the system is supposed to function.

Step 4: Introduction. Introduction is the actual ''turning on'' of the service system to interact with consumers.

Step 5: Audit. Audit is a series of feedback mechanisms and controls that allow fine-tuning or necessary modification of the service. The audit function is responsible for maintaining design integrity and is an essential ongoing monitoring activity.

## Why a Diversified Team Is Important

Service development requires the participation and involvement of many individuals who bring different expertise and experience to the process.

In assembling a development team, one person should be designated the captain or team leader. He or she is responsible for pulling together all the people and expertise needed to address issues related to design, implementation, documentation, introduction, and audit. The team itself should be structured around four critical functions: Design, Process, Means, and Evidence. Figures

14-7 and 14-8 show these functions of and relationships among the team members.

Design.    This team member will be the keeper of the service design itself as it progresses through changes and refinement. He or she will also be responsible for incorporating market research into the design specifications, integrating consumer and operational feedback into the design, and analyzing the impact of all proposed changes in process, means, or evidence.

Process.    This team member will focus on operational issues and constraints that affect the design, and will oversee operational implementation.

Means.    The means by which services are rendered are only two: people and goods. This team member will concentrate on people issues (skills requirements and training) and facilitating goods and services, such as computers and other goods and services needed to execute the service.

Evidence.    This team member will address all consumer encounter points. Service evidence means everything the consumer will be exposed to regarding the service. It includes advertising, collateral material, telephone dialogues, person-to-person interaction, environments, direct mail, and all other forms of visible, aural, or tangible evidence.

Team members may not carry the titles described previously, but may be drawn from marketing, operations, personnel, information services, and other areas in the company. However, by organizing the team around these categories—design, process, means, evidence—developmental issues will cluster together naturally in a way that corresponds to the main elements of all service systems. The four areas relate logically to one another. This logical relationship helps ensure that no important issue is omitted as cross-boundary tasks emerge. As development progresses, others with even more specialized knowledge will be drawn into the process.

### The Importance of Shared Understanding

Because many people will ultimately be involved, service design requires a high degree of shared understanding at each developmental stage. To provide a basis for this understanding, a technique called *service blueprinting* is suggested and described throughout this chapter. It is a way of diagramming and describing the total system and total concept to ensure that all issues and areas necessary to the successful development of a service are addressed.

## Benefits of Service Blueprints

The benefits associated with service blueprints can be understood in terms of the traditional management tasks—planning, organizing, directing, and controlling:

**Figure 14-7.** Service development functions of the team.

| Design<br>Management | Process<br>Management | Means<br>Management | Evidence<br>Management |

**Figure 14-8.** Functional interfaces of the team.

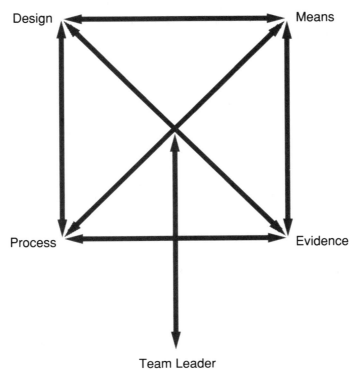

1. A service blueprint is a *planning* tool for visualizing or depicting the service concept in concrete terms, thus facilitating market research and concept testing.

2. The service blueprint is an *organizing* tool for assisting managers in assembling appropriate resources for effective implementation of the service concept:

   - *Human resource:* By answering the question, "What exactly will service providers do?" blueprints provide a task-oriented basis for job descriptions and employee selection criteria.

   - *Technological resource:* By answering the question, "How will the service be provided—that is, using what equipment?" the blueprint guides selection and design of appropriate equipment. In the event the service system design process *begins* with innovative technology, the blueprint assists managers with the process of developing rational, systematic human support (work flows, procedures) designed to maximize the technological benefits.

   - *Evidence:* By answering the question, "What evidence do consumers require to (1) select the service in the first place; (2) have service experiences consistent with their expectations; (3) select the service again?" a service blueprint guides the development of advertising and promotion, visual environment, consumer materials, printed forms, and even suggested "scripts" for verbal interactions.

   - *Process:* By answering the question, "How does the service work?" a service blueprint is the objective basis for development of service policy, work-flow design, and operating procedures.

3. The service blueprint is a *communication* and *training* tool that helps service providers relate their specific job to the service overall. By answering the question, "How does my job serve consumers?" a service blueprint can foster employee commitment to the marketing task.

4. The service blueprint is a *control* device that makes it possible to structure monitoring and feedback devices at job, system, and management levels. Service blueprints facilitate quality control through analysis of fail points, which is the first step in identifying meaningful checkpoints for statistical control of quality.

The service blueprint is thus a technique for assisting marketers to identify and manipulate service elements in order to create barriers to entry by the competition. Similarly, the service blueprint enables marketers to isolate the explicit elements that distinguish competitive service offerings.

## How to Blueprint a Service

In the beginning of a service project, the service definition is usually vague and only a skeletal indication of what the final service will be. Often no written definition exists at this first stage, only a verbal or mental concept. Even when a written description does exist, it is frequently a brief, abstracted statement.

The definition usually describes the main results or benefits of the service concept, rather than what service delivery entails. As shown in Figure 14-6, an iterative service design and development process is required to realize the service concept.

### Phase 1 Design

To initiate development, the team should begin by writing as complete a description of the concept as possible. A preliminary blueprint should also be created, even though it will appear primitive.

To illustrate the stages of the process, we will use the discount brokerage example.

This service concept might be stated as follows: Discount brokerage is a service through which people buy and sell stocks without paying for brokerage advice. The concept might be blueprinted as shown in Figure 14-9. To proceed from this stage to the creation and successful introduction of a new service requires a progressive program of refinement and detail.

### Phase 1 Analysis

Having defined the concept, the information-gathering process begins. A search is made for data and examples relating to the proposed service concept. Competitors are analyzed. Various approaches to implementation are identified. Dialogue with knowledgeable internal and external parties is initiated. As alternative approaches and features for the service are identified and as new ideas surface, the inadequacy of the Phase 1 definition becomes apparent.

### Phase 1 Synthesis

At this stage, basic boundaries for the service are drawn. A considerable amount of dialogue and discussion must take place in order to sort out the many alternatives and, more important, to achieve a common understanding of the basic

**Figure 14-9.** Definition for a discount brokerage house in Phase 1.

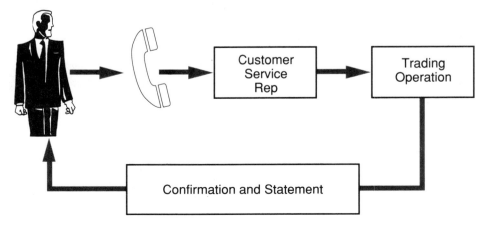

profile of the service to be built. The project team should meet on a regular basis, so that the viewpoints of various parties can be clarified. The team will make a number of decisions at this stage. The cumulative effect of these decisions is to clarify the service definition and limit the issues that remain to be considered.

Some of the many decisions requiring definition, analysis, and synthesis in discount brokerage include choosing among the wide variety of securities that are potential candidates for inclusion. Each type of security requires staff expertise, has cost implications, and involves computer systems development time. Some possibilities require joint effort with other operating areas.

Decisions about whether all or part of the service should be done in-house are needed. In one alternative, custody of customer securities would remain with an external broker. In another, it is maintained in-house. Automatic cash sweep to a money market fund is a possibility, but requires contracting with outsiders. Literally hundreds of issues, small and large, will surface in Phase 1.

### Phases 2 Through N

These three steps—design, analysis, and synthesis—must be repeated until the team has developed a complete and detailed service system blueprint. Shortcuts in the design phase inevitably lead to problems in implementation and introduction due to oversight, hasty conclusions, and erroneous assumptions.

The use of the service development checklist shown in Figure 14-10 can help team members ensure that they have considered all aspects of the service system. The process of answering questions on the list requires team members to refine and clarify the service system as a whole.

Each of these phases demands thorough and careful work. Different team members may focus on parts of design that match their areas of expertise, which is one reason why a diversified team is important. From these exercises come creative answers and unique solutions that lead to differentiated and successful introductions.

The reason for such thoroughness in the design stage is that no two services are the same. Even when the outward or superficial evidence appears similar, every service is different. Services are processes. As such, they are variable. Two firms offering the same service will, upon investigation, be found to have established different designs, and each design will pose different constraints and opportunities for changing, expanding, and controlling the service.

For example, the choice of computer system to produce customer statements may seem to be a mechanical rather than a marketing issue. Yet one computer may allow linkage to other service systems, while another does not. Computer linkage can allow new service combinations to be created, which can differentiate an organization's offerings to the market. One computer may allow free-form statement messages, while another does not. One may use a laser printer, while another does not. One may be formatted to fit window envelopes, while another requires that envelope labels be produced. Each of these choices affects the final service's design, and each is a marketing issue.

One firm's customer contact employees may be required to fill out forms, while another firm's employees enter information directly into the computer.

**Figure 14-10.** Service development checklist.

---

### Design Questions to Ask

* Have we described all the steps necessary to execute this service?
* Have we described completely the *order of* and *connections between* these steps?
* Have we described the *means* by which these steps will be rendered (i.e., people, computers, consumers)?
* Have we identified each point at which the service could fail?
* Have we described all the consumer encounter points identified with this service?
* Have we identified all the tangible evidence this service will present to the consumer?
* Have we defined all the facilitating goods and services required by this service?
* Have we identified the time/cost components of the service?

### Analysis Questions to Ask

* What consumer research can assist us in evaluating this service?
* What do we know about competitive services (quality, price, evidence, structure)?
* How do we know our operational design will work?
* What kind of people are needed in this system?
* What kind of technologies or facilitating goods are needed?
* Are our cost/time assumptions valid?
* Is our choice of encounter points optimal?
* Have we chosen the best forms of evidence?

### Synthesis Questions to Ask

* What parts of the blueprint have to be changed as a result of our definition and analysis?
* What impact do these changes have on other parts of the service system?
* What additional definition and analysis do we need to do?
* Have we revised the blueprint?

---

Each requires different training and different process standards, and potentially will yield different employee morale and different customer satisfaction levels. This seemingly small difference in computer use as a facilitating good may affect pricing and competitive position and will certainly affect evidence.

### Pricing Issues

Pricing issues deserve special mention because pricing a service is different from pricing a packaged good. Marketers are familiar with the cost components employed in a manufacturing setting: raw materials, labor, and overhead. In a manufacturing context, labor is understood to be the number of widgets produced in a given time frame. Marketers, however, sometimes encounter difficulties in costing services because they do not recognize anything on the service side comparable to the "widgets" manufactured in the factory.

A different method is required to cost the labor associated with creation of a service. In Figure 14-1 each step in the shoeshine process has been timed. For each step, *standard execution* plus *deviation tolerance* yields a *total acceptable execution*. These discrete steps are comparable to factory widgets; taken as a whole, they comprise the labor cost associated with the total service. Service blueprints enable managers to develop accurate labor costs because blueprints depict the individual steps that make up a service.

For tasks and steps in which time cannot be rigidly controlled or measured as, for example, data entry, an acceptable norm must be developed based on average execution standards. Costing norms would apply to such variable tasks as customer dialogues, problem resolution, and other steps calling for diagnosis, judgment, and choices among possible courses of action.

Facilitating goods and services can then be amortized into the cost structure based on expected levels of service production. Evidence will be similarly costed.

These techniques will yield a blueprint cost at various production levels of the service, which will later be compared with actual costs under live conditions. To then set a price for the service, the marketer can begin by establishing a price based on a satisfactory profit margin or return. Next, the marketer should evaluate competition and, if the new service has unique advantages, decide whether these "value-added" elements might justify higher pricing. Research can be very helpful at this stage. Because all pricing is, at some level, partly subjective, the potential price flexibility of a service often is dramatically affected by customer perceptions of the total service's benefit. Whenever a service may be perceived as unique by the market, care must be taken not to underprice it at the outset.

## How a Completed Blueprint Looks

In the case of the discount brokerage house, Figure 14-11 shows a condensed version of the completed blueprint for the concept. Clearly, there is a big difference between this and the initial definition.

At each stage, the service proposal should be widely circulated, so that its specifics can be critiqued. Attention should be focused on operational factors, as well as on the identification of flaws in the design and any remaining issues or problems. The more detailed the blueprint, the easier it will be to respond with constructive and specific feedback.

Exposing the proposal to the rigor of criticism is vital. If the design is critiqued in a vacuum or in a "planning" laboratory, not only are the conclusions likely to be biased toward the planners' preconceived wishes, but the service is very likely to encounter implementation problems.

## Use Research to Help You Design

Focused market research should also be conducted to give prospective customers an opportunity to respond to the service concept and provide input to the design

# Figure 14-11. Blueprint for the discount brokerage house.

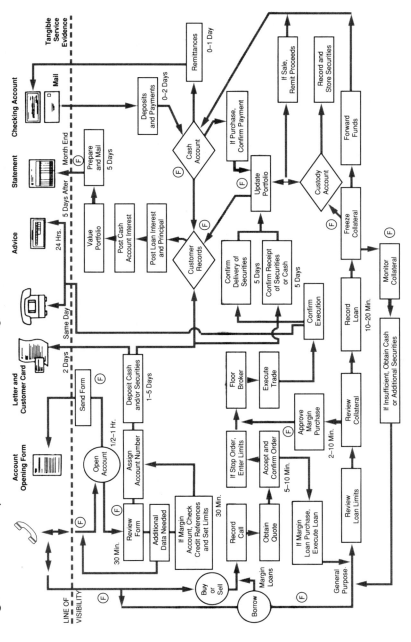

*Source:* Reprinted by permission of *Harvard Business Review,* exhibit from "Designing Services That Deliver" by G. Lynn Shostack, January/February 1984 issue. Copyright © 1991 by President and Fellows of Harvard College; all rights reserved.

Key: Ⓕ = Fail Point

process. Market research done at very early stages is usually worthless, because it only provides reaction to a vague abstraction.

When prospective customers are invited to respond to a service blueprint, however, abstractions give way to the concrete actions proposed to make up the service. A service blueprint used in a market research context enables prospective customers to enter imaginatively into the service process. Actionable feedback—valuable insights into customer needs and perceptions—is the likely result when the market is given actionable input in the form of a service blueprint.

From concept testing to price testing, from testing consumer response to statements to testing consumer response to uniforms on service representatives, each stage of development and operation benefits from well-crafted research.

## What Goes Into a Master Design

This stage represents the final pre-implementation blueprint. At this stage, the blueprint should be translated into a written document that includes a structural description of how the service system works, a pro forma financial projection based on pricing strategies derived from cost analysis of the functional design, an implementation plan that includes staff requirements, training, control and auditing standards, a market positioning and introduction strategy, including advertising/promotion, and a list of remaining issues. At this stage, issues become more and more specific, reaching to detailed levels such as design of customer statements, telemarketing, time/motion performance standards, selection of technologies, and mobilization of operating units. Even at this stage, hundreds of decisions remain to be made before the service reaches its final form.

The Master Design will trigger the preparation of detailed implementation sub-plans. A new team will be formed, consisting of all the accountable parties. Each area that will be involved in rendering the service will work from the final service blueprint, translating it to grass-roots levels in the organization.

The Master Design also triggers preparation of performance standards and development of Service System Audit instruments at both consumer and employee levels. The Service System Audit may be thought of as a series of still shots taken of the service system from a variety of angles and perspectives. The measurement devices mentioned here are commonplace. What distinguishes a Service System Audit is the *integration* of results geared to produce a comprehensive picture of service performance. The manager of design synthesizes audit measures to produce a composite evaluation of service performance overall.

In developing the Service System Audit, managers rely on performance standards enunciated in the Master Design. Development of the Service System Audit is a team effort. Managers of evidence and process prepare a Consumer Audit that focuses on pre- and posttesting of consumer encounter points, service fail points, and evidence. Managers of process and means prepare an Employee Audit that not only measures productivity (time and throughput) and quality (accuracy and timeliness) but zeroes in on internal, nonprocess issues as well. These issues involve assessment of the *means* by which the service is created:

systems, facilitating goods, and support service provided internally across departmental lines.

It should be noted that the Employee Audit mirrors the Consumer Audit. Where consumers express dissatisfaction with a given factor or service step, employees are in a position to identify *why* they were unable to perform as specified. Perhaps a computer system is inadequate, or a piece of evidence is missing or deficient. Because they are on the front lines of creating a service, employees are an indispensable source of service improvements.

The Service System Audit is the management tool for monitoring performance as conformance or deviation from standards established by the service system blueprint. Used imaginatively, the Service System Audit is also a useful tool for providing important performance feedback to employees. Such feedback lies at the heart of the self-monitoring of performance, which is often required in sophisticated service systems.

The blueprint will now be frozen until the post-implementation audit.

## Get Ready for Implementation

In this stage, the operational pieces of the service are put in place. Implementation requires a separate plan drawn from the Master Design. This sub-plan includes time and deliverable schedules based on working backward from the desired introduction date. As is true in all other phases of service design, hundreds of specific issues must be addressed, and every detail must be seriously considered. Staff must be housed and trained, procedures written, performance standards defined, and the entire process debugged. It is in this phase that delays, such as in telephone installations and delivery of the wrong equipment, occur.

If possible, pre-implementation planning should include an operating test of the service, using actual prospective customers. This is similar to product testing or market testing in a manufacturing environment.

## Be Sure You Document

After the entire implementation plan is established, the service is ready for market introduction. In this stage, advertising, direct mail, publicity, and service evidence such as customer statements are prepared. As is true throughout the service design and development cycle, each phase represents many complex processes. The development of advertising/promotion programs, for example, is a full-time activity that, for some services, may consume as much time as the design itself.

All standards for the system must now be specified, usually in the form of operating manuals, media programs, training plans, parallel computer tests, volume throughput standards, and such. Prices are set, quality expectations are defined, and evidence is produced. It is against this documentation that success or failure will be measured.

## You Are Ready to Introduce the Service

The service goes live. Telephones ring, inquiries are answered, accounts are opened, customers visit, representatives perform. Transactions are executed.

During the first stages of market introduction, it is vitally important that all parts of the service be closely monitored, which means that every phone call must be recorded and followed up to determine why accounts are or are not being opened. It means that every transaction is logged, every employee's performance is tracked, every glitch is isolated. This research should continue long enough to cover at least several complete cycles of the service. If the customer requires six months to experience all aspects of the service, then monitoring should continue six months before the next phase is reached.

Many services are thrown haphazardly into the marketplace. Whether they function as designed, or function well or poorly, seems to be of little concern. Considering the extraordinary labor involved in creating a service, it is unfortunate when a service is abandoned at the point of its birth. There are product analogs for this sort of sloppiness, but they are rare among goods companies, which have learned the value of and practice highly refined post-introduction research.

In this stage, data gathered in the Consumer and Employee Audits during the implementation stage are synthesized, and corrections to the service are made. Also at this stage, the next steps for modifying or enhancing the service are identified, and the design/development cycle begins again.

## Summary

The process of designing and developing a service is exceedingly complex. The description of actual events given in this chapter is a condensed one.

The first lesson to learn about services is that they are complex systems. All parts of the system must be addressed when developing a new service.

Second, the process is iterative and largely definitional. The objective of service design is to establish a totally specific and rational definition of the total system. Through iteration, decisions are made that make the profile increasingly specific, until all the means for creating the service have been laid down in an explicit plan.

Third, a great deal of the process is verbal. As the service is developed, an expanding circle of people becomes involved. This process and the dialogue that accompanies serve to construct successive and more refined service portraits.

It is important to control this expanding circle, so that each stage is properly completed before new parties are brought into the design process. One characteristic of projects that do not do well seems to be that too many people are involved in early phases. Conversely, projects that are developed entirely by staff or "planners" usually do not do well either. The key appears to be to start with a limited number of people and to add others only when their roles can be clearly defined. At each stage, the importance of translating verbal input into pictorial or quantitative terms is critical. This provides the objective benchmark for subsequent input and keeps the service clearly defined.

Fourth, every service is unique. The design process itself shows that the probabilities of any two services arriving at precisely the same design are virtually nil. Many factors—from environments to people—add variations. These subtle differences can be points of differentiation.

Finally, whether the process is fully documented or not, good service design seems to require that all stages be completed. Projects that fail often skip stages or gloss over them. And service problems appear to be traceable directly to stages that were not properly or thoroughly executed.

In sum, the design and development of a service can be made rational, objective, methodological, and precise. Such an approach to developing service systems is of great utility to all service marketers in ensuring success and quality in the marketplace.

\* \* \* \*

***G. Lynn Shostack*** *serves as chairman and president of Joyce International, Inc., a private $350 million company. She is a recognized authority on services marketing and the financial services industry. Ms. Shostack currently writes a column on innovation and entrepreneurship for* The Journal of Business Strategy.

***Jane Kingman-Brundage*** *is founding principal of Kingman-Brundage, Inc., a management consulting firm that is situated in North Salem, New York, and that emphasizes service system design and implementation. She specializes in the service blueprinting technique and has employed it on behalf of clients in major banks, investment institutions, and* Fortune 500 companies.

# 15

# Building Relationships
# That Last

Carole A. Congram

Does it cost more to attract a new customer or retain an existing one? Attracting new business is exciting, but it costs, conservatively, at least six times as much as retaining existing business. That's a pretty good reason to focus on keeping customers happy, but there are other significant reasons.

First, existing customers are easier to serve than new ones. Working relationships have been defined. People have gotten to know each other.

Second, your organization's revenues and profit potential increase. Continuing customers represent a revenue stream and, if your firm has a portfolio of related services, a base of cross-selling opportunities.

When a customer is lost, a new customer doesn't replace the lost customer immediately; there is a revenue gap. In addition, some services have start-up costs associated with new business that are borne by the service organization. For example, many accountants do not charge for the time spent learning about a client's business records and systems. These costs further erode revenues and profits.

Third, existing customers are sources of valuable ideas for your business. For example, if one of your objectives is to keep pace with customers' changing needs, customers can help you identify needed services that your firm can provide profitably. Another example: Customers can tell you the benefits they receive from your organization's services in terms that are meaningful to prospective customers. You can use this information to develop brochures or sales promotion materials that relate to prospective customers' concerns. Existing customers know your organization, including its people and service-delivery systems, very well. Their observations and insights can give direction to your marketing planning and implementation efforts.

A fourth reason to focus on existing customers is to develop advocates for your service organization. Customers who are satisfied with your firm's services speak well of the firm. They make good referral sources and can serve as references as well.

Fifth, a long-term working relationship improves the customer's situation. Communication lines are open, and there is minimal disruption to the customer's operations. Customers learn their role and responsibilities in the service-delivery process, as well as the ways in which your firm can help them achieve their objectives.

Finally, continuing relationships offer growth opportunities to your firm's employees. Their understanding of the customer's perspective increases with experience. Long-term relationships can be very satisfying, both personally and professionally. As customers' needs change, employees have stimulating opportunities to help customers solve problems. Productivity increases, and turnover goes down. Employees also learn that customer service is the core of marketing.

Considered together, these seven reasons provide the rationale, the impetus, for making retention an integral part of your service organization's mission statement or philosophy. Relationship building is the service counterpart of brand loyalty in consumer goods. The quality of your company's client relationships correlates directly with its level of service quality. In this chapter, we will answer critical questions about different aspects of relationship building:

1. What is the nature of the service relationship?
2. How can you manage long-term relationships?
3. How can you evaluate the effectiveness of retention programs?
4. How can your service organization support the relationship-building capabilities of service employees?

## The Nature of the Relationship

As readers of the "Personals" column know, there are relationships, and there are relationships. In services, there are different types of relationships, too. In this section, we will look at these types because they have implications for approaches to retaining (and attracting) customers.[1]

One way of looking at relationships is to examine the service encounter itself. Simply stated, the service encounter is the interaction between the customer and the service provider—the person or equipment delivering the service. In actuality, many services involve both people and equipment, but the combination varies by service. For example, a bank teller uses a microcomputer to support his service to a customer; people handle the exceptional situations in ATM services.

Another way of looking at relationships is in terms of the approach to service delivery.[2] One approach is the transaction-based relationship, characterized as having a defined beginning and ending, and minimal switching costs. Another approach to service delivery is the long-term relationship, characterized by loyalty (out of preference) or affiliation (imposed by regulation or limited choices), and high switching costs. Customers involved in long-term relationships are hard to lose, but, once lost, they are likely to be gone for good.

As shown in Figure 15-1, we can classify services simultaneously on these two dimensions—type of service encounter and approach to service delivery. The strategies associated with each of the four cells differ markedly.

In cell 1, the core service is dominated by equipment or technology, used in single transactions. An example is the ATM, a transaction based on a "black box." For services in this cell, strategic considerations concern accessibility, pricing, customer service for unusual situations, and mass communication regarding such features as location and ease of use.

In cell 2 are services, such as electrical utilities, rendered continuously

**Figure 15-1.** Services exemplifying type of service encounter in relation to service delivery approach.

**Service Delivery Approach**

| | Transaction | Continuous |
|---|---|---|
| **Equipment** | (1) ATM | (2) Utility |
| **Personal** | (3) Haircut | (4) Financial Planning |

(Type of Service Encounter — row label)

through equipment. Organizations in this cell need to concentrate on pricing, service for exceptional situations, and communications, particularly accurate, readable bills and information about the organization's approach to service quality. Like services in cell 1, these services exert a great deal of control over customers' experiences and perceptions of the service because of its automation. Interestingly, many cell 2 services remain unnoticed by customers until something goes wrong.

If your service is in cell 3, remember that first impressions count. Your customers have many alternatives to your transaction-type service, and they know it. Although your service may have a technical component, the personal interaction is just as important, if not more so. Thus, you want all your employees to make customers feel welcome, help them understand how your services can be tailored to their needs, and invite them to come back. Invest in helping your employees become more sensitive to customers' individual differences and more tuned in to two-way communication.

Services in cell 4 are particularly complex because they involve personal interactions over an extended period of time. These interactions could be face-to-face, by telephone, by correspondence, and through third parties. These interactions are further complicated by the individual differences of customers and service providers; by changing situational variables; and by the cultural influences imposed by the service organization.

The primary strategic concern of service organizations in cell 4 is internal marketing for two reasons. First, the service provider is integral to the service. Second, service providers not only must influence perceptions and expectations, but also manage them. We'll discuss relationship management in the next section.

Communication is especially important for organizations in cell 4. You want your customers to understand your firm's purpose or mission, as well as its range of services and their benefits. Thus, your communications must be focused and frequent. It is also important to focus on the service-delivery process so that (a) procedural components are well-defined and operating smoothly, and (b) components that must be handled personally are assigned to the appropriate people and performed correctly.

Can you shift your service from one cell to another? Yes, and no. If your service is in cell 3, it may be possible to move into cell 4 by tailoring the relationship management approaches to your situation and supporting employees in the development of relationship-building skills. In the remainder of this chapter, you will find examples of ways for your personal/transaction service to make the move.

For services in cells 1 and 2, profitability usually results from volume. High-volume customers of these commoditylike services are price-sensitive, and the low margins associated with equipment- and technology-based services make it difficult to add high-cost personalization. Although it may not be feasible or desirable for you to shift your service to another cell, you can use the relationship management techniques we will discuss next to develop strategies to retain your large or significant customers and to identify sources of added value for them.

Before moving on, consider what's in a name. If your organization is in cells 3 or 4, you may call your customers by another name. *Client* is the term used most frequently (and the term used in the remainder of this chapter), but *patient* (medical practitioners) and *guests* (hotels, hospitals, and long-term care facilities) are others. *Client* has the connotation of professional and personal; *patient,* professional; and *guest,* personal. Many services marketers think that all service companies should use *client* (or *patient* or *guest*), so you may want to review your organization's terminology.

## How to Manage Relationships

Relationship management is the process of ensuring the effective delivery of services to meet clients' needs. This definition implies that:

1. Service providers can have a positive influence on a client's expectations and experiences.
2. Relationship management is ongoing and systematic.
3. Relationship management involves identifying client segments and the services needed by these groups.

Here are three basic approaches to managing long-term relationships:

1. Managing critical incidents and periods
2. Client service planning
3. Integrating company and personal communications

They are the topics covered in this section.

## Managing Critical Incidents and Periods[3]

Relationships exist over time. Most relationships can be divided into two phases that have been compared to courtship and marriage[4]: pre- and postpurchase.

<u>Prepurchase Relationship Phase.</u>   During the prepurchase phase, the service organization uses marketing and communication tools and techniques to shape the expectations of prospective clients. These activities include public relations, community activities, advertising, personal selling, and word-of-mouth recommendations.

In many relationship-based services, prospective clients ask service providers to develop written and oral proposals in which they present their experiences working with clients similar to the prospective client, their approach to serving the prospective client, and the résumés of key service team members. The personal/transaction counterpart of the proposal might be an estimate, including a description of the service and a price quotation. When a proposal or estimate is well-prepared, the prospective client begins to understand the types of experiences he can expect with the service organization.

<u>Postpurchase Relationship Phase.</u>   Many service providers expend a great deal of energy on prepurchase (courtship) activities in the belief that:

1. The purchase cements the relationship.
2. The ongoing relationship will be maintained as a normal part of service delivery.

These assumptions are naive. Once the client purchases a service, he becomes an integral part of the organization's service delivery system. The client continually compares his experiences with the expectations formed during courtship.

Many clients have limited (if any) understanding of the technical side of a service. Over time, however, clients become astute observers of their service suppliers. Their perceptions of service quality stem from their experiences in the relationship aspects of service, for example, returning a telephone call promptly, delivering a report on time.

Every service delivery system—whether transaction or continuous—has critical moments when service employees can educate clients about the service delivery process. As a result, service providers manage their clients' expectations. Although different services have different critical moments, there are some points that recur across relationship-based services and may occur in handling exceptional cases in equipment- and technology-based services:

*The purchase.* Especially important to the client and service providers is the time of purchase. The client is apprehensive, asking himself, "Did I make the right choice?" Service providers must do something that communicates to the client, "You made the right decision."

Service providers can manage this critical moment by involving the client in some type of activity to reinforce the client's decision. For example, a private banker may send a small, thoughtful gift, accompanied by a personal note, to a new client. A consultant could schedule a planning meeting right away. Or, a hair stylist who wants to move her service from cell 3 to cell 4 could telephone new clients to inquire whether their new hairstyle is manageable. Once you identify the activity, you must build the system to make sure the activity happens—with every client.

*Before service delivery.* You can use the planning phase of any service line to educate your client about the service process. If your service is equipment-based, use printed communications, including monthly statements. Relationship-based services should use personal meetings, with written materials as support.

In your planning presentation, remember that although you may have done similar work many times, your client has not. Take the opportunity to explain the various phases you will go through and the reasons certain procedures are needed. If you can deal with misapprehensions or questions during planning, you can avoid surprises—something clients dislike—later on.

*During service delivery.* Give the client progress reports as a service is being delivered. You may want to relate these reports to the planning discussion. Or, as you complete a particular phase, you might call in one of your associates to review the completed work and help the client understand its benefits.

*After service delivery.* When the service is completed, be sure that the client understands the resulting benefits. In business-to-business services, prepare a written report, however brief, because it is something tangible for the client's personnel to keep. If you can arrange to make an oral presentation, do so. This face-to-face meeting will give everyone concerned opportunities to discuss the benefits of the projects and additional needs of the client.

If you are not working directly with top management on the project, find a way to let senior managers know about the benefits of your service. Suggest to the client's personnel with whom you are working that they include the project report (or a summary) in their management reports; or tactfully inquire if you can transmit your report directly.

*Periods of inactivity.* When your firm is not providing services to a client, it is important to communicate with the client. Personal communications could include telephone calls to keep in touch or to offer helpful ideas, sending articles of interest with a personal note, or invitations to social events. If a regular client does not respond, call. One owner of a four-star restaurant in New York calls patrons he hasn't seen in a month just to say, "How are you? We've missed you." If your firm has a newsletter, be sure that the client's personnel are on the mailing list. Your purpose is to keep your company's name in front of the client so that you continue to occupy a "share of mind."

Managing critical events or periods can be done by the single practitioner or the large organization offering clients a broad array of services. A specific service offers contact opportunities for all or most clients. Once these opportunities are identified, a separate ''critical event'' plan can be developed for each client, or the ''critical event'' approach can be incorporated into client service planning, the next topic.

## Client Service Planning

You may want to take a more formal approach to managing relationships with an individual client. Client service planning is a systematic approach to:

- Analyzing a client's situation
- Identifying the client's needs
- Tailoring your company's services to meet the client's needs
- Delivering the services
- Evaluating your company's effectiveness in helping the client achieve his goals

Although many service companies acknowledge the need for and value of client service planning, its execution is poor, especially when compared with the account management conducted by many industrial-product organizations.

First, we will look at points you should consider in developing a client service planning system. Then, we will move on to implementation.

How to Develop a Service Planning System. Five areas of activity are involved in developing a client service planning system:

1. Obtain top management's support.
2. Define the target group.
3. Use a team approach.
4. Design a client dossier.
5. Define marketing's role.

Let's consider each area:

*1. Obtain top management support.* If your organization's mission statement emphasizes client service, a logical extension of that commitment is client service planning. When top management needs to be persuaded, here are four ways to get attention:

1. Prepare an analysis of reasons for client loss.
2. Interview any significant clients lost unexpectedly.
3. Use client feedback, formal or informal, to gather information about service effectiveness.
4. Use third-party endorsement.

If all else fails, try to work within one service line headed by an interested manager. Then, use this success story to market client service planning within the organization.

*2. Define the target group.* In the best of all worlds, every client is a candidate for client service planning. In reality, that just is not possible. One approach is to use the 80:20 rule; that is, focus on the 20 percent of your clients who yield 80 percent of the revenues. Find that core group of clients that you do not want—and probably cannot afford—to lose, and you have your target group.

*3. Use a team approach.* In larger organizations, many client relationships are managed by the service provider who heads the service team. Other team members carry out their professional assignments, but they may have a limited role in managing any aspect of the client relationship. Yet, these service team members see client personnel often and have a great deal of information about the client—information that never goes beyond an individual team member.

By using a team approach, members of the service team can pool information. In this process, everyone gains a broader understanding of the client's situation. The team can discuss different approaches to meeting a client's needs and managing the relationship.

You may want to include other people on your service team. For example, someone in the marketing group may be knowledgeable about good ideas that have worked with other clients. Or, the team may uncover a unique service situation, which requires the experience and perspective of a guru in that area.

*4. Design a client dossier.* Information is critical in client service planning. Your dossier should include basic information about the client. You then can circulate this dossier to individual team members so that everyone has the same information base. You might include financial data, organization charts, plans, and information about services your firm has performed.

A very important section concerns the service team's evaluation of the quality of their relationships with key client personnel. They would include the chief executive officer (or top decision-maker), managers who influence the CEO, board members, professional service advisers, and other influential people. Each team member should evaluate his relationship with each person on the roster. Included in the plan should be action steps to initiate or strengthen relationships at all levels.

*5. Define marketing's role.* The marketing department has at least two roles in a client service planning system: administration and planning catalyst.

The administration of the system is best handled centrally. The responsibilities include:

- Identification of key clients
- Preparation of client dossiers
- Assembling and distributing action plans
- Evaluation

The first two areas have been discussed.

Action plans represent "to do's" generated during the implementation process, to be discussed in the next section. These "to do's" are critical because they are basic to any monitoring system.

The "to-do" system should be designed to give each team member a "tickler" of her assignments. Ideally, the system would allow the team member to report back as each assignment is completed.

Centralizing and computerizing the system allows for monitoring on a continuing basis. When to-do reports are not completed, a warning flag can be generated so that someone in the marketing group can follow up.

As planning catalysts, members of the marketing group can be helpful to service teams by suggesting alternative approaches to client service and identifying client-contact opportunities. A by-product of the marketing department's involvement is that marketing is perceived as linked to client service and to the work of service providers.

**How to Implement a Client Service Planning System.**[5]  Executing a client service planning system consists of three major sets of activities:

1. Developing strategies for each client
2. Defining and implementing action plans
3. Evaluating the results

*Develop client strategies.* It is very important for a service team to think through its objectives with a particular client. For most clients, the basic objectives include one or more of the following:

- Retain the client.
- Expand the relationship by selling more services.
- Build upon personal relationships.

For each of these objectives, certain key questions lead to specific objectives.

Retaining the client is important for all the reasons presented at the beginning of this chapter. You want to pose hard questions that indicate the strength of the relationship, such as:

- Have we kept our commitments and done what we promised?
- Does the client initiate discussions about service problems?
- What has the client liked about our service?

Cross selling is an important objective because a client becomes more dependent on your company as the number of services she purchases increases. In effect, it becomes harder for the client to switch companies. Key questions to answer include:

- What service ideas have we presented to the client in the past year?
- Why have these ideas been accepted? Rejected?

The objective of strengthening the relationship is critical; many service providers find out how critical when a client's CEO switches to a new company because the CEO has a solid relationship with that company's CEO. Service providers must give honest answers to such questions as:

- Would the CEO recommend our company to his peers? Has he done so? Why, or why not?
- Do we understand the CEO's long-term objectives for the organization? What are they? How can we help?

You may be wondering how the client service team obtains the information needed to answer these questions. Ideally, service team members have a continuing dialogue with key people in the client organization, and these topics arise frequently. Many service providers do not have this depth of knowledge because they do not have a broad-gauged relationship with the client's top people. If this is the case, consider having the top members of the service team meet with their counterparts in the client organization for a focused discussion. Alternatively, an outside consultant can interview the client's key personnel and bring this information back to the service team; the consultant could then act as a facilitator during the beginning stages of client service planning.

*Develop the action plan.* Once the dossier is analyzed and strategies are formulated, the team has an understanding of the client's situation and needs. Their task is to develop an action plan to meet those needs and solidify relationships with the client's personnel.

The plan is actually a set of action steps assigned to specific team members who are responsible for completing the actions by a set time. An example of a plan appears as Table 15-1. The service organization is a consulting firm, and the client is a communications company, ABC Corporation. Perry Jones heads the consulting firm's service team, and one of his top managers is Margo Liechty. Ellen Hanson is the executive vice president to whom Jones reports. Shown in the table are the activities that lead up to the presentation of service recommendations to the CEO of ABC Corporation.

*Evaluate results.* In terms of a specific plan, the service team can monitor its progress as specific activities are completed. Broader evaluation approaches will be discussed in a subsequent section entitled "Evaluating the Effectiveness of Retention Programs."

## Integrating Company and Personal Communications

In relationship-based services, communication is a given. Service providers contact clients personally on a regular basis, and firms generate messages through public relations and a plethora of print, including advertising and brochures. Yet, little planning is done to integrate these activities so that key people receive frequent communications, thus keeping the service organization's name front and center, and messages about the company and its services are focused and

**Table 15-1.** Example of an action plan.

| Activity | Responsibility | By |
|---|---|---|
| Meet with VP-marketing re planning process. | Jones | 9/15 |
| Set up luncheons with Hanson and | | |
|     1. ABC CEO and Jones. | Jones | 10/1 |
|     2. Jones and president of public relations unit. | Jones | 11/15 |
|     3. Jones and creative director. | Liechty | 10/1 |
| Invite Hanson to VIP dinner and seat with ABC CEO. | Jones | 10/15 |
| Prepare situation analysis. | Liechty | 11/16 |
| Review for brainstorming session on November 19. | Team | 11/19 |
| Draft recommendations for review with Jones. | Liechty | 11/23 |
| Revise and prepare presentation. | Liechty | 11/26 |
| Present service recommendations. | Jones | 12/1 |

reinforced. Your objective in communicating with clients is to have them conclude: ''The people at (company) keep me informed and pay attention to my needs. They care about me and my business (personal situation).'' Let's look at an example of how this integration process works.

An outplacement specialist has specific occasions to contact clients personally to develop business. One occasion is four months before the start of a client's fiscal year; that is when budgets are in preparation and positions to be eliminated are being identified. A second contact occurs one month before fiscal year-end when budgets are final (or are about to be). A third time is six months into the new fiscal year when financial projections indicate whether the client is ahead of or behind plan; clients having difficulty meeting their financial objectives might be eliminating positions.

Table 15-2 summarizes Laura Cole's communication plan for Tom Talbot, her contact at XYZ Corporation, a large client with a December 31 year-end. Her three business-development contacts are shown in June, October, and December. To complete her plan, Laura is taking advantage of firm-sponsored events and activities.

The firm is conducting a survey on a topic of interest to human resource professionals, and in February, Tom will be invited to participate; later in February, the survey will be delivered to him, and the results will be summarized in the firm's newsletter (April). In May the firm is sponsoring a seminar for clients to which Tom will be invited.

The November issue of the firm's newsletter will feature the benefits clients are obtaining from a new service that Laura described to Tom in September. (XYZ may not need the service, but Tom is a referral source, too.) The firm

**Table 15-2.** Example of a client communication plan.

| Client: | Tom Talbot |
| | Vice President—Human Resources |
| | XYZ Corporation |

| *Month* | *Activity* |
| --- | --- |
| January | New Year's card |
| February | Invitation to participate in survey Survey |
| March | Reprint of article of interest with FYI note |
| April | Newsletter featuring survey report |
| May | Invitation to attend firm seminar Seminar |
| June | Personal call re company situation |
| July | Social contact (lunch) |
| August | |
| September | Personal call re company situation |
| October | Newsletter: Feature on how clients are benefiting from a new service |
| November | Personal call re company situation |
| December | Holiday social contact (firm-sponsored event) |

purchases a New Year's card with a message about ''valuing our relationship with you''; Laura will sign the card personally. In addition, she will have lunch with him (July) and invite him to the firm's holiday social (December).

If Tom participates in the survey and attends the seminar, he will have at least thirteen contacts with Laura's firm during the year. Laura is managing only four of these contacts. The firm's administrative staff will orchestrate the others.

Notice that the service provider understands her client's business cycles. Her planned interpersonal contacts, which are what propel the relationship forward, are geared to the cycle. The firm-sponsored communications, which keep the firm's name in front of the client, usually invite the client to become involved with the firm in some way—for example, the survey and the seminar, activities that facilitate interaction between the client and the company's service providers.

A personal/transaction (cell 3) business could implement a similar plan tied to critical events. For example, an appliance-repair service could institute a process like this:

1. When a repaired item is picked up, the employee explains what has been done to the item in terms of how the repair will benefit the customer.

2. Two days after the item has been picked up, the repair service sends a thank-you postcard.
3. Four weeks later, an employee calls the customer to inquire if the item is working properly and say, "We want you to be satisfied with our work."

These examples demonstrate the significance of one of the most powerful resources available to relationship-based services: the database. Cell 4 companies are fortunate in knowing who their clients are. As a result, they can communicate with all clients or with specific subgroups for whom they have a special message. For organizations in cell 3 that want to move into cell 4, as well as for organizations in cells 1 and 2 that want to communicate directly with known customers, find a way to build a database of your best clients. When American Airlines designed the frequent flyer program, American created a "membership" database that allowed the carrier to communicate with a significant market and offer benefits that increased sales.

To sum up, relationship management is a powerful retention strategy, which "involves centering the organization on the expectations and requirements of *individual* customers and using information, technology, and management to meet more and more of their specialized needs."[6]

# Evaluating the Effectiveness of Retention Programs

Whatever type of relationship management or retention program you initiate, you will want to assess its effectiveness. Here are four indicators of your progress:

1. Financial results
2. Reduced client losses
3. Client feedback
4. Lost-client interviews

In this section, we will look at each approach.

## Improved Financial Results

The best financial reporting system would show you not only whether revenues are up or down, but also what is happening with individual service lines and individual clients. One basic report is shown in Table 15-3. This company offers four basic services. The figures in the table show the fees paid by a client for a particular service. Each row total shows the total fees associated with a client; the column totals show the total fees for each service line. A similar report could show variances from year to year. This type of information is especially valuable in client service planning because it shows what services a client is and is not using.

**Table 15-3.** Example of a financial report showing fees by
service line, by client, and in total.

| Client | Service 1 | Service 2 | Service 3 | Service 4 | Total |
|---|---|---|---|---|---|
| ABC Corporation | $ 11,750 | $ 22,000 | $ 0 | $ 0 | $ 33,750 |
| Baily Brothers | 0 | 52,000 | 0 | 0 | 52,000 |
| XYZ Company | 8,500 | 0 | 12,750 | 2,250 | 23,500 |
| Total* | $275,000 | $410,000 | $320,000 | $125,000 | $1,130,000 |

*Note that column totals reflect amounts for *all* the clients, not just for the three clients shown.

If your systems are not capable of this level of detail, another approach would be to look at total revenues. Have they increased or decreased? This indicator is not very satisfactory unless you understand how to use the data. One useful tool is a new-and-lost client tracking system.

## Reduced Client Losses

Although tracking lost clients is critical, many service organizations do not have a system to do this. Certainly it is more interesting to talk about new business (which does tend to be tracked), if only because new clients must be entered into the billing system. People avoid talking about lost clients, and it isn't unusual for them to stay in the client database long after their demise.

A new-and-lost client tracking system will help you determine whether lost-client volume is eroding your success at attracting new clients. If your company has been experiencing heavy losses, the data will tell you whether you have had fewer losses and reversed the trend.

## Client Feedback

Many service organizations have implemented client satisfaction tracking systems, which should incorporate data on relationship management, particularly because the information concerns day-to-day service delivery and interpersonal relationships, important indicators of service quality. Clients can provide you with valuable information about your strengths, as well as areas for improvement, whether your service organization is in cell 1, 2, 3, or 4 (see Figure 15-1).

In some service organizations, client satisfaction is not being tracked. In part, this results from service providers' reluctance to have management know what clients think about their service experiences and relationships. The service providers believe that negative comments would be used to evaluate them. In actuality, a two-track system could be developed that gives service providers confidentiality and specific constructive criticism based on client feedback, while giving management summary information that is useful in developing strategies for the organization.

### Lost-Client Interviews

Lost clients can be valuable sources of information about the way relationships are handled because of their firsthand knowledge and experience with your firm's service delivery systems. Find out what criteria were used in selecting the client's new company; it is likely that the decision-maker expects to have a strong working relationship with someone at her new company. The client debriefing can be the first step in your plan to salvage the relationship; the new association may not be successful.

### Evaluation Planning

As you undertake a client retention program, include evaluation in your program planning. In this way, you will have the information necessary to answer the question, "Is it working?" You also will have useful data to help you refine your program and improve its effectiveness. And, of course, the willingness of clients to continue and expand their relationships with your company indicates their satisfaction with its service delivery systems.

## How to Support Service Providers

Your organization's service providers need support in developing relationship-building and relationship-management skills and capabilities. This support may be offered through internal marketing, computer and manual systems, and client feedback systems.

### Internal Marketing

Relationship management skills can be learned on-the-job as well as in formal courses. Managers have a responsibility to help their staff understand a client's situation and why certain services are delivered in a particular way. Through such processes as client service planning, staff can gain insights into clients' concerns, not just the technical aspects of the company's services.

Formal educational programs that are relevant include all types of communication courses, including listening skills. In addition, business-to-business service providers should seek out programs related to their clients' business issues. Although it's important to maintain open communications with a client, it helps to bring some substance to the relationship—substance as defined by the client.

As you develop and refine your internal marketing programs (see Chapter 5), look for ways to tie them to client retention. Provide orientation programs for new services so that everyone in the organization has basic information about these services. Internal newsletters can feature clients so that the company's personnel become familiar with a client's business, including its products or services. Recognition programs can be designed to spotlight quality service; in fact, clients could nominate service providers with whom they have particularly constructive relationships.

### Computer and Manual Systems

As you formulate the type of relationship management process that is appropriate for your organization, identify the systems that will relieve service providers of time-consuming administrative tasks. Tickler systems can be helpful in reminding people to perform certain activities. If you want to integrate company-sponsored activities with personal-contact plans, design the company-sponsored activities in advance so that the integration process can be systematized.

Sophisticated software is available to help service providers keep track of client meetings, personal information about clients, and telephone conversations; the service provider can tap into a complete information file about a client and appear to have a remarkable memory.

Many relationship management systems can be administered by support staff. For example, the secretary to the head of a service team can take the minutes of a client service planning session and coordinate follow-up activities. By removing these administrative activities from your service providers' responsibilities, you free them up to spend more time with clients and prospective clients.

### Client Feedback Systems

Client feedback is an especially effective way to help service providers become more sensitive to client relationships. Feedback areas range from the client's knowledge of the organization's services to perceptions of the service provider's interest in the client's concerns.

Although feedback helps a service provider become more sensitive to a client's concerns, it doesn't help him understand how he can improve his relationship skills. That's one of the reasons why it is essential for the service organization to offer a broad range of educational and other support programs. In this way, if clients claim that service providers don't listen to their concerns, for example, the service providers can attempt to improve their listening skills.

## Relationships and Value

For many service organizations, retention means the difference between survival and profitability. It is important for service managers to understand the nature of their relationships with customers and clients, and to develop appropriate strategies for different types of relationships.

For services based on long-term, interpersonal relationships, the central role of the relationship should be reflected in their mission statements (or statements of philosophy) and substantive investment in developing the client sensitivity of service providers. Long-term relationships can be managed. For these relationships to endure, both clients and service providers must gain value from the relationship.

## Notes

1. For an interesting analysis of long-term relationships between industrial customers and their suppliers, see Barbara Bund Jackson, ''Build Customer Relationships That Last,'' *Harvard Business Review,* November/December 1985, 120–128.
2. Christopher Lovelock, *Services Marketing* (Englewood Cliffs, N.J.: Prentice-Hall, 1984), 53–55.
3. The description of critical points is based on ''How to Keep Clients Happy: Four Critical Points,'' in *The Accountant's Strategic Marketing Guide,* Carole A. Congram and Ruth J. Dumesic (New York: Wiley, 1986), 28–30.
4. Theodore Levitt, ''After the Sale Is Over . . . ,'' *Harvard Business Review,* September/October 1983, 87–93.
5. The section on client service planning is based on Carole A. Congram, ''Adding Value Through Client Service Planning,'' in *Add Value to Your Service,* ed. Carol F. Surprenant (Chicago: American Marketing Association, 1988), 175–178. Consult this article for more extensive information on the topic.
6. Lawrence A. Crosby, Kenneth R. Evans, and John C. Sack, ''A Strategic Framework for the Management of Service Relationships,'' based on a paper presented at the American Marketing Association's Financial Services Conference in Boston in June, 1988.

\*     \*     \*     \*

*Carole A. Congram, Ph.D., is the principal of Congram Associates, a consulting firm based in New York City and specializing in services marketing. She assists clients with a broad range of planning and implementation services. She also holds the position of associate professor of operations management at Bentley College in Waltham, Massachusetts. A frequent speaker on services marketing topics, she was on the national marketing staff of Touche Ross & Co. for eleven years, most recently as director of marketing communication planning.*

# 16

## How to Organize and Implement a Service Management System

Charmaine L. Ponkratz

The planning and implementation of services are becoming the riskiest activities a company can undertake. Not only are the costs of planning and research increasing, but also the complexity of many of the services that are being considered for implementation or introduction will result in skyrocketing investments. Under such circumstances, there is a great temptation to either stay with what a company is presently doing, or at the very least play the waiting game by letting the competition do it first. The implications of the latter strategy are far-reaching.

Realistically in managing the mix of services, a company has only two alternatives:

1. It can pursue its objectives and goals within the framework of a current mix of services, which basically means staying with what is already being done; this is a status quo decision.
2. Or, it can modify its present service mix either by adding new services, modifying current services, or by eliminating services that no longer meet its objectives and goals.

As simplistic as these alternatives may appear, they reflect the problem encountered not only by management in service industries, but by management in other industries as well. This problem is the failure to recognize that maintaining the status quo is, in fact, a decision—one that, like the decision to add, modify, or delete services, entails risks. Although certain kinds of risks can be avoided by staying with the status quo, or at least by letting someone else do it first, risks cannot be avoided entirely. The point is that obvious risks are associated with introducing new or modified services, but there are some not so obvious risks associated with the status quo.

## Service Life Cycle

To understand the less obvious risks, one needs to explore the typical nature of services as they move through the service life cycle. For purposes of this discussion, the service life cycle is divided into four stages. Throughout the discussion of the four service life-cycle stages it may be helpful to refer to Figure

**Figure 16-1.** The service life cycle.

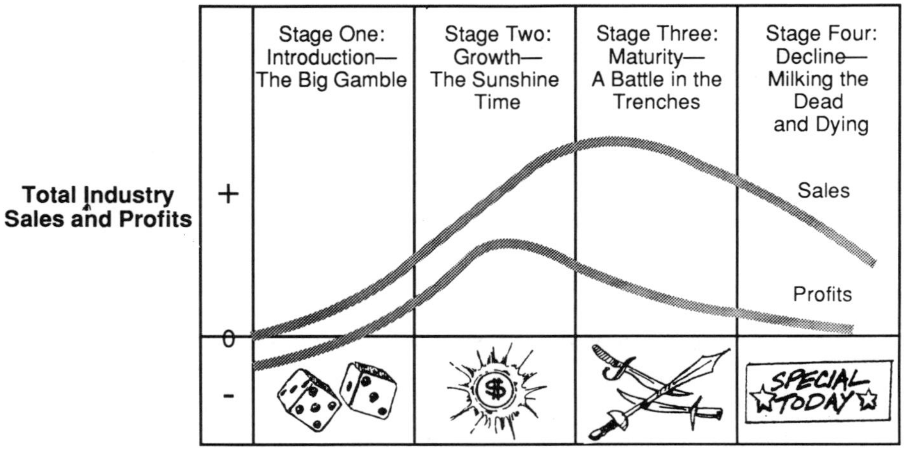

16-1 to gain a clearer understanding of the relationship between sales and profitability in each stage. The characteristics of each stage, which are described below, are summarized in Figure 16-2.

## Introduction—The Big Gamble

Calling the first stage The Big Gamble aptly describes the risk of introduction. Because the service is new and presumably unique, it is almost always introduced by a single company. Characteristics of the service in this stage can be described as follows:

- Since there is no competition at the introductory stage of a life cycle, significant product variations are not necessary to achieve a competitive advantage.
- Pricing tends to be influenced by the lack of major competition, and prices generally tend to be higher than they will be when the service matures.
- Because the new service is introduced by a single company, the market lacks awareness and understanding of the service. This problem puts a special burden on the promotional part of the firm's marketing strategy. To bring about market awareness, the promotional effort must be disproportionately heavy.
- Finally, the new service probably will lose money.

## Growth—The Sunshine Time

Why take a gamble? The answer is simple: To put the organization in the best possible position for taking advantage of the growth stage, appropriately called The Sunshine Time.

The characteristics in this stage are as follows:

**Figure 16-2.** Characteristics of each stage of the service life cycle.

| Typical Characteristics | Stage of Development | | | |
| --- | --- | --- | --- | --- |
| | Introduction:<br>The Big Gamble | Growth:<br>The Sunshine Time | Maturity:<br>A Battle in the Trenches | Decline:<br>Milking the Dead<br>and Dying |
| Industry sales | Start from zero and grow very slowly | Rapid growth, but start to level out toward end of cycle | Stable or grow slightly over time | Decline |
| Competition | Nonexistent or low | Some—grows as profitability in industry increases | Severe; heavy (large number, or vigorous) | Cutthroat |
| Segmentation | None, other than an attempt to find early adopters | Some on explicit characteristics | Heavy on explicit and implicit characteristics | Little emphasis; late adopters |
| Service diversity | Little or none; one-service concept | Increase in models; explicit or real differences based on function | Proliferation of models with short production run; implicit differences | Some reduction in models; weeding out the unprofitable |
| Promotion | Based on service function; heavy personal selling, highly educational, disproportionately heavy | Based on physical differences between models; some brand emphasis (explicit characteristics); personal selling; mass promotion | Emphasis on explicit characteristics more difficult; emphasis shifting almost completely to brand and to implicit or emotional factors | Emphasis on implicit characteristics; general withdrawal of promotion |
| Industry profits | Negative; market development | Highest level, but drop off at end of cycle | Profit squeeze; promotion cost up; distribution cost up; prices down | Small and declining |

*Source: Developing Bank Services: A Practical Guide,* © 1982 by the American Bankers Association. Reprinted with permission. All rights reserved.

- Significant growth occurs as others begin to introduce the service, general market awareness and acceptance has reached some critical mass, and sales become substantial.
- The new competitors at this point do not present a serious problem; instead, these new entrants into the market tend to expand the market at an even greater rate because of the increase in the general market awareness of the new service.
- Despite the competition, market sales will be increasing, so the major problems might be production and supply to keep up with the demand. Thus, price competition will be virtually nonexistent during this stage.
- Service diversity will begin to increase as competitors try to position themselves favorably within certain portions of the market.
- The character of the promotion effort will be different than it was in the introduction stage. During introduction it carried an educational burden, but in this stage it will emphasize brand or company recognition and preference.
- Perhaps the most important aspect of the life-cycle growth stage is that this is going to be the time of maximum profitability for the industry involved in delivering this service.

Before discussing the maturity stage of the life cycle, several key points need to be stressed. First, remember that the life-cycle discussion is being presented from an overall industry perspective. Division of sales and profits among competing firms within a particular industry is rarely equal. The organizations that make the investment during the introduction stage are usually in the best position to take advantage of opportunities at the growth stage and usually dominate market share and profitability throughout the life cycle. As a general rule, the later an organization enters a life cycle of a generic service, the more difficulty it has achieving market share and profitability.

Second, the industry profits for a generic service not only peak during the growth stage, but actually begin to decline toward the end of the stage, even though industry sales are still increasing. This is because the sunshine time attracts increasing numbers of competitors to the market, causing market saturation and the beginning of price competition. This brings home a key point: Sales are not profits, and increasing sales is not necessarily increasing profits.

### Maturity—The Battle in the Trenches

By the time a service reaches maturity, total industry sales have begun to level off, or they increase only slightly if the population increases.

In this stage the battle will be fought in the trenches, and some of the characteristics are as follows:

- Heavy competitive pressures will exist for the business, making the scramble for market share and profitability very difficult.
- Costs associated with diversifying the service will increase.
- Price competition will arise.
- Promotional efforts will become less effective.

*Decline—Milking the Dead and Dying*

One can assume that eventually all services will enter the decline stage, where:

- Sales will actually begin to decrease, probably as a result of the introduction of a new service or an elimination of the consumer need that justified the old service. Often this decline stage will be irreversible.
- Cutthroat competition will develop as companies desperately attempt to survive or to minimize their losses.
- The only organizations that actually profit in this stage are those that are skilled in milking the dead and dying to the end.

# Key Operational Components of Service Planning

With the foregoing as a background, we are in a position to review the key components of service planning. A nine-step approach will be discussed in the remainder of this chapter.

## Evaluating Present Service Mix

Placing a Service in the General Service Life Cycle.   Start out by placing a company's service(s) onto the life-cycle chart. It is not necessary to get involved in a complicated mathematical or market research project to determine their position within the life cycle. Take each service separately, analyze its characteristics, and determine whether that characteristic would indicate it is in the introduction stage, the growth stage, the maturity stage, or the decline stage. Table 16-1 may be used as a worksheet. The service charted in the example borders between the maturity and decline stages.

**Table 16-1.** Analysis of the life cycle of a service.

| Service Characteristics | Phases of Generic Service Life Cycle | | | |
|---|---|---|---|---|
| | Introduction | Growth | Maturity | Decline |
| 1. Industry sales | | | ● | |
| 2. Competition | | | ● | ● |
| 3. Segmentation | | | ● | |
| 4. Service diversity | | | ● | |
| 5. Pricing | | | ● | ● |
| 6. Promotion | | | | ● |
| 7. Industry profits | | | | ● |

*Source: Developing Bank Services: A Practical Guide,* © 1982 by the American Bankers Association. Reprinted with permission. All rights reserved.

Analyzing the Complete Service Mix Pattern.    After each service has been reviewed, transfer the findings to Figure 16-1 to determine whether the service mix is indicative of a bright future, a modest future, or a dead-end future. At least three benefits can be derived by completing this exercise:

1. It forces you to consider the most significant market factors and trends within your industry.
2. Based on where the service falls in the life cycle, it can help you anticipate the competitive environment.
3. Knowing what that environment is going to be like, you can make informed decisions with regard to modifications, cost cutting, and such.

Evaluation of the current service mix will provide a basis for the second phase of service planning.

### Establishing Objectives and Goals

Relationship to Company's Long-Range Plan.    A great deal of time could be spent on the subject of corporate goals and objectives, both long-range and short-range, as they affect marketing and specific services. Corporate goals and objectives need to be stated in a way that ties them directly to the marketing mix issues of product, price, place, and promotion. Market-driven companies will define their goals in terms of high-priority markets. It is the marketers' job to apply the marketing principles and develop appropriate objectives and strategies.

Four Strategies for Growth and Profitability.    Determining the marketing strategies to be followed to achieve company goals is a key step in the planning process. Four basic strategies can direct the company's future: market penetration, market development, service development, and service diversification. A clearer understanding of the components of these strategies can be gained by examining Figure 16-3. The strategy selection will determine the markets to be targeted—either present or new markets. For those companies planning for growth "(service) innovation is universally recognized as a strategy for building market share—in both mature and expanding markets." [1]

Regardless of the direction selected, turning strategies into action requires a written tactical plan.

Tactical Plans From a Service Planning Perspective.    There are three basic approaches: add a new service, drop a service, or modify a service.

Modifying a service entails changes of function, style, or quality. *Function* involves changes that enhance the usefulness or value of that service to the customer. Adding a capability or enhancement to a service is exemplified by financial institutions' shift from offering traditional second mortgages to offering contemporary equity lines of credit.

Modifications in *style* recognize that customers buy products or services for other than functional reasons; witness the success of designer blue jeans. A

**Figure 16-3.** Marketing strategies.

**Services**

|  | Present Services | New Services |
|---|---|---|
| **Present Markets** | Market Penetration | Service Development |
| **New Markets** | Market Development | Diversification |

**Markets**

change in style is demonstrated by the fact that a Gold MasterCard has a status value that a regular MasterCard does not have.

Modifications in *quality* involve altering the way in which a customer perceives the value of the service. Recently banks have begun rebundling or recombining services in order to create incentive pricing for customers who have more than one relationship with the bank. This is a way of adding quality or value to a service. Another example would be to assign a senior account executive to a customer relationship, which will add value to the service being delivered.

When developing the tactical plan, keep in mind the distinction between strategies and the related actions. Strategies are the *what,* the general path to be followed within reasonable time frames. Actions indicate the *how, with whom,* and *when* the strategy will be followed.

## Generating Ideas

Management teams often have a general idea about what kind of service addition or modification might be effective. No system for planning new services, however carefully designed and implemented, can produce winning services out of losing ideas. A company's ability to develop successful new services depends on its ability to generate good ideas for new services. Although these ideas occasionally appear out of nowhere, ultimately the success of a company's service planning system depends on developing a formal and rigorous procedure for generating ideas. Both external and internal sources of ideas must be nurtured and maintained.

External Sources of Ideas.   The external sources include primary research projects, unsolicited suggestions, secondary source research findings, and competitive offerings.

Internal Sources of Ideas.   Employee suggestions and established brainstorming sessions should not be overlooked as employees often hold the key to many product problems. When accepting ideas from internal sources, be careful to avoid passing judgment too early, because the net effect will be to stifle the number of ideas generated and thus affect future input. As ideas are presented, marketing management's job is to screen them.

### Screening Ideas for Services

Single out each one of the services submitted for consideration, measure it against the following criteria, and rate it as high, medium, and low. This will serve as a way of determining whether or not the service is worth pursuing. Any idea that fails to measure up to a significant number of these criteria should be eliminated immediately:

> *Customer transferability*—Will current customers utilize the new service?
> *Distribution system leverage*—Can current distribution systems be used to deliver this service? Will new facilities or new technologies be required?
> *Image*—Will this service be consistent with the kind of image that your company is trying to project?
> *Service synergy*—Will this service complement your company's current menu, or will it only confuse both the salespeople and the customers?
> *Skill similarity*—Does current staff have the skills required to deliver this service, or will training be a significant factor?
> *Personnel policy similarities*—Are compensation and benefit packages for the new employees hired to deliver this service similar to those of the current staff? Commission versus noncommission salary structures can create conflict and dissension within company units.
> *Risk to company*—What kind of capital investment is required? What kind of human resources investment is required? What is the risk level if the service fails and needs to be taken off the market?
> *Motivation for entry*—Is there a high motivation for entry? Is there substantial profit and growth for the future?

### Business Analysis: Determining the Levels of Volume, Price, and Profit

The service ideas that survive the initial screening should then be evaluated quantitatively. Estimates must be made of the expected costs, sales, and profits over some future time period. This will not always be easy, because the service prototype has yet to be developed and costs will be difficult to estimate (see

Chapter 14). Given the inability to determine the expenses of marketing, service production, and the uncertainty of market acceptance, it will be hard to estimate sales and profits.

Despite the uncertainties and the subjectivity that many of the estimates will require, it is necessary to come up with the best quantitative analysis possible. The reason for this is that the next step—actually developing the service—is likely to be very expensive, and only those services that appear quantitatively promising should make it to that step.

At this point the idea is under consideration, and assumptions should be made about how that service will look, how it will be delivered, how it will be priced, how it will be marketed, and how it will be received. This is not the stage at which the final service definition and specifications are developed.

When preparing these preliminary assumptions for the business analysis, it is important that the marketing and financial professionals meet with one another.

Determine the Costing Philosophy to Be Used.   The company's executive management background and culture generally dictate which costing philosophy is acceptable within the organization:

*Fully absorbed (average) costing.* This costing philosophy is based on the concept that unit costs should recover a proportionately fair share of indirect expenses and other fixed costs, as well as cover the incremental costs of the service.

The costing philosophy is probably more appropriate for use in repricing an existing service than in the pricing of a new one. Any company blindly following this philosophy in a highly competitive marketplace will potentially compromise its future for short-term profits.

*Incremental costing.* This costing philosophy suggests that unit costs should only recover the incremental costs directly attributable to the service offering. This costing philosophy is probably more appropriate for use in pricing new services than in the repricing of an existing one. Blind adherence to this costing philosophy will eventually lead to financial insolvency if all or most of the company's services are costed in this fashion to determine pricing. Some services must defray the nonallocatable expenses of the organization.

*Cost/volume average costing.* This philosophy advocates that unit costs should factor in the impact of volume on the costs incurred over a period of time. Cost reductions occur as a result of spreading the fixed overhead expenses over a greater volume of service usage. Additional cost reductions should occur because of the "experience curve" that results from volume increases. The "experience curve" effect suggests that "for each doubling in volume, the company should achieve a reduction in costs (typically 20–30%)"[2] as a result of experience-related operational and sales efficiencies.

This costing philosophy becomes more appropriate as the company's skills in forecasting volume growth or changes become more finely honed. This approach is likely to give the company a major competitive edge in the pricing of its services.

*Customer relationship costing.* This centers on the composite costing of a customer relationship rather than the individual service components. Few companies can employ this costing philosophy because of data processing limitations.

The heart of this costing philosophy is the presumption that the company can create and capitalize upon operational and marketing cost efficiencies, which will reduce the cost of servicing the customer relationship.

<u>Determine the Pricing Strategy.</u>   Once the costing approach has been defined and developed, the next step is to determine the appropriate pricing strategy (see also Chapter 17). In both cases it is important that senior management of the company agree on the technique or combination of techniques being used. At this point they must be given all the information they deem necessary to have confidence in their decision regarding adoption or rejection of the project. Several pricing strategies are commonly used:[3]

*Cost plus.* The basic strategy here is to determine service cost and price above that cost to provide an acceptable profit margin. The advantages to this method are straightforward: it is simple, easy to understand, and its execution is objective and analytical. The disadvantages of "cost plus" pricing are that it ignores customer needs, the marketplace, and competition.

*Competitive pricing.* Here it is important to determine what competitors are actually charging, which is not always as easy as it sounds. Quantity discounts and prices resulting from bidding situations, instead of true prices, are often quoted as a "going rate." Companies that use this strategy often reduce prices in order to attract more business. The advantages to competitive pricing are that it is simple and easy to understand, and it is easier to execute than the "cost plus" method. It focuses only on competition, however, and ignores costs and customer demand.

*Value pricing.* This pricing is based on what the market will bear and focuses almost exclusively on customer demands and other external factors. Value pricing can be very effective if the perceived value of services is properly identified. It focuses on customer needs and can result in ideal prices as defined by the customer. Because cost factors are ignored with this strategy, it is conceivable that despite an optimal market price, a product might not be profitable. This strategy requires significant data collection and research time, making it more expensive to develop services.

Once the business analysis of a new service is completed and the decision is favorable, it is time to shift from a research mode to an execution and implementation mode.

## Developing the New Service

The ideas that have made it this far have been screened and analyzed quantitatively and have survived the process. Now it is time to focus on the specifics of the new service.

Service Definition and Specification. Much of the basic service design work has been done in the analysis. Now each detail of the service must be examined critically from a market point of view to determine each feature and resultant customer benefit.

Operations and Procedures. Just as with service definition, much of the general framework will have been laid for operational procedures. At this point the focus will be on fine-tuning and testing. The service should be tested internally to ensure that it "operates" as it is designed to be marketed, to be sure service quality is at the desired level, and to correct any procedural problems.

Establishing a service task force or team is a particularly successful approach. This typically consists of two or three responsible individuals—one from operations, one from marketing, and one who is or will become the service expert or service manager. Each of the tasks relative to the service, from a marketing and an operations viewpoint, needs to be detailed and assigned with time lines.

Service Management. Each service will have its unique set of service management tasks to be completed:

*Information-gathering transfer system.* This involves creating the flow chart of information processing. This may be a paper process or an electronic entry. The process must track where and how information is gathered, how it is transferred, and how it gets reported back so management can track the service. This set of tasks must be completed before introduction because if demand is high, you will avoid many problems in this key area.

*Employee training system.* An employee training system must be established for this new service, and some of the important items that need to be presented to the employees are: A history of the service—where did this idea originate? What are the strategy and rationale behind introducing the service? What are the features of the service and, more critically, what are the benefits from the customer's point of view? What pricing and profitability information is relevant to the employees? Who are the priority target markets? What clues might they see and hear to indicate a sales opportunity?

Establish a cross-sales alert to include a list of services complementary to the one being introduced. Where does this service stand relative to the competition? How does this service fit into the current mix of services? What kind of service tracking information needs to be gathered from employees? What agreements, documents, and contracts are needed for implementation? And, what are the service or account-opening procedures? All these factors must be anticipated in order to help employees understand the new service and be responsive to customers.

*Promotion.* In the introduction stage of a service, it is critical that the promotion and service strategies are integrated, and that the elements of advertising, publicity, and personal selling are used with maximum effectiveness. During this stage education is critical if the market is to become aware of the product. All resources should be tapped to penetrate the market.

As a service moves through its life cycle, the factors that influence customers to purchase the service change. For example, price usually becomes more important in each successive stage, as shown by the progressively larger boxes for price in Figure 16-4, which also indicates shifts in other relevant factors. Marketing strategies must reflect these shifts.

*Service quality.* Much is being written about service quality. A company that is committed to quality in ''production'' or the delivery process will have the following philosophy: Quality will be defined by the customer. It will become a profit strategy for the company. Quality must be viewed as a journey, not an event. It must become everyone's job, with leadership and communication provided by top management (see also Chapter 1). It is a design issue, and talking about service implies establishing a corporate environment that can keep the service promise.[4]

### Testing the Service

Basically, there are three approaches to testing a service. A separate market may be selected, perhaps a branch office location. A separate segment may be tested, perhaps the senior market first. Or, the concept can be tested through the use of focus groups or other research mechanisms.

Although consumer input has been an integral component of the development process to this point, the service has not yet been offered in a real-time environment. This is the goal in the testing phase. Because some executives believe that test marketing exposes the new service to the competitors prematurely, in some cases services have not been test marketed and have been taken to commercialization without that step.

### Commercialization

The most exciting step of the product planning cycle is commercialization. The execution of this phase is the result of the marketing mix issues that were described earlier in this chapter. At this point the service development task force steps into the coach's role to support and encourage the company to achieve success.

### Management of Service Performance

After the service goes to market, the challenge is to manage and monitor its performance relative to the business analysis that was completed, and to oversee the new service problems and opportunities that arise. This requires the skills and leadership of the service manager. At this point the management information system must provide relevant and meaningful data so that service improvements and enchancements can be acted upon quickly to prevent the premature demise of a service.

There is one caution relative to new service development: If a company decides to go with a new service, it should fully commit to it. Do not expect a new service to take off by itself. It requires strong promotional support at the front end. A manager who discovers that full commitment never materialized,

**Figure 16-4.** Shifts in the marketing mix.

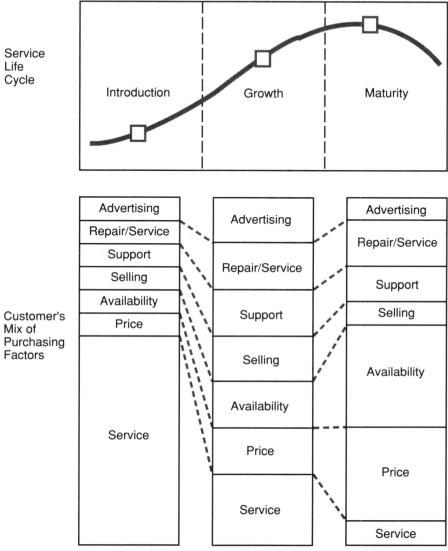

*Source:* Dick Kerndt, Value-Added Marketing Seminar, May 1987. Used by permission of The Richmark Group, Chicago, Illinois.

that the service is only marginally successful, and that the decision to continue or terminate is a toss-up is in an unenviable position. Give absolutely all of the resources the company can allot to the effort. Give the service the collective best, and if it does not work, scrap it. But if it does, it may be the service that keeps a company profitable for the next five years!

The length of a service's life will vary depending on many factors. A service that is faddish in nature may move through its entire life cycle in months, whereas others may last for 100 years or more.

Projecting the length of the stages within the life cycle is critical, because the ongoing service management strategies need to change during the different stages. This is particularly important during the decline stage when competition becomes fierce and the profit picture dims. It is at this point that service managers must plan for the careful elimination of the service line. Declining services need to be replaced by new services, and so the service development cycle begins again.

## Notes

1. Robert D. Buzzell and Frederick D. Wiersema, ''Successful Share-Building Strategies,'' *Harvard Business Review,* January/February 1981, 140.
2. Financial Institutions Marketing Association newsletter, December 1984.
3. ''Deregulation Brings Choices in Pricing of Financial Services,'' *American Banker,* October 1987.
4. ''8 Keys to Top Service at Financial Institutions,'' *American Banker,* August 1987, 4, 18.

*      *      *      *

***Charmaine L. Ponkratz*** *is vice president of marketing for Valley Bancorporation in Wisconsin. In this capacity she is responsible for the development, implementation, and review of corporatewide marketing strategies and programs. She has supported the introduction of many new services to customers. She also supervises departmental staff and the bank's advertising agency. Formerly Ms. Ponkratz worked in other banks in the areas of commercial loans, customer service, and new accounts.*

# PRICING AS VALUATION

The chapter in this section deals with pricing, one of the least understood elements in the marketing mix. Given that *every* service has a price, it is ironic that the price variable is used so ineffectively as a marketing tool. All too often a simple formula approach is taken to price determination (roughly, cost plus some add-on amount), while the critical factors of customer perception and response are left out of the calculation.

In this chapter you will be exposed to a much richer, deeper, and more profitable meaning of price than quantitative, monetary terms can begin to capture. Although certain costs (direct, indirect but traceable, variable, and semivariable) must play a role in pricing decisions, other more market-focused considerations must enter into the final price determination process. These market-focused considerations are the tools of what the author calls the *proactive pricer*—one who takes control of price and makes it work effectively in the marketing mix. Some of the market-focused pricing considerations covered in the chapter are price-quality perceptions, customer perceptions of value, and customer sensitivity to price levels and price changes.

The author concludes with the presentation of several common pricing strategies. Skimming/penetration options for new services are discussed. Pricing multiple services and the idea of bundling, or recognizing the symbiotic effects among demand and among prices for a group of several services, are also covered. Finally, contingency pricing, where some of the risk is removed from the price, is addressed; this strategy is particularly relevant for services given the fact that services are generally difficult to evaluate prior to purchase.

This is a chapter you will probably want to read more than once. Do not expect to be handed on a silver platter a neat and compact process for price determination. Service pricing does not work that way. You can reasonably expect to have full appreciation of all the information you need to make sound pricing decisions—information relative to consumer perceptions and behavior, to competitive actions, to the environment, and to cost classification. This information, then, is applied to a price determination process that starts with straightforward objectives, proceeds through development of price strategy, and ends with a price rooted in objective analysis and managerial judgment.

# 17

# The Pricing of Services

Kent B. Monroe

Pricing a product or service is one of the most important decisions made by management. Pricing is the only marketing strategy variable that directly generates income. All other variables in the marketing mix—advertising, product-service development, sales promotion, distribution—involve expenditures. In recent years, economic and competitive pressures have led to new marketing approaches and strategies, particularly in the area of pricing. Pricing practice still remains largely intuitive and routine, however, and the pricing literature has not produced enough new insights or approaches to stimulate most businesspeople to change their methods of setting prices.[1] Indeed, companies often determine prices by marking up cost figures supplied by the financial division, and do not bring pricing into their marketing strategies. However, the pressures of adapting to today's deregulated economy have placed additional burdens on the service industries. The purpose of this chapter is to offer some new insights and approaches to help service companies become active rather than passive pricers while adjusting to this new economic environment.

## The Meaning of Price

We often think of price as the amount of money we must sacrifice to acquire something desired. That is, price is considered as a formal ratio indicating the quantities of money needed to acquire a given amount of services:

$$\text{Price} = \frac{\text{Quantity of money or services received by the seller}}{\text{Quantity and quality of services received by the buyer}}$$

To illustrate the complexity of pricing, there are several ways to change this ratio. Moreover, the following discussion illustrates a major error made by many organizations. That is, many organizations focus only on the numerator of the ratio and forget the denominator. Also, by focusing on the numerator, they encourage their customers to think of price only in actual monetary terms, that is, as a cost or sacrifice to be minimized. However, firms that take a value orientation to pricing consider both sides of the ratio, and they encourage their customers to think in terms of the value of the quantity and quality of the services received relative to the monetary outlay. Thus, instead of promoting low prices, they promote better or more value for the required monetary outlay. For example, the price of a first-class hotel room in a major southeastern city varied between \$32 and \$178 for a one-night, single occupancy. The airlines sell the same commodity, a coach seat between two cities on the same flight, at different prices. The reason for the different dollar price involves differences in the buyer's perceptions of value received for these seemingly similar services.[2] Indeed, airlines or hotels sell a seat or room at different prices depending on when payment is made, when the trip or room is booked, the buyers' willingness to accept use constraints, whether a single individual or group is involved, and whether cancellation without penalty is possible.

Looking at the ratio, there are three obvious ways to change price: *change the quantity of money or services to be received by the seller, change the quantity of services to be received by the buyer,* or *change the quality of services provided.* A seller may change the quantity of services by changing the number of offerings. For example, a cable TV company may reduce the number of cable networks or premium channels to be included in the basic monthly package. Also, if the quantity aspect of the ratio remains unchanged, but the quality has been decreased, then the price has been increased because the buyer actually receives less. If quality is raised without changing the quantity ratio, then the price has decreased.

Price can be *changed by changing the premiums or discounts to be applied for quantity variations.* Offering discounts for quantity purchases, such as family rates for a health club, reduces the actual price to the individuals acquiring the service. Or, a lower group rate for a hotel reduces the price to each individual. Price can also be changed by offering premiums with purchases, such as trading stamps, toys, glasses, or frequent purchase rewards. In each case, if the quantity ratio remains constant, a premium serves to reduce the actual price paid, because the buyer receives additional goods or services.

Often the actual price is changed if the *place and time of payment are changed.* Being able to receive a service and having ninety days to pay without interest is an actual reduction in price over paying at the time of purchase. Because money has a time value, permitting customers to receive the service for a time without paying for it is a reduction in price. A reversal of this practice—purchasing an airline ticket sixty days in advance—leads to a reduction in the actual monetary outlay for the ticket, although because of the time value of money, it is less of a monetary reduction than customers may perceive. *Changing the acceptable form of payment* is another way to change price. Some organizations do not accept checks, others operate on a cash-only basis, whereas some accept credit charges for regular clients. Thus, *price is the amount of money and services (or goods) the buyer exchanges for an assortment of services provided by the seller.* The variety of ways to change price makes pricing a very important marketing decision. Focusing on both the numerator and denominator provides opportunities to make the offer more unique, even if the service otherwise is considered to be a commodity.

## Proactive Pricing

Pricing a service is one of the most important decisions made by management. During the 1960s the United States became a service-oriented economy, and the demand for services is still increasing. In virtually all instances this rapid increase in demand has led to rapid increases in prices, because pure services consist mainly of labor, and productivity gains have been low. Many of these price increases have resulted from a naive and unsophisticated approach to pricing without regard to underlying shifts in demand, the rate that supply can be expanded, prices of available substitutes, consideration of the price-volume relationship, or the availability of future substitutes. The demand for services remains strong, resulting in increased pressure on pricing decisions. A major impact of these pressures has been to make service pricing more delicate, more complex, more important. Organizations that have been successful in making profitable pricing decisions have taken what may be called a proactive pricing approach.[3] They have been able to raise prices successfully or reduce prices without competitive retaliation, and have become aggressive pricing strategists and tacticians.

There are two essential prerequisites for becoming a successful proactive pricer. First, it is necessary to understand how pricing works. Because of the complexities of pricing in terms of its impact on suppliers, salespeople, distributors, competitors, and customers, the simple prescriptions of traditional microeconomic theory are not appropriate for a modern market system. Indeed, companies that focus primarily on their internal costs often make serious pricing errors.

Second, it is essential for any pricer to understand how customers perceive prices and price changes. Often, price is used not only as an indicator of how much money the buyer must pay, but also as an indicator of service quality. Moreover, differences between the prices of alternative choices also affect buyers' perceptions. Thus, it is imperative that the price setter know how buyers perceive price information. Moreover, prices must be consistent with buyers' value perceptions. Failure to follow this basic prescription leads to some major pricing errors.

## Conceptual Orientation to Pricing

Five essential factors must be considered when setting price. *Demand* considerations provide a ceiling or maximum price that may be charged. The determination of this maximum price depends on customers' perceptions of value in the seller's service offering. Conversely, *costs* provide a floor or minimum possible price. For existing services, the relevant costs are the direct costs (costs to be incurred by and solely for the service) associated with the production, marketing, and distribution of these services. For a new service, the relevant costs are the *future direct costs* over the life of that service. The difference between what buyers are willing to pay (value) and the minimum cost-based price represents an initial pricing discretion. However, this range of pricing discretion is narrowed by *competitive factors, corporate profit and market objectives,* and *regulatory constraints.*

Primarily, competitive factors serve to reduce the price ceiling, whereas corporate objectives and regulation tend to raise the minimum possible price. Principally, corporate objectives translate into financial requirements that necessitate contribution margins to cover fixed costs and overhead and meet profit goals. Therefore, simply covering direct variable costs normally is an insufficient price level. Government regulation often forces the costs of production up (e.g., health-care requirements and safety standards). Regulation of certain marketing practices (e.g., nutrition labeling, and legal regulation against predatory pricing, as well as the need to protect a service from potential lawsuits) all have an upward effect on pricing.

Depending on the type of service and characteristics of demand and competition, the actual pricing discretion could still be relatively large, or it could be nonexistent. Nevertheless, several very important factors should be considered when setting prices. To focus only on costs obviously ignores many other important factors.

## Economics of Pricing

One of the most important cornerstones of price determination is demand. In particular, the volume of a service that buyers are willing to buy at a specific price is that service's demand. The discipline of economics provides the basic theory of how prices should be set, as well as some important analytical concepts for practical pricing decisions.

### Theory of Buyer Behavior

In economic theory, price influences buyer choice because price serves as an indicator of product or service cost to the buyer. Assuming the buyer has complete information concerning the prices and need satisfaction of comparable product alternatives, he or she can determine a product/service mix that maximizes satisfaction within a given budget constraint. Lacking complete and accurate information about the utility associated with the alternative services, however, the buyer assesses them on the basis of known information. Generally, one piece of information available to the buyer is a service's price. Other pieces of information about anticipated purchases are not always known, or are known less frequently than price, and the buyer cannot be sure how reliable and how complete this information is. And information not always available may introduce uncertainty about the buyer's ability to predict correctly the need satisfaction available through purchasing the service. *Hence, buyers may use price both as an indicator of service cost as well as an indicator of service quality (want satisfaction attributes).* This attractiveness attribute of a service's price will be discussed in a later section.

### Useful Economic Concepts

This brief outline of how price influences demand does not reveal the extent that price and demand are related for each product/service choice, nor does it help us to compare engineering services per dollar with accounting services per dollar. The concept of elasticity provides a unit-free measure of the sensitivity of one variable to another, and it provides a quantitative way of making comparisons across service choices. The first set of concepts from economic theory that is useful for pricing concerns the different types of elasticities.

Demand Elasticity. Price elasticity of demand measures the responsiveness of the quantity demanded for a product or service to a change in the price of the product or service. Specifically, *price elasticity of demand* is defined as the percentage change in quantity demanded relative to the percentage change in price. If it is assumed that quantity demanded falls as price increases, then price elasticity of demand is negative; if there is a positive relation between demand and price change, then elasticity is a positive value (i.e., demand increases as price is increased).

Often other measures of demand sensitivity are used to explore the implications of change. *Income elasticity of demand* is the percentage of change in quantity demanded of a service relative to a percentage change in personal income. If income elasticity is negative, this implies that as income goes up, fewer units are demanded. If income elasticity is positive, then demand increases as income increases, but there are two different possibilities. If income elasticity is a value between zero and one, then the demand for the service increases at a rate lower than the rate that income increases. But, if income elasticity is greater than one, then demand for the service increases faster than the rate that income increases (e.g., leisure and recreational activities).

A third measure of demand sensitivity is *cross-price elasticity of demand*, which measures the responsiveness of demand for a service relative to a change in price of another service. If this relation is negative, then in general the two services are complementary; if the relation is positive, then in general the two services are substitutes. Cross-price elasticity is often used as a measure of the effects of competitive price changes, and will be an important concept when discussing the price bundling of services later.

If the theory of consumer demand concerns the decision to choose to buy either of two services, A and B, and the quantities to purchase of each, we can describe the relations among these three elasticities. The ordinary price elasticity is composed of a substitution effect (cross-price elasticity) and an income effect (income elasticity). The income effect normally adds to the substitution effect, making price elasticity a more negative number (i.e., more price sensitive). Thus, other things remaining the same, a service with a low income elasticity (e.g., religious guidance) will have a lower price elasticity than will a service with a high income elasticity (e.g., nightclub entertainment).

Revenue Concepts. There is a relationship between sellers' revenues and the elasticity of demand for their services. To establish this relationship we need to define total revenue, average revenue, and marginal revenue. *Total revenue* is the total amount spent by buyers for the service (TR = P × Q, where P = price and Q = quantity). *Average revenue* is the total outlay by buyers divided by the number of units sold, or the price of the service (AR = TR/Q). *Marginal revenue* refers to the change in total revenue resulting from a change in sales volume.

The normal, downward sloping demand curve reveals that to sell an additional unit of output, price must fall. The change in total revenue (i.e., marginal revenue) is the result of two forces: (1) the revenue derived from the additional unit sold, which is equal to the new price, and (2) the loss in revenue that results from marking down all prior saleable units to the new price. Similarly, if price is increased, new revenue is derived by selling the marked-up items (force 1), but a loss occurs when the previously saleable items are not sold (force 2). If force 1 is greater than force 2, total revenue will increase; and total revenue will increase only if marginal revenue is positive.

To see how these forces operate, assume a data processing service increases its tape-handling fee from $100 to $120 per tape processed, resulting in a reduction of orders from 1,000 to 800. The gain in revenues is the 800 continuing orders at an increase of $20, or $16,000. The loss in revenue is the 200 lost orders at $100, or $20,000. In this example, the gain of $16,000 is less than the loss of $20,000, resulting in a negative marginal revenue of $4,000. Marginal revenue is positive only when the revenue generated from the new price is greater than the loss in revenue resulting from marking down all previously saleable items. It can also be shown that marginal revenue will increase if demand is price elastic and price is decreased, or if demand is price inelastic and price is increased.

Consumers' Surplus.    At any particular price, there are usually some consumers willing to pay more than that price in order to acquire the service. Essentially, this means that the price charged for the service may be lower than some buyers' *perceived value* for the service. The difference between the maximum amount consumers are willing to pay for a service and the amount they actually pay is called *consumers' surplus*. In essence it is the money value of the willingness of consumers to pay in excess of the stated price. This difference represents what the consumers gain from the trade. The difference is the money amounts of *value-in-use* (what is gained) minus *value-in-exchange* (what is given up), and for voluntary exchanges is always positive. Value-in-use always exceeds value-in-exchange simply because the most that anyone would pay must be greater than what they actually pay; otherwise they would not enter into the trade.

For example, assume that an orthodontist's fees for a two-year program of corrective treatment are $2,400, or $100 per month, and that 100 patients subscribe to the service. The aggregate value-in-exchange is $2,400 × 100 patients, or $240,000. Assume, however, that each of these patients would have been willing to subscribe to the service for up to $120 per month. That is, the maximum acceptable price is $120 per month, or $2,880 over the two years. The total amount these 100 people would have been willing to pay, or their value-in-use, is $288,000. The difference between the value-in-use and the value-in-exchange, $48,000, is their consumers' surplus.

The important point is that the price at which exchange takes place is not the equivalent of value as is so often assumed. Total willingness to pay (value-in-use) is comprised of value-in-exchange and consumers' surplus. It is that latter concept that becomes an important consideration in the determination of prices. Rather than concentrating on the cost considerations when setting price, the pricing problem becomes one of determining potential customers' perceived value-in-use, and pricing accordingly.

## Economics of Information

In 1944, Scitovszky concluded that "more often than not people judge quality by price."[4] He also argued that judging quality on the basis of price was rational behavior, because it merely represented a belief that the forces of supply and demand would lead to a natural ordering of competing products on a price scale, such that there would be a strong positive relationship between price and product quality. Thus, it is natural for price to be an appropriate *signal* of product or service quality.

In 1961, Stigler noted the seller may know the quality of the service, but buyers do not know its quality until after purchase and use.[5] Hence, in the interest of obtaining higher profits, a firm could set a high price that would not reflect the actual level of quality built into the service. Such a strategy could succeed only if buyers are unable to evaluate the service's attributes (and quality) prior to purchase, or not completely evaluate the service after a single purchase (or several purchases). Thus a situation in which the information about a service's quality is known by the seller but not known by buyers is a condition of asymmetric information. Emerging from this observation is the question of when it is in the firm's interest to signal to the marketplace the quality of its service using price, advertising, warranties, or other signals.

The managerial issue is how external information cues can be utilized by the seller to convey information about the service to the market. Specifically, a *signal* is an observable, alterable (by the seller) characteristic that may affect buyers' assessments of service quality. For this external cue to serve as a signal: (1) there must be discernible differences in a service characteristic or attribute across sellers; and (2) the quality level of services in the market must vary directly with the characteristic or attribute. This second requirement is critical, because if buyers know the quality does not vary as the signal varies, then the signal cannot be used to convey levels of quality. For example, at an international hotel chain, if a guest ordered a room service breakfast by 2:00 A.M., then delivery the next morning was guaranteed to be within fifteen minutes of the requested time or the breakfast was free. The hotel signaled the quality of delivery time with a strict time guarantee.

Economics of information or search theory provides a means of examining the elasticity of demand for services. One important idea stemming from this theory is that price sensitivity depends on the number of service alternatives about which the consumer is knowledgeable. The more costly it is to acquire information about alternatives relative to the benefits of having that information, the fewer alternatives consumers will seek and the more price inelastic will be demand. The number of alternatives that consumers will be knowledgeable about depends on whether the benefits of the product or service can be conveyed by search, experience, or credence attributes where:

- *Search attributes* are product or service characteristics that can be evaluated before purchase (dentist's fee, seat location at a performance, air travel time).
- *Experience attributes* can only be evaluated after purchase and use or receipt of the service (a hair permanent, dry cleaning, performance of a concert orchestra).

- *Credence attributes* usually cannot be evaluated immediately after receiving the service (legal advice, tax advice, many types of health services).

Demand is likely to be more price elastic for services that can be evaluated on the basis of search attributes, than for those that can be evaluated only after receipt of the service. Generally, the more that service personnel must exercise judgment in providing the service and the more the service can be customized across consumers, the less consumers are able to evaluate the quality of a service before receiving it and, therefore, the less sensitive will they be to price differences between alternatives. Moreover, under such circumstances, it is more likely that price may be used to infer service quality. This issue of when buyers may infer service quality on the basis of price will be discussed in a later section.

## Developing a Value Orientation for Pricing Services

As suggested previously, a successful proactive pricer sets price to be consistent with customers' perceived value. To understand how customers form value perceptions, it is important to recognize the relative role of price in this process. As a first step, however, it is important to understand how people form perceptions and how the perceptual process influences their perceptions of service quality and value.

### Perception

Perception basically involves the process of categorization; that is, we tend to place new experiences into existing classifications of familiar experiences. Thus, when buyers are confronted by a price different from what they believe they have previously paid, they must decide whether the difference between the old and new prices is significant to them. If the price difference is perceived to be insignificant, they may classify the two prices as similar and act as they have in the past. Similarly, when comparing two alternative services, if the prices of the alternatives are perceived as similar, even though they are not identical, some buyers may perceive the prices as equivalent and choose on bases other than price. Conversely, if the price differences are perceived as significant, buyers may classify the services as different, and make their choices on the basis of price.

### Price, Perceived Quality, and Perceived Value

Consumers' perceptions of a price derive from their interpretations of the price difference (real or implied) *and* from their interpretations of the cues in the offer. Consumers make their purchase decisions in a two-step process. First, they *judge* the value of an offer, and then they *decide* whether to make the purchase. It is also possible that they will postpone the purchase decision until they have more information about the offer and/or about other offers in the marketplace. Of concern here is how they use price information and other cues to judge the value of the offer, and how this evaluation influences their purchase decisions.

Buyers' preferences or choices depend on how they evaluate the quality or benefits to be received from a service relative to the cost or sacrifice inherent in the price. Thus, it can be argued that buyers' perceptions of value represent a trade-off between the quality or benefits they perceive in the service relative to the sacrifice they perceive by paying the price:

$$\text{Perceived value} = \frac{\text{Perceived benefits}}{\text{Perceived sacrifice}}$$

where perceived benefits are a function of perceived quality, and perceived quality and perceived sacrifice are positively related to price. Thus, in this formulation, price may have both attracting and repelling attributes. When price is used as an indicator of cost or sacrifice, then as it increases it tends to reduce demand for the service. However, if price is used as an indicator of quality or benefits, then as it increases, it tends to increase demand. Moreover, available research evidence indicates that buyers generally are unable to assess perfectly service quality (the ability of the service to provide satisfaction). Rather, *perceived quality* is the relevant variable, and under appropriate conditions, the perceived quality in a service is positively related to price. Perceptions of value are directly related to buyers' preferences or choices; that is, the larger a buyer's perception of value, the more likely that the buyer would express a willingness to buy or a preference for the service. Perceived value represents a trade-off between buyers' perceptions of quality and sacrifice and is positive when perceptions of quality are greater than the perceptions of sacrifice.

Recognizing this dual, conflicting nature of price leads to the question of how to determine the way price actually affects purchase decisions. It has been common to refer to the "irrational" way that price affects behavior as *psychological price*. For example, many restaurants and food service organizations set their prices to end in 9s or 5s because of the belief that these prices create an illusion of a discount to buyers. Despite the apparent acceptance of these "psychological" phenomena by many service providers, there is little evidence to support this "magical" or "illusory" nature of prices.

Spurred, in part, by business concern with product and service quality, there has been a renewed interest in the price–perceived quality relationship. Indeed, major business publications indicate that product and service quality can represent potent competitive advantages, and that "product and service quality [is] more important, if not everything."[6] Moreover, it is recognized that customers' perceptions of quality, benefits, and value are the reality faced by business and service organizations.

If buyers know that there is a positive price-quality relationship in the service market, then they are likely to use price as a quality indicator. If they know there is a weak price-quality relationship in the service market, however, they will be more likely to use other cues to assess quality. Thus, the strength of the use of price or other external cues, such as organization name, as signals of service quality depends on the relative perceived differences between different cues and on the degree buyers are knowledgeable about the service and actual price-quality relationships.

## Major Pricing Errors

In this section, we continue to develop important information about how people perceive prices and price differences. Primarily, we will be highlighting the second prescription for becoming a proactive pricer: *It is essential to understand how customers perceive prices, price changes, and price differences.* Initially, the concept of price thresholds will be developed and two major pricing errors will be illustrated. Then, the concept of reference price will be presented and a third major pricing error will be illustrated. Underlying the entire discussion is the key pricing principle: *Prices should be set so as to reflect customers' perceptions of value.*

Not Distinguishing Between Perceived Value and Price.  Humans have been shown to have upper and lower response limits to physical stimuli such as sound and light. For example, those of us who have taken hearing tests are aware that some sounds are either too low or too high for us to hear. The low and high sounds that we can just barely hear are called our lower and upper *absolute* hearing *thresholds*. A law from psychology, Weber's law, suggests that small, equally perceptible changes in a response correspond to proportional changes in the stimulus. This law applies to the perception of changes in a stimulus, that is, *to perceived differences between two intensities of a stimulus.* For example, if a service's price increase from $10 to $12 per hour is sufficient to deter us from buying the service, then another service originally priced at $20 would have to be repriced at $24 before we would become similarly disinterested. This law provides a basis for discussing the behavioral issues underlying the pricing error of *not distinguishing between perceived value and price.*

From the preceding discussion, we learned that a buyer has a lower and upper price threshold, which implies that he or she has a *range of acceptable prices* for a purchase. Furthermore, the existence of a lower price threshold implies that there are positive prices greater than $0 that are unacceptable because they are considered to be too low, perhaps because buyers are suspicious of the service's quality. This concept means that buyers have upper and lower limits for their considered purchases. Thus, people apparently may refrain from purchasing a service not only when the price is considered to be too high, but also when the price is considered to be too low.

To illustrate this issue, consider the plight of two local accountants who opened a local tax accounting service. They quickly gained a reputation of providing excellent service and enjoyed a competitive advantage over the nationally franchised tax consulting services. However, one of the national organizations upgraded its basic service package and offered additional service hours to meet the needs of the local community with a price premium over the local organization. Instead of raising its price to reflect its quality/value relationship, the local tax accounting service reduced the level of services included in its basic package to maintain its original price, thereby maintaining a lower basic price. Customers soon realized that the local organization now provided inferior service, and they shifted their patronage to the national organization. The important behavioral issue in this situation is to understand that there are limits or absolute thresholds to the relationship between price and perceived quality and perceived value. The local tax consulting service failed to recognize this relationship between price and perceived value, and that there is an important link between perceptions of quality and perceptions of value.

Not Distinguishing Between Absolute Price and Relative Price.   Usually a buyer has alternative choices available for a contemplated purchase and normally selects from among these choices. The prices of these alternative choices may provide cues that facilitate this decision process. Even if the numerical prices are different, however, it cannot be assumed that the prices are *perceived* to be different. As suggested earlier, the perception of a price change depends on the magnitude of the change. It has also been shown that people are more sensitive to price increases than to decreases.[7]

Generally, it is the perceived relative differences between prices that influence buyers' use of price as an indicator of quality. Similarly, relative price differences between competing brands, between different offerings in a service line, or between price levels at different times affect buyers' purchase decisions. The experience of a major snack food producer illustrates this *error of not recognizing the difference between absolute price and relative price.* Several years ago, the price of a specific size of this brand's potato chips was $1.39, whereas a comparable size of the local brand was $1.09, a difference of 30 cents. Over a period of time, the price of the national brand increased several times until it was being retailed at $1.69. In like manner, the local brand's price also increased to $1.39. While the local brand was maintaining a 30-cent price differential, however, the national brand obtained a significant gain in market share. The problem was that buyers perceived a 30-cent price difference relative to $1.69 as less than a 30-cent price difference relative to $1.39. This example illustrates the notion of differential price thresholds, or the issue of the degree to which buyers are sensitive to relative price differences.

As the potato chips example illustrates, relative price is a more important concept than absolute price. Further, the concept of price elasticity indicates how buyers perceive a price relative to another price, whether that price is the previous price paid, the price of the leading competitive offering, the highest or lowest price in the service line, or the expected price to pay. Thus, if buyers *perceive* that the service's price is different from the last time they purchased it, then the issue is whether this perceived price difference affects their purchasing behavior.

From behavioral price research, some important points about price elasticity have emerged. First, buyers, in general, are more sensitive to perceived price increases than to perceived price decreases. In practical terms, this difference in relative price elasticity between price increases versus price decreases means it is easier to lose sales by increasing price than it is to gain sales by reducing price.

Besides these important characteristics affecting a service's price elasticity, several other points should be considered. Sometimes a service may provide a *unique benefit* or have a *unique attribute* that buyers value. These unique benefits or attributes serve to make the service less price sensitive. Also, the *fre-*

*quency of past price changes* can influence buyers' sensitivity to price changes. If prices have been changing relatively frequently, buyers may not have adjusted to the previous price change, when a new change occurs. If buyers have not adjusted to the last price increase, then another price increase will be perceived as larger than it actually is, making them more sensitive to the increase. The issue this point raises is the concept of reference prices and the third pricing error.

<u>Not Distinguishing Between Pricing Strategies and Pricing Tactics.</u>   In the past few years, evidence has emerged confirming the existence of a reference price serving as an anchor for price judgments. It has been suggested that price will not serve as an indicator of service quality unless there is a perceptible difference in price from the buyer's reference price. Buyers may use as a reference point the range of prices last paid, the current market price or perceived average market price, a belief of a fair price to pay, or an expected price to pay to judge actual prices.

One of the most important points related to the concept of reference prices is that buyers do judge or evaluate prices comparatively. That is, to judge that a price is acceptable, too high, or too low, it has to be compared to another price. This other comparative price is the buyer's reference price for that particular judgment. Failure to recognize this important point has led to a third pricing error: *not distinguishing between pricing strategies and pricing tactics.*

Perhaps one of the most important points to understand when considering how buyers perceive prices is that perception is relative. That is, a specific price is compared to another price, or a reference price. The illustration for relating this important point to pricing strategy and tactics comes from a firm introducing a new service with an introductory low price. Initially, the service was targeted to sell at $17.50. However, the firm used the tactic of introducing the service at a temporary low price of $14.95. Later, when it was time to remove the introductory price, because of increased costs, the regular price was reset at $20.00. The service failed to sustain sufficient sales volume to warrant its continued existence. The error in this situation was that the pricing tactic of a low introductory price established a baseline or reference price of $14.95, rather than $17.50. Hence, the $20.00 price, when compared to $14.95, was perceived to be too expensive and people stopped buying. The short-term introductory price eroded the firm's ability to set a strategic higher price, and, in effect, the introductory tactic became the strategy.

When sellers advertise both the offered price and a (higher) comparative (regular) price, they are attempting to impose a reference price for consumers' comparisons. To make it easier for consumers to accept the higher price as a reference price, sellers may include such words as *formerly, regularly,* and *usually* to describe the higher price. Words can be used in a variety of ways to enhance consumers' perceptions that a sale is taking place and that the offer represents a bargain. Because prices are evaluated comparatively, the judgment of acceptability depends not only on consumers' price expectations, but also on information provided in promotions or advertisements. The perception of savings conveyed by price advertising leads to positive or favorable behavioral responses.[8]

# The Role of Costs in Pricing Decisions

It is important for the seller to know the determinants and behavior of service costs in order to know when to accelerate cost recovery, how to evaluate a change in selling price, how to segment a market profitably, and when to add or eliminate services. Even so, costs play a limited part in pricing. They indicate whether the service can be provided and sold profitably at any price, but they do not indicate the amount of markup or markdown on cost buyers will accept. Proper cost classification serves to guide management in the selection of a profitable service mix and to determine how much cost can be incurred without sacrificing profit.

Costs for pricing must reflect the future. Current or past information probably will not provide an adequate basis for profit projections unless it is valid to assume that the future is a mirror of the past. Service costs must be based on expected purchase costs of materials, labor wage rates, and other expenses to be incurred. In addition, information about development, promotion, and distribution costs is needed. Information on service costs should be regularly developed to determine whether changes have occurred that may affect the relative profitability of the company. It is planned costs that are important, not past costs, because profit planning necessarily deals with the future.

## Cost Concepts

To determine profit at any volume, price level, service mix, or time, proper cost classification is required. Some costs vary directly with the rate of activity, whereas others do not. When these different costs are mixed together in a total unit cost, it is not possible to relate volume to costs. However, if the cost data are properly classified into their fixed and variable components and properly attributed to the activity causing the cost, the effect of volume becomes readily apparent and sources of profit are revealed.

*Direct costs* (also called *traceable or attributable* costs) are those costs incurred by and solely for a particular service, department, program, or customer account. These costs may be fixed or variable. For example, material and labor costs may be traceable to a unit of service provided.

*Indirect traceable costs* can be objectively traced to a service, department, program, or customer account if the costs can be identified with that unit. These costs, although not incurred solely for a service, are objectively identified with the service. They may be fixed or variable. The time of an agent who serves several clients can be objectively traced to or identified by the amount of time spent on each client's account.

*Common costs* support a number of activities or profit segments. These costs cannot be objectively traced to a particular type of service based on a direct physical relationship to that service. The administration costs of a service facility are common to all units of service provided in that facility. A common or general cost does not change when one of the activities it supports is discontinued. Hence, discontinuing a service in the line will not affect the administration costs of the facility or of other general expenses such as market research or research and development.

### Cost Behavior

In addition to classifying costs according to ability to attribute a cost to a service, it is also important to classify costs according to variation with the rate of activity. As noted previously, unless costs can be segmented into fixed and variable costs, it is not possible to trace the effects of changes in price, volume, or service selling mix on costs.

*Direct variable costs* vary directly with an activity level. As activity is increased in a given time period, a proportionately higher amount of labor and materials is used. Assuming no changes in scale economies as the volume is increased, these direct variable costs will be constant per additional unit of service provided. The major criterion of a direct variable cost is that it be traceably and tangibly generated by, and identified with, the providing and delivery of a specific service.

*Semivariable costs* vary with activity rates but are not zero at a zero activity rate. Data processing costs are a good example of these costs. The costs of acquiring computer hardware and software are fixed, but the processing costs may vary with the amount of on-line time used. Hence, these semivariable costs consist of a base amount that is constant in relation to activity and a variable amount that varies directly with changes in the activity level.

*Fixed costs* do not vary with volume. Instead, they remain fixed over a period of time and do not increase as the quantity of services provided increases. Many costs for service organizations are fixed, ranging up to 80 percent of total cost. This means that volume shifts can have dramatic implications for the profits of a service organization.

Some directly attributable costs vary directly with the activity level, and some costs, although fixed, are directly attributable to the activity level. Hence, it is important to clarify specifically what is meant by the terms *direct* and *indirect. The directly traceable or attributable costs are those costs that we can readily determine as contributing to the service's cost. However, whether a direct cost is variable, fixed, or semivariable depends on properly determining the cause of that cost.* Perhaps, more than anything else, managers need to understand how costs are incurred and how they behave as activity levels change in their organizations.

## Profit Analysis

Virtually every planned action or decision in an organization affects costs and, therefore, profits. Profit analysis shows the effect of costs, prices, and volume on profits in order to determine the best course of action to follow. The goal of this analysis is to provide accurate and objective data about the contributions made by each service.

Perhaps the most important piece of data resulting from a profit analysis is the *profit-volume* (PV) *ratio*. The PV ratio is the percentage of sales available to cover fixed costs and profits after deducting variable costs. The formula for computing the PV ratio is [(price − variable cost)/price]. In the data below the contribution ratio or PV is the contribution of $35 ($100 − $65), divided by price, or 35 percent. Thus, 35 cents out of each sales dollar contributes toward paying fixed costs and providing a profit.

| | |
|---|---:|
| Price | $ 100 |
| Variable costs | 65 |
| Fixed costs | 2,500 |
| Contribution per unit | $ 35 |

If sales initially were $10,000 (100 units sold), then profit contribution is $3,500, and net profits are $1,000. Once the PV has been calculated, it is possible to determine the effects on profits of additional sales volume. If $1,000 of additional sales were generated, the additional profits would be $1,000 × 0.35, or $350. Since the fixed costs of $2,500 have already been covered by the original $10,000 of sales, additional volume contributes 35 cents of every sales dollar to profits. Thus, a 10 percent increase in sales produces a 35 percent increase in profits. Note that this analysis is possible only when all direct costs have been separated into their fixed and variable components.

Within a multiservice firm, each offering generates a different amount of volume, a different cost structure (including variable and fixed costs), different unit prices, and, of course, different revenues. Moreover, each service offering faces different competition, has a different demand elasticity, and perhaps depends for its sales, at least in part, on the sales of the other services in the line. Not only are these important factors different, but they are changing. The PV ratio can be modified and used to analyze the relative profit contributions of the service line. Each service has a different PV value and different expected dollar volume as a percent of the line's total dollar volume. In multiple-service situations the PV is determined by weighting the PV of each product by the percentage of the total dollar volume for all services in the line. For example, assume that the firm offers three services—A, B, C. The PV ratios of each product are 0.40 for A, 0.20 for B, and 0.10 for c. Additionally, service A generates 40 percent of the line's *dollar* revenues, whereas B and C generate 30 percent each. The composite PV ratio for the line is the sum of the weighted PV ratios: [(0.40 × .40) + (0.20 × .30) + (0.10 × 0.30) = 0.25].

What happens if the *dollar* volume mix of the three services changes? To illustrate, assume the PV ratios of the three services remain the same; that is, prices and costs do not change. However, service A now contributes 20 percent of the line's dollar revenues, whereas service B generates 50 percent of the dollar volume and service C continues to generate 30 percent. The composite

PV ratio for the line now is $[(.40 \times .20) + (.20 \times .50) + (.10 \times .30) = 0.21]$. Thus, unless there is a substantial increase in total dollar sales for the line, the firm will earn fewer profits with this shift in the dollar sales mix.

Often, when a shift in the dollar sales mix results in a poorer PV, management attempts to recover the profit level by an across-the-board increase in prices. Although the effect of this increase in prices helps to restore the original PV, this pricing reaction can lead to a further decline in profits because management has attempted to force the external factors of competition and demand to support the internal need for profit. When an across-the-board increase in prices leads to a substantial decrease in sales volume, it is quite possible that the remedy has aggravated the problem.

When there are differences in the PVs among services in a line, a revision in the service selling mix may be more effective than an increase in prices. That is, a company, by shifting emphasis to those services with relatively higher PVs, has a good opportunity to recover some or all of its profit position. Hence, profit at any sales level is a function of prices, volume, costs, and the service dollar sales mix.

## Developing Pricing Strategies

There are many kinds of pricing decisions that a company must make. Among these is the decision on what specific price to charge for each service marketed. But, the specific price to charge depends on the type of customer to whom the service is sold. If different customers purchase in varying quantities, should the seller offer volume discounts? The company must also decide whether to offer discounts for early payment, and if so, when a customer is eligible for a cash discount and how much to allow for early payment. Normally, the company sells multiple services, and these questions must be answered for each service. Additionally, the need to determine the number of price offerings per type of service and the price relationships among the services offered makes the pricing problem more complex.

### Pricing New Services

One of the most interesting and challenging decision problems is that of determining the price of a new service. Such pricing decisions are usually made with very little information on demand, costs, competition, and other variables that may affect the chances of success. Many new services fail because they do not possess the features desired by buyers, or because they are not available at the right time and place. Others fail because they have been incorrectly priced, and the error can as easily be in pricing too low as in pricing too high. The difficulty of pricing new services is enhanced by the dynamic deterioration of the competitive status of most services as they mature.[9]

The core of new product pricing takes into account the price sensitivity of demand and the incremental promotional and production costs of the seller.

What the product is worth to the buyer, not what it costs the seller, is the controlling consideration. What is important when developing a new service's price is the relationship between the buyers' perceived benefits in the new service relative to the total acquisition cost, and relative to alternative offerings available to buyers.

Alternative Strategies for Pricing a New Service.   The general presumption is that there are two alternatives in pricing a new service: "skimming" pricing, calling for a relatively high price, and "penetration" pricing, calling for a relatively low price. There are intermediate positions, but the issues are made clearer by comparing the two extremes:

*Skimming pricing.* Some services represent drastic improvements upon accepted ways of performing a service or filling a demand. For these services, a strategy of high prices with large promotional expenditure during market development (and lower prices at later stages) may be appropriate when:

1. Sales of the service are likely to be less sensitive to price in the early stages than when it is "full-grown" and competitive imitations have appeared.
2. Launching a new service with a high price is an efficient device for breaking the market up into segments that differ in price elasticity of demand. The initial high price serves to skim the cream of the market that is relatively insensitive to price.
3. A skimming policy is safer, in that facing unknown elasticity of demand, a high initial price serves as a "refusal" price during the stage of exploration.
4. High prices may produce greater dollar sales volume during market development than are produced by low initial prices. If so, skimming pricing will provide funds to finance expansion into the larger volume sectors of a market.
5. A capacity constraint exists.
6. There is realistic value (perceived) in the service.

*Penetration pricing.* Despite its many advantages, a skimming-price policy is not appropriate for all new services. Using low prices as a wedge to get into mass markets early may be appropriate when:

1. Sales volume of the service is very sensitive to price, even in the early stages of introduction.
2. It is possible to achieve substantial economies in unit costs by operating at large volumes.
3. A service faces threats of strong potential competition very soon after introduction.
4. There is no class of buyers willing to pay a higher price to obtain the service.

While a penetration pricing policy can be adopted at any stage in the service's life cycle, this pricing strategy should always be examined before a new service is marketed. Its possibility should be explored again as soon as the service has established an elite market. Sometimes a service can be rescued from premature death by adoption of a penetration price after the cream of the market has been skimmed.

## Pricing Multiple Services

Generally, a service organization has several service lines—a set of services that are closely related because they are acquired together, they satisfy the same general needs, or they are marketed together. Often some of these services are substitutes for each other, such as different types of checking accounts or different types of savings accounts. Other services complement each other, for example, a financial consultant who offers both tax advice and preparation services as well as investment advice. Because of the demand interrelationships inherent within a multiple service organization, as well as the cost interrelationships, and because there are usually several price market segments, pricing multiple services is one of the major challenges facing a pricing manager.

In services marketing one widespread type of multiple services pricing is the practice of selling services in packages or bundles. Such bundles can be as simple as pricing a restaurant menu either as dinners or à la carte items, or as complex as offering a ski package that includes travel, lodging, lift tickets, and ski rentals, as well as lessons. In either situation, some important principles need to be considered when bundling services at a special price.

Rationale for Price Bundling.    As observed earlier, most service industries are characterized by a relatively high ratio of fixed to variable costs. Moreover, several services usually can be offered using the same facilities, equipment, and personnel. Thus, the direct variable cost of a particular service is usually quite low, meaning that the service has a relatively high PV ratio. Thus, the incremental costs of selling additional services are generally low relative to the company's total costs.

In addition, many of the services offered by most service organizations are interdependent in terms of demand, either being substitutes for each other or complementing the sales of another service. Thus, it is appropriate to think in terms of relationship pricing, or the pricing of services in terms of the inherent demand relationships among them in order to maximize the benefits received by customers or clients. The objective of price bundling is to stimulate demand for the company's service line in a way that enhances achieving cost economies for the operations as a whole, while increasing net contributions.

Mixed Bundling.    In mixed bundling, the customer can purchase the services individually or as a package. Normally, there is a price incentive for the customer to purchase the package rather than acquiring the items comprising the bundle individually. In *mixed-leader bundling* the price of one service is discounted if the first service is purchased at full price. For example, if cable TV customers buy the first premium channel at full price, they may be able to acquire a second premium channel at a reduced monthly rate. Assuming that premium channels A and B are individually priced at $10 per month each, then B might be offered for $7.50 if A is acquired at its regular rate. In *mixed-joint bundling* a single price is formulated for the combined set of services. In this situation, the two premium channels would be offered as a set for one price, for example $17.50 per month. As should be obvious with these two examples, the net outlay for the customer buying either bundle is the same, but there is a difference in deciding which bundle to offer.

_Principles of Price Bundling._   Several economic concepts discussed earlier provide the basis for developing a set of price-bundling principles: consumer surplus, demand elasticity, and complementarity. Also, the behavioral concept of an acceptable price range plays an important role. Underlying the notion of bundling is the recognition that different customers have different perceived values for the various services offered. In practical terms, these customers have different maximum amounts they would be willing to pay for the services. For some customers, the price of the service is less than this maximum acceptable price (upper price threshold), resulting in some consumer surplus. For these customers, however, the price of a second service may be greater than they are willing to pay, so they do not acquire it. If the firm, by price bundling, can shift some of the consumer surplus from the highly valued service to the less valued service, then there is an opportunity to increase the total contributions these services make to the company's profitability.

Continuing with the preceding example, assume that a consumer would be willing to pay up to $12 per month to acquire premium channel A, but only $6 per month to acquire premium channel B. If each channel is priced individually at $10, then the consumer would be willing to subscribe to A only, and enjoy a consumer surplus of $2. Note, however, that a bundled offer of channels A and B for less than $18 ($12 + $6) would still provide the consumer with some surplus, while leading to an increase in revenues for the cable company from $10 to $17.50 per month.

The ability to transfer consumer surplus from one service to another depends on the complementarity of demand for these services. Services may complement each other because purchasing them together reduces the search costs of acquiring them separately. It may be economical to have both savings and checking accounts in the same bank to reduce the costs of having to visit more than one bank for such services. Services may complement each other because acquiring one may increase the satisfaction of acquiring the other. For the novice skier, lessons will enhance the satisfaction of skiing and increase the demand to rent skis. Finally, a full-service seller may be perceived to be a better organization than a limited-service seller, thereby enhancing the perceived value of all services offered.

As observed earlier, demand is likely to be more price elastic for services that can be evaluated on the basis of search attributes, than for those that can be evaluated only after receipt of the service, or not at all. Thus, services to be considered for a bundling strategy should have salient attributes that are search-based, because one requirement for successful bundling is that at least one of the services be price elastic.

Because the objective is to increase the overall sales level of the company, the services selected for bundling should be relatively small in unbundled sales volume to minimize losing revenues from effectively marking down a service that already has a high sales volume. For mixed-leader bundling, the lead service must be price elastic, have attributes that are easy to evaluate before purchase, be the higher volume service in the bundle, and be the lower margin service. The objective is to use a price reduction in the higher-volume service to generate an increase in its volume that "pulls" an increase in demand for a lower volume, but higher contribution margin service. The increase in volume of the second service will contribute more to profits than the loss due to the reduced contributions of the lead service.

For mixed-joint bundling, the per-unit profit contributions of each service should be about equal, the unbundled sales volumes should be about equal, their demand should be price elastic, and each should complement the other service. The objective is to increase demand for both services by packaging them together. In any case, these services should not be high sales volume services.

These principles suggest that companies should not pursue price-bundling strategies simply because others are doing it. As observed at the beginning of this chapter, me-too pricing likely will lead to serious pricing errors. Bundling can be an effective pricing strategy, but it should be applied in a limited way and only after a careful analysis of the nature of the services offered and an understanding of customers' perceptions of the value of these services.[10]

### Contingency Pricing

Sometimes it is unlikely that the value of the service can be calculated prior to delivery of the service. Even though the provider of the service is confident that the service will provide value to the client, it will be difficult to signal what its economic value is. One way to develop a pricing solution for this problem is for the seller to share some of the risks of delivering this value to the buyer through a contingency pricing arrangement. Several well-known forms of contingency pricing include: money-back guarantees, real estate agents' commissions based on a percentage of the selling price, and a lawyer or professional sports agent whose fee is based on a percentage of the damage award or contract negotiated. In the example developed below, the price is comprised of a fixed fee with a guarantee geared to the amount of the economic benefits realized by the customer.

The EMS Company was an engineering services firm providing means of controlling and reducing energy use in large buildings.[11] EMS was one of three companies submitting a bid to a school district that was interested in reducing its expenditures for energy (heating oil, gas, and electricity). In the most recent year of operation, the school district had spent nearly $775,000 on energy, and the proposed budget for the coming year was $810,000. The school board was interested in a long-term solution to its energy use problem, particularly using less of the district's budget on energy and more on direct education expenses.

EMS developed a proposal providing for a computer-controlled system that monitored energy use and operated on/off valves for all energy-using systems. The proposal specified a five-year contract with a fixed price of $254,500 per year, with a guarantee that the school district would save at least that amount of money each year or EMS would refund the difference. Included in the proposal was a carefully devised plan to take into account energy prices, hours the buildings were in use, and degree days so as to provide a basis of calculating the actual savings occurring. After five years the school district would own the system with the option of purchasing a management operating service for an annual fee of $50,000.

Although two other companies submitted multi-year bids of $190,000 and $215,000, annually, for three and five years, respectively, neither bid provided any guarantee for energy savings. Despite some questions about accepting the highest bid, the school board accepted the EMS proposal, because at worst the cost of the service was zero. During the first year, actual calculated savings exceeded $300,000. Had the company submitted a cost-plus bid, the bid would have been about $130,000 per year. The use of contingency pricing by EMS removed the risk from the school board's decision and added an additional $600,000 in profit contribution to EMS.

An example of another version of contingency pricing is the pricing practice of a restaurant in a suburb of Washington, D.C. Regular customers may order from a menu without prices, and after the meal they pay what they think the food is worth. Most people pay as much as, if not more than, the regular individual prices.[12]

## Managerial Recommendations

Value-oriented pricing can help prevent both the error of setting a price that is too high relative to perceived or delivered value, as well as setting a price that is too low relative to the value provided to and desired by customers. Pricing only from the viewpoint of satisfying internal profit needs often ruins attempts to gain a competitive edge and the ability to set prices above average market prices. In the preceding example, the EMS company developed a procedure for signaling the uncertain economic value to be delivered with a guarantee and successfully charged a premium price well above the cost-plus profit margin price.

As the sections on proactive pricing and major pricing errors indicated, many current pricing strategies of service companies may be inappropriate. However, there are a number of activities for developing appropriate strategies that can be accomplished leading to pricing practices and policies that are more consistent with the contemporary decision environment.

### Determine Consistent Objectives

Not all pricing objectives may be consistent. For example, increasing volume, improving cash flow, or improving margins may actually lead to very different pricing decisions. Yet, companies often indicate that they are attempting to accomplish each of these objectives simultaneously. Thus, it is important that pricing objectives be clearly stated, mutually consistent, and prioritized. Moreover, everyone concerned with the pricing decision, at any level in the organization, must understand the relevant objectives.

### Establish a Pricing Research Program

In terms of applied marketing research, the relative effect of price changes and price differences is the least understood and the least researched. The lack of data in this area has led to many inappropriate pricing strategies, as illustrated in this chapter. At a minimum, a pricing research program should develop the relevant cost classifications and determine how customers relate price to quality and value perceptions. Such an effort is necessary to understand the cost and volume effects of price changes and relative price differences.

### Maintain Feedback and Control

It is important that companies establish procedures to ensure that pricing decisions fit into their overall marketing strategies. Often, pricing decisions are made within the financial management function of the organization, and the potential for ignoring or minimizing the effect of buyers' perceptions is increased. Moreover, such a pricing approach tends to emphasize the cost aspects of the pricing decision. Yet, as this chapter demonstrates, buyers seek to maximize the value received from purchasing services. Typically, they are not interested in what it costs the seller to provide the services, but rather they are interested in the price-value relationship. Also, buyers are seeking benefits in the form of having certain functions performed, problems solved, or pleasures received. Value is created when the benefits delivered by the services match the benefits expected by customers/users/clients at a price consistent with this value. Customers' perceptions are important when developing a value-oriented pricing strategy. A service perceived to be of higher value than competitive offerings will be granted the privilege of obtaining a premium price by the market.

It is also important to provide for a feedback mechanism to ensure that all who should know the results of individual price decisions are fully informed. This prescription is particularly important for individuals who are in daily contact with customers and must quote prices to customers.

### Use Rigorous Thinking

Service companies also need to avoid me-too pricing strategies and tactics. A careful analysis of the organization's objectives, costs of providing specific services, competitors' offerings and costs, and the value perceptions of prospective and served customers must be completed before establishing specific strategies. Different service offerings compete in different markets facing different competitive environments while satisfying different benefits sought by customers. Thus, each service must be priced as an individual offering while understanding its inherent relationship to the other offerings in the service line. When pricing services as bundles, it is important to recognize that this strategy has limited usefulness and should be used for low-volume services having characteristics that buyers can evaluate prior to purchase. This prescription is simply an extension of value-oriented pricing that should be pursued in the development of any pricing strategy.

To summarize, pricing decisions should be made logically and should involve rigorous thinking. Recognize that judgment and prediction are needed about the future, not the past. Finally, pricing decisions should be made within a dynamic, long-run marketing strategy.

# Notes

1. Thomas Nagle, "Pricing as Creative Marketing," *Business Horizons* 26 (July/August 1983):14–19.
2. George F. Leaming, "Should You Price Your Unique Product or Service Like a Commodity? Or Your Commodity Like a Unique Product or Service?" presented at the First Annual Pricing Conference, The Pricing Institute, New York, December 3–4, 1987.
3. Elliot B. Ross, "Making Money With Proactive Pricing," *Harvard Business Review* 62 (November/December 1984):145–155.
4. Tibor Scitovszky, "Some Consequences of the Habit of Judging Quality by Price," *The Review of Economic Studies* 12(1944–1945):100.
5. George Stigler, "The Economics of Information," *Journal of Political Economy* 69 (June 1961):213–225.
6. Thomas A. W. Miller, ed. "31 Major Trends Shaping the Future of American Business," *The Public Pulse* 2, no. 1, New York: The Roper Organization, 4; see also "Top Management Takes Up the Challenge," *Business Week,* November 1, 1982, 68–69.
7. Joseph U. Uhl. "Consumer Perception of Retail Food Price Changes," paper presented at Association for Consumer Research Conference in Amherst, Mass., August 1970.
8. For more information on how customers perceive prices, see Kent B. Monroe, *Pricing: Making Profitable Decisions,* rev. ed. (New York: McGraw-Hill, 1990).
9. For additional reading on pricing new products or services, see Kent B. Monroe, "Techniques for Pricing New Products and Services," in *Handbook of Modern Marketing,* rev. ed., ed. V. Buell (New York: McGraw-Hill, 1986), 32:1–13; and Kent B. Monroe, Akshay R. Rao, and Joseph D. Chapman, "Towards a Theory of New Product Pricing," in *Contemporary Views on Marketing Practice,* ed. J. Sheth and G. Frazier (Lexington, Mass.: Lexington Books, 1987), 201–213.
10. For more information see Joseph P. Guiltinan, "The Price Bundling of Services: A Normative Framework," *Journal of Marketing* 51 (April 1987):74–85.
11. This example is adapted from Peter J. LaPlaca, "Pricing That Is Contingent on

Value Delivered,'' presented at the first Annual Pricing Conference, The Pricing Institute, New York, December 3–4, 1987.

12. "Paying What You Like," *New York Times,* August 3, 1988.

*     *     *     *

***Kent B. Monroe**, D.B.A., is Robert O. Goodykoontz Professor of Marketing at the R. B. Pamplin College of Business, Virginia Polytechnic Institute and State University, where he has pioneered research on the information value of price. He has served as a consultant on pricing, marketing strategy, and marketing research and also conducts executive training programs for businesses, nonprofit organizations, and universities.*

# DISTRIBUTING A SERVICE

The single chapter in this section deals with the means for getting a particular service to a specific customer. For products, distribution refers to the movement of the physical product from the manufacturer to the end user through intermediaries or "middlemen." The author points out that distribution means something somewhat different for services, given their intangibility. He argues that although goods producers have exclusive control over the quality and characteristics of their products, service producers must share responsibility for the "quality and characteristics" of their services with intermediaries who deliver the service.

Channel alignment—planning for the proper fit among intermediaries, services, customers, and corporate goals—is discussed as a necessary first step in distribution planning. Then, distribution considerations at each stage in the sales cycle—before, during, and after the sale—are discussed; issues covered include accessibility, location, facility design, personal selling, direct response marketing, quality, managing customer relationships, and cross selling. In conclusion, balancing retailing and wholesaling intermediaries and securing loyalty from your intermediaries are discussed, as well as the topic of multimarketing—using more than one channel arrangement to obtain maximum market exposure.

# 18

# Making Service Distribution Work

Donald H. Light

Like many concepts in services marketing, "distribution" comes from a product background. When 3M distributes its Scotch tape, it uses a variety of intermediaries (wholesalers and retailers), warehouses, and stores to move the tape from the factory to the ultimate customer. It is easy to see *who* does *what* and *when* they do it (see Figure 18-1):

- 3M makes the Scotch tape and ships it to the wholesaler's warehouse.
- The wholesaler stores the Scotch tape and on request ships it to an office supply store.
- The office supply store fills a purchase order for 100 rolls.

## How Do You Distribute a Service?

The intangible nature of services would appear to make the idea of "distribution" inapplicable to services. But there are more than enough similarities to make distribution relevant and important to service firms.

A hospital, which creates inpatient medical care, needs a way to distribute that service to its customers (the patients), just as much as 3M needs a way to distribute its Scotch tape. Where 3M uses office supply wholesalers and retailers, hospitals use doctors, health maintenance organizations (HMOs), and preferred provider organizations (PPOs).

And where 3M has exclusive control over the quality and characteristics of its Scotch tape, a hospital must share responsibility with its intermediaries to define and deliver inpatient care. The clean division of responsibility for each activity before, during, and after the sale of Scotch tape becomes much more complex for inpatient hospital care (see Figure 18-2):

- *Before the sale,* employers decide how to fund their employees' health care benefits, in this case choosing a PPO. The PPO in turn contracts with selected doctors and hospitals, from which the employees choose primary care physicians. The doctors decide to which hospital they will

The material in the sections "How Do You Distribute a Service?" and "Align It Properly" is based on D. H. Light Consulting Services, *Managing Life Insurance Distribution*, copyright 1987.

**Figure 18-1.** Distribution of Scotch tape.

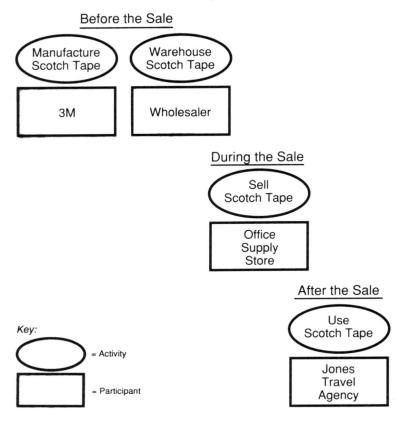

admit the patient, based on which hospitals have made agreements with the relevant PPO.

- *During the sale* (while the patient is in the hospital), how much and what types of inpatient care the patient receives is determined by the doctor, who is often guided by standards established by an HMO or PPO.
- *After the sale,* the doctor may recommend outpatient physical therapy provided by either the hospital staff or by an independent organization. The PPO reimburses the doctor and hospital for all services rendered, and in turn seeks payment from the employer.

## Is Distribution Just a Fancy Name for Sales and Marketing?

Clearly, services "distribution" is broader than service "sales." It is also different from service marketing. Service distribution strategy begins with the service and the customer as givens. It deals with the *means* that the service firm uses to get a particular service to a specific customer. Because of the intangible nature of services and the critical role that intermediaries play before and after the sale, distribution can be a potent competitive weapon for service firms.

**Figure 18-2.** Distribution of inpatient treatment.

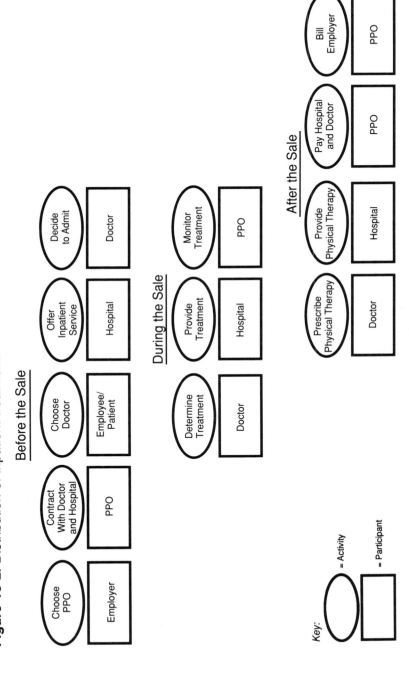

Before the Sale

| Choose PPO | Contract With Doctor and Hospital | Choose Doctor | Offer Inpatient Service | Decide to Admit |
| Employer | PPO | Employee/Patient | Hospital | Doctor |

During the Sale

| Determine Treatment | Provide Treatment | Monitor Treatment |
| Doctor | Hospital | PPO |

After the Sale

| Prescribe Physical Therapy | Provide Physical Therapy | Pay Hospital and Doctor | Bill Employer |
| Doctor | Hospital | PPO | PPO |

Key:

= Activity

= Participant

Source: Adapted from D. H. Light Consulting Services, *Managing Life Insurance Distribution,* copyright 1987.

*Making It Work*

To make its distribution system a truly effective competitive weapon, a service company should:

- Align it properly.
- Remember each part of the sales cycle:
  —Before the sale
  —During the sale
  —After the sale
- Balance retail and wholesale intermediaries.
- Make wholesale intermediaries effective product managers.
- Keep intermediaries loyal.
- Pay the necessary price to do multimarketing correctly.
- Control the pace of change.

# Align It Properly

*Channel Alignment*

A *distribution channel* is simply a specific set of intermediaries, products, and customers. *Channel alignment* is the fit among intermediaries, products, and customers (see Figure 18-3).

Products have many dimensions. For example, a residential mortgage is a complex and expensive product that is purchased infrequently. In contrast, a checking account is a simple and inexpensive product that is purchased rarely but used frequently.

Customers too have many dimensions. An unmarried, 32-year-old entrepreneur may have considerable wealth, but limited income, be quite sophisticated, and willing to pay higher prices for greater convenience. A married, 50-year-old mechanic with two grown children may have limited assets, but a good income, be financially unsophisticated, and seek the lowest price even if it means considerable inconvenience.

Proper alignment is a matter of using intermediaries that are appropriate for a given set of products and customers. Figure 18-4 shows four different banking service intermediaries—each appropriate for a given combination of product complexity and customer sophistication.

*Corporate Alignment*

Good distribution systems have another kind of alignment—between themselves and corporate goals. Corporate goals can be expressed in many forms: high profits, fast growth, rising market share, being customer-driven, and so on. A growth-oriented restaurant chain might choose to make its intermediaries franchisees. A profit-oriented chain might want to operate its own outlets.

Only new service companies have the luxury of designing their distribution channels from scratch. Most established concerns depend heavily on one or two

**Figure 18-3.** Channel and corporate alignment.

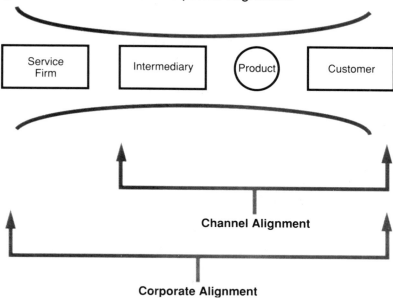

*Source:* Adapted from D. H. Light Consulting Services, *Managing Life Insurance Distribution,* copyright 1987.

**Figure 18-4.** Bank intermediaries for different product-customer combinations.

**Customer Sophistication**

|  | | Low | High |
|---|---|---|---|
| **Product Complexity** | High | Bank A<br>Loan Officer | Bank B<br>Private Banker |
|  | Low | Savings Bank<br>Teller | National Network<br>Automatic Teller |

*Source:* Adapted from D. H. Light Consulting Services, *Managing Life Insurance Distribution,* copyright 1987.

channels for the majority of their sales. Their challenge is to move the channel incrementally toward a better alignment with the corporate orientation.

For example, consider a profit-oriented owner of a cookie-store chain. If fixed equipment and rental costs are substantial, could profitability be improved by putting more volume through each outlet? And if so, could that higher volume best be achieved through advertising or through a "frequent cookie-eater club"? A growth-oriented owner might instead opt for simply increasing the number of outlets.

### Implications of Channel and Corporate Alignment

A service company should ask itself several alignment-related questions:

- How good is our current channel and corporate alignment? For example, are our intermediaries overskilled or underskilled for certain products or customer segments?
- Is our product or customer mix changing? If products are becoming less complex, or if customers are becoming more knowledgeable about the product, perhaps there is an opportunity to use less costly intermediaries. Are product and customer mix changes being driven by the distribution channel or vice versa?
- If our corporate goals are changing, should our distribution methods also change?

## Remember Each Part of the Sales Cycle— Before the Sale

Before a sale occurs, there is an initial contact between the service company and the customer. Some kinds of service companies—such as plumbers, restaurants, and barber shops—depend on customers to find them. Others—such as department stores, movie theaters and airlines—reach out to their potential customers.

### Helping the Customer Find You—Accessibility and Location

Choosing convenient locations is critically important for service companies that depend on their customers to find them. Convenience, though, is a relative term—otherwise there would be a bank on every corner (it only appears that there already is). The importance of ready access to a service company depends on transaction frequency and the acceptability of other forms of access.

People engage in some activities with great regularity, which explains the large number of grocery stores and gas stations. People engage in other activities only occasionally, which is why most travel agents are found in central business districts or in major shopping malls. People do still other things only once in a lifetime, which is why patients will travel across country for an open-heart transplant.

Many services do not require personal contact with the service company; for example, groceries can be bought over the phone, and cash is easily obtained through automatic teller machines (ATMs). Although technology has made these kinds of transactions possible, the real question is how many customers will actually use them. Although ATMs have been in existence for twenty years, fewer than half of all card-holding customers use them even once a month. To cite another example, the landscape is littered with failed attempts to sell consumer and financial goods through videotext (the IBM/Sears joint venture, Prodigy, is the major survivor).

Accessibility is also a matter of time. People have to see a movie at the times when the cinema shows it—unless they have rented the videocassette. Parents with sick children often have to take time off from work to take them to the doctor, unless they have access to a "doc in a box" (i.e., a walk-in urgent care center).

One of the most important decisions a service company can make is where to locate its intermediaries. In the 1950s and 1960s, Allstate Insurance Company located its new agents in Sears Department Stores, which was an innovative growth strategy as long as Sears kept opening new stores in demographically desirable areas. By the 1970s, however, Sears was opening few new stores, many of its older ones were (from an insurance point of view) in less desirable urban areas, and new Allstate agents had to compete with one another for time at the one sales booth in each store. During the past few years Allstate has begun to locate new agents in neighborhood sales offices, whose locations are selected without consideration of Sears store sites.

There is a substantial amount of market research that addresses the question of choosing locations. Much of it focuses on the demand side—the demographics and buying behavior of residents in zip codes, census tracks, and city blocks. Anyone undertaking this type of analysis should give equal attention to the supply side, that is, the costs and consequent profitability of maintaining intermediaries in various locations with the associated sales volumes and product mixes.

## Helping the Customer Find Your Products—Facility Design

Imagine waiting in a slow-moving line at an airport or railway station and seeing a fellow traveler walk to the counter to ask the agent a question. The agent informs the person that he must wait his turn like everyone else. When that person finally reaches the head of the line, the agent tells him he's in the wrong line.

As another example, a man needed to have a laboratory test done at his medical clinic, which occupies four different buildings. A directory near the main entrance listed the laboratory as being in Building A, but there was no map. The man remembered that there were red, green, and blue arrows painted on the floor to guide patients to the laboratory, X-ray, and rehabilitation departments. The arrows were still there, but no indication about which color led to which department.

The managers and staff who spend their days working inside a facility often lose sight of how confusing their facility can be to someone who does not know where to go or how to get there. Service companies can do several things to make it easier for customers to find their way:

- When building or remodeling, make key traffic paths easy to "read" from the main entrance.
- Post clear signs and maps.
- Provide a receptionist or staff specialist to greet and direct customers.

Facility design can also serve a promotional purpose. K mart's famous Blue Light Specials use that simple but effective beacon to guide shoppers to sale items. Many males have probably noticed how difficult it is to get in or out of department stores without weaving through a maze of cosmetics counters. Many restaurants wheel a dessert cart around to each table so that everyone nearby can see the high-calorie, high-profit selections.

### Finding the Customer Yourself

A service company can actively pursue its customers in several ways: advertising, personal sales, and direct marketing.

Advertising.   Advertising is its own discipline, and persons with an advertising budget will have no difficulty finding out everything they always wanted to know. The intangible nature of services does present a specific challenge. Merrill Lynch's corporate advertising department discovered this when it tried to substitute earnest account executives for its famous bull. The new campaign elicited a storm of protest, much of it from the account executives themselves.

Personal Sales.   Using personal sales methods to find leads, qualify them, and turn them into prospects can be very expensive. That is one reason why first-year commissions on most individual life insurance policies are so high. Professional services such as accounting, consulting, medicine, and law are also traditionally sold on a personal basis.

Personally sold services tend to be costly, technical in nature, and infrequently purchased. Personal contact is justified before, and sometimes even after the purchase, because it is difficult for the buyer to evaluate the quality and value of the product he has bought. Being eyeball to eyeball with the seller/creator of the service provides some reassurance.

Service companies that use personal sales methods can do several things to increase their sales productivity:

- Hire wisely—because personal relationships are very important, be sure that your intermediaries "fit in" with the people who will be buying from them (i.e., align the channel).
- Train well—quality will tell over time, especially if products, technologies, and the legal/regulatory environment are changing rapidly.
- Generate leads through advertising and direct marketing—personal sales

efforts are much more efficient if potential customers identify themselves.

    <u>Direct Response Marketing.</u>  Service companies using direct response
marketing (DRM) *contact and sell* to potential customers directly by mail or
phone—without using independent or commissioned intermediaries. Anyone with
a mailbox or telephone knows that DRM has increased in the past few years.

    DRM is not necessarily a low-cost distribution method. Three factors affect
its profitability:

- *The cost of developing, printing, and mailing:* Producing and mailing a
  DRM letter can run $200 to $500 or more per 1,000. Glossy, full-color
  catalogs with attractive layouts cost much more. (It is worthwhile being
  on The Sharper Image mailing list just for the entertainment value.)
- *Response rates:* The number of customer inquiries that result from a mailing
  can be under 2 percent.
- *Conversion rates:* The percentage of sales made to those responding can
  vary from as low as 1 to 5 percent to as high as 60 to 70 percent.

There is also the increasing danger of saturation. Response rates in particular may deteriorate substantially as more companies use DRM. How many
people routinely put bulk-rate letters directly into the round file?

    In terms of channel alignment, DRM is most appropriate for simple, me-
dium- and low-cost products and services. Not many people are willing to buy
a yacht or an estate plan over the phone, but some will order two $30 shirts or
even a $600 automobile insurance policy.

    Conversely, a few companies have shown that DRM can be used for higher
priced or more involved purchases. In 1986, USAA Life Insurance Company's
salaried ''financial services sales representatives'' sold an average of 1,200 policies with an average face value of $75,000. USAA's products include complex
universal life and variable universal life policies.

    DRM does *not* eliminate the human element is selling. Even when the
original solicitation is by letter or catalog, customers often purchase and try to
resolve problems by phone. Any service company that is serious about using
DRM has to be willing to provide high-quality customer service. A commitment
to customer service means paying for adequate telecommunications and computer systems. It also means hiring, training, and compensating people who can
sell and service—the same challenge facing personal sales-oriented service companies.

    A consumer once tried to purchase running clothes through a DRM catalog
company. Placing the order via the company's toll-free 800 number was easy,
but trying to find out why the order was not delivered required a toll call from
California to Washington, D.C. A few months later that company went out of
business. The owner claimed it was the victim of too much growth, but the
consumer suspects the real cause was a lack of commitment to quality customer
service.

## Remember Each Part of the Sales Cycle— During the Sale

### Achieve High-Quality Execution

How many times have you stood in a long line to rent or return a videocassette? How long have you waited for approval of a loan to finance or refinance your house?

Achieving high-quality execution at the time of the sale is largely a matter of completing the necessary transactions in a timely and accurate manner. The service company and its intermediaries share responsibility for doing this—although who does what, and how information is processed varies considerably.

Renting a videocassette should be a simple transaction—one that cries out for automation. But only recently has there been much movement toward the use of optical wands to scan each cassette's bar code, and point-of-sale terminals to record credit card data. In this case, the industry's fragmented structure and its fierce price competition slowed the introduction of available technology.

Financing a house appears at the other end of the size and complexity spectrum. Frequent delays in processing applications, coupled with the pressure to close within a specified time, have created a differentiation opportunity. The Travelers Insurance Company and other companies are trying to fill this need. Travelers Mortgage Services offers toll-free customer access to information, software to expedite loan processing, and, not coincidently, a bundled homeowners insurance product.

Here is a modest proposal for service companies that process complicated transactions. Publicize performance standards for:

- Turnaround time
- Accuracy *and*
- Actual results

## Remember Each Part of the Sales Cycle— After the Sale

### Manage Your Customer Relationships

What goes on after a product is sold is not typically thought of as part of "distribution." But services are intangible and often include a promise to perform at a future date. Consequently, the same intermediaries that sell the service may deliver it as well. Indeed, what actually produces satisfied customers in many service businesses is what the service company does *after* the sale (see also Chapter 15).

When service and product companies think about "service," it is often in the traditional sense of "We service what we sell." Software companies provide a good example of how widely the quality of this type of service can vary. WordPerfect, a popular word processing program, offers purchasers an 800 help line, which is answered quickly by knowledgeable staff. At the other end of the spectrum, some software firms expect customers to make a toll call and then wait interminably while listening to a recorded message offering access to a real person, in return for an additional fee.

Although servicing what you sell is important, a service company's focus after the sale should be on *managing the relationship* with its customers. Relationship management involves determining:

1. That there is a relationship to manage. An airline does have a manageable relationship with its frequent business flyers, but not with the person who flies once a year to visit Grandma at Christmas.
2. The important aspects of that relationship—for example, whether the frequent flyers book through a corporate travel department or an independent travel agent, what their hotel and rental car preferences are, and how they pay.
3. The relationship management goals—for example, to influence corporate travel department decisions, to obtain a higher proportion of the flyer's total travel, or to increase the number of bookings with affiliated hotels and rental car companies.
4. The specific steps to reach those goals—for example, developing a program for the airline's service representatives to call on corporate travel departments, offering incentives of lower prices or greater convenience to make the desired hotel or rental car reservations, or running a joint advertising campaign with American Express.

## Cross Selling

Selling additional products to your current customers should be fun, easy, and profitable. After all, you already have a satisfied customer—don't you? And everyone likes the convenience of one-stop shopping—don't they? However, cross selling, like peace and racial harmony, is easier to recommend than to achieve.

Allegis Corporation (nee United Airlines) provided a spectacular confirmation of the difficulty of cross selling in general, and one-stop shopping in particular. Allegis laboriously acquired Hertz Rent-a-Car and the Westin hotel chain—only to become the target of a corporate reorganization that changed management, put the new acquisitions up for sale, and did away with the name Allegis, which a detractor said sounded like the next world-class disease.

Barriers to successful cross selling are often rooted in distribution. UPS, which sells parcel delivery, wants to sell overnight delivery. However, most of its potential customers are satisfied buying overnight delivery from Federal Express. UPS may also discover that the shipping or traffic manager who decides to use UPS may not be the person who decides how the agenda packages for next week's board meeting are sent.

Another related problem is where the service company views two products as having good cross-selling potential because they are closely related, but the customer thinks they are quite different. For example, a bank might view certificates of deposit (CDs) as a logical cross sell to its savings account customers. But its customers might regard savings accounts as "savings" and CDs as "investments" that compete with mutual funds, real estate, and their own retirement accounts.

### Defending Your Customer Base

A related, though easier, after-the-sale task is to defend your customers against inroads from other companies. The basic techniques are to raise the costs to your customers of taking their business elsewhere and to provide better value (the relationship of benefits to price) than anyone else.

Information technology is a powerful tool for pursuing the first strategy. For example, a wholesaler might provide its retailers with inventory control and order systems that are conveniently tied to its own warehouses. IDS, a financial service company, prepares financial plans for its clients and sells them insurance and investment products. It recently began providing its clients with a consolidated quarterly statement summarizing all account activity, giving the clients a valuable snapshot of their financial status, and providing IDS's financial planners a platform for additional sales.

But even the best tools have to be used. In the insurance business, if an exclusive agent leaves the company, that agent's policyholders are known as "orphans." A surprising number of insurance companies, many of them with reputations as good marketers, have not systematically measured their orphan populations. And even fewer have developed "adoption" programs either to assign the orphans to new agents, or to service and market directly to them.

## Balancing Retail and Wholesale Intermediaries

*Retail intermediaries* work directly with the purchasers/end users of the service or product. *Wholesale intermediaries* work directly with the retail intermediaries. For example, Happy Hawaiian Holidays puts together package air, hotel, and rental car tours to Hawaii. A travel agent selling a Happy Hawaiian Holiday is in a retail position. Happy Hawaiian Holidays is in a wholesale position for TWA, the Waikiki Hilton, and National Car Rental.

Wholesale intermediaries are often independent contractors who can choose which service companies they will represent and how much business they will direct to one service company versus another. When choosing whether to use an external wholesaler or maintain an internal sales management organization, a service company must weigh the lower fixed cost and greater local knowledge of the former against the greater control and total dedication offered by the latter.

Service companies (such as airlines, hospitals, and insurance companies) that use independent retail intermediaries (travel agents, physicians, and insurance agents) face a classic dilemma. Is their "true customer" the intermediary or the end user? When the service company uses an independent wholesaler in the channel, it adds an extra level of complexity. The service company now must choose among three candidates for the "true customer" designation.

The answer to this riddle lies in the different skills and techniques that marketing to each level in the channel requires. Wholesalers are attracted to service companies that offer a broad array of products and provide strong systems support for sales and service. Retailers, on the other hand, consider how competitive products are (in terms of price, features, and quality) and their own compensation. Customers care about the product's price, features, and quality, but also about the image/reputation of the service company itself.

In order to identify its "true customer," a service company needs to match its own capabilities and goals against wholesalers', retailers', and customers' affiliation and purchase criteria.

## Make Wholesale Intermediaries Effective Product Managers

Retail intermediaries, like stockbrokers and life insurance agents, have to deal with a seemingly endless proliferation of products. Since one person cannot master the intricacies of 50 or 100 financial products, the brokerage firms and life insurers have thoughtfully provided product specialist wholesalers to support and promote the sales of nonmainstream products.

For example, The New England, a life insurance company, provides its field representatives (agents) with separate product specialists for group insurance, pension, and investment products. These product specialists in effect occupy a wholesaler position in the distribution channel, helping the agent to understand:

- The types of clients to which he or she might sell these products
- The intricacies of the products themselves
- The procedures for quoting and placing the business either inside or outside of The New England

There is one more level of complexity. The New England sells individual life insurance through a network of about ninety-two general agents (GAs), wholesalers who exclusively represent The New England. The GAs actually recruit, train, and supervise the agents. The New England distributes its group insurance and pension products through twenty-seven regional employee benefit offices, and its investment products through internal wholesalers employed by a subsidiary, New England Securities Corporation. The group, pension, and investment units also have appointed specialists within many general agencies to represent their own products at that level (see Figure 18-5).

If any of this seems complicated, consider what happens when a recently hired New England Life agent wants to sell an unfamiliar, complicated product like a split-dollar policy to fund a deferred compensation plan for a senior executive in a small business company. Figure 18-6 illustrates the number of spe-

*(Text continues on page 338.)*

**Figure 18-5.** Life insurance product specialists.

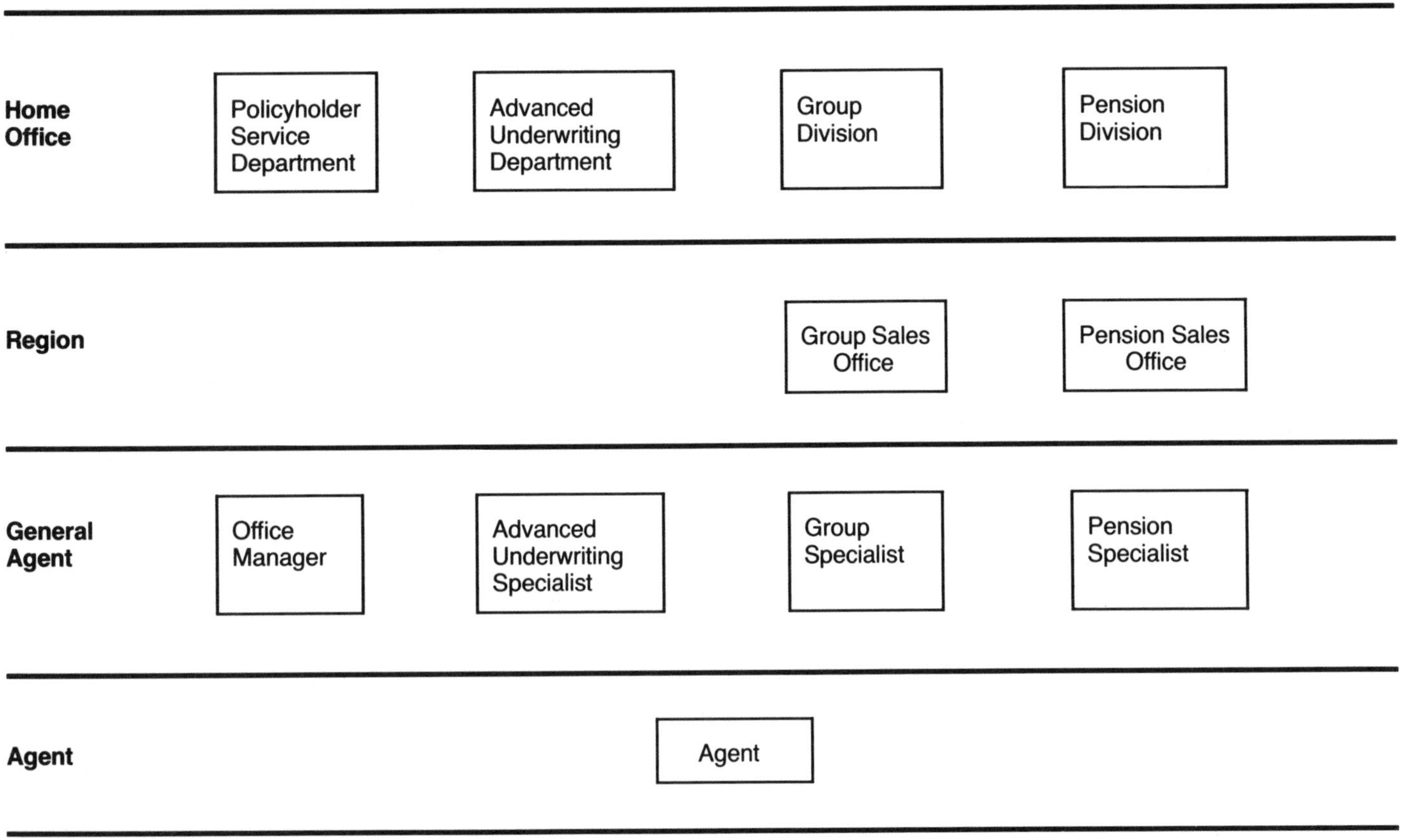

| Home Office | Policyholder Service Department | Advanced Underwriting Department | Group Division | Pension Division |
|---|---|---|---|---|

| Region | | | Group Sales Office | Pension Sales Office |
|---|---|---|---|---|

| General Agent | Office Manager | Advanced Underwriting Specialist | Group Specialist | Pension Specialist |
|---|---|---|---|---|

| Agent | Agent |
|---|---|

**Figure 18-6.** Selling a complex life-pension product.

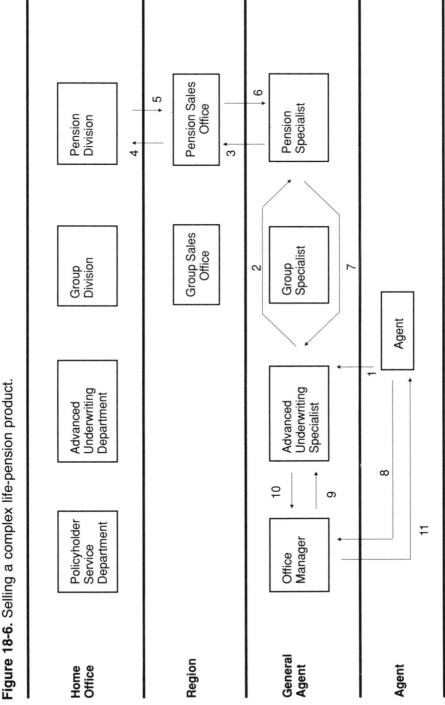

cialists and wholesalers located within the general agency, the region, and the home office with whom the agent may work in order to understand and sell the policy. (Incidentally, diagrams like the one in Figure 18-6 provide a good presentation of key business transactions in complex distribution channels.)

How can the agent and the product specialists navigate this maze? And how can The New England Life put enough good quality business through its wholesale and retail superstructure to exceed its fixed costs? One solution is to adapt a *product manager model* for wholesale intermediaries.

The product manager concept was originally developed by the consumer goods industry. The idea was to give one person responsibility (but typically not authority) for the production, distribution, and sales of a given product. Because they lacked direct line authority, good product managers became masters at:

- Developing an overall plan for their product
- Understanding the needs of each functional department
- Persuading each fiefdom to cooperate, notwithstanding the competing demands of all the other products flowing through the same channel

Channel wholesalers, such as the pension product specialist, are faced with a similar set of relationships. They must obtain products from the home office "manufacturer," that is, the actuaries and underwriters. They must facilitate the distribution of those products through the network of general agents. And they must promote the sale of those products through the retail agents. And they lack direct authority over any of these participants. Service companies that use wholesale intermediaries should consider recasting them into product managers—and giving those newly minted product managers proper training in planning, understanding, and persuading.

## Keep Intermediaries Loyal

### Three Levels of Loyalty

You are the new vice president of franchisee relations for "Yummy Corn," which currently operates twelve gourmet popcorn stores and plans to add 500 franchises over the next five years. Your mandate is to develop a set of objectives for Yummy Corn's relationships with its franchisees and to devise specific steps for achieving those objectives. Your job is made more challenging by the growth of three other gourmet popcorn chains: Tasty Corn, Hasty Corn, and Just Plain Corny.

Where to begin? It occurs to you that there are three levels of loyalty that a franchisee can display toward its franchisor:

- *Count me in* (or out)—deciding to continue or to terminate the Yummy Corn relationship

- *Nine to five*—doing an adequate job of meeting an average set of expectations
- *Pooling of interests*—strongly identifying with, and actively promoting, Yummy Corn's overall growth and profitability

So the first set of objectives comes fairly easily:

- Develop a relationship in which all viable franchisees wish to remain with Yummy Corn, and not defect to any of its competitors.
- Move as many franchisees as possible (half? two-thirds?) from a nine-to-five relationship to the pooling-of-interests level.

## Control Is Not a Dirty Word—It's a Two-Way Street

But the hard part is figuring out how to do it. The first step is to understand that in a relationship (between franchisor and franchisee, or bank and branch manager, or national television network and local affiliate) each participant has the ability to influence the other. Typically more of that power will rest with the franchisor/bank/national network. But the service company that tries to exercise its power too completely or arbitrarily will discover that its intermediaries are becoming less loyal, and perhaps easing out of the relationship altogether (taking as many customers with them as possible).

So how can a service company exercise the proper degree of control over its intermediaries? There are two basic techniques. The first technique is to establish carefully *the legal form* of the relationship. A service company can make its intermediaries employees, independent contractors, or franchisees. Each has its own advantages and disadvantages.

A service company exercises the greatest degree of control over employee intermediaries. The downside is that it is difficult to encourage innovation and initiative among employees, because employers, as large organizations, impose rules, predictability, and uniform compensation. In contrast a service company using independent contractors exercises less control over its intermediaries, but gains more entrepreneurial drive and creativity. The price for that drive and creativity may be substantially higher compensation.

Although franchisees are technically independent contractors, service companies can exercise a lot of control over them. McDonald's, to take an extreme example, tells its franchisees what food to sell, how to cook it, when to clean the kitchen, and what to wear while doing these tasks. Franchising also offers the service company a less capital-intensive way to expand, and a flow of revenue that is not directly related to the franchisees' actual profitability. As good as this sounds, franchisors need to remember that over time franchisees learn the business and establish their own customer relationships. Their ability to join another franchisor, or strike off on their own, gives the franchisees more power in the relationship—something the franchisors must acknowledge and respect.

The second technique available to the service company is to focus on *the quality* of its intermediary relationships. The service company can cooperate, coopt, or capture its intermediaries.

*Cooperating* with intermediaries means recognizing and supporting their autonomy—even when independent intermediaries can direct business from your own service company to another. Cooperation can take the form of:

- Supporting industrywide standards for systems and communications, making it as easy for the intermediary to do business with Service Company A as with Service Company B
- Promoting the intermediaries' identity through joint advertising campaigns
- Providing training, technical support, and financial assistance to individual intermediaries

*Coopting* intermediaries means tying them more closely to your own service company through subtle (or not so subtle) means that undermine their nominal independence:

- Developing proprietary systems (e.g., for sales and service as described earlier), a favorite ploy
- Developing joint advertising campaigns that promote the service company's identity at the expense of the intermediary (Ronald McDonald does not give the addresses of local franchisees)
- Providing superb compensation in return (explicitly or implicitly) for a large share of the intermediary's total book of business

*Capturing* intermediaries means establishing an exclusive relationship with your intermediaries—preferably at the nine-to-five or pooling-of-interests loyalty level.

## Pay the Price to Do Multimarketing Correctly

### What Is Multimarketing?

Multimarketing is the use of more than one channel to distribute one or more product groups to one or more customer segments. From a corporatewide perspective within the Fortune 2000, multimarketing is more the rule than the exception. Even within a division or business unit that obtains 98 percent of its revenue through a single channel, there is often pressure to reduce distribution costs (by using alternative channels) or to put more volume through the existing channel (by cross selling to current segments or making new sales to new segments).

The material on cooperating, coopting, and capturing is based on D. H. Light and G. Warfel, *Distribution Strategies for Services*, Business Intelligence Program, SRI International, 1984.
The material in the section "Pay the Price to Do Multimarketing Correctly" is based on D. H. Light Consulting Services, *Managing Life Insurance Distribution*, copyright 1987.

In 1988 Citicorp claimed a relationship with 17.5 million U.S. households. It reaches them through 288 retail branches in New York City, 136 in California, 60 in Illinois, 35 in Arizona, and 32 in Florida. It also uses its consumer finance arm, Citicorp Person-to-Person, with 66 nationwide branches. It is the largest issuer of Visa and MasterCard (about 18.3 million), and it owns the Diners Club card as well.

What about distributing banking services to its business customers? Citibank's Institutional Bank has its own calling officers, who sell services that are delivered by an elaborate worldwide electronic financial network, with more than 17,000 customer-product connections. It also provides an elaborate set of correspondent banking services to smaller banks, including loan syndications, participations, and processing services. Citibank's Investment Bank, with its own staff of investment bankers, underwrites and distributes securities for U.S. businesses in the Euromarket and is a primary dealer to other financial institutions for U.S. government securities.

Citicorp's profusion of products, channels, and customer segments might seem to be an extreme case. But consider American Airlines, which sells one product, air travel, through a multitude of channels. You can book your American flight from an independent travel agent, a corporate travel department, a tour operator, your personal computer, on the phone directly to American, in an American city ticketing office, or at an airport by using American's "Travel Teller" (a kind of airline ATM that makes reservations and prints tickets).

### What Is the Price?

Like many business concepts, multimarketing has a lot of surface appeal—"Hey, gang, let's get another distribution channel!" But there are pitfalls and costs.

Service companies that use different types of intermediaries to distribute the same product to the same customer face political problems. American Airlines gets most of its corporate business from independent travel agents. But what if American, hypothetically, were to deal directly with corporate travel departments *and* give them bulk discounts? The independent travel agents could retaliate by booking business travelers on other carriers.

Interestingly, though, the damage the travel agents could inflict is limited by several factors, including:

- Many business travelers' strong preference to fly American because of its reputation for quality service and dependability, as well as their participation in American's AAdvantage (frequent flyer) Program
- The fact that many travel agents use American's Sabre reservation system and have made significant investments in equipment and training
- The strength of American's schedule and hub-and-spoke route system

Other multimarketing service companies that face similar political problems may be able to defuse them by segregating the products or the customers. For example, national accounts may be handled corporately while local customers are handled in the field. Or, the product sold through direct marketing may be an economy version, with fewer options or less service support than the product sold by the field reps.

Potentially more serious is the frequent reluctance of corporate (or divisional) management to make an adequate investment in multiple distribution methods. The investment has two aspects:

1. Sufficient capital to finance the people, systems, and equipment necessary for making a new channel viable
2. A sufficient portion of senior management's time to *understand and support* the fundamental differences between a new channel and a dominant channel

The capital investment is the easier of the two. Good staff work, pro forma analysis, and/or the use of pilot projects should prevent serious underfunding.

Senior management's commitment of its own limited time is likely to be the larger stumbling block. Home-grown management will understand its own distribution system, but will have major blind spots looking at significantly different systems. Distribution chauvinism is exacerbated by the annoying tendency for some intermediaries to earn higher salaries than the senior corporate executives.

Although hiring managers with experience in a new channel may help, it doesn't really solve the problem, because the tasks of evaluating those managers' performance and allocating resources to competing channels still remain. In the end, the price that management has to pay for success in new channels is based on whatever is necessary to obtain direct, hands-on familiarity with what makes those unfamiliar channels work.

## Control the Pace of Change

Like any other important part of corporate strategy, "making service distribution work" depends on a combination of good planning, good execution, and good luck. Service firms have a basic choice: They can manage their distribution efforts, or they can let outside forces (their competition, technology, and regulation) do it for them.

Controlling the pace of change may mean taking small steps to fine-tune your channel's performance. Or it may mean taking major steps to restructure your intermediary relationships or shift toward new channels. But it always means understanding that distribution is a variable, not a given.

\*     \*     \*     \*

***Donald H. Light** is the principal of D. H. Light Consulting Services, Menlo Park, California, which he established in 1985. He consults to a wide variety of service companies, primarily in the areas of distribution strategy, planning, competitive analysis, and organization design. Previously Mr. Light was an internal consultant to business units within Allstate Insurance Company. He has also served as a consultant with SRI International's Financial Industries Center.*

# COMMUNICATING ABOUT AN INTANGIBLE

The two chapters in this section address the role of communications in your marketing program. The intangibility of services poses special communication challenges. Chapter 19, "Marketing and Communication Tools for Service Marketers," begins with a discussion of what you need to know before you can communicate effectively: what you need to know about your customers and what you need to know about your service. This information helps you understand what you need to communicate (what is unique about your service) and how you need to communicate (how customers see themselves and your product).

The bulk of the chapter is devoted to a comprehensive discussion of the various communication tools available—advertising and its different forms, including public relations, sponsorships, and promotions. The strengths, weaknesses, uses, and value of each communication tool are discussed. Communication effectiveness measures are included. Finally, the concept of a campaign is introduced—using the tools in an integrated and coordinated fashion to obtain the greatest positive effect from your communication dollars.

Chapter 20 describes how to put together an integrated communication campaign. An integrated communication program promotes the mission, positioning, and marketing goals of the organization. Additionally, all of the communication tools used in the program are designed to be mutually reinforcing. The value of an integrated program is discussed in terms of getting the maximum communication benefit given limited funds, staff, and time. Practical guidelines are provided to help you understand your target audience. Then, matching the appropriate communication tool to your target audience is discussed. Included in this matching effort is what the author calls a "communication review," where you examine your corporate identity, how it is working for you currently, how you would like it to work for you, and what you can do to improve and monitor it. Consistency and clarity in communication are stressed, as well as feedback and evaluation. The relationship between internal communication and external communication is emphasized.

# 19

# Marketing and Communication Tools for Services Marketers

Thad D. Peterson
K. Shelly Porges

So, you've done your homework. You've taken a look at your business, your objectives; you have a good sense of who your customers are and what your organization can provide them. You've developed a program that can be implemented and you're ready to build a promotion. What do you use? Television? Radio and newspaper? Direct mail and outdoor? Point-of-sale blimps? What, or more important, why? There are hundreds of different tools available, and almost every one is valid at one time or another. The question is which to use when, and why. In this chapter, we describe the basic tools available to a marketer for customer communication and briefly discuss their function, uses, strengths, and weaknesses. But before we begin with what they are, we start with who they are for—the customer. After all, marketing tools are simply the means by which you communicate your chosen message to your chosen customers at a specific moment in time. Fortunately, you don't have to think of the customers in the abstract. How do *you* react? What gets your attention? What's the process you go through?

After discussing the basic tools, we look at more sophisticated tools, such as special promotions and incentives. Another major section concerns measurement—how to assess your progress using these tools. Then we present ten rules of thumb that we have found useful in mounting successful campaigns. In the final section, we summarize the key points in developing a successful campaign. First, let's look at the marketing world through your customer's eyes.

## Know Your Customer

Customers are besieged with information. Commercials from morning to bedtime, outdoor boards on the way to work, direct mail in their mailboxes, posters, banners, promotions, key chains, magazine ads, newspaper ads, messages literally everywhere.

Because of this deluge, an information "noise level" has been created, which pervades our lives. Most of this information is barely noticed. It's only received by a customer when a combination of things happens:

1. The service being offered is of use or value to the customer.
2. The customer needs or wants the service at that particular time.

3. The customer perceives that he can pay for what he wants.
4. The customer sees or hears the message about the service.

Only then will a customer make a *choice* about the service being offered. And don't forget your competitors. They're out there trying to do the same thing. It's important to realize that in addition to the general noise level customers encounter, there's probably a service-specific noise level as well. It's up to you to overcome both.

Everyone knows it's a tough world out there. How can you improve the odds? *Know your customer!* Use all the information you can find. How old are they? What do they do? Where do they live? What are their goals? Are they married? Do they have kids? Grandkids? This is where your market research can help you make an informed decision about your communications.

There are several things to beware of as you analyze your customers. First, make sure you know why they are buying your service. Is it your service and a unique benefit? Or is it the *positioning* of your service? It makes a big difference in the way you communicate. If you have a unique benefit or service, your job is to communicate that uniqueness very clearly. If it's your position that's unique, your focus should be on the tools used to present the position and the dollars available to support it. Second, are you marketing to a stereotype? Be careful about labels like "mature," "upscale," "yuppie." They're almost never accurate. You have to get away from the stereotypes and understand the people. And, don't forget, regardless of the method of communication you choose, you always get customers the old-fashioned way—one individual at a time.

Now that you understand the people you want to talk to, it's time to decide what you want to say. What does the customer think about your service? Be honest: Is it really as good as you say it is? Customers are smart, so don't exaggerate. What's unique? What's better? Write up communication objectives that state your message clearly and simply. Then, take an honest look at your weaknesses and decide how you can counter them. Here's a sample format for laying out your communication objectives.

Communication Objective.   What is it, precisely, that you want to achieve with the communication? Sample: "Persuade customers to contact their local Smith Johns broker and inquire about the Smith Johns Money Market Fund."

Environmental Context.   *In the context of the customer,* why would it be logical for a customer to do this? Sample: "Current market fluctuations make investing in stocks and bonds a very high-risk proposition, and simultaneously, money market rates are at a two-year high. By moving to our Money Market Fund, customers can eliminate investment risk and still receive an excellent return."

Target Audience.   A precise definition of the customer. Sample: "Men, 35 years and older, with $25,000 in stocks or bonds. Married. Attended or graduated college and in a professional/managerial position."

Key Benefit. What is *the most compelling reason* for a customer to select the service? Generally, there should be only one benefit. If there is more than that, you get "main message dilution" and less impact. Sample: "With the Smith Johns Money Market Fund, you can eliminate the risk of stock market fluctuation and at the same time, earn a rate of return that exceeds inflation and bank rates."

Key Benefit Support. What is the proof of the benefit? Why is it believable? Sample:

The Smith Johns Money Market Fund is invested in government securities, the safest instruments available.

With the Smith Johns Money Market Account you have access to your money by check.

All you need to open the account is $5,000.

The current money market rate of xx percent is higher than current bank rates and better than the return on the Dow Jones for the last six months.

Tone. How do you want to say it? Sample: "Straightforward, understated, professional." Now, you're ready to think about *how* to use the basic communication tools.

## What Are the Basic Tools?

In this section, we'll talk about the communication tools that you use to promote your company's services. We'll start with those tools that are close to one-on-one contact with the customer in terms of communication and proceed from there. It's often advisable to use the same order when you are assembling your plan.

We are assuming that you have a clear idea of what you want to communicate, whom you wish to communicate with, and why they might be interested in your message. If you haven't done this, go back and do so. If you are not sure, the chances are that at best you'll waste a lot of money, and at worst, you'll fail *and* waste a lot of money.

Each different communication tool is described in the same format so that they can be compared easily. We'll start with the most direct and expensive tool: personal selling.

### Personal Selling

*Definition*—the effective creation of a customer through personal contact with another human being, a salesperson. How does it work? In services, there is always a modicum of information that must be conveyed in the process of making a sale. In some situations the information is so extensive or complicated that one-on-one selling is virtually the only way to make the sale. Brokerage services are a good example. In any service business, however, a competent, well-trained, and motivated sales force is critical to the success of any program. As marketers, we may or may not have control over the sales force, but there are several ways that marketing can assist the direct sales effort.

The most common criticism we hear from salespeople about marketers and their efforts is the lack of advance notice and information when a campaign is introduced. It's critical that salespeople feel that they are part of the program, because they're the most important part of the process. They need to know as much about the program as you can tell them. Tell your sales force what the program is all about, when it will start, who the target audience will be, what media will be used, and what the creative message will be. But most important: *Tell them why you are doing it!* It may be crystal clear to headquarters, and it may have been planned for some time, but that doesn't mean much to a person who tries to sell the product to real people day after day.

*When is it used?*—Direct sales is rarely *not* used. The primary reasons for using direct sales are: extensive information is required either by the customer or because a product or service is complex; the service is sold through a retail outlet; the service is sold through independent distributors; or the service is sold over the telephone.

*Strengths*—Direct sales can be one of the most effective methods of marketing because the sales process can be managed by the salesperson. It also allows for flexibility, so that although the service initially offered may not be exactly right for the customer and in any other communication medium would receive a solid ''no,'' in the hands of a capable salesperson, the situation can be adapted to suit customer needs. Direct sales can also lead to major cross-selling opportunities that wouldn't be available otherwise.

*Weaknesses*—The biggest limitation is cost. In most situations the direct sales process boils down to one salesperson and one customer and a certain amount of time. The cost-per-closed sale can be astronomical, particularly with a major business-to-business sale involving great expense and an extensive customer bureaucracy. It's not unusual for such decisions to take years in these situations.

Because of its one-on-one nature, the reach of a sales force is very limited and it's important that *qualified* prospects be identified for the sales force. Another weakness is consistency. Because a sales force consists of people instead of manufactured, homogenized messages, considerable variability is inevitable. Many service employees aren't yet comfortable with the concept of ''selling,'' so businesses are in the process of converting people who focused on service exclusively into salespeople. In this situation, it's not uncommon to encounter significant resistance from people who are neither interested in nor capable of direct sales. It's important for marketers to realize this and to work hard to build a good sales force as quickly as possible.

### Direct Response

*Definition*—There are two aspects of direct response:

1. Using any medium to reach customers in order to obtain an immediate sale or response, usually via telephone or mail. The communication medium could be: radio, newspaper, magazine, billing or other insert, and television, as well as mail or telephone.
2. Using the telephone or mail to qualify target prospects.

*How does it work?*—Direct response techniques are most often used for generating leads or actually making sales. Although the mail and telephone media are used by most service businesses on a daily basis, marketers who are not professionals often commit these "seven deadly sins":

1. *Not recognizing that you are already in the direct mail business.* Every piece of mail you send out could be working harder for you as a sales tool. By concentrating on who is getting your mailings (list) and what products or services might be appropriate to promote (offer), an information mailing can become a sales tool.

2. *Using the wrong mailing list.* List targeting has become almost a science. With the help of some outside vendors, you can focus on some very specific criteria, including:

| | |
|---|---|
| Geography | Purchase behavior |
| Age | Life-style indicators |
| Income range | Travel indicators |
| Gender | Marital status |

3. *Promoting a product that can't be sold by mail.* Not all products are created equal: That is, not all can be sold via mail. If you answer "No" to most of these questions, you may want to use a different medium:

- Is the target customer easily identifiable?
- Can the product be bought easily by mail?
- Can the benefits be fully explained in a simple letter?
- Can you overcome in writing the normal objections that might arise?

4. *Writing factual but unpersuasive copy.* Direct mail copy needs just one message: What's in it for customers? What are the benefits? What will happen to them if they accept your offer? What will happen if they don't? Here are some other tips:

- Make your copy personal.
- Make sure you're addressing an individual (not a group).
- Be brief.
- Ask for the sale.

5. *Omitting a call to action.* It's simple: You must ask for the order. And be specific: How should your prospect respond? Call you? Write? Fill out an application? Visit your store? The more direct the response device, the more

effective it is. That is, the phone tends to be more effective than mail, which, in turn, is better than an invitation to visit your store.

6. *Not giving a reason to act now.* Keep in mind that a prospect who gets your mail has two basic options: Act or toss. The more reason you give him or her to act now, the more likely you are to succeed. Here are some ways to create a sense of urgency:

* Create a time-limited offer.
* Use a natural time limit, e.g., pending holiday, tax time.
* Indicate that the offer is valid while the supply lasts.
* Make the offer to the first group (specify the total) of customers who respond.

7. *Giving up too soon.* Think of every mailing as a test—whatever the results. And build on your learning. That's one of the advantages of direct response: Because of the feedback received after each effort, you can improve each subsequent mailing.

*Strengths*—The key strengths of direct mail are as follows:

* Allows for specific targeting
* Can replace or support direct sales efforts
* Can be personalized
* Provides opportunity to deliver a detailed message at a precise time

*Weaknesses*—Its key weaknesses are:

* Costly to reach a large audience
* Costly to build frequency and thus, ineffective in building image
* Considered "junk mail" by some people

### Television Advertising

*Definition*—Any communication that is received by the consumer through television, including cable advertising and videocassette advertising.

*How does it work?*—Television is generally thought to be the most effective medium available because only TV can provide sight, sound, *and* motion. It can also deliver broad reach very quickly and is demographically adjustable. TV commercials can be bought in fifteen-, thirty-, and sixty-second units with the vast majority being thirty-second. The cost for TV time is based on the estimated number of people that are watching a particular show at a particular time. This estimate is measured in terms of "rating points," which is the percent of the total TV audience that is watching the program in question at the time. It's very unlikely that one would run one commercial one time, so the rating points of individual shows are added up for the week to arrive at the gross rating points (GRPs). So, if one ran a schedule in a week that had ten commercials that each received ten rating points, the total gross rating points for the week would be one hundred GRPs.

TV offers a great deal of flexibility to the marketer. You can be demographically selective with programming (such as buying all sports and news), thematically selective (such as sponsoring a particular program that your company is involved in), or time selective (such as all late-night).

When is it used? Television is used for a variety of reasons, but usually it is the lead medium in a major campaign or promotion. It can create more excitement than any other medium, and it can convey a message to a large group of people very quickly. It's especially effective with new products, services, or positions where maximum impact is a requirement. It is a broad-reach vehicle, so it's most effective when there is a distribution system that makes it easy for a customer to respond, or there is ready access to the product or service by telephone. It's often used for awareness advertising where it's important to convey a particular image associated with the company.

*Strengths*—No other vehicle allows the kind of creativity or intrusion that you can get with television, and there is no medium more universally seen and used. It delivers broad reach very quickly. It's perceived by employees and customers as "major league" advertising, and that can lend credence to the efforts of the sales force.

*Weaknesses*—TV advertising is expensive. Because of its broad reach, delivering thousands or millions of customers with one exposure, the absolute dollar cost is high. The cost per thousand people reached (CPM) can be low; however, production costs can be high as well. It's not unusual for a national brand ad to cost at least $250,000 or more. Also, it is becoming increasingly difficult for one program to reach a large number of people because of the increased use of cable TV and VCRs. When planning for television, keep in mind that the reach, frequency, and GRPs being presented are based on statistical estimates. Although these are valid, they don't measure a viewer's interest in the commercial being watched or whether anyone is in the room.

### Radio

*Definition*—Nothing fancy, advertising on AM and FM radio.

*How is it used?*—Like TV, radio is measured in terms of rating points, which can be accumulated to achieve reach and frequency. Aside from that, radio and TV are very different in terms of their ability to communicate and the way they reach the customer. Most customers select a few radio stations that they listen to almost exclusively. They can become very loyal to certain programs and formats, and listen to them on an almost ritualistic basis. Radio can be a very active medium when presenting talk-show formats, or it can almost disappear from consciousness when played as background music in an office. It is almost always a secondary medium to another activity (usually driving, but also other things such as reading and housework). Not many people just sit down and listen to the radio.

Radio time is usually bought in 60-second units, because it takes longer to make an impact without a visual component. Although radio can reach an audience very quickly, the relatively narrow audiences of each station means that in most situations time must be bought on many stations to attain significant reach. Because radio listeners tend to be loyal to a few stations and ritualistic in the time of day that they use the medium, most radio schedules include spots across the broadcast day in order to achieve as much reach as possible against that specific station's audience. Customers' habitual listening at certain times of the day (such as while commuting) means that if you have a spot on the same station at the same time for five consecutive days, you'll be getting excellent frequency against that customer. Radio is, therefore, a very good frequency builder in support of high-reach media like TV and newspaper.

*Strengths*—Radio is excellent for delivering frequency efficiently on a cost-per-thousand basis. It can reach both demographic and life-style targets, and it can do so with a longer message. A radio message is less easy to ignore than a newspaper ad, because it is part of the program format. Radio lends itself to interesting creative executions, and humor is particularly effective on this medium.

*Weaknesses*—There are no pictures! Radio can only convey its message through the sense of sound. It relies purely on the spoken word and other sounds to communicate, so its potential for total involvement is limited. The fact that it is often a background for other activities can also lessen its impact. Each radio station in a major market has a limited reach, and because customers are so loyal to their stations, you need to buy a lot of different stations to accumulate significant reach.

### Print Advertising

*Definition*—Print publications, including newspaper, magazines, Sunday supplements.

*How is it used?*—Print advertising is a varied and diverse area that can offer an advertiser broad reach, highly selective demographics, excellent graphic reproduction, and the opportunity for interesting and unusual approaches. We will break this section into three components: newspapers, magazines, and trade publications, because each is quite different.

Newspapers.   Newspaper advertising delivers very broad reach to a relatively nonselective audience. Space for newspaper is bought in standard advertising units (SAUs), or column-inches, depending on the publication. Virtually any size or shape ad can be run, depending on the printing limitations of the paper. Most major newspapers offer color reproduction, but the quality of the paper that is used generally results in poor color reproduction.

*Strengths*—No other print medium can deliver high reach in a market more quickly than a newspaper, and the immediacy of the medium increases the likelihood that your ad will be seen. Appropriate messages can be placed in specific sections, such as a sports promotion in the sports section, and regular weekly sections (such as food or entertainment) can be used to draw attention to your message and to deliver coupons effectively. Ads can usually be placed within forty-eight hours of an issue date, so newspapers can accommodate your placements very quickly if necessary. Production of newspaper advertising is relatively simple, fast, and inexpensive when compared to other media.

*Weaknesses*—Yesterday's ad is at the bottom of today's bird cage. Newspapers are generally read one day only and then the message is gone. And, because they are broad-reach vehicles, you're paying for circulation that you don't necessarily need. So the cost, both on a CPM and an absolute-dollar basis, can be very high. Reproduction can be a problem and quality varies significantly from publication to publication. Newspapers contain a lot of other advertising so your ad must compete in a cluttered environment.

Consumer Magazines. These publications deliver a visually appealing message to a demographically precise audience. Magazines are more restrictive than newspapers in the size and formats of advertising, with ad sizes being page units or fractions thereof. Advertising is frequently placed on consecutive pages, called "ad banks or ad wells," so that the integrity of the editorial material is maintained. Magazines are generally printed on high-quality paper that can easily accept four-color advertising.

Circulation is measured by the number of paid subscriptions plus newsstand sales the magazine has audited by an outside audit firm. Another measure is the circulation plus the number of people who read each issue, called "pass-along readership." Many national magazines offer regional advertising sections, and some companies insert ads in major national magazines on a market-by-market basis.

*Strengths*—Magazines have a unique ability to deliver a message to a very select audience that can be identified by such criteria as life-style, professional or personal interest, age, income, education, ethnicity, and language. They do an excellent job of reproducing four-color photographs that can add a patina of quality to a campaign. Because they can be demographically selective, they can be efficient on a CPM basis. Magazines tend to be kept, and some are reread or circulated to other people, thus increasing opportunity for exposure.

*Weaknesses*—Magazines require a lot of lead time to produce, and they can require that materials be delivered to them up to eight weeks in advance of publication. Four-color production is time-consuming and relatively expensive. If your ad is placed in an "ad well," it's likely that readership for your ad will be lower than if it appears by itself.

Trade Publications. In most industries, one or two trade publications are the lifeblood of the business. And, if you're involved in marketing a business-to-business service in one of these industries, you can't afford not to advertise in these publications. In many cases, the publications are delivered free to companies in the business, with all the magazine's revenue coming from advertising. In other cases, however, subscription price is very high to intentionally limit circulation to upper management. There are fewer controls or standards on trade publications than on consumer magazines, and it's important to check the audit statements to make sure they are delivering the circulation they promise.

*Strengths*—The greatest strength is that the people who are reading the magazine are interested both in the topic and the industry. And they'll be very conscious of the advertising, because it serves as the marketplace for the business. The quality of the color reproduction usually is very good. Many trade publications include reader response cards, so that customers or prospects can obtain information directly and thus you can get solid leads. Publishers of trade magazines tend to work hard to meet advertisers' needs.

*Weaknesses*—Although you may not be able to live without trade advertising, it's important to know who *really* reads these publications and why. Within your industry, there are probably only one or two magazines that everyone has to read to stay in touch with the business, while many others gather dust on someone's credenza. In this situation your input will be of significant value to your advertising agency in selecting media. This agency can help with circulation and cost, but what really matters is which publications are read. If you don't know, ask your sales force.

## Out-of-Home Advertising

*Definition*—Billboards, transit advertising, any advertising signage that is seen outside the home and is not printed or electronic.

*How does it work?*—Outdoor and transit advertising can convey a simple message to a large number of people on a daily basis. Thousands of cars pass outdoor boards each day and receive an impression. Outdoor advertising uses a system like Gross Rating Points (GRPs) to measure the audience reached, but in the outdoor business they use the term *showing* instead of GRP. Most billboards are a standard size called "30 sheets," reflective of the number of separate pieces used to make one billboard. Smaller billboards are also available (called junior panels or "10 sheets"), usually in high-density urban areas. In many markets oversized boards are available on which the message is actually painted onto the sign. Appropriately, these are called "painted bulletins" or "paints." Transit advertising varies by market, but most city buses carry advertising outside—the right-side ads cost more than those on the left. Many also carry advertising on the inside. Each market will have other opportunities for out-of-home advertising, such as bus kiosks and benches, subway advertising, taxicab advertising, and "moving billboards" (trucks that carry outdoor signs or displays through or to high visibility areas). Because of the diversity of the business, it's important that both you and your ad agency understand each local market so that you make the most efficient buy possible.

*Strengths*—Out-of-home is the undisputed champion of low-cost reach and frequency. It can generate millions of impressions on a monthly basis and can be selectively placed to reach only those customers in a certain area. Color reproduction is generally excellent, and, with the very large boards, you can get creative by using inflatable images that add three dimensions.

*Weaknesses*—Outdoor and transit advertising is not intrusive. It can be easily ignored and the impression it makes is minimal. Copy space is limited to the amount of time available for reading, which means that it must be very brief. In general, more than eight words of copy will be missed when traveling on a freeway at 55 miles per hour. Most outdoor boards must be posted for at least one month, and lead time is significant, which means it isn't conducive to short-term promotions. Many outdoor boards are not lit, so a significant percentage of your opportunity for reach can disappear at sunset. It's probably the most unpopular medium among consumers, many of whom consider it a blight. It is best used as a reminder in support of a major campaign in another medium.

## Collateral

*Definition*—Collateral materials are those delivered to the customer or prospect in direct support of the sale. This can include brochures, inserts into statements and invoices (stuffers), newsletters, catalogs—anything printed that ends up in the customer's hands.

*How does it work?*—Unlike other media, collateral is generally a direct selling tool that reinforces a sales presentation or amplifies a sales message. Brochures provide the opportunity to fully describe a product or service and potentially provide a sales opportunity after initial contact has been made. Catalogs can provide an array of products or services, and allow customers to control their own sales process. Statement or invoice stuffers can increase the visibility of a service among existing customers of another service at a very low cost.

For most services, there is almost nothing that the customer can physically handle, play with, or admire. In short, services lack *tangibility,* which can be a major limitation. Our brethren in package and durable goods don't have this problem. You can hold a can of tuna and look at the label, you can play games on a computer, and you can test drive a car; however, you can't kick the tires on a checking account, and mutual funds don't come in a box. Lack of tangibility is a problem that can be solved with collateral; well-designed, interesting, and attractive brochures can be a packaging substitute—a physical manifestation that customers can take home with them.

*Strengths*—Collateral is the only print medium in which every aspect of production is controllable. Size, shape, color, length, copy, and method of distribution can be custom-tailored to the specific needs of the organization. With collateral, you can deliver the sales message completely and logically, regardless of what the sales force is telling the customer.

*Sales support*—Collateral provides the sales force with support materials. It can be a valuable guide through the sales process.

*Weaknesses*—Intrusiveness: It's been said that the only people who read brochures from cover to cover are the writer and the lawyer. Unless customers are vitally interested and enthusiastic about the service, it's unlikely they will take the time to read all of your masterwork. Brochures are passive and generally ignored. To get a customer's attention, the copy must be arresting and well organized, and the brochure *must be visually interesting.*

*The "crutch" factor*—Brochures are no substitute for active selling by a salesperson. Too often, a good selling process is replaced by, "Look at this brochure, and call me if you have any questions."

## Public Relations

*Definition*—Public relations (PR) generally refers to any area of communication that reflects the public image of a company. As a tool, PR involves using public media to establish an image or communicate a message. PR consists of publicity, media relations, seminars, and other special events, any of which may entail coverage by the public media. Event marketing and sponsorships are discussed in a later section.

*How does it work?*—PR works because editors and columnists depend on information. Because news today comes from every area of the country, these people often rely on reports they receive from corporations and their PR representatives.

<u>Media Relations.</u>   Media relations is the process ensuring that the media covering your business are supplied with the information necessary to meet their reporting objectives while positioning your company and products in the most favorable light. Media relations is best handled when you initiate the contacts. Here are some tips:

1. Identify the media that reach your target consumer.
2. Identify the relevant reporters and editors who cover your industry or product area.
3. Meet with these journalists to introduce yourself as an industry or subject expert and to provide background on your company. The larger and more influential your company is, the more willing they will be to do this. However, even a small company with a distinctive point of difference can find a receptive audience.
4. Make sure to focus on the news value of what you're discussing with the journalist.
5. Make yourself readily available to reporters. If they call you, return the call immediately. Remember, they are usually working with deadlines.

Now, let's look at the key to successful publicity: providing honest, factual, well-written news stories. This is usually done via the press release. A properly written news release, just like a newspaper story, has all the points up front—the substantive facts, the descriptive detailing—the minor points come later. Here are some tips:

1. *Get to the point.* The prime rule in journalism is that the opening paragraph of a news article must contain answers to these five questions: Who? What? When? Where? Why? The assumption is that the reader may never get past the first paragraph, and you want to be sure that he gets all the facts before he stops reading.

2. *Make it news—not advertising.* No one is kidding anyone else. The editor knows you have prepared the PR story for the benefit of your company. But he or she will print it if the news offers benefit to readers and if it contains straight facts and no unsubstantiated allegations.

3. *A picture is worth a thousand words.* Send a photograph with your release if at all possible. It adds more interest to the story and gets you more space in the media.

4. *Controversy can be an excellent springboard for publicity.* The controversy over the infamous book *Satanic Verses* by Salman Rushdie ensured its success. A story is told about the great actress Sarah Bernhardt who in her day

was denounced by clergymen everywhere, thus ensuring massive attendance at her performances. After one minister delivered a particularly effective piece of publicity, she sent him a check with this note, "Your Excellency, I am accustomed, when I bring an attraction to your town, to spend $400 on advertising. As you have done half the advertising for me, I herewith enclose $200 for your parish."

Article Placement.   Another effective public relations technique is article placement. You can position your company or key individuals as subject experts by developing special-interest or newsworthy articles and circulating them to appropriate media contacts for publication. Some of the keys to success here are:

1. *Know your audience,* as always. The Home section editor is not interested in why home decorator stocks are rising. However, an article on how to decorate a bathroom for under $1,000 might be appropriate.
2. *Be flexible.* Some publications may want a 200-word summary of your piece and others may do a full-page version.
3. *Be succinct.* Short copy tends to get more pick-up.

*When is public relations best used?*—PR is extremely powerful when there is news value in a promotion, a new service, an innovative way to tell the story, a unique advertising approach, or a new position for a company. Reporters are always looking for new things to talk about, but they're also extremely skeptical and will shy away from "false news." Of course, PR is the major tool in the case of a serious problem or major political issue.

*Strengths*—PR allows you to place your message in the editorial section of a medium instead of advertising. It can allow you to increase market penetration by adding media at no advertising cost, and it can enhance the company's image and sell at the same time. When it works, it's very powerful.

*Weaknesses*—The trade-off is control. With PR you relinquish control of time, placement, and position. The danger is that the wrong thing will be said to the wrong person at the wrong time.

## What Are the Advanced Tools?

When appropriate, it's a good idea to add some energy to a program with promotions, event marketing, sponsorships, or incentives. Although they can be powerful additions to the marketing mix, these tools cannot be used alone, nor in most cases can they be the dominant message or effort. They are best used sparingly, strategically, and with a clear understanding of their true expense and real revenue opportunity.

### Promotions

Whether it's McDonald's Disney toy giveaway, MTV's weekend with a pop star, or Chrysler's zero percent loan offer, promotions can help to hype a service business. A promotion is a fixed-term campaign that highlights a specific offer or sales opportunity.

Promotions are most often used for leveraging sales in seasonal businesses, monitoring a sales blitz, and introducing new products or services.

A promotion works because it provides a focus for the sales effort and a "hook" or special emotional appeal for the customer. Successful campaigns are usually characterized by:

- *Fixed time period,* usually no more than three to four months (six to eight weeks is more common)
- *A special offer or customer incentive,* using any of the key promotional parameters, e.g., price, product, premium, enhanced service
- *Focused communication to prospects,* whether it's media advertising, in-store merchandising, or direct response
- *Promotional sales goal,* usually higher than sales goals during nonpromotional periods
- *Sales force incentive* (see section entitled "Employee Incentive Programs")

The key strengths of this tool are that it promotes heavy sales during a short period, provides customer and sales force focus, and allows for concentration of resources.

Its key limitations are that it does *not* necessarily support ongoing sales and, in fact, may displace sales that would have occurred before or after the promotion period. Additionally, it can create a "drag" on products or services not promoted.

Perhaps the most notable examples of promotions in service businesses are the "white sales" and holiday sales run by many retailers. Frequent buyer programs, whether for airlines or for gas stations, represent an attempt to extend the concept of a consumer incentive beyond the typical short promotion period.

## Event Marketing and Sponsorships

The 1984 Olympic Games dramatized the opportunities in event marketing and sponsorships. Millions of dollars were raised to stage this extraordinary event, as companies reaped the rewards of the attention the games received.

Event marketing is simply using an event and/or sponsorship (e.g., sports, cultural) to market a product or service. It is used for building awareness and a positive image, for promoting goodwill, and for providing a theme for a promotion.

Key strengths are that it provides a natural focus and can be perceived as *less* self-serving than a normal sales promotion, depending on the event. Event marketing does carry risks; if the event fails, for example, or if it is poorly attended, it can have a negative effect on image. The cost of event marketing can also be prohibitive because you incur the cost of the sponsorship in addition to the normal media and communications cost.

### Employee Incentive Programs

Employee incentives, used to focus the sales representatives on the promotional effort, can motivate them to close the sale at the point of purchase. This is especially true if your service is sold through an outside sales force that sells for many different companies. Since we're discussing promotional tools, it's not appropriate to discuss structural sales incentive and commission programs. We'll focus instead on tactical promotional incentives.

Incentives for employees can be cash, merchandise, travel, sweepstakes, and games to get the staff motivated to support a program. It depends on the situation and the objective. There are a few rules that apply to all programs, however:

1. *Make sure your program is legal.* Benefits from incentives are generally considered a part of an employee's compensation and so the tax implications of the program need to be considered. Also, if a contest is involved, check to be sure that it's being conducted in compliance with the law. Human resource specialists and lawyers should be involved in any incentive program.

2. *If at all possible, use goals.* People like to achieve and they like to know what achievement means. Set clear goals to give people something to aim for.

3. *Make sure someone, anyone, gets a payout.* It's critical that the promised reward is achievable. People will stop trying if they doubt their ability to achieve a goal. A well-balanced award structure with many awards for different levels of performance will increase interest and enthusiasm.

4. *Expect to be "gamed."* In every sales force there's at least one person who will take the time to figure out a legal way to "beat the program." The only thing to do is to accept this as fact and realize that most people will be perfectly content to participate as you planned. Ignore the people who don't, unless they actually cheat.

Employee incentives can be a major contributor to a program's success if they are well conceived, carefully implemented, and closely controlled. They can also involve a great deal of money but produce very little. It is advisable to seek professional assistance from an outside consultant or supplier to assist with the management of an incentive program.

## How to Measure Your Progress

Regardless of the type or size of campaign, there's a way to measure the results, and no marketing program should be considered complete without evaluation. Although the use of measurement-defining tools is important, what *really* matters is knowing if the campaign did what it was supposed to do. It's entirely possible to have a terrific advertising campaign with entertaining commercials that everyone loves, with no results in terms of sales or returns. So the first step is to measure the results against campaign objectives; then you can look at the individual components. Because measurement and research are covered in other sections of this book, we will concentrate on those measurement approaches that specifically evaluate marketing tools. And to keep things simple, we'll discuss them by type.

### Personal Selling

Tracking of individual sales efforts can be simple or complex, depending on the nature of your business.

In most cases, you will need a system that can link sales to a single office or individual. With commissioned salespeople, this is the basis of their compensation, so tracking must be both easy and effective. In other situations, tracking of individual efforts may be less important, but regardless of the circumstances, measurement of sales effort will show wide variation in performance and will help to identify weak and strong sales outlets. It's critical that individual sales results be tracked *and* reported back to the sales force. Specific items to be measured include sales closure rate, calls made, profitability, and customer service quality.

### Broadcast Advertising

Responsiveness to advertising can be measured by sales increases if a promotion is product- or time-specific. If it is not, research may be the only tool available to determine whether the desired objective was reached. This is particularly true if the objective is to increase awareness or change attitudes.

If the advertising objective is lead generation, then an 800 number or a reader response card can be included in the advertising to stimulate response and ensure accurate measurement.

### Direct Response

The results of direct response are the easiest to measure because this tool always includes a response device that can be tracked. In fact, there's almost a science to direct response tracking that can result in significant increases in response in subsequent efforts.

### Public Relations

It's difficult to track actual sales results from PR, because it is less controllable and more indirect. The first thing to be tracked is the placement of the story. Clipping services can provide copies of all published articles based on a press release or event. From there, either sales tracking or research can measure results. One thing to keep in mind is that customers frequently confuse the source of information on publicity. It's possible that a customer may respond to a survey by saying that he or she heard about something on television when, in fact, this person read an article about it somewhere else. Although this sometimes makes results difficult to read, it makes marketing an interesting profession.

## Promotions/Event Marketing/Sponsorships

Because these are usually used in conjunction with other marketing efforts, it can be difficult to identify the effects of promotional activity on actual sales. This, of course, is not true if the promotion is the primary message of the advertising effort. Regardless of the difficulty, every effort should be made to quantify the results of secondary activities, because they can be very expensive and their real value may be questionable.

# Ten Rules of Thumb for Success

In developing communication programs, certain guidelines or criteria ensure success. Here are ten rules of thumb that we think are critical to most programs:

1. *Define your goal clearly and focus.*
   * Make sure your goal is actionable and measurable.
   * Write it down.
   * Ask your employees to read it and then restate it in their own words to be sure they understand it.
   * Make sure everyone in your organization knows what the goal is.
   * Limit the number of major goals you have each year.

2. *Put yourself in the customer's shoes.*
   * Shop your company anonymously, if possible, to see how the average customer is treated.
   * Have friends do the same and give you honest feedback.
   * Read and respond to customer letters and phone calls.
   * Put yourself on all your mailing lists.

3. *Don't forget the emotional side of decision making.* Or, as Anatole France once said, ''It is human nature to think wisely and act foolishly.'' Packaging, graphics, casting, music—all can effectively influence the emotional side of a decision.

4. *Make sure you're not ''talking to yourself'' in your ads.*
   * You know what you mean, but will the customer? Have your ads reviewed by someone who is not familiar with your services.
   * After developing your ad, put it aside for a few days. Then review it. Does it still make sense?

5. *Time is a sales tool—limit it.*
   * Making time-limited offers is one of the best spurs to sales.
   * Use special occasions, such as national holidays and company anniversaries, to limit the time of the offer.

6. *Don't starve your media budget.*
   * If two-thirds or three-quarters of your ad budget isn't available to place your ad after production costs, rethink your advertising plan.
   * If funds are limited, concentrate your advertising in a niche to achieve a meaningful frequency, rather than spreading over a large audience.

*(Text continues on page 364.)*

**Table 19-1.** Guide to communications tools.

| Tool | Definition | Uses | Strengths | Weaknesses |
|------|-----------|------|-----------|-----------|
| Direct response marketing | Using any medium to reach customers and obtain immediate sale or response, usually via phone or mail<br><br>Using phone or mail to individually target prospect for response or sale | Lead generation<br>Direct sales support<br>Sales efforts<br>Very personalized message<br>Providing opportunity to deliver detailed message | Allowing for specific targeting<br>Can replace or support direct sales efforts for image building | Costly for reaching large audience<br>Too infrequent for image building<br>Seen as "junk mail" |
| Television advertising | Advertising on local network or cable television | Generating high reach, quickly<br>Conveying a message using sight, sound, and motion<br>Creating awareness<br>Image development | Intrusiveness<br>Opportunity for creativity<br>Delivering broad reach quickly<br>Seen as "important" to customers/employees | Production costs can be high<br>Media costs can be high<br>Cluttered medium |
| Radio advertising | Advertising on AM/FM radio | Targeting specific demographic segments<br>Generating frequency | Relatively low cost<br>Frequency building<br>Highly targeted<br>Can be very creative | Not visual<br>Generally passive<br>Limited reach for each station |
| Print advertising | Advertising in newspapers, magazines, and trade publications | Longer sales messages<br>Delivery of promotional vehicles, such as coupons<br>Advertising to highly specific groups | Visual, printed format good for long copy<br>Can be highly targeted<br>Can have broad reach (newspapers) | Can be wasteful<br>Cluttered environment<br>Passive |

| | Definition | Purpose | Strengths | Weaknesses |
|---|---|---|---|---|
| Out-of-home media | Advertising on billboards, buses, transit; advertising outside of the home | Broad reach<br>Communication of a simple message<br>"Reminder" or support | Very efficient (low cost per thousand)<br>Interesting creative possibilities | Very short message (8 words)<br>Not generally intrusive<br>Subject to weather, daylight<br>Long lead time on items not promoted |
| Public relations | Using public media to establish an image or communicate a message | Image<br>New product or other announcement | Offers credibility due to third-party reporting<br>Lower cost to reach large audience | Need to be newsworthy<br>Little control of message or placement |
| Promotions | Fixed-term campaign that highlights a specific offer or sales opportunity | Leveraging sales of seasonal businesses | Promotes heavy sales during short period | Does not guarantee ongoing strong sales |
| Event marketing and sponsorships | Using an event and/or sponsorship (e.g., sports, cultural event) to market a product or service | Building awareness<br>Building goodwill<br>Theme for promotion | Provides natural focus<br>Can be perceived as *less* self-serving than a normal sales promotion | If event fails, may incur *bad* image<br>Cost of event sponsorship usually added to advertising costs, thus expensive |
| Employee incentive | Providing dollar or other rewards to employees for generating sales or leads | Increasing sales<br>Motivating employees | Encourages employee support and participation in events<br>Usually increases direct sales | Can be costly to administer<br>May create tax liability for employees |
| Collateral | Primarily brochures, but also statement/billing inserts, newsletters, catalogs, and promotional signage | Sales support<br>Adding tangibility to intangible service | Complete control of size, shape, color, and distribution<br>A guide through the sales process for sales staff | Very low intrusiveness<br>Can be used as a crutch by the sales staff |

7. *Make sure all your media work together.*
   - During any particular period, all your media should communicate the same message for maximum impact.
   - The more ways you can manage to communicate your message, the more effective you'll be.
8. *Make the telephone your friend.*
   - There is no more direct, more effective form of remote communication than the telephone.
   - Use it to do everything from welcoming new clients to making a special offer to cross selling.
9. *Experiment with new approaches.*
   - No set of guidelines can ever be totally comprehensive. The only limit to ideas for success is your imagination.
   - Every great idea usually has three or four weaker precedents. Note: No one remembers how many strikeouts Babe Ruth had—only how many home runs!
10. *Break the rules—sometimes!*

## Coordinating Your Campaign

Now that you know of the tools available for the implementation of a marketing program (summarized in Table 19-1), you are ready to put everything together into a campaign. Where to start? At the beginning, of course, with the objectives of the program and the people you want to talk to. Is it a program that requires little explanation and involves something that most people are familiar with, or is it complex and little-known? Is this a major strategic effort or a short-term tactical program? Is the offer truly competitive, or does it need some promotional "sizzle" to get attention? The real secret to assembling an effective campaign is knowing precisely what you wish to accomplish. *All* decisions are based on that. If you have an advertising agency, its staff members can help you assemble the components of the program, but their input will be only as good as the direction they receive. The most effective programs seem to be truly collaborative efforts, where all those involved know the mission, understand their roles in that mission, and then are allowed to do their jobs. Vague instructions make for vague results.

Once people have their marching orders and a general idea of the campaign has been assembled, take the time to do a reality check. Is the program realistic? Is it too complicated? Can the sales force handle it? Does it still meet the original objectives?

If the program still seems right (and is approved), it's time to implement. Besides having a clear objective, execution is the most important component to campaign development. If you have a brilliant, strategic program that is badly executed, chances of failure are high. A simple program, well executed, will almost always produce the best results. Don't forget the ultimate law of business: MURPHY'S LAW. Program implementation requires strict control, realistic time lines, flexibility, and enthusiasm for the project if it is to succeed. Make sure that resources are available *before* they are needed.

So far, so good. It is a good program and it has been executed flawlessly. All program components work together and communicate one message consistently. Everyone has been informed, trained, and motivated, and the program launched. Time to relax? Not yet. Aside from making sure that everything is going smoothly after the program is launched, there's a chance to correct problems that were not anticipated, or to seize the exciting opportunities that the campaign creates.

\* \* \* \*

*Thad D. Peterson is senior vice president, director of marketing for the Eureka Bank, Foster City, California. Prior to joining Eureka, Mr. Peterson managed the marketing of Bank of America's travelers' cheques and savings and investment products, and served as senior business manager for savings and transaction products. While at Bank of America, Mr. Peterson was responsible for a number of successful launches of new services and products. He has also worked as an advertising account executive.*

*K. Shelly Porges is president of Porges Marketing, a San Francisco firm providing advisory services in the financial services and other service industries. Formerly she was senior vice president and head of retail product management for Bank of America, where she managed the bank's consumer and small-business products in the California Banking Group. Before joining Bank of America, Ms. Porges held key management positions at American Express.*

# 20

# How to Create an Integrated Communication System

Nancy L. Brenner

This chapter helps you create an effective, integrated communication system to support the marketing of your organization's services. It helps you to meet the *special challenge* of services marketing: how to communicate successfully to a variety of audiences something intangible—something they can't see, hear, taste, touch, or smell. It assists you in developing a communication program that:

- Supports your organization's mission and positioning.
- Achieves your organization's marketing goals and objectives.
- More effectively carries out your communication strategy—*without increasing your spending*.

You will find guidelines for developing an integrated communication system and examples of how other services marketers have used such an approach to meet their goals.

The key topics covered are:

- What services marketers can gain from formal communication programs
- Why you need an integrated program
- Why you need an active program
- How to create the communication plan
- How to take "inventory" of existing communication tools
- How to develop a "corporate identity"
- The role of internal marketing in developing and supporting an integrated communication program
- How to evaluate your communication program
- An example of an integrated communication plan

## What You Gain From an Integrated Communication Program

For most services marketers, expenditures on communication activities (whether labeled "communication" or not) form a significant portion of the overall marketing budget. Whether you are with an entrepreneurial firm or a Fortune 500 company, you probably use a variety of communication tools—and learn about

others daily. Yet no matter how large your organization, ultimately your resources—funds, staff, time—are limited. You want the best possible communication "package" to support your marketing efforts, but how do you get it?

One answer is an *integrated communication approach.* Such an approach:

1. "Fits" with the mission and positioning of your organization.
2. Is based upon a clear understanding of your marketing goals (general,
   nonquantified statements about your organization's future direction or
   rank vis-à-vis size, market share, profitability, and other key parameters
   to be achieved via marketing).
3. Supports the achievement of your marketing objectives (quantified versions of the goals).
4. Follows a clearly stated communication strategy.
5. Uses each element in the communication mix to carry out that strategy.
6. Helps make "real" or concrete to your audiences the abstract, intangible services that you are offering to them. Helps build their trust in
   something they cannot touch, see, or taste.
7. Ensures that each communication tool—advertising, public relations,
   collateral material—reinforces the others.
8. Allows you to measure and evaluate your progress.

The result: You get better value for your communication dollars.

## Why Do You Need an Integrated Communication Program?

All of us—including your current and prospective clients—receive and process
thousands of messages weekly. We are barraged by direct mail solicitations,
advertising, articles, letters, memos, and conversations. Your messages make
up only a fraction of the messages your clients receive.

As a marketing professional you need to determine:

* How to break through the communication "clutter"
* How to make sure that your organization's message is understood and
  acted upon by your target audience

### Why Your Communications Should "Fit" Your Organization

The style, appearance, tone, manner of your communications tell your audience
what to expect from your organization and its services. Just as a banker's conservative business suit suggests that he or she will handle your money prudently
and properly, a professional-looking, accurate, easy-to-read brochure can convey similar positive messages about the bank. (Conversely, a banker dressed in
T-shirt and blue jeans or a brochure that looks sloppy, contains errors, or uses

extremely informal language might suggest that the bank would be too casual in handling customers' money.)

In services marketing, these "subliminal" messages are perhaps even more important than they are in product marketing. Because services are intangible, are generally more expensive than the average consumer product, and may require considerable time and effort on the part of the *buyer,* they have special communication needs. The marketer must make his services as *real* and *specific* as possible for the potential client. The fewer "black boxes," the better. For example:

- Use pictures of staff and/or clients. Illustrate your service "in process" and/or the outcome, if possible.
- Use simple flow charts that list and explain the key elements involved in your services. Indicate approximate timing of key steps.
- Show examples of your "output," such as sample monthly statements for an asset management account.

In addition, give "proof" of how good your services are, such as:

- Client testimonials.
- Third-party ratings—industry awards, "reviews" in the business press, and such.
- Anecdotes that illustrate, give dimension to, or humanize your services.
- Information on the excellence of your resources (people and systems). For example, tell clients about the qualifications and experience of your consultants, as well as the information processing systems and hardware available to them.

For example, the purpose of a bank trust department is to manage its clients' assets in a prudent fashion. It needs to communicate that it is solid, strong, reliable, and trustworthy. Printed communications should have a high-quality look and feel. They might use rich, conservative colors (burgundy, gray, brown) and pictures of (satisfied) customers and staff to create a feeling of trust and confidence. The tone of written communications tends to be serious, educational. Even the offices of such organizations help create an image of dependability, permanency, and security, featuring wood paneling and furniture, carpeting, and rich fabrics.

Conversely, an entrepreneurial organization, or one in an industry where it is important to be on the "cutting edge," might want to appear innovative, fast-moving, modern. The tone and look of its communications would be bright, up-to-date, lively. Printed materials might feature bold, primary colors or current "high fashion" ones. Graphic design might be bold, "Eurostyle"; advertising might feature New Wave visuals and pop music; language would be more lively and informal than that used by a bank.

Of course, there is no one "right" communication style. But there *is* a style that is right for your organization and will help attract the types of clients you want. To determine which style is appropriate, you need to understand "who" your organization is (*mission* and *positioning*), and what it is trying to accomplish (*marketing goals* and *objectives*). Based on this understanding, you can create effective communications.

### Why You Need Focused Communications

To be heard, understood, and acted upon in today's "cluttered" environment, your communications need to be *focused*. Do not try to convey a dozen messages—stick to the most important one (or two).

One marketer suggests that you "pretend that you're trying to saw down a tree with a nail file." He says that "You can succeed—as long as you keep sawing at the same spot." In your communications, you can "keep sawing at the same spot" by focusing on a key benefit (better price, better turnaround, more protection, better expertise) or some service or feature that meets customers' specific needs. The more focused your message and the more targeted to your audience, the more effective your communications.

### The Key Role of Frequency

Frequency is the third key factor in communications. Ultimately, you want to influence the behavior of your clients and prospects. You want them to act: request information, set up a meeting, buy your services.

Research has shown that influencing behavior is a three-step process:

First, you must *generate awareness*.
Second, you must *change attitudes*.
Third, you can *influence behavior*.

For your communication program to change behavior—your ultimate goal—your audience must be exposed repeatedly to your message. Simply to produce measurable changes in awareness, the "target" viewer or reader needs to receive your message a minimum of three times within a period of approximately thirty days. Obviously, it is easier to generate the necessary frequency if your communications—advertising, brochures, articles, and such—all convey the same message.

## How to Develop a Plan for Integrated Communications

To embark on an integrated communication program, nine key steps need to be followed:

1. Understand your organization (mission and positioning) and its marketing goals and objectives.
2. Define your targets and understand their needs.

3. Develop a communication strategy, including identification of target audience and primary message, which will help to achieve your marketing objectives and goals.
4. Take inventory of your current communication tools/media. Look for gaps, opportunities to reinforce one communication mode with others.
5. Review your current communication "product." Seek consistency (or conflict) in look, message, tone, style.
6. Develop (or refine) your corporate identity. Create a stylebook that can serve as a guide in executing future communication projects.
7. Market your communication program within your organization to gain and maintain support.
8. Develop "action standards" and use them to evaluate your program on a regular basis.
9. Never stop testing and refining your communications.

Remember that the best communication programs are constantly evolving as the marketplace, the organization, and its marketing goals and objectives change.

## How to Understand Your Organization and Its Communication Needs

To understand the communication needs of your company, you must first understand "who" and "what" your organization is. Reread (or develop) the mission and positioning statements, which express (1) why your company is in business and (2) how your company is positioned versus its competition. Next, you must define what the company's marketing goals and objectives are—what your organization aims to achieve via its marketing efforts. By filling in Figure 20-1, you can develop or check the mission statement, positioning, marketing goal, and marketing objective(s) for your organization.

## How to Find Your Targets

Next, you need to zero in on prime prospects. A good starting place is among current clients. Who are your "best" current clients? Why? What needs does your organization meet for them and how? What "language" do they speak— what motivates them?

You must do some research, but you probably have many information sources available. Here's a partial checklist:

- Client contact and client service reports
- Client correspondence
- Industry directories
- Professional directories
- Association directories
- Corporate lists (e.g., the Fortune 500; Crain's list of leading banks, insurance companies)
- Articles in the business press

**Figure 20-1.** Fundamental organization descriptors.

1. *Mission Statement:* (brief statement of what the organization is, what services it provides, and to what sort of clients)

2. *Positioning Statement:* (brief statement of what is unique about the organization, its services, and/or the markets it serves)

3. *Marketing Goal:* (a general, nonquantified statement about the position or growth in industry rank, share, revenue, and/or profit that the organization plans to achieve via its marketing efforts; e.g., "substantial revenue growth in the United States")

4. *Marketing Objectives:* (a quantified expression of the marketing goal[s]; e.g., "25 percent growth in U.S. revenue next year")

- Articles in the trade publications
- Articles in the general press
- Discussions with your associates and staff

A consulting partner in a major CPA firm decided to prospect for new business. He started by analyzing his *current* client base, reviewing correspondence and contact reports, and talking with others in his firm about clients they had handled. Based on this analysis, he decided which clients were "Aces": highly desirable clients, who were realistic in their expectations, had good "chemistry" with his firm, offered visibility in a key company or industry, and generated good fees.

Next, he developed a chart profiling "Ace" clients. For each, he noted industry, size, and fees. He included key issues and needs for each, as well as the solutions his firm had offered and/or implemented. In addition, he noted and described the key decision maker at each client company, including functional area, level, seniority, and mind-set. This gave the consultant a profile of his most desirable clients.

Based on this profile, the consultant used the information sources listed earlier to compile a prospect list. His "first cut" was rather large—several thousand companies that he thought might be interested in his firm's services, based on their size, industry, products, and location. He narrowed this down to a target list of a few hundred companies, selecting those that seemed to have problems, issues, or needs similar to those of his "Ace" clients. Adding "key contact" name, address, and title, he created an "Action List."

With this Action List as a basis, he planned and implemented a simple, highly effective direct marketing campaign. He sent 200 of the decision makers on his list a well-crafted letter that outlined how his firm had solved problems similar to those of the addressee's firm. He included his telephone number and a business reply card.

More than thirty consulting engagements resulted from the consultant's efforts. The success of his marketing efforts is largely due to how well he understood the special marketing needs of a service organization. Specifically, he built the trust and credibility needed to "sell" an intangible by (1) developing a target list based on an understanding of their business needs and (2) tailoring the letters to "prove" to the recipients that his firm had been successful in meeting such needs for existing clients.

The target list (and his excellent understanding of his target market) will also guide the consultant in planning future marketing activities—advertising, by-line articles in business publications, seminars, and such.

## How to Communicate With Your Audience

Once you have defined your target audience, you must understand it. This may require further research. If possible, talk with current and prospective clients to learn their concerns, interests, and needs. Even a brief discussion can yield valuable insights into the right language, tone, and format for your target audience.

Your research can be surprisingly simple, quick, and conclusive. Interviews with only a dozen or so museum visitors helped one museum marketing director decide what to show on the cover of the holiday gift catalog. She showed each person catalogs from the museum and from three others, with the name of each institution covered. Each visitor was asked:

- Which museum does each catalog come from?
- Which cover do you like best, and why?
- Which cover do you like least, and why?
- Which cover is most appropriate for our museum's catalog; which is least appropriate, and why?

After these few interviews, the message was clear. Visitors and members expected to see a famous painting from the museum on the cover, rather than a piece of merchandise. This identified the catalog as coming from their museum and prevented it from being discarded as junk mail.

The research project took only a few hours. The out-of-pocket cost was nil. And the rewards, in terms of additional sales, (catalog and in-store) were excellent.

You can conduct similar informal research to develop or refine your hypotheses about your market. Such research can consist of a brief interview, either in person or by telephone, or a short questionnaire. Because you are marketing a service rather than a product, you will need to explore abstract (rather than physical) attributes and issues, such as:

1. Which of these key attributes does the client or prospect look for from companies like yours?
   - Specialized knowledge
   - High level of experience in the client's industry
   - Quick turnaround on proposals
   - Quick turnaround on projects
   - Price
   - Reputation
   - Your company's rank versus competition
   - Acceptability to board and/or top management
   - Availability of backup
   - Availability of a particular person or team
   - Prior professional relationship
2. How is your company perceived to "measure up" on these key attributes?
3. How is your competition perceived?
4. How would those who have used your services and/or those of your competition rate them overall against specific attributes?
5. Where and how do they learn about (or prefer to learn about) services such as those offered by your company?

Obviously, you will need to tailor your questions to your industry and marketplace, but this type of research can yield valuable information for your communication program. For example, the trust division of a major bank wished to expand its estates business, so its staff conducted focus group research among millionaires. The results suggested that wealthy individuals were most interested in having their estates handled by someone warm and caring, who understood their intentions and wishes, and who "would be there." Therefore, they had chosen as executors family lawyers, relatives, or even friends, rather than a bank.

Based on these findings, the bank revised its marketing strategy. To gain new customers, it promoted a "co-executorship" service through which people could select the bank and an individual to share the work of handling their estates. A series of brochures, letters, and sales presentations explaining this service was prepared. All communications were friendly in tone and inviting to read. They emphasized the bank's caring approach and the continuity of its personnel. To make the bank's services as concrete and "real" as possible to clients and prospects, communications used many specific anecdotes and pictures of staff and clients. One of the most useful tools provided to the salespeople was a simple flowchart that detailed key steps and timing for settling an estate. This helped prospects to grasp a fairly complex and abstract process. The trust department's technical expertise, previously the main message in communications, became a key support point.

The result? By addressing the needs and concerns of its market, making services and benefits comprehensible to intelligent laypersons, and communicating with them in their language, the trust department more than doubled qualified leads and sales in this area.

# How to Take an Inventory of Your Communication Tools

Now you have a clear idea of *who* and *where* your target audience is and *what message* you need to communicate to them. The next step is to determine what tools you have at your disposal. Your organization probably uses many forms of communication. Some may be obvious, like advertising or brochures. Others are not, like letterhead, signage, or even the decor of your offices. It is likely that some of these areas are your responsibility.

The following list should remind you of some of the major communication tools used by your organization:

- Advertising (magazine, newspaper, TV)
- Public relations (media placement, byline articles, seminars)
- Direct response (letters, direct mail, telemarketing)
- Seminars
- Sales presentations and leave-behinds

- Newsletters (internal and external)
- Flyers and brochures
- Market research (including publication of results)
- Letterhead
- Signage
- Business cards
- Posters
- Calendars
- Various sales promotion items (mugs, pens, lighters)

You can take inventory of your organization's communication activities by filling in the chart shown in Figure 20-2. Add other activities as appropriate. (Chapter 19 of this *Handbook* offers an excellent discussion of marketing communication tools.) Note that Figure 20-2 includes not only *what* the activities are, but also:

- Who is *responsible* for each communication activity
- Who has *authority* over each
- If your department has neither responsibility nor authority, what *other role* does it play

In looking over the completed list, you can identify valuable opportunities. For example, the museum marketing director completed a similar checklist before accepting the position and discovered that there was no paid advertising to announce exhibitions, nor any advertising or public relations support for the museum shop and other retailing operations. By filling these gaps, she generated substantial new revenues for the institution.

You can also uncover potential problems. In many organizations, no one senior manager has ultimate authority for key communications. Advertising reports to one manager, public relations to another, and direct response to a third. This can mean that your company is communicating too many messages, even conflicting ones, which is not the best way to support your marketing strategies. This is perhaps more of a problem in services marketing than in product marketing, because it is harder to give prospects "free samples" to try. You will need to work with others on the "communication team" to avoid such conflicts.

## How to Develop a Corporate Identity

You have now completed the first five steps to an integrated communications program:

1. You have reviewed the organization's mission statement, positioning, marketing goals, and marketing objectives.
2. You have developed a communication strategy based on the "promises" made in the preceding statements and have identified your "ideal" prospect.

**Figure 20-2.** Communication activities inventory.

| Communica-tion Activities | Department With Responsibility | Department With Authority | Other Role of Your Department | Budget |
|---|---|---|---|---|
| Advertising | | | | |
| Public relations | | | | |
| Direct response (list): | | | | |
| | | | | |
| Seminars | | | | |
| Sales presentations | | | | |
| Newsletters: | | | | |
| —Internal | | | | |
| —External | | | | |
| Flyers | | | | |
| Brochures | | | | |
| Market research | | | | |
| Letterhead | | | | |
| Signage | | | | |
| Business cards | | | | |
| Posters | | | | |
| Calendars | | | | |
| Sales promotion items (list): | | | | |
| | | | | |
| Other (list): | | | | |

3. You understand the key needs and issues in your target market.
4. You have a good profile of the key decision maker and how to communicate to him or her.
5. You have a good ''map'' of your organization's existing communication program.

Now you can begin to integrate the various communication efforts. First, take a good look at how you're currently communicating with clients and prospects.

### How to Conduct a Communication Review

Begin your review by collecting samples of every type of communication produced by your organization. Be as thorough as possible. Gather letterhead and
envelopes, business cards, newsletters, letters to clients, advertisements, brochures, flyers, direct mail packages, signage, press releases, byline articles,
seminar announcements, posters, sales promotion items, even samples of your
office decor. All are vehicles by which you communicate with your audiences.

Next, sort your samples by division, service area, target industry, or
whichever classifications are appropriate for your company. Spread out the materials in an unoccupied office, conference room, or storage room, and take time
to study them. Think about whether your communications are clear, user friendly,
and inviting. Do their message, tone, and look support the market strategy? Do
your communications speak with one voice? Have one look? If not, are variations, such as by service area, planned and appropriate? Or do you observe a
"Tower of Babel"? Are communications confusing or difficult to read? Do they
work at cross-purposes? Do they seem to come from one organization, or from
a dozen?

Even if you see room for improvement, don't despair! This is why major
corporations pay "corporate identity" or design consultants thousands—or
hundreds of thousands—of dollars to create and monitor their communications.
But even without such outside experts, you can improve your communications
simply by taking time to review a cross section and act on your conclusions.
See Figure 20-3 for a checklist of some of the key elements to review.

### How to Create a "Corporate Identity"

In developing a "corporate identity" program for a major cultural institution, a
nationally known graphic designer reviewed hundreds of items. Tacked up around
a conference room were materials ranging from glossy, four-color, multipart
direct response packages to relatively crude photocopied flyers. Noting the range
of quality, he observed: "The task is not to improve the 'top half'—it's to bring
up the 'bottom half.' "

When you review your own communications, remember that any program,
however good, can benefit from "bringing up the bottom half." It is encouraging to realize that you don't necessarily need to spend more. Rather, be more
consistent in positioning key information (company name, address, and logo),
in choice of typeface and colors, and in tone or voice. Be clear and focused in
communicating your message. Communications must be appropriate to your organization, goals, and audience.

Refer again to your mission and positioning statements and marketing goals
and objectives. Interview key management and staff to ensure that there is widespread agreement on them within your organization.

Then evaluate your communications against these yardsticks. Based on your
analysis, you can make some decisions (perhaps with the help of a graphic
designer) about standard ways of handling key elements. These can be recorded
in a reference notebook for future use by anyone involved in creating communications. With these basic decisions made, designers and other creative re-

**Figure 20-3.** Checklist of key communication elements.

1. *The logo or logotype:*
   —Is it standard for your division or area?
   —Is it used by the entire organization?
   —Is it distinctive?
   —Does it fit in with your organization's mission, positioning?
   —Is it placed consistently?

2. *The organization's (or division's) name and address:*
   —Is it placed consistently?
   —Are the size relationships of the key elements standardized?
   —Is it easy to find?
   —Is it easy to read?

3. *The overall "look" and quality of your communications:*
   —Is it consistent?
   —Is it appropriate to your organization?
   —Is it of high quality?
   —Are sizes of printed pieces standardized? Are sizes efficient in terms of printing and paper costs, interchangeability? Do the printed pieces fit in a modular system?
   —Have the following elements been considered?
     • Color
     • Typeface
     • Paper quality, texture, weight
     • Graphic style

4. *Tone:*
   —Is it consistent?
   —Is it appropriate to your organization, goals, audience? Think about how formal, complex, serious, educational or how informal, simple, amusing, entertaining the communications are.

5. *Readability:*
   —Do the size, weight, style, and color of *type* make it pleasant to read?
   —Is there enough "white space" in the *layout* so that pages aren't heavy, crowded, dense?
   —Are there *headlines* and *subheads* to lead readers into the material, to show them "where they're going," and to break up blocks of text?
   —Are there *visuals*—pictures, graphs, charts—to illustrate the material?

   Above all, is everything appropriate to and supportive of your company, its mission, and your communications strategy?

sources don't have to "reinvent the wheel" for every project. Instead, their time and effort can be directed toward developing the best communications possible.

Also, standardization of basics creates a consistent look and feel for your communications. It gives them more "stopping power" (e.g., the New York City Opera always uses the same unusual typeface in its advertisements). It saves time and money by allowing multiple uses of materials. (If all printed materials are similar in terms of color, size and shape, then major items can be incorporated into different marketing kits to meet different needs.)

## Internal Marketing—Why It's Key to Your Communication Program

Sometimes communication professionals are so focused on external audiences that they neglect the all-important *internal* ones. Yet there are important benefits to be reaped from communicating with these audiences as well:

1. *You gain valuable input, which can improve your communications.* For example, a financial services marketer was developing a direct mail package aimed at retail securities brokers. A colleague who reviewed a draft suggested adding a list of specific bonds insured by the firm. This addition helped increase the response rate substantially.

2. *You can identify potential problems early in the game.* For example, a recently hired marketing officer discovered that both he and his organization's new public relations officer planned to develop advertising. Because they had discussed their plans, they avoided duplication of effort.

3. *You can defuse corporate jealousy.* What marketer hasn't heard the complaint from other areas: "Why is so much money being spent on marketing when *we've* had to cut back on staff and programs?" A well-designed, internal marketing effort can educate your organization about the benefits of the communication program and reduce such interdepartmental backbiting.

4. *You can build organizational support for the communication program.* People like to feel that they are part of the team. Include your colleagues by informing them of upcoming plans and activities and explaining how your programs will support *their* efforts. Nothing irritates a salesperson more than learning about a new advertising campaign from his customers. Or worse, from his competitors!

5. *You can build your case for continuing (or increasing) funding for future communication programs.*

### The Key Steps in Internal Marketing

Internal marketing involves five key steps, from preliminary research to communication of results. You must:

1. *Involve others*—superiors, peers, subordinates—*at the outset,* when you are determining or confirming the company's communication needs and identifying client issues and concerns.

2. *Involve "key players"*—those who must approve and/or utilize your communications tools—*at the development stage.* For example, a marketer at a

financial services company made it a practice to review each draft of a market research questionnaire with the company's president and department heads (e.g., risk analysis, new business development, legal). In this way, each department began to "own" the questionnaire and study, rather than feeling that it had been imposed on them by the marketing department.

3. *Prevent "disasters."* Client contact people who know their customers and their product can help communications staff avoid embarrassing "over-promises." (For example, the advertising department of a hospital planned to advertise that emergency vehicles would always arrive at accident scenes in less than fifteen minutes. When the emergency rescue team warned them that this couldn't be guaranteed, the ad was changed and an "overpromise" avoided.)

4. *Inform and train those who use the materials.* When an ad, brochure, or mailing is completed, present and explain it to client contact personnel or salespersons. Teach them how to use the material or program to support their efforts. Otherwise, carefully crafted programs may remain on the shelf.

5. *Communicate positive results to your organization,* early and often. Remember, *frequency* is as important in this "market" as in any other. If you want to increase your organization's awareness of the communication program, generate positive attitudes, motivate employees, and influence management (e.g., to increase budget allocations), you need to be an active internal marketer.

Some specific techniques for internal marketing include:

1. *Displays.* Make it clear that your department is *active*. Prominently display samples in your office, other offices in your department, and nearby common areas. Also display recaps of current programs and announce new ones.

2. *Newsletters/announcements.* Develop a special letterhead for your area. It needn't be expensive—bond paper with a masthead printed in a distinctive color will suffice. The masthead could read "Communication News," "Communication Highlights," or "Communication Announcements." Use it to communicate planned activities or program results. For example, you might circulate:

- Announcements of new programs
- Articles or press mentions generated by your PR efforts
- Press releases
- Advertising schedules/media plans
- Copies of mass mailings
- Summaries of communication plans
- New brochures, advertisements, and other materials

3. *Presentations.* From time to time, you may wish to present plans or results to groups ranging from a few senior managers to client-contact staff to the entire organization. Presentations can be informal affairs, using handmade flip charts, or they can be tightly scripted multimedia shows; it depends on your budget, your audience, and your objectives.

Displays, communication newsletters, and presentations are all valuable tools. Unlike the organizational grapevine, they allow you to choose your timing and convey your message exactly as you wish. You can place your program in the context of the company's mission, goals, and objectives. You can explain your communication strategy and tactics. You can present activities and outcomes (even unexpected outcomes) in a clear and positive fashion. In a live presentation, in particular, your message is reinforced because it's presented visually *and* verbally. The communication of your message is also stronger if your audience can interact with you. And a Q & A session can provide *you* with valuable learning as well.

## How to Evaluate Your Integrated Communication Program

Make sure that your communication program is on track by monitoring and evaluating it on an ongoing basis. Make evaluation an integral part of your communication plan.

### The Organizational Context

As indicated earlier in this chapter, a successful and integrated communication program is one that:

1. Fits in with your organization's mission and positioning.
2. Supports the achievement of your marketing goals and objectives.
3. Executes a well thought out, clearly stated communication strategy.
4. Is consistent and of high quality.

You should evaluate your communications on an ongoing basis—while each element is being developed *and* when it has been implemented, to make sure that these four criteria have been met.

### The Communication Review

Conduct periodic reviews of your communications, to make sure that your efforts remain on track. If you work with outside resources—PR firms, advertising agencies, graphic designers, and such—have each conduct a formal review at least once a year. Also, repeat the "corporate identity review" described earlier in this chapter.

### How to Assess Results—Realistically

A wise marketer once said, "The proof of the plan is in the results." A communication plan that is appropriate to your organization and is focused on strategy, and of suitable quality, should be successful. It is tempting to define success for your *communication* program as the achievement of your *marketing* objectives; for example, "15 percent share growth" or "$20 million increase in revenue." But other factors (e.g., budgets, production bottlenecks, sales force activities) can affect *marketing* outcomes, so it is important to look at *communication* measures in addition to *marketing* measures. For example:

1. Advertising
   - Increase in awareness
   - Positive shift in attitudes
2. Direct response
   - Number of inquiries
   - Number of qualified leads
3. Public relations
   - Number and quality of press mentions
   - Number and context of stories placed
   - Client attendance at/reactions to functions
4. Brochures, advertisements, direct response
   - Does it communicate what was intended?
   - Is it read, understood, acted upon?

Be sure to set appropriate action standards up front. Otherwise, an excellent result may look inferior, and a useful communication tool could be scrapped. For example, a financial services marketer was told by his direct response consultant that a test market would generate 300 to 500 phone calls a month, because the advertising was designed primarily to generate awareness. Under pressure from management, he promised 1,000 to 2,000 phone calls per month. Management suspended the test market before its effect on awareness could be determined, because just under 300 calls per month came in. As a result, it was never determined whether the *primary* objective of the test was achieved. Finally, if budgets and circumstances allow, apply a principle of direct response marketing to all of your communications: Develop alternatives and test, test, test.

## Summary

The example starting on page 385 of a communication plan serves as a summary of this chapter. It illustrates the key points that have been made. The plan demonstrates how to begin developing an integrated communication program by stating and understanding the organizational mission and positioning and its marketing goals and objectives. The example illustrates a communication program that is formal (i.e., planned), integrated, and active. It contains a statement of communication strategy (one that demonstrates "fit, focus, and frequency") and explains the specific communication tactics/tools employed. It notes the application of a previously developed corporate identity to all materials created for the program. Finally, it indicates the methods that are to be used in evaluating the program.

*       *       *       *

*Nancy L. Brenner heads Brenner Consultants, a marketing consulting firm in New York City. Her experience includes management positions with Bond Investors Guaranty, Chemical Bank, and the Art Institute of Chicago.*

# Example of a Communication Plan for a Securities Insurance Company

## Background

Securities Insurance Corporation insures bonds against defaults. Because SIC is a relative newcomer to the industry, bond traders and bond buyers appear to perceive SIC-insured bonds to be worth slightly less than those insured by the competition. If this perception could be changed, it could mean millions of dollars in additional premium revenues for SIC.

The market for bond insurance is complex. Key players include:

- Issuers of bonds
- Investment bankers, who help issuers to structure and market new financings
- Bond traders
- Retail securities brokers
- Institutions that buy bonds
- Individuals who buy bonds

## Mission Statement

SIC is an insurance company that provides coverage for holders of municipal bonds in the event of default.

## Positioning

SIC is a leader in the financial guaranty industry because of the strength of its claims-paying resources and the innovative way it has serviced its clients' needs.

## Marketing Goals

To improve the market's perception of the "trading value" of SIC-insured bonds, which will permit increases in SIC's premium rates and a resulting increase in its return on equity.

## Marketing Objectives

To increase average premiums by 10 percent; to increase return on equity by 12 percent.

## Communication Strategy

To develop a multimedia communication program, which would include general advertising, direct response advertising, direct mail, public relations, collateral materials, and sales calls/sales presentations. Communications would be targeted to key audiences (retail bond buyers, retail brokers, bond traders, institutional bond buyers, bond issuers, and investment bankers) in order to generate increased awareness, favorable attitudes, and (secondarily) retail "leads."

## Communication Tactics

1. *Consumer advertising*
   - A national advertising campaign, to include newspaper, magazine, and TV.
   - To reach adults 35+, in households with $50,000+ incomes, who currently own municipal bonds.
2. *Direct response*
   - Direct response devices included in general advertising (above), including "offer" of free information about insured bonds and incoming toll-free telephone number and coupon to request "offer."
   - Fulfillment and database system set up to (1) send out consumer information kit, (2) collect key information on respondents, and (3) produce "lead" sheets and reports.
   - "Fulfillment package"/information kit included an envelope, which announced on the outside that the recipient had requested the enclosed materials, a personalized cover letter, an educational brochure on bonds, and a bond list.
   - Broker mailing, sent to retail brokers. Included personalized letter, educational brochure, bond list, samples of the advertising, a media schedule, and a business reply card (to be used to request quantities of brochures to give to customers).
   - Several mailings each to other key audiences: bond issuers, bond traders, and institutional bond buyers.
3. *"Institutional" advertising*
   Advertising in various trade publications (newspapers and magazines) aimed at "professional" audiences—issuers, investment bankers, bond traders, institutional buyers.
4. *Public relations*
   A multidimensional program, including:
   - Press releases.
   - Media tours, generating articles in business publications and in the business sections of daily and weekly newspapers, and appearances on "financial news" shows on TV and radio.
   - Byline articles in trade publications.
5. *Internal marketing*
   - A presentation was made to each department in the company to explain the marketing and communication plan, to show the communication materials, and to elicit questions and comments.
   - Existing "Communication Highlights" paper was used for company-wide distribution of changes in media schedules, copies of articles, announcements of upcoming broadcast appearances, and such.
6. *Cost/timing*
   A six-month test was launched, to cost approximately $1 million, with marketing/communication activities focused in one state with significant bond-issuing and bond-buying activity. Annual spending for the national plan was estimated at $3 to $5 million.
7. *Corporate identity*
   All materials adhered to the existing corporate identity, in terms of typeface, logotype, and placement/size of logotype and company name and address. To unify

the materials in each direct mail "package," all elements (envelope, letter, bond list, postcard) featured one simple graphic device—a thin red stripe that extended down the left side of each. This element had previously been used in other materials produced by the company (e.g., annual reports, brochures).

8. *Evaluation*

Four main means of evaluation were planned for the test:

- "Pre-" and "post-" telephone surveys on awareness and attitudes were to be conducted among retail investors and retail brokers.
- The number and quality of responses to the retail advertising were to be reviewed.
- The number of responses to the retail broker mailing was to be reviewed, as well as feedback from sales calls on brokerage offices.
- "Pre-" and "post-" telephone surveys on perception of trading value of SIC bonds were to be conducted among bond traders and institutional bond buyers.

# SERVICE AS A COMPONENT OF PRODUCT MARKETING

The final chapter of this section covers the topic of using service as a means to differentiate your product from all others. This chapter points out that *everybody* is in a service business because service is fast becoming the last source of differential advantage for product marketers. The chapter makes excellent use of the information that precedes it in this *Handbook*—market research, service encounters, positioning, internal marketing, service design and development, consumer evaluation of service, and communication. Hence it is a valuable integrative chapter for product and service marketers alike.

# 21

# Using Service to Differentiate a Product

Douglas C. Snyder
Barbara M. Zuppinger

Service. You know it's important to airlines, hotels, and financial institutions. But your company produces a range of excellent products and is well-established in its field. Do you really need to think about service?

Yes, you do. In fact, not only do you need to think about it, you need to take urgent steps toward introducing a service philosophy into your organization. If you don't, ultimately your company will lose out to competitors who have discovered that an excellent product teamed with top-notch service add up to an unbeatable combination.

## The Winning Factor—What It Is

These days, having thoughtfully designed, carefully made products just isn't enough. In today's fiercely competitive marketplace, most of the vast range of products available meet acceptable standards of price, performance, and reliability.

In many cases, it's extremely difficult to identify features that differentiate a product from all the similar ones on the market. So how do you make your company's offerings stand out from the crowd? Where do you find the winning factor that makes a product special and motivates consumers to choose it ahead of the competition's?

You find it in a place that many product managers overlook—in the relationship between you and your customers and in the service you provide. Remember, as customers look at you, they see a process that includes buying, acquiring, installing, and using your product. Product vendors tend to highlight product features in each of these individual stages. But the product itself only represents one element of the relationship you are building with the customer.

Service is the other element. And it is critically important to understand the relative importance of service and product features in each of the four stages. This relative importance will vary by product and by customer set. And, of course, some customers will never see all of these stages. Frequently, buyers may see only the front end, whereas people who use your product may see only the "using" segment. Understanding the relative importance of service in each segment will help you target your service efforts on the segment that gives you the best payback.

## The Winning Factor—How to Get It

In the following pages, we'll discuss how a company can make the transition from a product-based organization to one that is service-oriented. It isn't a simple step. In many cases it will mean shifting corporate philosophy and culture, redefining employee roles, and creating new systems, procedures, and measurements. But it will be worth the effort.

We'll describe how you get started, where you look for information and inspiration, and how to deal with the facts you uncover. We'll suggest how to arrive at a positioning statement outlining your service goals, and will show how some companies have reorganized to achieve their objectives. We'll review some change management techniques and talk about internal and external communications.

What we can't give you is commitment, which is far more vital than the cold facts. You must start thinking like your customers, seeing through their eyes, identifying their needs, and meeting their expectations. You need to set business priorities based on service quality, rather than just sales and manufacturing objectives. And you need to develop, sustain, and communicate a vision of what your new organization will become.

The information in this chapter will help you to differentiate your product in terms of service quality. Only you can decide if that's the route you want to follow.

But before you say, "Well, it's a good idea, but I don't think it would work in my operation," it might be worth looking at how a few companies have added service to their product offering. By examining the relationship between themselves and their customers, they were able to identify service needs that no supplier was meeting. You may be able to do the same!

## When You Can't Change the Product—You'd Better Add Some Service!

Linde, a division of Union Carbide, is a Toronto-based supplier of industrial, medical, and specialty gases and is the market leader in the $600 million Canadian industrial gas business. Customer surveys showed that in most cases, Linde's products were not differentiated from those of the competition. Customers naturally found it difficult to separate one brand of gas from another. Because of this, the surveys revealed, customers tended to be influenced by the level of service they received from different suppliers.

Simple facts. Yet they led to a reevaluation of Linde's marketing strategy and the growth of a new customer service culture within the company. Linde's management realized that service was the vital factor that could differentiate its products from its competitors'. And its research also provided the justification for reallocating resources to support the company's service initiative.

If you are engaged in a commodity-type business, where there may be no apparent rationale for choosing one supplier's product over another's, customer research could reveal similar facts. Later we examine Linde's experience in greater depth, describe the type of customer research required, and discuss how to use the data you obtain.

## When Customers Won't Assemble the Product— You'd Better Add Some Service!

When IBM announced its desktop publishing system, which uses industry-standard software, it realized that novice desktop publishers might not feel up to the challenge of putting together their new machines and loading in the system and publishing software. So the company offered its desktop publishing system as a ready-to-run package, with all hardware components installed and tested, and software preloaded into the machine. All that new users had to do was plug in connecting cables and the power cord, run the tutorial, and go to work on their first publication.

What IBM implied by this action was that, when everything else is equal, a product that was easier to set up, easier to understand, or easier to use would have a substantial advantage. Service, in this case, was used directly to enhance the product.

There are dozens of examples of products that could be improved by a little more attention to their service component, such as model kits that don't include the glue to put them together, or freshness codes on perishable items that the average shopper cannot interpret.

What these product features say to the customer is that the manufacturer doesn't care, and we have seen in earlier chapters that customers like to do business with people who do care.

Adding service to products can take place at every point along your product development, sale, and postsale cycle. Each opportunity should be looked at for its potential to add to your competitive position. Each person, at each point in the cycle, quite literally is in "marketing"!

## When Customers Aren't Sure They'll Like Your Product—You'd Better Add Some Service!

There are numerous familiar, well-documented methods of influencing buyers prior to the purchasing decision. Yet service is often overlooked as a way of managing customer expectations.

Merle Norman Cosmetics uses the slogan "Try Before You Buy" to sum up its sales approach. Free samples of most products are available, and cosmeticians give lessons and "make-overs" free of charge and help customers learn how to use various cosmetics before making a purchase. The result? Buyers who are unsure of their needs, who are confused by the vast array of cosmetics on the market, turn to Merle Norman cosmeticians for advice and invariably buy from them.

Giving customers an opportunity to try products before purchase is another way of using service to add value to your products. The sample eliminates the negative impact of a customer being impressed by your packaging, but disappointed with the product.

If your company produces a product that lends itself to demonstration, customer tryouts, or free samples, perhaps you should consider the value of service management concepts to your business.

## When Everyone Delivers Good Pizza—You'd Better Add Some Service!

A Toronto-based pizza franchise guarantees "Delivery Within Thirty Minutes or Free!" This is a risky promise, but with high potential payback. Combined with a catchy telephone number, the slogan has put Pizza Pizza on the lips of almost every adult and child in the Toronto area.

The entrepreneur behind the company understood that the key requirement for his customers was to get good pizza delivered to their homes in a consistently short time. While other pizza companies attempt to differentiate themselves on the basis of quality alone, Pizza Pizza has established a market position by concentrating on this key element of service.

It has demonstrated how the distribution process can be streamlined to provide a level of customer service that results in competitive advantage. By guaranteeing delivery time, the company offers its customers an additional benefit by ordering from Pizza Pizza and gives them measurable evidence of its commitment to service.

We've given a few examples of where service opportunities are found in some businesses. Our list is just a beginning! There is no limit to the creative ways that service can be added to your product to give you a strong competitive advantage.

When you understand the expectations of your current and prospective customers, and how they compare you to your competition, you will find new opportunities for adding value to your product through service. And you will be able to imagine how your organization could change to become more responsive to the customer. Read on, and we'll show you how to transform that vision into reality.

## How to Make It Happen

You've decided the best way of adding value to your product in the eyes of the customer is to improve the service you offer. That's the easy part. Now comes the challenging job of transforming your product-based management perspective into one that is service-oriented.

## Where to Start

Where do you start? There is a logical, step-by-step sequence you can follow (which we will describe shortly), but there is no one correct starting point. Each business is unique in its background and its current challenges.

Your best success will come if you begin with current business problems or opportunities. If you can demonstrate that improved service will result in new market opportunities, improved customer loyalty, improved employee morale, increased productivity, or stronger competitive positioning, people will listen to you.

## The Process

The process for enhancing the service offered with your product draws on all the same service marketing concepts you will find discussed in greater detail in other chapters of this book. As we go along, we'll refer you to the appropriate chapters so that you can enrich your background knowledge in these areas. Our job is to apply these concepts to product differentiation. We will do this by focusing on your total business, its relationship with your customers, and the marketing, distribution, and post-delivery services it provides to complement your product sale.

Using Figure 21-1, let's take a look at each of the major components of this process in that logical sequence that we referred to earlier:

1. *Service Encounters.* Every day there are thousands of episodes in which customers come into contact with some aspect of your company, and thereby have the opportunity to form an impression. By identifying and analyzing these moments of truth, or service encounters, you will start to define your interactions with your customers (see also Chapters 5 and 15).

2. *Research.* You will also want to know what your customers want from you and what your competition currently delivers. This insight is best gained through a carefully planned and executed research plan. Both customers and your own employees are excellent sources of information (see also Chapters 9 and 10).

3. *Positioning.* Once you understand what your customers want and what your competition is delivering, you can determine how to position your products and services. A clear and concise positioning statement that captures your new service vision begins the process of communicating your differentiation strategy internally and, eventually, to your customers (see also Chapter 3).

4. *Alignment.* It is critical that your management and employees now transform their missions, operational goals, and attitudes to be consistent with the new positioning statement (see also Chapter 4).

5. *Design.* It is not enough that your people really want to deliver high-quality service and that their work attitudes are truly aligned with your positioning statement. The hard work now is to redesign the current processes that govern their daily activities. These processes—your service offerings—must be

**Figure 21-1.** Components of service marketing.

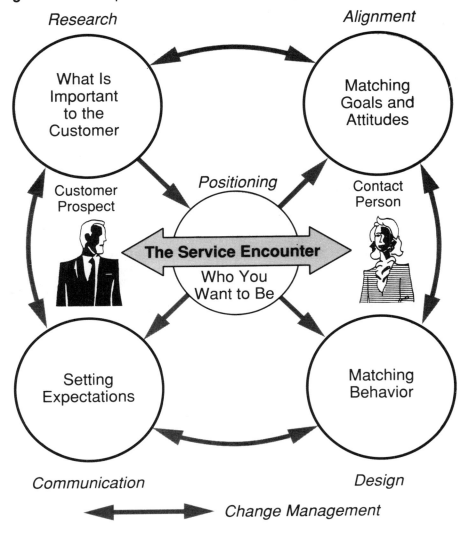

designed from the customer's viewpoint, not just to meet your internal business management needs (see also Chapter 14). Measurements must be refocused on committed customer service levels and should allow you to compare your performance with your customers' perceptions of value (see also Chapter 13).

6. *Communication.* Communicating your new service vision and positioning statement to your employees and involving them in the design of your new service offerings are key to your success. Once you can consistently deliver the service levels that differentiate your products from those of your competitors, tell the world about it. Tell your own people. Tell your customers. And tell the people who have not yet become your customers. Catchy slogans have only short-term payback. Well-designed communication campaigns backed up by good

service will pay long-term, high-value dividends. In our experience, you cannot communicate too much (see also Chapters 19 and 20).

7. *Change Management.* To ensure that all of the changes that result from the new service vision are well implemented, you will need a management process that is highly responsive. You'll find that your employees become advocates for the customers and their changing expectations. Your internal processes must be flexible enough to respond to this new input and to integrate it into the design of new product and service offerings (see also Chapter 7).

The interaction of all of these components of service marketing (as illustrated in Figure 21-1) is dynamic. Where you choose to place emphasis initially will depend on your current business needs, including current service levels. But all of the components will come into play in the sequence that you need them as you work to differentiate your product by adding service. We will discuss each of these components in more detail in the balance of the chapter.

Don't feel that you have to become expert in all these areas—or that the resources of a large organization are required to establish a service philosophy. The American Marketing Association has an entire division dedicated to services marketing, and you will find that an increasing amount of information is becoming available through material written by academics and businesspeople who specialize in this area. Also, a growing number of experienced consultants are available to help you work through the process.

## How to Identify Your Service Encounters

Because the success of your mission hinges on enhancing the service encounters customers have with your company, the first step is to understand the nature of these occasions, and exactly where and when they take place. You will find they exist to support your product management processes, that is: sell, order, supply, distribute, settle, and support. These processes are the basic components of any company's operations.

As shown in Figure 21-2, you can place all your employees into two broad categories—those who have direct contact with your customers and those who support these contact people. Examples of the former are employees involved in such departments as marketing, administration, and production maintenance, who are engaged in such activities as providing product information, coordinating delivery, collecting payment, and handling complaints. We will refer to these as your "contact" employees. Examples of those who support your contact employees are people involved in such departments as supply and inventory management, physical distribution, billing, and technical competency centers.

When customers decide to deal with your company, they bring along a wide range of expectations about your performance. These have been formulated from a variety of sources, including word-of-mouth communications, their personal needs, past experience with your company, and competitive alternatives. All these influences lead customers to expect a certain level of service from your organization.

**Figure 21-2.** Managing the service encounters.

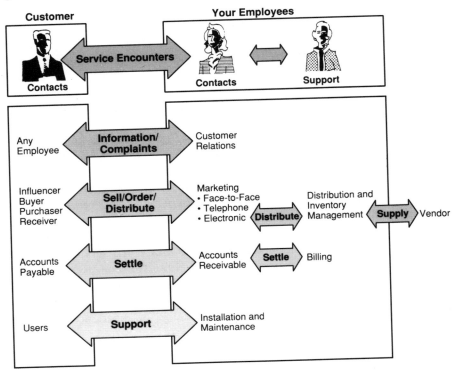

Meanwhile, the contact employees we've just discussed, all fulfilling different roles in the business, are each making a contribution to your company's performance at their point-of-service contact, wherever that may be. This service encounter is the critical point at which your level of service is visible and judged. Remember, it takes years to build a reputation, but only moments to ruin it.

There are people at your customer's end of the service encounter as well. For instance, your salespeople usually talk to buyers and decision influencers; employees involved in collection are in contact with your customer's accounts payable department; your customer relations department talks to anyone in your customer's organization with a complaint or query; and your product service people could have contact with any user of your product.

It's important to define these key relationships and also to determine how they differ with the size of your customer's business. If you are selling to a small company, one customer employee might play a number of roles, from purchasing to accounts payable.

In a larger organization, your customer contacts will be more numerous, perhaps including the company president, a group of senior managers, a larger group of middle managers, and numerous technical and administrative people. Eventually, all of these customer employees will be involved in a service encounter with one of your company's contact people, and you want to ensure that each of them leaves the encounter with a high opinion of your company's service.

Don't forget that the customer's view is of your total service offering. Customers know little and care less about the demarcation of responsibilities within your organization. They only know whether they like doing business with you. So when you examine your service encounters, try to see each encounter through your customer's eyes. However well an internal hand-off procedure seems to work, it doesn't work at all if it frustrates your customers—the people who keep you in business.

One of the difficulties here is that you are dealing with perceptions. You may examine a service encounter and decide that your company delivers a high level of service. And you could be right. But if the customer doesn't perceive this, you will gain no advantage from it.

Zeithaml, Berry, and Parasuraman have developed a model that is useful in understanding the quality of the service encounter. In Figure 21-3, you'll see that the measure of service quality is the size of the gap between the expected and the perceived service, labeled Gap 5. This gap is the result of four different internal gaps that affect a company's ability to deliver consistent, high-quality service. If you can eliminate these four internal gaps, you will have eliminated Gap 5—your customers' perceptions will now match their expectations, they will be more satisfied, and you will be actively building loyalty and repeat business.

When an organization sets out to enhance its service encounters, its first job is to tackle Gap 1, between management's perception of customer expectations and what those expectations really are. What do customers actually want? What do they expect to receive from each of those important service encounters? How do they judge your performance compared to that of your competition? There's only one way to find out—and that's by asking your customers directly.

## How to Research Your Customers' Expectations and Priorities

Research is the key to uncovering your customers' real expectations. In fact, there are a number of excellent reasons for committing time and effort to obtaining reliable customer data.

A research study provides you with hard facts on which to base decisions and establish priorities for action, bringing objectivity where before there might have been emotional subjectivity resulting in wasteful interdepartmental contention. Research can reveal shortcomings in your operation, from the customer's point of view, and highlight how you are viewed in relation to the competition. With this information in hand, you'll be able to see how you can use service to differentiate your product in its market.

Good research helps set a framework for tracking and measuring your on-

**Figure 21-3.** Model of service quality.

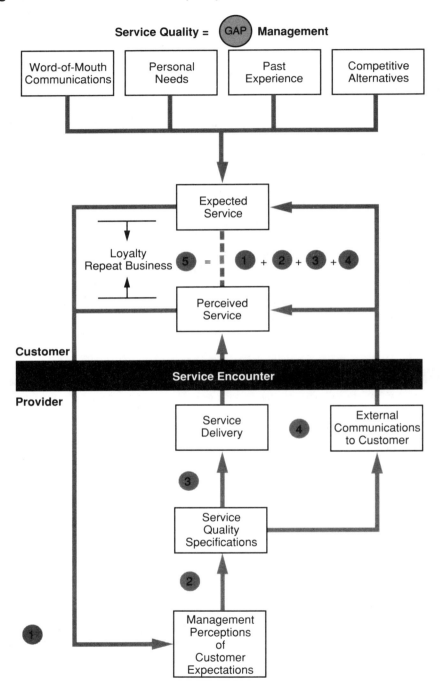

*Source:* Adapted from the "Conceptual Model of Service Quality" created by Valarie Zeithaml, Leonard Berry, and A. Parasuraman, published by the Marketing Science Institute in Report #87-100, June 1987. Used by permission of the publisher.

going performance. It also provides tangible evidence to customers and employees that you're committed to improving your service encounters. And it will yield insights about the most effective ways to communicate with your customers, prospects, and employees. If you only do one thing to get started, we recommend research, because these new insights will give you the arguments necessary to gain support for the other components that make up a complete service marketing plan.

It's important to define exactly what you need to research. You want to know more than just your customers' opinions of the services your company offers. You want to know what kind of relationship is important to your customers and how they view your current levels of service. For instance, you might believe that having your telephones answered by the fourth ring is an acceptable and, for you, a very manageable level of service. Testing your customers' perception of this might reveal that a large number of current and potential customers don't wait for four rings and hang up after three. You might be losing business. By understanding how your service levels are perceived, you now have the data required to take corrective action.

Linde, a division of Union Carbide, differentiates between its focus on *service* and its focus on *services*. Linde's management believes that you get the opportunity to establish a customer relationship because of your products and the services you provide that complement your products. However, you build customer relationships because customers prefer doing business with you—not the competition—because of your service.

The first step in a customer survey is to give customers, rather than your company management, the opportunity to define what is important in your relationship with them. This is normally achieved through focus group sessions where the identity of the sponsoring company is not revealed and customers can air their views in a relaxed, unstructured environment.

An important factor in the research process is evaluating the company's performance against your competitors'. Your lowest cost sale is to an existing customer, but you can only increase your market share by keeping your own customers and capturing some of your competitors'. By using research to find out how you stack up against major competitors in key areas of importance to the customer, you can decide how to adjust service levels to be competitive overall. Remember that to be "best of breed," you only have to be slightly better than the competition.

Employees can also provide valuable data about the key factors that influence your customers to purchase from you. In a survey relating to computer workstations, IBM Canada Ltd. asked two groups of employees the same questions they asked customers about its performance in key areas. One group of employees consisted of marketing representatives who had face-to-face contact with customers on a daily basis. The other group included administrative people in telephone sales positions or in positions that support the face-to-face marketing force.

By developing a matrix (like the sample in Figure 21-4) showing the opinions of these three different groups on each factor researched, priorities for

**Figure 21-4.** Satisfaction with service factors defined as important in supplier selection.

| | | Audience Satisfaction | |
|---|---|---|---|
| Important Factors | Customers | Employees Marketing | Administration |
| Knowledgeable Contact | + | − − | − − |
| Immediate Delivery Information | + | − − | − |
| Immediate Pricing Information | + | + | − |

*Key:*
+  =  Positive Rating
−  =  Negative Rating
− −  =  Very Negative Rating

action can be developed leading to projects that change operational procedures and/or raise awareness of the other groups' point of view.

Once you know which factors influence the customer's buying decision and how you compare to the competition in these key areas, you can make informed decisions about changing or redesigning your offerings. This doesn't mean you have to meet customer expectations (which aren't always practical for you), but you have to aim for a "higher score" than your competition on these key factors identified by your research. You may not be best at everything, but you do want to achieve a position of overall competitive advantage.

Surveying employees also provides valuable feedback for the communication programs that are required when the company is working toward new service quality goals. The action of involving employees promotes awareness of the service marketing philosophy, and it also builds commitment as people begin to visualize their own roles in the delivery of high-quality service and understand that management values their ideas and efforts. Teamwork and a sense of joint ownership develop as different departments make their contributions to the research questionnaire, and management becomes aware of the company's preparedness for change.

This type of formal research lays the foundation for a disciplined system of service quality management.

## How to Develop Your Positioning Strategy

Once the first customer and employee survey results are in, review your strengths and weaknesses and decide how to differentiate your company from its competitors. (Chapter 3 discusses differentiation and positioning in greater detail.)

When you want to differentiate your product on the basis of service, you need to identify key areas where your company can excel in the eyes of the customer and which you are confident the company can achieve. Then you embody these in a positioning statement that sums up your service marketing opportunities and how your company will capitalize on them.

Linde Canada undertook customer research to help determine how to differentiate its products in the marketplace. The survey revealed that buyers were heavily influenced by the quality of a supplier's service, rather than price alone, and that customers perceived little difference in the level of service offered by Linde and its competitors.

These findings made sense when the company reviewed its products from the customer perspective. "Customers see service as a value-add, and it's something you already have—it doesn't cost you any more to treat the customer better," says Lana Korb, manager of service positioning and marketing communications at Linde—a program that is "positioning" Linde as a customer-focused organization. "We set out to put Linde above the crowd in terms of service by encouraging employees to care about customers and exceed their expectations."

At the outset of its service positioning program, Linde Canada expressed its service goals in the following mission statement.

> Our commitment in Linde Canada is to be the leading manufacturer and marketer in our industry. Our products, services, and technologies will meet or exceed the needs of our customers. We will create an environment which fosters innovation, teamwork, personal growth, excellence, and integrity. In all we do, we will visibly differentiate ourselves through service. As a result, we expect Linde Canada to achieve superior financial performance.

With the help of its advertising agency, Linde then summarized this mission statement into its positioning statement:

### *Linde: Your Source for Special Service*

This statement emphasized the role of Linde people in meeting customer needs. It also changed its product-oriented advertising, which had looked much like that of its competitors, to a more "friendly" style that first and foremost highlighted the Linde organization and its service commitment.

Customers' perceptions are based on the sum total of their interactions with your company, and on the behavior of many employee. When you have learned what key factors influence customers to do business with you, the next step is to realign your organization to refocus employee efforts in the right direction and deliver what customers want. A tall order? Perhaps. But Linde did launch a realignment program to deliver the best possible service that is proving highly successful. Let's take a closer look at it.

## How to Align Your Organization for Service

Linde believes that one of the keys to success is its senior management's support of the service positioning program. When trying to introduce a service philosophy, the old maxim of starting at the top holds true. Using the research you have obtained, convince senior managers of the importance of the customer perspective, and then ask them to work together toward a mission statement. Each manager in turn then works with his or her own work groups to express their mission and goals in terms of the overall mission. Before long, you will have created an imperative for going through the alignment process and will have the organization working with a common purpose from the top down. As Linde found through research with customers, employees must bring empathy to the customer relationship. And the key to ensuring that they do this is the way that their managers support them and reinforce their service skills. So management training and development are crucial. Your employees are "responsible" for the quality of their service encounters, and management must learn to be "responsive" to employees.

"Management can't control every move employees make," says Korb. "You have to empower employees by giving them the space, and the skills, to react to customer needs."

Linde's employee empowerment process involved having all Linde employees attend workshops that taught value-added service skills, particularly for high-pressure situations, and how to deal more effectively with others. Key managers, whom Linde characterized as "leader-managers," went through an intensive training program in managing performance and change. All other managers then completed three-day sessions on managing service skills. And every other employee received two days' training in specific service skills.

Linde believes that not only is the quality of every interaction between employees and customers vital, but also that the quality of interactions between employees and their own internal clients is equally important. For this reason all employees, whatever their job level or salary status, attended the service workshops.

The service program was launched across Canada with special kick-off meetings at which all managers took responsibility for communicating the message that customer service is paramount. The shift in Linde's culture began with these meetings and workshops.

Now that the program is under way, service assignments and skill reviews are used to reinforce the concepts taught to employees and work unit managers by applying techniques to real situations. The company's quarterly employee publication continues to tell the service story, and a special newsletter, entitled *Winning Moments,* details service successes.

The company has created a service program team reporting to the vice president and general manager of Linde to plan and manage the strategies for shifting the culture to a service orientation. This involves introducing the service focus into activities like goal setting, establishing measurement criteria, providing feedback, and developing rewards and support systems.

At the same time, Linde's ongoing activities in advertising, customer communications, and media relations are being refocused to reflect the company's service orientation.

"Most of the program start-up has been about bringing people on board," says Korb. "Marketing is the easy part of the job—it's getting every employee fully behind the program that's the tougher job. It takes time to create a new culture."

# How to Design Services to Differentiate Your Product

In designing service offerings to complement your product, you must keep in mind all the elements of your total service commitment. You need to identify exactly what your service offerings are and win visibility for them in the day-to-day management system, which, in the past, has often been product-oriented. And your design must address the findings of your customer research and support your positioning statement.

Try looking at it through the following manufacturing analogy that IBM developed to help manage the design of services. The service offerings your customers experience can be compared to "service production lines" that support each of your lines of business. Within each service production line, your end-to-end relationships with your customers are managed, allowing them to order, buy, receive and pay for your products. Within each service production line are people in jobs or workstations where the tasks of selling, ordering, shipping, collecting, and servicing are performed.

At the same time, new automation technology allows either an individual workstation or the total service production line to produce higher quality output, become more productive, or both. Finally, quality control measurements are put in place to ensure that every individual job and every production line is operating to achieve the customer expectation of quality and price.

In manufacturing you find engineers who support the design of each of these production lines, workstations, automation changes, and quality control measurements. Similarly, in the world of service, you need to assign process engineers to ensure that service offerings are designed, with equal care, to meet customer requirements.

## How to Design a Service Production Line

By looking at its business processes in relation to products, customers, and competitive strategy, IBM identified a number of separate service production lines, which it named process paths. Each of these paths represents a separate source of revenue generation—a different group of products with its own customer set and competitive focus.

In IBM's case, the original "big ticket" path evolved into many different paths. This evolution came about because, like many large manufacturing organizations, IBM had built its business on custom-built products, characterized by long lead times and high unit prices. Constant employee effort was required to bridge the gaps between the basic processes of sell, order, supply, distribute, settle, and service.

Then things changed. With the advent of the commodity-like personal computer, and a business environment characterized by extremely short lead times and lower-priced products, it soon became apparent that internal procedures would have to be streamlined.

A different management view was needed. It was no longer possible to manually bridge the gaps between the basic processes. Attention had to be focused on what the customer experienced across the whole cycle, and service levels had to be defined for each point of interaction. By taking the customer's view, rather than the traditional internal management view, IBM was able to develop specific process paths for each of its many lines of business.

You can evaluate the effectiveness of your process paths by using a technique known as blueprinting.[1] A blueprint is essentially a process flow diagram that uses an imaginary "line of visibility" to separate the activities customers see during service encounters from internal operations (see Figure 21-5). By producing a blueprint of this kind, you can trace exactly what has to happen to deliver customer satisfaction, and you can identify obstacles along the way.

Even better, you can now plan the process, setting time constraints (shown across the top of Figure 21-5) and changing procedures where necessary to make the path smoother, improve service levels, and, possibly, reduce workload and costs. At the same time, you create a framework that allows you to manage service levels versus cost trade-offs. Later, we'll give you an example of how IBM management used this approach to solve a practical problem.

Obviously, to make process path management work, you must assign specific people to manage your process paths and give them customer service level accountability. When these design engineers are successful, they will have closed Gap 2 in the service quality model (Figure 21-3) by matching quality specifications to customer expectations.

### How to Design Service-Oriented Workstations (Jobs)

Once the process path design is complete, the next step is to design the specific jobs each contact person will perform during the service encounters (see Figure 21-2). Because each job plays a unique role in the process path, each must be carefully designed to meet a number of objectives. If you look at Figure 21-6, you'll find a list of the job design factors you should consider. And remember, any change in service levels or in the supporting automated systems will require redesign of the jobs involved.

It's critical, as well, that management set authority levels that empower employees to bridge the gap between the inflexibility of the company's policies

**Figure 21-5.** Process path blueprint.

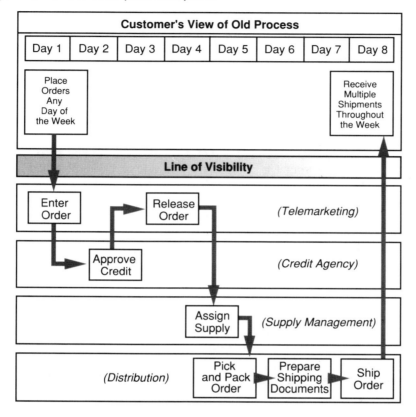

and procedures and the uniqueness of each customer situation. Review each service encounter again, and ask yourself how many other employees your front-line contacts have to deal with in order to satisfy the customer. Ideally the answer is zero!

As with process path management, someone in your staff organization must be responsible for managing the definition of authority, processes, skills, and automation required for each job.

## How to Design Service-Oriented Automation

In a service environment you must be geared for change, so the automated systems you design have to be flexible. This is most easily done by setting up a requirements-gathering process that is driven by the need to improve service levels, and that reflects the service quality and productivity needs of each contact job as it supports each process path.

There's also an opportunity here for electronic data interchange between your customers and yourself, but keep in mind that not all customers are comfortable with a "high-tech" medium for their service encounters. Some of them will always want a "high-touch" alternative that allows them face-to-face (or at least telephone) contacts with your employees. Careful process path design

**Figure 21-6.** Job design—key analysis factors.

---

1. What service encounters are employees in this job accountable for?

2. During the service encounters, what process path service levels does the employee in this job have responsibility for or set the expectations for?

3. What has customer research revealed about the service characteristics necessary for each service encounter?

4. What is the current performance in terms of customer satisfaction, productivity, morale? Plan versus actual?

5. What dialogue sequences are required to define the service encounter? What are the prerequisite information, knowledge, skills, activities, and response times necessary for these dialogues?

6. How many other people does the employee in this job need to interact with to get the job done? How can this number be reduced to as close to zero as possible?

7. What empowerment does this employee need in order to maintain customer satisfaction during the service encounters (e.g., credit approval, reship approval)?

8. What opportunities are there to introduce increased tangible evidence into each service encounter?

9. What is the optimal design of the workstation to support each employee in this job (e.g., procedures, furniture, computer terminals, telephone)?

10. What are the three most important changes required to improve both service quality and productivity on this job?

---

can ensure that these alternative contact methods are considered and properly managed.

## How to Design Measurements That Really Measure Service

Thanks to your research, you have insight into your customers' expectations and an understanding of how you measure up to the competition. As a result, you have been able to select key factors that position your company to be competitive. But how do you measure your operations to check that you're achieving your objectives?

In fact, you will need to measure three different aspects of your operations: the end-to-end performance of your process paths; the performance of people in the core jobs that support each path; and your customers' perceptions of each path's effectiveness.

IBM has subdivided its customer service level measurements for a process path into three categories: fill rate (how often you have what customers want), cycle time (how long it takes customers to get what they want), and service quality (what it is like to deal with you—for example, timely information, courtesy, accurate shipments). IBM's research program indicated what levels of fill rate and order cycle time were necessary and which aspects of service quality to focus on in order to achieve the objectives of the company's positioning statement.

When you are in an industry that relies on high customer loyalty and repeat business, you must develop an efficient way of measuring how well you are meeting those customers' needs. One company that has done this very successfully is GTE Service Corporation. In conjunction with Total Research Corporation, GTE developed a Business Customer Opinion Survey,[2] which combines an annual census that reaches all of GTE's medium and large business customers, and samples of small businesses and competitors' customers. Telephone interviews lasting ten to fifteen minutes are conducted monthly, with more than 35,000 customers interviewed each year. Each interviewer gathers the customer's perceptions of the key factors identified through earlier research, thus providing external quality measurements that can be linked to the internal operational measurements described earlier.

An analysis of the differences between your target and actual service levels, and between your internal performance and external customer perceptions, will reveal the need for operational change, or improved communications with your customers, or both.

Whatever your business, customer service level measurements are vital to the health of your service program, because they provide service targets, as opposed to just product-oriented targets. You can now make your managers accountable for both.

## How to Improve Service Without Increasing Resources—An Example

A situation was uncovered at IBM that required a readjustment of one of the company's process paths. Feedback from dealers indicated that there was an opportunity to increase their satisfaction by reducing the time required to process their orders and ship their products.

Like all other customers, dealers called in whenever they needed a product, and orders were shipped as soon as prerequisite procedures had been completed (see Figure 21-5). Investigation of the process revealed that as the order moved through order entry, credit approval, and inventory allocation, each department had independently decided to handle dealer orders first thing each morning. The result was that it took eight days from the time the order was received until the product was shipped (see Figure 21-7).

The company improved the situation by having each dealer call in the orders on a specific day of the week. The work in each of the separate departments was reorganized so that it is now done at a different time on the same day. Products are now shipped to dealers on their specific day of the week, thus establishing a shorter, reliable delivery time of three days!

The benefits of the changes are that dealers get products more quickly and they know exactly when to expect them, so they can make commitments to their customers and, when necessary, schedule extra manpower for receiving and stocking. And the benefit to IBM is that its service level in one process path

**Figure 21-7.** Redesigning the process path.

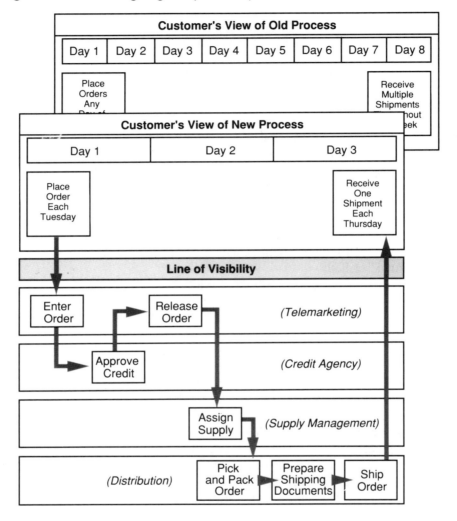

has been dramatically improved, without causing additional workload, hiring more staff, or affecting the achievement of existing business targets. The change could only be made because the company had established a process path view of service delivery and was monitoring service fulfillment.

## How to Use Communications to Energize the Organization

As Linde's experience showed, communicating the service message to both customers and employees is central to the development of a service philosophy. External communications, like advertising and media relations programs, achieve awareness of your service image, set expectations, and help create preference for your service. They tell customers how you are striving to give them better service and provide tangible evidence of your service commitment. But communications are not self-fulfilling. It is key to communicate only what you know you can perform. If you look back at Figure 21-3, you'll see that when your external communications activities are conveying service messages consistent with your performance, you have eliminated Gap 4, the gap between service delivery and customer expectations.

Credible communications are achieved by involving your contact employees in the formulation of customer material, because they have a good understanding of the kind of language customers will relate to and will know whether your performance expectations are realistic. In this way, you ensure that employees feel a sense of ownership for the service vision and are committed to achieving it.

Internal communication supports positioning and alignment, keeps your contact employees informed about your product and service offerings, and ensures behavior consistent with service level targets. You can find the most appropriate means to accomplish this from such approaches as employee publications, service discussion groups, special videos, presentation tours, and early exposure to customer advertising.

Your communication will be ineffective unless carefully planned to take your target audiences—employees and customers—through the steps of awareness, knowledge, liking, preference and commitment to your key service messages. These messages will be developed from the results of your research, your positioning statement, your progress in improving service quality, your directions, and upcoming changes. To be effective, this communication support plan must be carefully developed and implemented as a single, integrated plan, by your services marketing manager in conjunction with your process path, job, and product managers.

## How to Enable Change

In today's environment, constant change is the norm. As you develop the management system for your service offerings, a change management approach is essential. It will help you keep the focus on your customer's service requirements and priorities, while ensuring synchronization between announcements of new products, and changes in process paths, employees' jobs, and automated systems. The following will be some of the drivers of change:

1. Announcements of new products
2. Productivity requirements resulting from competitive pressures
3. Opportunities to use new technologies to increase the automation of the process paths and jobs
4. Your customers' changing needs and expectations, perhaps driven by new levels of service offered by your competitors
5. Your step-by-step plan to migrate from current processes into a disciplined set of process paths

**Table 21-1.** Staff management roles.

| Responsibility | Services Marketing Manager | Process Path Manager | Job Manager | Automation Manager |
|---|---|---|---|---|
| Service encounters | S | S | P | |
| Research | P | S | S | |
| Positioning | P | S | | |
| Alignment | P | S | S | |
| Design | S | P | P | S |
| Communication | P | S | P | S |

Key:
P = Primary role
S = Secondary role

To effect a smooth transition, the interactions between the six key components of service marketing (see Figure 21-1) must be well managed. In large, complex organizations it may be helpful to designate four different managers; the process path manager, the job manager, the automation manager, and the services marketing manager. In smaller businesses, one person can assume all of these separate roles, as long as each role receives specific attention.

Shared responsibility for each of the six components of service marketing should then be assigned, either as a primary or a secondary role, to each of these people, as shown in Table 21-1. In addition to the core roles described in Table 21-1, the following change management groups are recommended (see Table 21-2). At IBM, they meet monthly to review new requirements for change and to review implementation status.

## Product Announcement Review Board

This board is made up of all corporate departments necessary to launch a new product (e.g., finance, legal, marketing, administration). This is a key meeting for your process path managers to ensure that new products can be handled

**Table 21-2.** Change management.

| Participant | Change Management Groups | | | |
|---|---|---|---|---|
| | Product Announcement Review Board | Process Change Review Board | Systems Change Review Board | Customer Advisory Council |
| Customers | | | | X |
| Product manager | X | | | X |
| Job manager | | X | X | X |
| Process path manager | X | X | X | X |
| Automation manager | | | X | |

adequately by existing process paths at existing service levels, or that appropriate changes are made to the paths to accommodate them.

### Process Change Review Board

This board is made up of the managers responsible for each of the core jobs and each of the process paths. In their meetings, members review common projects representing the process changes necessitated by new product announcements, correct processes that do not work effectively, or improve the level of service provided by a core job or a process path. The board ensures that all aspects of each change have been planned for and that any implementation problems are identified and resolved.

### Automated Systems Change Review Board

This board is made up of the managers responsible for each of the core jobs, each of the process paths, and each of the automated systems. Members review the status of projects that are implementing changes to automated systems. They check progress, ensure that all implementation plans are synchronized, and are specifically accountable for ensuring that priorities for automation are driven by a customer-oriented view of the process paths.

### Customer Advisory Council

In addition, it can be very helpful to set up a Customer Advisory Council consisting of representative customers and your product, process path, and job managers. This group will help you gauge the impact on your service encounters of any changes you may make.

Depending on the size of your company and the scope of your service offerings, you may choose to combine the Product Announcement, the Process Change, and the Automated Systems Change Review boards into one. These groups may seem, at first, like a major investment in time, but once you understand your current processes and your desired new service offerings, you will recognize the benefit of the boards in maintaining control. In fact, establishing groups like these is the only way that IBM has found to ensure that quality and productivity targets are consistently achieved.

## How Far? How Fast?

Changing people's attitudes tends, by definition, to be a slow process. You can't implement change by using strategy like a baseball bat and beating people over the head with it. If your service philosophy is to take hold, you must nurture people in order to unleash their commitment and inherent creativity.

Most people—and organizations—resist change. But they do change, often dramatically, when change becomes essential to relieve pressure of some kind. You can use this phenomenon to bring about change in your organization.

Find, or create, a pressure point, and then suggest how service quality management techniques can help ease it. The customer research you've done may highlight problems people don't know they have, until you point them out, together with the service philosophy required to solve them.

If your pressure point is market share, explore research and positioning. If it is competitiveness, explore research and design. If it is customer satisfaction, explore service encounters. If it is productivity, explore design. If it is morale, explore alignment and communication. Eventually, these individual achievements will come together to result in the overall success of your vision—your services marketing plan.

## Start Now

First steps tend to be the hardest—and the first steps toward establishing a service philosophy in your business will demand a great deal of determined effort. The aim of this chapter was to make those first steps easier. We've described the research we think is required to set positioning and design goals. We've described some changes that will probably be needed in your organization, and some ideas on measuring achievement. We've suggested how to get started and outlined the benefits you might expect from a fully implemented service orientation program.

We've taken what we think is a logical step-by-step approach. If you have not yet established a service philosophy in your organization, it's worth remembering that our sequence isn't the only way of doing things. There may be a number of valid entry points into a service culture, and you must identify the one appropriate for your business.

The important point is not where you start adding service to your product offerings, but that you do start. Those hesitant first steps may be difficult, but they're necessary to get you on the road to competitive advantage in the next decade.

## Notes

1. Lynn Shostack, "Planning the Service Encounter," in *The Service Encounter: Managing Employee/Customer Interaction in Service Businesses,* ed. John A. Czepiel, Michael R. Solomon, and Carol F. Surprenant (Lexington, Mass.: Lexington Books, 1985).
2. Total Research Corporation, *A Total View* 1, no. 29, 1986.

## Further Resources

Albrecht, Karl, and Ron Zemke. *Service America! Doing Business in the New Economy.* Homewood, Ill.: Dow Jones-Irwin, 1985.

Berry, Leonard L., A. Parasuraman, and Valarie A. Zeithaml. *Communication and Control Processes in the Delivery of Service Quality.* Cambridge, Mass.: Marketing Science Institute, 1987.

Grönroos, Christian. *Strategic Management and Marketing in the Service Sector*. Cambridge, Mass.: Marketing Science Institute, 1983.

Lovelock, Christopher H. *Services Marketing*. Englewood Cliffs, N.J.: Prentice-Hall, 1984.

Shostack, Lynn. "Designing Services That Deliver." *Harvard Business Review*, January/February 1984.

Zeithaml, Valarie A. *Defining and Relating Price, Perceived Quality, and Perceived Value*. Cambridge, Mass.: Marketing Science Institute, 1987.

\* \* \* \*

***Douglas C. Snyder*** *currently serves as manager of direct marketing and integrated distributed support in the information and marketing services organization of IBM Canada, Ltd. in Toronto. During his twenty-two years with IBM, he has worked in a variety of positions, including systems engineer, marketing representative, systems engineering manager, product manager–software, and marketing strategy manager.*

***Barbara M. Zuppinger*** *is vice president of the Ontario Training Corporation. In this capacity she has overall responsibility for marketing the corporation's services. She is also responsible for specific brand management of SkillsLink, an on-line database of training resources and support services available to employers in the province. She was previously program manager, services marketing, at IBM Canada, Ltd.*

# PART VI

# STATE-OF-THE-ART MARKETING IN ELEVEN SERVICE INDUSTRIES

# About This Part

The chapters in this final part address marketing issues and practices in various service industries, as well as marketing in the entrepreneurial service business. The major theme throughout these final chapters is the idea that marketing is not only an attitude, but also an array of activities. Be aware that the authors who contributed these chapters were given free reign on content. They were invited simply to write about how to be successful in their respective service industries. Therefore, the fact that there is consensus on the dual nature of marketing is real, not contrived. The difficulty seems to be making attitude and action consistent—moving from saying you are a customer-centered organization to *being* a customer-centered organization.

Another common theme you will discover throughout these chapters is that the impetus for marketing is from external rather than internal pressures. External pressures such as deregulation, increased and diverse competition, and technological innovation have been the catalysts, not enlightened top management. Thus the initial marketing response in most service industries has been reactive rather than initiating. All eleven chapters prescribe a move away from a fatalistic approach, to planning your destiny and then marketing your way toward it.

These chapters are provided to foster the cross-fertilization of services marketing ideas and strategies. Basic marketing texts traditionally have presented fundamental marketing concepts and activities and have drawn examples and illustrations from across diverse goods-producing industries. Services marketing knowledge has grown in an industry-specific manner. Many new journals and books address services marketing—a marketing journal for the health-care industry and another for professional services, and books for financial services marketers and for the transportation industry. For maximum understanding of marketing and spread of useful marketing information, however, industry fences need to be torn down, or at least scaled. The information here can be used to begin that process.

Read the ten industry-specific chapters with an open mind. Expose yourself first to what is happening in service industries seemingly unlike yours. For example, if you are in the financial services industry, read that chapter last. Commit yourself to reaping at least one idea that is transferable to your own situation from each chapter that describes a service business "foreign" to you. You must look beyond your industry because there is a marketing maturation process that results in "me too" marketing at some point—perhaps four to six years after companies in your industry "discover" marketing. It is then that you must be prepared to break away from what has become precedent and expected in your industry to what is new and innovative and what will afford you a differentiated position of strength.

Forcing yourself out of familiar situations will help you generate new ideas and strategies to help meet the marketing challenges in your industry.

Chapter 22, an upbeat look at the emergence of a growth industry, information services, kicks off this part of the *Handbook*. The information explosion, coupled with new needs for information and technological advances in making information available, has created some lucrative service business opportunities for the astute and able marketer. This first chapter describes how to create a new customer-focused service business, using marketing attitudes and activities to take maximum advantage of the combination of fortuitous trends. The author points out that self-service can sometimes be a formidable competitor.

The following three chapters—telecommunications, transportation, and financial services—are grouped together because these are all longstanding services that have been subjected to tremendous change in the form of deregulation, rapid technological advances, and new competition, both domestic and foreign. In these service industries the old attitudes and activities are inappropriate in the new competitive environment. The traditional inward focus on operations and all the activities that support internal efficiency is having to give way to a focus on the customer and his or her needs and on activities that support increasing customer satisfaction. A basic shift is needed from evaluation of historical financial data as the major indicator of performance to performance evaluation in terms of how well customer needs are anticipated and satisfied in comparison with the competition. Each of these chapters helps you decide how to reorient the attitudes and activities in your organization toward greater customer sensitivity.

Chapter 26 focuses on professional services, which represent some of the best examples of the special nature of services:

- Professional services are produced and consumed simultaneously.
- Clients participate actively in the service delivery process.
- Professional services are intangible, although many have tangible elements.
- Quality is difficult to manage and control because of the uniqueness of each encounter between a client and a professional.

This chapter describes how a firm can achieve a consistently high level of service quality with a twofold strategy: (1) Focus on the service delivery process, and (2) raise the sensitivity of every employee in a professional service firm.

The next two chapters, marketing in education and marketing arts services, illustrate industries that have been relatively resistant to marketing. Educators resist marketing because they believe it may compromise academic freedom and artists because they believe it may compromise artistic integrity. Changing demographics and psychographics, however, are propelling these industries into marketing activities, like it or not. Both of these industries have a public relations tradition, and so initial marketing efforts have a strong brochure-writing bent. Furthermore, the emphasis in communication is on individual events rather than on an integrated and ongoing promotional plan. The authors of these chapters advocate the move toward more comprehensive, coordinated, and enduring marketing programs.

Chapter 29 deals with retailing. Change seems to be a given in retailing. The author borrows the term *creative destruction* to describe the constant cycle of change evident in retailing. Traditional sources of differentiation in retailing, such as price and exclusive brands, are being examined more closely, and so service is moving to the forefront as a viable differentiator. The author describes how to gauge service levels on variables such as credit, atmosphere, and image to meet the expectations of various market segments. This chapter echoes the admonition to measure success not only in terms of sales and profits, but also in terms of customer satisfaction and other customer-designated criteria.

Chapter 30, marketing in health care, describes, again, an industry resistant to marketing. There is a traditional public relations planning role in health care, and so fitting marketing into the organizational structure becomes an important issue that the author discusses. Health care stands out as a unique service industry in terms of the tremendous diversity in customers and customer needs—physicians, referral specialists, employers, insurance companies, relatives of end users, and so on. Also, consumer decision making in health care runs the gamut from routine, low-involvement decisions to the most complex and highly involved decision-making processes. The author discusses how the health-care industry has accommodated the marketing function.

The last industry-specific chapter in this final part concerns marketing in the hospitality industry, which is a 24-hour-a-day, 365-day-a-year business that exemplifies the fact that marketing needs to be continuous and ongoing. This chapter brings us full circle to discussing marketing in terms of attitude and activities. The author describes the entire process of moving from a "marketing department"-driven hotel to a market-driven hotel. An infinity sign is used to illustrate the process, a symbol that could not be more appropriate to show the ongoing flow of marketing activities. The need for marketing to permeate every nook and cranny of a service organization—hospitality business or otherwise—is stressed in this chapter.

Finally, recognizing that much growth in our economy comes from entrepreneurial service businesses, Chapter 32 is devoted to the special planning and management issues within these smaller service organizations. A planning system is presented that includes such components as analysis of the environment in which your business operates, clear specification of your mission, enumeration of the areas in which you must plan strategy (customers, service offering, price, distribution, communication), and putting it all together into an actionable plan. This chapter provides a concise summary of the key elements and processes in marketing planning.

The advice offered in the eleven chapters that make up the final part of this *Handbook* can be summarized as follows:

- Define what you do and how you benefit the customer in terms that are market-, not operations-oriented.
- Segment your market to zero in more accurately on customer needs.
- Perform situation analyses, both internal and external.
- Design customer-sensitive internal and external marketing programs.
- Develop customer-driven rather than financially-driven evaluation systems.
- Plan strategically; avoid reactive measures.
- Organize in a manner that supports marketing activities.
- Lead and manage by example, not by rhetoric.

This last point is of particular importance—a "Do as I say, not as I do" philosophy produces an ineffective, unfocused service organization. Service providers will serve customers with care and respect if they are led and managed with care and respect.

# 22

# Information Services

Fred O. Jensen

In his landmark book *Megatrends*,[1] John Naisbitt convincingly makes the case that the United States today is truly an information society. As a result of the United States' transition from an industrial society to an information society, information has become a strategic resource needed by all businesses, governments, and individuals to successfully conduct their affairs. Reflecting this transition, the number of companies selling information services in the United States increased sixfold from 1960 to an estimated 1,500 companies in 1988, and their revenues grew, on average, about 12 percent annually, a rate well above the average for American business.

Although there is a strong and growing demand for information, organizations and individuals alike are paradoxically suffering from "information overload." The volume of scientific and technical data available now doubles in three to four years! At the same time, suppliers of information services are encountering unprecedented levels of competition. Both of these trends, information overload and heightened competition, have created an urgent need for more effective marketing by companies providing information services. Through greater excellence in marketing, information suppliers can gain a better understanding of their customers' needs and develop information services that are more relevant, accurate, and timely. Similarly, today more than ever before, marketing may be the only area in which an information supplier can develop the competitive edge needed to profitably win market share.

This chapter discusses the unique attributes of information services, describes the U.S. information services industry, and provides practical and powerful guidelines for planning, developing, and marketing these services.

## What Is the Information Services Industry?

Because of the complexity of the "information business," defining the information services industry is not a straightforward task. For example, Samuelson's *Economics* textbook, *Playboy* magazine, CBS-TV's news broadcasts, and Dun & Bradstreet's Business Information Reports all provide their users with information of some sort. Thus, on this basis, they could all be considered participants in the information services industry. However, there are critical differences in the characteristics of these businesses, which give rise to very different marketing environments. As a result, it is not practical to consider these businesses as being in the same industry. This section defines an information services company and provides an estimate of the size, composition, and recent growth of the industry comprised of such companies in the United States.

## Defining the Information Services Industry

The four information services mentioned earlier actually serve very different primary user needs—an education need, an entertainment need, a general information need, and a specific decision-making information need, respectively. They also differ in their primary source of revenue. TV news programs and *Playboy* magazine are paid for primarily by fees from advertisers. Their primary business mission is to deliver an audience to their advertisers, rather than to deliver information to their viewers and readers. The *Economics* textbook and Dun & Bradstreet's Business Information Reports, conversely, are paid for entirely by user fees. Their primary mission is to deliver information to their users, who will expect greater benefits from these services because they are paying for the entire cost of the service. This is unlike the situation for a controlled circulation magazine or a network TV news broadcast, which are essentially free to the user.

Because of the differences in user needs served and source of revenue, these four services call for significant differences in marketing practices. This chapter focuses on the marketing practices used by companies and units of companies that provide a service that has information as its core ingredient, is paid for primarily by revenues derived from the information users or their organizations, and is used ultimately to assist in making decisions.

Using this definition,[2] the information services industry includes such services as Dun & Bradstreet Business Information Reports, F. W. Dodge Construction Project News, Mead Data Central LEXIS, Dialog Information Services, IMS International Sales Territory Reports, and *Consumer Reports* magazine. Perhaps equally important, this definition excludes from the information services industry companies producing such products and services as mass media publications, trade magazines, data processing services, computer hardware and software, and communications equipment and services.

## Size and Composition of the Information Services Industry

In 1988, the U.S. information services industry included some 1,500 companies that generated an estimated $17.7 billion of revenue in the United States. Compared with other major U.S. industries, most of these companies are small. In 1988, about 90 percent of these companies had revenues of less than $20 million. Today, the largest information services company is the Dun & Bradstreet Corporation, with 1988 revenues of more than $4 billion. Since 1982, when industry revenues totaled about $9 billion for an estimated 1,250 companies, the industry has enjoyed an average growth in revenue of approximately 12 percent annually.

Table 22-1 shows the revenues for each of the industry's six major information subject areas. Information to serve the needs of the marketing function

**Table 22-1.** 1988 U.S. market for information services by subject area.

| Information Subject Area | Estimated 1988 Revenue ($ bil.) | Estimated 1988 Share | Average Annual Increase in Revenue From 1982 to 1988 |
|---|---|---|---|
| Market/Marketing/Media research | $ 6.6 | 37.3% | 13% |
| Economic/Financial/ Securities | 3.9 | 22.0 | 16 |
| Credit/Check authorization | 2.4 | 13.6 | 11 |
| Product/Price | 1.5 | 8.5 | 9 |
| Legal/Regulatory | 1.4 | 7.9 | 10 |
| Medical/Scientific/ Technological | 0.8 | 4.5 | 12 |
| All other | 1.1 | 6.2 | 8 |
| Total industry | $17.7 | 100.0% | 12% |

Estimates have been made by the author and are based on the Information Industry Association's 1982 survey of information providers, the results of which are contained in the report "The Business of Information 1983," prepared by A. C. Nielsen Company.

of businesses is now the largest segment of the information services industry. During the six years from 1982 to 1988, this segment grew in terms of revenues by some 13 percent per year. Only information services directed toward the financial services industry grew more rapidly.

Not apparent from the data in Table 22-1 is the growing importance of on-line and personal computer (PC) diskette delivery of information services. As a result of the continuing dramatic gains in the price-performance characteristics of computers and the proliferation of personal computers throughout U.S. businesses, revenues from on-line and PC diskette delivery of information have increased by some 25 percent per year since 1982. In 1988, information services delivered in this manner accounted for almost $7 billion of revenue, with print media accounting for essentially all of the remainder. The large and growing installed base of personal computers, both in businesses and in homes, is a key factor to be considered in the marketing of information services.

## The Market for Information Services

Businesses, professional firms (e.g., accounting and law firms), and government units are far and away the major buyers and users of information services today. Although a number of information services are offered to consumers (e.g., The Source and *Consumer Reports* magazine), these account for only a small fraction of the industry's revenues. The information services business is predominantly a "business-to-business" service today. As the installed base of personal computers in homes expands and consumer awareness of the availability and value of information services increases, however, the consumer market will grow in relative importance in the future.

## Who Are the Prospects for Information Services?

Virtually every business and professional firm, no matter how large or small, in every sector of the economy is a prospect for information services. Furthermore, within businesses, each of the major functions is a prospect for different information services. For example, marketing, sales, production, purchasing, finance, and corporate planning all have their special and distinct information needs. What's more, the specific information required by some of these functions often differs from one industry to another. For example, the marketing function of a building products manufacturer such as Owens Corning Fiberglass has information needs that are very different from those of the marketing function of a computer manufacturer such as IBM.

The market for an information service is generally viewed not as just a set of companies, but as a specific function within that set of companies. For example, the market for a service that reports on the buying intentions of data processing departments would consist primarily of the marketing and sales functions of manufacturers and developers of computer hardware and software. (Such a service is provided by Computer Intelligence Corporation of La Jolla, California). Of course, it is this industry-specific nature of information needs that limits the potential size of the market for most information services. Hence, information services typically tend to be relatively small businesses.

Although the information required by the marketing and sales function tends to be very industry-specific, other functions are often quite similar in their information needs across industries. The purchasing function in many industries, for example, may need credit information on the same suppliers. Similarly, legal departments and data processing departments within businesses have many of the same information requirements regardless of the industry in which their companies participate. Information services that can serve a function across many industries generally enjoy a far larger market. Thus, it is not surprising that the single largest information service in the world is Dun & Bradstreet's U.S. Credit Report Service, with 1988 revenues estimated at over $400 million.

## Why Are Information Services Purchased?

As with any tangible product, information services are purchased because the customer perceives that the benefits received from the information amply justify the price paid for it. Unlike a tangible product, however, information consists of symbols on a page or a video screen. It has no inherent value of its own. The benefits of information are determined solely by the perceived impact that the information has upon the customer's decision making. Hence, for marketers of information services, it is critically important to understand how information is used by customers in order to assess its value to them. Such understanding, of course, is key to setting an appropriate price for an information service.

In many instances, a company buying an information service could develop the same information on its own. Customers of information services "buy" rather than "make," however, because the key index of value—the benefit/price ratio—is usually much greater for the purchased service. This is because the price of the information service is generally a fraction of the cost that the company would incur to develop the same information on its own. In marketing information services, it is generally helpful to know the typical customer self-development cost because this sets a theoretical upper limit to the price of an information service. Similarly, the greater the spread between customer self-development cost and the price of the information service, the greater will be the appeal of the information service.

# Market Selection and Service Planning

There are never any guarantees that a new business will be successful. However, in planning and developing new information services there are several useful guidelines that, if followed, can enhance your chances of success. This section describes the attributes of a winning service-market combination, presents a technique for segmenting the market, and outlines a practical approach to identifying and developing new information services.

## Attributes of a Winning Service-Market Combination

The most successful information services tend to have certain attributes in common. Similarly, the markets served by the most successful information services also tend to have certain characteristics in common. In developing plans for new information services, careful attention should be given to determining the extent to which these attributes are likely to be present.

Looking first at the service, an "ideal" information service would score high on all of the following attributes:

• *High value added.* The service provides information that is derived from a proprietary database involving a large quantity of data items. A "large quantity" is one that would require a significant time and dollar expenditure on the part of any one user of the service to create and maintain the database on its own. The service, therefore, has a high value added, and there are substantial barriers to the entry of competitive suppliers. Dun & Bradstreet's U.S. Credit Report service, for example, maintains credit information that is gathered by some 1,000 field reporters on more than nine million U.S. companies.

• *Frequent changes.* The contents of the database change frequently (e.g., hourly, daily, monthly) and, therefore, must be updated. This creates the opportunity to provide an ongoing service with continuing revenues. The larger the proportion of the database that changes in a given time period and the greater the magnitude of change in individual data items, the more frequently users will require updated information.

• *Critical information.* The service provides information that is essential to the operation of the customer's business. The more immediate and measurable the benefits of the information, the more likely a customer is to continue using the service. For example, current and historical prices of common stocks are absolutely essential to stockbrokers in serving their customers. By contrast, forecasts of interest rates over the next six to twelve months, although very relevant, are far less essential.

• *Large customer base.* The service has a large number of customers; of course, large is a relative concept and difficult to quantify. However, information services with more than 10,000 subscribers will not be seriously affected if several customers discontinue the service. On the other hand, if there are only fifty customers, for example, the loss of several customers could have a serious impact on the service's profits. In addition, a larger customer base generally results in lower unit costs for the service, thereby strengthening the competitive position of the service. In this case, share of market should be an important strategic objective.

Turning now to the demand side of the equation, an ''ideal'' market for an information service would score high on all of the following attributes:

• *Large prospect universe.* The market contains a large number of prospects for the service. Many information providers serve markets with more than 10,000 prospects for their service. Other things being equal, this will clearly be a more attractive market than one with, say, only 1,000 prospects.

• *Growing prospect universe.* The number of prospects is growing or is, at least, not declining. This is key because the number of customers for the service ultimately depends on the number of prospects.

• *Profitable prospect universe.* The prospect universe, in the aggregate, has an adequate level of profitability, with the outlook that this will continue in the future. Profitability ensures that customers and prospects will continue to be able to pay for the service.

• *Dynamic business environment.* Key aspects of the business environment of companies in the prospect universe are changing rapidly and significantly. This situation generally gives rise to a strong demand for information services that help in coping with the changing environment. For example, information systems departments in all industries must be knowledgeable about the ever-increasing capabilities of the latest computer equipment and software available. The need for such information is created by the continuing advances in information technology. Similarly, producers of telecommunications equipment and communications services have had to operate in an increasingly competitive environment as a result of deregulation. This has given rise to a sharply increased demand by these companies for information about their marketplace.

It's not likely that a specific service-market combination will have high scores on all of these attributes. However, the extent to which these attributes are present, together with the competitive environment, will be the key determinants of success for an information service.

### Segmenting the Market

An effective approach to segmenting the market for information services is to first identify one or more industries you think might contain potentially attractive markets for information services. Typically, these industries are large, include thousands of prospects, and have dynamic business environments. Keep in mind that prospects for information services include both the manufacturers or producers of an industry's output and the buyers or users of the industry's output. Examples of such industries are construction, health care, computers, and communications.

As noted earlier, the user of an information service resides within a particular function of a company. Therefore, the actual potential markets for such services are the company-type/user-function combinations that exist in the industry. These combinations or market segments can be conveniently portrayed in a market segmentation matrix such as the one shown in Figure 22-1. In this matrix, the construction industry is segmented into seven types of companies. These are manufacturers of building products for use in residential and nonresidential construction; architectural, engineering, and interior design firms; and general contractors and subcontractors.

In addition to grouping companies by type of business, it is often useful to further segment them by size. In the construction industry, for example, this is particularly true for contractors. Such companies can vary in size from one with only three employees serving a local area to one with more than 1,000 employees operating worldwide. Clearly, these two companies will have different requirements for construction-related information services.

Three user functions within the construction industry's companies are also shown in Figure 22-1. These functions—product and market planning, sales and marketing, and construction product selection and purchase—are illustrative of potentially large users of information services within these companies. The selection of such user functions must be based on a thorough understanding of the organization of each company type and the roles the various user functions play in each. Which user functions are most important will, of course, vary from industry to industry and will not necessarily parallel this construction industry illustration.

As shown in Figure 22-1, there are nineteen market segments that represent potential target markets for information services. Prospects within each of these target markets can be expected to have similar information needs. Once this segmentation process has been completed, each of these segments should be further evaluated for its potential attractiveness in terms of specific information needs, number of prospects, outlook for growth, competition, and your company's capabilities and objectives.

## Identifying Information Service Opportunities

Once a target industry has been appropriately segmented and several potentially attractive target markets selected, the next step is to identify specific information services to offer to these markets. To do this successfully, marketing personnel (e.g., a market manager) of the information services company must complete four key tasks. These are:

1. Develop an in-depth understanding of the business of the companies in the target market. This is essential to carrying out steps 2 and 3.

**Figure 22-1.** Example of a market segmentation matrix for the construction industry.

Type of Company

| User Function | Building Product Manufacturers | | Design Firms | | | Contractors | |
|---|---|---|---|---|---|---|---|
| | Nonresidential | Residential | Architects | Engineers | Interior Design | General | Subcontractors |
| Product and Market Planning | | | | | | | |
| Sales and Marketing | | | | | | | |
| Construction Product Selection and Purchase | Not Applicable* | Not Applicable* | | | | | |

*Building product manufacturers are producers, not buyers, of finished construction products and materials.

2. Acquire a thorough knowledge of the decision-making process within the companies in the target market.
3. Evaluate how effectively key decisions are currently being made and determine if improvement opportunities exist.
4. Establish development priorities, if two or more specific opportunities are identified.

The basic elements involved in carrying out these four steps are described on the following pages. For the purposes of this discussion, the construction industry market segmentation matrix in Figure 22-1 is used and the target market is assumed to be the sales and marketing function of nonresidential building product manufacturers.

Understanding the Prospects' Business.   To gain an adequate understanding of the business of the companies in the target market, the market manager must first analyze the economics of these businesses. In simple terms, the market manager must know how these companies make money. What are their major sources of revenues and costs, and what has been happening to revenues and costs in recent years? Also, how will current trends and developments affect the outlook for revenues and costs?

The managers should also have a solid grasp of the key factors required for success. What are the four or five areas in which these companies must perform exceptionally well to be outstanding in their field? Finally, the market manager must know how companies in the target market are typically organized and the general responsibilities of the major departments. In particular, the interface between the sales and marketing departments and other departments must be well understood. With this understanding of companies in the target market, the market manager can talk knowledgeably with executives in these companies to learn the anatomy of their marketing decision-making process.

Understanding the Decision-Making Process.   To develop this understanding, the market manger must: (1) identify the key marketing decisions, (2) determine who influences and makes each decision, and (3) evaluate the importance of each decision. As a first step, a list of key marketing decisions made within most industries should be prepared. This would include such decisions as changing product price, setting sales quotas, assigning sales compensation levels, and setting advertising budgets. This list should be expanded based on the manager's acquired knowledge of the companies in the target market and then confirmed in interviews with key marketing personnel in this market.

The best opportunities for providing improved marketing information services will, of course, generally be where the most critical decisions are made. Thus, the market manager must evaluate each of the key marketing decisions for its importance. One approach is simply to rate each decision high, moderate, or low in importance relative to the ''key factors for success'' and its probable impact, in qualitative terms, on the company's business. Another approach is to estimate the dollar impact of these decisions as a measure of importance. The frequency of each decision should also be considered in assessing importance. The more often a decision must be made, the greater the dollar impact associated with that decision in a given period of time. These measures of importance also aid in evaluating the benefit of new or improved information and help provide an indication of the potential price that companies might be willing to pay for such information.

Next, it is important to know who influences, as well as makes, the key marketing decisions. This involves knowing the departments and personnel who have a role in the overall decision-making process—that is, who approves, recommends, provides input, and such. This information will help pinpoint to whom an information service should be marketed. Table 22-2 presents an illustrative summary of an analysis of the marketing decision-making process for a large manufacturer of building products.

<u>Evaluating How Effectively Decisions Are Made.</u>   This evaluation is the next step in identifying opportunities to provide information services to the target market. It involves: (1) identifying the information currently being used in making a decision, (2) evaluating how effectively the current information enables the decision to be made, and (3) developing an "overall customer need" rating based on the effectiveness of current information and the importance of the decision.

*Identifying information used to make key decisions.* As a first step, the information used for making each of the key marketing decisions identified earlier should be determined. This should include not only the specific content of information used, but also its source. Decisions may be based on information that is obtained entirely from sources outside the company, entirely from sources within the company, or from a combination of external and internal sources. It is important to understand how information from external sources is integrated with the company's own data for use in decision making.

*Evaluating the effectiveness of the information.* This step involves an appraisal of five key factors:

1. *Completeness of information.* Is there additional information that would improve the quality of the decision on a cost-effective basis? In assessing completeness, it is critical to distinguish between information decision makers *need* as opposed to what they *would like to have.* Generally, managers will only pay for information they truly *need* for decision making.

2. *Accuracy.* Is the level of accuracy of the information used sufficient in light of the nature of the decision being made?

3. *Timeliness.* Does the information arrive in the hands of the right people in time to be effective in making the decision? Also, how much time has elapsed between the time the information is used and the time the information was last updated? Is the information sufficiently current?

4. *Ease of use.* Is the information relevant to the decision readily identified and easily interpreted? Is the delivery format—print, computer terminal—as convenient and cost-effective as it can be? If the decision requires information from both internal and external sources, are these two sets of information easily and conveniently combined for the decision maker?

**Table 22-2.** Example of a summary analysis of the marketing decision-making process.

| Key Marketing Decision* | CEO | Marketing VP | Participants in Decision Sales Manager | Product Manager | Market Manager | Importance of Decision |
|---|---|---|---|---|---|---|
| Change pricing on product category | Approves | Approves | Input | Recommends | Input | Very important |
| Set sales quotas | Delegates | Approves | Recommends | Input | Input | Moderately important |
| Set advertising budgets | Approves | Approves | Input | Recommends | Input | Very important |

*Add other decisions as appropriate.

5. *Cost.* What is the current cost of the information and how does this compare with the importance of the decision?

Each of these five factors represents potential areas for improving current information. Each key element of information used in making a decision should be rated according to these factors. Again, ratings of low, moderate, and high in terms of acceptability can be used for this purpose. For cost, actual dollar estimates should eventually be developed.

*Identifying opportunity areas.* This step requires comparing the importance of a decision with the completeness and accuracy of current information. For decisions of lesser importance, less complete or accurate information is acceptable as long as the cost is reasonable. Important decisions will require better information and be less sensitive to higher costs. These evaluations, of course, ultimately require sound judgment. However, this judgment can be developed by talking with the people involved in the decision-making process.

Table 22-3 presents an illustrative summary evaluation of how effectively marketing decisions are made in a large company in the target market. In Table 22-3, the right-hand column, "Overall User Need," gives an estimate of the company's need for better information for each major decision.

In the search for information service opportunities, a market manager should also be looking for opportunities to provide computer software or systems that will facilitate the cost-effective use of the information. Such a system should also enable a customer company to easily enter its internal data into the system where appropriate.

**Establishing Development Priorities.**   To complete the process of identifying information service opportunities, each information need should be assigned a development priority so as to focus efforts on those areas having the greatest new business potential. This involves considering not only customer need and potential new revenue, but also:

• *Ease of entry into the business.* For example, does the information services company already have the basic data required and would the proposed new service merely involve reorganizing it somewhat? Or, would entry involve a major new data collection effort? Also, does the company already have a presence in the proposed target market?

• *Barriers to entry.* How easy would it be for a competitor to enter the business? This would influence the future profitability of the service.

• *Risk.* Does the program require heavy upfront investment, new technical skills, or expertise that the company does not possess?

Table 22-4 provides a simplified example of how development priorities might be set, taking into account these considerations. The right-hand column gives a recommended development priority for each of the two identified information needs.

An assessment of a large target market in the manner outlined here could

**Table 22-3.** Example of a summary evaluation of the effectiveness of marketing decision-making.

| Decision* | Market Information Used | Evaluation of Information | | | | | Importance of Decision | Overall User Need |
|---|---|---|---|---|---|---|---|---|
| | | Completeness | Accuracy | Timeliness | Ease of Use | Cost | | |
| Change pricing on product category | Competitive prices | Low | Low | Low | Moderate | Expensive | Very important | High |
| | Market share trends | Moderate | Moderate | Low | Low | Expensive | Moderately important | Moderate |
| Set sales quotas | Market potential | Low | Low | Low | Low | Moderate | Very important | High |
| | Current and past sales | High | High | High | High | Low | Moderately important | Low |

*Add other decisions as appropriate.

**Table 22-4.** Example of how to set development priorities.

| Information Need* | Overall Need | Ease of Entry for Company | Barriers to Competitor Entry | Profit Potential | Risk | Recommended Development Priority |
|---|---|---|---|---|---|---|
| 1. Competitive prices (for pricing) | High | Difficult | Low | Low | High | Low |
| 2. Market potential (for sales quotas) | High | Moderate | High | High | Low to Moderate | High |

*Add other factors as appropriate.

be expected to require about six months to complete. This assumes that a competent market manager, with some familiarity of the target market, is assigned to this task on a full-time basis.

## Developing a New Information Service

The previous section describes a program by which a market manager can identify bona fide information needs that represent potential opportunities for new information services. With such opportunities identified, the next challenge is to design and develop a specific service that will respond to these customer needs. This is the task of the service planning function.

Service Design. Working with the market manager and drawing upon that manager's acquired understanding of companies in the target market, the service planning manager must first create an initial design for the proposed new information service. In doing this, six key factors should always be considered to help ensure achieving a sound service design. These factors are:

1. *End user*. Who will use the information, and how will it be used? Knowing this is essential to developing a service that meets the customer need.

2. *Editorial content*. What specific text or data will be provided by the service, and how will it be organized and displayed? Can this information be readily developed or acquired? Also, if economically and technically feasible, the organization of the data should be customized to meet the needs of each specific customer. For example, if the service is to report total industry demand for a product by geographical area, these areas should, ideally, be the same as each customer's sales territories.

3. *Frequency of update*. How rapidly does the usefulness of the information deteriorate? This will generally depend upon the rate of change of the situation to which the information pertains. The proposed service should provide updates of the information as frequently as necessary to properly support decision making by the user. This can range from continuous, real-time updating to daily, monthly, or annual updating.

4. *Delivery media*. What delivery media will meet the customer needs most cost-effectively? Information service providers have a wide array of media available today, including printed reports, looseleaf services, bound directories, diskettes, CD-ROM diskettes, and computerized on-line services. In choosing the media for a new service, an awareness of the extent to which the prospect universe is able to use information delivered on PC diskettes or via on-line computer is critical. If, for example, only a small percentage of prospects have personal computers with modems, then an on-line service is not likely to be the appropriate medium for distributing information to these prospects. In this instance, it may be necessary to provide the service via printed reports. Of course, it may still be desirable to offer the service on-line as well.

5. *Ease of use*. Is the information displayed in a convenient, easy-to-read format? Attractive layouts of text and data on printed pages and video screens

can contribute greatly to the success of the service. Also, for PC diskette and on-line services, the ease and speed with which a customer can search, retrieve, manipulate, and display information are critical to the success of the service. Moreover, where necessary, a computerized service should enable the user to easily combine internal company data with that provided by the service.

6. *Customer support.* What support services will be provided to customers? The scope and quality of these can have a significant effect on customer retention and renewal. This is especially true for services distributed via PC diskette or on-line. For such services, it is vital to provide adequate user training, easy-to-follow user manuals, and a toll-free telephone number that customers can call to obtain assistance in the use of the service.

Economic Feasibility and Market Testing.  With the initial design and specifications of the service complete, the next steps in the development process are (1) evaluating the economic feasibility of the service and (2) conducting a market test of a prototype or simulation of the service to help estimate market potential. In evaluating the economics of the service, the planning manager should develop cost estimates for the service at a low, moderate, and high level of sales. The major functions for which costs must typically be estimated include data acquisition, production (i.e., data entry, computer operations, systems development, and communications), editorial review, sales and marketing, and administration. These costs, together with the company's profit goals, are the determinants of the minimum price that must be charged for the service at each sales level. If these prices seem unduly high compared with the benefits of the service, either a lower cost design must be developed or the development of the proposed service should be dropped.

Assuming that the minimum prices that must be charged for the service appear reasonable, a prototype or simulation of the service should then be tested in the market. The main objectives of this test are twofold: (1) to confirm the appropriateness of the service design and (2) to assess the prospects' willingness to buy the service at various price levels, including the minimum prices established by the economic evaluation. In conducting this market test, it is essential to use a prototype or simulation that is as close as possible in appearance, format, and content to the actual service. The more accurately the prototype portrays the actual service, the more valid the results of the market test will be. In general, for a new service, this test should consist primarily of personal interviews that include a thorough demonstration of the service and its benefits.

With the results of the market test (assuming they are favorable), the planning manager makes additional changes to the service design as appropriate, establishes an initial pricing structure for the service, and updates the business plan preparatory to launching the service.

# Pricing Information Services

The factors that must be considered in setting the price of an information service are essentially the same as those for most other products and services. These are the demand for the service, the availability and prices of substitutes, the direct cost of producing the service, the pricing objective (e.g., market penetration versus market skimming), and the company's profit objectives. There are, however, three guidelines for pricing that are particularly pertinent to information services and that generally should be observed. These are discussed in the following sections, together with several special factors that should be considered in pricing on-line services.

## General Pricing Guidelines

First, the upper range of price for a new information service should always be based on the value of the perceived benefits of the service to the customer and not the cost to produce it. For example, if an information service providing sales leads might enable a user to earn an additional $100,000 of annual profit, a price of $5,000 or $10,000 a year for such a service may viewed as a good value. The incremental cost of providing the service, however, may be less than $1,000. This value-based approach applies to any information service used in making a decision. Here, the magnitude of the dollars involved in the decision and the potential improvement in the decision outcome, which might result from the use of the information, are key determinants of the value of the service. Of course, in spite of a high value, the price of an information service will still be limited by the availability and price of substitute services, or by the customer's self-development cost.

The second guideline that should generally be followed in pricing a new information service is to pursue a market penetration strategy rather than a market skimming strategy. Information services typically have high fixed costs and relatively low incremental costs per customer. By setting a lower price, more customers can be expected to buy the service. This results in greater market penetration and lower unit costs, which will deter potential competitors from entering the market. Moreover, if the demand for the service is elastic, as is often the case, the market penetration strategy will generate increased revenues and profits vis-à-vis a higher price.

A final point that should be considered in pricing an information service deals with the definition of a customer and the limitations upon the use of the information by the customer. Customers of an information service must be prohibited from reproducing, giving away, or reselling to others, either in print or machine-readable form, the information they purchase from the service. If this is not done, customers, in effect, can become competitors, and the revenue potential for the information service may be seriously eroded.

The definition of who is a customer (i.e., one who is entitled to receive and use the information provided by the service) can also affect the size of the potential market for the service. For example, a customer may be a single employee who is billed for the service, or all employees at a single location of the customer organization, or all employees at all locations of the organization. Admittedly, enforcement of these restrictions is often difficult in practice. Nevertheless, they should be spelled out clearly in the subscription agreement for the service. Because such agreements are legal contracts, you should seek legal counsel on this matter.

**Figure 22-2.** Price schedule for a leading on-line financial information service.

| | |
|---|---|
| Initial Subscription Fee | $ 29.95 |
| Annual Service Fee | $ 12.00 |
| Minimum Monthly Charge | None |
| Hourly Connect Charge | |
|     Prime Time (1200 baud) | $165.60 |
|     Nonprime Time (1200 baud) | $105.60 |
| Hourly Communications Charge | Included in connect charge |
| Special Charges per Document | |
|     for Selected Databases | $2.00–$85.00 |

*Pricing On-Line Services*

On-line information services derive essentially all of their revenue from sub-scribers who are active users. Inactive subscribers receive little or no value from the service and are not likely to continue as subscribers. Thus, the pricing structure for an on-line service should be geared to acquiring new subscribers and encouraging them to become active users of the service.

With this in mind, as well as the pricing guidelines outlined earlier, the pricing structure for an on-line service should, ideally, charge a user only for value received. This means that period charges unrelated to usage of the service should be kept to a minimum. Also, the level of price should be set to achieve maximum market penetration consistent with the service's costs and profit goals. Further, in addition to making it easy for a prospect to decide to subscribe to the service, the pricing structure should encourage usage. A key means of doing this is to provide new subscribers, at little or no charge, thorough training and support in the use of the system via seminars, on-line tutorials, user manuals, and an 800 telephone number for assistance. These support services enable the subscriber to use the service more effectively and efficiently and thereby increase its value.

The key charges for a leading on-line financial information service are shown in Figure 22-2. This pricing structure is typical of most on-line services. As shown in this figure, there are special additional charges for accessing certain databases in the system. This is an effective means of obtaining additional revenue from selected databases that provide greater value to the subscriber.

## Selling Information Services

Most information services have three characteristics in common that should be considered in developing a sales approach. First, information services generally involve an ongoing service and are sold on a subscription basis. Second, given the business-to-business nature of most information services, the prospect universe for such services is usually identifiable and reachable. Finally, because the service is information, it can readily be described and illustrated in words and pictures.

The first of these characteristics means that renewing the subscriptions of existing customers represents a significant revenue opportunity in addition to acquiring new customers. The next two characteristics indicate that information services lend themselves well to direct marketing methods, and these should be employed to the maximum extent. Guidelines for selling to acquire new customers and for winning renewals from existing customers are reviewed in the following sections.

## Acquiring New Customers

In developing plans for selling to new customers, information services companies should evaluate the cost-effectiveness of both personal selling and direct marketing. Depending upon the scope of the company's line of services, the complexity of the services, and the prices of the services, one of these sales approaches will prove to be more cost-effective for a given service. Typically, personal selling is difficult to justify economically if the dollar unit of sale is less than $10,000 to $15,000 per year. Although a number of information services involve units of sale ranging well in excess of $20,000 annually, most services have prices under $5,000 per year. Hence, direct marketing will be the preferred selling method in a majority of cases.

Although the specifics of any direct marketing program will depend upon the services to be sold and the nature of the prospect universe, there are three guidelines that should be observed in most situations. These are:

1. In planning a direct marketing program, at least three approaches should be evaluated: direct mail, direct mail combined with telephone follow-up, and direct response advertising in appropriate trade journals. Direct mail will typically be most cost-effective for lower-priced services that can be clearly and convincingly described in print. Direct mail followed by a telephone call will generally be best for higher-priced services and for services that are more complex and require greater explanation. Trade journal advertising, depending upon the service, may be used to generate either sales or requests for additional information that can serve as qualified leads for telephone selling or personal selling.

2. The copy in ads and mailing pieces must clearly explain what the service is, what its benefits are, and how the information should be used. In addition, the overall appearance of an ad or mailing piece should convey an image of authoritativeness and reliability. Such an image will enhance the perceived quality of the service.

3. The fulfillment operation should perform flawlessly, whether responding to an inquiry requesting additional information or delivering the service to a new customer. Prompt and efficient performance here can significantly enhance customer satisfaction and reinforce a decision to purchase the service.

*Winning Renewal Business*

Renewing the subscriptions of existing customers is often the most important source of revenue for an information service provider. For some services, renewal rates can range as high as 60 to 90 percent of the customer base. Because the cost of renewing an existing customer is significantly less than that required to acquire a new customer, a high level of renewal can dramatically reduce the overall cost of revenue development.

To achieve the highest possible renewal rates, information services companies must, prior to renewal time, pay particular attention to the quality of their performance in three areas. First, the core service must "deliver" in terms of serving customer needs; that is, the perceived benefits of the service must meet the customer's expectations. Second, the fulfillment operation must continue to provide prompt and efficient delivery of the service. Finally, customer inquiries and complaints should be handled courteously and promptly by a well-trained customer service staff. Through the use of a toll-free telephone number that customers can call for assistance, this staff is the company's primary contact with customers during the subscription period. Hence, excellent performance here can greatly enhance the value of the service in the eyes of customers and increase their willingness to renew subscriptions.

The selling of subscription renewals to existing customers should be initiated at least two to three months prior to the end of a customer's subscription period. Either direct mail or telephone selling may be used to solicit renewals. Keep in mind, however, that the prospects are current customers. Consequently, the economics of telemarketing will be much more favorable here than when soliciting new customers.

An excellent strategy in selling subscription renewals is to offer the renewal at a discount. Such discounts may range from 5 to 15 percent off what a new subscriber would be charged, thus providing existing customers with an attractive incentive to renew. The revenue loss resulting from these discounts can usually be totally offset by savings in new customer acquisition costs.

The responsibility for selling subscription renewals, together with that for acquiring new customers, should generally be assigned to the sales organization. Customer service should not be directly involved in the selling process because providing service typically requires an orientation very different from that of selling. However, the customer service staff must work closely with the sales organization and should maintain a database of key information on customers, which will be helpful to the sales organization in selling renewals.

# The Outlook for Information Services

The prospects for information services companies are exceptionally promising. Opportunities for new and expanded information services will abound in the 1990s as the markets for information become more global and businesses, professionals, governments, and consumers increasingly recognize the strategic value of information. At the same time, advances in information technology will continue to yield more powerful and easier-to-use information processing capabilities at lower cost. This will increase productivity and create new opportunities for both users and providers of information.

The coming decade will also bring unprecedented challenges to most information services companies because of rapidly changing markets and intensifying competition. Those companies that stay in close touch with their customers and can move quickly to adapt and expand their service offerings to meet evolving customer needs will be the most successful.

## Summary

Companies that provide information services sell their services primarily to businesses, professionals, and government units. They derive essentially all of their revenue from the users of information, not from advertisers.

Users of information services generally buy such services to assist them in making specific decisions. Hence, in order to develop new or enhanced information services, information providers must have an in-depth understanding of the customer's decision-making process and how information can be used to improve the quality of decision making. Guidelines for identifying new information service opportunities are presented together with suggested approaches for pricing and selling information services.

## Notes

1. John Naisbitt, *Megatrends: Ten New Directions Transforming Our Lives* (New York: Warner Books, 1982).
2. This definition is essentially the same as that used by the Information Industry Association in its report "The Business of Information 1983," prepared by A. C. Nielsen Company.

\* \* \* \*

*Fred O. Jensen* *is president of Jensen Associates, a management consulting company specializing in strategic and marketing planning for organizations in the service sector. He is also professor of management and head of the department of management at Stevens Institute of Technology. Previously he served as vice president of planning and development at McGraw-Hill Information Systems Company, a major publisher and provider of information services.*

# 23

# Telecommunications

Rusty Campos
Mary Cain

The AT&T divestiture changed the fundamental way of doing business for the largest and arguably the most successful corporation in the world. The federal order known as the Modified Final Judgment (MFJ) broke up the Bell System in 1984 by separating seven regional holding companies or "Baby Bells" from AT&T. Because the MFJ stated primarily what AT&T and the Baby Bells could not do, each of these eight multibillion-dollar companies had to reestablish what businesses they were in and—within the constraints of regulation, tradition, and the continued operation of the telephone network—decide how to operate these businesses.

The telecommunications industry has seen unparalleled rates of change both in regulation and in technology. When the airline industry was deregulated, airlines weren't making the change from propellers to jets simultaneously. In telecommunications, changes in technology and business needs are revolutionizing the industry as much as the changes in regulation.

The links between computers and communications are much closer than before. Growing numbers of businesses are connecting computers inside their companies by building their own private voice and data networks. An entire industry is developing around the technological requirements of these private networks. The preference for companies to buy and operate their own networks indicates that the telecommunications industry is not meeting all their needs.

This chapter focuses on marketing issues in this highly regulated industry. Regulation has the power to distract companies from their customers. The focus is on the marketing issues that endure despite regulatory constraints: defining your business, identifying competitors, keeping your customers, and managing your culture.

## Define the Business

Before the 1980s, everyone knew that the "telephone company" was the only place to go for telephone service. For customers, divestiture meant that services had been unbundled, and they needed several suppliers to do what had been done by AT&T. Divestiture meant that everyone in the telecommunications industry had to look carefully at how AT&T and the Baby Bells would define their businesses before examining their own businesses.

## Service Means Relationships

The word *service* has several meanings within the telecommunications industry. In most cases, *service* is used to mean dial tone, or delivering uninterrupted telephone service to paying customers. *Service* now refers to the functionality sold to customers, such as call waiting or 56 kilobit data channels. These services are often called *products*.

To define a business, the appropriate meaning of *service* is this:

### *Everything you do for, with, and to your customers*

In defining a business, the first two meanings of service are limiting. It is myopic to say you are in the business of delivering dial tone or providing products, but this is occasionally the inside-out perception of regulated companies: Here is our network, and this is how you use it.

The third meaning of *service* leads to a useful business definition. A telecommunications service business should:

### *Help customers be more effective through telecommunications*

This definition is broad enough to apply to residential and business customers. More important, it defines the underlying basis for the customer-supplier relationship: a mutual interest in accomplishing the customer's objectives.

## Making Customers Effective

A rationale for a service business is to make its customers more effective in ways that are meaningful to them. This includes not just the service itself, but also acquiring the service and keeping it functioning in a productive way for the customer. Delivering service effectiveness includes helping the customer order it, maintaining the continuity of service, and changing the service when the customer needs change.

A service business must meet different criteria for effectiveness by knowing how businesses and consumers measure it. Effectiveness means different things to different customers. Businesses may find their success in handling large quantities of telephone orders, in timely negotiations for the best price on materials, or in coordinating several suppliers to meet high-quality standards.

Customer effectiveness is one of several themes that can guide a business definition. Two other examples are low-cost provider and high-quality niche provider. These themes lead to substantially different business definitions that have good potential for success.

## Customer Needs Lead to Segments

Customer groups that differ in their effectiveness goals should be handled differently. How you define the groups reflects the way you want to do business with them. Customers with similar needs should be in a group that is handled by employees who know those needs and how to meet them.

Industry classifications are a common basis for segments, but they may not reflect underlying telecommunications needs. Companies in the same industry may use different telecommunications strategies to achieve advantage. A few differences in telecommunications applications can establish unique competitive advantage. When telecommunications can provide superior inventory control, service allocation, or cash management, the impact on profits can be substantial.

These unique applications can be profitable for both parties. Although the applications may seem unique within an industry, good marketing can identify similar opportunities in other industries. Establishing your market segments prepares you to identify these opportunities.

Successful segmentation must go beyond a cursory look at customer needs. Customers cannot place themselves in your segmentation scheme, nor can customers always articulate their needs. Systematic market research is essential to overcome the predisposition to the ''obvious'' segmentation.

## Identify Needs-Based Segments

Segmentation requires that you first identify customer needs, then group customers according to the needs they share. How do you go about understanding customer needs? The four-step process is first to listen, then analyze what you heard, tell the customer what you heard, and finally listen again. In this way, you hear what customers say and verify what they mean. The critical step is to put customer needs in your own words, then see if customers believe you have captured their meaning.

The next step in segmentation is to group customers with common needs into segments. Even with only a few sets of needs, there is an immense number of possible groups. You can try different groupings yourself or use statistical clustering rules to produce groupings. You know that you have a good set of segments when two criteria are met:

1. You can make an educated guess about which of these segments will include a new customer.
2. You can visualize the different business problems and the solutions you would offer to each segment.

If you can't provide a solution to customers in a segment, this segment may not be part of your business definition. If you are sure this segment is included in your definition, you may have found a good target for development.

Can you do your own market research using this approach? Consultants find it easier to be objective than do people inside the company. Objectivity is a matter of perspective, not a bias or character flaw. Your job is to view situations based on the interests and objectives of your company, and it's difficult to change your perspective. If you find yourself thinking that your customers don't understand you, then a consultant can bring you a fresh perspective on understanding your customers.

*Technology and Needs Interact*

Telecommunications services are valuable in helping businesses meet their customers' needs. The role of technology in helping to determine business needs is a two-way street. Technology can fill communications needs, through voice mail or smart PBXs (privately owned, computerized telephone switching equipment). It is also true that the use of technology can create the need for telecommunications services. For example, faxes (or facsimile machines) create needs for higher-quality lines and for more lines dedicated to the faxes, but the technology doesn't justify itself. It's the fundamental business need that has to be met, and faxes appear to be meeting this need at present.

Other technologies may replace the fax and its accompanying telecommunications needs. Companies that understand the underlying business needs are prepared for the telecommunications requirements that will follow the new technology.

## Identify Your Competition

The Bell companies have been slow to identify their competitors, partly because the Baby Bells are still defining their businesses and partly because they are still denying serious competitive threats to their local telephone business. Current competitors and potential rivals are very much aware of how they can compete with the old monopoly companies and are making significant inroads.

One of the difficulties in identifying competition is that customers don't always take telecommunications problems to telecommunications companies. Computer companies that build data networks often face telecommunications problems. How computer companies solve the problem depends on their vested interests in the solution. In any case, the telecommunications company has lost control over the customers.

*Profits Are Vulnerable*

Relatively small companies are chipping away at the most profitable and vulnerable pieces of the business. Some key examples of niche suppliers are:

• Alternative operator services (AOSs) are hired by hotels to handle long-distance calls placed by their guests. The AOS resells the long-distance service and splits the profit with the hotel.

• Systems integrators are companies adept at taking dissimilar systems and making them work together. They pick up where telecommunications companies leave off, building complete systems of computers, phones, PBXs, and myriad other devices.

• Companies ranging in size from IBM and Honeywell to the "ma and pa" shop in the local shopping mall are entering into competition for "smart buildings." They can provide all the wiring for a given building or area (campus, office complexes, hospitals, and so on) so that a single vendor can handle an array of services, including telephone, electronics for heating and air-conditioning systems, computer, and security systems—services that make the building "smart."

Growing numbers of small companies are trying to capitalize on the tremendous changes occurring in the industry. Some resemble the numerous small computer companies that sprang up (and often quickly died) before the computer industry shakeout.

Another threat to the telecommunications companies is the trend for large businesses to self-provide—that is, to build their own telecommunications networks—in hopes of obtaining better service, better integrated systems, lower costs, or other advantages. Most of these companies begin with the idea of providing for their own needs, but often start new businesses by selling their excess capacity to other companies, thereby competing with the phone companies. Companies as diverse as Merrill Lynch and Boeing have entered the telecommunications business. The phone companies lose to companies that self-provide and also to companies that buy from self-providers.

## Recognize Global Competition

The U.S. telecommunications industry has yet to recognize its greatest potential threat—the companies outside its borders that have learned to listen to customers. Some telecommunications companies are moving into international ventures from their traditional domestic markets at the risk of ignoring foreign competition in the United States.

Several European and Japanese companies can provide formidable competition to domestic telecommunications companies. For example, British Telecom is upgrading its network to compete more effectively with AT&T for international business from the United States. Other international companies are using their private networks to compete with domestic companies. Employees of Honda Ltd. can use Honda's private network to check parts inventories throughout the United States and Japan.

## Dealing With Partial Deregulation

No discussion of the telecommunications industry is complete without some mention of the effects of regulation. The Baby Bells want to compete on what they consider to be a "level playing field," with the same freedoms and restrictions as their peers. The consequences of the present state of regulatory affairs will not be fully known for years to come.

Regulation prevents the Baby Bells from delivering complete solutions to customers' business problems. For example, data systems solutions cannot be provided if they cross LATA (local access transport area) boundaries. Regulation restricts Baby Bells from manufacturing or providing many products and services outside of their geographic territories. Another result of regulation is a complex set of pricing schemes throughout the industry. Until these restrictions are lifted, the industry will continue to operate in a partially free marketplace, with consumers' dollars carrying less influence than they would in a purely competitive environment.

## How to Keep Customers

It is now common to claim that it's cheaper to keep a customer than to find a new one and that it's even easier to keep a satisfied customer. The question is how to keep customers satisfied, and the answers differ for each customer segment.

The key to finding the answers is to make systematic measurements of service quality. Although this has all the appeal of a dental examination, it also has one of the benefits: You get to keep what's being examined.

Satisfying customers depends on several factors: their needs, their expectations about your filling those needs, and their perceptions of your service performance. Measuring customer satisfaction isn't enough to diagnose problems—you have to know what's important to customer segments and make improvements where they will count the most.

Many companies have conducted customer research to measure service satisfaction and used those results to determine bonus levels for employees. In many cases, customers are simply asked whether or not they are satisfied with the service. However, customer expressions of satisfaction don't tell the whole story. Satisfaction has a broad range of connotations, and customers who claim to be satisfied have not shared the same service experiences. Some customers relate tales of prolonged difficulties, then finally admit that they are satisfied—that is, that their expectations have been lowered to the point where they are no longer disappointed.

For example, late one afternoon, I called the customer sales and service department of my local exchange carrier to change one of my service options. I got a recording saying my call would be answered soon, then music. I put the call over my speakerphone so I could work while I waited. After about five minutes, the music stopped. Thinking that my speakerphone had somehow disconnected me, I dialed the number again. This time I got a recording saying that office hours were eight to five; looking at my watch, I saw that it was one minute after five.

Valid expectations were met—the office did not close early—and my request was handled the next day. The question is whether this practice leads to satisfied customers who, given a choice, would continue to do business with this carrier.

### What to Measure in Service Quality

First, customers need to express their priorities about a comprehensive set of needs that could apply to them. Next, they should say how well your company fills those needs. As a check on the competition, it is worthwhile to ask customers how they feel (or know) your competitors perform in meeting these needs.

These measurements lead to a valuable set of information about product development, competitive threats, and other marketing information. The most critical information is this:

**For each segment, which needs are important, and how do customers feel you are meeting those needs?**

This information provides a check on your customer assets, which assesses the health of your business and helps you set priorities in dealing with the most critical problems.

### How to Interpret Service Quality Data

Valid feedback on service quality must measure customer expectations and the degree to which they have been fulfilled. Average scores are not very useful in these situations, so it's important to know the percentages of people whose expectations were met or exceeded. For those whose expectations have not been met, it's critical to measure which service elements have fallen short. Answers to open-ended questions can be insightful, eloquent, and persuasive, but they can also detract from the real issues. Quantitative measures, observed over time, provide a sound look at how systems, incentives, and practices can be improved.

### Developing Value in Services

If you develop your understanding of customer needs, you can provide improved value in two ways. First, you can identify service elements that better meet communications needs. As an example, remote activation of call forwarding is important for a customer who needs to turn on his or her telephone answering service while at an unexpected location away from the office—for example, the operator of an appliance repair business.

Second, you can better aggregate services so the whole has more value than the sum of its parts. For example, working parents can be offered a package that includes:

- Call waiting so parents can get through when the children are talking to friends
- Speed dialing so work and emergency numbers are easy for children to use
- Message service so parents can record instructions for children arriving home after school

This group of features can be sold as a working-parent package with videotape instructions on how to use it, labels so the children can use speed dialing, and a hot-line number for help with the service for both children and parents.

### Demonstrate Value in Services

Telecommunications services provide value by helping businesses serve their customers, reduce costs, and improve quality. Marketers need persuasive measures of productivity to communicate the benefits of telecommunications services. For example, a fax can save up to twenty-four hours compared to Federal Express, but a skeptic might question the value of the savings.

The key marketing issue is to translate communications benefits into productivity improvement that justifies the investment of time and money.

## Manage the Corporate Culture

One of the key challenges facing the telecommunications industry today is the need to build on the strengths of the past and yet free up a company's creative capabilities. Although corporate culture is not totally within the control of a corporation's management, it can be nurtured to produce several critical elements in great demand in telecommunications today: systematic planning, a new definition of service, and innovation.

### The Need for Planning

Because of the rapid pace of change in telecommunications since divestiture, many companies have been forced to recognize the need for systematic planning. Planning starts with a clear picture of who your customers are, what your company provides them, and what your company wants to achieve for its stockholders and employees. As in any other industry, planning includes definitions of goals and objectives established by top management. It continues with detailed plans for operational units, requirements for market research, new product development, technology deployment, advertising, and all other aspects of the business. The plans must then be integrated to ensure compatible strategies that can be implemented across operating units for both the short and long range.

What makes telecommunications different is that these skills are scarce in this industry. Most of the experience of telecommunications managers comes from a regulated and operational environment, as opposed to one that is competitive and strategic. The most successful telecommunications companies will be those that break out of old molds, learn to set goals based on future needs instead of past results, and meet those needs through innovation and risk taking.

### The New Meaning of Service

As noted previously, the term *service* can have several interpretations. Part of the cultural change centers around redefining service quality from electronic quality (availability of circuits and sound transmission) to meeting customer needs and expectations. Although technical measurements are necessary, they are not sufficient to produce satisfied customers.

Telecommunications companies have begun to redefine service quality. In addition to traditional technical measurements, they are taking a customer perspective. Although companies must continue to provide high-quality technology, they must do so within the parameters of the customer's needs and expectations. Increasingly these needs are for packaged services, greater flexibility in pricing, and a more complete understanding of the customer's problem.

### Risk Plus Innovation

Another massive shift that needs to occur is in the way telecommunications companies view risk. Before divestiture, it was considered good business to avoid risk. Now it is preferable to maintain a portfolio of projects that range from high to low risk.

Much of the focus of Baby Bells' strategies has been to capitalize on their networks as investments that they can leverage to great advantage. Newer entrants, such as MCI and US Sprint, are building networks with the goal of providing such leverage over the long term. Although this strategy of leveraging the network is valuable, you must look outside the network for additional value to offer customers.

One example is to develop a related technology, such as network management systems, to sell in situations that don't necessarily relate to the public switched network. By focusing too closely on what has been a valuable and enormous investment, you may press up opportunities outside that investment that may pave the way to the future.

With the network as a base of investment, risk was unwise. In the past, risk was to be avoided in the regulated environment. Today, with the onset of competition, risk and reward go hand in hand. Assessing acceptable levels of risk requires systematic, ongoing market research and, more important, a recognition that risk is essential to success.

Because risk cannot be avoided, the objective is to manage it. Once risk management is the issue, it becomes easier to encourage innovation and creativity in a work force that has not always been rewarded for these behaviors.

To manage risk you must first separate the outcome of a project from the likelihood of achieving that outcome. As an example, put your projects in a $3 \times 3$ matrix, with one dimension representing risk as the likelihood that a project might be successful. Use three categories of risk: high, moderate, and low probabilities of project success. The other dimension measures the outcome of the project as the size of the anticipated profit if the project is a success: high, moderate, or low, based on your company's expectations.

Good risk management indicates that projects should be distributed among the nine cells and not only in the high-reward, low-risk categories. Separating risk from reward clarifies the distinction between the merits of the solution and its potential profitability. Placing projects in a portfolio of risk and reward allows you to refine the ways you compare projects and monitor their progress.

## Summary

Divestiture has redefined the telecommunications industry. To succeed, a business must look carefully at how it serves its customers, then examine how it makes its customers more effective. Identifying segments based on needs is the fundamental step toward understanding and serving customers.

Once you have defined your business, you can identify and guard against competitive threats. Niche suppliers and self-providers can rival international competition in their threats to profits.

Keeping your customers depends on meeting or exceeding their expectations for value. A systematic program of measuring service quality can help you set priorities for current services and service development efforts.

Since divestiture, telecommunications marketing requires a balance between keeping the best parts of the old culture while energizing the new culture with a customer orientation, a balanced approach to risk, and a willingness to meet the twin challenges of changing technology and more demanding customers.

*    *    *    *

*Rusty Campos, Ph.D., serves as vice president, research, for Sundel Research, Inc. He was formerly president of Campos Research and Analysis, a market research and consulting firm specializing in telecommunications products and services for businesses and consumers. Prior to that, he was director of strategic market research and analysis at U S WEST, Inc., a regional holding company that owns a number of telecommunications and diversified companies.*

*Mary Cain is director of competitive analysis and the corporate library within the U S WEST strategic marketing group. While at U S WEST and one of its predecessor companies, Ms. Cain has been responsible for a variety of marketing, human resources, and planning functions. Her previous experience encompasses health services, human resources training and development, and consulting.*

# 24 _____

# Transportation

Craig E. Cina

During the last decade, the transportation industry has experienced unsettling change. The era of government regulation has given way to a new era of deregulation, bringing with it marketing challenges that are unfamiliar to most transportation professionals. The only constant in today's dynamic transportation environment is change, and for strategically oriented companies, change presents a continuous flow of marketing opportunities. Transportation companies have a unique opportunity to establish a competitive advantage, not just settle for parity as they had to in yesterday's regulated environment.

This chapter presents a blueprint for taking advantage of an unsettled marketplace. It shows how to take advantage of change through strategic thinking, how to keep close to the customer, and how to turn knowledge of the customer's buying motives into lucrative results. Although this chapter focuses on the transportation industry, the suggested course of action is also pertinent to other service industries as well—whether consumer or business-to-business.

The transportation executive will gain several important benefits from reading this chapter. The reader will:

- Have a clear understanding of how to use strategic thinking for uncovering the key factors of success in his or her industry.
- Learn how to use the key factors of success for establishing a competitive advantage.
- Know how to get closer to the customer and to use this familiarity to an advantage.
- Learn how to translate visions into profitable realities.

Quite simply, the chapter will show how companies become leaders through insightful strategic and market planning.

## Transportation Services in Transition

During the late 1970s and early 1980s, the federal government began dismantling the complex system of air, rail, and motor carrier regulation. The era of deregulation legislated by the Airline Deregulation Act of 1978, the Staggers Rail Act of 1980, and the Motor Carrier Regulatory Reform and Modernization Act of 1980 created uncertainty within the transportation industry and presented new, unfamiliar marketing challenges. Since deregulation, the transportation industry has weathered more change than in any other decade. The transition from a strictly regulated industry to one where companies can haul and charge virtually whatever they want has been troublesome for many transportation service providers.

## What Pre-Deregulation Was Like

Before deregulation of the transportation industry took effect, the transportation world was an idyllic place with a virtual guarantee of income for a limited number of companies that provided their constituencies with a limited number of services at top rates. Regulation protected inefficient operations and rewarded high-cost companies with regular rate increases. There was no need for marketing prowess in this business environment. Because prices and routes were fixed, the only thing transportation companies had to sell was service performance and promotional and giveaway items. However, transportation companies didn't concern themselves with service performance because competition was restricted to specified geographic territories. As a result, consumers were paying too much for too little service. But then, deregulation arrived with a vengeance—radically changing the once stable transportation industry.

## What Happened After Deregulation

The great wave of deregulation during the late 1970s and early 1980s was predicated on the belief that deregulation would spur competition, enhance productivity, and reduce prices. And that belief came true. Transportation companies are now free to go where they want and charge what they want. However, these newfound freedoms created havoc within the transportation industry. Transportation companies just didn't command the marketing prowess necessary to cope in a truly competitive marketplace. As evidence to this fact, here's what has happened since deregulation.

  • Transportation companies first tried to maintain a market presence by undercutting each others' rates. As a result, prices plunged as companies vied for market share. Pricing was the tool transportation companies turned to because of its simple execution and instant but short-lived paybacks. Overall, the nation's freight bill as a percent of GNP dropped from 7.8 percent in 1980 to 6.5 percent in 1987—a direct reflection of the intense price competition occurring across all transportation modes.[1]

More specifically, airline fares, when adjusted for inflation, have declined 20 percent since deregulation in 1978, and only 10 percent of their customers are now flying on a nondiscounted fare. Trucking rates have also fallen sharply. Today's discounts on many classes of freight are routinely 30 percent or more, and on others, they go much deeper. In like fashion, the railroads' revenue per ton-mile, when adjusted for inflation, dropped from 2.61 cents per ton-mile in 1979 to 1.98 in 1987—a decline of almost 25 percent. The results are clear: Deregulation has produced lower prices for customers, prices at which many marginal transportation companies could not survive.

Deregulation has spurred a large increase of entrants into the transportation industry, but at the same time has created a stronger control of freight (or passengers) by the top-tier carriers. For instance, since deregulation, 17,000 new companies have entered the trucking industry, whereas 6,500 have failed. However, the top twelve motor carriers accounted for 59 percent of the 1987 trucking market, up from 45 percent in 1978. Similarly, more than 120 scheduled airlines (excluding commuters) have entered the market since 1978, whereas more than forty have exited. Nevertheless, the five largest airlines control about 70 percent of passenger traffic today, versus 60 percent a decade ago.[2]

Conversely, due to high capital requirements for entry, deregulation fueled a major consolidation in the rail sector. Mergers have reduced the ranks of large rail-freight carriers from thirteen in 1978 to six huge systems that carry 86 percent of the railed freight. Furthermore, rail carriers took advantage of deregulation by purchasing truck lines. For example, Union Pacific acquired Overnite, Norfolk Southern purchased North American Van Lines, and Burlington Northern has purchased six trucking companies.

What this all means is that deregulation created a flood of new entrants, mergers, and acquisitions. So although the smaller upstarts captured small segments of the business, the larger, well-heeled companies bolstered their positions through mergers, acquisitions, and facility expansion. The bottom line is that the competitive environment has intensified, and with it, a need has emerged for professionals who can market transportation services.

## How Other Forces Are Shaping Transportation Services

Innovation and creativity are becoming part of the transportation services landscape. Stodgy, operations-driven companies are slowly giving way to more market-driven approaches. Never before has the shipper had so many options from which to choose. If shippers need time-sensitive overnight delivery, they can get it with a high degree of reliability. How about delivery to foreign nations? The shipper can choose from a variety of options, including all air, land-ship-land, or a whole host of other combinations. Companies, realizing shippers' needs range from expedited and time-definite to more economical service, are increasingly offering services to meet those needs.

Moreover, shippers desire to employ transportation companies that can service all their shipping needs—commonly referred to as one-stop shopping. No company has been able to offer its customers true one-stop shopping service, but several companies such as UPS, Federal Express, and CSX are moving in that direction. The challenge is to integrate all the transportation logistics under one roof so that the customer doesn't have to deal with several different entities within the same transportation company—a challenge that has proved formidable.

Rising customer expectations is an emerging trend that is negating much of the transportation industry's progress. No longer will customers settle for less than satisfactory service. They are finding several small "niche" companies that can serve their special needs more effectively than larger transportation organizations. In addition, just-in-time, service quality, and customer satisfaction have all been popular topics in transportation journals—demonstrating to shippers that there is a better way. Opportunistic companies will recognize this trend and offer services that meet these higher expectations.

### Why Services Marketing's Importance Is Growing

Companies must adapt to change or face the inevitability of failure. Unfortunately, at a time when transportation companies need to strengthen their service, service quality has been less than satisfactory. The "war stories" of service failures are all too common. Flight delays, rude drivers, and freight claims are just a few of the problems that plague the customer—wasting precious time and money. For instance, consumer complaints with the airline industry rose from 23,609 in 1978 to 44,845 in 1987. Although no one expects transportation service always to be perfect, steps must be taken to improve the quality of service or face customer dissatisfaction and, ultimately, a loss of customers.[3]

This means that transportation companies must shift from a traditionally operations-driven orientation to a more market-driven one. Thus, transportation service organizations must gain a firm grasp on how to plan and market their services more effectively. The next sections present a blueprint on how transportation companies can become better service providers.

# How to Take Advantage of Change

A changing marketplace presents transportation service companies with both opportunities and challenges. The key determinant of a transportation company's success or failure will be the ability to establish a well-conceived strategic vision to guide its decision making. The strategic vision will provide the company with a key element differentiating it from the competition. Transportation executives need to understand the important trends shaping the transportation environment and the strategic responses necessary to gain a competitive advantage.

Unfortunately, the majority of transportation service providers seems to have lost sight of, or even worse, fails to recognize the value of strategic thinking—the understanding of where a company is today and a vision of what management wants the organization to become in the future. A rowboat race is a fitting analogy to understanding what is meant by strategy and execution. The navigator begins by setting the course for a successful race (the strategy). The navigator's sense of direction is critical because if the rowboat strays off course, it will miss the target and lose the race. Equally important are the people manning the oars. If they do not row synchronously (execution), the boat will move along slowly and be overtaken by more efficient crews. Thus, strategy and execution must work in unison.

Theodore Levitt, renowned marketing professor from Harvard University, wrote a classic article entitled "Marketing Myopia," in which he stated that railroads were "myopic" because they defined their business improperly (i.e.,

"We're in the railroad business" instead of "We're in the transportation business"). As a result of this narrow focus, the railroads lost market share to other forms of transportation. That narrow business focus is still prevalent in today's transportation industry.[4]

The transportation industry's mind-set has been on the "numbers," which means focusing on past financial and operating statistics. This misdirected focus leads to a perpetuation of the status quo. Transportation executives need to study the competition, the customer, and their own corporations and to capitalize on marketplace opportunities with a well-conceived game plan—leading with their strengths and exploiting their competitors' weaknesses.

## How to Facilitate Change

Strategic thinking is a very disciplined process. It relies on intuition and creativity and often calls for a departure from the status quo. This does not imply that the strategist rejects rational analysis; rather, he or she uses it to stimulate the creative process—a process that often calls for change. This disruption of the status quo is at the heart of the issue. Leading companies accept it as a normal outcome of strategic thinking, and it is a natural part of their way of doing business. Conversely, too many transportation companies take comfort in maintaining the status quo and relying on the "numbers" to guide their course of action. This narrow focus makes these companies vulnerable to change and competitors with new customer-satisfying approaches.

Most of today's transportation organizations are not organized for innovation and change. They reward their people for "doing things right" as opposed to "doing the right things," which is a necessary ingredient of managed change. Strategists who advocate a departure from the status quo may find themselves at odds with traditional management philosophy. Success is often tied closely to the manager's willingness to perpetuate past practices. The culture of most companies rewards logic and rationality; hence, analysts, rather than the forward thinkers, tend to get attention. The bottom-line outcome is that longer-term strategic thinking takes a backseat to short-term concerns—resulting in a loss of vision and sense of purpose. Management readily directs attention to answering why sales were off by 2 percent last quarter, but determining if or how their present service offering will still be viable over the next five to ten years may be shelved for a rainy day.

## How to Gain the Vision

Transportation companies can increase their ability to think strategically—a competitive weapon that has proved formidable to many "by the numbers" companies. Here's how it is done:

• First, strategic thinking and strategy formulation are within the domain of top management. The CEO or president should begin by establishing a formal strategic planning process. This does not necessarily mean hiring more staff or adding new procedures. What it does mean, however, is taking the time to think about the competition, the customer, and the company's own resources in a holistic fashion. If the company is uncertain how to get started, it may wish to seek the expertise of a reputable strategic planner.

- Second, the company must gain knowledge of:

  The competitive environment and how the company is positioned relative to the competition
  The driving forces of change in the marketplace from both a customer's and an industry perspective
  How the company's resources compare with those of the competition
  What the customer's buying motives are

From this analysis, the company must determine what the key factors for success are in the industry. This analysis will provide the basis of the strategic planning process but will not determine it.

- Third, after considering the market's driving forces and key factors for success, top management should then set forth a strategy to guide the future direction, decision making, and tactics of the corporation—the outcome of which should be a sustainable advantage over the competition. The strategy should address three simple questions:

  1. Where are we now? (answered in the second step)
  2. Where are we going? (mission statement/strategy)
  3. How are we going to get there? (tactics)

Executives must remember to keep their rational thinking (what is) and creative thinking (what could be) in balance.

Here are a few tips to make sure your strategy is on target:

1. If you had to read it twice to get the message, that's once too many. For example, instead of saying, "Our organization will stress the importance of being customer-driven by reinforcing the critical nature of our customer-employee encounters," why not say, "We are committed to making every one of our customer contacts count"? Keep the strategy simple.
2. If your strategy already describes a competitor or can readily be adopted by a competitor, it will be of little lasting value. The strategy must be "different" from the competition in some meaningful way and provide the company with a competitive mental angle in customers' minds.
3. The strategy must be actionable.

- Finally, the strategy must be put into action. The CEO or president must convey its importance to the long-term success of the company. The CEO's demonstrated commitment to the strategic plan will speak louder than just words. Many CEOs form an implementation task force to ensure that the strategy's intent is realized. The more people who are involved in the process from its conception, the more likely that the strategy will be executed successfully.

### What's the Benefit?

Strategic thinking has the power to produce a sustainable competitive advantage in almost every marketplace. It does this by spawning ideas that go beyond traditional analysis and by producing strategies that put the company back in control of its destiny. Even though strategic thinking can't guarantee a company's success, it can give the company a better-than-even chance for future competitive viability in this world of day-to-day business practice.

## How to Keep Close to the Customer

One of the most important management responsibilities that is being ignored in today's business world is staying close to the customer to satisfy his or her needs and to anticipate future wants. Strategic planning and thinking are not enough. To succeed, products and services must meet a customer need, and the organization must be flexible enough to adapt as the marketplace changes. That means a company's personnel must constantly interact with customers through observing, listening, and talking. As Yogi Berra claimed, you can see a lot by observing. Thus, keeping close to the customer complements the strategic planning process and helps ensure that longer-term thinking is consistent with shorter-term actions.

After thorough research, Tom Peters and Robert Waterman, authors of *In Search of Excellence,* discovered that excellent companies really are close to their customers. Although other companies talk about it, the excellent companies do it. Unfortunately, the transportation industry does not bring to mind many companies that are touted as being close to the customer—*In Search of Excellence* mentioned only American Airlines and Delta Air Lines.[5] Federal Express has also been recognized for its approach to service. Beyond a handful of companies, transportation service organizations still have a great opportunity to bridge the gap between the customer and the company. Here's how it can be accomplished.

### How to Get Started

As study after study has shown, keeping close to the customer starts with senior management. Senior executives demonstrate their commitment to keeping close to the customer through personal example. According to the old cliché, "Actions speak louder than words."

A good place to start is to make keeping close to the customer an explicit part of the company's mission statement. Although an excellent start, simply mentioning it within the company's mission statement doesn't make it happen. Senior executives must get out from behind their comfortable desks and visit customers. Corporate officers at IBM still make sales calls to customers on a regular basis. Sam Walton, founder of the eminently successful Wal-Mart Corporation, still makes regular visits to his stores and talks with customers. Furthermore, successful companies such as 3M and Hewlett-Packard encourage their employees to visit customers. This provides the company's employees with tangible evidence of senior management's commitment to keeping close to the customer. Close customer contact is everybody's business.

### How to Listen More Effectively

Excellent companies are better listeners. They have learned that real innovation and success come from the external environment, not from the people behind the company's desks. Here are a few techniques that enhance listening power:

Toll-free phone numbers have proved their worth to a great number of companies. Procter & Gamble was the first consumer goods company to put a toll-free 800 telephone number on all of its packages—and with great results. In its 1979 annual report, P&G stated that it received 200,000 calls on the toll-free line. P&G responded to every one of those calls, and reports were prepared for board meetings based on those calls. These calls have provided P&G with new product ideas, in addition to the public relations value of the number.

Another approach is giving out home phone numbers for key company personnel. This tactic demonstrates a company's total 24-hour commitment to the customer. One division of Trus Joist, a $200 million high-technology forest products company, used this approach. Even though its toll-free number received all of the calls, the company's dedication to the customer was clearly evident.

A similar approach is being applied by Yellow Freight System, Inc., a $2 billion trucking service company. It calls its approach the Answers Team. Here's how it works. Customers are given an Answers Team brochure that contains a list of key local contact personnel by function and direct-line phone number. So, if customers want to know where their freight is, they call the tracing clerk directly by name and phone number. Yellow's Answers Team is another way companies can bridge the gap between the customer and themselves.

Many companies have found visits to their "lead users" particularly beneficial. These cutting-edge users are often great sources of new ideas for service enhancements and new service offerings. Even more beneficial is inviting a group of six to eight individuals from "lead user" companies for a round-table discussion. The interaction among a group of cutting-edge individuals can be informative and stimulating.

### How to Use Customer Research and Surveys

Less direct methods of gaining customer information consist of formal market research and customer surveys. Customer research can be broken down into two major types—qualitative and quantitative. Qualitative research provides a company with "directional" information since sample sizes are small. Conversely, quantitative research provides executives with statistically valid findings on which to base business decisions.

Qualitative Methods.   There are several ways in which companies can get qualitative information from customers. First, the company can conduct a depth interview, which is a one-on-one personal interview in which the interviewer attempts to get subjects to talk freely and to express their opinions on a specific topic. Depth interviews are an excellent way to get information on sensitive topics or to gain a good understanding of a particular issue. They are very expensive to conduct, however, and the results are not necessarily representative of the market being studied because of sample issues.

A more popular approach to qualitative research is the focus group. In a focus group interview, a small number of individuals (six to ten) are brought together rather than being interviewed individually, as in a depth interview. In this group setting, individuals are asked their opinions on key marketing issues by a nonbiased professional moderator. The advantage of the focus group is that each individual is exposed to the ideas of the others and submits his or her ideas for consideration by the group. Focus groups provide a company with a wealth of ''directional'' information on specific issues. Because of sampling limitations, however, the results gained from focus groups should be employed cautiously, or, preferably, for support for quantitative research that is projectable.

<u>Quantitative Methods.</u>   Well-designed quantitative customer surveys provide managers with statistically sound answers to their marketing questions. Generally speaking, a representative sample of customers is selected from a company's marketplace. This sample of customers is asked to answer several questions of interest to the company. The results are then tabulated and analyzed for management's use. Although a detailed discussion of quantitative methods is beyond the scope of this chapter, here are several key studies that transportation service companies should conduct to stay in sync with their marketplace.

First, and most important, transportation service companies should undertake a customer segmentation and positioning study. This type of study will provide the company with such information as:

- The key decision maker in service selection.
- The key determinants in transportation service selection.
- How the transportation provider performed relative to the competition on the key determinants in selection.
- Identifiable groups of customers whose needs are similar to one another within the individual group but whose needs are distinct from customers within the other groups. These groups of customers are typically referred to as customer segments.

Armed with this information, the transportation executive can determine the key factors for success in the marketplace, how the company is positioned relative to the competition, and the customer segments that are targets for marketing efforts.

Another type of study gaining popularity within the business community concerns customer satisfaction and service quality. These studies attempt to:

- Determine what factors influence perceived service quality.
- Identify the factors creating dissatisfaction.
- Determine how satisfied customers are with a company's service relative to the competition on factors associated with perceived quality.
- Assess the payback for service quality improvements.

With these results in hand, the transportation executive should be able to determine a course of action that increases customer satisfaction and consequently improves revenue growth.

Finally, these two studies should be performed on a regular basis in order to track the success of marketing programs. It is important to observe changes in the company's position relative to competition. Furthermore, many companies are now turning to customer satisfaction measurement and feedback systems to track their progress in improving their service package as perceived by the customer. Customer satisfaction measurement and feedback systems are a particularly effective way to gain information on customers' perceptions down to the individual transportation terminal level. It must be emphasized that the performance that the company measures and rewards is the performance that it will get. Thus, careful consideration of the measurement system is warranted.

### What Are the Benefits?

The bottom-line benefit of getting close to the customer is this: Strong evidence indicates that the majority of innovations comes from the customers and that those companies that are closer to the customer reap the rewards. As Peters and Waterman discovered, the top performers in an industry are often better listeners. Transportation service companies that employ the techniques described previously have a better chance of formulating programs and tactics that are meaningful for customers and help separate the company from its competition.

## How to Turn Research Into Reality

Knowledge of the customers' needs and wants is meaningless unless the transportation service provider uses this knowledge to improve employee and company performance. Translating research into reality is where most companies falter. Executives take comfort in knowing what the customer thinks, but turning this knowledge into a game plan for action is where the real work begins. Implementation is often difficult, frustrating, and tedious. It's much easier to sit back and relax or ask for more research. Concrete action is the only way to make the changes necessary to stand out from the competition and to establish a sustainable competitive advantage. Assuming a marketing game plan based on strategic thinking and customer feedback is in place, here's what is left to be done.

### How to Gain Senior Management Commitment

As mentioned previously, in order to change research into reality, the proposed course of action must receive explicit endorsement and commitment from senior management, particularly the president and CEO. The research and resultant course of action must clearly demonstrate to senior management the rewards for undertaking the action. In addition, the presentation to management must answer the proverbial ''What's in it for me?'' question.

Senior management must do more than give tacit approval and lip service to the course of action—leaving implementation to the staff. Senior managers must actively convey support through their own actions—actions that establish priorities for implementing the game plan. Senior management backing will certainly get the course of action off to an excellent start, but it will require more than that.

## Why Employee Communication Is Important

Good communication is an extremely critical dimension to successful execution of a marketing game plan. Employees must know:

- What the contents of the game plan are
- What's expected of them
- How the game plan will affect them
- What's in it for them and the company

The best way to communicate this information to employees is through face-to-face meetings. The message should also be reinforced through videos, newsletters, personal correspondence from senior management, and public relations. At this point, the employees understand the game plan and management's commitment to it. However, they still haven't assumed ownership for its success.

## How to Get Employee Ownership

Employees must feel a part of the game plan, particularly front-line employees, who are often the most underpaid and undertrained in the organization. However, these people have more contacts with customers than any other group of employees. Understandably, upper management is often surprised when they learn that front-line employees have the most influence on their customers' perceptions of the company's service quality. In the eyes of the customer, at the point of contact, the employee is the company. It is hard to believe that many companies still do not recognize this relationship and, as a result, fail to involve front-line employees in the game plan and its execution.

Employees will assume ownership for the game plan if they are involved in the process and personally feel that they will benefit from its success. Properly executed quality circles, companywide surveys, and persuasive communications clearly demonstrate the company's concern and commitment to the game plan. Actions always speak louder than words. Employees must also believe that their cooperation in implementing the game plan will be recognized and rewarded by management—an extremely critical element to employee ownership and success.

Excellent service is rare because many managers fail to recognize and reward front-line workers for delivering service excellence that is on target with the game plan. Top managers must ask themselves what the incentive is for the employee to go the extra mile for realizing the game plan. Relatively few transportation service providers have installed a performance management system that rewards employees for implementing the game plan—whether it be specific customer-satisfying actions or behaviors that raise the customers' perceptions of the company. Desired performance expectations should be an explicit part of front-line employees' job models, and their performance appraisals should reflect how well they meet those expectations. Implementing the game plan will then become an expectation and the desired outcome of employees' performance.

Leading service organizations realize that the performance they reward and recognize is the performance they receive. Therefore, it is imperative that the performance is linked directly to implementing the game plan. Frequently, companies reward employees for actions that are not in line with game-plan objectives, only to realize later that these actions do not support the plan.

One additional point should be noted. Although money is a strong motivator, other ways are available to inspire employee performance. They include praise, time off, preferred work assignments, advancements, prizes, awards, and company-paid excursions. Performance management systems are an excellent way to get desired behaviors from employees.

### Why a Feedback System Is Important

Executives, managers, and employees need to understand how employee performance is perceived by the customer. A customer feedback system provides the report card that the company's employees receive as a result of their performance. The feedback system helps management determine whether or not their efforts in realizing the game plan are paying off and, if not, what refinements are needed.

Marriott's Guest Service Index (GSI) is a good example of a successful customer feedback system in action. Through the use of "in-room" questionnaires and "mail out" surveys, Marriott is able to continuously monitor their employees' performance in meeting expectations. Other companies have found telephone surveys a more desirable method to obtain customer response. Regardless of the methods employed, customer feedback systems are growing in popularity, and many service companies now install them. However, relatively few transportation companies have a system in full operation.

The customer feedback system is of limited value unless it is shared with employees who are responsible for the results. Feeding the results back to the front-line employees provides them with a good indication of how well they are hitting the desired target and what they need to do to improve. This feedback system relates directly to the performance management system and provides the basis for employee appraisals. It also can serve as the means by which employees are rewarded, either singly or in groups.

Interestingly, keeping close to the customer starts and ends with research. The process begins by determining what drives the customer's buying decision and how the company is positioned relative to the competition. After program implementation, customer satisfaction should be measured on an ongoing basis.

# Marketing Transportation Services in Perspective

The transportation industry has undergone dynamic change. Deregulation of the industry fueled a change in the traditional business environment that presented a continuous flow of new opportunities for enterprising companies and serious challenges to companies unwilling or unable to make the transition. Those companies that approached this new environment opportunistically are still competing today; those that didn't have become a part of history.

The transportation industry's shakeout is still in progress. The weak players have already exited the marketplace, leaving the stronger ones to compete. Competition will intensify as the remaining companies continue to vie for market share.

The key to future success and long-term viability in the transportation industry is marketing prowess. There are several important steps that transportation service providers must take in order to enhance their marketing prowess. They are:

- Strategic thinking and planning
- Keeping close to the customer
- Turning market knowledge into concrete actions

These steps must be viewed as one blueprint for marketing success as opposed to three unrelated steps. These three links in the marketing chain start with the strategy, move into the tactical, and then finish with implementation.

First, strategic thinking and planning should be considered the "germination of ideas" phase. It is the time for creative thinking. Transportation executives must focus their thoughts on "what could be," as opposed to "what is." Thinking within the context of "what is" will lead to traditional solutions to transportation problems. A fresh approach is needed where exploring the "what could be" path opens up new vistas for competitive advantage.

To be effective, the strategic planning process must answer three questions:

1. Where are we now?
2. Where are we going?
3. How are we going to get there?

If a company invests its time and energy in answering these questions, it will have created the blueprint for the future that provides it with a unique position in the marketplace.

Once transportation service managers have created the strategic plan, they must next develop a practical course of action. The best way to develop practical ideas for action plans is to stay close to the customer. By staying in close contact with the customer, the company not only discovers whether or not its strategic plan is on target, but also if its tactical programs are effective. This means that the company's personnel must:

- Get out into the marketplace and meet with customers on their turf to find solutions to their problems.
- Perform customer research studies to find out what the key factors of success are, how the company is positioned relative to the competition on these factors, and how the market is segmented relative to different buying motives.
- Employ toll-free numbers, visit "lead users," and provide customers with phone numbers of key customer service personnel.

Finally, with the strategic and tactical ideas in place, the transportation service provider must turn these ideas into realities, which requires:

- Commitment from senior management
- Communicating that commitment to employees
- Rewarding and recognizing employees for helping to realize the game plan
- Implementing a customer feedback system that keeps the company and its employees on target

If a transportation service company employs this blueprint, it has a better chance of succeeding in these tumultuous times because it will have established a distinct course of action that will create a competitive advantage in its marketplace.

## Notes

1. "Focus: A Decade of Deregulation," *Traffic World,* supplement to December 5, 1988, issue, A–N.
2. For related discussions, see "Focus: A Decade of Deregulation," *Traffic World,* supplement to December 5, 1988, issue; and "The Frenzied Skies," *Business Week,* December 19, 1988, 70–80.
3. "The Frenzied Skies," *Business Week,* December 19, 1988, 71.
4. Theodore Levitt, "Marketing Myopia: HBR Classic," *Harvard Business Review* 53 (September/October 1975): 24–39.
5. For further details, see Thomas J. Peters and Robert H. Waterman, Jr., *In Search of Excellence* (New York: Harper & Row, 1982).

*            *            *            *

***Craig E. Cina*** *is vice president of marketing and sales with NTS, Inc., a credit card company servicing over-the-road trucking companies. Previously he was director of market planning at Yellow Freight System, Inc., where he was responsible for the company's strategic market planning, marketing research, business analysis and forecasting, competitive intelligence, and service analysis efforts. He also directed marketing research and planning at Zale Corporation.*

# 25

# Financial Services

John A. Czepiel
A. Dawn Lesh

The two major factors that shape the practice of marketing in financial services organizations are (1) the environment and (2) how the specific business views and organizes its marketing efforts. Both factors are equally important in creating and constraining managers' opportunities for effective action. Successful service marketers possess one key quality—the ability to understand the complexities of the external environment as opportunities to be exploited, rather than as problems to bemoan. The strong and sometimes capricious economic, political, social, and international forces that impinge on and constrain the actions of financial services companies are not likely to abate. Success will go to those managements that recognize this and consider constant change as part of the rules of a very complicated game.

The relative newness of marketing in financial services companies requires marketing managers who are organizationally savvy—as well versed in selling their ideas as they are in selling their company's services. This requires that financial services marketers be able to conceptualize and create marketing as it is needed within their company. This chapter concerns both of these issues. It presents an overview of the current strategic environment, identifying those few, important trends that are affecting the ways in which financial services must and can compete. It also addresses the specific issues faced by marketers as they attempt to lead their companies to success within that environment.

## How to Win in the New Competitive Order

The reality of life in any business is the inevitability of change. Although financial services managers may believe that theirs is a business that gets more than its fair share of change (they may be right), the company that takes strategic advantage of change is the one that succeeds. This section presents an overview of the three major external forces that affect competition within the financial services industry. These three forces are the increasing internationalization of all financial products and players, the continuing change in the regulatory environment (which is removing many barriers to open competition and to the types of companies allowed to compete), and the accelerating impact and pervasiveness of information technology. Overriding these three substantive forces is the recognition that the change they create is ever-increasing. This suggests that the race will be won by those companies that react the most swiftly *or* by those that anticipate or even create the change that affords the opportunity.

*Internationalization*

Just as financial services have begun to adjust to the existence and pace of domestic change, the internationalization of financial services and competition has added new dimensions. Whether one is in banking, investments, currency trading, financial instruments, or investment banking, the effect and pace are the same. And one need not be directly involved to be affected. Every manager needs to be a global manager these days. The next few paragraphs will identify some of the major international trends that will present opportunities for those with the foresight to turn them to advantage.

Around-the-Clock Markets.   The new financial order is beginning to take shape. London, Tokyo, and New York are leading the way, but Frankfurt, Singapore, and Hong Kong are not far behind. The 24-hour financial market is rapidly developing, along with the ability to profit and the need to manage the risk that accompanies round-the-clock trading. It matters little whether that trading concerns equities, currencies, or commodities; the effect is the same. Global communications are making it possible for alert managers to react to events at any time of the day or night. The concept of releasing news ''after the close of the market'' will soon be meaningless. A market will always be open somewhere. The questions are how to position oneself to take advantage of the new reality, what customer groups can profit most, what products can be created, and how the organization can seek to capitalize on the reality, rather than practicing damage control after the fact.

Floating Exchange Rates.   Fluctuations in the exchange rate have made many people aware of the interconnectedness of the world economy. No matter what the geographical distance from national borders or the seemingly domestic nature of one's business or local economy, the changes have been felt by all. And despite the occasional official posturing in the media for a return to fixed rates or, worse yet, tighter controls on international trade, neither is likely to happen. Too many economies have too much to lose to return to the old days. The opportunities are there for all. The question is how any given institution should participate, not whether it should participate. The future of almost every financial services institution will be determined by its ability to provide its customers with the necessary capabilities to cope with both the fluctuating exchange rates as well as their consequences.

Getting Started Internationally.   One need not be a major player to be affected by or to capitalize on the international front. And because internationalization will be an increasingly larger part of all economies in the future, those that learn soonest will garner the most. One exercise that any player can perform is to make a systematic evaluation of the real and potential impact that international forces can have on it. Calculating your company's ''international connectedness score'' can be a revealing exercise. Answer the following questions to find out just how connected you are:

- What effect has the international economy had on my community, my business, my customers?
- What international products and services are my current customers now buying, which do they need, which do they want, which ones should we offer or not offer, and what revenues are we missing by not offering those services?
- Which of my competitors is providing these services, and how is that ability affecting my strategic position?

The secret for the company that has little experience in the international arena is not to make a big splash, create a major task force, or even announce a "program," but simply to take one step at a time with its existing customer base. If you are a local bank, for example, it may not be necessary for you to create special "international" services to participate. The local presence of your institution in your market and your knowledge of the needs of the markets and decision makers are appealing characteristics to the larger foreign company's expert in the international arena, which needs representation in local markets such as yours. In this way both your needs and the needs of your clients for greater international services are served.

## Domestic Regulatory Change

Although the rapid changes occurring in the international scene sometimes seem overwhelming, the continuing changes that have been buffeting the domestic arena are no less important just because they have become more familiar. Although for many the prospect of staying alive another year may seem to be the biggest problem, the proactive are able also to recognize the opportunities that change presents.

Predicting actual change is difficult, but the direction is clear: Wherever the economics favor the actions of free markets is where the pressure for deregulation will be. The only force that prevents this from happening is the political power that the various financial industries possess. Although the freeing up of financial markets is the long-term trend, that does not mean there will not be occasional backsliding. However, wise managers will not base strategy solely on political influence or on the possibility that legislation will be reversed. The next several paragraphs present an overview of the major trends affecting financial services institutions.

Banking and Thrifts. After a long period during which bankers felt that their preserve was opened up to all comers, while restrictions on the banks themselves were maintained, it appears that some greater freedom may be in the offing. Only a few institutions are likely to be able to capitalize on the opportunity, however, because of the current low profitability levels in the industry. In addition, it is still unclear whether bankers have acquired the entreprenurial talent required to move beyond their current province.

Overall, the banking industry continues to lose in terms of the share of the nation's financial assets it controls. And because the factors that drive that share are largely due to its regulatory inability to serve customers' broadened needs, marketing can do very little to prevent that erosion. The increased financial sophistication of both consumer and business markets and the increased availability of services and products from new competitors, such as insurance companies or the financial subsidiaries of manufacturing companies, are strong forces that the banking industry has found difficult to counter.

Competition within the industry for that declining share of the nation's financial assets is increasing, however. The interesting marketing battle is not so much between the commercial banks and the thrifts as it is between the large money center banks, the bank holding companies, and the larger regional banks. To business clients, making a choice among these suppliers must sometimes seem to require trade-offs between relationships and economics, trust and products, or service and efficiency. It remains to be seen how both clients and banks reconcile the need for long-term relationships with the realities of economics. Neither party can afford to subsidize the other or to take actions against their own best economic interest, yet the functions served by true relationships must still be performed if both parties' needs are to be served.

Brokerage and Investment Banking.    Because of the thinness of margins in the banking industry, it is not surprising that one major trend in the securities business is the continued incursions being made by bankers hungry for higher margins. In fact, the traditional wisdom that the Glass-Steagall Act (which restricted the legal range of banks' activities) was designed to ensure the stability and integrity of the banking system has been challenged by revisionists. These revisionists state that it was simply one more barrier to entry designed to maintain the profitability of the securities industry. And, indeed, the entry of banks into the underwriting and distribution of municipal securities has resulted in the lowering of the profitability of that business, causing some traditional securities companies to exit the business. Of course, to remind these companies that such all-in-one accounts as the Merrill Lynch Cash Management Account had directly impinged on the bankers' territory in the first instance might be seen as irrelevant.

The second trend affecting the securities industry is the lingering uncertainty about market stability. This is an opportunity that remains to be exploited. New services and the positioning of companies as sensitive and capable in this regard would do much to attract institutional and individual investors.

Insurance.    This remains one of the most regulated of the major financial services industries, at least insofar as its base product is concerned. The biggest threat is within the industry's own control, and that is to refrain from the commodity price wars that erupt when investment income returns become attractive. The industry must continually change its products in line with the continuing changes in the tax code and other major economic variables. The periodic eruption of "hot products" offers opportunities to those who move fast before the most profitable and prime prospects are sold.

Large insurance companies have been moving to take broader roles within the financial services industry—witness Prudential's acquisition of Bache (to become Prudential-Bache) and John Hancock's diversification into stockbroking, investment management, and home loans. To date, however, these activities have resulted mainly in a financial supermarket approach to the business. The real rewards, however, will go to the visionary marketer who can combine the awesome financial, technological, and distribution advantages these companies possess to create entirely new competitive forms.

## Technology

Of all of the changes that affect the financial services industry, the continued impact of technology is without equal. The investments in hardware and software are becoming a significant barrier to entry. In fact, the investment level in technology is becoming such that the large institutions are increasingly distancing themselves from smaller ones across all sectors. In response, smaller institutions, in banking especially, are taking part in various technology-sharing networks. First seen in the guise of regional ATM systems, shared electronic financial delivery systems are growing in popularity as a defensive strategy. In fact, some people regard such systems sharing as a form of strategic alliance that provides the benefits of merging without the loss of individual identity.

It will be interesting to see if the smaller companies in other financial services sectors are able to adopt similar technology responses to counter the increasing dominance of the largest companies. Conversely, the company that has the technology has the opportunity to sell its expertise and technology to smaller companies. Such actions will not only allow the company to achieve greater economies of scale in its own system but will help ensure that its approach becomes the dominant design—the one that is accepted as the technological standard in the industry. The marketing implications of achieving such a result are real in both a positive and negative sense. The company that becomes odd man out technologically will suffer on all fronts, especially in customer acceptance.

Technology in financial services is an interesting interplay between those companies that are willing to accept the risks of innovation and the willingness of customers to accept the fruits of that innovation. Financial services have used electronic access to put the customer into the operations system to a degree that surpasses that of any other industry. The experience that has been gained in achieving this is a valuable resource. The important marketing question is how to capitalize on this knowledge base to create additional value for customers as well as to determine how the expertise itself can be sold.

One important reminder: Customer acceptance of technology is still evolving. Despite the seeming presence of ATMs on every street corner, fewer than 50 percent of all bank customers use them, and that number is closer to 30 percent in smaller institutions. As a percentage of transactions in banks, tellers still account for the majority of deposits and withdrawals. In other words, it is not an imperative that all be leaders in technology. Clearly the pioneers will reap the rewards of their successes, but they will also have accepted the risks. Experience has shown that a follower strategy in technology is still viable. How long such a strategy will remain viable is an open question, however.

# Achieving Marketing Success in Financial Services

It takes time to achieve real change, especially when that change is as much attitudinal as it is substantive. Marketing is a concept that derives from the recognition that the real source of power lies with customers. However, it is frequently difficult to gain that understanding in institutions and with individuals who have seldom had to compete except in the most rudimentary fashion. Whether it was simply location and price, white shoes and an old school tie, or "trinkets and trash" as one bank marketing officer put it, the old ways and attitudes toward what marketing consists of are still around. Overcoming old conceptions and implanting new ones are still the primary tasks for many marketing officers in even the most advanced, most seemingly marketing-oriented financial services businesses.

There are three major tasks that a marketing-oriented manager in a financial services organization must accomplish in order to achieve success. The first of these is to identify the key strategic success factors operating in the specific industry and to build the company's unique strategy around those factors. Second, the manager must be able to establish an organization and system capable of creating and implementing plans built around the company's strategy. Third, the manager must be able to free marketing of its departmental base and infuse and diffuse it throughout the organization.

## Making Key Strategic Success Factors Work for You

In the early 1800s, Carl von Clausewitz, a Prussian military strategist, was able to distill the essence of military strategy to its single key factor—the principle of force. His insight enabled military strategists to focus on what it took to win wars, which was to put two soldiers ready to fight in the place where the enemy had only one. The marketing strategist's task is very much like a general's; it is to distill the essence of competition in a given industry and to devise plans that incorporate the essence in quantities that overwhelm the efforts of competitors.

On one level the task is easy. The business is financial services. The key factors for success are finance and service. The business that delivers these to customers at a better rate than a competitor can or does wins the war. Taking it one step further, economics is the determinant of the financial part—true economic value will always win. The competitor who devises a way to profitably deliver more for less always gains. Perceived value—that combination of the quantitative dollars-and-cents economic value the service provides plus the qualitative social and psychological value added by the particular supplying company—is the force underlying the service part of the business.

In terms of a specific business, this definitional task becomes more difficult. Definitions of economic value differ among market segments, and there are large numbers of features and attributes that combine to define good service for any market segment or even for an individual customer. Suburban customers define *service* one way, rural customers another way. Small businesses focus on advice and flexibility, whereas larger businesses value rates over "service." The essential twist that marketers can bring to the seeming intractability of this problem is to let the answer depend on customer perceptions. It matters little how those within the company define value. Good customer-based research answers the question in the only valid way—the way the marketplace defines it.

The truly difficult issue in financial services is that in each and every sector of the industry, large numbers of competitors all seem to be able to deliver equivalent economics and perceived service value. Such situations reduce competition to one variable—price—and the only winners are customers. In this situation, the company's task is to do what any good general would do—either to manipulate the situation to favor his army or to leave the battlefield and find a war he *can* win. This task is not as difficult as it sounds. The company can move along any of three fronts to accomplish this end: Improve the economics, improve the service, or move on to find a specific segment of the market where the company's current abilities are superior to those of the competition.

In sum, then, the strategic positioning of the company is the key task of the marketer. It is the marketer's responsibility to use market-derived data in order to guide the company to understand what it takes to win customers and overtake competitors. The marketer's next task is to organize so that the strategy gets implemented.

## How to Organize for Successful Marketing

Building a marketing organization is not very difficult. The strategy that has been developed for the company or particular subunit explicitly demands certain kinds and levels of performance. These imperatives are translated into a strategic marketing plan that specifies objectives, market and service pairings, and the general directions that the marketing mix should take. In simpler terms, the strategic marketing plan defines the steps that the company will take to achieve the kind of competitive edge specified in its overall strategy. Such a plan defines the kind of organization needed to achieve this edge.

A marketing strategy that defines the company's competitive edge in terms of unique, high-quality service offerings that deliver true performance benefits to a wide portion of the market will organize around the "product manager" concept. Because the company's edge comes from the strength of its offerings, these offerings must be the focus of the organization. Alternatively, if the company defines its edge to be based on the specific knowledge and expertise it has acquired in servicing the needs of selected market segments or niches, then the central organizing concept ought be that of the "market manager." In each instance the company will still likely have managers of the "other type" (a predominantly product-management organization may still have and need market managers and vice versa).

Perhaps the most difficult position for the marketer is in the company that has defined its competitive edge in terms of being the low-cost producer of basic, adequate quality services. Here the competitive edge comes from a dedicated pursuit of cost through simplification and scale economies. Here the marketer's task is not the precise delineation of segment needs and carefully crafted segment-by-segment plans, but rather the need to look across segments for customers who can be swayed by economics and be aggregated into the large markets dictated by the strategy. The selling function becomes the central focus in this instance.

Across all strategies the role of the research function is central, for without data the company must operate on the intuitive feelings of key managers. Intuition is not bad, provided it is correct. However, not all managers are capable of the insight that correct intuition demands. Research allows the company to succeed without depending on that difficult-to-judge (and hire for) skill. Hiring into the research function those who can communicate the need and value of data-based decision making is key to the success of the entire function.

### Making Marketing the Company's Way of Life

At any professional meeting of financial services marketing executives, the question of how to diffuse marketing ideas throughout the organization is always on the agenda. And there is no simple answer. There are, however, two techniques that experienced managers in financial services companies report using successfully.

The first technique is to promote marketers into the line organizations they support. Clearly, such actions might seem to require the marketer to be recruiting more than usual, but the rewards are reported to be worthwhile. In the first instance, line managers familiar with marketing use it more and spread the word to their peers. Second, over time, as the success of those who have moved out of the function into broader responsibilities becomes known, the function comes to be regarded as the best place to learn the business.

The second technique is to become a better marketer. A number of experienced financial services marketers report that they have a regular "calling" schedule within their companies. Part of their personal measures of performance is to have lunch once a week with their peers and clients in other functions. At these informal meetings, the manager has the opportunity to discuss how the marketing function has been able to help line managers achieve success and to develop the personal relationship that makes it easy for the client to seek the marketer's help.

## Putting It All Together

There's no secret to doing successful marketing for and in financial services businesses. The first task is to be able to translate the larger financial, economic, and political environment into the opportunities and constraints relevant to your own business. Financial services is about finance and economics, and the ability to adapt rapidly to changes in the supply and demand factors that drive the business is essential. Change is now a major element in the business just as it has now become international in character. The ability to understand and act in such an environment is the price of entry.

Success in financial services comes not only from reading the signs of change but in interpreting their meaning in terms of the key strategic success factors in your business and in those of your competition. The marketer must isolate the key strategic factors for the company based on customer responses to its offerings and actions and on the analysis of competitive abilities and strategies. Translating this insight into a strategy and the plans that implement that strategy are the major tasks of the marketing function. The shape that the organization takes follows from the strategy. Those companies that are best organized to deliver true value—financial/economic value and service value—win. It's that simple.

\*     \*     \*     \*

*John A. Czepiel, Ph.D., is an associate professor of marketing at the Graduate School of Business Administration, New York University. The author of many books and articles, he is also an active consultant to a wide variety of companies in both services and manufacturing industries.*

*A. Dawn Lesh is a managing director and head of market research with J. P. Morgan & Co. Previously she served as vice president, strategic planning and marketing research, for the New York Stock Exchange, where her responsibilities included product and market research, strategic development, and marketing research/decision support systems.*

# 26

## Professional Services

Carole A. Congram

Professional services is one of the newest service industries to turn to marketing, largely as a result of increasing competition and a growing awareness that professional service organizations must operate more like businesses if they are to be profitable. Within this industry are some of the best examples of the special characteristics of services, as we will see in this chapter. But, first, what professions comprise this industry?

Traditionally, *profession* refers to those fields that require an individual to obtain some type of certification in order to practice and that impose a code of ethics, violation of which prohibits a professional from further practice. It is noteworthy that, in some professions, the code itself has prohibited such marketing activities as advertising and reinforced the widely held belief that professionals are above the competitive fray.

Among the professional service disciplines are architecture, accounting, law, medicine, and engineering. Although this chapter focuses on these professions, it also applies to several fields in which certification is not required, but in which practitioners consider themselves to be professionals and develop similar types of service practices. These fields include consulting, investment banking, advertising, public relations, market research, design, and data processing.

Communication is important within all of these professions, and professionals understand its significance in business development. Typically professional service firms have begun their marketing efforts with a promotion project, usually a brochure describing the firm's array of services and capabilities, as well as listing its clients. While communication is a critical part of a firm's marketing efforts, many firms have minimized the potential benefits of their initial investment by not expanding their activities into other areas of the marketing mix. Success in achieving marketing's goals—to acquire and retain clients*— demands more than developing communication tools.

Success depends upon understanding that every activity of a professional service firm influences people's perceptions of the firm, whether they are current or prospective clients, current or prospective employees, referral sources, the press, or the community at large. Success depends upon achieving the consistently high level of service quality that is expected by clients. The purpose of this chapter is to describe how a professional service firm can deliver high-quality service consistently.

---

*A purchaser of professional services may be called a *customer, patient,* or *client.* Because most professions use the term *client,* this term will be used throughout this chapter to refer to purchasers.

This chapter begins by considering some of the special characteristics of professional service firms; characteristics differentiating among professions will be presented first, and then characteristics common to most firms will be discussed. A second section focuses on the professional, the service provider. Finally, two strategies are proposed that offer the most effective means of achieving a firm's quality objectives:

- Design an effective and efficient service delivery process.
- Raise the service sensitivity and capabilities of all employees.


## Key Characteristics of Professional Services

In this section, the characteristics that can influence the strategies a professional service firm might use to achieve its objectives are examined.[1] First, we look briefly at two characteristics that differentiate among services. Then we look at some characteristics that cut across professions so that strategies applying to a broad range of professional service organizations can be discussed.


### How Professional Services Differ

Two basic characteristics differentiate among professional services: the nature of the service act and the distribution method.

<u>What Is the Professional Service Act?</u>  Extracting a tooth, writing a will, developing architectural plans—these three examples illustrate how widely professional service acts can vary. The first requires physical strength, as well as knowledge of several principles of physics; the second, knowledge of precise legal terms and, at times, social psychology; and the last, the ability to translate a dream into a working blueprint—in scale. Because of the strong technical underpinnings of professional services, professionals understand the technical aspects of the act they are performing. The act has been proceduralized. In developing strategies, professionals must go beyond the procedures and understand two basic elements in the service act: its recipient and its degree of tangibility.

*Who or what is the recipient?* The first key element in the service act is the recipient of the service. Is the recipient a person or a thing? Health care services are provided to people; engineering services to things. When the recipient is a person, most professionals can improve their service by understanding the client's role in the service act, as well as his or her expectations. Professionals need to focus on such questions as:

- When does the client need to be present physically? Why?
- What are the benefits that the client is receiving as a result of the service act?

The answers may lead to streamlining certain parts of the service delivery process, communicating more effectively with current and prospective clients, or identifying new services.

*Tangible or intangible?* Can you see, touch, hear, or smell a service? Although professional services are largely intangible, they are often accompanied by tangible elements.[2] Consider the battery of shots a veterinarian gives your pet or the decor of an interior decorator's office. Clients use these tangible elements, or evidence, in evaluating a service.

Professional services differ in type of evidence. For example, in a medical practice, tangible elements include the decor of the reception area, staff uniforms, and technical equipment; a management consulting firm's evidence includes written proposals and reports, as well as portable microcomputers used at clients' offices. Professionals must identify the evidence that clients use in evaluating services and manage the presentation of that evidence so that clients' perceptions are influenced positively.

There is one type of evidence common to all professional services—the service provider. For many clients, the service and the professional or administrator are inseparable. The service provider is perceived as having the depth of experience or high level of expertise that is the essence of the service. Firms must help their employees understand their impact on customers' perceptions, especially in the area of service quality.

## What Is the Distribution Method?

Closely related to the service act is the approach used to deliver the service—that is, accessibility and location. Professional services differ in both areas, and the increasing availability and use of technology have had an enormous impact on the way professionals deliver services.

With regard to accessibility, sometimes a client must visit a professional's office. For example, patients must go to a medical facility for certain types of surgery. At times, however, it is more efficient for the professional to visit the client, as in the case of accountants, who must meet with several people in a client's organization and review certain internal documents and computer files. Usually professionals do not routinely go to a client's premises because of the expense to the client. For example, if your tax consultant came to your house, the billing for his or her travel time would add a considerable amount to your fee, based on an hourly rate.

When clients must travel to the firm, another important factor is location, which includes convenience, parking, and safety. As a firm grows, the number of locations may increase. Advertising agencies, for example, may establish offices in proximity to their major clients. Or, through mergers, firms may gain additional geographic coverage; for example, one reason for the recent consolidations by major accounting firms was to improve their international coverage. Developing a formal network of independent firms is another alternative; law and accounting firms have forged international affiliations in order to provide geographic coverage to clients.

Technology is changing the ways professionals deliver their services. For example, with a telephone and a fax in his or her briefcase, a management consultant can be in contact with a client instantaneously; laser technology makes sophisticated surgical techniques routine; and clients now transmit data electronically to their accounting firms, thus speeding up the processing of financial statements. Professionals must keep abreast of the technology that is relevant to their practice and adopt these advances when they support a firm's objectives.

These two characteristics—differences in the service act and the method of service distribution—are key differentiators among the professions. Next we will consider their similarities.

## How Professional Services Are Similar

Professional services are alike in several significant ways:

- The service delivery process is complex, and quality is difficult to control.
- The client often has difficulty making the purchase decision.
- All employees have a marketing responsibility.

In addition, organizational characteristics influence the likelihood that a firm will achieve its service quality objectives, and some of these characteristics recur across firms. In this section, these similarities are described in more detail.

The Complexity of Service Delivery and Quality.    Professional services are produced and consumed simultaneously. For example, an architect helps a client define the style of house desired, as well as the special features to be included in the house. Site surveys and budget must also be considered before the architect can secure the client's approval to move forward in developing a set of plans.

This simultaneity feature is confounded by a second characteristic: The client must be involved in the service delivery process. For example, the client must provide background information for the personal financial planner; hip replacement surgery requires the patient's physical presence and participation.

Because clients' needs vary, professional services usually are customized, further complicating service delivery. For example, when prescribing a medication, a physician must consider other medications a patient is taking; or a tax-planning specialist must review the regulations of the specific jurisdictions in which a client does business. This customization process can involve a high degree of analysis and judgment from professionals.

These three characteristics make it difficult, if not impossible, for professional service firms to control quality. Why? Basic to the delivery of a professional service is the service encounter—that is, the interaction between a client and a professional. Both parties bring to the interaction different needs, experiences, expectations, and characteristics, and the encounter is also influenced by the organization's culture, including its procedures. Additionally, for relationships that continue over time (as do most professional relationships), the encounter is influenced by the changing needs and expectations of both the client and the professional.

The multitude of variables involved in the service encounter makes it difficult to ensure encounters of consistently high quality for both clients and professionals. The most important question for a firm's management to address is not "How do we control service quality?" Rather, it is "How do we manage the quality of our services?" Other key questions that must be answered include:

- Do clients understand their role in service delivery?
- How can professionals manage client expectations effectively?
- How can professional and administrative staff members become more knowledgeable about and sensitive to their influence on clients' perceptions of service quality?

The Difficulty of the Purchase Decision.   Another significant factor is the difficulty clients have in making the decision to purchase a professional service. Many clients do not have the background to evaluate professional service providers' technical capabilities. In fact, in selecting a professional service firm, clients assume that a certain level of technical excellence exists. Instead, clients consider whether the firm has a good reputation, is recommended by a respected person, or can demonstrate relevant experience or specialized service. A challenge to professional services marketers is to identify the right market segments, communicate with them efficiently, and become the firm for them to consider and prefer.

The Marketing Responsibility of Each Employee.   In a professional service firm, every professional—in fact, every employee—has a marketing role.[3] Everyone serves clients directly or indirectly. That a physician or an architect serves clients directly is obvious. Less so is the service role played by the technician or bookkeeper who may never meet a client, but whose work is visible in reports or bills, which form part of a client's experience with the firm. Frequently, these behind-the-scenes employees have as their clients the front-line service providers. The challenge in professional service firms is to develop a cadre of professional and administrative staffers who understand how clients define service and who recognize their individual roles in delivering service of consistently high quality.

The Effects of Organizational Characteristics.   The professional organization is a service system that must be kept in balance if service quality is to be consistently high. Professional service firms have many organizational characteristics that influence strategy development—implicitly or explicitly, and positively or negatively.

The organizational hierarchy of professional service firms is relatively flat, a characteristic sought by many multilayered corporations. As a result, professional service firms have fewer layers of decision making, and it is possible for professionals to be extremely responsive to clients' needs. In addition, because most professionals serve clients in some capacity, they have an opportunity to establish close working and, often, personal relationships with their clients.

The large majority of professional service firms are solo practitioners, whose pressures stem from needs common to all firms: to develop billable time, to respond to clients' requests and service needs, and to maintain technical skills and capabilities. Time pressures make it difficult for the single practitioner to do much comprehensive planning.

As firms increase in size, partnerships predominate, introducing new pressures. First, partnerships tend to foster a committee approach to addressing issues. When managed well, committees can be effective in the planning phase of an effort, with the implementation left to one or two people. In practice, professional service firms' committees tend to have "too many cooks"; as a result, their "products" lack imagination or creativity. A committee approach is one of the reasons clients have such difficulty differentiating among competing firms—they all look alike.

Second, each profession encourages specialization, and the number of specialty areas within a profession makes it easy for a firm to organize by area. Thus, a law practice might be composed of groups specializing in litigation, corporate issues, real estate, and taxation. Similarly, a group medical practice might comprise internal medicine, gynecology and obstetrics, pediatrics, and gerontology. Within a firm, one subgroup may become dominant, perhaps because of its profit contribution, the seniority or reputation of its professionals, or the significance of its clients. Turf issues can result, causing the professionals to be internally focused, rather than market-focused. Clients in need of a generalist to help them synthesize specialists' recommendations and give them an objective viewpoint remain confused.

Third, the culture of a professional service organization is critical for attracting and retaining clients and staff. Most management groups have not studied their culture to see how it influences service quality. Yet, clients, who are keen observers of the professionals with whom they work, are aware of such basics as whether a firm gives top priority to billable time or client service. They know when their telephone calls are being answered promptly, when a professional is suggesting a new approach to solving a nagging problem, and when they are on the receiving end of a thoughtful gesture. Clients and staff know the degree to which service quality is integral to the firm's culture. In firms that truly focus on quality, the culture will be characterized as quality-oriented.

## The Challenge Facing Professional Service Marketers

Clients have difficulty understanding what a professional service is, even when the service has tangible aspects or products, such as filling a tooth or rendering the design of an interior. This difficulty comes from the process nature of a service. From the client's point of view, experience is key to understanding how the service delivery process works and evaluating the quality of a professional service. From the professional's point of view, the technical component of service delivery is highly structured, whereas those service aspects related to clients' experiences are left to the discretion of professionals. Therein lies the challenge to professional service firms: How can professionals define *quality* in a substantive way so that clients, prospective clients, employees, and other significant audiences understand how quality is practiced in a firm? For a firm's management and marketing and other functional personnel, the challenge is to develop the systems that efficiently and effectively support the delivery of a consistently high-quality service.

## The Professional and Service Quality

Professionals are highly educated; many are excellent analysts, some are creative, and others are entrepreneurial. In their practices, the pressures are many and great. Top management is pushing for billable time and new business; clients have questions or require attention; involvement in professional organizations is time-consuming; bookkeepers want time reports. And, family and friends want them to participate in leisure activities and social events. In some professions, regulatory agencies impose standards that must be followed to the letter. Professionals are pulled in many directions.

As they begin their careers, young professionals equate service with technical prowess; their education and professional affiliations have emphasized it, and they believe that technical proficiency is what clients want. This view is reinforced by the amount of time spent on client work and frequent interaction with clients; it is easy to equate time spent with service. Many marketing activities that are appropriate for younger professionals—for example, speaking opportunities or participating in community organizations—seem unrelated to day-to-day client service activities. It is easy, then, for a professional to think of service and marketing as two discrete areas.

Ideally, as professionals mature, they realize that clients regard technical expertise as a given and that clients value the professional who understands their needs and objectives—the person who can mobilize resources to help the client achieve his or her objectives. (In fact, when a client retains a professional because of his or her high level of expertise, the client frequently equates the professional and the service.) Professionals learn that service is a process, that their firm cannot be successful in the marketplace unless it is perceived as offering service of consistently high quality, and that service is the heart of marketing in a professional service firm.

Senior professionals have responsibility for the client relationship; in client meetings, they play the key role in influencing clients' expectations about the firm, its professionals, and the service delivery process. Clients' perceptions of the service experience, however, are influenced by professionals at every level— and especially at junior levels[4] because these professionals have many interactions with clients in the course of service delivery. The discrepancies between promises made by senior professionals and actual experiences—with professional and administrative staff at all levels—that do not measure up to expectations represent important indicators of service quality. To manage clients' perceptions, a firm must invest in supporting front-line professionals so that they develop and manage constructive client relationships.

## Strategies for Service Quality

Service quality strategies for professional services must focus on two areas: clients' perceptions and professionals' attitudes and behaviors. Because the service delivery process is the basis for clients' experiences and for professionals' provision of service, the process deserves strategic focus. And, because the service is delivered through professionals, assisted by support personnel, a second strategic concern is their development as excellent service providers.

### Strategy 1: Attain Superior Service Delivery

The service process encompasses more than the proceduralized technical component. To clients, service also includes their experiences with the professional service firm, and these experiential aspects are often left to the discretion of the individual professional. We will look at two planning approaches that offer a more focused means of managing this process: service blueprinting and relationship management.

Service Blueprinting.   One approach to viewing a service as a system is the service blueprint, "a holistic method of seeing in snapshot form what is essentially a dynamic, living phenomenon."[5] (See also Chapter 14 of this *Handbook.*) The blueprint brings a discipline to service delivery systems. The blueprint is divided into two sections by a horizontal "line of visibility." The area above the line shows a client's experiences, in sequence, during the service delivery process—that is, the ways in which the service organization is visible to the client. The area below the line shows the flow of those activities that support the "visible" elements.

The blueprint is especially valuable for professional service firms because it:

1. Focuses on the client and his or her experiences.
2. Shows how the technical procedures relate to the administrative and relationship-building activities conducted as part of service delivery.
3. Shows activities that may be proceduralized, as well as those that must be individualized and, thus, deserve special attention.
4. Provides a basis for identifying gaps in the service process that need to be rectified or improved.
5. Shows opportunities to increase or decrease client involvement in the process.
6. Shows professional and administrative staff members how their activities relate to the client and to each other.

In addition, when the needs of a specific market are known, an analysis of a blueprint may suggest ways to tailor the service to that market.

The blueprint represents not only a significant approach to achieving service quality, but also a means of identifying characteristics that differentiate, or could differentiate, your service in the marketplace. According to Shostack,

". . . every service is unique . . . [and] so complex, the probabilities of any two services arriving at precisely the same design are practically nil."[6]

For example, a tax specialist whose clients own small, growing businesses observed that his clients hate surprises. In analyzing the blueprint for his service, he spotted an opportunity to simulate alternative tax strategies several months prior to year-end. This simulation would help the client understand the effects of different approaches on his or her tax situation and make decisions more effectively. Not only could this approach eliminate surprises, but it would also offer one or more opportunities for the tax specialist to meet with clients to help them achieve their objectives. He expected that clients would pay standard rates for the added value. He also anticipated that the additional contacts and service would strengthen client relationships even more and provide excellent professional development experiences for the professional staff. Furthermore, he planned to use the "no surprise" approach as the focus of communications to new and prospective clients.

Relationship Management. Client retention deserves strategic consideration. When a professional service firm loses clients, it may indicate that the firm is not maintaining a consistently high service level. In progressive firms, the importance of client retention is recognized, and relationships are managed systematically. Among the approaches used are client service planning and critical incident management. (For further information, see Chapter 15, which discusses long-term relationships and has sections on each of these approaches.)

Client service planning is particularly effective with larger clients of professional service firms that have an array of services that may be useful to a client. This process is designed to ensure that a client's needs are understood by the service team, that the firm's services are tailored to meet the client's needs, and that services are delivered effectively. The objectives of this approach include retaining the client, expanding the client relationship by providing more services, and building upon personal relationships with decision makers and other key employees in clients' organizations.

For professional service firms having limited resources and service offerings, as well as for larger firms, a critical incident approach is beneficial. In this approach, experiences that recur across a firm's services are identified, and activities are designed to reinforce the relationship. For example, when a prospective client chooses a professional service firm, he or she may be apprehensive about the decision because of the intangibility of the service. A professional can reinforce the decision by planning some activity that causes the client to conclude, "I made the right decision." The professional might send a small gift, perhaps a book on a favorite topic, or call to arrange a planning session.

Continuing attention to the service development and delivery process helps a professional service firm focus on the client in terms of both needs and participation in the process, identify new service or cross-selling opportunities, and differentiate itself in the marketplace. In addition, the firm's employees more fully understand the meaning of *service* and their role in high-quality service delivery.

## Strategy 2: Develop Excellent Service Providers

Every employee in a professional service firm should understand how the firm's clients define *service quality* and what part his or her activities and attitudes play in this definition. In addition, an employee should be able to describe the firm's purpose, services, significant clients (if appropriate), and his or her role in the service delivery process. This process is called *internal marketing*. (See Chapter 5 for an in-depth discussion of this process.)

The premise of internal marketing is that the firm regards its professional and administrative staff as a market or an audience. A senior person within the firm is responsible for internal marketing; this responsibility includes developing a plan similar to the type used to reach a market of prospective clients.

The plan might cover such objectives as:

- Increasing sensitivity to clients' needs
- Helping professional and administrative staff understand their role in client service (a service blueprint could be useful here)
- Helping all staff understand the firm's basic services
- Helping all staff understand firmwide strategies

Among the tools and activities that might be useful in internal marketing are:

- Orientation programs for new employees
- Orientation programs regarding new services
- Firmwide communications, including newsletters and copies of general mailings to clients
- Educational programs concerning:
  —Communication skills
  —Technical topics
  —Marketing issues and programs
  —Topics of interest to clients (e.g., financing for small business)

It is important to encompass the whole firm in internal marketing. Administrative staff, who usually have no technical background in the profession, should be included. Firms that have done so have found that employee turnover is reduced and that staff members do make client referrals because of their knowledge of the firm.

Internal marketing is a cooperative effort among marketing, human resources, and operations. Recruiting and compensation programs should reflect the firm's focus on service quality and marketing.

## The Challenge of Balancing Strategies

According to Maister,[7] managers of professional service firms must "balance the often conflicting demands and constraints imposed by . . . two markets": current and prospective clients for a firm's services and professionals who can provide the firm's services to clients. The key to attracting and retaining clients is to deliver consistently high-quality service, achievable by designing an effective and efficient service delivery process. Simultaneously, the firm must invest in internal marketing in order to develop employees who are sensitive to clients' needs, take satisfaction in their delivery of high-quality service, and receive support for managing the quality of the firm's services.

## Summary

The premise of this chapter is that professional service firms can achieve their service quality objectives through two primary strategies:

1. Focusing on the service delivery process, that is, the interaction between the client and the professional and the broad range of firm activities supporting that interaction and other client experiences
2. Raising the client sensitivity of all professional and administrative staff, who serve clients directly or indirectly by supporting contact employees

Firms that adopt these strategies and translate them into substantive ongoing systems recognize that (1) it is the client's definition of *quality* that counts, and (2) employees shape a client's experiences with the firm and thus influence his or her perceptions of the firm's quality of service. The benefits to these firms include identifying ways to differentiate themselves in the marketplace, improving client and employee retention, gaining value-added pricing advantages, and increasing opportunities for new business with both current and prospective clients.

In successful professional service firms, marketing and operations are interdependent. A firm that delivers service at a consistently high level of quality will achieve its marketing objectives.

## Notes

1. The characteristics differentiating between professional services are based on a classification scheme presented by Christopher H. Lovelock in *Services Marketing: Text, Cases and Readings* (Englewood Cliffs, N.J.: Prentice-Hall, 1984), 49–63.
2. G. Lynn Shostack, "Breaking Free From Product Marketing," *Journal of Marketing,* April 1977, 73–80.
3. Evert Gummesson coined the phrase *part-time marketer* to describe employees' marketing roles in "The New Marketing—Developing Long-Term Interactive Relationships," *Long-Range Planning* 20, no. 4 (1987):10–20. He described the marketing responsibilities of professional services firms' employees in "The Marketing of Professional Services—25 Propositions," in *Marketing Services,* ed. James H. Donnelly and William R. George (Chicago: American Marketing Association, 1981), 108–112. See also his comments in Chapter 7.
4. For a description of the role of staff accountants in influencing clients' perceptions, see W. R. George and K. W. Wheiler, "Practice Development—A Services Marketing Perspective," *The CPA Journal,* October 1986, 30–43.
5. G. Lynn Shostack, "How to Design a Service," in *Marketing of Services,* ed.

James H. Donnelly and William R. George (Chicago: American Marketing Association, 1981), 221–229.

6. G. Lynn Shostack, "Service Designs in the Operating Environment" in *Developing New Services,* ed. William R. George and Claudia E. Marshall (Chicago: American Marketing Association, 1984), 41.

7. David H. Maister, "Balancing the Professional Service Firm," *Sloan Management Review,* Fall 1982, 5.

## Further Resources

Congram, Carole A., and Ruth J. Dumesic. *The Accountant's Strategic Marketing Guide.* New York: Wiley, 1986.

Connor, Richard A., Jr., and Jeffrey P. Davidson. *Marketing Your Consulting and Professional Services.* New York: Wiley, 1985.

Wilson, Aubrey. *Practice Development for Professional Firms.* London: McGraw-Hill (UK), 1984.

\*    \*    \*    \*

*Carole A. Congram, Ph.D., is the principal of Congram Associates, a consulting firm based in New York City and specializing in services marketing. She assists clients with a broad range of planning and implementation services. She also holds the position of associate professor of operations management at Bentley College in Waltham, Massachusetts. A frequent speaker on services marketing topics, she was on the national marketing staff of Touche Ross & Co. for eleven years, most recently as director of marketing communication planning.*

# 27

# Education

Laurence N. Smith
Rita Abent
Dennis Lefond

Marketing education services has taken on new emphasis in recent years as institutions at all levels strive to cope with changing demographics and increased competition. Although all institutions engage in marketing activities, whether intentionally or not, most do not use a marketing planning process, and most do not realize their marketing potential.

Educators seeking to make an immediate impact on the marketing function at their institution will find this chapter helpful. It is organized into four major parts:

1. Assessing your organization's marketing status and defining next-step activities
2. Defining ten marketing elements as they apply to educational organizations
3. Introducing market research as the key to marketing planning
4. Focusing on promotions as a means of establishing an immediate marketing presence

## Assessing Your Organization's Marketing Status

Marketing exists at all educational institutions from preschool through professional schools. At only a few institutions is marketing a highly sophisticated, fully integrated process in which data and resources are managed to produce results. At many more, it is a piecemeal approach to solving specific fundraising or admissions problems. Unfortunately, at even more institutions, marketing is simply what occurs as a result of day-to-day activities.

The reasons for such variance most likely have to do with an institution's responses to three factors:

1. Perceived need
2. Ethical question of whether or not educational nonprofit institutions should be marketing
3. Ability to mobilize for action

For many years educational institutions existed in a sellers' market and as such had a ready supply of buyers for their product. They defined what was sold, when, where, to whom, and at what price. If buyers didn't like what sellers were offering, they could go elsewhere or adjust their needs. Although this is not to imply that institutions were totally customer-insensitive, it does recognize that for many years customers' needs were weighed against the needs of those providing the service—and those providing the service generally prevailed.

Changing demographics, the requirements of a technological society for retraining and retooling its workers, and increased interest in leisure learning are all reshaping the American educational sector.

### Does Your Organization Need Marketing?

Institutions are now in or are facing a buyer's market. Too few traditional students, strong competition in the marketplace, and increased societal demands are forcing institutions to review their entire marketing portfolio.

Institutions are having to step up their customer service initiatives in order to maintain their market position. Fortunately, educational institutions don't have to start from zero. For decades, whether they were aware of it or not, institutions have been engaged in the marketing and exchange process. Marketing, as you'll recall from earlier chapters, is creating desired exchanges with targeted publics for the purpose of achieving organizational objectives. Exchanges in this context are what the organization offers (classes, credits, degrees, socialization) in return for a price (funding, tuition, time).

As Figure 27-1 illustrates, educational institutions, regardless of function (preschool, K–12, college, university) or designation (public, private), are practicing marketing. Because marketing was seen as unacceptable or irrelevant, however, these exchange functions had to be disguised as public affairs, public relations, and/or student affairs. Institutions that are further along in developing integrated marketing functions are those that were able to recognize the marketing implications of these activities and expand upon them.

### Should Nonprofits Be Marketing?

Herein lies the crux of the marketing dilemma facing educational institutions. Our position is that marketing is already taking place. The real question facing institutions is the degree to which they wish to establish their own preferred future and to use available tools to achieve their goals.

Marketing, which is both a science and an art, provides managers with a wide array of tools, as well as strategic and tactical approaches that have proved successful for diagnostic and prescriptive purposes. As institutions adopt marketing, they will strengthen their organization and better manage their future.

Developing this marketing management mode requires visionary leadership. It calls for recognizing that marketing is a critical and central form of modern educational enterprise. It implies knowledge that, no matter what you call it, the marketing function must be managed to ensure that goals are realized.

**Figure 27-1.** Traditional exchange functions in education marketing.

| Indirect Publics | Give | Receive |
|---|---|---|
| Boards | Consent to manage | Visibility, influence |
| Legislature | Funding | Educational programs, societal progress |
| Taxpayers | Taxes | Education for children Education/socialization for next generation of taxpayers |
| Foundations | Grants | Recognition |
| Parents | Tuition | Education for self, family |
| Employers/Industry | Taxes | Skilled work force |

| Direct Publics | Give | Receive |
|---|---|---|
| Students | Time, effort, tuition | Training, degrees, credits, skills, attitudes, knowledge, social opportunities, enjoyment |
| Athletic fans | Price of ticket, time | Excitement, entertainment |
| Theater-, concertgoers | Price of admission | Entertainment, cultural enhancement |
| Parents in PTA | Time, effort | Influence, better programs |
| Students using services (housing, food, bookstore, health center) | Money, time | Products or services (housing, food, supplies, health care) |

## Can Your Organization Be Mobilized for Action?

Mobilizing the educational community to embrace a marketing philosophy and orientation requires an enormous commitment of energy, resources and institutional readiness to respond. An institution's readiness to embrace a marketing culture is generally characterized by four stages:

| | |
|---|---|
| *Stage 1* | Passive |
| *Stage 2* | Awakening |
| *Stage 3* | Energized |
| *Stage 4* | Internalized action |

In Stage 1 (passive), most administrators and faculty do not understand marketing or its potential benefits. They view it as an inappropriate activity. The organization may have a number of marketing activities going on (e.g., promotional publications, fund-raising campaigns), but it is not conscious of what they are or does not know how to maximize their effectiveness. When a marketing initiative is generated, it is often a reactive response to an immediate problem, such as a decline in enrollment or the need to generate funds to offset budget cuts. Marketing tends to be promotion-oriented. Materials are written and distributed without regard to any marketing plan. Promotional publications are written to satisfy internal needs—to please or at least not to offend the administration or faculty.

Stage 2 (awakening) is characterized by the existence of a small core group that understands marketing and advocates its use. There seems to be a great deal of activity as people realize marketing's potential, collaborate, and mobilize resources. Stage 2 is usually triggered when there is an erosion of program/ product vitality. In Stage 2 there is a great deal of unevenness across the institution in understanding and applying marketing principles. Consultants are hired to teach, train, and recommend action.

In Stage 3 (energized), you will find institutions that have formalized marketing roles and responsibilities. Resources are committed. Marketing is seen as an integral part in developing action plans. In Stage 3 the marketing strategy has been developed, and long-term contracts are arranged with vendors who implement specialized activities, such as interviewing, printing, mailing, or telemarketing. An annual marketing plan is part of the institution's strategic plan. Stage 3 usually evolves when the expectations for success are so high that marketing must be included.

In Stage 4 (internalized action), an intact organizational marketing structure is part of the formal operation and organization of the institution. The marketing structure is vertically integrated and horizontally linked with structured reporting relationships across departments, providing the appropriate marketing management matrix for success. Each area within the institution is tied into the marketing planning, execution, and management networks.

## Moving Your Organization Forward

Institutions need to assess their level of readiness and then initiate activities that will facilitate moving them toward Stage 4.

Your institution is at Stage 1 if the prevailing attitude is "If people don't like it here, they can go elsewhere"; if suggestions for new and/or different programs face stiff opposition; and if marketing and promotions are not recognized as separate and distinct activities. If you don't know who your consumers are, or what they want, you're at Stage 1.

Stage 1 behavior is fine providing you stay in a sellers' market. If you wish to have any success in responding to new market challenges, however, you'll need to initiate activities that will move you away from Stage 1 behaviors.

If you are in Stage 1, you need to:

- Increase institutional awareness of marketing benefits.
- Forge links with professional marketers.
- Form collaborative task groups to share information and solve problems.

- Scan the literature and profession for marketing ideas and practices you can emulate.

You are at Stage 2 if there is a growing awareness that change is necessary. The organization is awakening to the fact that new approaches are critical if vitality is to be maintained or regained. Task forces and committees have been appointed, but they tend to deal with the peripheral marketing issues rather than marketing planning.

To move your institution out of Stage 2, you should:

- Look for models and develop pilot projects.
- Engage consultants to assist in training and program development.
- Consolidate marketing teams.
- Seek out new approaches and take risks.
- Test marketing results.

You are in Stage 3 if people have stopped apologizing for using marketing terms in the everyday life of the institution. Accountability and responsibility for marketing functions have been institutionalized. Marketing research is the basis for institutional decision making, and marketing planning and execution are major factors for success.

At Stage 3 you should:

- Refine marketing initiatives based on results and research.
- Contract for services you need but have not used.
- Continually develop systematic marketing plans.

At Stage 4 goals and tracking mechanisms have been developed and subscribed to throughout the institution. The marketing structure has a high ranking administrator who commands institutional respect and support and who is seen as a vital link to the organization's success.

If you're at Stage 4, you should:

- Document marketing practices.
- Contribute to the literature.
- Serve as a mentor for institutions in Stages 1 through 3.
- Celebrate your success.

## Ten Key Elements of Education Marketing

Because most for-profit businesses have integrated marketing organizations that can analyze, apply, and evaluate the marketing mix relative to their unique situation, and most educational institutions do not, we find it helpful to expand the traditional mix to include ten elements, listed in Figure 27-2.

The educational marketer can use these ten elements as the basis for developing a situation analysis and research base. Once you have determined which

**Figure 27-2.** Ten key elements of education marketing.

1. Publics—All the constituencies with which education has an exchange process:

   - Students
   - Parents
   - Vendors
   - Legislators
   - Taxpayers
   - Boards
   - Foundations
   - Employers
   - Unions

2. Products—The offerings being exchanged with publics:

   - Courses
   - Curriculum
   - Entertainment
   - Services
   - Programs
   - Enrichment

3. Price—The cost of the offering to the publics:

   - Tuition
   - Time
   - Child care
   - Deferred earnings
   - Financial aid
   - Taxes/millage

4. Place—Where and when the buyer can obtain the offering:

   - On-site
   - Off-site
   - Weekend/sunrise programs
   - Seminar cruise packages
   - Day programs
   - Evening programs

5. Promotions—The processes by which the organization creates attention, interest, desire, and action and communicates information about the offer to the buyer:

   - Letters
   - Telemarketing
   - Personal contact
   - Sales promotion
   - Advertising
   - Direct mail
   - Giveaways
   - Videos

6. Preparations—The processes by which the organization creates a marketing environment and marketing management systems for analysis, planning, implementation, and control:

   - Formal organizational structure
   - Translating available data into market data
   - Designating human and financial resources
   - Using results management

7. Performance—How the organization measures its effectiveness in terms of its delivery systems:

   - Formal training
   - Outcomes assessment
   - Consumer satisfaction surveys

8. Planning—The processes by which the organization determines goals, objectives, and desired outcomes, and the management systems established to ensure achievement of these goals and objectives:

   - Strategic thrust and tactical development
   - Operational monitoring
   - Outcomes management

9. Personnel—Those individuals who have accountability and responsibility for the marketing function:

- Full-time
- Part-time
- Contractual
- Volunteer

10. Politics—The driving and restraining forces in the environment in which the marketing function takes place:

- Boards
- Numbers of participants
- Institution's image
- How institution wants to position itself
- Budget
- Informal process by which decisions are made

of the ten elements are critical to the development of your marketing plan, you must conduct market research to obtain information that will help you develop strategies to reach your goals.

# Market Research

Marketing is managing the exchange process. To do so with insight and intent requires that you know and understand the process from both sides of the exchange—the organization's and the constituent's. Market research is one of the most objective methods to assess the exchange process from the constituent's perspective because the key ingredient of market research is data collection.

Educators collect mountains of data about constituents, although it is seldom in a format conducive to making marketing decisions. Educators collect, obtain, and use three types of data:

- Proprietary organizational records
- Trend data and published research
- Original research

## Proprietary Organizational Records

Educational organizations are drowning in data about their students and course enrollments. The following is a brief list of information that is usually collected, but is seldom used in the marketing sense:

- School enrollment
- Grades
- Addresses
- Financial aid
- Disciplinary records
- Activities
- Course enrollment
- Test scores
- Family size
- Gender
- Attendance
- Race

By examining these data you can identify who your students are and what courses or classes they desire. By examining these same data over a period of years, educators can identify trends that will help them alter the organizational offerings to meet needs. For example, colleges should track their students' secondary schools so that enrollment patterns can be identified. These patterns can then be compared to enrollment projections from those same sending institutions to help project potential market share. Grade-point averages and standardized test scores can be analyzed over several years and correlated to college performance and graduation rates to determine the validity and reliability of the admission department's entrance criteria.

Existing data can also provide leads for new market segments. For example, families with small children might be prime users of a new child-care program or might be interested in summer youth camps.

### Trend Data and Published Research

Other sources of data available to educators include state and national enrollment and achievement reports, which can provide direct insight into the exchange process. To stay ahead of the competition and benefit from changes, beginning educational marketers need to mirror their more experienced colleagues in the for-profit sector by constantly scanning a wide variety of topics and sources and asking specific questions. It is likely that educators know the types of information shown in Figure 27-3. To be effective, educators need to assess the marketing implications of this information. The lists specify topic areas, sources of information, and questions to ask when reviewing information.

### Original Research

Some information will not be available and will have to be collected by the educational organization or a market research supplier. Some educational organizations such as colleges and universities have staff and faculty who can conduct sophisticated research. All educators, however, can interview their students, either individually or in groups. In this way, they can begin to gain greater insight into the perspectives and needs of students, parents, and other constituents. The following types of questions are illustrative of those asked by market research studies in education:

- What services do students need, want, demand?
- What courses do students need, want, demand?
- When should courses/events be offered?
- What is the best price to charge?
- Will a new course or degree sell?
- What types of students are we currently serving?
- What is our image with various constituents?
- How satisfied are the publics with our offerings?
- What specifically contributes to satisfaction and dissatisfaction?

**Figure 27-3.** Scanning events, developments, and trends that influence institutional success.

---

### Topic Areas

| | |
|---|---|
| Population changes | Learning technology |
| Lifestyles | State and local finance |
| Family composition | Religious institutions |
| Education—same level | (parochial) |
| Education—other levels | (Youth) values and lifestyles |
| Economy | Marketing |
| Technology | Management/Business |
| Labor projections | |

### Sources of Information

| | |
|---|---|
| Television news | Friends |
| Newspapers | Seminars |
| Magazines | Colleagues |
| Newsletters | Census reports |
| Professional journals | Federal publications |
| Future-oriented publications | State and local reports |
| Books | Federal, state, and local officials |

### Questions

How accurate is this information?
How direct/indirect is the impact on education?
How significant is the impact on society?
What are the training implications?
Where will this impact my marketing mix? Product? Price? Place?
  Promotion? Will it alter the type of customers I serve?
Will the impact be felt in the immediate or in the distant future?
Is the information privileged or hard to obtain?
What is the likelihood my competition will respond?

---

- Where should we offer classes?
- What benefits do constituents believe they receive from our classes?
- Is our advertising noticed, effective, and efficient?
- What media do our constituents use?
- What do employers and colleges or educational organizations that will be working with our students want them to know?

Informal qualitative research that involves asking students their opinions is an excellent starting point. If educators plan to make major changes in the manner in which they market educational services, it is usually advisable to conduct objective, quantifiable research with carefully selected samples. Market research helps you develop successful strategies for reaching your marketing goals, particularly strategies for the critical area of promotion.

# The Promotional Plan: Building a Competitive Advantage

Research is the best starting point for designing an effective marketing plan. Promotion is the best starting point for establishing a marketing presence. Promotions help:

- Establish image and positioning congruence (in other words, the way the institution is viewed by the public matches the way it wants to be seen).
- Create awareness.
- Mobilize involvement.
- Move people to action.

Unfortunately, education has been narrowly focused in its use of promotions. At best, promotional plans have consisted of personal contact (counselor visits to schools, parent-teacher conferences, and college fairs) and the development of print material featuring faculty and facilities (brochures, newsletters, prospectuses).

Although these are important components of a promotional strategy, they are only a beginning. Fortunately, academic institutions are moving beyond the question of whether or not they should be promoting (economics has helped in that regard) to how to promote most effectively.

## First Steps in Developing a Promotional Plan

Before mapping out a plan, assess your current situation and how well it's working. Figure 27-4 offers a brief checklist that can be used for both internal and external activities.

Once you've assessed your current situation, determine the goals and objectives of the promotional plan. Do you want to:

**Figure 27-4.** Promotional pulse check.

|  | Yes | No |
|---|---|---|
| Do you have a promotional plan? | ____ | ____ |
| Do you have a balance of promotional components: personal contact, advertising, public relations, and direct marketing? | ____ | ____ |
| Do you measure the effectiveness of each component? | ____ | ____ |
| Is the promotional plan integrated with other sections of the marketing plan? | ____ | ____ |
| Are your promotions achieving the desired results? | ____ | ____ |
| Are your promotions cost-effective? | ____ | ____ |
| Do your promotions use different approaches for different market segments? | ____ | ____ |

**Table 27-1.** Strengths and weaknesses of selected promotional techniques.

| | Promotional Technique | | | |
|---|---|---|---|---|
| *Characteristic* | *Personal Contact* | *Advertising* | *Public Relations* | *Special Events* |
| Audience type | Small | Mass | Mass | Varies |
| Dominant impact | Action | Attention | Attention | Varies |
| Expense | High | Moderate | Low | Moderate |

- Increase market penetration?
- Expand your market?
- Introduce a new program or service?

Understanding whom you want to reach and why is critical to the success of any marketing initiative, especially promotions. The one rule that educators must remember is: *You can't be all things to all people!*

Marketers use the mnemonic AIDA when describing the steps for successful communication. First you have to get their *A*ttention; you have to hold their *I*nterest; you have to arouse *D*esire; and you have to generate *A*ction.

Certain types of promotional components are better for creating attention than for generating action. A hot-air balloon, for example, attracts a great deal of attention, but is a limited means of communicating high-content information and thus moving people to action. You need to balance use of these components to achieve maximum effectiveness.

Table 27-1 highlights the relative strengths and weaknesses of four promotional components. It's easy to see that personal contact (e.g., visits to counselors) far outpaces any other area for effectiveness in "moving people to action." It also costs the most and reaches the least number of people. Advertising can reach thousands and costs less per person reached than personal selling, but it is less effective in moving people to action.

A classic marketing tool that combines the best elements of both personal selling and mass advertising is direct marketing. *Direct marketing* is an interactive system of advertising that uses one or more media to effect a measurable response. Two highly successful formats of direct marketing are telemarketing and direct mail. Educational institutions have been slow to embrace direct marketing. As institutions that use direct marketing will testify, however, direct marketing works. It is targeted and numbers-driven and, if done properly, it moves people to action.

Direct Mail.   Direct mail is the classic example of direct marketing. Direct mail reaches people in a personal way by putting your message in their hands. To be effective as a direct response mechanism, however, the piece must be more than pretty pictures and institutional self-adulation. It must:

- Highlight benefits of your institution.
- Identify and trigger a desire.
- Instill a sense of urgency.
- Prescribe action.

To determine whether your copy is market-response driven, see how it measures up against the following guidelines:

1. *Is it prepared for a specific market segment?* Alumni and freshmen recruits have different needs. A piece written for one probably won't be effective with the other. Tailor pieces to the audience.

2. *Does it use language people will understand?* "Interdisciplinary," "matriculate," and "curriculum responsiveness" may sound very academic, but will the audience understand these terms? Keep the words simple and the message concise.

3. *Does it get to the point?* People are bombarded with thousands of messages daily. You have only a few seconds to attract attention. Don't bury the point.

4. *Does it highlight benefits, not features?* The most important element in the direct response formula is the reader. And the reader wants to know, "What's in this for me?" Focus on what the reader will gain. For example, being an accredited institution is a feature—the benefit to the readers, if they attend, is that their degree has respectability and marketability or if they transfer, their courses are recognized.

5. *Does it offer an easy way to respond?* Always provide a means of interaction, with either a response card or a toll-free number. Make the card stand out. Use postage-free cards if possible for the best return rate.

6. *Does it thank the reader?* Time is a precious resource. When you've used people's time, thank them. People need to know you value them and their time. As a bonus use the thank-you to restate your offer or to invite your reader to visit, call, or return the card.

Direct mail pieces don't need to be elaborate, expensive formats. The classic format consists of an envelope, a personalized letter, and a brochure that supports the contents of the letter.

The letter is the key component. To make sure it's effective, remember AIDA (attention, interest, desire, action). To be most efficient, direct-mail letters should:

- Be personalized.
- Use short paragraphs.
- Use bullets and/or underlining to emphasize points, direct the reader, and emphasize action.
- Make an offer.
- Use a P.S. to restate the offer.

Telemarketing.   Another cost-effective direct marketing tool institutions can employ is telemarketing, which uses telecommunications technology as a channel for implementing sales and service programs. Effective use of telemarketing can help institutions accomplish these objectives:

- Open up new territories.
- Improve response time.
- Conduct primary research.
- Qualify inquiries.
- Generate leads.
- Increase contacts.
- Expand service hours.
- Add a personal touch to mass marketing.

Every contact with the public you serve should be a marketing promotions opportunity. Correspondence, business cards, flyers, brochures, special events, personal contacts—everything you and your faculty do needs to focus on putting your best foot forward. Every contact should be used to enhance your image and position. You're already marketing. The trick is to do it better, to make it work for you.

## Summary

In terms of markets reached, people served, and resources expended, education is among the most critically important service sectors. It will continue to play an increasingly vital role in our society as we retool and retrain America to maintain and enhance our competitiveness in the world community.

Education remains the vital link between where we are and where we want to be if we are to secure the future we envision for ourselves. We believe that the marketing strategies and techniques explored in this *Handbook,* together with the special focus of this section, are among the most appropriate tools to be mastered if we are to maintain our effectiveness and fulfill new expectations.

Strong marketing management, together with full implementation of the marketing concept as an exchange process, will afford the education service sector the opportunity to remain sensitive and responsive to individual needs while also serving larger societal needs. The tools and skills inherent in the marketing planning and execution processes will enable those of us in stewardship roles to execute them with maximum results.

## Further Resources

*The Admissions Strategist Series.* College Board Publications, 45 Columbus Avenue, New York, NY 10023-6692.

*American Demographics Magazine.* American Demographics, Inc., 108 N. Cayuga Street, Ithaca, NY 14850.

*College Marketing Alert: How to Compete for Students and Funds.* Business Publishers, Inc., 951 Pershing Drive, Silver Spring, MD 20910-4464.

Hossler, Don. *Enrollment Management: An Integrated Approach.* New York: College Entrance Examination Board, 1984.

Ingersoll, Ronald J. *The Enrollment Problem.* New York: Macmillan, 1988.

Kotler, Philip, and Karen F. A. Fox. *Strategic Marketing for Educational Institutions.* Englewood Cliffs, N.J.: Prentice-Hall, 1985.

*The Nonprofit Times.* Davis Information Group, P. O. Box 7286, Princeton, NJ 08543-7285.

Smith, Virginia Carter, and Susan Hunt, eds. *The New Guide to Student Recruitment Marketing.* Washington, D.C.: Council for Advancement and Support of Education, 1986.

Topor, Robert. *Marketing Higher Education.* Washington, D.C.: Council for Advancement and Support of Education, 1983.

The following associations and organizations provide a wide array of programs, activities, services, and publications:

American College Testing Program. 2201 N. Dodge Street, P.O. Box 168, Iowa City IA 52243.

The College Board. 45 Columbus Avenue, New York, NY 10023.

Council for Advancement and Support of Education (CASE). 11 Dupont Circle NW, Washington, DC 20036.

\* \* \* \*

*Laurence N. Smith is vice president for university marketing and student affairs at Eastern Michigan University in Ypsilanti. He has overall leadership responsibility for strategic marketing planning and management in these areas. He is well-known as a pioneer in the marketing of nonprofit institutions and organizations and for his work in transformation management, which involves mobilizing organizations for renewal.*

*Rita Abent is the editor of the* Hollywood (Florida) Sun, *a South Florida Newspaper, Inc., daily that serves South Broward County. Prior to that she held the position of director of marketing media at Eastern Michigan University.*

*Dennis Lefond, Ph.D., is director of university market research at Eastern Michigan University. His responsibilities include conducting quantitative and qualitative market research for the university and its departments and using statistical software, sampling procedures, data analysis, and report writing to improve decision making.*

# 28

# The Arts

William M. Dawson

Although the preceding chapters have discussed various aspects of market planning, a common theme throughout has dealt with identifying and understanding consumers. This article describes consumers of the arts from one point of view that has proven highly successful in reaching that understanding: the Values and Lifestyles program (VALS*) at SRI International. It discusses the major competition for a potential arts consumer: a shortage of discretionary leisure time. Finally, it focuses on recognizing the arts and consumers as being part of an "Experience Industry"[1] and the implications for more effective communication.

## Product or Sales or Consumer Orientation?

The first comprehensive overview of marketing the arts appeared in 1980.[2] It was prompted by the realization that resources that had been taken for granted were no longer as readily available. Competition for audience, for earned revenue, and for external funding had increased significantly, and rarely were arts organizations utilizing marketing skills. Since that time increasing attention has been devoted to finding out what motivates arts consumers. As people are being urged to use their free time more creatively, a general recognition has begun to emerge that simply citing coming events or putting more money into advertising and promotion is not enough. It is now understood that the consumer determines whether a transaction is to occur and that a wide variety of factors enters into that determination. When supply exceeds demand, the consumer determines when and at what price the transaction will be made; today the supply of arts products far exceeds the demand.

Kotler and Andreasen have succinctly differentiated between a product orientation, a sales orientation, and a customer orientation, noting that "marketing planning must *start* with customer perceptions, needs and wants."[3] Both product determination and the means of communication in the arts have been driven largely by the narcissistic desires of the arts organization and by a theorized image of who the consumer is. Product selection, whether the season's repertoire or calendar of events, is too often based on the desires of an artistic director who has little concern for or understanding of the needs of a presumed audience. Communication is usually addressed to a faceless mass, much like

---

*VALS is a registered trademark of SRI International.

casting a net into the waters and hoping that upon retrieval, there will be a catch.

Most arts organizations tend to be product- and sales-oriented, focused on satisfying their own needs, rather than being market-oriented or focused on satisfying the needs of a consumer. There is a fear of sacrificing one's artistic integrity if the thrust of programming is consumer-oriented. To alleviate this fear, a balance needs to be established between what the consumer wants and what the organization wants. It is not a matter of either/or; it is a matter of market analysis and using creative judgment in both program selection and communication.

## Know Thy Consumer

Many arts organizations have undoubtedly conducted demographic surveys in an effort to identify their current consumers. The results have provided a rather flat profile of such factors as education, age, sex, income, and occupation. Demographics tell us who is there, but not why. Lacking in dimension, these studies have rarely revealed descriptive information about the values and lifestyles of consumers and the factors that motivate their purchase and consumption of the arts product. Little information has been gathered that identifies the role or roles that the arts play in the consumer's life.

Equally important is a lack of understanding of members of the general public and their attitudes about the arts. Other researchers have designated arts-aware people as Crafts, Intellectuals, or Ego-Recognitions;[4] Culture Patrons;[5] Peak Aesthetic Experiencers or Cultural Aspirants;[6] Hedonic Consumers;[7] or, merely, the "arts sample."[8] The few studies that have dealt with lifestyles have been helpful, but perhaps the most significant have been those conducted by researchers at SRI International and the Association of College, University, and Community Arts Administrators (ACUCAA),[9] now known as Association of Performing Arts Presenters.

VALS is a systematic way of viewing people on the basis of their attitudes, needs, wants, beliefs, self-images, aspirations, demographics, and the products they use. The program was created by the late Arnold Mitchell and SRI International in 1978 in an effort to gain a better understanding of people, their buying habits, and the trends of our times. Regularly updated since its inception, VALS has been a fluid and flexible monitor of the changing motivations in people's behavior and purchasing habits. (For a detailed explanation of the VALS program, the book by Arnold Mitchell is recommended.)[10] More than 100,000 Americans have been classified into the VALS type.

In essence, VALS is a program that helps marketers get closer to the people they are trying to reach. The typology is divided into four major categories, with a total of nine distinct lifestyle types. Although it is oversimplified, the program nonetheless has provided new insights into characterizing the lifestyles of Americans. The system is being applied currently in many areas of business, and more than 150 leading corporations, advertising agencies, and media companies are using its findings.

In conjunction with SRI, ACUCAA conducted two U.S. studies relating the VALS typology to the performing arts. The purpose was to better identify by lifestyles those people most likely to attend performances, those most likely to be marginal consumers, and those least likely to attend, or the "hardest sell."

It became evident that only three of the lifestyles could be identified clearly as primary target markets: Achievers, Experientials, and Societally Conscious. Comprising 38 percent of the adult population, these three groups form the vast majority of attenders, real and potential.

Demographically, Achievers have a median age of 41.7 years, are predominantly male, and are usually married; 56 percent have attended or graduated from college, and their household income is the highest of any of the groups.

Experientials are younger with a median age of 27.1 years, are predominantly female, and are usually single; 75 percent have attended or graduated from college, and they generally have sufficient affluence to afford what they want.

Societally Conscious have a median age of 37.2 years, have a more even ratio of males to females, and are usually married; 91 percent have attended or graduated from college, and their household income is only slightly lower than that of the Achievers.

Knowing these demographics reveals very little about what is important in the lives of these types of people and reveals almost nothing about the kinds of products or messages that address their needs. Not surprisingly, and like most demographic studies, this study indicated the most likely arts consumers are well-educated, relatively affluent, and employed in professional, technical, or managerial positions.

A brief overview of some of the characteristics of these types may be more helpful. Achievers are materialistic, comfort-loving, and oriented toward fame and success. That success is evidenced in consumer terms by their homes, cars, clothing, jewelry, clubs and organizations, and vacations—all of the external symbols that spell success to others. Rewards for their hard work are important to them.

Experientials are more concerned with a rich, inner life. Intellectual and spiritual matters are important to them. They are more concerned about what a product does for them than about how it portrays them. Actively involved in outdoor activities, they seek direct experience and deep involvement in any of their activities.

Societally Conscious have many of the same concerns and interests as the Experientials, but have less of a hedonistic need. These are people who want to live in a socially responsible way and who take an active role in many social issues. They, too, are concerned about their own inner growth, and they are less concerned about style and various forms of self-display than either of the other types.

All of these and many other characteristics, attitudes, and beliefs are cues that provide us with a better understanding of our target markets. Although not intended primarily to determine product decisions, the results of the studies also indicated definite audience preferences in music, theater, and dance. More significantly, clear distinctions became apparent regarding the benefits sought. In the national studies and in succeeding local studies, it was evident that pleasure, diversion, amusement, and fun dominate the expectations of those who consume the arts frequently, infrequently, or not at all.

Although the benefits sought are generically identical, each takes on a distinctly different meaning for each of the lifestyles. For example, pleasure for an Achiever might be interpreted as being seen by the right people, the social nature of the occasion, the ''star'' quality of the performers, and practical problems such as parking and getting a good seat. For Societally Conscious, the same word might take on substantially different meanings; seeing a ''star'' may not be as important for members of this group as for Achievers, but experiencing something new, being moved emotionally, fulfilling oneself, and witnessing the creativity are more important.

The VALS and the ACUCAA studies provide a sense of the need for still deeper and fuller knowledge of consumers. Learning about audiences and defining them result in better understanding. If we understand them better, we can deliver better services and messages to them.

## "I Don't Have the Time. . . ."

In 1970, Staffan Linder[11] became aware of the increasing lack of leisure time, particularly for what he called the "leisure class." His thesis then was that the economic growth in America was not resulting in a greater amount of free time and a leisurely life for many Americans. Rather, it was resulting in a scarcity of time and in lives lived at a more hectic tempo. In the ensuing years, other studies and journals have noted the increased competition for those hours we call our own.

A study conducted by Lou Harris for the American Council for the Arts[12] noted that leisure time for the average American declined from 26.2 hours a week in 1973 to 18.1 hours in 1984, and to 16.6 hours in 1987. A wide variety of newspaper and magazine articles has reported on this trend in American lifestyles. When queried, most people feel they have fewer hours to spend at their own discretion. With the increase in the number of working mothers, for example, there is a desire for more guilt-free leisure hours, and this desire is even stronger for single parents. The increase in the number of families in which both spouses work has also resulted in a loss of leisure time.

As those free hours have declined dramatically (whether in reality or in perception), there has been a corresponding increase in the kinds of service being used to protect those precious hours. The increase in such services— including lawn-care services, restaurants, convenience stores, microwaves, automatic teller machines, house-cleaning services, take-out, mail order, and home shopping—bears testimony to people willing to spend more money in order to save time.

Consider the target markets identified by the VALS study; each of those lifestyles is primarily engaged in a professional, technical, or managerial occupation, and it is likely that the demands of those occupations have increased rather than decreased. Consider also that 55 percent of married Achiever women work full-time and 12 percent work part-time, 22 percent of married Experiential women work full-time and 34 percent part-time, and 57 percent of married Societally Conscious women work full-time and 13 percent part-time. The AC-UCAA studies have shown that women are the primary purchase decision makers and that overall they attend arts events on a ratio of 3 to 1 as compared to men. Harris also noted that women's leisure hours per week declined from 15.6 hours in 1984 to 14.0 hours in 1988. For the typical arts consumer, time has become more precious than money in many ways. This may be partly why Harris showed an overall decline of 12 percent in arts attendance since 1984. The decline was even greater for music, theater, and dance.

Coupled with this are more recent trends such as "caregivers" and "cocooning." Caregivers are those people who provide nonprofessional health care, usually to a family member. Increasingly this burden is being assumed by working women who are providing such care for their older, ailing parents. Because 62 percent of American women are now in the work force, the additional burden of caring for an ailing family member puts even greater demands on time.

*Cocooning* is the term being used to identify those people who, having experienced the daily rat race, are electing to stay at home during their hours of discretionary leisure time. One indication of this is the fact that between 1984 and 1987, VCR ownership has increased 234 percent, and this trend is expected to continue as more people opt to find more of their entertainment at home. Other indications include the previously mentioned use of take-out and convenience foods and microwaves.

Given the wide variety of reasons for the decline in discretionary leisure time, the arts marketer's challenge is to make the arts appealing enough so that they become preferred among the many options people have for spending that time.

## The Experience Is the Product

If the evidence points toward less leisure time, particularly for those people most likely to be arts consumers, and if arts attendance is declining, what will make people say, "I want to be there" or "This is how I want to spend an evening"?

Obviously, the quality of the actual product is of critical importance. The consumer needs to be able to recognize it as one that will provide pleasure, diversion, amusement, and fun. Is it, however, the actual product or the benefits sought that are paramount? What people are truly seeking is a meaningful use of the limited leisure time at their disposal. The experience to be gained is the major criterion for the choice that is made.

The experience in the use of leisure time can take many forms: After a particularly difficult day at work, the most meaningful use of leisure hours may be to stay at home with a stereo playing softly and read a good book. It may be a ski trip, a movie, scuba diving, shopping, gardening, a nature walk, an evening out with friends, a museum or gallery visit, a concert, or a religious service. The range of options is infinite.

Nor is this experience limited to the use of time. The cars we buy provide a driving experience; where we dine is frequently based on the atmosphere and experience of the restaurant; clothes are often purchased on the basis of the way we want to look and how others will view us—the experience. It is difficult to think of any product that is not experience-related. Not only must the experience be meaningful and the benefits strong enough to satisfy one's values, but the intensity of the experience is an essential factor.

In short, the experience is the product. The actual product—the car, restaurant, or arts event—is merely a means to the experience, which truly is the end product.

In the arts, it is not heresy to say that the art or artist is a means to an end. If the art or artists can provide a meaningful experience for the consumer, the artistic mission is fulfilled. This view requires a real shift in the arts marketer's thinking—a shift in emphasis from the actual product to the experience of the product use. A person must have the actual product—the art—but it is the perceived experience he or she will have that determines whether that person will or will not make the attendance decision.

## Communication Implications

Given the understanding of consumers, the demands for their time, and their desire for meaningful experiences, how can we communicate more effectively for their attention and attendance?

The first commandment is: Know thy product. This may seem obvious at the outset, but an analysis of brochures, advertising, and other promotional efforts reveals that many arts marketers apparently have little understanding of the nature of the product. Obviously, one must know the actual product, but what is the product the consumer seeks? The experience!

As an example, one might seek escape as the experience, but consider that it is less likely to be an escape "from" and more likely to be an escape "to." The latter is more suggestive of the product's potential experience—an escape to the private and often unspoken emotions, dreams, and aspirations of one's inner being. If life is complicated and complex, perhaps the product experience is an escape to greater simplicity and "less noise."

Know thy product: Is it emotional or logical, feeling or thinking, right- or left-brained, utilitarian? It is a promise, a promise of an experience providing benefits valuable to the consumer.

The second commandment is: Know thy consumer. Seeing the actual product through consumers' eyes, understanding what they seek and desire, and showing them what the experience will be are the keys to more successful communication.

Know whether your purpose is to inform, educate, or motivate. Each has its appropriate role, but where and when each is used requires some thought. It seems appropriate to say that one has to motivate people to attend, and although this may include some information, the emphasis needs to be on the experience one will have. Give more attention to the 95 percent of the people who are not knowledgeable about your product than to the 5 percent who are familiar with it. Once people are in attendance, the roles of information and education can be utilized more fully.

The third commandment is: Visually and verbally show and tell people what the experience will be. Most efforts to inform are attribute-laden; when one does not know the product, the tendency is to fall back on facts. The emphasis is on pictures of each and every artist or attraction with lengthy biographical detail. When was the music written? Under what circumstances? When was it first performed? Where? For whom? When was the group formed? Where were the artists trained? How long have they been performing? What kind of special instruments do they play? What special awards have they received? What works have they commissioned? What have they recorded? The backgrounds of the conductor, playwright and director, major performers, choreographer—all are in abundant evidence. Regardless of the art form, this is the usual tendency. What this emphasis on facts seems to reveal is that the marketer has little or no understanding of the experience provided by the art, or if that knowledge is present, it is buried under correct, cerebral, proper journalistic style.

The pictures used are static profiles or photos lacking any kind of dramatic intensity. Often, the artists shown are not recognized by the majority of viewers, and names under the pictures could easily be switched with little loss of impact. Visually, it is an old but true adage that a picture is worth a thousand words. Must that visual, however, be a literal representation? Photos of faces with few having any kind of name recognition do little to excite the viewer's imagination. Consider using nonrepresentational visuals. We have a visually literate society; can't we give them something that creates a mood, something that stirs the imagination, something that awakens inner values? The visual is a symbol of the experience to be had.

The arts are emotional in nature, yet the visuals we use do little to capture the emotion of the art. When people can't try the product in advance, metaphor can be synonymous with the experience. The nonrepresentational image can be provocative, and although it may have no apparent connection to the actual product, it can establish a generalized impression, feeling, or attitude. A picture can convey emotion far more rapidly than words and allows people to find their own meanings. Research indicates that pictorial stimuli are stronger than verbal, and that visual information is processed before the verbal.[13] Research is also revealing that if a picture creates positive feelings, more positive thoughts are activated, which can result in more positive thoughts about the actual product. Thus, the visual sets the stage for the verbal. It dominates initial impressions, and its final importance determines how much of the verbal will be processed.

When we write, we tend to write for ourselves. An in-depth analysis of brochures usually shows an abundance of copy containing the previously mentioned attributes. Rarely does it capture the excitement of an event; even less frequently does it capture the experience.

Do we make it easy for people to make a decision? We tend to believe that people will read everything we write. Achievers will not wade through a lot of copy, and although Experientials and Societally Conscious are more apt to read, even they will not spend large amounts of time perusing our hyperbole. How much information do we need to make a decision about dining out or going to a movie?

We have a tendency to be overly serious about our art, and that serious attitude dominates most of our promotion. Don't be afraid to be warm, human, and even to have a spirit of playfulness in the copy.

In individual copy, rather than saying how good "they" are, say what the experience will be. The focus needs to be on the consumer, not on the artists. We know that if copy is complex, has awkward syntax, and demands use of prior knowledge, it does not capture much attention. Shorter copy, the use of bullets, open-ended messages, and experience-based messages that can evoke an emotional satisfaction of values will be more effective than the "W's" of journalism. Think of it this way: If our communications are dull and boring, what will the event be like? The communications have to be as enjoyable as the event.

## Summary

This chapter has focused on the importance of understanding consumers. The purpose is not merely to give them what they want, but to understand them— their personalities, situations, attitudes, aspirations—so as to demonstrate how the artistic offering can meet and fulfill their needs.

The real competition for the arts is people's time, and some very sophisticated marketers are competing with us for that time. We can best compete by viewing the actual product as a means to an end that provides a meaningful and satisfying experience.

## Notes

1. James Ogilvy, *The Experience Industry* (Menlo Park, Cal.: Values and Lifestyles Program, SRI International, 1985).
2. Michael Mokwa, William M. Dawson, and E. Arthur Prieve, eds., *Marketing the Arts* (New York: Praeger, 1980).
3. Philip Kotler and Alan R. Andreasen, *Strategic Marketing for Nonprofit Organizations* (Englewood Cliffs, N.J.: Prentice-Hall, 1987).
4. George E. McKechnie, *Leisure Activities Blank—Manual,* Research ed. (Palo Alto, Cal.: Consulting Psychologists Press, 1975).
5. Alan R. Andreasen and Russell W. Belk, "Predictors of Attendance at the Performing Arts," *Journal of Consumer Research,* September 1980; *Audience Development: An Examination of Selected Analysis and Prediction Techniques Applied to Symphony and Theater Audiences in Four Southern Cities,* report 14, research division, National Endowment for the Arts, Washington, D.C., January 1981; *The Arts Public in the South,* report 17, research division, National Endowment for the Arts, Washington, D.C., 1984.
6. George Mialouis and David Lloyd, *Marketing the Arts in a Rural Environment,* monograph series 4 (Dayton, Ohio: Wright State University, 1979).
7. Elizabeth C. Hirschman and Morris B. Holbrook, "Hedonistic Consumption:

Emerging Concepts, Methods and Propositions,'' *Journal of Marketing,* Summer 1982.

8. John R. Nevin, *Leisure Attitudes and Participation in the Bay Area,* Center for Arts Administration, Graduate School of Business, University of Wisconsin-Madison, Madison, Wis., 1983.

9. Arnold Mitchell, *The Professional Performing Arts: Attendance Patterns, Preferences, and Motives,* vols. I and II (Washington, D.C.: Association of College, University, and Community Arts Administrators, 1984, 1985).

10. ———, *The Nine American Lifestyles* (New York: Macmillan, 1983).

11. Staffan B. Linder, *The Harried Leisure Class* (New York: Columbia University Press, 1970).

12. Lou Harris, *Americans and the Arts* (New York: American Council for the Arts, 1988).

13. Sidney Hecker and David W. Stewart, eds., *Nonverbal Communication in Advertising* (Lexington, Mass.: Lexington Books, 1988).

\*    \*    \*    \*

**William M. Dawson, Ph.D.,** *is a consultant to the arts. In that capacity he has worked with arts agencies at the regional, state, and local levels. Based in Madison, Wisconsin, he has planned, coordinated, and taught more than 200 training sessions for arts administrators throughout the United States and Canada. The topics have included strategic planning, consumer behavior, and creative advertising. He previously served as executive director of the Association of College, University and Community Arts Administators, Inc. (ACUCAA).*

# 29

# Retailing

Donald A. Hughes

The last song has not been composed. The last novel has not been written. And, the last retailing format has not been invented—nor will it ever be.

The history of retailing has been a chronicle of change. This change has not been a complete version of Joseph Schumpeter's theory of "creative destruction," in which ". . . industrial revolution . . . incessantly revolutionalizes the economic structure *from within,* incessantly destroying the old one, incessantly creating a new one. This process of Creative Destruction is the essential fact about Capitalism."[1] As new forms of retailing emerge, they inhibit the growth of old forms and sometimes cause an absolute decline in them. But the old forms never disappear completely. Individual retailers such as B. Altman, W. T. Grant, Korvettes, and Woolco may fade away, but the form survives, even though in a diminished state.

The small specialty shops of the nineteenth century were elbowed aside in the latter part of that century by the emerging department stores, but specialty retailers managed to reemerge as a strong growth segment in the 1970s and 1980s. Small neighborhood grocery stores were dealt a heavy blow with the growth of supermarkets beginning in the 1930s but still exist in many places today. Their natural offspring, the convenience store, has been a growth segment in recent years. In the 1990s, more changes will result from the recent spate of acquisitions, consolidations, and bankruptcies.

## Forces for Change

Change in the retail industry evolves from a variety of forces:

- *Concentration of population.* The general store is the best a small community can expect. As the population grows, the variety of retail outlets grows with it. In the early years of our nation, isolated farms were dependent on the itinerant peddler; today pedestrians in the Chicago Loop need walk no more than a block or two to find a shop specializing in nothing but cookies.

- *Distribution.* The advent of parcel post brought big city variety to rural communities through the Sears, Roebuck and Montgomery Ward catalogs. Similarly today, smaller communities benefit from distribution innovations such as Wal-Mart's "hub-and-spoke" distribution system, which provides one-day replenishment to stores within a 300-mile radius of the centralized distribution center.

• *Technology*. The explosion of communication alternatives and the dramatically lowered cost of data processing and storage can be seen in the proliferation of 800 numbers, computers, scanners, videoconferencing facilities, electronic tie-ins with suppliers, and interactive kiosks. Atop all this we have the emergence of J. C. Penney's Telaction, combining telephone and cable TV, and the Sears/IBM entry, Prodigy, which offers shopping through the home computer.

• *Labor force*. During the 1930s, 1940s, and 1950s, department stores thrived with a plentiful supply of relatively low-cost but talented labor as educated women found working in these stores to be one of the few careers open to them. More recently, the ''Baby Boom'' poured millions of teenagers into the labor force as baggers, stockers, and cashiers and helped fuel the growth of mass merchants and fast-food outlets.

• *Sociological changes*. The family, paramount in the fifties, supported the general merchandiser that offered everything the family needed—including credit. Today the traditional family shares the spotlight with a more rapidly growing array of household types, including single parents, single renters and home owners, childless couples, elderly widows and widowers, and unmarried cohabitators.

Although the household consisting of a married couple with at least one child is still a powerful economic force in our society, it has not experienced any significant growth in numbers from 1977 to 1987. Conversely, some nontraditional types of households have grown rapidly during this period (see Table 29-1). The number of married homeowners with at least one child present grew slightly less than 3 percent over this ten-year period, whereas total households increased by 20.7 percent. On the other hand, home ownership among those divorced or separated and those single–never married has increased rapidly. Households that are renters have increased more rapidly than home owners, and the increase has been spectacular among the divorced/separated and the single–never married.

The difference in the needs of these nontraditional households with generally lower incomes means that retailers cannot expect a given level of household growth to produce a corresponding level of growth in their traditional merchandise mix.

• *Legislation*. As Fair Trade Laws were abandoned, the protection afforded to the retailers of national brands eroded and discount stores pushed their way into the retail scene. To complicate the changing situation, national chains could no longer undercut the Fair Trade price with their private labels to the same degree as they had in the past.

Blue Laws have also been slowly disappearing from state after state to make shopping a seven-day-a-week possibility and, for some retailers, a 24-hour-a-day operation.

• *Credit*. Prior to the advent of the bank card, credit was very much a local service with the exception of a few national chain stores. Consumers who traveled or moved their residence were either restricted to cash transactions or forced

**Table 29-1.** Changes in numbers of households by residence, marital status, and presence of children.

| Type of Household | Units (000's) | | Change (%) |
|---|---|---|---|
| | 1977 | 1987 | |
| Homeowners | 48,083 | 56,823 | + 18.2 |
| Married—one or more children | 23,115 | 23,792 | + 2.9 |
| Married—no children | 13,428 | 16,623 | + 23.8 |
| Widowed | 6,441 | 7,796 | + 21.0 |
| Divorced/separated | 3,333 | 5,494 | + 64.8 |
| Single—never married | 1,766 | 3,118 | + 76.6 |
| Renters | 26,058 | 32,221 | + 23.7 |
| Married—one or more children | 6,606 | 7,322 | + 10.8 |
| Married—no children | 5,074 | 4,675 | − 7.9 |
| Widowed | 3,399 | 3,495 | + 2.8 |
| Divorced/separated | 5,420 | 7,777 | + 43.5 |
| Single—never married | 5,559 | 8,952 | + 61.0 |
| Total Households | 74,141 | 89,044 | + 20.1 |

*Source:* Adapted from the Bureau of Census, current population surveys, March 1977 and 1987.

to go through the process of opening new credit accounts. Bank cards have changed all that. Consumers can have instant credit at hundreds of thousands of retailers throughout the country.

• *Shifting channels for national brands.* The relative ease of entry into the retail field by entrepreneurs with new ideas has been aided by the changing position of brands in the industry. Brands formerly helped to structure the industry in a fashion that was understood by the consumer and the retailer. Today brands that were once the province of the department stores and higher priced specialty stores are available in off-price outlets. National chains are supplementing their private labels with national brands, while department and specialty stores try to compete with the off-price outlets with *their* own private labels.

## Service Moves to the Forefront

With price cutting rampant in the field and exclusivity of brands a thing of the past, retailers are turning to service as a means of differentiating themselves from the competition.

Service in the retail industry is not a new subject. Richard Sears built the platform when he advertised "Satisfaction Guaranteed or Your Money Back," and Marshall Field put the finishing touches on it when he said, "Give the lady what she wants." The retail industry has become so enormous, fragmented, and specialized, however, that the retailer must ask, "Satisfaction with what—the goods, the service, the price, or the convenience?"

Today, understanding what the "lady" wants is far more complicated than it was in Marshall Field's day. The customer wants it all, of course, but most are willing to compromise at some point in the consumption process. Traditionally, retailers have looked at their relationship with the customer as based upon the delivery of *value,* which was loosely defined as:

$$\text{Value} = \frac{\text{Quality}}{\text{Price}}$$

Many retailers understood intuitively that this was an oversimplification of a complex process. Consumers do not choose to purchase from one retailer rather than another on the simple comparison of the price and the perceived quality of the merchandise. One retailer may have the lowest price in town for a standard piece of merchandise, but he will never capture 100 percent of the market. Other retailers will win business by "wrapping" the merchandise in differing levels of:

> *Breadth of offerings.* Some consumers prefer a supermarket approach to shopping so as to minimize time spent whereas others like the specialty store approach.
>
> *Depth of offerings.* Some consumers prefer an outlet that has a complete selection within a few lines of merchandise.
>
> *Convenience.* A location close to the consumer's home or place of work will often be an overriding consideration in the purchase of some items. In addition, the hours that a retailer is open sometimes negate any price disadvantage.
>
> *Atmosphere.* Stores vary in the ambience they provide. For some consumers and for some occasions, a plain pipe-rack atmosphere is sufficient, whereas for other consumers at other times and locations, surroundings that better suit their moods or the spirit of the merchandise are more appropriate.
>
> *Credit.* Although bank cards have made credit almost universally available, some retailers also offer their own plans, which may be more attractive to some consumers.
>
> *Image.* The mental image evoked when the retailer's name comes to mind may be sufficient to overcome any price difference when choosing among retailers.
>
> *Service.* Finally, the level and quality of assistance given to the customer in the search, acquisition, and consumption process can outweigh raw price in many instances.

**Figure 29-1.** Examples of levels of service.

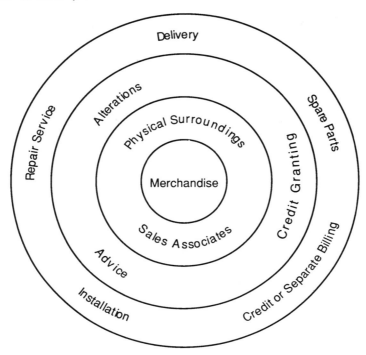

## All Retailers Are Not Created Equal

Service levels need not reach the heights of a Fifth Avenue specialty store to be successful. What the customer wants in that store is not necessarily what she wants when she stops to buy *The New York Times* and a half-dozen bagels on a Sunday morning. Service excellence is delivering what the customer is led to expect given the mix of price, quality, convenience, and ambience.

Retailers vary in the service levels they offer (see Figure 29-1). Consumers shop at the store for the merchandise, but that merchandise is surrounded by levels of service offered by the retailer. At the first level is the minimum service required to direct customers to the merchandise and accept their payments. In the second ring retailers may assign employees to offer advice and provide such services as altering clothing, cutting glass, mixing paint, or granting credit. The next circle involves such after-sale services as delivery, installation, monthly billing, and merchandise repair or replacement. Placing a retailer in one or the other rings is not a value judgment. Some stores that have built their business on selling at the lowest prices will achieve higher satisfaction levels in industry surveys than conventional department stores. They do this by providing a minimum level of service in a consistent and friendly fashion. Their marketing plan execution is highly efficient. Thus, there are successful retailers at each of the three service rings shown in Figure 29-1. The consumer is the final judge of whether the "bare bones" level of service provided by low-cost retailers is sufficient or whether he or she prefers a more complete level of service for a given product at a given time.

Several consumer surveys have shown that their primary reason for seeking out a retailer is (and it comes as no surprise) the merchandise carried by that retailer. What may be surprising is that the prime reason for ceasing to patronize a retailer is not the merchandise but the service provided.

## The Retailers' Challenge

The task for retailers is to decide what level of service is appropriate for the consumer needs they elect to serve and then ensure that this level of service is maintained by the organization. It is a rare retailing organization that does not stress the importance of customer satisfaction in annual reports, public speeches, and communications to employees. The following quotations are representative:

> . . . customers are truly the boss, and everything is done to provide the service the boss deserves.

> We are very excited about our capability to provide increased customer service, a strategy which is a requirement for excellence.

> [We are] committed to providing the customer with the best possible service. Taking care of the customer is a major reason for our existence.

> To our customers, we will offer unsurpassed customer service. . . .

> We introduced innovative programs that raised standards for customer service.

> . . . [we] have implemented a broad-based customer service program.

Despite this commitment it is the daily sales report and the monthly profit and loss statement that receive top billing in staff meetings and that count the most in compensation throughout much of the organization, from the commissioned sales force to the CEO.

The day-to-day emphasis on sales and profits is not a product of insincerity on the part of executives who preach putting the customer first. Customer satisfaction statistics are produced (often at best) once a year. The review of those statistics becomes an "event" similar to the annual golf outing. All assemble to hear the news (good, bad, or indifferent) and return to those measurements that are built into the day-to-day operations.

The following conditions set the stage for successful execution of a customer service orientation:

1. The commitment must start at the top. If the CEO makes speeches extolling the supremacy of the customer and then measures the success of the components of the business only on sales and profit growth, the troops get their message from the measurements—not the rhetoric. If the CEO personally reviews the sales and profit figures at management gatherings but sits in the audience while a subordinate reports on the latest customer satisfaction readings, the priorities are impressed upon the group.

2. The CEO needs a central point to which he or she can go in order to obtain all data relevant to customer service and satisfaction. All CEOs know where to find information on the progress of sales and the components of the profit-and-loss statement. Pulling together similar information concerning customer service, customer satisfaction, and customer complaints is an extended project.

3. Reporting on customer satisfaction levels must be built into the system in the same manner as sales and profit reports are built in.

4. The choice of an executive to head up a department responsible for customer satisfaction (or consumer affairs) is crucial. It should be someone on the way up the company ladder, not someone appointed to meet a need for affirmative action in promotions or hiring. One study of consumer affairs departments reported, "A relatively high proportion [32 percent] of the [consumer affairs] executives were females, especially in the retail [61 percent] and consumer non-durable [60 percent] categories." The study went on to ask, "Are the consumer affairs departments really integrated units within the corporate decision-making structure?" The answer was ". . . no—generally not."[2] The implication of "window dressing" is there.

## An Effective Measurement Program

Measuring effectiveness in customer service programs involves four types of measurements (see Figure 29-2). Measurements can be either *objective* (e.g., speed in answering the phone) or *subjective* (e.g., the customer's perception of the courtesy expressed by an employee when the phone is answered). In either case measurements can be *internal* (involving only a retailer's own customers) or *external* (involving all consumers so as to provide comparisons with other retailers.)

Objective measurements vary from retailer to retailer, depending on the merchandise carried and the retailer's place in the circle of services described in Figure 29-1. For some retailers, objective measurements include the length of lines at checkout counters, for others the length of time required for clothing alterations, and for still others the time taken to answer a call for in-home repair of an appliance. Care must be taken in establishing and measuring standards. Employees are always tempted to "beat the system." Given a list of measurements that will affect their income and promotion opportunities, employees understandably will devote their efforts to maximizing those measurements by all possible means. Possible neglect of other areas is a very real danger.

**Figure 29-2.** Measurements of customer service.

**Scope of Measurement**

|  | Internal | External |
|---|---|---|
| **Objective** | Waiting time in line<br><br>Time required for repairs<br><br>Out of stock | Industry averages and standards<br><br>Observations |
| **Subjective** | Perceptions of customers | Perceptions of consumers |

**Type of Measurement**

Subjective measurements involve surveys of customers and of consumers in general. Experimentation with various questionnaire formats and interviewing methodology is recommended so that a program that is financially feasible and, at the same time, produces a good managerial tool is chosen. Once a program is selected, however, it should not be changed without very good reasons, because a comparison over time is desired and even small changes can destroy comparability.

Of the various methodologies available, telephone or mail interviews hold the best promise of balance between cost and reliability. Interviewing customers in the store or consumers in the mall is fraught with the hazards of interviewer bias in selecting respondents and the vagaries of weather and promotions in changing the customer mix from one interviewing period to another.

Whatever the interviewing methodology selected, the retailer will face the problem of the "halo effect" in interpreting the responses—consumers tend to rate a store highly for all aspects of operation if they like one or several key aspects of the operation.

Care must be taken in establishing the measurement program to make sure that the costs involved are not so high as to invite a scrapping of the program at the first sign of a profit squeeze or a slowdown in sales. Changing customers' perceptions, which have been formed over a long period of time, is not an easy task. Management may become disenchanted with the lack of change in measurements over the short term and be tempted to shift funds to obtain more visible results if a program that is too elaborate and expensive is installed.

For retailers having a large base of credit customers, some experimentation with two or three questions on the monthly bill would be worthwhile. This program is inexpensive and can be supplemented with more detailed surveys from time to time if the situation warrants their use.

## What to Do With the Measurements

Linking compensation with measurements of customer service is the best way to ensure continued emphasis on this aspect of the operation. Where feasible, the link should be at all levels, including the CEO. A portion of the incentive compensation, or bonus, should be based on improvements in measures of customer service until an acceptable level is reached. Thereafter, compensation should be tied to the maintenance of this level. Other forms of recognition for outstanding personnel or units should be used together with adjustments to compensation. These could include plaques, merchandise awards, recognition banquets, and trips.

## What the Future Holds

Service appropriate to the retailer's marketing mix is the key to survival and growth in the future. Service is the glue that holds together the successful marketing mix—the old reliable four P's—product, price, promotion, and place. New forces for change will continually develop, and the successful retailer will meet them with a top-down commitment to service.

To be successful, the retailer must first identify and understand the service level desired by customers through a systematic approach to measuring customer satisfaction. The complementary challenge, which is more difficult, is to ensure that this level of service is delivered consistently throughout the organization.

## Notes

1. Joseph A. Schumpeter, *Capitalism, Socialism and Democracy* (New York: Harper & Row, 1976), 83.
2. Claes Fornell, *Consumer Input for Marketing Decisions* (New York: Praeger, 1976), 33, 166.

\*     \*     \*     \*

***Donald A. Hughes*** *is visiting associate professor at DePaul University in the marketing department, where he teaches marketing research, consumer behavior, and retail management. He also serves as a consultant to the corporate law department of Sears, Roebuck and Co., and to The Perlen Company. He formerly held the positions of national manager of merchandising research, and manager, consumer research division, at Sears, Roebuck.*

# 30

# Health Services

Robin Scott MacStravic

As an identifiable discipline or profession, health services marketing is more than a decade old. Although it is difficult to pinpoint its beginning, the year 1977 has a lot to recommend it. That was the year that the American Hospital Association sponsored its first conference on hospital marketing and published its first guidelines on hospital advertising. It was also the year in which the first health services marketing executive was named—a physician given the title of marketing vice president at Evanston Hospital, Evanston, Illinois. Moreover, 1977 was the year that the first text on health care marketing was published, even though articles had been written on the subject since 1969.

Since 1977, hospital services marketing has grown dramatically. It is estimated to have reached an expenditure of $1.6 billion by hospitals alone in 1986, roughly half of which was spent on advertising. Most large hospitals have marketing staff, as do many large clinics. There are four separate organizations to which health service marketers may belong: the Academy of Health Services Marketing, a subsidiary of the American Marketing Association; the Society for Hospital Planning and Marketing and the Society for Hospital Marketing and Public Relations, both sponsored by the American Hospital Association; and the College of Health Care Marketing, an independent association.

Despite its growth, however, health care marketing does not enjoy the stature or even the acceptance that is found in other industries. Many respected professionals, especially in the fields of medicine and nursing, believe that marketing is too commercial an approach for what should be a vital social service. Chief marketing officers, although well paid, are rarely on a par with chief financial officers or chief operating officers in health care organizations. While budgets for advertising alone represent an average of 3 to 5 percent of total expenditures in other industries, overall marketing expenditures, including advertising, don't amount even to 1 percent of total health care expenditures, although they are growing rapidly.

Health services marketing represents a particular challenge both to health care professionals and to marketing professionals. It illustrates all the typical challenges of services marketing plus the unique complexities of health care. Health care is dependent on government sources for almost half its revenue, yet purchasing choices are made primarily by individual private citizens. Patients use health services, yet physicians decide how many of which types on their behalf. Employees and their dependents demand health services while employers pay for them through fringe-benefit health insurance coverage. Hospitals are required by some laws to provide some services and prohibited by other laws from providing other services unless they obtain a Certificate of Need.

This chapter examines health services marketing as both a typical and unique example of services marketing. It describes how health services are currently being marketed, discusses some of the issues being addressed by the organizations and individuals engaged in marketing, and ventures some guesses as to how health services will be marketed in the future.

## Who Is the Health Care Customer?

One of the unique aspects of health services marketing is the complex nature of the health care "customer." Even though the use of the word arouses anger in some health care professionals, it is both appropriate from a marketing standpoint and necessary to encompass the wide variety of individuals and organizations that participate in "buying" decisions. For hospital services, both personal physicians and referral specialists are primary customers. Family members, friends, and acquaintances may be powerful influentials. Employers, insurance companies, and government and private agencies may dictate where patients go for service or decide how much will be paid for specific services.

For nursing home care, the most typical "customer" is the daughter or daughter-in-law of the actual consumer or nursing home resident. Other family members, legal guardians, spouses, children, parents, or even grandchildren may participate in deciding whether nursing home care will be sought and which home will be chosen. Hospital discharge planners, social service agencies, physicians, clergy, and other nursing homes may be important participants in making choices for particular residents. In only a minority of cases do residents themselves select the home where they will be accommodated.

For mental health and substance-abuse services, family members, physicians, schools, and the courts are important customers in addition to the clients or patients who are actually served. Many patients are committed involuntarily, although only short-term commitments are usually accommodated in private facilities. Although psychiatrists and nurses are dominant providers of such services, clinical psychologists and social workers, psychotherapists, and volunteer counselors are also active as participants and competitors.

For most health services, "purchase" is a high-involvement situation. For some, however, it is a low, even no-involvement case. Routine employment, school, camp, and insurance physicals may be sought from the most convenient source without much consideration. At the other extreme, for trauma victims or unconscious patients, provider choice may be made by the ambulance driver, police or fire personnel, or passersby. The more urgent the need for care in many cases, the less say the patient has in choosing where to get it.

The trend, however, has been to move away from an old-fashioned model in which decisions were made by health service professionals on the patient's behalf. The consumerism movement of the 1960s, together with growing competition in the 1970s and 1980s, has increased the importance of consumers in making health service decisions. Patients have more rights to refuse treatment, even if it means they are likely to die as a result. Providers are addressing more consumer concerns by providing services at convenient places, hours, and prices. Services that are particularly sensitive to consumer choice, such as maternity care, substance-abuse services, cosmetic surgery, and eye treatment, have seen the greatest use of consumer-directed marketing and advertising.

This trend is likely to continue. Inpatient hospital care is a declining "product" as its life cycle is threatened by employer and government reluctance to pay for its high costs. Long-term care in nursing homes, senior citizen centers, and the home is a growing product as the population ages and as the numbers of those in the over-75 and over-85 categories grow even faster.

The greatest growth opportunities, however, are in ambulatory "retail" service aimed at improving people's quality of life through better health. Much of the growth in weight management, smoking cessation, physical fitness, and similar health-promoting services has occurred outside the formal health services system. Health care has become aware of this growing market, however, and is rushing in to fill any gaps available, or to compete for viable markets where possible. As the physician-dominated, high-cost service markets diminish, consumer-dominated, low-cost markets are expanding. The importance of consumer-directed marketing is growing accordingly.

## Where Does Marketing Fit in the Organization?

Because marketing is such a recent addition to health services administration, it functions in an organizational environment in which there is uncertainty about where it belongs and anxiety about having to give up power to marketers. As a result, there is a vast difference between the marketing function and formally identified marketing activities and responsibilities. Only gradually are health care marketing professionals beginning to participate in, influence, and coordinate most marketing functions.

Consider the market research and analysis function. Planners had authority and responsibility for market analysis and new-product development before marketers arrived on the scene. Customer satisfaction was often the responsibility of patient relations professionals with backgrounds in nursing or social work. Relations with physicians are typically the responsibility of medical directors who are themselves physicians. Employees, who are key to the satisfaction of both patients and physicians, are surveyed by personnel rather than by marketing departments.

Decisions about what will be done for whom and how it will be done have traditionally been made by operating officers. Marketers typically are not included in executive councils and are invited only when top administration considers them necessary. Chief financial officers dominate pricing decisions. Most product, price, and place choices are made without any input from marketing.

The one area where marketing has had the most freedom is in promotion. In most instances marketers have been given authority to design and implement advertising campaigns, and they were often supplied with substantial budgets, although allocations were still modest compared with other industries. Even in

marketing communications, however, marketers faced the reality that public relations professionals had preceded them and in most cases were firmly entrenched with their own strategies and budgets.

Marketing began in most hospitals as a staff function, reporting most often
to the CEO, but lacking clear mission or authority. (This is still the most common approach to marketing.) In recent years, product management has become
a popular approach, with individual managers having profit responsibility for
particular service programs, such as maternity care, cancer care, rehabilitation
services, outpatient surgery, and the like. Where this approach is employed,
marketing professionals are often assigned as staff to particular product managers, joining them in aiming at product-specific success.

A third approach, segment management, seeks to promote lasting and successful relationships with selected market segments, as opposed to selling particular products. Women's health centers, clubs for those over 65, diabetes management programs, and similar population-focused approaches are being employed. Where providers sign contracts with particular employers, government,
or insurance purchasers of care, each beneficiary population becomes a separate
market segment to be managed. Managed care programs aim at integrating and
controlling the costs and use of services by particular populations. Case management services aim at integrating and controlling the costs and use of services
by specific individuals who need a wide array of care over an extended period.

In segment management, marketing may be a line or a staff function, depending on who is assigned market-specific responsibility. In product management, responsibility has typically been given to those who are actually managing
the individual service programs; these persons have usually risen from the ranks
and have no marketing background. Segment management offers marketers an
opportunity because there are no people already entrenched with responsibilities
for particular markets. Whether staff or line responsibility applies, segment
management performance will indicate how much and how well marketing contributes to the fulfillment of the organization's mission.

The trend will probably be toward a combination of product and segment
management. Given the need of current organizations for short-term financial
success, product management is appealing internally and has often proved to be
effective externally. Given the importance of retaining good customers and selective contracting by purchasers, segment management will increase in importance. Marketers will have to be flexible to accommodate either approach or a
combination of both and, as the opportunities arise, to adopt staff or line authority.

## Developing a Comprehensive Internal Marketing Process

As in most services organizations, internal marketing is vital to successful health
care marketing. Individual physicians, nurses, technicians, and service employees deliver the health care product. Marketers can design the health service
experience and describe it in glowing terms for promotion purposes, but they

don't deliver it. Getting all those who produce the health care experience to recognize and optimize their opportunities to satisfy customers is a constant challenge.

Because patients and their family members can be vital partners in delivering health care, they are part of the internal market as well. Training patients to seek care at the right time from the right people is key to both managed care and case management. Enlisting patients and their family members to participate as partners in the care process promotes both good medical outcomes and higher satisfaction and can reduce costs of care as well. Engaging patients in lasting customer relations, such as scheduling follow-up visits, complying with medical advice, and returning for use of other services (i.e., cross selling), promotes financial as well as mission fulfillment for the organization.

All internal "customers," including physicians, employees, and patients and their significant others, are key human resources for the health care organizations. All must be satisfied and, if possible, pleased with their experiences in the organization in order for them to maximize their potential lifetime contribution. All physicians and employees should be recruited, trained, directed, evaluated, and rewarded based on what they can and do contribute to objectives and financial success. Marketing can play a vital role in designing and implementing ways in which exchange relationships with all these customers can be optimized.

## The Challenge of Differentiating Through Quality

Where segmentation is being approached through segment management, service differentiation is a critical and difficult challenge in health care. The environmental factors of government, employer, and insurance purchasers are forcing providers to compete on price. Where differentiation by price is possible, offering discounts without compensating increases in volume simply reduces provider revenues. It is vital for providers to develop ways of effectively differentiating on the basis of service quality or place convenience, rather than on price alone.

Health care has maintained a traditional public position that all licensed providers offer good quality care. Health professionals have strong opinions regarding which providers are better than others, but making public comparisons is not acceptable. The American Medical Association warns its members against making any such comparisons, suggesting unique or superior service qualities, or even discussing the outcomes that might be achieved. The American Hospital Association recognizes, but does not endorse, comparisons, suggesting that any comparative statements be backed by objective documentation.

Quality has traditionally been an internal affair in health care. The prevailing doctrine calls for peer review, review of physician performance by other physicians, and assessment of hospital performance by Joint Commission on Accreditation of Healthcare Organizations, made up of physicians and other health professionals. Such reviews are intended not to indicate which providers are best buys, but merely to identify those that meet peer standards and those that do not.

Increasingly, external groups are developing their own approaches to quality assessment. The federal government's Health Care Financing Administration began publishing observed versus expected mortality rates for hospitals in 1986. Various state and local consumer groups have developed consumer guides to hospitals, physicians, and nursing homes. In all such cases, these groups use publicly available data or their own surveys and their own standards of quality to rate hospitals. In some cases, hospitals have incorporated such ratings in their advertising messages, suggesting that they had the lowest open-heart-surgery mortality rate in the country or were the only area hospital on a list of top hospitals.

Health service organizations face the challenge of developing quality indicators that are meaningful to each of their distinct customer constituencies and market segments. Armed with indicators that can be measured and communicated, providers can then manage their operations so as to maximize their demonstrable quality, or to stay ahead or abreast of the competition, at least in the eyes of some segments. They can then use their quality indicators in approaching prospects in order to increase their patient volume, or to protect what they already have.

Marketing professionals should play a dominant role in meeting these challenges. Market research techniques can be used to discover how particular constituencies define and gauge quality. Armed with such information, marketers can assess internal operations and particular customer experiences and suggest ways to improve both. Knowing how customers judge quality and how well operations meets customers' expectations, marketers can design and implement effective marketing communications that focus on service or place distinctions rather than on price.

As the number of competitors continues to increase for hospitals, physicians, managed care organizations, home health agencies, and other providers (nursing homes being one possible exception), the demise of the less effective and the survival of the more effective are clearly inevitable. Marketers who can help deliver and *demonstrate* high-quality service (at reasonable cost, of course) will help determine who survives. In making such a contribution, marketers will be in a superior position to demonstrate their own value to the organization.

## Marketing as Service

In *Service America,* Albrecht and Zemke champion the notion that managers should serve those who serve customers and should act as coaches rather than bosses.[1] This idea would require radical reform in health care management where traditional bureaucracy holds sway. This is despite the fact that health services organizations, as Drucker noted, are made up of precisely the kinds of professionals who fit into his new organization model in which employees make most decisions on their own, without managerial direction.[2]

If it is or should be true that managers in health care serve the servers, it must be equally true for marketers. Whether health organizations are divided into fiefdoms by function, by product, or by segment served, marketers should act to integrate and support the marketing function, as well as perform their independent responsibilities.

Market research and communications should serve and be served by operational managers. Research should guide their choices regarding which services to offer and how to manage individual customer experiences and lasting relationships. Communications should maintain or increase patient volumes and promote customer satisfaction. Operational managers should keep marketers informed of changes they make so that research can monitor the effects and communications can incorporate the results.

Marketing has yet to prove itself in health care. In spite of anecdotal evidence of significant successes, a healthy skepticism remains as to the benefit versus the cost of marketing departments, programs, and specific campaigns. Marketing passed from being considered an unworthy, unnecessary, and inappropriate intruder in the 1970s to being hyped as the savior of a troubled industry in the 1980s. Neither characterization is accurate, and marketing has yet to prove what it really is or to demonstrate what it actually can do.

Perhaps the greatest present challenge facing health care is to demonstrate its quality and benefit to its wide variety of customers and other constituencies. After spending hundreds of millions of dollars advertising how caring they are and how effective they are in delivering state-of-the-art service, health care organizations now face public demands that they prove these claims. Where marketers can help their organizations assess, manage, and demonstrate high (preferably superior) or unique quality, they can promote their organization's success and their own survival.

Proving their effectiveness is a challenge to marketers as well. Most health care marketing and advertising efforts were carried out without explicit goals or even precise plans of where to begin. In many cases the motto was fire-ready-aim, with new programs initiated and advertising campaigns implemented before market analysis developed assessments of what should and should not be changed.

To evaluate marketing's contribution, it is essential to show what changed because of what was done in a different way. It is not enough, for example, for a hospital-sponsored physician referral service to count how many people called the service, made appointments, saw a physician, or even were admitted to the hospital. The marketers who developed and advertised the service must be prepared to prove that those patients were above and beyond the number who would have seen the same physicians and been admitted to the same hospital had the referral service never existed.

Marketing's challenge is both to contribute meaningfully to the success of product and segment management strategies, and to demonstrate that its contribution warrants the cost. Just as health care organizations must prove their levels of excellence to their constituents, so marketing must prove its value to the organizations that invest in it. Marketers need to develop methods of tracking customer knowledge, attitudes, and behavior to show the impact and value of their efforts. In tracking these factors, marketing professionals can also help show where they are doing the most good and thus improve the possibility that their evidence and arguments will be accepted.

## Summary

Marketing in health services has had a dramatic though rocky beginning. It has the potential to become as valuable to health care organizations as it has in consumer and industrial goods and some other service industries. To realize this potential, marketing professionals should be prepared to demonstrate their organization's value to the community it serves, as well as their own importance to the organizations they serve.

## Notes

1. Karl Albrecht and Ron Zemke, *Service America: Doing Business in the New Economy* (Homewood, Ill.: Dow Jones-Irwin, 1985).
2. Peter Drucker, "The Coming of the New Organization," *Harvard Business Review* 88, no. 1 (January/February 1988): 45–53.

*    *    *    *

*Robin Scott MacStravic, Ph.D., serves as vice president, marketing and strategy, at St. Anthony Healthcare Corporation in Denver. Previously he was vice president for planning and marketing with Health and Hospital Services in Bellevue, Washington. He also has taught planning and marketing at the School of Public Health at the University of Washington in Seattle, and served as editor of the journal* Health Care Planning and Marketing.

# 31

## Hospitality Services

Fletch Waller, Jr.

An old adage holds that the three key elements in marketing a hotel are location, location, and location. It's false. No hotel sells itself over a sustained period. Those who abdicate their marketing roles and rely only on great location are soon displaced by the hotelier who builds a property close by, provides tailored services, and hustles out to the market in inviting and compelling ways.

Similarly, the lodging establishment, whether hotel, motel, conference center, or resort, that relies on international chain headquarters to do its marketing is setting itself up for being outperformed by the competitor who manages his or her own marketing, including using corporate activity to the full advantage of the individual unit.

Marketing is both a point of view and an activity. Both viewpoint and activity are necessary to achieve success, and nowhere more so than in a hotel that concurrently serves different groups of customers 24 hours a day, 365 days a year.

Marketing must be a property activity; the key marketing leader must be the general manager of the hotel, motel, resort, or conference center. The first section of this chapter, then, addresses how an individual property might be managed to incorporate a marketing point of view and to execute marketing activities that increase its revenues, gross margins, share, and customer satisfaction—the objectives of marketing. The chapter then goes on to explore how to assess a hotel's marketing situation; the difference between the marketing department and a market-driven hotel; what a hotel marketing process entails; managing that process; and the future of hotel marketing.

## How to Measure Marketing Performance

Marketing activities that increase revenues, margins, share, and satisfaction all imply measurements. A leader in this industry once said, "I know there are accounting rules and I have an outside auditor to tell me whether my accountants are following the rules. What are the rules for marketing? And how do I know you are following them?" This is a healthy dilemma. There are no rules; every time some professor codifies shall's and shall-not's, some marketer breaks those rules with spectacular success. The essence of marketing is dynamic response to changing marketing situations. Measurable results are what matter, not rules, standards, or conventions.

What are the results of hotel marketing? There are five that, over time, are the measure of marketing success:

1. Gross operating revenues grow faster than inflation.
2. Room revenues per occupied room grow faster than inflation.
3. Market share of room revenues exceeds share of room supply.
4. Unaided awareness among relevant market segments increases to equal that of any competitor's.
5. Preference among the relevant market segments rises steadily, eventually surpassing all competitors.

In any given year, there will be other goals related to budgets and to laying foundations for future business: future group bookings, repeat customer ratios, development of a new promotional tool, and such. But over time, the five listed here will be the core measures.

Ideally, each should be defined numerically at the beginning of a year and measured at year-end, with compensation adjusted to reflect the degree to which they were attained.

## What Is Your Hotel's Marketing Situation?

Effective marketing of a hotel proceeds from an up-to-date, realistic look at its *marketing situation,* a combination of three sets of factors:

1. *The physical property.* Is the hotel old or new; tired or fresh; large or small; with ample or very little meeting space; with a famous restaurant or a no-name dining facility; with modest or luxurious rooms; and so on?
2. *The streams of potential customers flowing past its doors.* Do possible patrons include conventioneers, traveling families, tourists, weekend escapists, traveling professionals, foreign tour groups, or others?
3. *The competition for those customer streams.* Is the hotel the only one in the area, or one of three, or one of ten major competitors within a mile?

When one multiplies the possible permutations of set one times set two times set three, it is little wonder that no two hotel marketing situations are identical. Each hotel must view its own situation with a fresh outlook in order to make effective marketing decisions about service levels, pricing, allocation of resources (salespeople versus advertising versus convention service or catering staff versus publicity versus frequent guest programs), market segmentation strategies, and inventory control to manage yield.

Don't be casual about assessing the marketing situation, and don't delegate it to the marketing director. At least once a year, engage the entire management team or executive committee in a disciplined assessment. And then review it regularly to make sure it's still accurate.

To gauge the competition, assign someone to monitor each competitor and write a report. Stay in and walk around each competitor's property, and look carefully at restaurants and public spaces.

Track competitors' rates and occupancies, and calculate share indices of occupied rooms and rates. (This is a sensitive area. It is far better to subscribe to an industry service than to trade information with all the attendant questions of legality, ethics, and reliability.) Make telephone inquiries of competitors' rates and promotion availabilities; don't rely solely on rate lists. Track lost group business, and try to gauge available meeting space in the market's future.

For the market demand, start with those competitive data on occupied rooms, but augment them with data from an audit/feasibility company, the local chamber of commerce, port authority, and convention and visitors bureau.

Be realistic about your own hotel. Step back and take a critic's view of your strengths and weaknesses. Use your own tracking and rating information. Listen to your guests carefully and objectively. Most important, ask your employees who have direct contact with guests—in the restaurants, at the door and desk, in the housekeeping department—what they see and hear about how you are perceived by customers. And how is this hotel perceived by the community? Do people refer visitors here? Is this the preferred luncheon spot or banquet venue? And what of your employees? Do they see trouble spots you've overlooked? Are they proud of this establishment?

With all this information in hand, reach a consensus among members of the management team on what this hotel's marketing situation really is. Then, and only then, should the team begin its marketing planning for whatever future period is in question.

## Marketing Departments and Market-Driven Hotels

Marketing, the activity, is normally delegated to a marketing department. But isn't marketing, the point of view or process, too important just to be left to people with marketing in their titles?

Theodore Levitt stated that the purpose of a business is to create a customer and keep him (or her).[1] A hotel creates and keeps customers by fulfilling their wants, needs, and expectations. Hearing and seeing what the market wants and needs; matching the hotel's services and facilities to best fit the optimum number of prospects' wants and needs; managing their expectations so that they will be satisfied and will return (be kept)—this is marketing. And, yes, it is too broad and too important to be left solely to the marketing department. In any enterprise, but especially in a hotel that is selling personal performance, the market point of view must be everyone's point of view. One hotel can be dominated or driven by finance, another by marketing, and another by operations. But the most successful, over time, will be the market-driven hotel in which each employee, regardless of function and responsibility level, is conscious of and trained to see his or her job in terms of helping to create and keep a customer. That hotel will develop a marketing process that yields loyalty, perceived value, high revenues, and market-share leadership.

# How to See and Communicate the Hotel's Marketing Process

If marketing is so broad, what part of the process is the responsibility of the marketing department? Let's examine the process and see what is logically a marketing activity.

The marketing process of a hotel is, like the infinity symbol, a never-ending loop of activities that involves everyone. It starts, perhaps, when the hotel is conceived, when what to be and offer are first decided. Figure 31-1 represents the process.

## Deciding What to Be and Offer

From the first realistic assessment of the marketing situation, one decides what to be and offer, and *to whom*. Of the three elements of the marketing situation— physical property, prospect streams, and competition—the second is usually where the key to the marketing puzzle is found. The challenge is to discern the wants and needs of each market segment and decide how to speak to each prospect in each segment and meet each expectation.

Much has been written about product proliferations, such as conference centers, all-suite hotels, catering halls, family resorts, long-stay facilities, and the rest. Yet there is always more than just one market segment that must be attracted and held if a property is to maximize its revenues. Whether for a full-service hotel or a property targeted at a particular need, multiple segment marketing programs will produce more than a single, generic approach.

Any broad market category can be subsegmented. Consider meetings, for example. A training meeting is different from a conference; an association meeting planner has an entirely different set of problems and needs than does a corporate meeting sponsor. Consider vacationers—families are different from vacationing couples; young weekenders are different from midweek retired couples. In other words, each subsegment has its own needs, responds to promises differently, is reached individually, and buys in its own way. So segment and resegment to identify opportunities. Recombine segments only when it is inefficient to serve or communicate or make yourself available in an individual way.

Pricing.   Pricing is a key element in deciding what to be and offer. How do you set published rates? What guidelines do you provide for group negotiations? How do you set promotional prices? Restaurant prices? Volume discounts? Pricing is part art, part science, consisting of critical judgments that should not be delegated to directors of marketing or food and beverage. General managers, with their experience and intuition, must provide the art. They must be involved and vigilant; it's often tempting for departments to call for price rises to make margin percentages look better or to propose discounts to close a sale. The directors of marketing and of food and beverage must provide the science, using such sources as comparative price shopping, *each week;* customer surveys of price and value ratings; sensitivity models; and probes of nonusers.

The goals of this constant reviewing, tightening, and loosening are to in-

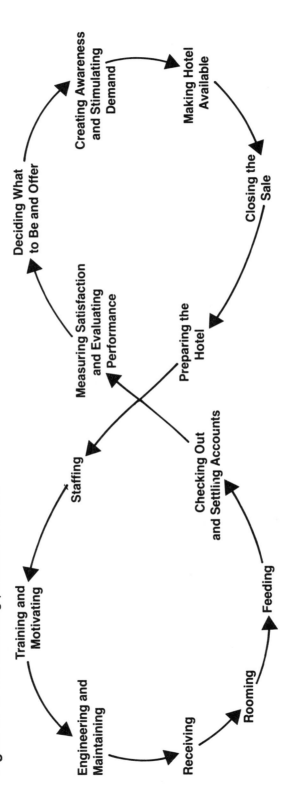

**Figure 31-1.** The marketing process for a hotel.

crease (1) the customer's perceived value and (2) incremental margin dollars (not percents). There are no other goals.

The hotel industry is beset with an overemphasis on price. It is the most convenient yardstick with which to compare hotels, especially for meetings. Customers have been trained by their associations, travel agents, and corporate controllers to negotiate for deals, discounts, and special rates. And hotel people have fallen into step, willingly citing price before features and benefits. Is price a valid yardstick?

No. A hotel is not a commodity. Each one is distinctive. And what is value? Is a smoothly executed business trip worth $10 more a night than one where the customer suffers an uncomfortable bed, poor room service, a late wake-up call?

Stand firm on price, and make it clear how your hotel can provide value. Sell services, features, and benefits before responding to the customer's constant "How much?" But remember that, in the end, it is the customer who values your hotel. Listen and watch for signs that tell you how you are valued and what you must do to increase your value in customers' eyes.

In summary, the decisions on what to be and offer are best developed collegially by your management team in a way most likely to create uniform understanding and commitment. Then, each department can be market-driven, fully responding to the wants, needs, and expectations of your guests.

## Creating Awareness and Stimulating Demand

Once what to be and offer to whom is determined, the marketing department assumes the task of creating awareness among the relevant segments and stimulating their demand for the hotel's services and facilities.

Advertising.    Advertising is one of the most perplexing of a hotel's marketing tools. Some hotels advertise extensively, others almost never. Some advertise locally, others out of market. Some advertise offers and deals, others only image. All are poor accounts because media budgets are small and fragmented, while considerable service and production effort is required. The chain's corporate director of advertising is constantly seeking control of the hotel's budget; the general manager and owner always complain that the corporate ads aren't selling their property enough.

Keep in mind that advertising works differently with different market segments. Advertising does not create demand among business travelers and meeting planners or catering event sponsors because their decisions are dependent upon business needs. It can only help create temporary awareness and may influence brand selection for an upcoming trip or meeting. Conversely, primary demand for weekend escapes or resort package purchases can be stimulated by advertising.

As with any product or service, the discipline of precisely defining the currently held belief of a particular prospect is the first step toward effective advertising. Then, the new belief that you would like to have the prospect hold should be described, so that he or she would then act in a certain way—by calling, inquiring, making a request of a secretary or travel agent, and so on. Then ask whether this (or any) advertising is likely to establish that new belief.

Direct Mail and Collateral.   As with other forms of advertising, the same current belief/new belief/action process works as a guide for and test of direct mail and collateral pieces. The advantage of direct mail and brochures over other forms of advertising is that you have a better idea who will see the piece and with what interest. But the questions must still be asked: ''Do we really know what the prospects now know of and believe about us? What do we want to have them believe? So that they do what? [Only action rings registers.] Is it likely that this ad/piece/brochure will create that new belief?'' If the answers are negative, send the agency back to the boards or save the money.

Publicity.   Publicity has long been an important part of hotel marketing, especially locally where it is often as important to the customer as to the hotel. Purposeful publicity is worth far more than advertising. Much publicity, however, is merely opportunistic—a mention of the hotel because of a newsworthy event taking place there. Rarely is that purposeful.

What is purposeful publicity? It is publicity that plants in a prospect's mind a belief about the hotel that will lead to a desired action. The belief might be as simple as ''There's only one place to hold a charity event'' or as complex as ''XYZ has the best value weekend packages in the five-state area.'' The slant of the story and its placement should be designed to change beliefs in targeted minds. Otherwise, publicity mentions fill scrapbooks but not sales books. Targeted, purposeful publicity is hard to generate but is well worth the effort. Any hotel with considerable catering activity, and every resort, should put at least as much effort into planning and executing publicity as it does into advertising.

Customer Clubs.   Customer clubs, especially frequent-guest programs and local dining clubs, are powerful tools for retaining customers. With lodging supply outrunning demand in most places, and with competitive advantage so transitory, retaining customers is much more productive than struggling to attract new ones, which usually requires luring them away from a competitor. As in any retail business, your best prospect is your most recent customer. Build and maintain a good guest history system, and use it aggressively to thank, to remind, to inquire, to offer. This is a business of building relationships, and there is no better way than customer histories and customer clubs. These should be the primary marketing tools for the hotel's individual traveler market segments.

Sales.   Nothing pleases some traditional general managers more than weary salespeople with bloody knuckles. Yet nothing is so wasteful as frenetic, unfocused sales calls.

The sales force is the primary and necessary tool for generating meeting and group business. For individual travel, however, sales calls may have only a secondary effect; the productivity of individual travel accounts should be examined and justified, account by account, at least quarterly. The fact that the hotel receives several hundred reservations from travelers calling on ABC Company does not, by itself, make this company an active sales account. Does a sales call attract more business? That is the difficult but necessary question.

Although it is easier to demonstrate results with business meetings, no less diligence is required to assure sales productivity. There is no secret to hotel sales. All the modern sales techniques are applicable: qualifying customers, pre-planning to understand their wants and needs, discerning between prospecting and closing, active sales management review of account files and status of tentatives, and training in presentation and closing.

There are two common failings in hotel sales. First, and appallingly frequent, is a salesperson pitching his or her hotel for an upcoming meeting before finding out the purpose of the meeting! How can one best present the features and benefits of the hotel without knowing the prospect's situation? The purpose of the meeting reveals a great deal about wants and needs and about the planner's/buyer's/sponsor's concerns.

The second failing is carrying too many files. Reclassify account lists at least annually. Position accounts on a grid, rating them on value (size of meetings, frequency of meetings, lavishness of meetings) and loyalty (are they predisposed to our hotel, do they call us first, do we get only their secondary meetings?). Have the sales team rate them on a ten-point scale judgmentally; no great quantification is required. The grid might look like the one shown in Figure 31-2.

The boundaries between cells are arbitrary, but they should be rational.

**Figure 31-2.** Knowing whom to and not to call upon.

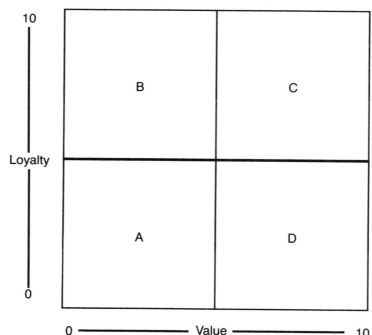

Accounts in cell A are too small and use the hotel infrequently. Drop them, even though "Joe is a great guy." B accounts, although small, are loyal; they should be serviced only often enough to retain their loyalty and to monitor changes in their status. The C accounts are the family jewels—of high value and loyal. Do whatever is necessary to keep them this way.

D accounts are the challenge. How do you increase share of these high-value accounts? Each one presents unique problems and opportunities. One by one, assign them to a salesperson and have them studied. What do they need? Why do they use hotel XYZ? Have a campaign laid out to move them from cell D to C. Consider setting up an incentive program for D account businesses. Engage the entire executive committee in planning the campaign to win them away from other hotels.

This is targeted selling. It is amazingly productive because, unfortunately, poorly focused salesmanship is the rule rather than the exception in the hotel business.

Promotions.    Promotions are a marketing tool for creating awareness and stimulating demand. The word covers a multitude of offers: continuing deals, such as 50 percent off weekends; seasonal arrangements, such as summer family plans or winter business travel discounts; annual events, such as Mother's Day brunch or a New Year's package; one-shots, such as a chocoholic or murder mystery weekend.

To be effective, promotions must be advertised, if not in media then via direct mail or telephone. Yet, the special efforts and the ad costs frequently are not charged against the promotion! For each promotion, a pro forma statement should be prepared that includes all applicable costs, including occupied room costs. The incremental volume required to produce the room and food and beverage margins necessary to break even should be calculated before any commitment to the promotion is made. This simple discipline will focus attention and get the entire hotel behind the effort. It will avoid a lot of wasteful churning with no profit result.

## Stimulating Demand for Catering

The preceding sections have addressed advertising, publicity, customer clubs, sales, and promotions from the perspective of creating awareness of and stimulating demand for lodging, that is, room sales. The tools apply equally well to catering, restaurant, and lounge sales, however. The incremental contribution margin in catering is smaller than in rooms; that of food and beverage outlets is smaller still. The typical hotel accounting system does not charge ads, promotions, brochures, catering salespeople, or customer club discounts to the food and beverage department statements. To a food and beverage director, such support seems "free." Only when all costs are included can intelligent pricing be done to assure proper margins. Develop the discipline to prepare pro forma statements on these tools as they apply to catering and, especially, to outlets, to make sure that marketing resources produce incremental margins. You can model various levels of support (see Chapter 17 for thoughts on pricing services) and prices to see what reasonable expectations produce. This discipline by the hotel executive committee develops commitment and assures that limited marketing resources are being allocated so as to maximize gross profits.

## Making the Hotel Available

After creating awareness and stimulating demand, how does the hotel make itself available to travelers and their agents, to meeting planners, to catering event sponsors, and so on?

The salespeople, in the hotel and backed up by chain or representation offices in major markets, make the hotel available to meeting planners. Are rooms and meeting spaces available on the desired dates? At what rates? The catering sales team makes the hotel available for banquets and events. Will the Blue Room be available that evening? At what rate? Such simple questions.

Management frequently complains that the director of marketing isn't looking ahead far enough, that all she's doing is shuffling papers; that the director of sales isn't making his own sales goals; that salespeople are in the office rather than out making sales calls. Eighty percent of these complaints are grounded in the difficulty of managing availability and answering those simple questions: Is there space? At what rates?

How Do You Maximize Revenues?    Ellen and Jim are both working tentative groups for June 8. Jim's is big; he's put a "hold all space" on the book. Suzy needs the ballroom that night for a United Way banquet. John's customer is on the phone, asking for two meeting rooms and luncheon for a midsized group. What's John to say? How much can he get, and is it worth enough to bump Jim's group? Is Ellen's a "firm tentative"? What's the latest, and when will she hear back from the client? Does John's customer really need the ballroom after 5 P.M.? How fast can the banquet be set up? Can United Way be charged for the labor to change the room, and can it then be reset before 8 A.M. if Jim's group books? What's the reservations office forecasting for individual demand? At what average rate? What's going on?

What is going on is the most valuable part of creating hotel profits, and often one of the worst managed. The need of the prospective catering or meeting customer is information: Is the XYZ hotel an option for me? The need of the salesperson is also information: What space and rate can I offer? And the need of the marketing director and general manager is information: What are the alternative uses of our perishable space? How do we avoid having space producing no revenue that day? How do we avoid leaving money on the table by underpricing to demand?

The information necessary to foresee the future is in customers' offices, in the catering department, in the group sales office, and in the reservations department. The task is to integrate it and constantly revise it as transient demand ebbs and flows, as tentative bookings close or are lost, as competitors' available meeting and banqueting spaces are booked. (Yes, forecast competitors' available capacity, day by future day!)

The integration of these sources of information and the ease of resolving conflicting demands for spaces are the reasons for consolidating catering, reservations, and group sales into the marketing department. Hotels that keep them apart—catering in food and beverage, reservations in rooms, and sales in marketing—are sure to underutilize their assets and to fall short of their full revenue potential. Consolidation of the activities under the marketing director does not guarantee realization of full potential. He or she needs training and a system.

It is possible to run a manual system with paper sales and event calendars. It is risky to do so because cancellations, confirmations, and lost business may not get entered. Usually the calendars lag commitments sufficiently to cause uncertainty and confusion. Poor response time to customer inquiries is one result.

Far better is a computer system that gives each salesperson easy access to the latest daily availabilities and the hurdle rates required to justify space commitment. Such systems are hard to create, to tailor to one's particular needs and to revise with ease; it takes effort and time to train computer illiterates. But the effort is definitely justified by increased profits. It is not possible to discuss such systems in depth in this chapter; suffice to say here that this subject deserves the keen interest of owners and general managers.

One last word on making the hotel available to catering and meeting planners: Get rid of "hold all space" notations on tentatives and definites. That is lazy selling. Make the salesperson work the account to specify each and every meeting room need, by time of day. This not only allows catering an opportunity to fill in with revenue-producing events, but also forces the group salesperson to learn the wants, needs, and expectations of his or her meeting planner and sponsor. It enriches the file and will help convention services fully deliver when the meeting takes place. In other words, it makes the hotel more efficient and increases the likelihood of a satisfied customer; everyone's a winner.

How to Generate Profits in the Reservations Office.　How is the hotel made available to individual travelers? Through the reservations office and its extensions—that is, an 800 number reservations center, general sales agents in foreign countries, and airline reservation systems that incorporate hotel booking packages for the convenience of travel agents.

No other marketing activity has so immediate and direct an impact on hotel profits as does reservations. One cannot speak of availability in a vacuum; the question is, what rooms are available in what rate categories? Opening up discount and promotional offers at the right time can increase occupancy and total revenues. Closing off promotional availabilities and filling high-rated rooms yield higher average rates, and each additional dollar drops right to the bottom line. But if timing is wrong, out of sync with demand, unoccupied rooms and lower revenues result.

Reservations is a dynamic process of inventory control and demand forecasting, not a static process of merely receiving requests. Reservation tools are changing fast. Automated yield management and elaborate real-time reservations networks are under development. After a decade of relatively static technology, a new generation of systems is about to appear.

Two points are important. First, no one is so undervalued and so central to hotel profits as a skilled reservations director, especially because the technology of the field is changing faster than most general managers and marketing directors can accommodate. Second, each year, lodging consulting firms publish reports that track the loss of the independents' market share to chain-affiliated establishments. The primary cause of this loss is the availability of a wide variety of chain rooms and prices through real-time, dynamic reservations systems. Distribution power is bringing about industry concentration, so the independents must find a widely available, real-time reservations system to hook into if they intend to retain share and offer competitive service. Unique resort and destination independents may be able to hold out, but they do not disprove this reality.

## Closing the Sale

Is the sale closed when space is booked or room availability is acknowledged? No. There are upselling opportunities all along the line. Individual travelers should be upsold by the reservations agent before confirmation of a reservation. An agent can open with the highest price and can suggest deluxe rooms or executive floors. If your hotel is not training and managing agent sales techniques, you are underperforming. Too many hotel managements focus on reservation costs (talk time, handled calls per employee hour, and such), and too few pay attention to conversion ratios and average rates booked per employee. But sales training is not enough; empathy is required as well. How well do your reservations agents understand the world of the traveler? Few of them stay in hotel rooms, and, in the case of upscale properties, few can relate to the ability to pay $100 or $200 per night. Have your agents stayed in your rooms? Have they been coached on the value perceptions of your clients? If not, your sales training may be for naught, blocked by the agent's inherent lack of empathy.

After confirmation, there is still opportunity—and risk. What happens when the traveler arrives to check in? Well-trained and motivated front-desk agents can upsell again—to a better view, to a larger room, to an executive floor or junior suite. Again, every extra dollar falls right to the bottom line. But there is also revenue risk at the front desk. Arriving guests may ask, even badger, for lower rates and discounts than their reservation confirmed. At one hotel where this was measured, the drop from confirmed to realized revenues was more than $20,000 in some months! Agents must be trained to provide service, but to courteously and firmly resist revenue decay.

In some hotels, the front desk entails such sufficient profit impact and guest service potential that it has been made part of the marketing department. This strategy is still quite radical, but chains such as Red Lion and Hilton International have made front-desk support staff part of their corporate marketing team.

Upselling meeting planners can be done when convention services begins to work with the planner on the upcoming meeting. Creative theme parties, themed coffee breaks, special banquets, and hospitality suite entertainment all offer ways to serve both the client's interest in a memorable, successful meeting and the hotel's interest in generating maximum contribution margins. Convention services people need to understand (from a complete sales file and hand-off of the account) the purpose of the meeting. Their efforts might be increased with an upsell incentive program and clear goals stated in terms of ancillary revenues per group room night.

Closing the sale is a part of the marketing process that is too easily taken for granted once a meeting is booked or a reservation confirmed. At this juncture, do not fail to find opportunities to serve creatively and add value and, thus, to reap the increased profits such service and value perceptions generate.

## Preparing the Hotel

For hoteliers, forecasting is an ongoing struggle. At weekly forecast meetings, department heads confer on upcoming occupancy levels, staffing needs, and so on—all of which are vital concerns. But our focus here will be on qualitative rather than quantitative forecasting, on marketing's opportunity to help prepare the hotel employees to meet the wants, needs, and expectations of the arriving guests and customers.

Leonard Berry's work on relationship marketing[2] suggested that a hotel is selling neither a product nor a service; rather, it is selling a relationship between its employees and its guests/customers. This is a powerful concept. It promises that higher rates of repeat business and lower rates of employee turnover both result from satisfying, fulfilling interactions between employees and customers. It suggests that marketing's task is to nurture that healthy relationship. This means, in turn, that marketing must look inward, at the employee end of the interaction, as well as outward toward the potential customers. For every marketing program, then, there are properly two audiences—employees and prospects.

This is sound philosophy, but how does it translate into action? What can the marketing director do to help prepare the hotel? First, he or she should make sure that the latest information on the hotel's prospects, and their wants and needs, is communicated to all employees and incorporated into training videos, course materials, and employee newsletters.

Second, the marketing director should make quarterly presentations of ads, promotions, publicity, and new collateral so employees are conscious of the expectations of being planted in the minds of prospects. It should be asked of all program materials, how will this play in the employee cafeteria?

Next, the marketing director should try to describe in weekly forecast meetings the qualities and expected behavior of guests. Is the Sunday check-in group traveling across time zones, and are members of that party likely to go to their rooms immediately? Or, are they likely to congregate in the lobby bar and greet their fellow attendees? Will there be heavy Monday morning room service breakfast demand from spouses, or will they be attending an event? Are many women travelers expected, with room service dinners heavier than normal? Will there be a large influx of foreigners, with demand for fax and business services? Ebullient salespeople? Inexperienced travelers? And on it goes; whatever information that can help forewarn departments and employees about the style, tastes, needs, wants, and expectations of the customers they are about to encounter will increase the probability of a satisfying interaction for employee and guest.

Management's role is to nurture that relationship. As it strengthens, as employees and customers are mutually fulfilled, repeat rates rise, marketing efforts become ever more productive, and hotel profits increase. The burden of marketing the hotel is on the service employees, and marketing's task is to help them succeed in it.

## Operations Loop

This brings us onto the left-hand loop (Figure 31-1) of the marketing process—those activities traditionally called operations. Here are staffing, training, purchasing, engineering and maintenance, and the other jobs to be done to receive guests, house them, feed them, respond to their needs, settle their accounts, and send them away happy. The people working in these delivery areas are not "operators" but the true marketers of the hotel. They are serving your customers and guests. They, together with the employees serving those guest-contact people, carry the primary marketing responsibility, for only they can *keep* a customer.

Are they selected for their common sense and willingness to serve others? Are they trained only in how to do a job or also in why, in the customers' wants, needs, and expectations? Are they empathic? Interested? Motivated? Are they rewarded and recognized and given feedback on how the guest/customer has responded?

Is your best prospect your most recent customer? If the true marketers of your hotel have been properly prepared to do their jobs, then your repeat customer rate will be high. High repeat rates yield lower marketing expense-to-sales ratios, higher marketing productivity, and higher profits.

## Tracking Satisfaction and Evaluating Performance

The last step in the marketing process is to close the loop. How did we do? What do we need to do better? What should we be or offer next time to better satisfy, to retain our customers, to provide more value, to increase our share and revenues?

This is a 24-hour, 365-day-a-year retail business. It never stops. Competition introduces new facilities and services, perhaps in a totally different market, and the expectations of your customers are suddenly slightly different. You must stay in touch.

There are several ways to do so. A continuing audit of guest reactions can give accurate, detailed tracking by service and department, month by month. This audit is expensive and requires precise management to get a reliable sample of guests. But it provides sensitive and projectable scores around which employee motivation and management incentive programs can be designed.

Guest comment cards, voluntarily submitted, are timely indicators of trouble. Beware of using them as indicators of absolute satisfaction levels, however, because they represent a small percentage of guests and tend to be biased toward the infrequent traveler.

Finally, have the executive committee stay in touch. Some hotels assign ''lobby lizards''—managers who stand at the check-out area each morning—to chat with and thank guests. Others have a weekly general manager's breakfast round table or a general manager's cocktail reception. These contacts are no substitute for tracking; they are not customer research. They are valuable, however, as stimulants to generate ideas and challenge assumptions.

## Managing the Marketing Process

From the foregoing description of the marketing process, it is evident that effective marketing of the hotel depends not just on the marketing department. Rather, it is a function of all departments sharing a coherent view of what they are trying to be and offer to whom—in other words, being a market-driven team. The marketing department is responsible for some parts of the process, such as *creating awareness and stimulating demand.* Marketing should be responsible for *making the hotel available* and *closing the sale,* although many hotels do not recognize this yet and hold other departments accountable for some of these duties. The marketing department is merely a participant in *preparing the hotel.* It doesn't matter who is accountable for *tracking satisfaction and evaluating performance,* provided they are done. But the continuing and fundamental task— *deciding what to be and offer*—ultimately belongs to the general manager. This responsibility cannot be delegated; it is the general manager who must lead the team to adjust, improve, refine, and commit to the current raison d'être of the hotel.

The general manager must also see that the marketing plan, operating plan, human resources plan, and financial plan of the hotel are coordinated and spring from common customer focus. Planning is a team process that involves every functional manager: The marketing plan yields the revenue targets; expense and operations planning yields the operating profit targets; the human resources plan yields the management development, turnover, and staffing targets; and financial planning yields the cash flow, investment, and net profit targets. Each plan must reflect the assumptions and realities of every function.

Too much has been written about the importance of an annual marketing plan. Planning by segment is what matters; the plan is merely the communication of what has been decided so that all understand and so that the goals and key actions for each market segment and revenue source can be monitored. The marketing plan should be simple and specific, unencumbered with extraneous marketing data, job descriptions, and vague generalities. The plan should be quickly understandable to a new marketing director or general manager. It should also include marketing department budgets, which reflect the responsibilities of the marketing director in this hotel.

Now it is evident why the general manager is the key marketing person in the hotel. For the marketing process to be cohesive and integrated, the sponsorship of the general manager is required. Only he or she can provide the inspiration and leadership to create a truly market-driven hotel team.

## The Future of Hospitality Marketing

The role of the hotel marketing department has been evolving over the last decade from group sales to the diverse and complicated job described herein. Some hotels added convention services, whereas others added advertising, promotions management, and publicity. Marriott was the first chain formally to define the job as what is called "creating awareness and stimulating demand" with a heavy emphasis on planned allocation of advertising, sales, promotion, collateral, and publicity resources. Westin was the first major management company to integrate those marketing activities with catering and reservations in order to be able to "make the hotel available," "close the sale," and maximize revenues per available room. Many hotels have yet to adopt this integrated view of marketing's role; none has moved to the next logical step of incorporating the front desk arrival process into marketing's job of "closing the sale."

Management development, of course, has lagged in this evolution. Few marketing directors are prepared for supervising reservations, running yield management and space utilization systems, or stimulating catering creativity. The traditional path from group salesperson to group sales manager to director of marketing is still the norm. More must be done to vary the path and to cross-train in advertising, front office, reservations, catering, and convention services.

In addition to broader experience, marketing candidates also need skills in problem analysis, creative problem solving, and influencing others to build consensus. This is not only necessary for a director of marketing, but also for the key marketing person in the hotel, the general manager.

Hotels' management generally value most highly the skills of spotting problems and quickly solving them. This crisis management mentality reflects a 24-hour, 365-day retail business in which hundreds of different kinds of problems can derail the flow of customer transactions and services. Today's business must be dealt with promptly and efficiently.

As hotels compete in mature, increasingly competitive markets, however, the analytic, conceptual, creative, and leadership skills required to manage an effective marketing process will become equally esteemed.

Marriott has long recognized that an effective marketer can be just as attractive a candidate for general managership as is an experienced operator. In the future, all general managers will have to be skilled in the marketing process as well as in operations and control. A general manager candidate will at least have a marketing viewpoint if not hands-on experience in a marketing activity.

The marketing process is integrative, bringing operations, human resources, marketing, and finance together in a market-driven orientation. Yet to be tried is actually organizing a hotel this way, with only four key directors reporting to the general manager. Marketing might have the front desk. Operations might have housekeeping, the chef, restaurant operations, engineering, security, and so on. Finance would have accounting, control, and purchasing. Human resources would have what will in this decade be the hotel's most challenging and critical area of all—recruiting, training, motivating, and retaining competent people.

In a truly market-driven hotel, customers and employees reinforce each other and are happy, and owners are content, enjoying market leadership and optimal, long-term profit returns. And such a hotel is never dull, for the marketing process itself is a renewing, dynamic one of constant challenge and continual change.

## Notes

1. Theodore Levitt, *The Marketing Imagination* (New York: Free Press, 1983), 48.
2. Leonard L. Berry, "Relationship Marketing," in *Emerging Perspectives on Services Marketing,* ed. Leonard L. Berry, G. Lynn Shostack, and Gregory D. Upah (Chicago: American Marketing Association, 1983), 25–28.

\*　　\*　　\*　　\*

***Fletch Waller, Jr.,*** *serves as a consultant to services management, mainly international lodging businesses. Based in Seattle, he specializes in marketing effectiveness and productivity, with an aim toward integrating his clients' marketing and operations to yield customer-conscious employees and satisfied repeat customers. Prior to this, Mr. Waller was executive vice president of Westin Hotels, accountable for all marketing operations, and senior vice president of marketing for Marriott Hotels.*

# 32

# The Service Entrepreneur

Adrienne Margules O'Hare
Carole A. Congram

You have done it. You've taken the big step and set up your own business. You are doing your own thing. It's risky, but you love it. You wonder, at odd moments, whether you could ever work in a big organization again.

You also find yourself thinking more and more about business development. Perhaps your former employer gave you some work that helped you get started. Or perhaps you had been doing some consulting in the evenings or on Saturdays. And you have gotten some new clients. But you know that you aren't doing enough to attract new business, and you must do something about it— soon.

The purpose of this chapter is to support and reinforce your entrepreneurial spirit and success, and to help you assess your options, design strategies for winning clients/customers, inform the community of your capabilities and skills, and evaluate your progress. Your success as a service provider will depend on your ability to:

1. Assess the needs of your market (clients/customers).
2. Deliver services that meet those needs.
3. Communicate the benefits of your services.
4. Provide follow-up to keep a loyal and satisfied client base.
5. Develop a professional network as a referral and support system.

Your fierce commitment to "having it happen and having it happen now" will be the force behind your business development success.

## How to Plan for Success

EMSOC is a strategic planning process with the following components:

**E**nvironment
**M**ission
**S**trategies
**O**perations
**C**ontrol

The authors thank Elizabeth Capen for her insightful comments about and suggestions for this chapter.

**Figure 32-1.** Strategic market planning: the EMSOC approach.

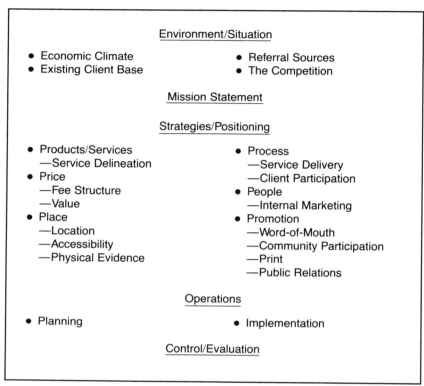

You can use EMSOC to create a marketing plan. The goal of the process is to discover and describe a niche that you are uniquely qualified to fill and focus your energies on communicating with that segment of the market.

The EMSOC process was developed to help service entrepreneurs sort through conflicting demands and opinions about how they should move forward. EMSOC has been used for several years in hundreds of service enterprises, and it has worked well as a systematic planning tool for developing service businesses.

Figure 32-1 outlines this process and also corresponds to the organization of this chapter.

## The Environment: How to Define Your Market

Your environment, the real world in which you operate, holds the key to defining your market.

### Economic Climate

To identify your market, you will need to be aware of any local, national, or regional governmental policies that could impact your business. You also must be able to assess what elements of the national, regional, and local economy will affect your market.

### Existing Client Base

Who are the people and businesses to whom you have sold your services? These customers represent your present market. Why did these people need your services? What benefits did they receive as a result of working with you? Your experience with them represents a valuable asset in defining your market opportunities. One of the things you can do is to interview some of your clients to find out what attracted them to you, whether you have services that they would recommend to others, and what benefits they received from your services.

You also want to identify the characteristics of your client base. Success in your service business may depend on how effectively you sort existing and potential clients into groups or market segments. Characteristics such as age, income, occupation, hobbies, activities, or lifestyle and personality variables emerge when you analyze the clients you know and can serve.

Look at your existing client base. Can you identify high-profit and low-profit clients and customers? If you can, do these groups have a profile? Client data can be extremely valuable in identifying the market for your services.

Your objective is to establish a position for yourself in your community as an expert in a particular market (e.g., people 55 years of age or older, new businesses started by people with scientific or technological backgrounds). You then will develop strategies to reach these specific groups.

### Referral Sources

Referral sources are essential for many service entrepreneurs because they can influence decision makers. In fact, for many service businesses, the principal market is composed of referral sources.

There are two rules you must remember when establishing a referral network. One, referrals come from relationships. Each person with whom you have a relationship—from the neighbor you see in the supermarket every other Thursday to your best friend from high school—is a referral source. The second rule is that you have to ask. It is not intrusive to tell people what you are doing and ask them to refer others to you.

### Competitors

It's easy to think that you have no competitors because your service is unique, but that probably is not the case. If you do not have direct competitors, there may be indirect ones.

Direct Competition.   Who are the people who sell the same services that you offer? They are your direct competitors. You should identify them and obtain as much information as possible about them. Try to obtain their brochures. When you compete with them, ask the prospective client to give you information about other companies under consideration, as well as the range of fees proposed.

Indirect Competition.   Who are the people who sell services that can substitute for the services that you offer? These indirect competitors often are difficult to identify because their services seem so different from yours. Yet, from your clients' viewpoint, these services may be acceptable alternatives to your service offering.

If you are an interior decorator, for example, your indirect competitors include staff people at a local department store; they may offer free decorating services to customers who purchase the store's furniture. Or, if you are a personal financial planner, your indirect competitors include software development companies offering packages a potential client can use at home.

Whenever your potential client has a choice of ways to meet a need, you have a competitor. You must understand the advantages and disadvantages of your indirect competitors' services—from the client's point of view—so that you can develop strategies to respond to potential clients' objections and make your service the preferred choice.

### Sources of Market Information

Much of the information that you will need to analyze the composition of your potential market is available free or at low cost. Your chamber of commerce, local library, and the business and marketing departments of your local colleges and universities have market studies of your area.

The local chapter of your professional organization can help you with research studies or reference material on the purchasers of your services. And, don't overlook the Yellow Pages; they are gold mines of information about your market and competitors.

To sum up, there are a number of activities that will help you define your environment and your market. Joining the key professional organizations associated with your field will keep you abreast of the shifts in market trends and the economy. Understanding your client base is the best way to understand the needs of your market.

Make sure that you know who your direct competitors are. If possible, create opportunities to network with them. Use your indirect competitors as a referral base. Become known in your community as a professional, a leader, and a colleague. It's good marketing.

## How to Define Your Business Mission

A mission statement is your vision of your business. Before we look at ways to develop a statement, let's consider the reasons why you want to have one.

### Two Benefits of a Mission Statement

Why do you need to formulate your vision? One reason to have a mission statement is to help everyone you work with, including partners, employees, clients, and suppliers, to have a clear understanding of what is important in your organization. For example, if your mission statement emphasizes client service, your secretary will follow up on a client's query before ordering supplies, and clients will know that their needs get top priority.

The second benefit of a mission statement is that it can help you evaluate how new opportunities relate to the core of your business. Your resources—time and money—are limited, and you must use them for activities that help you reach your goals. With a mission statement, you have a framework for answering such critical questions as: How does this opportunity fit into the business I want to build? How will this opportunity help us attain our vision? As new opportunities arise, you will have a reason to say "Yes" to those that fit—and "No" to those that do not.

## How to Develop a Mission Statement

> At Black & White, client service comes first. We help our clients achieve their business and professional development objectives by designing meeting formats that reflect a client's corporate personality and by unobtrusively handling the thousands of details that make a meeting run smoothly.

There is no right way or wrong way to create a mission statement. Good statements do share some characteristics. They are short, easy to understand, memorable, and believable.

To get started, think about your professional track record. What are you really good at? What compliments do clients make repeatedly about your services? What do you really enjoy doing? What is your single driving force? The president of Black & White, a meeting management consulting firm, responded: "We are dedicated to helping clients succeed. The meetings we manage are run professionally; we are sticklers for details, and people notice how everything is taken care of."

Next, look at the list of factors in Figure 32-2. This list will help you consider the broad range of factors that may shape your vision. As you review the list, think about the importance of each factor to your company. You may want to add some factors, too.

Identify the three or four factors that you consider significant, and, in the space provided, write a sentence summarizing why the factor is important. They represent the core of your company's mission statement. What is the significant point about each factor?

Next, consider how these significant factors relate to each other. When you see these relationships, you are ready to write a first draft of your mission statement. Find something that addresses your commitment. Find that magic combination of words that gets your juices flowing.

Remember: Keep it short and simple. Anyone who reads the statement—an employee, a client, a prospective client—should know what's important in your firm.

You will want to revise your mission statement not only now, but also as your company develops and expands. If you have a partner or key employee, the process of developing a mission statement can help you identify the points on which you agree and disagree, and develop a shared vision. Developing a good mission statement frees you to devote your energy to attaining your vision.

**Figure 32-2.** Ranking factors to develop the mission statement.

*Rank*

_____ The Client                    _____

_____ Community Involvement         _____

_____ Creativity                    _____

_____ Growth                        _____

_____ Information                   _____

_____ Innovation                    _____

_____ New Business                  _____

_____ New Services                  _____

_____ Profitability                 _____

_____ Quality                       _____

_____ Service                       _____

_____ Technical Proficiency         _____

_____ Technology                    _____


Other (list):

_____ _____

_____ _____

_____ _____

_____ _____

_____ _____

_____ _____

_____ _____

_____ _____

## Strategies: Positioning Yourself for Success

For strategy development, the EMSOC process uses the traditional marketing mix—product/service, price, place, and promotion. The special nature of services requires the addition of two more P's—process and people. The six P's represent the basis from which you will develop strategies for achieving your goals.

As we discuss the P's, consider each one in relation to your mission, strengths, and interests. Because the time you have to invest in marketing is limited, it's crucial that you develop strategies that lead to activities you enjoy and do well (with the help of educational programs, if necessary). Be honest with yourself. Planning is the easy part. Making the plan happen is hard work, and you want to set yourself up to succeed by leveraging your strengths.

### How to Define Your Product/Service Line

What is it that you actually do? How do people see your services? The reason we start with a product/service strategy is to ensure that, as a service provider, you match your services to what the client or customer actually needs—and will buy. Frequently you are doing something that clients don't like to do or don't have the time or staff to do.

You want to determine an appropriate mix of service offerings. First, write a description of the services you currently offer. What are the features and benefits of each service you can deliver? Ask people you have worked with to define what you did for them. Why do they value your work?

Now consider the market information you have. What services do you offer that are heavily used in your community? What service features provide an advantage over your competitors? Can some of your services be modified or redefined so that they could substitute for existing services? Is it possible to adapt an existing service or set of skills into a new service offering? Is it possible to modify or enhance an existing service to become more competitive and profitable?

Your goal in assessing your service portfolio is to uncover that unique combination of services that will set you apart from your competitors. You want to create a distinction, a favored position, between you and everyone else.

Developing new services, as well as eliminating useless or unprofitable ones, is an integral part of managing your business and can keep you out in front of your competitors. This ongoing process of differentiation keeps you current and competitive.

### Price: How to Set Fees

As a service provider, you are selling your time. In establishing a fee structure, you need to determine how many billable hours you can generate, as well as the nonbillable time you will need for job research, business development, and administrative chores. Keep in mind that each hour of billable time pays for your unbillable office time, staff time, and overhead.

The existing fee structure in your community will set your upper and lower limits. Your fee structure will fall somewhere within this range. What position do you want to have within that range? Do you want to be the low-cost provider? How would that appeal to your preferred clients? A credible fee structure rests on the perceived value of your services.

It is quite common for service providers to spot needs that the client has not recognized or considered as work that someone else could perform. Addressing unarticulated or untapped needs is one of the most difficult marketing challenges because the client has no reference to gauge value. The client is taking a risk in dealing with an unknown. The service entrepreneur can build perceived value by relating services to analagous service categories so that the client has a reference point. For example, the very first accountants faced tremendous obstacles in persuading businesspeople to entrust their financial affairs to them. Yet, today, this service is taken for granted.

## Place: How to Project Professionalism

In the marketing mix, place refers to location, accessibility, and physical evidence. Do you go to your clients, or do they come to you? If they come to your office, where are you located in relation to them? How accessible are you? Do you have adequate parking, and do clients get the best spots?

Consider the role of technology in accessibility, too. If your clients use a fax to do routine business with suppliers, you should have one. If you are out of your office frequently and many of your clients want to speak with you regularly, perhaps you should have a telephone in your car.

People judge you by your surroundings. Is your office neat and attractive? If you are just setting up shop or using shabby discards, consider renting attractive furniture from a rental company. This can be an inexpensive way of delaying significant expense and avoiding a decor that is inconsistent with the image you want to convey.

Physical evidence includes your printed materials—business cards, stationery, mailing labels, report covers, invoices, brochures, and signs. You want these items to have a consistent look in terms of color, typeface, and other elements. This consistency is your firm's identity, a systematic way of presenting your business visually. Your goal is to have clients and others recognize any printed communication, or physical evidence, from your firm because of the consistency in appearance.

## Process: How to Understand What You Do

It's very important for a service entrepreneur to understand the delivery process that is the foundation of each service offered. Why? First, clients evaluate your service on the basis of their experience in the service delivery process. You want to know where the fail points are so that you can take preventive action or have backup support when you need it.

Second, clients participate in the service delivery process. When they understand this process, they can be better clients. They know what their role is. And there are no surprises.

For each service you offer, map out the steps in delivering the service. One useful tool is the service blueprint described in Chapter 14. A blueprint will give you a good picture of your operations as they affect the client's experience with your company. You will find duplicative efforts, potential trouble spots, and ways to be more efficient. Another benefit is that the blueprint will help you explain a service to employees and show them how their work relates to client service.

## People: How to Be More Sensitive to Clients

Clients of service businesses expect to be treated exactly like that—clients. They expect you to become increasingly familiar with their business so that you understand it thoroughly and can discuss it knowledgeably.

They expect your staff to be interested in their business concerns and to be courteous, helpful, caring, and knowledgeable about your business. All too often, service entrepreneurs think that their representatives understand what they are supposed to do and say without the benefit of any direction.

Do your employees understand what your business is? Can they speak intelligently with people in the community and communicate what services you provide? Unless you have taken steps to help them, in all likelihood your employees are working in a vacuum.

You can help your employees be more sensitive to clients and others by giving them a clear picture of what services you offer and making sure they understand some of the benefits of those services. If you are an image consultant, your staff should be able to say something like: ''At Color Magic, we help people look their best. People look different, depending on the colors they wear, and we help them identify the colors that harmonize with their natural coloring.'' It's simple, it's clear, and it's better than ''We help people improve their image.'' What does that mean?

You can help your employees understand how to be more sensitive to clients. The person who answers your telephone should know that clients who want to leave a detailed message should be able to do so, rather than being asked to call back later. If your mailing list is maintained by a service bureau, those who update your list should know that you expect ''zero defects'' because clients want to be addressed correctly, and any errors reflect on your firm.

When your organization is small, your employees or representatives model their behavior on your behavior. Thus, client sensitivity may be part of your firm's culture now. Your objective is to have everyone who represents your firm understand his or her relationship to your clients—even if the representative never sees or speaks with a client.

## Promotion: How to Help People Know About Your Services

Last, but by no means least, is the area of promotion. Here is where you express everything you've learned—about yourself, about how you deal with people, about the special service mix you can offer, about your service delivery process, and about fees. Your objective here is to develop strategies to communicate your capabilities. Recognize that implementation is time-consuming. As we discuss the different types of promotion, try to identify those activities you enjoy—so that they get done.

In developing your promotional campaign, remember that services are intangible. As a result, your capabilities will usually be evaluated by subjective criteria. You can help prospective clients be more objective by giving them tangible evidence of your capabilities. This evidence might be a sample of your service. If you offer landscaping services and call on a prospective client who has an overgrown shrub, you might trim it—on the spot—to a more attractive shape, thus demonstrating your initiative, responsiveness, creativity, and interest in solving the client's problem. You also can give prospective clients evidence of community acceptance—press releases, seminars, community activities, brochures, and portfolios.

Remember, too, that people tend to buy services on the basis of recommendations from peers and friends. The most effective promotional strategy is to obtain recommendations from people who can substantiate their recommendations.

The goal of your communication program is to be one of the three or four firms prospective clients consider when they need services like those you offer (or to be one of the three or four firms recommended by referral sources). To reach this "preferred" status, you must familiarize prospective clients, referral sources, and significant others with your firm's name and services. This familiarization process takes time. People must see information about you and your firm frequently over a period of eight to twelve months. Remember that people are deluged with communications every day; look at your own in-box for starters. Your promotional campaign must stand out from these competing communications by addressing topics of interest in an attention-getting manner. In this section, we'll describe four types of promotion: the "word-of-mouth" campaign, community participation, the paper campaign, and public relations.

Your Word-of-Mouth Campaign.    A word-of-mouth campaign is very powerful once you decide what "word" you want to spread. Intangible qualities like commitment, integrity, experience, reliability, and trustworthiness work well in these campaigns. Review your mission statement carefully because your word-of-mouth message must be consistent with it. If your landscape services are geared toward people who want unusual plantings and design, you want people to use words like *creative, spectacular,* and *follows through,* not *inaccessible* and *low priced.*

To create a word-of-mouth campaign, give people something positive to say about you. Making speeches and slide presentations creates the visibility and credibility you need to generate a successful campaign. Behind a podium, you're an expert. You reach not only the audience you're addressing, but also those who hear about your speech or read about it in the press.

Don't wait for an invitation to speak. Most organizations have program committees looking for speakers. Let them know that you are available, and discuss the subjects their members are interested in. Then give them a list of topics that you are prepared to present.

Audiences expect a logical, accurate presentation on a topic that is meaningful to them. If it's appropriate, illustrate your talks with slides and other graphic materials, including handouts. If you think you need help with presentation skills or speech writing, get professional assistance—it will pay off.

At the presentation, be sure to collect business cards. One way to obtain these cards is to offer something—an article related to your presentation, perhaps, or a copy of your presentation. Those cards represent valuable information—names for your mailing list, people you should telephone about their interest in your presentation and need for your services.

Your Community Participation Campaign. Active participation in the community can help you promote your services. Organizational involvement is one important alternative. Identify the organizations that represent professional and business development opportunities. There may be some in which you should retain a membership without a commitment to participate actively. The important organizations are those that add to your professional capabilities or give you opportunities to meet prospective clients and referral sources. Consider joining groups in which your clients are active as a way to meet people with needs and interests similar to those of your clients.

Once you have identified organizations in which you are interested, get involved. Do things that will expand your network; get on the program committee or volunteer for the board. Organization involvement is related to your word-of-mouth campaign; the work you do with an organization should support the "word" about your business.

Teaching is another activity in which to demonstrate your expertise and expand your network. If you have an idea for a course or seminar, submit it to your community college or university, extension program, or continuing education center. The title of "adjunct professor" or "instructor" will add to your credibility even though the pay isn't high. Once your clients' demands on your time increase, you will have to decide if the contacts and satisfaction warrant it.

Sponsorship is another source of visibility. Sponsor an athletic team in your town. If you own a photocopy shop, every T-shirt or sweater team members wear will advertise the name of your company. It might sound corny, but, in combination with other activities, this identifies you as a community-minded citizen. Other suggestions: Provide a prize for the high school homecoming queen, a local or county exhibit, or Junior Achievement. A small trophy goes a long way in establishing you in the minds and hearts of neighbors.

Your Print Campaign. Complement your activities in the community with the written word. In designing any written communication, remember that you are persuading and giving tangibility to an intangible service. Be specific: This is not the time to use generalities or vague words. Keep it simple. Simplicity reaches people directly. Be clear about what you can do. Define your services concisely, and include examples of how you have helped clients. With every word you write, you are trying to earn the reader's respect.

Keep your copy focused on matters that concern your clients. They want to know what benefits they will receive as a result of retaining you, as well as the specific features of your services. Yes, you are being motivational. You want readers to take action.

Get all the help you can in designing your promotional materials. Some sources are free from your professional association and your local business organizations. You may want to get help from a marketing consultant, a public relations firm, or an advertising agency. It's important to develop the best materials possible because they are a tangible representation of your business.

Most service entrepreneurs develop some type of brochure that presents their mission, highlights their areas of expertise, and outlines the breadth of their services as well as the benefits clients can expect. Think about how you will distribute a brochure. You can use a brochure to respond to inquiries or mail one directly to prospective clients. Referral sources should have a copy, too. And, if you are giving a presentation, you could hand out copies to the audience.

Your paper campaign may include advertising in local and specialty publications. Before you advertise, weigh its benefits for your business carefully. Many people equate advertising with marketing, and they are disappointed when no new business results. Advertising presells; it starts a dialogue, particularly when you offer the reader something—a brochure, for example. Advertising also requires a commitment to a campaign. One-shot advertising isn't effective. People must see your message several times if they are to remember it.

Writing articles for publication is another source of print promotion. If you enjoy writing, submit articles to local or national publications. When an article appears, send reprints to current and prospective clients. If you enjoy speaking, tape your presentations, and develop them into publications. Hire an editor to turn a transcript of the tape into an article for publication and reprints.

Your Public Relations Campaign.    In media relations, it is important to be aware that the editors at your local radio station, newspapers, and magazines may be interested in the *concept* of your business, not your business per se. Small newspapers and local radio stations frequently cannot find interesting stories on their own because of time constraints, but they are interested in unusual stories with a local slant to help fill space or time. Although you have no control over timing or content, you are getting free publicity.

You can call an editor or a program director and try to set up a meeting. Usually the editor will ask you to send a press release. In developing a press release, type the information on 8½ × 11 bond paper with the name of your business in the *upper left* and the address and date in the *upper right*. Under the name of the business, write CONTACT, and give the name and telephone number of the appropriate person in your business to contact.

In the middle of the page, type in caps FOR IMMEDIATE RELEASE. If the material is time-dated, include the date when you would like the story presented. Create a headline that announces or describes the main idea of the release. Try for impact by writing an opening sentence that grabs the reader's attention.

Follow-up is critical. Call the editor, and ask if your release arrived. If it has, ask if the editor has had a chance to read it. If not, ask if you may call back at a later date. You may want to point out why the article is timely or important to readers or listeners. If you are told that your timing is off, send a new release at a better time. If your release isn't being run, try to find out why. Don't be discouraged. Keep trying.

Articles in the media are very effective in creating visibility and credibility. An article about your business can be useful in your promotional package for prospective clients. Remember to send each article to current clients, too.

# Operations: How to Create a Plan and Make It Happen

Planning is the easy part, so we'll discuss that first. Implementation is the hard part. As an entrepreneur, you have a lot of demands for your time, and juggling these demands is a job in itself. Thus, you need to focus on how to turn the plan into reality. What time can you commit? And you must make the commitment. Do you need help? What kind? When? As we discuss planning and implementation and you consider your situation, you must be brutally honest about your strengths, shortcomings, and interests.

## Developing a Marketing Plan

Figure 32-3 presents some key questions relating to the EMSOC process. Review these questions; they represent the major points in a marketing plan.

You probably are concluding that you have some work to do. Perhaps you need more information. Maybe you need to look at your service delivery process a little more closely. You may need to revisit your marketing materials. Before you move on to these activities, let's look at an example of a marketing plan and how it was developed:

Janet Jones, a single practitioner, offers accounting and tax services. In the past three years, she has built a stable, profitable practice. Her best clients are small businesses, some of which are owned by growth-minded entrepreneurs. The personal and business finances of small-business owners are intertwined, and Ms. Jones has invested considerable effort in understanding small-business issues, particularly tax issues. She is using off-the-shelf software, as well as a service bureau, to streamline the technical side of her work, and she employs two part-time accountants who understand her operations well.

Ms. Jones is eager to keep her clients happy. She knows that there are other firms that would like her clients' business, and she has decided that one good way to retain her base of clients would be to add a service they know they need. In talking with them about their long-term objectives, she learned that clients wanted assistance with financial planning. Her younger clients are concerned about financing their children's education. Older clients wonder how they will be able to retire.

Although there are financial planning consultants in the community, their services are expensive, or they sell financial products. No other small accounting firm appears to be offering the service, so Ms. Jones believes that she can attract new clients, some of whom would be candidates to purchase accounting and tax services.

While Ms. Jones was enrolled in a series of personal financial planning courses, she defined the service she will offer and designed the service delivery process, which she tested on members of her family. She is ready to introduce the service to her clients.

Her goal is to increase her firm's revenues by $51,000 through the addition of this new service. Ms. Jones knows that she must get the word out that she

**Figure 32-3.** A strategic EMSOC inquiry.

Environment/Situation

- Is there a need for your services in your community?
- What is the local economic climate?
- Who are your clients? Potential clients? What are their needs?
- Who are your referral sources?

Mission Statement

- Do you have a mission statement that helps people understand the essence of your business?

Strategies/Positioning

Products/Services

- What services can you offer?
- How do these services meet the needs of your market?

Price

- Is your fee structure realistic?
- Why do clients value your service?

Place

- Are your facilities accessible to your clients?
- Do your office and staff represent you well?
- Do the materials and collateral you use represent you well?

Process

- Do you know where the fail points are in service delivery?
- Have you developed routines for those aspects of your service that can be standardized?

People

- Do the people who represent you understand their relationship to your clients—even if these representatives have no client contact?

Promotion

- What do you want people to say about your business?
- Is the concept of your business newsworthy?
- How are you going to let people know about your services?
- Do your words communicate the benefits of your services?
- How will you keep your name in front of target audiences?

Operations

- What goals and priorities should you focus on?
- What is the best plan for achieving your goals?
- Who will do what by when?

Control/Evaluation

- How will you evaluate your progress?

can help people with financial planning, and she wants to use her presentation skills to accomplish this. At a meeting of a local business group, she spoke with the newspaper's business editor. Her enthusiasm for her new service and its benefits convinced the editor that his readers would be interested in knowing more about the process. His newspaper will sponsor a round-table discussion about personal financial planning. Ms. Jones will take part in the round table and will help the editor scope the discussion and identify participants. The round-table discussion will be summarized in the newspaper, and Ms. Jones will mail a reprint to clients, prospective clients, and referral sources.

In addition, Ms. Jones has lined up two speaking engagements where she will discuss you-know-what. Her presentation to a trade association will generate publicity in the trade press, and she can use the clippings in presentations to prospective clients. She also will speak before a local business group. A summary of this presentation will be mailed to clients, prospective clients, and referral sources; many of these people will be invited to the luncheon, also.

Figure 32-4 shows when these presentations, as well as other mailings, will occur. Ms. Jones is also going to experiment with a listing/advertisement in the directory published by the local chamber of commerce, of which she is a member. In reviewing the listings, she noticed that there was no entry for Personal Financial Planning. She knows that many members use the services of other members, so she is going to create the category. (You'll note that the second part of the example here bears a similarity to the client communication plan in Table 15-2.)

### Seven Rules of Thumb

Ms. Jones's plan is based on some basic rules that you can use in evaluating the plan you develop:

1. *Make your objectives specific and measurable.* Ms. Jones will know when she has acquired new business totaling $51,000.
2. *Build on your strengths and interests.* Ms. Jones enjoys public speaking, and this activity is the core of her communication program.
3. *Try to use any marketing activity several ways.* Ms. Jones's speaking activities are turned into reprints, publicity, and summaries that can be used in mailings and qualifications materials.
4. *Find ways to keep your name and services in front of key people.* Ms. Jones's six mailings (see Figure 32-4) to clients, prospective clients, and referral sources help her occupy "a share of mind."
5. *Keep the logistics simple.* The mailings in Ms. Jones's program can be administered by her secretary, if she has one. A mailing house can take care of the mailings, too.
6. *Aim for the best quality—within your budget.* Ms. Jones may have thought it would be nice to have a newsletter for clients and others, but she found that newsletters take a lot of time to prepare and are expensive on a unit basis when relatively few are needed. Thus, she opted to send

**Figure 32-4.** Example of a marketing plan.

Jones & Company
Marketing Plan
19xx–19xx

Mission:      At Jones & Company, we help clients achieve their business and personal financial planning objectives.

Environment:   Competition among accounting firms is increasing, and many companies are switching firms to reduce fees. New tax regulations are complex, and laypersons have a hard time understanding the effects of these changes on them.

Goal:       To increase revenues by $51,000 in the current fiscal year.

Strategy:    To retain and attract clients by offering a new service, personal financial planning (PFP), that includes educational and retirement planning. Specific targets are to provide PFP services to:

        6 current clients at total fees of $16,000
        15 new clients at total fees of $35,000

To develop a communication program emphasizing PFP.

Communication Plan:

| Month | Activity |
|---|---|
| January | Mailing:  New Year's card |
| February | Publication:  Round-table feature |
| March | Mailing:  Round-table reprint |
| April | Speech:  Trade association; publicity |
| May | Mailing:  Article of interest |
| June | Advertisement:  Chamber of Commerce membership directory |
| July | |
| August | Mailing:  Invitation to luncheon (Sept.) |
| September | Luncheon speech:  Local business group |
| October | Mailing:  Summary of September speech |
| November | Mailing:  Article regarding taxes |
| December | |

reprints and summaries, which could be reproduced on quality paper and personalized with a cover note.

7. *Keep your plan short, specific, and manageable.* Entrepreneurs don't need fifty-page plans.

## *Making the Plan Real*

Implementing a marketing plan requires the creation of operational procedures. In our example in the previous section, we mentioned some approaches: having your secretary administer mailings, including the development and maintenance of your mailing lists, or using an outside service, such as a mailing house. In this section, we will describe some of the resources you might consider—once you have exhausted your employee(s), family, and friends. First, we'll describe consulting resources—then, support services.

<u>Retaining Consultants.</u>  As you develop your plan or as your practice expands, you may need the assistance of marketing and communication consultants. Whom should you choose? Specialists in marketing, public relations, or advertising?

Marketing consultants may specialize in a particular area (e.g., planning, communications), but many are generalists who can help you develop and implement your plan. They can help you write and produce a brochure, survey your clients to find out why they value your services, and help your staff become more sensitive to clients' needs.

Public relations consultants work well with the press and excel at the publicity aspect of marketing. Many public relations people have excellent networks, and they can be very helpful in introducing you to referral sources and building your network. Some public relations firms employ communication specialists who can help you with brochures, speeches, and newsletters.

Advertising consultants specialize in getting your message across through paid placements in print, radio, and television. Some advertising agencies have public relations capabilities, as well as people who can write and produce brochures and other support materials.

If you are interested in hiring a consultant, try to find one with expertise in your area. By doing so, you save yourself the costly and time-consuming process of educating its staff from scratch. One warning: Check to see if the firm has any of your competitors as clients—you want to avoid conflicts.

Interview the consultant at length to see if you get along with one another and whether your strategic and implementation thoughts are compatible. Ask to see brochures, catalogs, or advertisements, and have the consultant explain how this material fits into the client's overall plan. Speak to the consultant's clients, too.

Make sure the consulting firm is the right size for you. You want to deal with a firm that is small enough to consider your work profitable and worth its best efforts, but large enough to offer the services you need. An example: A $10,000 advertising account represents only 0.1 percent of a $10-million agency's income, and may receive only 0.1 percent of its management attention and 0.1 percent of its creative effort.

To test the working relationship, you might want to hire a consultant to work on a single project. On an ongoing basis, you want to work with someone who is on your wavelength. Most consultants work on both types of fee arrangements: fee per project, and ongoing fee, usually paid monthly for a specified period of time.

    Finding Support Services.   Once you develop your plan, list the activities you can handle in-house and those you cannot. Then define the kinds of help you need: someone who can edit your speech so that it can be published; a typist who transcribes speeches; a designer to devise a new look for your firm. Whatever type of help you need, someone in your community can do it.

    How do you find this help? Ask your clients whom they use. Your suppliers may know someone. Check with the chamber of commerce and other business groups. Someone in your network knows this source of help.

## Control: How to Measure Progress

The issue of control can be summarized very briefly. What did you want to achieve? By when? If you have defined your goals in measurable terms within a certain time period, you can answer these questions at appropriate time intervals—weekly, monthly, or quarterly.

    If you are getting the results you wanted, why is it happening? If you are not, why not? Have you and your staff performed as you said you would? What should you do about it? What have you learned in the past few weeks (or months) that will make you a better service entrepreneur? Create a new plan, or revise your existing plan, and act on it. The discipline of marketing works; make it work for you.

## Set Yourself Up to Succeed

You have your own business. You are doing what you do best, doing it the way you always knew it should be done, and you're being paid to do it. It's an adventure, and it has its rewards.

    Marketing can help you achieve your goals. As we have seen in this chapter, creating a marketing plan of action requires a systematic analysis of your environment and your situation, a strong sense of mission, and well-conceived strategies. And, success means having a strong plan and an even stronger implementation approach.

    As your business succeeds and expands, use the discipline of marketing to help you develop an ongoing approach to evaluating your progress. Continually challenge yourself with such questions as: Are there new markets for our services? Are we meeting our clients' needs? How can we differentiate our services even more from those of our competitors?

    You will want to explore some of the concepts and processes described elsewhere in this *Handbook*. As your staff expands, internal marketing will become even more important. As you introduce new services, blueprinting will be helpful in defining each service and differentiating it. These are only two examples of the ways in which marketing can help you achieve your objectives through ongoing planning and self-evaluation.

## Further Resources

Davidson, Jeffrey P. *The Marketing Sourcebook for Small Business.* New York: Wiley, 1989.

Phillips, Michael, and Salli Rasberry. *Marketing Without Advertising: Creative Strategies for Small Business Success.* Berkeley, Calif.: Nolo Press, 1986.

\*    \*    \*    \*

*Adrienne Margules O'Hare is owner of The Marketing Company, a multiservice marketing and management firm in Tucson, Arizona. Her clients include retail stores, manufacturing and trucking companies, real estate and financial planning companies, and home health care and consulting services. She previously served as a public awareness consultant to the Department of Education in central Massachusetts, where she helped achieve passage of the first statewide program for the handicapped.*

*Carole A. Congram, Ph.D., is the principal of Congram Associates, a consulting firm based in New York City and specializing in services marketing. She assists clients with a broad range of planning and implementation services. She also holds the position of associate professor of operations management at Bentley College in Waltham, Massachusetts. A frequent speaker on services marketing topics, she was on the national marketing staff of Touche Ross & Co. for eleven years, most recently as director of marketing communication planning.*

*The authors contributed equally to this chapter.*

# The Service Marketer's Bookshelf

Albrecht, Karl. *At America's Service*. Homewood, Ill.: Dow Jones-Irwin, 1988.

*Focuses on the issues and problems in implementing many of the service strategies introduced in Albrecht and Zemke's* Service America: Doing Business in the New Economy *(described below).*

Albrecht, Karl, and Lawrence J. Bradford. *The Service Advantage: How to Identify and Fulfill Customer Needs*. Homewood, Ill.: Dow Jones-Irwin, 1990.

*Presents a step-by-step guide to conducting customer research and using the results to differentiate a service company from its competitors.*

Albrecht, Karl, and Ron Zemke. *Service America: Doing Business in the New Economy*. Homewood, Ill.: Dow Jones-Irwin, 1985.

*Describes service companies in which management has made the "service transition" and achieved success through excellent service; emphasizes customer retention.*

Bateson, John E. G. *Managing Service Marketing: Text and Readings*. Chicago: Dryden, 1989.

*Examines traditional marketing concepts and marketing-mix variables in service settings exclusively; contains many excellent readings.*

Carlzon, Jan. *Moments of Truth*. New York: Ballinger, 1987.

*Written by the insightful chief executive officer of Scandinavian Airline System; describes the process of turning a troubled organization into an industry leader through the implementation of service quality and internal marketing processes.*

Czepiel, John A., Michael R. Solomon, and Carol F. Surprenant, eds. *The Service Encounter: Managing Employee/Customer Interaction in Service Businesses*. Lexington, Mass.: Lexington Books, 1985.

*Explores the face-to-face meeting between customer and service provider in various service settings and from various points of view; discusses measurement techniques, cross selling, and other topics related to the service encounter; focuses on the ways service is delivered.*

Desatnick, Robert L. *Managing to Keep the Customer: How to Achieve and Maintain Superior Customer Service Throughout the Organization*. San Francisco: Jossey-Bass, 1987.

*Focuses on ways to improve employees' sensitivity to customers; describes educational programs, supervision, evaluation, and other critical areas.*

Fisk, Raymond P., and Patriya S. Tansuhaj. *Services Marketing: An Annotated Bibliography*. Chicago: American Marketing Association, 1985.

*Annotates references in conceptual areas (e.g., service strategies, service mix elements, management issues); lists references in ten industry groups, including health care; financial services; professional services; government and nonprofit services; telecommunications; hospitality, travel, and tourism; and arts and entertainment.*

Grönroos, Christian. *Service Management and Marketing: Managing the Moments of Truth in Service Competition.* Lexington, Mass.: Lexington Books, 1990.

*Incorporates a number of practical models and case studies that explain the nature of market-oriented management; analyzes the impact that service-dominated competition has had and will continue to have on management decision making. Special attention is devoted to service quality and internal marketing.*

Grönroos, Christian. *Strategic Management and Marketing in the Service Sector.* Cambridge, Mass.: Marketing Science Institute, 1983.

*Presents a profit- and market-oriented theory for managing and marketing service organizations; emphasizes service strategy, service quality, and internal marketing.*

Heskett, James L. *Managing in the Service Economy.* Cambridge, Mass.: Harvard Business School Press, 1986.

*Discusses strategies for success in service businesses and presents a practical framework for developing strategies; includes many examples from various service industries; considers challenges to multinational service companies.*

Langeard, Eric, John E. G. Bateson, Christopher H. Lovelock, and Pierre Eiglier. *Services Marketing: New Insights From Consumers and Managers.* Cambridge, Mass.: Marketing Science Institute, 1981.

*Reports the findings of a major research effort that examines customer participation in the service delivery process, management's understanding of customer needs, and the relationship among operations, marketing, and human resources in service companies.*

Lovelock, Christopher H. *Managing Services: Marketing, Operations, and Human Resources.* Englewood Cliffs, N.J.: Prentice-Hall, 1988.

*Structures readings and cases to help managers in service organizations understand the need to integrate these three functions on an ongoing basis; covers a wide range of service industries.*

————. *Services Marketing.* Englewood Cliffs, N.J.: Prentice-Hall, 1984.

*Presents the basics of services marketing, with many examples from a wide range of industries; includes cases and readings, some of which are classics in the services marketing literature.*

Normann, Richard. *Service Management: Strategy and Leadership in Service Businesses.* Chichester, England: Wiley, 1984.

*Presents a framework for managing service organizations—the Service Management System; emphasizes quality as integral to the system.*

Rathmell, John M. *Marketing in the Service Sector.* Boston: Winthrop Publishers, 1974.

*One of the first books on services marketing; discusses the special needs of service organizations in terms of the marketing mix.*

Sasser, W. Earl, Paul R. Olsen, and D. Daryl Wyckoff. *Management of Service Operations: Text, Cases, and Readings.* Boston: Allyn & Bacon, 1978.

*Examines the unique demands imposed by the service delivery process on managers; emphasizes the need for continuing interaction between marketing and operations; focuses special attention on the multisite service company.*

*Service Management. Harvard Business Review* Reprint Series, no. 18051, 1979.

*Comprised of twelve articles from* Harvard Business Review *on service strategies, the service delivery system, and motivation, control, and organization.*

Shaw, John C. *The Service Focus: Developing Winning Game Plans for Service Companies.* Homewood, Ill.: Dow Jones-Irwin, 1990.

*Discusses key differences between industrial and service organizations; presents concepts, tools, and processes to help the management of service organizations develop and implement strategies.*

Spechler, Jay W. *When America Does It Right: Case Studies in Service Quality.* Norcross, Ga: Industrial Engineering and Management Press, Institute of Industrial Engineers, 1988.

*Presents key strategies and success factors in improving a company's performance in service quality; authors from thirty-seven companies representing twenty-seven manufacturing and service industries describe their approaches to service quality and the resulting benefits.*

Zeithaml, Valarie A., Leonard L. Berry, and A. Parasuraman. *Communication and Control Processes in the Delivery of Service Quality.* Cambridge, Mass.: Marketing Science Institute, 1987.

*Presents a conceptual model of service quality; examines four gaps that occur in service organizations and impede the delivery of high-quality service; discusses organizational factors that affect the delivery of service quality.*

Zemke, Ron, and Dick Schaaf. *The Service Edge.* New York: New American Library, 1989.

*Describes five principles of service quality and how they are exemplified in 101 companies.*

## American Marketing Association Conference Proceedings

Berry, Leonard L., G. Lynn Shostack, and Gregory D. Upah, eds. *Emerging Perspectives on Services Marketing,* 1983.

Bitner, Mary Jo, and Lawrence A. Crosby, eds. *Designing a Winning Service Strategy,* 1989.

Bloch, Thomas H., Gregory D. Upah, and Valarie A. Zeithaml, eds. *Services Marketing in a Changing Environment,* 1985.

Czepiel, John A., Carole A. Congram, and James B. Shanahan, eds. *The Services Challenge: Integrating for Competitive Advantage,* 1987.

Donnelly, James H., and William R. George, eds. *Marketing of Services,* 1981.

George, William R., and Claudia E. Marshall, eds. *Developing New Services,* 1984.

*Service Excellence: Marketing's Impact on Performance,* 1989.

Surprenant, Carol, ed. *Add Value to Your Service: The Key to Success,* 1988.

Venkatesan, M., Diane M. Schmalensee, and Claudia Marshall, eds. *Creativity in Services Marketing; What's New, What Works, What's Developing,* 1986.

# Index

# About the Editors

A veteran services marketer, **Carole A. Congram** is the principal of the consulting firm of Congram Associates in New York City and an associate professor of operations management at Bentley College in Waltham, Massachusetts.

As a consultant, she assists clients with a broad range of planning and implementation services, including strategic planning, internal marketing, client retention systems, and communications.

As a teacher, she helps undergraduate and graduate students understand the special nature of service organizations and the need for functional integration in these settings. Her research interests center on the service encounter and client retention.

Previously, she was with Touche Ross & Co., the international accounting and management consulting firm, for eleven years. Most recently she was the firm's director of marketing communication planning. Previously she headed the firm's marketing services group.

Ms. Congram speaks and writes frequently on services marketing topics and issues. She is the co-author (with R. J. Dumesic) of *The Accountant's Strategic Marketing Guide* (Wiley, 1986). In 1988, the American Institute of Certified Public Accountants published *Developing and Implementing an Effective Marketing Program,* a self-study course she created. She is also the co-editor (with J. A. Czepiel and J. B. Shanahan) of *The Services Challenge: Integrating for Competitive Advantage—Proceedings* (American Marketing Association, 1987).

Active in the American Marketing Association, she served on the national Services Division Planning Council from 1984 through 1987. She was a co-chair of the fifth national Services Marketing Conference, held in Boston in 1986. In addition, she was a co-chair of the first symposium on the marketing of accounting services, held in Chicago in 1984.

She was a member of the board of directors of the American Marketing Association's New York chapter from 1988 to 1990. She served as chair of services marketing programming for the chapter from 1985 to 1989 and now heads its Services Leadership Council.

A member of the board of reviewers of *The Journal of Services Marketing,* Ms. Congram has a Ph.D. from the University of Wisconsin-Madison, an M.Ed. from the University of North Dakota, and an A.B. from Tufts University.

**Margaret L. Friedman** is currently an assistant professor in the marketing department of the College of Business and Economics, University of Wisconsin-Whitewater. She teaches courses in consumer behavior and personal selling and has developed an undergraduate course in services marketing. She is an advisor to the Whitewater student chapter of the American Marketing Association.

Prior to her current position, she was director of service sector marketing programs at Management Institute, the continuing education unit of the School of Business, University of Wisconsin-Madison. In that capacity, she developed and implemented one- to three-day programs, covering such topics as market planning, communication effectiveness, and nonprofit marketing, targeted specifically at service sector businesspeople.

Before pursuing her academic career, Ms. Friedman worked in the consulting division of Arthur Andersen & Co. (now Andersen Consulting) in Milwaukee, where she specialized in the design and installation of information systems for the health care industry.

She consults with various service sector businesses, including CUNA Mutual Insurance Group, the Pupil Services Division of the Janesville, Wisconsin, school district, and several entrepreneurial organizations. She has published several articles in services marketing in both academic and trade journals.

Ms. Friedman's undergraduate degree, from Smith College, is in sociology. She holds M.B.A. and Ph.D. degrees from the University of Wisconsin-Madison. In her dissertation she pursued her interest in service sector/health care marketing through an investigation of the patient-physician interaction from a sales effectiveness perspective.